THE THEOLOGY OF MAN AND GRACE

CONTEMPORARY COLLEGE THEOLOGY SERIES

GENERAL EDITORS: J. FRANK DEVINE, S.J.
                    RICHARD W. ROUSSEAU, S.J.

THE THEOLOGY OF MAN AND GRACE is one of the volumes in
the Historical Theology Section of the Series

The Theology of Man and Grace: Commentary

Readings in the Theology of Grace

EDMUND J. FORTMAN, S.J.

PROFESSOR OF THEOLOGY

BELLARMINE SCHOOL OF THEOLOGY, NORTH AURORA, ILLINOIS

THE BRUCE PUBLISHING COMPANY / MILWAUKEE

IMPRIMI POTEST:

IOANNES R. CONNERY, S.I.
Praepositus Provincialis
Provinciae Chicagiensis, S.I.

NIHIL OBSTAT:

JOHN A. SCHULIEN, S.T.D.
Censor librorum

IMPRIMATUR:

✠ WILLIAM E. COUSINS
Archbishop of Milwaukee

March 18, 1966

Library of Congress Catalog Card Number: 66–19970
© 1966 THE BRUCE PUBLISHING COMPANY
MADE IN THE UNITED STATES OF AMERICA

EDITORS' INTRODUCTION

The Contemporary College Theology Series

THIS series begins with the presupposition that theology is necessary. It is necessary if Christian intelligence is to search for meaning in its dialogue with God, man, and the world. Since Christian intelligence is not the exclusive possession of the theological specialist or the cleric, the search must be carried on in all those areas of life, secular as well as religious, including the college situation, where meaning is to be found.

This search is a peaceful one for in some mysterious way it has already achieved its goal: the vision of faith and the fullness of love. Still it remains a relentless and universal search. Its inner certainty must radiate out not only to the edges of the mind but also into the farthest recesses of the world. We could call it "lay" theology but this word seems too pale a description for such an exciting enterprise of the Christian life.

In view of this the editors of this series are convinced that new questions had to be asked, new structures created, and new books written. These books would be neither catechetical nor apologetic. They would be purely and simply theological. The primary audience would be believers, but all thinking men would find them useful. In scope they would be broad enough to insure perspective. They would be scholarly enough to be intellectually relevant. They would avoid pedantry. In short, they would try to present a rich and deep understanding of Christian revelation in such a way that today's college students would be able to respond with a Christian faith and life that are both culturally mature and scientifically precise. Finally the authors of these books would be, for the most part, teachers in colleges and universities where much of the contemporary theological dialogue is now going on.

The series falls into four parts: biblical, historical, ecclesial, and ethical. The divisions were not predetermined by the editors. They follow the shape of the most vigorous theological work now being done.

The books in the biblical section are intended to go beyond the traditional treatment of Bible history and the now familiar perspectives of salvation history. They concentrate on various books of the Bible. Their method has been especially designed for college work. Tentatively it might be called "exegetical theology." Every verse is not considered after the fashion of a commentary, nor are narratives developed as a biography, nor is there any attempt to create large theological syntheses. Rather the individual books are studied in chronological sequence; key passages are treated in detail and the rest are summarized. At the same time some attention is paid to the growing theological synthesis.

Since scholastic theology is already represented by individual works and sets of textbooks, the books in our historical section study dogmatic questions from a developmental point of view. In this way the editors hope to make the college students more aware of the great wealth of theological thinking that recent historicotheological studies have uncovered. This method, which is more inductive than deductive, should happily coincide with the thought processes of the college students. The three basic poles for synthesis are: God, Christ, and Man. In each area the historical development will be studied and a significant number of basic source texts presented. The problems raised in these studies will range all the way from Augustinian pessimism to Teilhardian optimism.

The textbooks for the third part of the series will deal with issues of great contemporary importance. They will examine questions discussed by the Second Vatican Council. As the name implies, ecclesial theology must first concern itself with the Church, what the Church knows herself to be as expressed in the insights of the new *Constitution on the Church* and with the more significant of the Church's allied concerns: other world religions, American Protestantism, its history, its motivating forces and spirit, and finally the new sacramental theology so enriched by the many magnificent liturgical advances. All of this growth has brought a wider and deeper appreciation of the nature of the Roman Cath-

olic Church and her relationship, rooted in understanding and love, with the whole world.

The fourth and final section of the series is devoted explicitly to Christian moral response. The editors subscribe to the position that the proper place for the Catholic college or university to examine ethical questions is in a revelational rather than in a purely philosophical context. In addition to the "virtue" divisions of the *Summa* or the classic moral theology text, designed primarily for confessors, there is a need and a place for a "Christian ethics" that reflects the new insights which both biblical and dogmatic theology can provide. These books will strive to be openly Christian in spirit, eclectic in approach, up to date in scholarship, and they will address themselves to those ethical problems which are most real to the modern American mind.

In this volume Father Edmund J. Fortman, S.J., professor of dogmatic theology at Bellarmine School of Theology in North Aurora, Illinois, presents a history of the development of a Christian understanding of man or, better, of the mutual relationship between God and man. It is hoped it will stimulate fresh insights into this vital theological area. Over the centuries it has acquired the name of grace, and it is under this heading that Father Fortman assembles a number of commentaries on the various historical periods of that development, written by Catholic, Orthodox, and Protestant authors.

The first four chapters are dedicated

to the problem as seen in Scripture, with whole chapters devoted to St. John and to St. Paul, whose contributions are, of course, so important. The patristic tradition is summed up well in two chapters, one on the Eastern and the other on the Western Fathers. The Council of Orange, the key council in the earlier history of the Church in this area, is given a full chapter, as it deserves. The medieval period is summed up as leading to the Council of Trent. The ideas of the reformers are balanced by a chapter on Trent, and the developments of the sixteenth through the eighteenth centuries, not always the most interesting segment of this development, are gathered together in an intriguing way. Finally, developments through the nineteenth and twentieth centuries in Protestant, Orthodox, and Catholic circles respectively are treated in the concluding section.

In a series such as this, with its limitations of space, a certain choice has to be made in the selection and length of documents, but despite these admittedly difficult restrictions, those chosen by Father Fortman admirably

fulfill their purpose of illuminating one of the great problems of Christian theological history, as well as of interesting the college reader.

Finally, the editors would like to express their thanks to all those whose interest, advice, and cooperation have made this series possible. They are especially grateful to Mr. William May of The Bruce Publishing Company, who not only initiated the project and sustained it through the inevitable disappointments and complications, but contributed so much of his editorial skill to its final shape. To the individual authors who so graciously added to their heavy burden of academic responsibility by undertaking these books, we can only express the hope that their share in the shaping and influencing of the American Catholic community of today and of tomorrow will be far more meaningful to them than any meager thanks of ours.

The Editors,

J. Frank Devine, S.J.
Boston College

Richard W. Rousseau, S.J.
Fairfield University

ACKNOWLEDGMENTS

THE editor and publishers of THE THEOLOGY OF MAN AND GRACE are grateful to the following for permission to reprint copyrighted materials:

Beauchesne et ses Fils, for excerpts from H. Rondet's Gratia Christi;

Cambridge University Press, New York, for excerpts from C. H. Dodd's The Interpretation of the Fourth Gospel;

The Clarendon Press, Oxford, for excerpts from Nigel Abercrombie's The Origins of Jansenism and from H. Wheeler Robinson's Inspiration and Revelation in the Old Testament;

T. & T. Clark, Edinburgh, for excerpts from Karl Barth's Church Dogmatics;

The Clergy Monthly, India, for P. De Letter's "Contemporary Theology of Grace";

Yves M.-J. Congar for excerpts from his article "La déification dans la tradition spirituelle de l'Orient," La Vie Spirituelle (Mai, 1935);

Desclée et Cie, Tournai, Belgium, for excerpts from Ch. Baumgartner's La Grâce du Christ and from F. Cayré's Manual of Patrology;

Helicon Press, Inc., Baltimore, Md., for excerpts from Karl Rahner's Theological Investigations, Vol. I;

B. Herder Book Company, St. Louis, for excerpts from J. Tixeront's History of Dogma and from The Church Teaches;

Herder & Herder, Inc., New York, for excerpts from L. Cerfaux' Christ in the Theology of St. Paul and from F. Amiot's Key Concepts of St. Paul;

Independent Press, Ltd., London, for excerpts from Henry David Gray's The Christian Doctrine of Grace;

Letouzey et Ane, Paris, for excerpts from E. Portalié's A Guide to the Thought of St. Augustine;

Longmans, Green & Co., Ltd., London, for excerpts from Leonard Hodgson's The Grace of God in Faith and Philosophy;

A. R. Mowbray & Co., London, for excerpts from G. W. H. Lampe's The Doctrine of Justification by Faith;

The Newman Press, Westminster, Md., for excerpts from Joseph Bonsirven's Theology of the New Testament and from Joseph Lortz' The Reformation: A Problem For Today;

Oliver & Boyd, Ltd., Edinburgh, for excerpts from T. F. Torrance's The Doctrine of Grace in the Apostolic Fathers and from his article on Justification in The Scottish Journal of Theology, Vol. 13 (1960);

The Oxford University Press, New York, for excerpts from Robert McAfee Brown's The Spirit of Protestantism;

Prentice-Hall, Inc., Englewood Cliffs, N. J., for excerpts from P. Gregory Stevens' The Life of Grace;

ix

The Presbyterian and Reformed Publishing Co., Philadelphia, for excerpts from G. C. Berkouwer's *The Conflict With Rome* and from C. Van Til's *Christianity* and *Barthianism;*

Priory Press, Chicago, for excerpts from J.-H. Nicolas' *The Mystery of God's Grace;*

SCM Press, London, for excerpts from W. T. Whitley's *The Doctrine of Grace* and from John Macquarrie's *An Existentialist Theology;*

Seabury-Western Theological Seminary, Evanston, Illinois, for excerpts from Frank Gavin's *Some Aspects of Contemporary Greek Thought;*

The Society for Promoting Christian Knowledge, London, for excerpts from C. K. Barrett's *The Gospel According to St. John;*

W. Spemann Verlag, Stuttgart, for excerpts from Metropolite Seraphim's *L'Eglise Orthodoxe;*

Theology Digest, for excerpts from A. Feuillet's article "The Incarnation: Mystery of Salvation;"

Theological Studies, for P. Le Letter's "Sanctifying Grace and the Divine Indwelling" and "Grace, Incorporation, Inhabitation."

CONTENTS

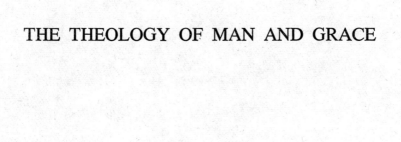

THE THEOLOGY OF MAN AND GRACE

I

GRACE IN THE OLD TESTAMENT

1. T. F. Torrance[1] sees the substance of the doctrine of grace in the Old Testament, in its clear-cut expression of God's free, unlimited, unsolicited, unaccountable love for men. He finds no single word for "grace" there to correspond to *charis* of the New Testament, but in three of its words, *'āheb*, *hēn*, and *hesed* he sees varying approximations to the New Testament *charis*.

THERE is no one word for grace in the Old Testament as there is in the New, nor are the precise lineaments of the New Testament thought manifest, but

---

[1] Thomas F. Torrance was born in 1913. He was educated at the University of Edinburgh and received his D.Theol. at the University of Basel. He is a minister of the Church of Scotland, and at present is professor of Christian dogmatics at the University of Edinburgh. He is the author of numerous books and articles. It is from his book, *The Doctrine of Grace in the Apostolic Fathers,* that this excerpt has been taken, selectively, from pages 10–18. It was published by Oliver and Boyd (Edinburgh, 1948).

1

the substance of the doctrine is there. In fact there is no language that expresses so profoundly and so tenderly the unaccountable love of God as the Hebrew of the Old Testament. This is not thought of abstractly but in intensely personal terms as the active love of one who is essentially the living and loving God of Israel. The dominant thought throughout is the amazing choice of Israel by God as grounded in His free and unlimited love and as creating a community in fellowship with God who bestows Himself upon them as Father and Saviour forever.

The word generally used to express this unsolicited and unaccountable love is *'āheb*, which is rare in any of the Semitic languages except Hebrew. It is usually kept to refer to a love in God which is unconditioned except by His love and by His will to love. This is brought out with particular clarity in Deuteronomy. "It was not because you were more in number than any other people that the Lord set his love upon you and chose you, for you were the fewest of all peoples; but it is because the Lord loves you, and is keeping the oath which he swore to your fathers. . . ."[2] "The one thing," a recent scholar has said, "of which all the Old Testament writers are certain is that God's love for Israel was not because of anything that Israel had or was."[3]

The sovereign and gracious character of this love is emphasized by the

use of another word and its derivatives: *hānan*. . . . Comparing *hēn* with *hesed* Mr. Snaith has said, "It tends to carry with it, to a greater extent than does *hesed,* the idea of unmerited favour, or of supreme graciousness and condescension on the part of the giver, who is the superior. There is not the slightest obligation on the part of the superior to show this *hēn*. It is all his generosity. . . ." The standing translation of *hēn* in the LXX is the word *charis,* particularly in such expressions as "to find favour," or "to obtain favour," but in those passages where *hēn* is related to the very nature of God as gracious and merciful and full of pity, *charis* is significantly not used at all. . . . The reason for this seems undoubtedly to lie in the fact that *charis* in its classical and hellenistic usage has a sensuous substratum in its meaning, a semi-physical sense of charm or gracefulness as something aesthetically pleasing, while the Hebrew *hēn* never has this sense.[4] It seems therefore that the shrewd translators of the LXX wanted to avoid the possibility of *charis* corrupting the Old Testament thought of the grace of God into something semi-physical and aesthetically pleasing, the very tendency that later became so rampant in the second, and third, and fourth centuries of the Christian era, and has ever since left its mark on the doctrine. Thus practically the only real significance that *charis* derives from

---

[2] Dt 7:7 f.; see also 9:4; 10:15; 23:5.

[3] Norman H. Snaith, *The Distinctive Ideas of the Old Testament* (1944), pp. 135, 128.

[4] Nor does *hēn* have the sense of gratitude or thanks as *charis* does. Cf. W. H. Lofthouse, "*Hēn* and *Hesed* in the O.T.," in *Zeitschrift für alttestamentliche Wissenschaft* (1933), 30.

its Septuagintal association is that it may be related to the divine favour, but not in expressions which are of intrinsic religious import. It is, however, when we take the Hebrew words *'āheb* and *ḥēn* together that we see the true beginnings of what a reminted *charis* came to express in the New Testament. If, as the late H. R. Mackintosh once wrote, "Grace is love in its princely and sovereign form, love to the indifferent and the disloyal, whose one claim is their need,"[5] then we have that clearly expressed in *'āheb* and *ḥēn*.

The Old Testament approaches still nearer to the New Testament *charis* in another of its great words, *ḥesed*. This is a word upon which recent research has thrown a flood of new light. The usual translation of the Authorized Version is loving kindness, but it is now generally recognized that while this does convey a large part of the meaning, it leaves out what is most distinctive in *ḥesed*, which does not refer to any act or relation of kindness indiscriminately but to one "where there is some recognized tie"[6] and in which the emphasis is laid upon the persistence and devotion of love.[7] It is closely bound up with a two-sided relationship within which covenanted kindness is a sure bond if not also a duty. . . .[8] *Ḥesed* is therefore not to

be regarded as a virtue among virtues, or even as one at the top of the scale, but rather as the fundamental relationship upon which the whole structure of Israelite society and religion rested. As such it embraces all social and personal relationships, but primarily is a relationship between men and God which includes also men's relations with one another because they are all related to God in *ḥesed*. . . .[9]

Writing of Isaiah 54:8, Mr. Snaith has said:[10] "here undoubtedly, as in all these cases, *ḥesed* has to do with mercy and forgiveness, but its true significance, as the *ḥesed* of God, is that it is everlasting, determined, unshakable. Wonderful as is His love for His covenant-people, His steady persistence in it is more wonderful still. The most important of all the distinctive ideas of the Old Testament is God's steady and extraordinary persistence in continuing to love wayward Israel in spite of Israel's insistent waywardness."

Ḥesed is the act of kindness by which God chooses Israel and promises therewith blessing and salvation. God promises to bring Himself into such a relation with Israel that His mercy and might are, as it were, at their disposal. Thus *ḥesed* is really the selfgiving of God to Israel, a promise which is confirmed by an oath and established in a definite covenant. . . . God's mercy remains true, and even

---

[5] H. R. Mackintosh, *The Christian Apprehension of God* (1934), p. 212.

[6] W. F. Lofthouse, *art. cit.*, 30.

[7] N. H. Snaith, *op. cit.*, p. 94 f.

[8] Dr. Nelson Glueck had defined *ḥesed* as "die dem Rechts-Pflicht-Verhältnis entsprechende Verhaltungsweise," *Das Wort Hesed im altt. Sprachgebrauche als menschl. u. göttl. gemeinschaftsgemässe Verhaltungs-*

weise (Giessen, 1927). A better German expression would be *Gemeinschaftstreue*.

[9] Cf. the expression "the *ḥesed* of God" or "the *ḥesed* of the Lord," 2 Sam 9:3; 1 Sam 20:14; see Sellin, *ad loc., Theologie des alten Testaments*, p. 28.

[10] *Op. cit.*, p. 102.

though Israel prove faithless and break the covenant, God will still hold fast to His loving purpose and will not be thwarted.[11] In this light ḥesed must be viewed as the great sacramental word of the Old Testament faith, while the covenant itself must be looked upon as the sacramental pledge of God's unaccountable love. Ḥesed is therefore not only the great presupposition of men's relations with God constitutive of all their life, but it is the decisive and eternal deed of God's love which makes the ground of men's approach to God an act and a promise in which He is irrevocably committed. . . .

Ultimately the sure and unswerving love of God finds a righteous way of forgiving the sinner, and in spite of his apostasy of turning him back with a new heart and a new righteousness into the bond of divine love. The major point here, so difficult for us to grasp and to express in any other language than Hebrew, is that righteousness and love, grace and justice, are held together as differentiations within the same unity, and even within the unity of a single thought or word. . . .

2. **Ch. Baumgartner, S.J.,[12] presents principal themes of grace in the Old Testament. He sees the Old Testament giving witness to the salvific justice of God and the Alliance prefiguring the definitive communion of God with men. More particularly he discerns grace in the gratuitous favor and benevolence of God, in a spiritual transformation of man effected by the spirit, the creator of the new Alliance, as well as in salvific justice and the gift of wisdom.**

"But now the righteousness of God has been manifested apart from law, although the law and the prophets bear witness to it."[13]

The death of Jesus Christ is the manifestation in the fullness of time of the saving justice of God. According to St. Paul the Old Testament gives witness to this saving justice, announces, and prepares it. The Alliance prefigures the definitive communion of God with men. The God of the Alliance is already a God of love, of goodness, of fidelity, of tenderness. And the prophets announce a transformation of men by the gift of the spirit and of justice.

Grace, favor and benevolence of God. A text of Exodus, wherein Yahweh Himself reveals to Moses that He is a God of grace, will often be taken up by the prophets and psalms. "Yahweh, Yahweh, God of tenderness [rahamim] and of grace [ḥēn], slow to anger, rich in kindness [ḥesed] and

[11] Is 54:8 f.; Ps 89:1 f. This is the theme of Hosea.
[12] Ch. Baumgartner, S.J., was born in 1900. He is professor of theology at the Jesuit College of Engheim. He is the author of *Jesus Christ, centre de la vie du chrètien* and editor of the *Dictionnaire de Spiritualité*. This excerpt was taken from his book, *La Grâce du Christ* (Desclée & Co., 1963), pp. 15–19.
[13] Rom 3:21.

in truth [*emet*], showing kindness [*hesed*] to the thousandth generation."[14]

For Hosea the history of Israel is the history of God's love for it, despite its ingratitude and infidelity. The prophet compares this love to the love of a spouse or a father. . . . "And I will betroth you to me for ever; I will betroth you to me in righteousness [*sedeq*] and in justice [*mihpat*], in steadfast love [*hesed*], and in mercy [*rahamim*]. I will betroth you to me in faithfulness ['*emunah*], and you shall know the Lord."[15]

This formula embraces at the same time the relations of men to one another and their situation before God; the movement of the creature that aspires to encounter his Creator and the generosity of Him who out of love loves His creature; the renewing of hearts and the coming of a new world.[16] It appears to suggest further that grace in the new humanity of the future will be this same faithful love that God communicates as a gratuitous gift.

Like Hosea, Jeremiah is the prophet of the God who is smitten with love for His people. For him too this love is like the passion of a man for a woman and of a father for his children.[17] While Hosea reserves the word *rahamim* for God, for Jeremiah, God's proper attribute is rather *hesed*.[18]

These same themes we find in Ezekiel and Isaiah.[19]

Grace, spiritual transformation of men. Yahweh's love for His people, His grace, is the source of many temporal and spiritual benefits. It is especially the principle of a profound renewal of hearts that purifies them from sin and gives them the strength to accomplish Yahweh's law. The two principal themes that announce this interior transformation are those of spirit and of justice.

Spirit. It is almost always in the perspective of messianic announcements that the prophets predict a spiritual regeneration in the community and individuals. Its mysterious source is the spirit, the creator of the new Alliance. For Jeremiah the new Alliance consists essentially in the renewal of hearts,[20] but he does not speak of the spirit of Yahweh nor does he relate the renewal of hearts to Him. That will be done by Ezekiel. . . .[21]

Saving justice. "It is especially in second Isaiah that justice becomes synonymous with grace and salvation. Justice for him is not only the deliverance of the oppressed and the restitution of their normal state, but the gift of a new reality which is superior to that which existed heretofore. This new aspect of justice is due less to the exilic experience . . . than to the eschatological and messianic perspective that dominates all his message: justice is a communication of grace and glory, and its beneficiary will be not the innocent and oppressed but

14 Ex 34:6-7.
15 Hos 2:19.20.
16 J. Guillet, *Themes bibliques* (2 ed., Aubier, 1954), p. 56. [Eng. tr. *Themes of the Bible* (Notre Dame, Ind., 1964), pp. 51-54.]
17 Jer 3:19-20, etc.
18 Jer 9:23; 16:5; 31:3; 32:18; 33:11.
19 Ez 16; Is 49:14-15; 54:4-10; 62:4-5.
20 Jer 31:31-34.
21 Ez 36:25-28.

the people whose only merit is to be the elect of Yahweh. The limits of the Alliance are enlarged for justice and will extend not only to the Israelites but to all peoples."[22] The last prophecies will repeat this theme of saving justice,[23] a justice that is at the same time divine and human and that is both a gift of the just God and in man a new attitude of docility to God![24] Thus in Isaiah II and III justice is interiorized and becomes docility to the law of God and connects up with the new heart of Ezekiel. It is the human aspect of the justice of God.

The theology of saving justice will be taken up again by St. Paul, particularly in the epistle to the Romans. In the Old Testament the justice of God is fidelity to His promises of salvation but it also has an eschatological and interior character and supposes the previous destruction of sin. In St. Paul all these aspects will reunite in the person and work of Christ. The death on the cross is the definitive revelation of the justice of God and the place where it manifests and accomplishes itself once for all. It is at once judgment and grace, condemnation of sin and justification of sinners.[25]

The Gift of Wisdom. The interior law of love written in hearts (Jeremiah), the effusion of the spirit as principle of moral and religious regeneration and creator of the new Alliance (Ezekiel), saving justice with its human aspect of docility to God (Isaiah II and III), all these themes lead us to the threshold of the New Testament. It seems that Wisdom, the last book of the Old Testament, takes still a further step toward the revelation of the mystery of grace, which is the mystery of God's self-communication to men.

According to the prophets God will give Himself in the messianic future but He will do this by His gifts. They do not suspect that God will give Himself, though perhaps they suggest this obscurely. But the book of Wisdom lets us hear this more clearly, for Wisdom does not merely communicate its gifts, it comes itself into the just.

Wisdom is "nothing less than God Himself communicating Himself to the spiritual creature. By Wisdom God gives creatures a reflection of His beauty[26] and the internal cohesion that makes everything subsist.[27] But to man God communicates Himself in a more intimate way, a way which supposes a welcoming response from the free creature, and thus man enters into participation in the divine nature and its immortality.[28] Wisdom enters into the soul that opens up to it, and renders it lovable to God.[29] It leads it in the ways of service of God to the eternal life of God.[30]

"Here we are at the threshold of the New Testament. St. John and

---

[22] E. Jacob, *Théologie de l'Ancien Testament*, pp. 80–81. [Eng. tr. *Theology of the Old Testament* (London and New York: Herder and Stoughton; Harper and Row, 1958).] Is 45:8; 46:13; 51:5; 54:13–14; 54:17.

[23] Is 59:17; 61:10–11; 62:2.

[24] Is 51:1–7.

[25] J. Guillet, *op. cit.*, p. 91.

[26] Wis 7:22–8:1.

[27] Wis 1:7.

[28] Wis 1:1–15; 2:23.

[29] Wis 9:10–12; 10:16.

[30] Wis 6:9–21; 10.

St. Paul will use the same formulas to tell of the spirit that God sends into the heart of His faithful to make them pleasing in His eyes, and to make charity and all the virtues germinate there. The glory of the Word too will be described in terms borrowed from Wisdom.[31] We must not ask more of our author than he knows: the Trinity is not revealed to him. But he has pushed as far as possible the preparation of the human spirit to receive this revelation."[32]

Prayer. In the prophets the gifts of grace appear especially as benefits of the messianic era, reserved to a far future. . . . But grace in the Old Testament is not only the object of the hopes of the prophets or of the pious reflections of the wise. It is at the center of the piety of the Jewish people, as many prayers of the psalmist show.[33]

The God of the psalms[34] is the almighty God who has created heaven and earth. He is especially the God of the Fathers, of Abraham, of Isaac, and of Jacob, the God of the Alliance. He is the God of kindness, fidelity, tenderness, and love. This is the leitmotif of many prayers of praise and thanksgiving and supplication.

The benefits the faithful ask of God are not merely deliverance from sickness and persecution, from calumny and a premature death. They confess their sins and implore pardon in repentance and confidence.[35] And the gratuity of this gift is sometimes implied, sometimes insisted on expressly.[36] In one of the oldest recitals of the Bible,[37] which relates the adultery of David, the essentials of the doctrine of the prophets and psalms are already apparent: To the sinner who confesses his fault and repents of it, God graciously accords pardon. In many collective or individual supplications for the remission of sins that have been committed, we find formulas expressing the desire to be preserved from sins of word and bad desires,[38] while a certain number of psalms even ask for the grace of perseverance in good[39] and of observance of the law. . . .[40]

[31] Col 1:15; Heb 1:3.

[32] A. Lefevre, *Introduction à la Bible,* 2 ed., p. 770.

[33] Cf. P. Grelot, *Sens chretien de l'Ancien Testament* (Desclée, 1962), p. 141 f.; 151 f.; 159 f.

[34] Pss 33:5, 22; 48:10; 98:2–3; 100:5; 103; cf. 89; 113; 117; 118; 135; 136; 138; 145.

[35] Pss 51:1–6; 12–13; cf. 19:13; 25:7.

[36] Pss 25:11; 79:9; cf. Esdr 9:6 f.; Neh 1:5 f.; 9:16 f.; Dn 9:4 f.

[37] 2 Sam 11 and 12.

[38] Pss 19:14; 141:3–4; Sir 23:1–6.

[39] Ps 51:12.

[40] Pss 25:4–5; 119.

3. F. L. Moriarty, S.J.,[41] touches on some interesting aspects of grace. He points out the utter gratuity of Abraham's election, his deep faith, and his justification by faith, and offers us a glimpse of the economy of grace which begins with Abraham and reaches its climax in the death and resurrection of Christ. In Jeremiah he lets us see the new covenant Yahweh makes with Israel. In it there is the same divine initiative as before, but now the emphasis is not on external precepts but on man's interior renovation and response.

Abraham believed God. When Abram was ninety-nine years old, Yahweh appeared to him and said, "I am God Almighty. Walk in My presence and be perfect. And I will make My covenant between Me and you, and will multiply you exceedingly." Then Abram fell prostrate, and God said to him, "This is My covenant with you; you shall be the father of a multitude of nations. You shall no longer be called Abram, but your name shall be Abraham; for I have made you the father of a multitude of nations. . . ."[42]

In this excerpt from the sacerdotal tradition there is an almost monotonous insistence on the divine election of Israel. No less than thirteen times in this chapter the word "covenant" occurs and the writer is telling us that God was binding Himself to Abraham at the same time that He made the Patriarch an instrument of His designs for mankind. Abraham could only dimly grasp the ultimate meaning of this covenant and the promises. Sufficient to believe that God would accomplish them.

There will be more to say about the covenant when we consider the place of Moses in Israel's history. In general it can be said that the covenant is a dominant idea in the story of God's dealing with man, and the free selection of Abraham rather than anyone else underlines the truth that God is not subservient to any established pattern in His action but sovereignly free in His election. Another expression of the promises to Abraham is found in a brief passage: "In blessing I will indeed bless you and multiply your descendants like the stars of heaven and the sands on the seashore. Your descendants will possess the gate of their enemies."[43] The divine liberality stands out in every phrase. The promises are the gift of God, not a payment for fulfilling legal obligations. If the promises had depended on observance of the Law, faith would have little meaning. . . .

[41] F. L. Moriarty, S.J., was born in 1913. He received his L.SS. from the Pontifical Biblical Institute of Rome in 1949. He has contributed articles to *Theological Studies, America, Catholic Biblical Quarterly,* and is also the author of *The Book of Numbers.* It is from his book, *Introducing the Old Testament,* that this excerpt has been taken, selectively, from pp. 16–18, 153–155. The book was published by The Bruce Publishing Company of Milwaukee in 1960.

[42] Gn. 17:1–5.

[43] Gn. 22:17.

No one has insisted on the gratuity of Abraham's election more than St. Paul. The Apostle recognized in the call of Abraham the beginning of the history of salvation. Inchoatively, at least, the great patriarchal figure heard the "Good News," and he was not only justified by his belief in the promises but that faith made him the prototype of all those who believe, the "Father of the Faithful." In two of his Epistles, to the Romans and the Galatians, Paul draws out the continuities between the believing Abraham and the Christian who is justified by faith and not by the works of the Law. Man's right relation with God is not based on his own goodness and accomplishments; it is based on God's goodness and is His achievement. This is an economy of grace which begins with Abraham and reaches its climax in the death and resurrection of Christ. Such an economy manifests the unity of God's design, its universality, and the continuity of the divine action in history. It is only in the New Testament, the time of fulfillment, that the grandeur of Abraham becomes most apparent. He has become the point of departure for the Pauline doctrine of justification; his faith is seen as a total adherence to a Person and not as a purely intellectual assent. What was asked of Abraham — that he walk before God and be perfect — is asked of the Christian who would be a true heir of the promises made to our Father. Obedience to law in a spirit of empty legalism does not satisfy the demands of God. What God desires is that inner integrity, an epitome of

virtues, not the least of which is the humble acknowledgment of our own nothingness apart from Him. The man of faith is the true Israelite called to live, not under the constraint of law, but in the liberty of a Christian.

Jeremiah. In the vision of the New Covenant, Jeremiah reached the climax of his teaching: "Behold the days are coming," says Yahweh, "when I will make a new covenant with the house of Israel and the house of Judah. Not like the covenant which I made with their fathers. . . . But this is the covenant which I will make with the house of Israel after those days," says Yahweh. "I will put My law within them, and I will write it upon their hearts; and I will be their God, and they will be My people."[44]

A bridge between the two covenants is constructed in this passage. It is not a prophecy that the Law of Sinai will be repudiated, but rather that new means will be given to fulfill the Law once given. The covenant relation is not ruptured, but brought to a higher level of perfection. For, under the New Covenant, the grace of God, as contrasted with external precepts carved on the tablets of the Law, will act directly on the mind and heart of man, bringing him into a more perfect and interior relation to the will of God. In both the Covenant of Sinai and the New Covenant God takes the initiative, but there is advance in several directions.

The inward character of the new relation is expressed by the phrase, "I will put My Law within them, and

---

[44] Jer 31:31–34.

I will write it upon their hearts." Good and evil are rooted in the heart of man. Just as a man's sin involves more than an external act of disobedience, as Jeremiah recognized so well, so his union with God involves more than an external conformity to law in a spirit of pure legalism. Jeremiah knew well, from personal observation of Josiah's reform, how impossible it was to legislate men into a proper relation with God. The prophet envisaged an interior transformation of man, not unlike the regeneration which is so prominent in the doctrine of St. John. This transformation was not to be the work of man but a mystery of grace which enables a man, through self-renunciation, suffering, and obedience, to share in the very life of God. The optimism of Jeremiah was grounded on his faith in God and God's fidelity to the promises made long ago; he had no illusions about his country's natural capacity to bring about a spiritual reform. A corollary of this interior renovation would be the personal response of the individual who would do God's will by a spontaneous surrender of his heart to the promptings of God's grace. Here was a foreshadowing of that Christian liberty which has replaced the service of a slave with the freedom of God's children, living under the New Covenant of grace.

It would be a mistake to conclude, from Jeremiah's emphasis on a personal relation to God, that he was concerned exclusively with the individual or that he should be called "the father of individualism." Aside from the fact that the individual, as a responsible

agent, appears in some of the earliest sections of the Old Testament, notably in the Ten Commandments with their categoric "thou shalt," we should not forget that Jeremiah set his vision of the future in the context of a community, the New Israel. Individualism and collectivism were nicely balanced in the thought of Jeremiah, and one should not be stressed to the exclusion of the other. The personal, individual elements were there, notably in the promised "knowledge of Yahweh."[45] They were present as well in the promised "forgiveness of sins," but in the age of the New Covenant men were still to remember that they were members of a community and that it was through life in a community that they were to be saved. Excessive individualism has no place in either the Old or the New Testaments. The failure of his own people to make return of Yahweh's love tore at the heart of Jeremiah. But if the original community had shut its eyes to its true vocation, Yahweh could still create a New Israel with which He would enter into a New Covenant.

The Church has, from the beginning, seen the fulfillment of this vision in that solemn scene in the Upper Room when Christ told His Apostles that the New Covenant was being inaugurated in the blood He was

[45] This "knowledge," which appears frequently in the Old Testament, is a dynamic thing which combines intellectual apprehension of the truth with the fulfillment of God's commands. It embraces much more than what we are accustomed to associate with the term. To know God is, above all, to do His will.

about to shed for the redemption of all men. Through the blood of Christ would come forgiveness, extended to the whole race of men, a New Law inscribed in the heart of man, and an outpouring of grace through which men could know God in all the richness of that biblical word.

4. **H. Wheeler Robinson**[46] **studies grace and repentance in the Old Testament. If we take** *hesed* **as best denoting the deep-seated relation of God to Israel, which it is His "righteousness" to carry into effect, we are at once pointed to "repentance" as the corresponding attitude in man, which it is the purpose of God's** *hesed* **to arouse and maintain.**

Grace and repentance. If we were analysing the conception of God for its own sake, rather than His characteristic interrelation with man, we should naturally be led for one member of our contrast to His "righteousness," as denoting the moralization of the concept of holiness through the great prophets and most explicitly through Isaiah. His teaching in this respect is epitomized in the words:

Yahweh Zebaoth is exalted in judgment (*mišpat*),
And the holy God shows Himself holy[47] in righteousness (*zedakah*) (5:16).

The Hebrew word translated "righteousness" is, however, chiefly forensic in its primary associations, and had to share in the same process of prophetic moralization as the term "holiness." As Robertson Smith says:[48]

the Hebrew always thought of the right and the wrong as if they were to be settled before a judge. Righteousness is to the Hebrew not so much a moral quality as a legal status.

Probably Kautzsch is correct in deriving the term from the fundamental idea of conformity to a norm, an idea developed in the juristic, ethical, and theocratic realism. We need something more positive and intimate to characterize the interrelation of God and man than the implication of "righteousness" that He will conform to the true standard of that relation. Now the outstanding word to describe its content rather than its form is *hesed,* which when ascribed to God may often be rendered "grace" rather than "loving-kindness" or "mercy." But even the rendering "grace" does not suggest the element of loyalty, of moral obligation, of social bond, which the Hebrew word includes, an element finding parallel expression in the quite

---

[46] H. Wheeler Robinson, D.D., late principal emeritus of Regent's Park College, Oxford, and speaker's lecturer at the University of Oxford. This excerpt is from his book, *Inspiration and Revelation in the Old Testament* (Oxford Paperbacks, Oxford at the Clarendon Press, 1962), pp. 57–61.

[47] The verb is from the same root as "holy" and in the reflexive form. R.V. "sanctified" obscures the point of the phrase.

[48] *The Prophets of Israel*, p. 71.

different word translated "redeemer," properly kinsman-vindicator.[49] The root-meaning of *hesed* is brought out very effectively in the Arabic equivalent, which means promptitude to help, or, as a verb, "to gather with a view to help."[50] Thus in Hosea 2:19, 20 (Hebrew text 2:21, 22), where the prophet is characterizing Yahweh's future and lasting betrothal to Israel, its qualities are given as those of righteousness, justice, grace, compassion, and fidelity. The spontaneous character of Yahweh's grace, which springs from His deep-seated loyalty to Israel, is seen in Jeremiah's striking anticipation of the parable of the Prodigal Son:

The people found favour[51] in the
    desert —
A people escaped from the sword.
While Israel marched to his rest,
From afar did Yahweh appear.
"With a love from of old I love
    thee;
Therefore in *hesed* I draw thee"
    (31:2, 3).

In the parable the penitent son is already returning, "But while he was yet afar off, his father saw him, and was moved with compassion and ran and fell on his neck and kissed him."[52] The spontaneous loyalty of the father to his son is even more marked in the

prophecy than in the parable, for there God takes the initiative.

If, then, we take *hesed* as best denoting the deep-seated relation of God to Israel, which it is His "righteousness" to carry into effect, we are at once pointed to "repentance" as the corresponding attitude in man, which it is the purpose of God's *hesed* to arouse and maintain. The fundamental idea of "repentance" in the Old Testament is expressed by the verb *šub* which means to "turn" or "return." It is unfortunate that the Authorized and Revised Versions should have used the term "repent" in a now archaistic sense, to express regret or sorrow without any moral connotation, as when we read that "it repented the Lord that he had made man on the earth, and it grieved him at his heart."[53] Here and elsewhere, "repent" renders another Hebrew word meaning "be troubled";[54] but we are concerned with the verb rendered "turn"[55] or "return"[56] in repentance. This occurs very frequently, although it is actually rendered "repent" only three times in our Authorized Version[57] and even these three disappear in favour of "turn again" or

---

[49] Jb 19:25; Pss 19:14, 78:35; Prv 23:11; Is 41:14.

[50] Kazimirski, *Dictionnaire Arabe-Francais*, I, p. 549. Robertson Smith, *The Prophets of Israel*, p. 408.

[51] Skinner, whose translation in *Prophecy and Religion*, p. 300, is here followed, renders *hēn*, a related term, by "grace," and *hesed* by "kindness."

[52] Lk 15:20.

[53] Gn 6:6.

[54] *Naham*, apparently connected with an Arabic root having the fundamental meaning "breathe heavily" (Cf. Kazimirski, IV, p. 468, "groan deeply" as under a heavy burden). Hence the two apparently inconsistent meanings of the root in Hebrew, viz., "be grieved" and "be comforted," i.e., draw a deep breath either of distress or of relief (so König, *Heb. Wörterbuch*, s.v.).

[55] E.g., 2 Kg 17:13: "Turn ye from your evil ways."

[56] E.g., Dt 1:45: "Ye returned and wept before Yahweh."

[57] 1 Kg 8:47; Ez 14:6; 18:30.

"return" in the Revised. It may seem a little curious that there is no corresponding noun in the Old Testament with the meaning "repentance"; the derived word *tešubah,* so frequent and important in later Judaism,[58] has not yet acquired that meaning. We may see in the use of the verb a characteristic emphasis on action, the volitional emphasis of Hebrew morality, which clings to the verb "turn" in preference to an abstract noun.[59] Repentance does not mean simply the passive state of being sorry about sin (or its consequences); it denotes a positive turning away from it with new resolution and direction. This, of course, is the ultimate demand made by the prophets, even when they are simply announcing a divine judgment on sin. We think of Amos as the outstanding prophet of judgment and little else; yet we find as the repeated refrain to one of his utterances which reviews the disciplinary judgments of God, "Yet ye have not returned unto me, saith Yahweh."[60] Such judgments and such warning were already an exhibition of grace apart from Yahweh's *hesed;* why should He trouble any more with a rebellious people, or raise up prophets at all? But the grace which was for the most part implicit in pre-exilic prophecy[61] became explicit in the religion of the exilic[62] and post-exilic periods,[63] and repentance becomes more definitely the proper response to that grace, as sin now becomes the churlish refusal of it. The ultimate definition of sin is always in terms of grace.

The *locus classicus* for repentance is the 51st psalm. Here we find the appeal from the inevitable frailty of flesh, prone to sin, to the Holy Spirit of God, thus incorporating our two previous antitheses of Spirit and flesh, Holiness and sin. But the psalmist reaches a new level of insight in his conceptions of grace and repentance. Doubtless he would not have been able to realize the grace of forgiveness without the removal of the physical penalty for sin, as we may see from the words, "that the bones which thou hast broken may rejoice." But his repentance is moral and spiritual, and his appeal for forgiveness is primarily to the *hesed* of God, and not to his own merits or to ritual sacrifices. So he begins:

> Be gracious unto me, O God, according to thy *hesed.*

He also reaches the profound truth that man's relation to God must be initiated by God Himself:

> Create in me a clean heart, O God,
> And renew a right spirit within me.

That is the thought of Jeremiah's "new covenant" of God with Israel, in which God will write His *torah* on the hearts of individual Israelites;[64] it

---

[58] Cf. Moore, *Judaism,* i, p. 507 ff.

[59] LXX regularly translates by *èpistréphein,* but in later Jewish writers and translators we find *metanoein,* "giving a somewhat different turn of meaning to an established idea" (Dodd, *The Bible and the Greeks,* p. 181).

[60] Am 4:6, 8, 9, 10, 11.

[61] It becomes explicit in Hos 14, which can claim to be a genuine outcome of his personal experience.

[62] E.g., Is 43:25.

[63] E.g., Ps 103:3, 4, 8 ff.

[64] Jer 31:33

is also the thought of Ezekiel's more drastic remedy for sin:

A new heart will I give you
and a new spirit will I put within
you (36:26).

The significant thing here is that grace and repentance are not separate abstractions; they are unified in the living experience of the penitent believer, which overcomes the sharp antithesis of holiness and sin by its transformation of both. It is this inwardness of the new relation which characterizes the higher levels of Israel's religion, and enables us to understand something of the height to which the close of the 73rd psalm reaches — the Old Testament equivalent to the close of Romans 8 — or the paradox of the Shema' in Deuteronomy 6 when the impossible command to love God is made possible by the disclosure of a God whom to know is to love, since He is a Redeemer. By the same inwardness, the apparent externalism of Torah-religion was transcended for the devout Jew, the Jew who learnt to say, "Thy statutes have become my songs in the house of my pilgrimage."[65] Obedience and the routine which directs it and trains for it must have its essential place in every religion that outlives its early enthusiasms. But its fulfillment is reached only in the love that finds its perfect freedom in service.

[65] Ps 119:54.

II

GRACE IN THE NEW TESTAMENT – SYNOPTICS

1. T. F. Torrance[1] considers grace in the New Testament as the most characteristic element of the Christian Gospel. The intervention of God in the world out of sheer love and His personal presence to men through Jesus Christ are held together in the one thought of grace. Torrance sees in the Gospels not grace in the abstract but in concrete manifestations in the person and work of Christ, so that grace is identical with Jesus Christ in person and word and deed. This he finds normative to all New Testament doctrine.

GRACE in the New Testament is the basic and the most characteristic element of the Christian Gospel. It is the breaking into the world of the ineffable love of God in a deed of absolutely decisive significance which

[1] Ch. I, n. 1. This excerpt is from *op. cit.*, pp. 34–35, 20–26.

cuts across the whole of human life and sets it on a new basis. That is actualised in the person of Jesus Christ, with which grace is inseparably associated, and [is] supremely exhibited on the Cross by which the believer is once and for all put in the right with God. This intervention of God in the world and its sin, out of sheer love, and His personal presence to men through Jesus Christ are held together in the one thought of grace. As such grace is the all-comprehensive and constant presupposition of faith, which, while giving rise to an intensely personal life in the Spirit, necessarily assumes a charismatic and eschatological character.

Under the gracious impingement of Christ through the Spirit there is a glad spontaneity about the New Testament believer. He is not really concerned to ask questions about ethical practice. He acts before questions can be asked. He is caught up in the overwhelming love of Christ, and is concerned only about doing His will. There is no anxious concern about the past. It is Christ that died! There is no anxious striving toward an ideal. It is Christ that rose again! In Him all the Christian's hopes are centred. His life is hid with Christ in God. In Him a new order of things has come into being, by which the old is set aside. Everything therefore is seen in Christ, in the light of the end, toward which the whole creation groaneth and travaileth waiting for redemption. The great act of salvation has already taken place in Christ and has become an eternal indicative. The other side of faith is grace, the immediate act of God in Christ, and because He is the persistent Subject of all Christian life and thought, faith stands necessarily on the threshold of the new world, with the intense consciousness of the advent of Christ. The charismatic and the eschatological aspects of faith are really one. In Christ the Eternal God has entered into this present evil world which shall in due course pass away before the full unveiling of the glory of God. . . . Throughout all this the predominating thought is grace, the presence of the amazing love of God in Christ, which has unaccountably overtaken the believer and set him in a completely new world which is also the eternal Kingdom of God. . . .

We do not meet with *charis* in its distinctive New Testament sense in the Synoptic Gospels. St. Luke does use the actual word some eight times, but in each case it may be interpreted adequately in accordance with contemporary usage.[2] In the fourth Gospel it occurs three times in the prologue where the significance is strongly coloured both by the Old Testament and by "Pauline thought." . . . Grace is received on the ground of sheer grace, whereas one might have expected, in continuity with earlier and current Jewish thought, it would be on the ground of conformity to Law.

Though it is not recorded that Christ Himself ever spoke of grace, it

---

[2] Lk 1:30; 2:40, 52; 4:22; 6:32, 33, 34; 17:9. The only possible exception is 4.22 to which the Lucan use of *charis* in Acts 14:3; 20:24, appears to lend a Pauline coloring.

is quite clear, as the prologue to St. John's Gospel indicates, that Christ who was "full of grace" was in His own person the source of the whole conception. In this sense, too, the teaching of Christ is full of grace, and out of that fullness has the rest of the New Testament received. It is upon the person and the work of Christ, therefore, that emphasis must be laid in any account of grace in the Gospels. It matters little that the word *charis* in its significant sense is wanting, for there it is not in the abstract that we encounter grace, but in concrete manifestation: in the glad spontaneous fashion in which our Lord received sinners as in the instances of Matthew and Zaccheus, of the sinful woman in Simon's house and the woman brought before Him to be stoned, freely forgiving them; and in the eager compassion in which He healed the sick and suffering, as in His constant demand for mercy and forgiveness among men because of the love of God. Quite as compelling in presenting the features of grace is His teaching on the merciful and forgiving love of God, especially in parables such as the lost coin, the lost sheep, the lost son, the labourers in the vineyard, or the good Samaritan.

All this might well be put under two main points: (1) God's love is bestowed spontaneously and freely, and is not evoked by anything in His creatures. Indeed God's love has all its reason within Himself. It is its own motive. . . . Such initiative in the divine love completely takes man by surprise. God is among men with redemptive purpose before they are aware of it.[3]

Another important element here is that before the unconditioned will of God for men's redemption the notion of merit disappears. Indeed the Gospel as Christ proclaims it is directed to the very folk who, it might appear, have the least right to expect it. That is evident, for example, in the Beatitudes,[4] but also in the attention Christ persisted in directing throughout His ministry to demerit: "They that are whole need not a Physician, but they that are sick. . . . I am not come to call the righteous, but sinners to repentance."[5] . . . All notions of human achievement, of having claims on God, or of bargaining with God, and of self-esteem are ruled out of the Kingdom where God deals with men only on the basis of His astonishing generosity. . . .

However, though the love of God is not conditioned by merit or demerit that does not mean that it is arbitrary or capricious in any way, that God is not concerned whether the objects of His love are good or bad, for the love of God as Jesus proclaims it is essentially holy love,[6] and therefore, though He never bribes nor bargains with men, Christ does give reward and punishment a real place in the Kingdom.[7]

---

[3] Mt 24:42 f.; 25:6; Lk 12:39 f.; 17:21; Mk 13:33 f.

[4] Mt 5:1 f.; Lk 6:20 f.

[5] Mt 9:12, 13, etc.

[6] See H. R. Mackintosh, *The Christian Apprehension of God*, 183 ff.

[7] Mt 6:19 f.; 10:41 f.; 10:28; Mk 10:21; etc.

That is apparent when Jesus tells His disciples what is laid up for them in reward,[8] but He makes it very clear, when they, and in particular the two sons of Zebedee, misunderstand Him, that the reward is not a question of merit but of the good will of God,[9] and that in the Kingdom of God the standards of men are quite reversed: humility and service displace competition and achievement. It is interesting to note that here as at the Last Supper our Lord directly bases this teaching on humility on His own self-surrender to the point of death which cuts across all human distinctions and makes all men alike. Following Him the disciples are to give themselves to others in service, not seeking to be ministered unto, that is, not seeking reward. This means that Christ holds to the conceptions of reward and punishment precisely because of grace which is so absolute that, with all legal ground and human claims forfeit, man is thrown into a position of real responsibility. Therefore His demand for obedience (including ideas of reward and punishment) is always set in the context of grace. . . .

(2) The second main point in the Gospel about grace is that Christ definitely identified the gracious and decisive movement of God for the redemption of men with His own person. In Him the grace of God became evident and confronted men as a *fait accompli*. That is everywhere apparent in His life and teaching, though it is particularly clear in the incident at Nazareth, where, after reading from the book of the prophet Isaiah of "the acceptable year of the Lord," He said, "Today this scripture has been fulfilled in your hearing. . . . " "And all spoke well of him and wondered at the gracious words which proceeded out of his mouth."[10] . . .

The astonishing thing to so many of His contemporaries was that Jesus spoke with such power, for His word was deed, and His deed was word. Thus Jesus deliberately confronted men with His own person as being identical with the Word of God.[11] It is this identification of the grace of God in word and action with His own person and action that is so highly significant, for that became normative to all New Testament doctrine. Furthermore, as in the rest of the New Testament this is particularly related on the lips of Jesus to His own death and resurrection as of divine redemptive significance for men. Again and again Jesus related the will of God for men's salvation to His passion, especially at the Last Supper, though it was only after the event that this action was seen by the utterly astonished disciples to be identified with the pure grace of God. In Christ's death and resurrection they realised that God had given Himself fully to them in spite of their sin and quite independently of human efforts or plans. It made clear once for all that the saving initiative was absolutely with God. It was therefore impossible for man to approach God or face Him

---

[8] Mt 19:28; cf. 21.
[9] Mt 20:23, etc.

[10] Lk 4:16–37.
[11] Lk 24:19. Cf. Acts 1:1; 2:2; 10:36–38.

on the ground of achievement or merit or in the hope of reward. The whole basis of religion was altered — men now approached God because in Christ He had committed Himself to them, and was already among them forgiving and saving. It was in the resurrection of Christ, as Jesus Himself foresaw, and as all the evangelists make clear, that the grace of God broke in upon the mind and heart of the disciples, so that they understood that in the cross and resurrection of Christ the amazing deed of God in holy love was a creative act which invaded human flesh and blood, transforming it and filling it with spiritual power.[12] It was, as they came to say, "The grace of the Lord Jesus Christ and the love of God and the communion of the Holy Spirit."

2. **William Manson[13] considers** charis **in classical usage, in the Septuagint and Philo, and in the Greek speech of the first century as background for the Christian adoption of the term. He thinks the term might not have been adopted apart from certain potentialities it was developing before and during the first age of Christianity.**

"Grace" (charis) represents the central and fundamental conception of the Christian religion of the New Testament. The word is used in the New Testament writings upwards of 150 times, and of these occurrences no fewer than 100 are in the Epistles of St. Paul. In the Gospels the term is extraordinarily infrequent. Instances occur as follows: St. Matthew: 0; St. Mark: 0; St. Luke: 8; St. John: 3.

None of the eight examples in Luke shows charis in its distinctive New Testament sense.

In later times consideration of the nature and necessity of grace gave rise to deep and serious cleavages in Christian doctrine. These differences, though cutting deeply into contemporary theology, did not always extend downwards to the rock-floor of the New Testament. But even in the New Testament certain unevennesses, indicative of minor divergencies of thought, are found emerging. Primarily an expression for the generous love of God to man by which salvation is constituted and the era of redemption opened, "grace" acquires a relation also to the spiritual life of Christians, and is conceived as working in immanent fashion in the Christian nature, in the gifts and for the offices with which Christians are endued.

---

[12] Cf. J. Moffat, Grace in the New Testament, p. 91: "Grace is a meaningless word apart from the resurrection." See also pp. 82, 87, 89, 95.

[13] Rev. William Manson, D.D., was born in 1882. He was professor of biblical criticism at the University of Edinburgh, 1946–1952. Among the many works he published are: Christ's View of the Kingdom of God, Jesus the Messiah, The Epistle to the Hebrews. This excerpt is taken from his article, "Grace in the New Testament," in The Doctrine of Grace, ed. W. T. Whitley (SCM Press, London, 1931), pp. 33–40.

The Christian adoption of the term — whether by St. Paul or by the pre-Pauline Church — involved a high ennoblement and extension of the Greek word *charis*. This becomes evident when regard is had to the previous philological history of the term.

"Charis" in classical usage. *Charis* in classical Greek has as its original sense "beauty," "attractiveness," "loveliness," literally, "that which delights or charms." In this sense the word occurs from Homer downwards with reference to beauty of person or to charm and winsomeness of speech.[14] Thence, by an interiorising process which is a regular feature in the history of language, *charis* acquires the sense, secondly, of "that which is attractive in disposition or character," therefore "favour," "goodwill," "graciousness." Hence — again by a natural transition — it designates, thirdly, an objective mark of favour, i.e., "a boon conferred," "a kindness done." Finally, since it is of the nature of such favours to evoke a response, *charis* becomes equivalent to "gratitude" or "thankfulness."

None of these senses of the term is unrepresented in the New Testament. At the same time none of them explains the religious force which the word has acquired on Christian lips. One reason of this is that nothing in Hellenic religion answered to, or anticipated, the Christian sense of the goodness of God to men. The Hellenic mind might believe in propitiating the gods, averting their wrath, and earning their favour — its principle was, indeed, *Do ut des* — but Hellenic reason rejected the idea that God could love man with a love equalling, not to say excelling, man's love to God. "It would be absurd," says a writer of the Aristotelian school, "to accuse God because the love one receives in return from Him is not equal to the love given to Him."[15] . . . The Platonic Socrates prays to the gods that he may be made beautiful "in the inward parts,"[16] and a Stoic in Cicero asserts that "No man ever became great without some Divine afflatus."[17] But such sayings, though common enough, are very far from basing Greek religion on such a conception of supernatural grace as we find in the New Testament. Seneca's *"Sacer intra nos spiritus sedet"*[18] is not equivalent to any statement of St. Paul regarding the Holy Spirit.

"Charis" in the Septuagint and in Philo. Many of the classical words adopted by Christianity for its self-expression had passed through an intermediate stage of development in the Septuagint, where they had been wedded to Hebrew and Jewish religious ideas. But in the general development of language thus marked by the Septuagint, *charis* has but little share. One special capacity indeed the word acquired in its Septuagintal use, and that was that now for the first time it came into relation to the Divine Being through being applied to His

---

[14] E.g., *Odyssey* VI, 235; VIII, 175.

[15] *Eudemian Ethics*, 1238B.
[16] *Phaedrus*, 279B.
[17] *De Nat. Deor.*, II, 66.
[18] Seneca, *Ep.*, xli, 2.

favour and to the blessedness which that favour imports. But *charis* never in the LXX attains the constitutive fundamental sense which it bears in the New Testament. While the mercy of God is a constitutive part of the Old Testament religion, while God is revealed as "merciful and compassionate, patient, and very pitiful, and true,"[19] this mercy or loving-kindness is nowhere expressed by *charis*. The latter in the LXX answers to the Hebrew *ḥēn,* which means "favourable regard," "inclination to favour." It occurs mostly in the phrase "to find favour," and therefore scarcely takes us beyond the circle of an Oriental sultan's court where suppliants wait for concessions from the monarch's will. The mercy or *ḥesed* of God is in the LXX rendered not by *charis* but by *eleos.*

As an indication of the relative insignificance of the first of these terms in the religious vocabulary of the LXX we have the fact that, though the Psalms abound in experiences of what we would call the grace of God, the word *charis* occurs only twice, and then merely with reference to grace of speech or other outward excellence,[20] while in Isaiah and Jeremiah the word does not occur at all!

In Philo and other Jewish religious writers the word plays no distinctive part. Philo indeed uses *charis,* chiefly in the plural, to signify Divine gifts or bounties. But these are conceived regularly on the natural plane of life. They are indeed none other than the ordinary constituents of the Greek conception of well-being. God, the Maker and Father of all, gives to men sight, hearing, health, earth, air, water, fire, etc. which are all "gifts" of His, or "charities." Moreover, Philo tends to the view that these bounties are conditioned by human merit; at any rate, when sin came into the world, "the ever-flowing springs of the favour of God were stayed, when evil began to prosper above the virtues."[21]

Not even the higher conception of the Divine *ḥesed* or mercy is able in Judaism to achieve the place occupied by *charis* in Christianity. While the gracious love of God to men had been the real foundation of the prophetic religion of the Old Testament, particularly in Hosea, in Jeremiah, and in 2 Isaiah, it has to be noticed that even there the salvation of God was based not upon *charis* but upon the sovereign power and glory of God, upon His "righteousness," or "judgment," or "torah." In post-prophetic Judaism, where religion was hardening into legalism, the relations of God and men were regulated ordinarily upon a basis of merit and reward. Men kept the Law of God, and so earned the favour of God. The mercy of God was at best subsidiary, a supplement to His justice, a reserve of goodness available for such as, striving to satisfy the demands of righteousness, had fallen short of that end.[22]

[19] Ex 34:6.
[20] Pss 45:2; 84:11.
[21] *De Mund. Opif.,* 168.
[22] Cf. R. Bultmann, *Jesus,* p. 137: in Judaism: "ist der Gedanke der Gnade Gottes nicht radikal gedacht: denn Gottes Gnade erscheint hier als freundliches Übersehen der Sünden, als in Gegensatz stehend

Something outside of Judaism proper, then, is necessary to explain the central and fundamental significance of "Grace" in Christianity, and this something is the Christian *experience* of redemption. This Christian experience in Paul and others called for a new medium of expression, a new Christian linguistic. Yet even here the term *charis* might not have been adopted apart from certain potentialities which the word was developing before and during the first age of Christianity.

"Charis" in the Greek speech of the first century. In the . . . treatise of G. P. Wetter,[23] and also in the article on *charis* in the Moulton-Milligan *Vocabulary of the Greek New Testament* will be found evidence from Imperial inscriptions of the first century which reveals better than any other material at our disposal the kind of potentialities which the term *charis* had developed in the age of St. Paul. *Charis* in these inscriptions constantly designates the imperial favour as shown in some deed of gift or benefaction bestowed on some city or community, and in many of these cases, as Wetter points out, the favour is magnified by the addition of such epithets as "divine" or "immortal" or "godlike" or "eternal." Indeed the language of such inscriptions often bears an extraordinarily close resemblance to that in which St. Paul praises the

riches of the Divine "grace.". . . Such uses of the term approach with remarkable closeness the sense borne by *charis* in the Christian vocabulary, all the more because of the epithets "divine," "eternal," "immortal" which are so often conjoined with it.

It would seem reasonable, therefore, with Wetter to regard this style – a style which merely extends a current Greek signification of the term – as supplying the linguistic starting-point for the Christian use of *charis*. "Grace" on Christian lips will be primarily the "gift" or "benefaction" of God to man, the generous favour by which the Supreme Being makes men recipients of His salvation. The expression registers not simply a will to give but a deed of gift, not only an attitude of favour but an outflowing of favour in largess, not a mere benevolence towards men or cities or states, but an enriching of them with real blessings. For St. Paul it means the whole self-giving of God to men in Jesus Christ.

But attention should be called to a second and different significance which the same term *charis* was acquiring in the New Testament age. In religious and mystical circles in the Hellenistic world *charis* was sometimes charged with the sense of "charm," "magic potency," "mystic power." In such a sense it is found in some of the magical papyri which have recently come into our possession[24] where *charis* appears in company with "dynamis," "nike," "pneuma," "tyche," and "praxis" as one of the forms under which supernatural or demonic agency

zu seiner Gerechtigkeit." ("The idea of God's grace is not radically thought out: since God's grace appears here as a friendly overlooking of sins standing in opposition to his righteousness.")

[23] *Charis*, pp. 15–19.

[24] Cf. Wetter, *op. cit.*, pp. 130–137.

or help was invoked. Wetter does not contend that *charis* in a *magical* sense would have appealed to any Christian writer, but he supposes that the debased sense which the term bears in magical circles points to a *higher* mystical or religious sense which it possessed in other circles, and he considers that this higher sense may have commended it in Christian quarters. Whether, however, *charis* bears such a sense anywhere in the New Testament seems to the present writer very doubtful. The meaning "power" or "potency" is in any case not to be derived from the older Greek signification of the term but marks a new development.

3. P. G. Stevens, O.S.B.,[25] sees our life of grace depicted in the Synoptic Gospels as one of sonship in the kingdom of the Father that is established in and through Christ for the salvation of men. This kingdom is the central point of the gospel message. It is a reality always associated with the inner transformation of grace. To enter it men must be reborn in faith and baptism into a new life so as to become in a new and radical way sons of the Father in union with Christ.

Grace: the kingdom of the Father. The synoptic gospels present the reality of a loving Father in heaven. . . . Christ calls God His Father, but also directs us to see God as "our Father."[26] The essential feature of the reign of grace is a filial spirit in which through the mediation of Christ we address the sovereign God as truly a loving Father to us. Our life of grace is one of sonship: "Be children of your Father in Heaven."[27] It is because of the power and efficacy of the Father's love and forgiveness that the Christian is not only freed from sin but is welcomed into his Father's home. There he is a son who partakes of the joy, the peace, and the blessedness which the Father bestows in the kingdom of His only-begotten Son.

This kingdom is the central point of the message of the synoptic gospels. . . . It is established in Christ, but is meant to be spread to the hearts of all men in all ages. . . . This kingdom or reign is not primarily one in heaven but is something established here on earth by Christ.

The individual's relationship to Christ. Membership in the kingdom is determined by the relationship of the individual to Christ. "He who would save his life will lose it; but he who loses his life for *my sake* and for the sake of the gospel will save it."[28] Even if we must await the second coming of Christ for the glorious mani-

---

[25] P. Gregory Stevens, O.S.B., is professor of religious education at the Catholic University of America, and of moral theology at St. Anselm's Priory. This excerpt was taken from his book, *The Life of Grace* (Prentice-Hall, Inc., 1963), pp. 2–8.

[26] Mt 6:9, 15.

[27] Mt 5:45.

[28] Mk 8:35.

festation of this kingdom, the decisive age has arrived in this life; the Church is the present organ of the Father's glorious rule. Her life, the life of faith and grace, is hidden, though it contains the seeds of glory. It is God acting in Christ who has established this kingdom. Man entering the kingdom must always be aware of this primacy of the divine initiative. . . . This does not mean that the members of the kingdom are incapable of life and action but that a new life and activity enables them to share in Christ's work of establishing His kingdom. Only then can they achieve the destiny of being fully sons of the heavenly Father.

The individual's relationship to the Father. In preaching the kingdom, Jesus makes clear that the basic reality underlying it is God's fatherhood. The frequent designation of God as Father[29] is a way of presenting to us the secret of God's action toward us in the order of salvation: *God is a Father who wishes us to become by grace His sons.* . . . God is the Father of all men, but there is a sense in which men must *become,* must change into sons. To accomplish this change they are invited to enter into the kingdom[30] . . . for not all men are inheritors of the kingdom. Although God is the Father of all, not all have answered His call to the kingdom. The members of the kingdom have received God's distinctive vocation and have responded by fidelity in a childlike disposition. They have thereby ob-

tained the newness of life as sons. Only those who have been called to be sons and who have renounced the obstacle of sin can enter into this kingdom of grace. The quality of son pertains first and in a unique way to Christ, the beloved Son. Through Him it is extended to the members of the kingdom in a real process of filiation and adoption.

A new life and faith. To receive Christ is to receive the kingdom, and this involves a certain inner disposition of heart. Man's receiving of the kingdom means welcoming a person, Christ,[31] as well as receiving a message,[32] the gospel of grace. . . . The effect of grace is to assure to man all that can fulfil him: salvation and beatitude. The grace of life in the kingdom is none other than the gift of salvation. . . .

The inner reality of grace and the kingdom is thus incorporated into the external and visible organization of the Church, a society which has the spiritual goods of grace at its disposition. The life of grace is never a purely internal or purely individual reality. It is by its very structure the grace and kingdom of Christ established in this world on the foundation of the apostles. The kingdom begins with Jesus. To its establishment all His work is directed. . . .

This doctrine — the kingdom which is the gospel — is received in faith. Those who profess this faith are united in a single society which is the Church,

---

[29] Cf. Mt 5:16, 45, 48; 6:1, 4, 6, 8 f.; 7:11, 21.
[30] Mt 5:45.

[31] Mk 9:37.
[32] Lk 8:13.

the Israel of God founded on Peter.[33] Into this kingdom all men are invited with divine insistence,[34] even to the eleventh hour.[35] The same recompense of grace is offered to all who answer the call of Christ. The kingdom is at once personal and social. Each man must enter it on his own account and live a personal life of justice, seeking at the same time that holy community which is the kingdom of God.[36]

God gives the aid of His grace to those who have been given the first grace of entrance into the kingdom.[37] The kingdom is thus a totally gratuitous gift; it is also a task or burden to be carried. All the works, the good deeds and activities of the kingdom are from God;[38] cooperation with His grace brings the reward of new graces.[39]

In Jesus and through Him, therefore, is established the new and eternal rule of God which is a new covenant of the Father with the men who become brothers of Christ and truly sons of God. The whole purpose of the establishment of the kingdom is to institute a new order of salvation. . . .

Receiving the kingdom. The reception of grace means first of all the repentance always demanded by Christ,[40] that is, a renouncement of sin, a turning away from evil, a regret for past faults. But the reception of grace is also a movement to a new life, to Jesus, in fact, accomplished in faith. Faith in turn is the acceptance of His witness, the assent to His doctrine, and the acknowledgment of Jesus as the Christ: through Him there is acceptance of the Father.[41] . . . By faith and baptism man enters into the kingdom.

The kingdom mentioned by the synoptic authors is a reality always associated with the inner transformation of grace. It is the infusion of a new life into the Christian, a fulfillment of the prophecies of a "new heart" and a "new spirit" in the Old Testament.[42] Before this transformation man is spiritually lost and dead, but now like the prodigal son he is found again and is revivified.[43] A new life is given by God. The justified man, like a good tree, bears new fruit[44] since he has become a "son of the kingdom" who has received the "good seed" sown by the "Son of Man."[45] He is become a child of the Father in heaven.[46] Because of this new life the members of the kingdom are to imitate the Father[47] as the model of their new life. Grace is to grow by a process of constant development and assimilation, that is, likeness to God Himself. . . .

Christ did not come merely to preach a new code of behavior, nor merely to reassert a proper conception of the true God: He came to found

---

[33] Mt 16:19.
[34] Mt 22:2–10.
[35] Mt 20:1–6.
[36] Mt 6:33; Lk 12:31.
[37] Lk 12:32; Mt 13:11.
[38] Cf. Mt 19:11.
[39] Cf. Mk 4:24 f.; Mt 13:12; 25:29; Lk 8:18.
[40] Mt 4:17; Mk 1:15; Lk 3:3, 5; 5:32; 24:47.

[41] Cf. Mk 1:15; 11:31; Mt 18:6.
[42] Ez 11:19; 36:25–27; Jer 31:31–34.
[43] Lk 15:24, 32.
[44] Mt 7:17.
[45] Mt 13:38.
[46] Mt 5:45.
[47] Mt 5:48.

that kingdom through which salvation would be definitively offered to all men. Entrance into the kingdom means more than a pledge of allegiance to Christ . . . it means truly becoming sons of the Father in union with Christ. . . . Becoming in a new and radical way a son of God is not merely a matter of acknowledging God's dominion and mercy. It is truly to become a member of His family, to enter into a personal relation with Him, to be reborn in faith and baptism into a new life. . . .

4. **J. L. McKenzie, S.J.,**[48] studies the word *charis* and its cognates in the New Testament and sees it closely identified with the entire Gospel and even in the New Testament a characteristic description of the New Testament message. In some passages of the New Testament he finds the conception of grace as something given, received, a reality in the Christian soul and in the world in which the Christian lives, and hence grace cannot be conceived in these passages as exclusively the saving will of God.

The frequency of the word *charis* and its cognates in the NT stands in contrast to the simple and undeveloped idea of favor in the OT. It is closely and fundamentally identified with the entire gospel and ultimately becomes a technical term, a key word. It does not acquire all the connotations which it has acquired in the development of Christian theology; but it is, even in the NT, a characteristic description of the NT message.

The verb *charizesthai* is comparatively weak in theological content. It means to grant freely as a favor. With God as the agent, the object of the granting is all things in Christ (Rom 8:32), the inheritance to Abraham (Gal 3:18), unspecified gifts of God (1 Cor 2:12), the gift of faith and of suffering with Christ (Phil 1:29). As effects of the saving will of God these are more clearly seen in the use of the noun *charis;* cf below. Jesus granted sight to the blind (Lk 7:21). He Himself is the indirect object of divine good will when He is granted the name which is above all names (Phil 2:9).

Charis occurs frequently in the introductory and final greetings of the epistles; here it has clearly become a key theme word, almost a slogan, of the early Christian communities (Rom 1:7; 16:20; 1 Cor 1:3; 16:23; 2 Cor 1:2; 13:13; Gal 1:3; 6:18 . . .). It is usually joined with peace in these greetings; it is the atmosphere of the early Church and the condition which one Christian wished for another.

[48] John L. McKenzie, S.J., is an eminent Scripture scholar and teacher. At present he is teaching at the University of Chicago. He is the author of several books, *The Two-Edged Sword, The Power and the Wisdom, Myths and Realities.* This excerpt is from his *Dictionary of the Bible* (Milwaukee: The Bruce Publishing Company, 1965), pp. 324–326.

Charis is used in the profane sense of attractiveness, charm (derived from *charis*), the quality which wins favor. Its characteristic theological use in the NT designates the good will of God, sometimes in the general sense: The good will of God was upon Jesus, i.e., God was pleased with Him (Lk 2:40); Paul and Barnabas are recommended by the brethren to God's good will (Acts 14:26; 15:40). In particular and most frequently it means the saving will of God executed in Jesus Christ and communicated to men through Him. It is not easy to draw a precise distinction in the NT between this saving will conceived as the act immanent to God and the effects of the saving will as they appear in the life of Jesus and in the Church; hence the term "grace" is better as a translation than "favor" or "good will," since, like *charis*, it designates the reality of God's saving will both in its principle and in its effects.

This grace of God is the totality by which men are made righteous (Rom 3:24; Ti 3:7). By grace Paul was called (Gal 1:15). God bestows His glorious grace on us in His Son (Eph 1:6). The grace of God has appeared (in the incarnation of Jesus Christ) for the salvation of all men (Ti 2:11). By the grace of God Jesus suffered death for all (Heb 2:9). The throne of grace is the point from which Christians should seek help (Heb 4:16). The grace of God is not distinguished from the grace of Jesus Christ, for only through Jesus does grace reach men. Paul speaks of the grace of Jesus Christ who became poor to enrich us (2 Cor 8:9). The grace of our Lord has overflowed with faith and love which are in Christ Jesus (1 Tm 1:14); the speech here is somewhat obscure, but it is clear that faith and love, communicated through Christ, are the fruits of grace.

Elsewhere the emphasis falls rather on that which is given through grace than on the saving will which gives it. God is the God of all grace (1 Pt 5:10), of every deed of grace. Grace is something which is given (Ja 4:6; 1 Pt 5:5). The Word is full of grace, i.e., of saving deeds, which we receive (Jn 1:14, 16). Grace is a store to which we have access through Christ (Rom 5:2). It is a state or condition in which we stand (Rom 5:2). It is received in abundance (Rom 5:17). The grace of God has abounded more than sin (Rom 5:15, 20; 6:1). It is given us in Christ (1 Cor 1:4). Paul has not received it in vain (2 Cor 6:1). The surpassing grace of God is within the Christian (2 Cor 9:14). It extends to more and more people (2 Cor 4:15). Christians are called in the grace of Christ (Gal 1:6). It can and should be obtained by the Christian (Heb 12:15). The prophets foretold it (1 Pt 1:10). By a rather singular turn of phrase it is described as coming in the revelation (i.e., the Parousia) of Jesus Christ (1 Pt 1:13). The Christians are heirs to the grace of life (1 Pt 3:7). They should grow in the grace and knowledge of Jesus Christ (2 Pt 3:18). Some have perverted the grace of God to licentiousness (Jude 4). The spirit is called the spirit of grace (Heb 10:29); grace is received with the spirit.

Wide as may seem to be the range of these passages, they have in common the conception of grace as something given, received, a reality in the Christian and in the world in which the Christian lives. Grace cannot be conceived in these passages as exclusively the saving will of God.

Grace stands in opposition to works, which lack the power to save; if they had the power, the reality of grace would be annulled (Rom 11:5 f.; Eph 2:5, 7 f.; 2 Tm 1:9). Grace stands in opposition to the law. Both Jews and Gentiles are saved through the grace of the Lord Jesus (Acts 15:11). To hold to the law is to nullify grace (Gal 2:21); and when the Galatians accept the law, they have fallen from grace (Gal 5:4). The Christian is not under the law but under grace (Rom 6:14 f.). Grace is opposed to what is owed (Rom 4:4).

The gospel itself, which is the good news of grace, can be called grace. It is the true grace in which the Christian should stand (1 Pt 5:12), in which he should continue (Acts 13:43). It is the grace and knowledge of Jesus Christ (2 Pt 3:18) in which the Christian should grow. The gospel is the gospel of the grace of God (Acts 20:24) or the word of His grace (Acts 14:3; 20:32).

Grace is a principle of Christian life and action. This appears first of all in the concept of mission; Stephen was full of grace and power by which he spoke (Acts 6:8). Paul speaks several times of his apostleship as a grace which he has received (Rom 1:5; 12:3; 15:15; 1 Cor 3:10; 15:10; Gal 2:9; Eph 3:7 f.). In this grace his hearers are partakers (Phil 1:7). He has the stewardship of God's grace for those to whom he preaches (Eph 3:2). The grace of the apostleship is something which the apostle must communicate and share. But it is not merely a static quality: it is dynamic, the grace by which the apostle performs his apostolic functions (Rom 12:3; 1 Cor 3:10; 15:10; Eph 3:7 f.). Grace is also a principle of Christian life and action even when the apostleship or other particular offices are not in question. Grace fructifies in good works in the churches of Macedonia (2 Cor 8:1). The grace of God is sufficient to enable Paul to resist temptations; it is the power of God in contrast with the weakness of men (2 Cor 12:9). The grace of God and not earthly wisdom is the principle which guides Paul's conduct (2 Cor 1:12). The law and its works are replaced by an entirely new principle of activity. The Christian, while he is absolutely a recipient of grace, is not an inert recipient; the saving good will of God enables him to hear the gospel, to believe it, to become one with Jesus Christ and to live in union with Christ according to the ideals proposed by Christ.

The verb *charitun*, to bestow *charis*, is rare. It occurs with *charis* as its object in Eph 1:6. The participle *kecharitomēnē* is addressed to Mary (Lk 1:28). The common version "full of grace" is correct as long as the word is not made to bear the entire weight of a theology of grace which is subsequent to the NT. Literally the word means "highly favored"; but in the NT context of God's favor as "grace," described above, it signifies the saving will of God and all its effects, here in particular the first step in the process of salvation, the incarnation of Jesus Christ.

Strictly speaking, the Gk word *charisma* as the favor granted should be distinguished from *charis,* the good will by which the favor is granted. Actually the NT uses this word rather rarely in a general sense. Paul wishes by his letter to impart some spiritual *charisma* to the Romans (Rom 1:11), and he observes that the Corinthians lack no spiritual *charisma* (1 Cor 1:7). In Rom 6:23 the *charisma* of God is life everlasting in Jesus Christ. The *charismata* of the OT are all the gifts of God to Israel (Rom 11:29); such gifts are irrevocable. But rather early the term *charisma* is used to designate a particular type of spiritual gift which enables its receiver to perform some office or function in the Church. These are the gifts which each has received and which are to be employed for speech and service (1 Pt 4:10). The *charisma* is conferred upon Timothy by the imposition of hands, the rite by which he is ordained to his office (1 Tm 4:14; 2 Tm 1:6). Celibacy or marriage is each the fruit of a *charisma* (1 Cor 7:7).

There are several enumerations of these offices or functions. Rom 12:6 mentions prophecy, service, teaching, exhorting, contributing, helping, works of mercy. Eph 4:11 mentions apostles, prophets, evangelists, pastors, teachers. Historians of the Church no longer distinguish between the primitive "charismatic" age, in which such offices were presumably filled only by some charismatic manifestation, and the later "hierarchical" age, in which they were filled by organizational methods. The Church has never forgotten that her offices, which are not secular, cannot be filled without the saving will of God, which she believes is still directed toward her.

A particular problem is presented in 1 Cor 12–14, where Paul speaks at length of charismatic manifestations in the church of Corinth which are not paralleled elsewhere. These are enumerated in 1 Cor 12:8–11 as wisdom, knowledge, faith, healing, thaumaturgy, prophecy, the distinction of spirits, tongues, and the interpretation of tongues. The gift of tongues (glossolaly) is mentioned also as an effect of the spirit in Acts 10:46; 19:6; the account of Pentecost, Acts 2. To Paul all of these are inferior to love (1 Cor 13); prophecy is superior to the rest, and Paul frankly seems to regard tongues as a less desirable gift.

Of the *charismata* in general, most of which can be easily identified, it must be said that the effusion of the spirit in the primitive Church should not be measured according to western European standards; and this is said with no concession to the excesses of some Christian sects. The spirit, as

Paul says, has different gifts but is the same spirit; and the atmosphere of religious exaltation which was normal in the Hellenistic world could scarcely have been irrelevant in the primitive development of Christianity. Such external manifestations were a visible sign that a new force, a new spirit was at work. It is evident from the NT and from the literature of the postapostolic age that these phenomena were elements of the birth of the Church which did not endure once it was securely established in communities.

What is meant by the gift of tongues is somewhat perplexing. It may help to recall that to the Gk speaking world all foreign languages were "barbarian," literally "babbling." One who spoke a foreign tongue spoke unintelligibly, and one who spoke unintelligibly spoke a foreign tongue. The speaker of tongues needed an interpreter; it is probable that the tongues spoken at Corinth were the utterances of ecstatic speakers who expressed their exaltation in unintelligible cries. The glossolaly of Pentecost (Acts 2) is described more precisely as speech understood by a number of foreign visitors mentioned by name. Here the tradition has no doubt employed symbolism. . . .

5. **J. Bonsirven, S.J.,**[49] **studies the "kingdom of God" as it appears in the Synoptics, why Jesus used the expression, what He meant by it, how this kingdom may be defined so as to bring out its essential characteristics, and what the coming of this kingdom demands by way of purification of heart.**

The whole mission of the Son of Man was to establish the kingdom of God. At the very beginning of His ministry He proclaimed: "the kingdom of God is near at hand"[50] and He defined His message as "This Gospel of the kingdom."[51] What is this kingdom of God? The recent controversies have tended to obscure the meaning of the expression and the idea behind it so much that one hesitates to define them. Still, as Büchsel points out, the term is a simple one: the kingdom of God must be a kingdom of which God is the king. . . .

We can . . . confirm that "kingdom of God" is a theocratic expression, but

[49] Joseph Bonsirven, S.J., is an eminent Scripture scholar. He is the author of *Exégése rabbinique, Enseignements de Jésus-Christ, Palestinian Judaism in the Time of Christ.* This excerpt is from his *Theology of the New Testament* (Westminster, Md.: The Newman Press, 1963), pp. 34–59.

[50] Mk 1:15; Mt 3:2; 4:17; 10:7; Lk 10:9, 11. The words "is near at hand" are a translation of *eggiken* which many take to refer also to a design of Providence brought to present fruition: Jouon, *Recherches de Science Religieuse* (hereafter

RSR), 1927, p. 138; Lagrange, *Saint Marc*, p. 16 f.; Preisker, *Theologisches Wörterbuch zum Neuen Testament* (hereafter TW), II, p. 330.

[51] Mt 24:14 (the Evangelist defines the preaching of Jesus in the same way: 4:23; 9:35).

used less in a Messianic than a moral and religious sense; it was a fully comprehensive term and "pregnant with a wealth of meaning,"[52] it was tolerably widespread, and every mention of it was bound to arouse an echo in men's hearts.

Given this background we can see why Jesus used the expression. He came to establish an order which would embody the religious ideal of the Old Testament. He could not have found a better term to express it, profoundly evocative yet somewhat indeterminate as it was. His disciples would define the notion for themselves stage by stage as they saw the new order developing, and more particularly as they adopted the new way of life and made it their own.

And so we must clearly understand that under cover of a phrase which was in general circulation at the time, Jesus was promulgating an entirely new doctrine of His own, one which many were to regard as revolutionary.[53] . . .

At no time did Jesus give a defini-

tion of this "kingdom of God," and this gives our contemporaries an opportunity to credit Him with a wide variety of conceptions of it. These can be classified into two diametrically opposed types: according to one of them, Christ had in mind a spiritual kingdom, already existing at the time and progressive — an *evolution;* according to the others, He was looking forward to it as something which had to come into existence suddenly as the result of an eschatological *revolution* which would shake the whole world. . . .

To round off these ideas about the kingdom, let me briefly indicate certain benefits it confers; later, we will consider them at some length. We shall see that the object of the kingdom is to raise up many brothers for Jesus, to give men an opportunity of becoming the sons of God. Equally, we can accept it as true that in the kingdom a new and eternal covenant, providing for all sorts of spiritual blessings, is entered into with God. We already know that these divine graces are imparted to us by Jesus and in Jesus, the only mediator between God and man.

We can now define the kingdom and bring out its essential characteristics. It is a system of salvation which begins with Jesus, but continues the order of the Old Covenant. It assumes several aspects: it is a doctrine, a mystery, which only the faithful can assimilate; it is also a society in the form of an organism developing continually in accordance with the laws of

---

[52] L. de Grandmaison, *Jesus Christ,* I, pp. 281–291; Balmain Bruce, *The Kingdom of God in Christ's Teaching according to the Synoptical Gospels* (Edinburgh, 1897), p. 41; Garvie, *Exp. T.,* XLII, p. 194; K. Lake and F. Foakes-Jackson, *Beginnings of Christianity* (London, 1920), I, pp. 270–278; Kuhn and Kl. Schmidt, TW, I, pp. 570–573; J. Boehmer, *Der religionsgeschichtliche Rahmen des Reiches Gottes.*

[53] TW, I, p. 593; ed. Koenig, *Geschichte des Reiches Gottes bis auf J.C.* (Leipzig, 1908), p. 317 ff.; Dewick, *Christian Eschatology,* p. 226 (different from the Jewish apocalypses); Bruce, *The Kingdom of God,* ch. 1.

its being. It exists on earth, incarnate to some extent in the Church, a militant and imperfect state. It is to come into full existence only in the kingdom of God, the final state from which the worthless elements have been eliminated, where the divine blessings are received without any hindrance or reservation. It is in fact the type (and, as it were, the sum total) of all the supernatural benefits which are granted to us even on this earth, but only appear in all their glory in heaven. There is no opposition between these two states, at once similar and diverse. They give rise to a constant and irresistible dynamism, the dynamism of life itself; it is seen at work in the material creation. How much more active it is in this new creation than the impetus of the divine life in the world, since grace rises unceasingly to glory.

Can we now give a definition of the Reign (the sovereignty) of God? It is grace and glory,[54] "the whole epic of salvation."[55] God uniting with His creation in mutual love, eventually eternal love."[56] It could be put more fully, though less elegantly: "It is the society of men who possess in Jesus Christ the gift of divine sonship, preserved and developed by strife in this life, thanks to the mediation of their Saviour, and reaching its triumphant fulfilment in the next by total assimilation to their Lord."[57]. . .

"Repent, the kingdom of heaven is at hand." This is how St. Matthew (4:17) sums up the earlier teaching of Jesus. The coming of the kingdom demands, first of all, a complete purification of heart. Of necessity, therefore, sin occupies an important place in the teaching of Jesus. His mission had as its main objective something more than a negative purpose, but it could not afford to lose sight of the enemy who was always on the alert or grow weary of throwing him off the track and putting him to flight. . . .

Because He feels and understands the universality and gravity of sin as no one else does, Jesus alone is fitted to be our Saviour. In the Gospels only the angels (Lk 2:11; Mt 1:21) and the Samaritans call Him by this title. But He does make it clear more than once that He has come to bring salvation to all who are lost.[58] In so doing, He fulfilled the hopes of the Jews and gratified the profound desire of the Jewish heart for salvation, though it was often thought of in too material a sense. The salvation that Jesus brought was eminently spiritual; in a negative sense at first — deliverance from sin — but afterwards something more positive; access to the good things that make real life possible and that make up real life, participation in the divine life which was then assured,

---

[54] Bonnetain, "Grâce," *Dictionnaire Biblique* (Vigouroux), *Supplement* (hereafter DBS), III, c. 951, 959 f.

[55] Y. de la Briere, *Dictionnaire Apologetique de la Foi Catholique* (hereafter DAF), I, c. 1247.

[56] L. de Grandmaison, *Jesus Christ*, II, pp. 78–79.

[57] This overacademic definition is explained in my *Enseignements de Jesus-Christ*, p. 359.

[58] Lk 19:9, 10; 5:32. Mt 10:6; 15:24. Jn 3:17; 5:24; 10:9; 12:47.

though it was only to be enjoyed in its fullness, without fear of loss, in the next world.[59] . . .

The soul which has good dispositions can obtain pardon for its faults: that is one of the benefits the Messianic age brings with it;[60] it is one of the essential elements of the New Covenant.[61] It is also a part of the mission the risen Lord assigns to His disciples: "that repentance and remission of sins should be preached in his name to all nations" (Lk 24:47; Jn 20:22, 23). And Jesus pronounces these absolutions in advance, as it were, exercising a divine power, for the benefit of the palsied man whose faith was so meritorious (Mk 2:1–12; Lk 5:17–26; Mk 9:1–8), and then for

the sinful woman of the city (Lk 7:36–50). Notice in the second of these accounts the phrase "If great sins have been forgiven her, she has also greatly loved." True contrition springs from love, and it is by love that it brings health to the soul.

This indicates the full extent of the remission of sins which is granted to us in Christ. He is "the lamb of God who takes away the sin of the world," and He it is again who baptizes with "water and . . . the Holy Spirit" (Jn 1:29, 33; 3:5). In neither case is there any question of an absolution that simply wipes out stains. What is involved first and foremost is an outpouring of the means by which men become the children of God. Jesus left to His Church the task of defining this positive aspect of the two sacraments, the one that admits us to the body of Christ and the other that confirms us in our union with Him. The place He reserves in them for love makes it clear that Christian repentance is the door by which we enter fully into the kingdom of God in the full enjoyment of our prerogatives as children of God.

---

[59] The word "salvation" (to save) often corresponded in the vocabulary of Jesus to the verb "to give life." Mk 10:17, 23, 25, 26, 27 is a good illustration of this salvation, at once eschatological and present; cf. Mk 8:35; 13:13; Lk 13:23 f.; 9:24; 17:33; Mt 7:13 f.; 10:22; 16:25; 24:13.

[60] Mi 7:18, 19; Is 1:18; 33:24; 44:22; 43:25; Jer 33:8; Za 3:9; 13:1; Dn 9:24.

[61] Jer 31:34, commented on in Heb 8:6–13; 10:17, 18.

III

GRACE IN ST. JOHN

1. H. Rondet, S.J.,[1] prefers to study St. John's grace-doctrine before St. Paul's. The idea of life synthesizes the Johannine doctrine of grace. This is a superior life, a supernatural life that comes from on high by a new birth, and it connotes a divine presence, that of the Father and the Son and the Holy Spirit. It is a life fed by the Eucharist, a participation in the very life of God, an eternal life.

IN THE teaching of Jesus as it appears in the Synoptics, the theology of grace does not yet seem explicit.[2] To discover it, we must look to the doctrine of St. John. For him theology is only

[1] H. Rondet, S.J., was born in 1898. He was a member of the faculty of theology at Lyon-Fourviere. Among the many works he has published are: *St. Joseph, Mère de la divine grâce, Notes sur la théologie du péche, Le Sacre Coeur*. This excerpt is taken from his superb *Gratia Christi* (Paris: Beauchesne Et Ses Fils, 1948), pp. 43–47.

[2] E. Tobac, "Grâce," in DAF, t. II, col. 333. Cf. W. Manson, "The Doctrine of Grace in the New Testament," in Whitley, ed., *The Doctrine of Grace* (London: SCM Press, 1931), p. 40; P. Bonnetain, "Grâce" in DBS, t. III, col. 716, 950.

a long commentary on the teaching of Jesus. Despite its late redaction it is here that the Johannine doctrine of grace must be situated.[3] It takes us back to the source of the Christian revelation. Though it is not always possible to distinguish the original message from the expression the apostle gives it,[4] it is truly Christ who is speaking to us by the intermediary of the beloved disciple.

At the center of this theology of grace we must place the discourse after the Supper and the allegory of the vine. Its axiom, "Without me you can do nothing,"[5] will dominate the whole history of the notion of grace, and St. Augustine will develop it. . . . The doctrine of the Mystical Body is there in its entirety.[6]. . .

This supernatural grace, considered as a superior life, pervades the whole fourth gospel. It also appears there as a light, and no one better than St. John has put into relief the supernatural character of faith as a gift of God.[7] It is in St. John that Christ

refutes the Semipelagians in advance.[8] . . . Grace also appears as a supernatural force which gives the justified man the power to avoid sin.[9] But it is really the idea of life that synthesizes the Johannine doctrine of grace. . . . Some have at times wished to oppose the Pauline theology of grace to the Johannine theology, but at bottom there is no difference between the two apostles, for each in his own way is only repeating Christ.[10]

The grace which unites us to Christ is not only a principle of life.[11] It also connotes a divine presence, that of the Father and of the Son, and of the Holy Spirit who, thanks to the sacrifice of Christ, will be given to all who abide in His love,[12] in such a way that the Holy Spirit will be in them as a spring of living water,[13] that water which the Lord, sitting on the edge of Jacob's well, had made the woman of Samaria desire.[14]. . .

This life which Christ gives to those who give themselves to Him is already

---

[3] Historians of dogma are accustomed to present the doctrine of St. Paul before that of St. John. This is to forget that John is before all a witness of Christ and that Paul's doctrine, without ceasing to give us new lights on Revelation, is already a theology in the precise sense of the term.

[4] J. Lebreton, *Histoire du dogme de la Trinité* (6 ed., 1927), t. I, pp. 487–488; M.-J. Lagrange, *Evangile selon saint Jean*, (Paris, 1925), pp. cxlv–cxlvii.

[5] Jn 15:1–8.

[6] E. Mersch, *Le corps mystique du Christ* (2 ed., 1936), t. I, pp. 249–250. [Eng. tr. *The Whole Christ* (Milwaukee: Bruce Publishing Company, 1938), Part One, pp. 179–181.]

[7] Lagrange, *op. cit.*, p. clxvi; Lebreton, *op. cit.*, t. I, pp. 510–515; Bonnetain, *art. cit.*, col. 1116–1119; J. Huby, "La connaissance de foi dans saint Jean," in RSR, 1931, pp. 400–403.

[8] Jn 6:44.

[9] 1 Jn 3:6.

[10] Cf. the brilliant study of P. Rousselot, "La grâce d'après saint Jean et d'après saint Paul," in RSR, 1928, pp. 87–104.

[11] The idea of new life necessarily supposes that of a created grace, principle of knowledge and action, but it would be an anachronism to wish to find this notion explicitly in St. John.

[12] Jn 14:23, 26; 16:13.

[13] Jn 7:38–39.

[14] Jn 4:8.

eternal life, anticipated resurrection, eternity in time.[15] Those who are united to Christ, submissive to the Spirit of Christ, cannot die.[16] The second death will have no influence on them, for death according to the flesh will only reveal what they are: authentic sons of God.[17] If we add to John's doctrine of eternal life his magnificent development of the eucharistic nourishment of life[18] and all the sacramentalism that is so strongly marked in the fourth gospel, we begin to comprehend the profound sense of the word that the beloved disciple heard fall from the lips of the Good Shepherd: "I came that they may have life, and have it more abundantly."[19]

2. A. Feuillet, S.S.,[20] sees the end and purpose of the Incarnation as the revelation and communication to men of divine life. For St. John the Incarnation signifies a descent into this world of divine life, divine in its origin and nature, so that the Christian is born of God and is able to act as a true child of God. The synoptic theme of the kingdom and the Johannine theme of life are not so remote from one another as might appear at first glance.

The fundamental orientation of Johannine theology differs considerably from that of the synoptics. Matthew, Mark, and Luke emphasize the restoration of the kingdom of God by Jesus; John accents almost exclusively the Person of Jesus as the revelation made to the world of the very mystery of God. In contrast to St. Paul whose soteriology rests entirely on the death and resurrection of Christ, the soteriology of John refers first of all to the Incarnation.

But this difference should not be exaggerated. John remains faithful to the essentials of the primitive Christian message. Christ saves us first and foremost by His death and resurrection, that is why this period is the *hour* par excellence of Jesus. But this decisive hour is prepared by everything which precedes, including the mission of the Son of God into this world by the Father and the assumption of human nature by the Son. Whereas Paul has in mind above all the cross and the paschal mystery, John contemplates the Incarnation as being already in itself a mystery of salvation. . . .

John speaks of the redemptive In-

[19] Jn 10:10.

[20] A. Feuillet, S.S., is a professor of New Testament exegesis at the Institut Catholique in Paris and a frequent contributor to *Revue Biblique* and *Nouvelle Revue Théologique*. Among his books are *Le Cantique des Cantiques* and *Le Livre de Jonas*. This excerpt is taken from his article in *Theology Digest*, Spring, 1960, pp. 76–79. The article is entitled, "The Incarnation: Mystery of Salvation."

[15] Bonnetain, *art. cit.*, col. 1122–1124. In St. Paul eternal life is more explicitly eschatological.

[16] Jn 8:51.

[17] 1 Jn 3:1–2.

[18] Jn 6:51–58.

carnation in terms of the initiative of the Father, the gift of the Son by the Father, and the God of Love in the Old Testament. The Father "consecrates" His Son and sends Him into this world. The Father entrusts man to the Son; He gives Him a work to do and a message to give. He permits Christ to be the source of life for humanity. . . .

The end and purpose of the Incarnation is the revelation and the communication to men of the mysterious riches of divine life, a communication which presupposes the redemptive work of Christ. While John maintains that salvation depends above all on the death and resurrection, he is unique in affirming that Christ, by His mere presence among men, frees them by giving them His light. "You shall know the truth, and the truth shall make you free."[21]

Looked at in itself the salvation brought by Christ has the following aspects: (1) a deliverance from slavery caused by sin and the gift of divine sonship; (2) a deliverance from darkness and the gift of light and truth; (3) a deliverance from death and the gift of life.

In the Old Testament, the word "life" expresses the highest good that man can possess, but life and its beatitude are never seen as distinct from God. Yahweh, the living God, is the tree of life, the path of life, the source of life, the book of life, the light of life. Obedience to the law of God and conformity to His wisdom is the path

of life; disobedience to the divine will leads to death. In the Old Testament God gave the manna; in the New, through the Incarnation, He gives Himself.

In the mind of John, since life belongs properly to God, the Incarnation of the Son of God signifies a descent of the divine life into this world which is normally given to corruption and death. Moreover this life which Christ bestows is not only divine by its origin, it is divine by its very nature. The Son communicates to the baptized essentially the same life communicated by the Father to the Son. The eternal divine life is opposed to human life as the spirit is to the flesh; it cannot be obtained except by the power of regeneration.

Divine life is received not only after the resurrection of the dead; it is given now as an imperishable good and as an interior principle of action. Whoever believes in Jesus has passed from death to life. Though he die, he has assurance not only that he will be raised up on the last day, but that he will never lose the supernatural life which brings about his union with Christ, the resurrection and the life.

The discourse on the bread of life distinguishes between the offer of eternal life in the present and the resurrection on the last day. The existence of a current of life actually binding Jesus to His disciples is stated in the allegory of the vine, which is closely related to the discourse on the bread of life. The Son's dependence on the Father during His human life is an

---

21 Jn 8:31.

example for the disciples. Modeling themselves on the Son and receiving from Him a life which is truly divine, they are able in turn to act as true children of God: "to them he gave the power to become children of God."[22]

Hellenistic influence? The First Epistle of St. John defines Christian existence as a vital and ontological relation with God. The Christian is actually in communion with God: He is born of God, possesses God, knows Him, and dwells in Him. Some exegetes deny any properly mystical significance to Johannine thought in the sense that men here and now actually possess divine life. Bultmann, for example, would say that John has only "radicalised" traditional eschatology by making its various manifestations (death, judgment, resurrection, eternal life) just so many actual events which happen at the very moment Jesus is speaking.

Actually many authors recognize in John a reflection of Hellenistic mysticism. To a certain extent John attempted to adapt the Christian message to the Greeks. For example, when John emphasizes that Jesus is the only qualified revealer of the divine world, because He alone has seen the Father, he did so with Hellenism in mind. The Greek mysteries, *gnosis,* and even philosophy laid claim to lead to the knowledge and the vision of God. We may suppose with Bultmann that John purposely used terms that were current among the Greeks, but gave them a new content.

A profound Semitic and biblical foundation anchors the whole of Johannine thought. The mysticism of John, like Paul's, remains fundamentally irreducible to the Greek mysteries, understood as the ecstatic contemplation or vision of the divinity. The Greek mysteries claimed a substantial union with the divinity without demanding on man's part any moral effort. Gnostic salvation consists actually in freeing man from matter, from time, and from fate.

Mysticism of John. Johannine mysticism, completely different from mystery religions, is bound up with the history of salvation. It is not man who undertakes to advance toward God; it is God, whom no one has ever seen, who at a certain determined point in history takes the initiative to make Himself known to the world through His Incarnate Son. Everything comes from the gratuitous love of God for man. As Nygren says, such a love was totally unknown to the Greeks.

The great obstacle to man's union with God is not matter nor fate; it is sin. Besides, this union can never be a strict becoming-divine. John carefully maintains the immeasurable distance that separates man from God, even in those passages where he teaches the life-sharing of Christ and Christians. No matter what may be the experiences of the divine here below, man remains essentially orientated toward the parousia. The indwelling Spirit cannot replace, but only prepare, man for the parousia.

Christ in the synoptics. If the

---

[22] Jn 1:12.

Johannine Christ teaches an actual participation of His disciples in the very life of God, how can we explain a doctrine that at first glance seems completely foreign to the synoptics? Does it actually fit in with the Jesus of history? In the synoptics the fundamental theme is the kingdom; in the fourth gospel the theme is life. A solution can be found in a relationship between these two themes.

In the synoptics, the kingdom is far from being purely eschatological. If the kingdom is first of all a dynamic reality, the decisive intervention of God in history announced by the prophets, then because of the coming of Jesus and because of His ministry, His teaching, His expulsion of demons, and His cures, this sovereign intervention has begun here and now. Because He is the Son of God per-

fectly submissive to the Father, Jesus Himself is the kingdom of God. The choice that He proposes for or against the kingdom is a choice for or against His Person. Actual access to the divine life is an idea less distant from the synoptics than might have appeared at first. They themselves equate the ideas: "entering into the kingdom" and "entering into eternal life."

Can we go further and maintain that the Christ of the synoptics, just as the Christ of John, already promises access here and now to the divine eschatological goods, from the time that a person consents to follow after Him? We think so. The salvific goods (pardon for sins, divine sonship) bound up with the kingdom of God are salvific goods which one enjoys right now.

3. C. H. Dodd[23] also sees life as a major theme of the Evangelist. It is the life of God, accessible to men here and now, though it implies for its fulfillment an order of existence beyond space and time. It consists in "knowledge of God" which is union with God but not metaphysics, nor direct super-sensuous vision of the absolute, nor yet mystical ecstasy or "enthusiasm." It takes the form of faith, which is both acceptance of the fact that Jesus Christ is the revelation of the eternal God, and a personal attachment to Him.

In an earlier chapter I drew attention to the use of formulae coupling "life" and "light" in Hellenistic religious language, and observed that in the Fourth Gospel the same conjunc-

tion is to be found. Our present investigation of the leading concepts of Johannine thought started with the concept of life. We found that John conceives zōē aiōnios, the life of God,

---

[23] C. H. Dodd was born in 1884. He was Norris-Hulse professor of divinity at Cambridge, 1935–1939. Among his publications are: The Gospel in the New Testament, The Coming of Christ, The Bible Today, Parables of the Kingdom, New Testament Studies. This excerpt was taken from his book, The Interpretation of the Fourth Gospel (Cambridge University Press, 1960), pp. 201, 185b, 198c.

to be accessible to man here and now, though it implies for its fulfilment an order of existence beyond space and time. It consists in "knowledge" of God, which is also communion with God, or "dwelling in" God. So far, he speaks the common language of Hellenistic mysticism. But for him the knowledge of God which is union with God is not metaphysics, nor direct super-sensuous vision of the absolute, nor yet mystical ecstasy or "enthusiasm." It is conditioned by a relation to the historical manifestation of the Logos. It is here that *alethēia*, absolute reality as revealed, is to be found. Hence knowledge takes the form of faith, which is both an acceptance of the fact that Jesus Christ is the revelation of the eternal God, and a personal attachment to Him. It is not a stage preliminary to knowledge, but is itself the knowledge of God which is communion with Him and constitutes eternal life. It is a way of "seeing" God. . . .

In these passages we discern a certain conception of a relation between faith and vision. In the first place, there is a form of vision, simple physical vision, which may exist without faith. Many of the contemporaries of Jesus saw Him in this sense, but without any saving effects. But when simple vision is accompanied by faith, it leads to vision in a deeper sense. No one, it is true, has direct vision of God; but he who has faith has eternal life; faith therefore is the equivalent of the life-giving vision, or knowledge of God. Finally, in the

Thomas-episode we have the transition: Thomas is of those who have seen Christ, physically, and, having faith, he has seen Him in the true sense: but more blessed are they who, without the physical sight of Him, have faith. "If you have faith, you will see the glory of God," Jesus had said to Martha (11:40). In the prologue it is said *etheasametha tēn doxan autou*: the evangelist speaks for those who have faith, and therefore vision. We may now recall Philo's equation of *pistis* with *aphanous upolepsis*, and the Hermetic association of *pistis* with knowledge, life, and light.

Faith, then, is a form of vision. When Christ was on earth, to have faith was to "see His glory" — to apprehend and acknowledge the deity through the veil of humanity. Now that He is no longer visible to the bodily eyes, faith remains the capacity for seeing His glory. This conception is vital to the evangelist's whole conception of the incarnation. Eternal life is the knowledge or vision of God. But no man has seen God at any time, as the mystics do vainly talk. He who has seen Christ has seen the Father. What, have the unbelieving Jews who saw Jesus seen the Father? No; to see the Father in Christ, to see His glory, was and always is the part of faith, *aphanous upolepsis*, and this is just as possible, and just as necessary, for us as for those who saw Him in the flesh. Thus *pistis* is that form of knowledge, or vision, appropriate to those who find God in an historic Person of the past, a Person who nevertheless, through it, remains the object of saving knowledge, the truth and the life. . . .

If the mystic is one whose religious life is expressed in ecstasy, or one who experiences an impersonal absorption in the divine, then Bauer is certainly right in refusing the name to the Fourth Evangelist. But to suggest that he was merely using stereotyped terms in vogue, without attaching any particular meaning to them, is precarious; and to reduce his conception of the Christian life to a kind of legalism ("keeping the commandments") is certainly to misunderstand him. His thought has two inseparable strains. On the one hand we have the language of *gnosis theou*, of vision, of the indwelling of man in God and of God in man. On the other hand we have the insistence on the deed, the fruit. Both these strains must be taken seriously. They do not lie side by side unassimilated. They are so fused that both acquire definition and fullness of meaning through their combination. It is not by denying, or emptying of real meaning, either the one set of concepts or the other that we are likely to understand the teaching of the Fourth Evangelist. It is his special characteristic that he combines these two aspects of the religious life in so remarkable a way. The idea in which they meet is that of the divine *agapē*. That such *agapē* will express itself in acts of brotherly love, to the laying down of life, is for him in the nature of the case. But while it expresses itself in obedience to the law of charity, the love of God is not to be identified with . . . law-abiding obedience.

The term *agapē* differs in meaning from *eros*. . . . *Agapē* is characteristically the love which gives itself. It has its origin in God, the highest of beings, who, loving His creatures, raises them to Himself. . . . The glory of God is manifested wherever His love becomes effective: supremely in the self-offering of Christ; and also in those who through Christ live by the love of God.

If now we are thinking in terms of union with God, is not love, as a matter of fact, the only kind of union *between persons* of which we can have any possible experience? Cosmic emotion is not very uncommon, and it is possible for the philosopher to interpret it as unity with "God" in a pantheistic sense, and so to give a religious colour to what is really a theory of the universe. It is also possible to interpret certain abnormal psychical states as "possession" by the divine Spirit. But in neither case have we evidence that union with a personal God is attained. For the only kind of personal union, I repeat, with which we are acquainted is love. John says that this is in truth the kind of union with God given in the Christian religion. He makes use of the strongest expressions for union with God that contemporary religious language provided, in order to assure his readers that he does seriously mean what he says: that through faith in Christ we may enter into a personal community of life with the eternal God, which has the character of *agapē*, which is essentially supernatural and not of this world, and yet plants its feet firmly in this world, not only because real *agapē* cannot but express itself in practical conduct, but also because the crucial act of *agapē* was actually performed in history, on an April day about A.D. 30, at a supper-table in Jerusalem, in a garden across the Kidron valley, in the headquarters of Pontius Pilate, and on a Roman cross at Golgotha. So concrete, so actual, is the nature of the divine *agapē*; yet none the less for that, by entering into the relation of *agapē* thus opened for men, we may dwell in God and He in us. Whether this should be called "mysticism" I do not know.

4. C. K. Barrett[24] is interested in John's recording of the history of God's saving activity. He sees John's description of the Christian salvation as richer than the synoptic presentation not because he has enriched it from non-Christian sources but because he has used non-Christian and non-Jewish terminology to bring out what was from the first implicit in the primitive faith.

Salvation. God did not send His Son into the world to judge it but to save it;[25] those who believe in Jesus as the Christ, the Son of God, have life in His name;[26] to receive Christ is to become a child of God.[27] That salvation was in fact effected by Jesus Christ, and could be offered through Him to men, is a point John scarcely troubles to demonstrate; the history he records is the history of God's saving activity, directed to the need of man, and he never thinks of it in other terms. But what did he mean by salvation?

In the world in which Jesus lived more than one notion of salvation was current. For example, within Judaism there was more than one form of the hoped-for messianic salvation. It might occur within the present world order as a reversal of political and military fortunes; or it might be a purely apocalyptic event taking place on the boundary between this world and the unseen other world. The elect might become prosperous rulers of a fruitful land, or as the angels in heaven. There is much variety here, but there is within Judaism a general tendency (not without exceptions) to regard salvation as the fruit of a future act of God, for which men may hope, in which they may believe, but upon which they cannot at present set their eyes. Outside Judaism the futurist, eschatological, outlook was not unknown, but it was not prevalent. Salvation was a present experience given by God to men, either through sacraments or through knowledge, *gnosis*. Each of these non-Jewish lines of

[24] C. K. Barrett has contributed articles to the *Journal of Theological Studies*, both the old and new series. This excerpt is taken from his book, *The Gospel According to St. John* (London: S.P.C.K., 1960), pp. 65–74.

[25] Jn 3:17; 12:47.

[26] Jn 20:31.

[27] Jn 1:12.

thought generally included a descent of a redeemer God into the otherwise abandoned world of flesh, sin, ignorance, and death. On his return to the heavenly world from which he came, he left behind him means (sacramental or intellectual) by which men might follow him and so escape through the circle of destiny into the upper divine world. This was salvation.

There is good reason to conclude that John was acquainted with both worlds of thought, the Jewish and the pagan. He also makes clear the provenance of his own doctrine of salvation: Salvation is of the Jews.[28] . . . The Old Testament furnishes the essential thought-forms, and the essential language, too, for the conceiving and expressing of salvation.

John, then, takes a decidedly Jewish viewpoint, and takes his stand upon the Old Testament. This fact must not, however, be allowed to obscure the complementary fact that he also uses language akin to that which we have noted as proceeding from Hellenistic and gnostic sources. "This is eternal life, that they should know thee, the only true God, and him whom thou didst send, Jesus Christ."[29] Through knowledge comes salvation. The gospel has also a strong sacramental interest; there is no doubt that a non-Jewish flows beside the Jewish stream. This is no accident, nor is it due simply to the fashionable eclecticism which sought to make the best of all religions. . . . The old eschatological notion of salvation was not adequate for Christian use, because the promised salvation was now partly fulfilled, and could no longer be described as purely future. Moreover, it was really true that the Redeemer had come down from heaven to earth, and had wrought His saving work and returned to heaven. It was true that to know Him in the biblical, not the gnostic, sense of knowing[30] was to have eternal life, and that He had left behind Him sacraments by which He communicated Himself to those who believed. The partial realization of the Jewish eschatology opened to John a field of thought and vocabulary which was closed to orthodox Judaism. Consequently John's description of the Christian salvation is richer than the synoptic presentation not because he has enriched it from non-Christian sources but because he has used non-Christian and non-Jewish terminology to bring out what was from the first implicit in the primitive faith.

Salvation is the fruit of the whole incarnate life of Jesus Christ, including His death and resurrection; consequently it is revealed in all His actions. The miracles in particular show figuratively what salvation is — the curing of the sick, the feeding of the hungry, the giving of sight to the blind, and the raising of the dead. Salvation, that is, means the healing of the ills of mankind, and the imparting of light and life; in other

---

28 Jn 4:22.
29 Jn 17:3.

30 John's characteristic use concerns knowledge of divine persons, of the relation between them, and especially of the mission of Jesus to the world.

words, Jesus deals with sin, and gives men knowledge and life. These aspects of salvation are seen from time to time in the course of the gospel, but appear pre-eminently in the death and resurrection of Jesus. . . .

Salvation and knowledge. The word *gnosis* does not occur in the gospel. . . . To know God is to have eternal life;[31] to know the truth is to be set free.[32] Knowledge, then, is a way of entrance into salvation and life. Jesus Himself knows the Father and His ministry may be summed up as the communication of this knowledge.[33] The Johannine picture of Jesus corresponds in these respects with that of the gnostic redeemer; but important differences remain. The key of knowledge is not used for unlocking the various doors of the surrounding heavens so that man may escape from his prison house, nor does John give any indication that he shares the belief that man's wretchedness is due simply to ignorance; it is due rather to sin. Man cannot be saved by the acquisition of cosmological secrets; no such secrets are given in the gospel. In fact that parallelism between the Johannine and gnostic language may be misleading; in John as in Paul the real medium of salvation is faith. The verb *pisteuein* is used almost synonymously with *ginōskein*[34] and knowledge itself implies relationship in addition to cognition: to know God is to be united with Him. . . .

Sacraments. Unlike the synoptic

[31] Jn 17:3.
[32] Jn 8:32.
[33] Jn 1:18; 17:26.
[34] Jn 6:69; compare 3:15 with 17:3.

gospels, the fourth contains no specific command of Jesus to baptize, and no account of the institution of the eucharist; neither rite is explicitly mentioned. Yet it is true that there is more sacramental teaching in John than in the other gospels. . . . The sacraments, then, so far as they appear in John, are means by which Christians are incorporated into the saving work of Christ, sharing thus in the descent of the Redeemer to an obedient death, and in His ascent through death to the glory He enjoyed with the Father before the creation. There is thus a close relation between the Johannine teaching and Paul's baptismal doctrine of crucifixion, burial, and resurrection with Christ, and his eucharistic doctrine of a rite based upon the proclamation of the Lord's death and continued in hope of His return in glory, though there is no literary ground for supposing that John had heard of Paul's terminology. These observations go far towards answering the question which no discussion of John's sacramental teaching can avoid: To what extent is John dependent upon Hellenistic, or other non-Jewish, sacramental theory? The answer is, substantially very little, formally a good deal. The sacraments in John are, as we have seen, extensions of the fundamental sacramental fact of the incarnate life of the Son of God and interpretations of the primitive eschatological sacraments; they arise out of what is regarded by John as a unique Psalms, confident in their own monofact, and are themselves unique. But, just as the writers of some of the theism, employ the language of polytheism in the praise of God,[35] so John, confident of the distinctively Christian quality of the sacraments, uses extrabiblical religious language in expounding them. . . .

Mysticism. Of mysticism in the proper sense ("a tendency of religious feeling marked by an effort to attain to direct and immediate communion with God," *Chamber's Dictionary*) there is nothing in John. There is no communion with or knowledge of God save that contained in the Old Testament tradition and mediated through Jesus Christ. This is stated in the baldest terms;[36] but it is also implied throughout the gospel. . . .

For many reasons it is impossible to classify John with the mystics of his age, or of any age; but at the same time it must be admitted that there are mystical elements in his thought. In particular, he teaches the abiding of the Father and the Son with the believer[37] and of the Spirit with and in him;[38] conversely the abiding of the believer in Christ is emphasized in the allegory of the Vine.[39] The relation is in fact reciprocal,[40] and of course is essential to the conception of salvation which is taught in John; but it remains controlled by the notions of faith and knowledge referred to above. John knows no special class of "mystic" Christians any more than

he knows a special class of "gnostic" Christians. The state which is described in this semi-mystic terminology is simply the state of Christian salvation, perhaps most simply represented by the *enephusēsen* of 20:22. Jesus sends His apostles as He has Himself been sent by the Father; He breathes into them the Spirit that has rested upon Him.

John's "mysticism" does not closely resemble, though it may be said to presuppose Paul's "eschatological mysticism," in which being "in Christ" means that the believer shares in the messianic kingdom inaugurated by the suffering and triumph of the death and resurrection of Jesus. Paul's mysticism rests upon a Christ who is primarily the eschatological redeemer, standing upon the boundary of this age and the age to come. The Johannine Christ may rather be described as Himself the one true mystic. He is essentially one with the Father;[41] He is the Son of God, and thus makes Himself equal with God.[42] His communion with God is so constant and so close that no worded prayer is necessary.[43] . . . If John has borrowed from contemporary mystical thought he has done so not in his description of Christians but in his portrait of Christ. The "mystical" life of Christians (the word is misleading) is derivative and rests upon the essential relation of Jesus with the Father.[44] . . .

35 Ps 97:7.
36 Jn 1:18; 14:6.
37 Jn 14:23.
38 Jn 14:17.
39 Jn 15:1–6.
40 Jn 15:3.

41 Jn 10:30.
42 Jn 5:18.
43 Jn 11:42.
44 Jn 17:23.

5. Ch. Baumgartner, S.J.,[45] sees the center of St. John's theology as the Word made flesh, the source of eternal life, of grace-life to the believer even now. This life means a new birth from God, the mutual immanence of God and the believer, communion with God. For St. John the idea of life, like its synoptic equivalent of the kingdom, presents two phases, a beginning in the present world and an expansion in the world to come. To the kingdom of the Synoptics St. John gives a more profound theological explanation and to the kingdom's interiority he gives its ontological foundation.

1. **The Word made flesh, source of life.** Jesus is the life.[46] This life He holds from the Father.[47] But He receives it from Him to give it to men. He is its unique source for them. . . .

For St. Paul it is the Christ who died and rose again, the Christ who has become vivifying spirit by His resurrection, whose influence extends to the members of His body. The union with the Paschal Christ is at the center of his theology. St. John's point of view is different.

The mystery of the Incarnation commands all his thought. Not in the sense that he considers the earthly Christ, before His death and resurrection, as the source of life. For him too this source is the glorified Christ.[48] But we do not find in St. John the contrast that is so fundamental in St. Paul between the two successive states of Christ who, from the sphere of sin to which, in his "emptying of self" He

pertains through His body, must pass to the divine sphere by His obedience to death. The Christ of St. John is the Word made flesh, the unique Son who manifests progressively to the eyes of faith, by His words and His works, a glory that He possessed always and which He will reveal in all its lustre in the hour of His elevation, i.e., of His death and resurrection.

Eternal life and kingdom. Life and eternal life are synonyms for St. John, as for the synoptics. Among the synoptics it is a purely eschatological reality, that begins at the resurrection of the dead and the judgment. It is otherwise for the kingdom, whose annunciation is at the center of the preaching of Jesus. The kingdom begins already here below, before its definitive establishment at the end of time. It begins in humility and in secret, it increases and develops slowly and progressively on this earth by the Church. St. John speaks of the kingdom of God in only one passage.[49] But what for him corresponds to the reality of the kingdom and takes its place is the idea of life . . . which, like its synoptic equivalent,

[45] Ch. Baumgartner, S.J. Cf. Ch. I, n. 12. This excerpt is taken from *op. cit.*, pp. 33–39.

[46] Jn 1:4; 11:25–26; 1 Jn 1:1–2.

[47] Jn 5:21, 25; 6:38–40.

[48] Jn 7:37–39; cf. 12:32; 19:34.

[49] Jn 3:3, 5.

presents two phases, a beginning in the present world and an expansion in the world to come.

The eschatological character of the Johannine eternal life has no need to be underlined. In the context in which it appears, there is question of the resurrection at the end of time for life or damnation.

Present and interior reality. At the same time in these same texts and elsewhere this life is considered a present reality. It is put in relation with faith. To believe is to have eternal life.[50] Eternal life is not only an actual and present reality, it is a reality that is interior to the believer, a life of the soul, a life of grace, a supernatural or mystic life. It corresponds to the initial phase of the Kingdom of the synoptic gospels, of which it is a more profound theological explanation. To the interiority of the kingdom, to the new manner of life of the children of God, to the filial spirit, the interiority of the Johannine life gives the ontological foundation. St. John hardly stresses the increase and development of this life; he insists on its perfection and its superabundance.

When St. John affirms that he who believes has eternal life, that he who eats the flesh of Jesus and drinks His blood has eternal life, that Jesus dwells in him and he in Jesus, he does not mean merely to affirm that the faithful are sure to receive eternal life at the end of time, that they have a right to it as to an inheritance they will enjoy in a distant future. He means

to say: the believer lives because he has received the gift of Life. This interpretation is confirmed by some texts that relate to the passage from death to life.[51] Beside the resurrection of the dead at the last day[52] there is question of another resurrection that does not bring the body from the tomb. It is the passage from spiritual death, the death of sin, to the life given now by Jesus.[53] As spiritual death is an actual and interior reality, so is the life to which the word of Jesus calls those who are buried in the tomb of sin.[54]

2. Communion with the Father and Son in the Spirit. According to the gospel of St. John, faith is needed to have eternal life. The first epistle rather envisages this faith as a consequence of this eternal life in him who truly possesses it. Faith,[55] the flight from sin,[56] fraternal love[57] are the effects and the criteria of eternal life, the signs that permit us to recognize its presence in the community and in individuals. Whoever avoids sin, practises justice, walks in the light, loves his brethren, believes that Jesus is the Son of God and the Messiah, he is certainly in communion with God, he is born of God. God dwells in him and he dwells in God; he "knows" God. These formulas: communion with God, immanence of God in the faithful and of the faithful

---

[50] Jn 3:14; 5:24–25; 6:47, 53, 54, 56; 10:10.

[51] Ap 3:1–2; Jn 5:24; 1 Jn 3:14–16.
[52] Jn 5:28, 29.
[53] Jn 5:25.
[54] Cf. Jn 8:51; 10:28; 11:26.
[55] Jn 5:13.
[56] Jn 5:18.
[57] Jn 4:16.

in God, birth "from God," knowledge of God: all designate eternal life. They all express it under different aspects. This doctrine is not new in relation to the fourth gospel, but as the first epistle seems more explicit on these points, we take it as our point of departure in expounding these themes.

Communion with God. "But if we walk in the light . . . we have fellowship with one another."[58] The term *koinonia* is used only at the beginning of the epistle. This communion is with the Father and His Son Jesus Christ. The communion of man with God is at the same time a communion among the faithful. Being united to the Father and the Son the faithful are united among themselves, and are animated by the same life. Communion with God and communion among the faithful are two aspects of the same reality; participation in eternal life. If the vocabulary of *koinonia* is absent from the gospel, the doctrine is there, particularly in the sacerdotal prayer.[59]

Immanence of God in the faithful and of the faithful in God. "No one has ever seen God. If we love one another, God abides in us."[60] "God is love, and he who abides in love, abides in God and God in him."[61] It is a presence of the Father and of the Son.[62] In the epistle St. John especially considers the presence of God as a principle of action: faith and fraternal

love are its effect and sign. This point of view is also that of the gospel in the allegory of the vine.[63] The inhabitation of the Father and Son, of which there is question in the preceding chapter, appears rather as a consequence of the observance of the commandments.[64]

Besides faith and fraternal love there is still another criterion of the presence of God the Father and Son: it is the Spirit.[65] The faithful know that they have the Spirit, for the Spirit manifests Himself by His charisms.[66] His favors are the proof of His presence, which is the principle of the life of God in us.[67]

Birth "from God." "If you know that he is just, know that everyone also who does justice has been born of him."[68] Participation in the divine life, communion with God, presence of God in the faithful and of the faithful in God are realised in fact when they are born of God and become children of God,[69] that is to say, at baptism. In the epistle John does not say when this birth takes place. This image, applied to the gift of divine life, recalls the conversation of Jesus with Nicodemus.[70] To see the kingdom of God, to enter it, in other words, to have eternal life, one must be born from on high. This new birth is realised in baptism which is a bath

---

[58] 1 Jn 1:7.

[59] Jn 17.

[60] 1 Jn 4:12.

[61] 1 Jn 4:16.

[62] 1 Jn 2:5–6, 24; 5:20; cf. Jn 6:56.

[63] Jn 15:1–5.

[64] Jn 14:23.

[65] 1 Jn 3:24; 4:13.

[66] 1 Jn 4:1.

[67] 1 Jn 3:9.

[68] 1 Jn 2:29; cf. 3:9, 10; 4:7; 5:1, 4, 18.

[69] 1 Jn 1:12–13; 3:1–2.

[70] Jn 3:3–8.

of regeneration in the Spirit. To make us understand the nature and necessity of this rebirth Jesus insists on the absolute difference between natural life and divine life. There is a radical discontinuity between the flesh and the Spirit. The flesh is, for St. John, human nature considered in itself, in its feebleness as creature. The Spirit is God Himself or the supernatural order. From the flesh to the Spirit, from man to God, no passage is possible without the intervention or coming of the Spirit, without the regeneration of man by God. Nicodemus must comprehend the impotence of man to pass to God by his own powers. There is no evolution of man to the condition of son of God. As mysterious and unseizable as the wind that passes, the regeneration of man by the Spirit is not less real.

Whoever is born of God cannot commit sin. This is what distinguishes the child of God from the child of the devil. He becomes thus like God. To be like God is to act as God acts, to love as God loves. The reason for this likeness between God and His children, is the gift of a vital principle received at their birth, a principle of action that comes from God. To the expression "to be born of God" corresponds the expression "to be of God."[71] This last formula signifies a divine origin, the communication of something properly divine, a certain community of life. This theology resumes and explains, by assigning to it its ontological foundation, the Matthean norm of Christian life: "You therefore are to be perfect, even as your heavenly Father is perfect."[72]

6. **P. Gregory Stevens, O.S.B.,[73] sees in St. John a profound revelation of the doctrine of grace. The Christian becomes a son of God, a child of truth and light, by a communication of divine life and truth which transfers him from the world of sin and darkness into the glorious kingdom of God. This communication of divine life, effected in the rebirth of baptism through faith and constantly renewed in the Eucharist, is a real beginning here on earth of the life of glory.**

The new life. The profoundly theological reflections of St. John present the reality of the kingdom of grace primarily under the symbol of a divine life communicated by the Father in Christ.[74] Indeed, this is the purpose for which Christ Himself entered the world: "I came that they may have life, and have it more abundantly."[75] The theme of life is the most prominent one in John's thought about Christ and His work. It is in

[71] 1 Jn 3:10; 4:4–7; 5:19.
[72] Mt 5:47; cf. Lk 6:36.

[73] P. Gregory Stevens, O.S.B. Cf. Ch. II, n. 25. This excerpt is from *op. cit.*, pp. 8–18.
[74] Jn 3:16.
[75] Jn 10:10.

terms of John's teaching on life in Christ and Christ's life in the individual Christian that his doctrine on grace will be developed.

First of all, Christ the Word is Himself life.[76] . . . In the imagery of the fourth gospel, God Himself is life: "For as the Father has life in himself, even so he has given to the Son also to have life in himself."[77] Through the Word men have the power to become sons of God.[78] Thus does John trace the great lines of his vision of the divine plan for man's salvation. God the Father who is love is the source and first principle of salvation. This divine love is manifested in the Word who is light and life, and the Word "became flesh" and entered the world in order to communicate to men the richness of grace, to bestow on man life and light, rescuing man from death and darkness. Thus does John summarize the essentials of the theology of grace: its source is the divine life itself, in the love and life of the Father and of the eternal Son; its realization comes in the course of human history by the incarnation of the Word of life, through whom we participate in the divine life itself.

Christ: the new life. Christ Himself is a gift of grace, indeed *the* gift of grace.[79] So too is the life of God communicated to man.[80] The Father thus communicates His life, light,

grace, and truth through the mediation of his only-begotten Son.[81] . . . To those who receive Jesus, life is given. The life consists in knowing and loving Christ and the brethren.[82] To come to this life, sin must first be destroyed by the power of "the lamb of God, who takes away the sins of the world."[83]

John does not deny that man can lose grace by his weakness, pride, and sinfulness. He does affirm in a positive strain that grace is a new life so powerful in and of itself that it gives man the power to resist sin, and thus to remain in the light. The Christian is in principle free of sin. Sin no longer has power over him. Man is still able to refuse the power of life and to succumb to death and evil, but this is not possible for the Christian who maintains his love for the Word who destroys sin.

New birth in Christ. The destruction of the power of the evil one in the life of the Christian is accomplished by a new birth. John stresses above all else the positive aspects of grace by which we are reborn to a life of light, truth and love. From the first chapter of his gospel, John affirms that Christ "gave the power of becoming sons of God: to those who believe in his name."[84] He emphasizes that this is not a mere figure of speech but a realistic description of a living, spiritual entity.[85]

This is a new birth "of water and

---

[76] Jn 1:4–17.
[77] Jn 5:26.
[78] Jn 1:16 f.
[79] Jn 4:10.
[80] Jn 5:21.

[81] Jn 6:40; 8:31 f.
[82] Jn 17:3.
[83] Jn 1:29.
[84] Jn 1:12.
[85] 1 Jn 3:1.

the Spirit"[86] by which man is born again just as really as he was born by physical generation. . . . Man shares in the life of God by becoming a son of God.[87] This doctrine of a new creation is taken up again in forceful style by St. Paul, who stressed the redemptive aspect of this dramatic transformation of man. . . .

The true light. If the reality of grace is presented in John in terms of the great symbol of life, it is also a part of the Johannine symbolism to see Christ as the light, the true light,[88] the light of the world.[89] . . . John sees light and life as interchangeable concepts in speaking of the Word.[90] Those who receive the light have the knowledge of God which makes them sons of God and partakers of His life. Those who receive the light become sharers in the true light that God Himself is from all eternity. . . . If this great symbol of light in John has an intellectual dimension — so that the life of grace is defined in terms of a knowledge of the Father and the Son[91] — we must see in the Johannine doctrine of light a profound reality which sees the light as God Himself. Our participation in this light is thus another way used by John to reveal the mystery of the Christian's sharing in the ultimate reality which God is, by way of a decisive regeneration. This rebirth separates him from sin and darkness. It introduces man into the

life of God who is light and truth. . . .

The notion of eternal life was of course present in the synoptics.[92] However, it is only in John that the reality of life is treated so thoroughly and with such depth. What was implicit in the synoptics becomes the core of John's profound theological meditations.

Grace and glory. We have seen in the synoptics the doctrine of the kingdom presented in its two distinct phrases: that of establishment and beginning on earth in this life, and that of completion and fulfillment in the next life at the last judgment. John does not deny or even overlook this distinction between the life of grace and the life of glory. "He who loves his life, loses it; and he who hates his life in this world, keeps it unto life everlasting."[93] More often, however, John sees the whole Christian life as a unity, and stresses the mystery that eternal life is already present, has already begun, here on earth. In a sense, then, John sees the last days as already accomplished in what has been called his "realized eschatology." That is to say, John sees the essentials of life in God and union with the Word as a realization here and now of the glory to come. The life of grace is a real anticipation of the life of heaven. . . .

The third chapter of the first epistle expresses the conviction that the divine life is now present as a result of the new generation by God. . . . The whole passage insists on the difference

[86] Jn 3:3, 5.
[87] Jn 3:6.
[88] Jn 1:9.
[89] Jn 8:12; 9:5.
[90] Jn 1:3 f.
[91] Jn 17:3.

[92] Mt 19:16 f.; 25:46,34; Mk 9:43, 45.
[93] Jn 12:25; cf. 14:2 f.

between those who possess life, who are living, and the sons of the world or of Satan who do not possess this life and cannot manifest its sign which is fraternal love. There is then a real inner transformation that makes the Christian a son of the Father who, in all that he does, manifests this inner life. The life of grace is a force leading to a mode of activity proper to it. We may say that John sees the total Christian reality as a process which has its beginning and its progressive unfolding in love, and its consummation in glory. There, our sonship will be fully manifest in the vision of God.

Life in God. The complete reality of the inner transformation of the life of grace is brought out by St. John in his repeated mention of the new presence to the Christian of the Father and the Son: that is, the real indwelling presence of the persons of the Trinity.[94] Not only is the Christian given life, which later theology will call created habitual grace, but he is given "uncreated grace": the actual presence of the persons of the Trinity.

It is this life in the presence of the Son which will be consummated in glory but which is now hidden in faith.[95] The principle of deathless life is already communicated to the Christian who lives in Christ. The physical reality of this mutual presence of the Christian and Christ is placed in a strong light by the parable of the vine and the branches.[96] The whole

parable teaches that the life which Christ is, is transmitted to us, the branches, so that there is a communion in the same life. This vital and intimate connection involves a *mutual presence of man to Christ and Christ to man* which is the constant condition of the life of the Christian. This life furthermore fructifies and expresses its dynamic nature by the good works which manifest the life of the branches in vital communion with the vine. Indeed, one text in this parable: "without me you can do nothing," will be constantly present to the theological awareness of the Church in her doctrinal development. . . .

All men may receive this life if they are not so attached to sin and darkness as to refuse the light. For those who receive this life there is entrance into communion with the divine persons, a sharing by grace in the life which is proper to God alone. This union with Christ perfects the union among those men who are joined in fraternal charity. The union which binds Christians together is an imitation of the unity which unites Father, Son and Spirit, and the result of the wonderful presence to the Christian of the Father and Son.[97] In these words John seeks to express the inexpressible mystery of shared life which incorporates man into the divine life of the Trinity.

This incorporation is at once individual and personal as well as social. As the parable of the vine and the branches indicates, our union with Christ is also a union in the reality

---

94 1 Jn 2:23–25; 5:11 f.
95 Jn 11:25 f.
96 Jn 15:4 f.

97 Jn 14:23.

of the one life of the Church. This union which the Christian expresses by keeping the commandments, and above all by loving the brethren, unites him in a profound union with his fellow Christian. The ecclesial aspect of grace is thus one of the aspects of the divine life in man which John clearly teaches.

Conclusion. St. John presents us with a profound revelation of the doctrine of grace: the result of his penetration, in the Spirit, into the mysteries of our relationship with the triune God. The Christian thus becomes a son of God, a child of truth and light, by a communication of divine life and truth which transfers him from the world of sin and darkness into the glorious kingdom of God. This communication of divine life, effected in the rebirth of baptism through faith and constantly renewed in the Eucharist, is a real beginning here on earth of the life of glory to come. This life of glory will be but the flowering and the open manifestation of the inner transformation which has already taken place in the life of grace.

IV

GRACE IN ST. PAUL

1. **T. F. Torrance[1] sees *charis* in the New Testament as primarily a Pauline word. It expresses God's lavish self-giving to men in the person and death of Jesus, and not an inward quality of Christian life adhering in the human soul. Paul deliberately avoided using *charis* in the sense of an energizing principle.**

Charis in the New Testament is primarily a Pauline word, but there is no doubt at all about the fact that the source of the Apostle's doctrine of grace goes back to Jesus Christ Him-self in teaching and life,[2] though it was the wonder of such grace manifested by the risen Christ that first overpowered Paul and then held him

---

[1] Cf. Ch. I, n. 1. This excerpt is from *op. cit.*, pp. 26–33.

[2] See J. Weiss, *Das Urchristentum* I, p. 350; *Paulus und Jesus*, p. 22 f.; H. A. A. Kennedy, *The Theology of the Epistles*, p. 54.

captive for life in the bonds of ador-
ing gratitude and love. The extreme
zeal of his Pharisaic piety and the
circumstances of his life at the time
of his conversion, when he was en-
gaged in persecuting the followers of
Jesus, served to throw into bold relief
the absolute initiative of God in salvation, for this same Jesus in boundless
love intervened in his career and for-
gave him outright, and even sealed
this gracious pledge of pardon by calling him to be an Apostle of this grace
to the Gentiles.[3] "And last of all," he
says to the Corinthians, "he appeared
to me also as to one born out of
due time. For I am the least of the
Apostles, because I persecuted the
Church of God. But by the grace of
God I am what I am."[4] . . . That God
should stoop to the Cross out of love
for men was well-nigh incredible, but
that was the truth that broke out of
darkness into Paul's mind. Jesus Himself was the deed of God's unspeak-
able grace, God in a self-giving to men
that was infinitely lavish.

To express that Paul uses the word
charis. Whether or not he coined it,
as seems likely (some word had to be
coined), it is certainly he that gives
it its distinctive sense, putting into it
the basic message of the Gospel.
Henceforth it becomes on the lips of
redeemed sinners[5] the great word of

the evangel: the grace of our Lord
Jesus Christ. Two elements are always
cardinal to the use of the word in
St. Paul: the person of the risen Lord,
and the Cross. . . . In the background
there is always the thought that *charis*
is the grace of God, but in the foreground it is the person of Christ, and
the act of Christ that fill the focus
of vision. Grace reigns through Christ
in God. God manifest in grace is Jesus
Christ, and that manifestation is essentially (not incidentally) through the
Cross. "The grace of God," he says,
"was given to you in Christ Jesus"[6]
and the gift took the form of a reconciling sacrifice.[7] . . .

It would be safe to say that Paul
never speaks of grace except as
grounded in the self-giving of God in
the person and death of Jesus, and in
every instance it is the objective side of
its content that predominates. There is
no hint of any psychologising in his
use of the word *charis*. He does, however, use the word in an applied as
well as in a primary sense, but these
correspond, from the point of view
of the redeemed sinner, to the two
main aspects in which grace was seen
to be manifested in the gospels.

(1) In its primary sense in St.
Paul's epistles grace has to do with
the act of divine intervention rather
than with our receiving of it. *Charis*
is now the presupposition of all man's

---

[3] Eph 3:1 f.

[4] 1 Cor 15:8–10.

[5] If our Lord did not speak of grace in
this way, that is to be expected because He
was the Redeemer, and not a redeemed
sinner, and as Redeemer supplied in His
own person and work the glorious content
of the word *charis*. Hence we find it in

the Epistles rather than in the Gospels, that
is, on the side of the joyful receiver, rather
than on the side of the gracious giver,
which is in line with the etymology of
the word itself.

[6] 1 Cor 1:4.

[7] Rom 3:24–26; 5:1–21; cf. Ti 2:11.

relations with God and constitutive of the whole Christian life. . . . An entirely new perspective is given to human history through which everything is thrown into a new light. Thus Paul thinks of grace as disclosing a new world which has broken through by the Cross into our world and is now operative in the Gospel.[8] . . .

(2) In its applied sense Paul's use of *charis* is more elusive, though it is perfectly clear that there is no real difference between this and the fundamental sense of the word. Even here the primary sense predominates, though the focus of attention is upon a particular application of grace. Just as Paul thought of the grace of God as having actualised itself among men in Jesus, so in an applied sense Paul thinks of that same grace as laying hold of men in an act of forgiving and creative love. . . .

In all this Paul is careful to lay the emphasis on grace as the gift of God. It is his only in an applied sense, and he is vividly conscious that it is none other than the risen Christ who confronts men through the word of his Gospel. *Charis* is not here, therefore, in any sense a quality adhering to Paul, but a particular manifestation of the gracious purpose and power of Christ. It is in this sense too that Paul speaks of others as being in the grace of God, or as standing in grace, or falling from grace, or as being under grace.[9] Grace is here the new supernatural order which breaks in upon men, but which manifests itself in their faith, and in their Christian life. *Charis* is the word used for the cause and the source of the Christian status, but it is *charis* essentially in its fundamental sense even here, and not as a transferred quality.[10] . . .

There can be no doubt that Paul did think of the impact of grace upon men in terms of power, for "the kingdom of God," he said, "was not in word only, but in power."[11] The Gospel was not in word only, not a fiction, but in power and reality, creating its own results in righteousness and truth. This is no doubt the most elusive point about Paul's conception of grace, and it is at this point that later divergencies first arose. Paul thinks of grace acting dynamically upon men, but he never allows his thought of it, in this applied sense, to stray from its original transcendent character. Grace comes from beyond the self, and is quite other than man or anything human. As power acting on men it is not impersonal, but intensely personal, as personal as Christ Himself, for it is Christ acting in person, and not in any sub-personal fashion. Hence the close attachment of grace and Gospel. Grace is possessed as Christ is possessed, by faith. And grace is a gift in the sense that Christ is a gift, in His personal self-giving, which is gift in the sense of *dandum* rather than *datum*. Thus grace is never a private possession in the sense that it can be pocketed or handed on.

---

[8] 2 Cor 4:6, 15; 5:17; 1 Cor 2:12; Col 1:13.

[9] Rom 5:2; 6:14; 12:3; 15:16; Gal 5:4; cf. Eph 2:5.

[10] Cf. 1 Cor 3:10; 15:10; Gal 2:7; Rom 12:3; 15:15.

[11] 1 Cor 4:20.

When Paul does use *charis* in such a way that it makes us wonder whether he is not after all using it to indicate the effect of redeeming favour in an inward quality of Christian life, we must remember that his doctrine of the Christian life is thrown into eschatological form. "You are dead and your life is hid with Christ in God."[12] The Christian's righteousness, wisdom, sanctification, and redemption are to be found in Christ Himself,[13] and so Paul can speak of these as differentiations of *charis* even when they are manifest in the believer, without really using *charis* to denote qualities adhering in the human soul. *Charis* is never adjectival on the lips of Paul, but always dynamic. . . .

Thus any attempt to detach grace in a transferred sense from the actual embodiment of God's grace in Jesus Christ is to misunderstand the meaning of the Pauline *charis* altogether. It was doubtless for that reason that whenever Paul spoke of grace-gift in a detached sense it was not *charis* he used, but *charisma,* and what is more, he did not derive *charisma* from *charis* but from *Pneuma.*[14] That means that Paul deliberately avoided using *charis* in the sense of an energising principle, though that is the way in which *charis,* due to Hellenistic influences, came to be used in later Christian literature.

2. **William Manson**[15] **sees St. Paul's doctrine of grace starting from the position that the whole life of salvation rests upon God's free gift. This gift or generous love of God by which in Christ salvation is bestowed on man and a new world of blessings is opened is grace for St. Paul. Thus grace in its fundamental sense refers to God's self-giving rather than to man's receiving, and hence grace is not properly to be thought of in quantitative rather than dynamic terms.**

St. Paul's doctrine of grace . . . starts from the position that the whole life of salvation rests upon God's mercy or free gift. Power, happiness, peace, achievement, bliss are conditional upon open-hearted receptivity towards God through the self-surrender of faith. With his mind fixed upon the Cross,

St. Paul will stake everything upon God's self-giving as the presupposition of all religion, and this he styles *charis,* taking up and extending a contemporary usage of the Greek expression. We must here think not merely of a Divine attitude of favour or mere willingness to bless but of a Divine self-giving that exerts itself in action, and that dynamically creates its own results in righteousness.

I. Grace for St. Paul signifies the

[12] Col 3:3.
[13] 1 Cor 1:30.
[14] 1 Cor 12:4–11.
[15] Cf. Ch. II, n. 13. This excerpt is from *op. cit.*, pp. 43–52, 59–60.

generous love or gift of God by which in Christ salvation is bestowed on man and a new world of blessings opened. It implies that what saves man is not something proceeding from himself or from his own nature, or from his own will or effort, but something "wholly other," which proceeds from God and which is "exhibited"[16] on the Cross of Christ.

Here we have the fundamental Christian sense of grace to which all uses of the word in the New Testament go back, and by which in the last resort all these other uses must be justified. The simplest expression of the idea is in Rom 3:24 where St. Paul speaks of Christians as "justified freely by his grace through the redemption (or deliverance) effected in Messiah Jesus."

It is plain from the character of the allusions here that God's grace, God's free giving, has for its object to disclose and to bring in for Christians a higher world of spiritual good, in which we must see the translation into present actual experience of *eschatological* promise of salvation. This is a thoroughly characteristic aspect of the thought of grace in St. Paul. Grace creates the conditions, the new world, in which it operates. It effects deliverance from the tyranny of darkness and confers entrance into the Kingdom of God.[17] . . .

II. The term "grace" is also used by St. Paul with reference to the new Divine influence or influences which operate from within the Christian nature. The gracious initiative of God in salvation appears as taking effect in human hearts in immanent fashion and under differentiated forms. . . . In some of his sentences St. Paul seems to mean by *charis* not God's redeeming favour as such but the results of this favour in Christian character and conduct. For example, in the passages above refererd to,[18] it seems as if "grace" possessed a new sense, referring less to the Divine graciousness in giving, than to an inward quality possessed by Paul for fulfilling his office. But this differentiation of ideas in St. Paul is more apparent than real. While the language in such sentences as "I say by the grace given to me"[19] indicates that the reference is to something communicated to Paul and now possessed by him, yet even here he is thinking not of any special apostolic endowment but of a particular manifestation of the Divine grace which called him into the service of Christ. . . .

It seems best then to say that St. Paul, keeping steadfastly to the original sense of the word, thinks of the grace of God as becoming effectual in various ways, now as giving men a new status, now as conferring various special gifts, now as inspiring to fresh tasks and responsibilities. . . . From this a very important conclusion follows. If grace in its fundamental sense refers to God's self-giving rather than to man's receiving, it is not properly to be thought of in quantitative rather

---

[16] Rom 3:25–26.
[17] Col 1:13.
[18] 1 Cor 3:10; Gal 2:7; Rom 12:3; 15:15.
[19] Rom 12:3.

than dynamic terms. The quantitative idea of grace, as if given en bloc, was as foreign to St. Paul as was the quantitative idea of faith to Jesus.[20]

III. Yet St. Paul recognizes in the Church various spiritual aptitudes and functions which have their source in God's will to give, and which using a term connected with *charis* he therefore calls *charismata,* i.e., "grace-gifts."[21] . . . It is to be noticed, on the other hand, that while the word *charisma* is etymologicaly dependent upon *charis,* the efficient power or principle from which St. Paul directly derives the various *charismata* is not grace but the Spirit.[22] . . . It would appear, therefore, that "grace" has undoubtedly an immanent and dynamical quality in St. Paul's teaching, but that at the same time, when he thinks of the power which is at work in Christians, he speaks of the Spirit rather than of "grace." When he speaks of the latter, while he has in mind the effects which spring from the operation of grace on the Christian soul, he thinks even more primarily of the unmerited love of which Christians are the objects. The fact that he does not call it *charis* when this term lay so close to his hand in connection with the *charismata* is strong evidence that St. Paul meant by the grace of God something prior to, and conditioning, the energy of all "grace-gifts."[23] . . .

Conclusion. The predominating sense of grace in the New Testament is that which the word bears in the writings of St. Paul, who thinks of the Divine salvation primarily as a "boon" flowing from the generous, unmerited graciousness of God to sinful, lost humanity as expressed supremely on the Cross of Christ. For St. Paul the free outgoing and self-imparting of the redeeming love of God to man in Christ is constitutive of the whole of salvation. God deals with men in Christ purely on a basis of infinite, undeserved mercy. In defence of this conception St. Paul fought for the admission of the Gentiles into the Church upon a basis of faith or trust alone, and in his teaching grace has constant reference to this incorporation of the Gentiles into the people of God. The evidence, whether in St. Paul or in the rest of the New Testament, of any departure from this primary conception, of a less sure grasp on grace as the whole Divine *a priori* of salvation, is inconsiderable.

Thus grace remains, strictly speaking, undifferentiated, as being the entire presupposition of the Christian life, from which everything in that life flows, and by which everything in that life is inspired. As such it assumes, by taking up and raising to a higher power certain capacities native to individuals, the special form or "grace-gifts" or *charismata.* Yet even such gracious "inworkings" of God's Spirit are not viewed as concrete entities or inherent powers. Still less does the New Testament speak of "means" of grace, or connect *charis* explicitly with any sacrament. The tendency to connect grace specially with the sacra-

---

[20] Lk 17:5 f.
[21] Rom 12:6.
[22] 1 Cor 12:4-11.
[23] Rom 5:8 ff.

ments arose later as the result of a disposition in the Hellenistic Church to fix attention less on God's great redemptive act in Christ than on special means whereby Christians are helped to live the spiritual life. In St. Paul such need for prevenient power and direction is dealt with rather in terms of the Spirit, for Christians are not all alike "spiritual." His thought of grace remains distinctively one of new status or relation to God, as in the words: "You have been saved by grace through faith, and that not of yourselves; it is the gift of God."[24]

3. F. Amiot[25] studies the new man of justification and the way to justification through faith and baptism. He finds the notion of grace, like all the great Pauline themes, complex. As it appears in man, it seems like a new quality molding the soul inwardly. The transformation it effects in the soul Paul describes as being in a special way the work of the Holy Spirit.

The new man: justification. If it be true, as St. Irenaeus asserted, that Christ "brought complete renewal in giving himself"[26] there is no room for surprise that St. Paul should present a share in salvation as a renewal which reaches to the very depths of our being. The Christian is a new man, built on the ruins of the old or sinful man. This is a fundamental theme, acting as a corollary to the theme of salvation and to that of Christ the new Adam who came to make superabundant reparation for the ravages caused by the fall of the first man. . . .

To put the matter precisely, the new self is none other than Christ whom we put on in baptism[27] in a complete submission to His divine influence. The change is so radical as to result in a divine creation in Christ Jesus[28] — in other words, a new creature.[29] It would be impossible to conceive a more striking expression of the idea. At all events, what was old has passed away and something new has appeared.[30] There has been a regeneration, and a renewal of our nature in the Holy Spirit,[31] the ultimate effect of which is to form Christ in the Christian by a process of spiritual birth.[32] It is not a question of a static condition, perfect from the start, but

---

[24] Eph 2:8.

[25] F. Amiot, S.S., was born in 1889 and is professor of Scripture at St. Sulpice Seminary, Paris. He is the author of various works, such as *La bible apocryphe, The History of the Mass,* etc. This excerpt is taken from his book, *The Key Concepts of St. Paul* (New York: Herder and Herder, 1962), pp. 120–123, 126–130, 133–137, 141, 150–157, 166.

[26] *"Omnem novitatem attulit seipsum afferens."* Adv. haer., 1. 4, c. 34, n. 1; P.G., VII, 1083.

[27] Gal 3:27.

[28] Eph 2:10.

[29] Gal 6:15.

[30] 2 Cor 5:17.

[31] Ti 3:5.

[32] Gal 4:19. Compare the rebirth announced by Christ to Nicodemus (Jn 3:3–5).

of a state that the life of the neophyte must confirm and complete in an un-interrupted spiritual progress, calling forth "such good actions as he has prepared beforehand, to be the employment of our lives."[33]. . .

Paul once more uses various metaphors to describe the new state of the Christian. The debt of sin has been remitted to him and his sin forgiven.[34] He has been ransomed — and at a great price[35] — by the outpouring of the blood of Jesus.[36] He has thus been reconciled to God[37] and no judgment now stands against him.[38] From being God's enemy, he has become a son by adoption.[39] To resume then, he is justified — and this is the expression most frequently used — by the completely free granting of divine justice.[40] This not only puts an end to the state of sinfulness but also has the positive effect of sanctification.

Justification is thus, at one and the same time, destruction of sin and communication of a new life. The first aspect is adequately shown in the passages in which the apostle deals with the stripping and crucifixion of the old self, forgiveness of sins and reconciliation to God, but there is no forgiveness that is not accompanied by the transmission of new life, that is without positive justification or sanctification, without the formation of the new self.

The texts already quoted all indicate in some degree this two-fold aspect. There are others even more characteristic: "Christ Jesus, whom God gave us to be all our wisdom, our justification, our sanctification, and our atonement."[41] "Now you have been washed clean, now you have been sanctified, now you have been justified in the name of the Lord Jesus, by the Spirit of the God we serve."[42]

We shall show further on how it follows clearly enough from the gift of the Holy Spirit, from the life of Christ in us, and from the adoption of sons, that it is a question on all sides of interior realities and that justification is not, as Luther would have it, a simple imputation of divine justice, or a reconciliation still leaving a state of sin. This interior character is, moreover, implied by the antithesis between our solidarity in Adam and our solidarity in Christ. In Adam, all are made sinners, and in Christ, all are made just. . . . To regard justification as nothing more than an ineffective declaration or a purely formal imputation is to adopt a view diametrically opposed to St. Paul's.[43]. . .

The way to justification: faith and baptism. For the apostle, faith is not simply the assent of the intelligence to the word of God and of Christ but is a total gift, a complete change of direction, which makes thought prisoner in order to bring man entirely into the obedience of Christ.[44]

---

[33] Eph 2:10.
[34] Col 1:14.
[35] 1 Cor 6:20; 7:23.
[36] Rom 3:24.
[37] Rom 5:10–11; 2 Cor 5:18–19; Col 1:22.
[38] Rom 8:1.
[39] Gal 4:5; Rom 8:15; Eph 1:5.
[40] Rom 1:17; 3:24.
[41] 1 Cor 1:30.   [42] 1 Cor 6:11.
[43] For a Semite particularly, the word of God has a creative effect. If God declares a man just He renders him truly so.
[44] 2 Cor 10:5.

In this way, not only does the believer give up the autonomy of his own thinking[45] but he deliberately abandons the idea that he is himself a centre. He is ready to put on Christ, allowing himself to be penetrated with Christ's life.[46] In the light of his knowledge of Christ, he deliberately chooses to look upon as refuse what he was once wont to consider enviable privileges, to give up his own justice in favour of that which comes from God and is founded in the faith of Christ.[47] Embracing the highest form of liberty, he is ready to make himself God's slave.[48] In short, he is willing to become a new creature.[49] Understood in this way, faith extends to every aspect of life. It can be described as a paschal action because, with baptism to which it leads, it unites to the death and resurrection of Christ. Does not becoming a new creature in fact mean crucifying the flesh with its passions and offering oneself as a sacrifice with the Saviour?[50] But death with Christ enables us to share in His life and guarantees salvation.[51]. . .

Some texts already quoted might lead us to suppose that St. Paul attributes justification to faith alone but he does not in fact speak of justification by faith except to contrast it with the works of the law. In his mind, faith presupposes a desire for baptism and should lead the person concerned to ask for it,[52] so that justification is both by faith and baptism. Even in his discussions with the Judaists, he occasionally mentions them together.[53]. . . He was himself baptized by Ananias, immediately after his conversion.[54]. . . Baptism is not only a rite of purification and renovation, but also constitutes an illumination. . . .

The fundamental thought in Paul is the one referred to above, linking the baptized with the death, burial and resurrection of Christ. He sets it out in a well-known passage which provides the Lenten and Easter liturgy with frequent inspiration.[55]. . . Christian baptism unites the catechumen to the bloody and glorifying baptism of Christ which, by anticipation, procured for all believers pardon for their sins and glorification. By the reception of baptism the recipient is plunged into the death and burial of Christ at the same time as he is immersed in the water, and is linked with His resurrection on emerging from the baptismal font. The two actions are in reality one and are inseparable for the catechumen as they were for Christ. By them, the catechumen becomes one plant with Christ. . . .

---

[45] Intellectual humility, which is a constituent of faith, is clearly brought out in the famous passage in which St. Paul contrasts the false wisdom of the world with *Christian wisdom:* 1 Cor 1:17–3:16.

[46] Gal 2:20; 3:27.

[47] Phil 3:7–9.

[48] 2 Cor 10:7; Rom 6:17–19.

[49] Gal 6:15.

[50] Rom 15:16; Phil 2:17.

[51] Rom 10:9–11.

[52] St. Paul does not deal with the situation in which baptism has been deferred or is impossible, but it follows from his teaching that faith saves before baptism if it is perfect and includes a desire for baptism with an acceptance of the demands that baptism makes. . . .

[53] Gal 3:26–27.

[54] Acts 9:18.

[55] Rom 6:3–13.

It can be seen from what we have said that baptism and faith imply each the other. Faith enlightens and already justifies. Baptism incorporates into the Christian community and into the body of Christ. Baptism provides an entry into the visible Church and gives faith its full extension by virtue of the public and solemn proclamation of the sacrament which accompanies reception and by the action of the sacrament throughout life. Baptism and faith are divinely ratified by the gift of the Holy Spirit, which makes the person baptized an adopted child of God, destined for resurrection. Baptism reminds the neophyte that it is God who has made him die to sin in union with the death of Christ and that God will complete His own work. It provides certainty of entry into the kingdom and of a share in the new life. As it makes the catechumen capable of receiving the other sacraments and able to share in the worship of the Church, baptism constitutes an invitation to spiritual growth in order to attain the future kingdom. Through it, there is a marvellous sharing in the redemption, which is static from the point of view of spiritual regeneration, and dynamic considered as a gift of supernatural life, vivifying and strengthening the soul.[56] If the newly baptized submits himself to divine action, the influence of Christ's resurrection will be unceasingly at work in him until the day he enters into glory. . . .

Grace: the Holy Spirit. The word grace, *charis,* is one of those dear to St. Paul who uses it to describe supernatural gifts. It is such a happy choice that theologians have retained it unchanged, giving it the same meaning as in the epistles. The term *charisma* is also to be met with on occasion, either in the same sense or to denote the extraordinary gifts of the Holy Spirit, which are designed for the common good of the Church rather than the sanctification of the recipient and are often miraculous.

The word grace, which is equivalent in many respects to salvation, justification and sanctification, has the advantage of emphasizing that we are concerned with a gift. It underlines the absolute gratuity of spiritual life. The redemption is grace par excellence,[57] the source of salvation for all men alike.[58] Grace is the powerful gift that abounds still more where sin abounded and which reigns through justice to bring eternal life.[59] As a fruit of the preaching of the gospel[60] it is of such richness that it brings us salvation,[61] redemption and the remission of sins through the blood of Christ.[62] It constitutes the new economy, the new dispensation, one which liberates from sin and is very different from the dispensation of the law with which

---

[56] The passage in Acts 19:6; 1 Cor 12:13, and Heb 6:2 may refer to confirmation, but the interpretation is the subject of debate. For a further consideration of baptism see the review *Lumière et Vie,* March and May, 1956. . . . Cerfaux, *The Church in the Theology of St. Paul* (New York: Herder and Herder, 1958), pp. 127–129.

[57] Rom 3:24; 5:15.
[58] Ti 2:11.
[59] Rom 5:20–21.
[60] Col 1:6.
[61] Eph 2:8.
[62] Eph 1:7; Heb 2:9.

St. Paul contrasts it.[63] It is the affirmation and the beginning of the supreme gift, of the consummation of salvation which is eternal life in Christ our Lord.[64]

Like all the great Pauline themes, the notion of grace is complex. As it appears in man, it seems like a new quality moulding the soul inwardly. It is distinct from justification, understood in the strict sense as the passage from a state of sin to one of justice. It is a new mode of being which follows upon justification. In other words, it constitutes the "new creature." . . .

Theology labels it final justification to distinguish it from initial justification, which is the act itself whereby the sinner is justified. It also refers to it as sanctifying grace, because it is the source of holiness. It is the fruit especially characteristic of the redemptive sacrifice. . . . Like the redemptive act from which it springs, grace is completely gratuitous and merciful, and it supernaturalizes the whole of Christian life, from the first call to faith onwards. . . .

Sanctifying grace, the habitual state of holiness and of peace with God, is accompanied by the transient supernatural aids that are equally gratuitous and necessary and that theologians refer to as actual graces. No act of faith can be accomplished except through the movement of the Holy Spirit.[65] . . Grace is necessary at the beginning of the apostolate and for the effective preaching of the gospel,[66] but it is no less so for the whole exercise of the apostolic ministry and for the building of the Church.[67] . . . But grace is freely offered. God in His goodness produces in us the will to do, and the accomplishment of that will,[68] and our ability to perform supernatural works comes from Him.[69]

The fabric of graces from which God mercifully makes the web of our lives clearly does not dispense us from the need to accept the advances He makes. God wishes to respect our freedom and will exercise no constraint on unsubmissive instruments. Thus it is that the epistles are full of invitations to faithfulness and effort. . . . It is everywhere a question of grace and we might say that Pauline teaching is centred on grace. Grace and merit, mysteriously and harmoniously linked, both have as their final end eternal life, which is the gift of the heavenly heritage, man's supreme happiness and God's great glory.

The transformation effected in the soul by grace is referred to by Paul as "spirit" and he describes it as being in a special way the work of the Holy Spirit, the third person of the Trinity. The sanctifying and transforming action of the Spirit began with the resurrection and Pentecost — at least in its full and final form — and has never ceased. . . .

---

[63] Rom 6:14; Gal 2:21; 5:4.

[64] Rom 6:23.

[65] 1 Cor 12:3. [66] Eph 3:7–8.

[67] 1 Cor 3:10.

[68] Phil 2:13.

[69] 2 Cor 3:5. This passage relates to the apostolic labors. Applying it more generally, theologians have legitimately deduced the need for grace in the fulfillment of all supernatural actions.

The Spirit is primarily and essentially a gift. His outpouring is the fruit of the redemptive sacrifice. . . . He has also been called the soul of the Mystical Body in so far as He is the element interior to the Mystical Body whereby Christ unites the faithful with Himself. His action is infinitely varied and can be considered from many points of view, which should nevertheless not lead us to overlook the fundamental unity of this divine activity. . . .

These varied operations of the Spirit show that He is, in the highest degree, a principle of life. He is the agent of the resurrection for Christ and for the Christian and, in spite of the inevitable occurrence of bodily death, He does not cease to vivify our spirit by the justice and sanctity that His presence brings.[70] This life, imperfect here below, will blossom forth later in eternal life.[71] Full possession will take the place of the first-fruits.[72] And from the time at which St. Paul is speaking onwards, the Spirit is infusing into men's hearts a life that is truly divine. . . .

But, that being the case, it must be recognized that the life of grace constitutes a participation in the life of God Himself, or, to be more specific, in the life of the Trinity. The Christian who is justified and sanctified is the adopted child of the heavenly Father and the temple of God, the brother of Christ, the temple of the Spirit who acts in him.[73] It is through the Spirit that this marvellous union is effected.[74] It is the presence of the Spirit, the Spirit of the Father and the Son, that brings about our adoption and proves its reality.[75] There is, therefore, the particular action of the Holy Spirit giving rise to new relationships with the divine persons and the presence in the soul of these three persons. The persons are, moreover, inseparable. The change brought about in the soul in this way was to be later described by St. Peter[76] as participation in the divine nature, common to the three persons. St. Paul is saying in effect the same thing when he shows that the Christian is assimilated to God by knowledge and love,[77] in a way that remains imperfect, but will blossom forth one day in perfect knowledge, in the vision of God face to face and in a charity that will not pass.[78] Nevertheless, it is by the Spirit that we can penetrate to the very depths of God's nature and that His love is spread in our hearts. We can see that the whole of the New Testament looks towards the gift of the Spirit as towards the supreme good and the greatest fruit of the redeeming blood. . . .

---

[70] Rom 8:10–11.

[71] Gal 6:8; Rom 6:22.

[72] 2 Cor 1:22; 5:5; Rom 8:23; Eph 1:14.

[73] Gal 4:5–7; Rom 8:15–17, 29, 9, 14; 1 Cor 3:16; 6:19.

[74] 2 Cor 13:13.

[75] Gal 4:6.

[76] 2 Pt 1:4.

[77] 1 Cor 2:10; Rom 5:5.

[78] 1 Cor 13:12, 8.

4. Ch. Baumgartner, S.J.,[79] sees the theology of St. Paul dominated by the doctrine of the Two Adams and the two humanities of which they are the principle. It is in becoming a member of the Church by baptism that the believer puts on the new man and becomes a new creature. Holiness and justice, life in Christ, participation of the Spirit, are ecclesial. The gift of the Spirit is ecclesial and personal. Received in and by the Church He produces a profound transformation in the regenerated man and makes of him a new creature.

The theology of St. Paul is dominated by the doctrine of the Two Adams and the two humanities of which they are the principle. The first, psychic and terrestrial, is at the origin of the old and carnal humanity; the second, spiritual and celestial, is the source and exemplar of the new humanity,[80] of the people of God, of the Church formed of pagans and Jews reconciled with one another and with the Father, thanks to the blood of Christ.[81]

It is in becoming a member of the Church by baptism that the believer puts on the new man and becomes a new creature. Holiness and justice, life in Christ, participation of the Spirit, are ecclesial. The Spirit who animates the Christians is the Spirit of the Church. They receive Him only as members of this Church to which they are aggregated so as to serve it and find there their proper fulfilment. The gift of the Spirit is in its entirety ecclesial and personal. Received in and by the Church He produces a profound transformation in the regenerated man;

He makes of him a new creature.

Life in the risen Christ. Grace is a participation in the death and resurrection of Christ by faith and baptism.[82] . . . It is in this risen Christ, spirit, power and life, that the baptized exist and live. They have quit their old existence in sin, world, flesh. They live a life of the risen one which is communicated to them by Christ.[83]

If someone is in Christ, he is a new creature, the old being has gone and a new being is there.[84] The formula "in Christ Jesus" is very frequent in St. Paul. It designates a personal relation with Christ. To live in Christ, to exist in Christ signifies that the life of the Christian is a life flowing from his union with Christ, who is its source, exemplar and author by His active presence in the believer. . . . Just as the Christian exists and lives in Christ, Christ lives in the Christian and is in him.[85] The two formulas express from two different points of view the same relation and the same

---

[79] Cf. Ch. I, n. 12. This excerpt is from *op. cit.*, pp. 23–32.

[80] 1 Cor 15:45–49; Rom 5:12–21.

[81] Eph 2:14–22.

[82] Gal 3:26 ff.; Rom 6.

[83] Rom 6; 1 Cor 1:30.

[84] 2 Cor 5:17.

[85] Gal 2:19–21; cf. 4:19; 2 Cor 13:5; Eph 3:17; Rom 8:9–11.

union of Christ and believers. He is the efficient and exemplary cause of this new life but in such a way that He is also, in some manner, its unique subject. That which the formulas of reciprocal immanence of Christ in Christians and Christians in Christ tend to suggest, St. Paul also expresses directly. "For you are all the children of God through faith in Christ Jesus. For all you who have been baptized into Christ, have put on Christ. There is neither Jew nor Greek, there is neither slave nor freeman, there is neither male nor female. For you are all one in Christ Jesus."[86]

The "putting on"[87] goes beyond the plane of a simple moral conversion. At baptism a new ontological relation is created. In "putting on Christ" the neophyte becomes really "one" with Him, not by a juridical fiction, but by a communication of life. He is inserted into Christ to such an extent that Christ becomes for him the principle of supernatural being and in some fashion transforms him into Himself, making him a son of God and rendering him a partaker in his own right of the divine inheritance. . . . From the baptismal water there rises a reconciled humanity that is one with a unity that is not the abstract unity of a unique category but the concrete spiritual unity of a multitude become "one" by the presence of one in all.[88]

The gift of the Spirit. The Spirit of

filiation. The identification of believers with Christ is realized in the Spirit. He who has not the Spirit of Christ does not belong to Him.[89] The person of Christ and that of the Spirit constitute one single and same principle of the spiritual life. But because they are distinct persons they are not this principle in the same manner. First it is the risen Christ who sends the Spirit whose power transforms us.[90] Then the role of the Spirit is to liken and unite us to Christ. He is the Spirit of filiation. . . . It is by His Spirit that Christ incorporates and identifies us with Himself.[91]

The Father is the One whose children we are. St. Paul, as elsewhere in the New Testament, always refers the adoptive filiation to the Father, from whom all paternity in heaven and on earth draws its name.[92] Our filiation is a resemblance to that of the Son by nature, and it reproduces the image of the Son so that He should be the eldest of a multitude of brothers. Adoptive filiation is related to Christ as to its meritorious, efficient and exemplary cause.[93] It is also related to the Holy Spirit as its principle and witness. The Father adopts us by the Son in the Spirit. . . .

Liberating grace. The old man gave way to a new creature. That is to say that St. Paul envisages the newness of being and of life essentially as

---

[86] Gal 3:26–28.
[87] Gal 3:27; Col 3:9.
[88] D. Mollat, "Symbolismes baptismaux chez saint Paul," in *Lumière et Vie*, mars 1956, p. 72.

[89] Rom 8:9.
[90] Ti 3:6.
[91] Eph 1:3–5; Rom 8:14–18, 29; Gal 4:4–7.
[92] Gal 4:6; Rom 8:15–16; Eph 1:3 ff.; 3:15.
[93] Rom 8:29; Gal 4:5; Ti 3:6.

the term of a deliverance, opposed to an anterior state of servitude. One of the characteristic traits of Pauline theology is the liberating role of grace or the contrast between two forms of existence, carnal and spiritual, and the consequences of this, i.e., the necessity of being delivered from the one to enter the other and the impossibility of passing from the one to the other without the power of the Spirit. This theme we also find in St. John.[94]

The liberating action of the Spirit is profoundly rooted in the soteriology of the Apostle. According to him Christ operates the redemption of men by accomplishing first in Himself the painful and meritorious passage from existence in the flesh to existence in the Spirit, from the kenosis to the glory of the resurrection and the lordship.[95] . . . By His obedience, He has merited to triumph over sin, over the law, over death, over His existence in the flesh by the power of the Spirit who has resurrected Him. He has thus become the new Adam, living and vivifying spirit[96] and source of the Spirit for men. . . .

St. Paul opposes the humiliation and glorification of Christ. This point of view commands the Pauline theology of grace. It will be a participation and an imitation of the death and resurrection of Christ. The apparition of the new being has as condition the previous disappearance of the old be-

ing.[97] In being liberating grace is vivifying.[98] To live in Christ the Christian must, as did He, abandon his anterior existence in the flesh. A painful transformation, this, by reason of the opposition in man and even in the Christian of two principal enemies, the flesh and the spirit. The spiritual life thus becomes the stake in a dramatic struggle. It can grow and develop only at the price of a constant victory of the Spirit over the hostile powers. . . .

Justice and justification. Justification is the judgment by which God declares the sinner just and renders him effectively just and holy. It is an event that is at the same time juridic and mystic. It is a justification that gives life.[99]

God justifies the sinner by faith. St. Paul defends this thesis against the Judaizers in the epistle to the Galatians and exposes it more fully in the epistle to the Romans. The act of faith is indispensable to the justification of man.

It is the very action of God that operates justification by Jesus Christ, but this is not done independently of an act of faith which it stirs up in man.[100] The "objective" redemption is evidently independent of the faith of the subject, but the subjective appropriation of this redemption is not realized without it. It is then by faith that the sinner becomes just. Faith is the means by which the justice of God manifested in Jesus Christ becomes effectively the justice of man.

---

[94] Jn 8:36.

[95] Phil 2.

[96] 1 Cor 15:45. Cf. F. X. Durrwell, *The Resurrection* (New York: Sheed and Ward, 1962).

[97] 2 Cor 5:17.

[98] Rom 8:2.

[99] Rom 5:18.

[100] Rom 1:16–17; 3:21–22; 10:9–10.

This faith, an indispensable condition of justification, is an act of knowledge. It is not merely the confidence of the sinner in the mercy of God who pardons his sins; it is first of all an intellectual adherence to the Christian message.[101] However, the faith that conditions justification is not a pure intellectual adherence; it is knowledge and confidence and the homage of obedience and an engagement of the whole being. It is an active faith operating by charity.

It is the active faith that is the necessary condition of justification.

At first glance this seems to contradict the very enunciation of the Pauline thesis: "For we reckon that a man is justified by faith independently of the works of the Law."[102] The works of the law are the observances that it prescribes. It would seem then according to St. Paul that justification is independent of all the good works of man. . . . But we must distinguish two affirmations in St. Paul's thought. On the one hand pagans and Jews who are converted to Christ are justified independently of their previous works, since instead of accomplishing the law (natural or positive) they have all sinned and are deprived of the glory of God.[103] Are they also independent of present and future works? St. Paul teaches the contrary.[104] God who pardons past faults demands for present and future justification the practice of the law inasmuch as this

is the permanent expression of the will of God. Hence the exhortations that terminate the epistles.[105] And the same doctrine about the relation of justification and works is found in Eph 2:1–10.

On the other hand at the same time that St. Paul affirms the necessity of works of faith for justification he proclaims that the law has lapsed and that the Christian is freed from it. Yet in the same context of the anti-Judaizing polemic he repeats his teaching about the necessity of practising the law.[106] The law as it is summed up in charity remains obligatory for the Christian. It is the "law of Christ"[107] and its practice is the condition of final salvation at the last judgment.[108]

In the verses that immediately follow Rom 3:28 there is question of liberation from the Jewish law in its particularity and not of liberation from the law in its permanent value. Man is justified by faith alone if we understand this as St. Paul does: the faith that acts by charity.[109] Justification that is independent of the "works of the law" is not independent of the works of faith. Charity, the work of faith, is an integral part of it as the necessary exercise of the faith by which man advances to justice and holiness.

Justification is a reality actually present and interior to the man whom it transforms into a new creature. The justice of God reaches man only by

---

[101] Rom 10:9–10.
[102] Rom 3:28.
[103] Rom 1–3.
[104] Rom 2:6, 13; 8:3–4.

[105] Rom 13:8–10, etc.
[106] Gal 2:15–21; 3:23–29; 5:1–6, 13–14.
[107] Gal 6:2.
[108] Gal 6:7 ff.
[109] Gal 5:6; cf. 6:15; 1 Cor 7:19.

means of living faith. It transforms him interiorly. In Jesus Christ who is the justice of God, man becomes himself the justice of God.[110] One can and even must say that the justice of God reaches us in Jesus Christ as an alien justice since in fact it does not come from us. But coming from God it reaches us in truth as a personal gift always supported on the active faith with which it is born and progresses and decreases and dies. It does not cease then to depend each instant on the salvific action of God in Jesus Christ, for if faith is a free act of man it is first a gift of God.

Justification or the divine justifying sentence is not simply declarative but efficacious: it transforms the human situation, destroying the old man and creating the new one. God is not content to close His eyes to the sin and to regard the sinner as if he were just. He really delivers him from the sin and makes him veritably the son of God. Justification, in its subjective realisation by means of active faith, implies then a rebirth, a transformation, an interior change of the very being of man.

First the justified man ceases to be the sinner that he was.[111] Then the justified man is not simply just in the sense that he will be so one day in virtue of the divine promise. Just as the justified man is no longer now the sinner that he was, so he is not simply the just man that he will be. In other words remission of sins and divine filiation are not a mere promise and equivalent to a presence in virtue of a divine guarantee. They are an actual reality. St. Paul often designates justification as actually existing, even as past.[112] It is true that he also speaks of it as a reality to come, as an object of hope[113] but this is because he is always thinking of the last judgment and the final redemption. In this respect we are saved only in hope.[114] Nonetheless we are already children of God and heirs.[115]

5. P. Gregory Stevens, O.S.B.,[116] thinks St. Paul is expressing a fundamental New Testament theme when he sees the purpose of God's creation as making all men His children by uniting them to His Son, Jesus Christ, as brothers. The process of assuming man into the life of God involves first the negative aspect of freeing man from all that separates him from God and holiness, then the positive aspect of incorporating man into Christ through the Spirit so that he may live for the Father. Grace for Paul is both in God and in man.

---

[110] 2 Cor 5:21; 1 Cor 1:30–31.
[111] Rom 6:17–18; Col 1:21–22; cf. Eph 2:1–6; 5:8.
[112] 1 Cor 6:11; Rom 3:24; 5:1; 8:30.
[113] Rom 2:13; 3:20; Gal 2:16; 5:4–5.
[114] Rom 8:23–24.
[115] Rom 8:16–17.
[116] Cf. Ch. II, n. 25. This excerpt is from op. cit., pp. 18–39.

St. Paul surely expresses a fundamental New Testament theme when he sees the purpose of God's creation as making all men His children by uniting them to His Son, Jesus Christ, as brothers. "He predestined us to be adopted through Jesus Christ as his sons, according to the purpose of his will, unto the praise of the glory of his grace, with which he had favored us in his beloved Son."[117] The process of assuming man into the life of God involves first the negative aspect of freeing man from all that separates him from God and holiness, then the positive aspect of incorporating man into Christ through the Spirit so that he may live for the Father. These two elements, while inseparable in Paul's thought, are dramatically distinguished in the description of the work of redemption.

Christ and Salvation. The divine plan of the salvation of man is accomplished in the work of Christ; He thus becomes the center of the whole reality of mankind and human destiny. "He [the Father] has rescued us from the power of darkness and transferred us into the kingdom of his beloved Son, in whom we have our redemption, the remission of our sins. He is the image of the invisible God, the firstborn of every creature. For in him were created all things in the heaven and on earth, things visible and things invisible, whether Thrones or Dominations or Principalities or Powers. All things have been created through and unto him, and he is before all creatures, and in him all things hold to-

gether."[118] The reality of Christ appears thus as the climax of all creation, as the goal of God's action from eternity. The coming of Christ, and the subsequent elevation of the faithful man into Christ and His life, does not appear, in the light of this text, as a divine afterthought to the creation of the universe. . . .

Grace for Paul: in God and in man. It has been usual in the history of theology to speak of the difference between the Greek Fathers, who emphasized in the work of Christ the realization of the eternal divine will for the divinization of man, and the Western Fathers, notably St. Augustine, who stressed the historical reality of the redemptive purpose of the incarnation. It may be said that both these elements are found in St. Paul and that it is well to see all aspects of the mystery of Christ if we are to understand what God has accomplished in Him. Through the incarnation Christ realizes to the full God's expression of Himself to His creatures by assuming humanity unto Himself. Thus, by bringing man into the divine life, God washes away the sins of man and bestows on him the life of grace. The word salvation may be used to signify this whole process, or better perhaps, the term *grace*.

Grace means both the loving benevolence of the Father manifested in Christ and the divine gifts bestowed on us in Christ by which we are saved, that is, sanctified in being made like to Him. . . . Grace, then, is a word which can be applied both to

---

[117] Eph 1:5 f.

[118] Col 1:13–17.

the loving mercy of the Father and to those redemptive works of Christ which make God's love operative in the world. . . . Grace and redemption can thus refer to what happened in and through Christ; "the work of grace" can refer to the central reality of saving history; the redemptive actions of Christ. These actions may be called grace or graces, for they are in themselves the merciful, "gracious" effects of the totally gratuitous love of the Father for us. . . .

The grace by which we are saved can refer to the supernatural realities of our transformation into Christ, that is, our "subjective" and personal assimilation of the saving effects of Christ's objective redemption. . . . Grace . . . within man . . . is, quite simply, the sanctification of man incorporated into Christ by faith and baptism. We thus consider not so much what has taken place in and through Christ as what happens, through Christ and in the Spirit within man himself. This distinction will enable us to consider grace insofar as it refers to the realities of the process of our Christianization.

Positive and negative aspects of grace. . . . Paul continually emphasizes that we are saved only in Christ and through His grace; moreover, he sees this salvation as effected first in a rescuing or liberation from sin and darkness, and then as the reconciliation or transfer of man into Christ. Catholic understanding has always seen in these Pauline expressions assertions of a real and radical transformation. The change takes place in

man as the result of the bestowal upon him of the benefits of Christ's redemptive action. In other words, our incorporation into Christ involves a real conversion from one state or condition of reality to a new one. An actual change is effected within man[119] – a Liberation from Sin . . . a Liberation from the Flesh . . . a Liberation from the Law . . . a Liberation from Death . . . and Life in Christ.

Life in Christ. "If then any man is in Christ, he is a new creature."[120] Because the Christian is in Christ he is a new being: not new in his natural being as such, but new in the life of God and in the supernatural order. Because he is possessed of a new life, he is in Christ, and thus in a new relationship with God. The positive aspect, then, of the work of grace, will involve an inner transformation which amounts to a new creation. It will mean a new presence of God to man and of man to the loving God who saves him.

Justification. St. Paul often uses the words "just" and "justice" of genuine religion and its true followers. This use is in accord with the usual and general scriptural meaning of these terms. Justification, especially in Paul's epistles to the Romans and to the Galatians, is the process or the action by which God sanctifies man, that is, by which God makes man pleasing to Him. The notion may be extended to the use of the term justice as a designation of the whole inner reality of the Christian life of grace. St.

---

[119] Ti 2:11–14.
[120] 2 Cor 5:17.

Paul recalls the sanctification or justification of Abraham who appears as the symbol or the great example in the Old Testament of the bestowal of gratuitous grace by God; "Even thus 'Abraham believed God, and it was credited to him as justice.'[121] Know therefore that the men of faith are the real sons of Abraham."[122]

Paul is writing to oppose those Jews and Christians who saw justification as something to be accomplished by a person through his own good works. In this aberration man was seen as bringing about grace as a reward or even as a salary from God for good deeds done. Paul vigorously opposes this religion of human self-sufficiency, denying, as we have seen, man's power to perform the good works of the Law and constantly affirming that justification is a work of God bestowed on faithful man as a free gift. . . . It is in this context that the example of Abraham is proposed. . . . Abraham was truly a just man before God. How had this come about? St. Paul describes two ways of receiving something: in the first, recompense is given for work accomplished; in the other a pure gift is bestowed. The justice of Abraham was a gift that was bestowed as really as a payment rendered for services, but was nevertheless in no way dependent on Abraham's merits or his work. Not even faith was a good work meriting grace: "For by grace you have been saved through faith; and that not from yourselves, for it is the gift of God;

not as the outcome of works, lest anyone may boast."[123]

Faith in St. Paul is indeed hearing the divine message and accepting it;[124] it is an obedience to the divine authority.[125] It is, moreover, the commitment and surrender of all that a man is to God, this commitment and openness to God is *itself* the work of grace. Faith, then, becomes the act of grace by which a man is enabled to cooperate with the justifying power of God. . . . God makes man pleasing to Himself only in and through man's free cooperation in faith, by which man opens himself to the gift of God and accepts it wholeheartedly.

What is the reality of the justification accorded by God when man cooperates in faith? Is it merely like a statement of God declaring the sinner just? Or is it a divine act by which the sinner is internally transformed and becomes a new reality before God? Catholic thought has always been that the justice bestowed on man is a gratuitous gift[126] and a true justice which actually transforms man into a person pleasing to God. St. Paul links justice and justification with sanctification and purification[127] and sees the justified man as living a new life in Christ.[128] The liberation from sin and death, already described, is a spiritual reality which is accomplished in man

---

121 Gn 15:6.
122 Gal 3:6 f.
123 Eph 2:8 f.
124 Rom 1:17; 10:14–21; 1 Thes 1:3–10; 1 Cor 2:5; Eph 1:13.
125 Rom 1:5; 16:26; 2 Cor 10:5 f.
126 Gal 3:6 ff.
127 1 Cor 6:11.
128 Rom 3:21–26; 6:15–23.

by grace at the moment of justification. Its effect is to introduce man into a genuine state of justice. This new life is indeed life in Christ, so real that Paul can say: "With Christ I am nailed to the cross. It is now no longer I that live, but Christ lives in me. And the life that I now live in the flesh, I live in the faith of the Son of God."[129] . . . The whole of Romans 6 may be read at this point. It summarized Paul's realistic understanding of the incorporation into Christ, dying to sin and rising to a new life, which is accomplished in the process of justification.

Newness of life. Justification is thus synonymous with the communication of new life in Christ to the Christians. St. Paul frequently contrasts the "old man" of sin and the flesh with the "new man" who is spiritual and dedicated to a fundamental holiness. "If any man is in Christ, he is a new creature."[130] Because God has created us "in Christ Jesus"[131] the Christian is to live this new life. "But be renewed in the spirit of your mind, and put on the new man, which has been created according to God in justice and holiness of truth."[132] The liturgy of Easter is especially devoted to this theme of new life won for us in Christ, and communicated to us in the sacraments. Entrance into the Christian life is truly a "regeneration" and a "renewal": the equivalent of being "justified" by

His grace.[133] . . . Paul stresses this point, that the Christians to whom he writes may be thoroughly convinced of the mysterious and hidden, yet actual, presence of grace. This conviction in them will lead, in turn, to their living in the light,[134] to action which gives expression to the new "reality" which Christians have become. . . .

Sons of God by adoption. The reality of the new being of the Christian is also portrayed by St. Paul as an extension or participation in Christ's personal being as Son of the Father. The Christian, united to Christ, is truly a son of God in virtue of possessing the divine reality of grace. That he is a son of God is the result of a rebirth by which the divine life is communicated to him. "But when the fullness of time came, God sent his Son . . . that he might redeem those who were under the Law, that we might receive the adoption of sons. And because you are sons, God has sent the Spirit of his Son into our hearts crying: 'Abba, Father' so that he is no longer a slave, but a son; and if a son, an heir also through God."[135]

Just as the synoptic gospels presented our Lord inculcating the notion of God as Father, so does St. Paul insist on the fact that by grace we have entered into new relations with God in virtue of an adopted sonship in Christ. By grace we are joined to Christ and thus related as sons, as children to the Father in heaven. . . . The Christian has relations with God which go

---

[129] Gal 2:19 f.
[130] 2 Cor 5:17; cf. Gal 6:15.
[131] Eph 2:10.
[132] Eph 4:23 f.; cf. Col 3:10.

[133] Ti 3:6 f.
[134] Eph 5:8 f.
[135] Gal 4:5-7; cf. Rom 8:14-17.

beyond those of creature to Creator. They are those of son to Father, of two persons who enter into mutual communion which is a genuine friendship. . . .

In Christ. If we are related as sons to the Father, it is because of a union with Christ so intimate that it appears to St. Paul as an identification of Christ with each Christian.[136] Thus the Apostle realizes that Christ lives in him and that the Christian is "in Christ." "For you are all the children of God through faith in Christ Jesus. For all you who have been baptized into Christ have put on Christ."[137] Sharing in the reality of Christ is the innermost principle of the Christian life; it is, in terms of later theology, a sharing in the being of God Himself, in the reality of Christ through the power of the Spirit. All Christian life is but an expression of this fundamental reality, so that the basic morality of the Christian is found not in the Law but in being true to what one is through the grace of Christ. To be "in Christ" according to Paul is not merely to profess faith in Him, to adhere to His teachings, or even to be attached to Christ by personal admiration. It is much more profound. *It is to be one with Him.* . . .

A new existence has been received by the Christian, so that he lives in Christ.[138] This does not mean, of course, some sort of mystical or real absorption into Christ so that the human self disappears. It does mean a

real sharing in the life which is proper to Christ alone, the Son of the living Father. It means a new creation in man by the reception of grace, and a new, conscious mode of existence in which Christ becomes in a real sense the center and focus of the Christian's life.

All this is the work of the Spirit.[139] The Spirit who lives in the Christian makes him a son with the Son. He is made in the image of the Son according to the eternal will of the Father.[140] This new life is consciously realized in faith and love, though it is rooted in the transforming adoption of the Christian into Christ in what theology calls "the bestowing of sanctifying grace." . . .

Life in Christ is thus realized in the radical transformation of the Christian from a son of wrath and sin into a son of the Father, a brother of Christ. This new being is consciously expressed by sharing not only in the knowledge of Christ, but in His sentiments, and in His conscious love for the Father. The Christian is constantly alert to this reality. His life becomes progressively more deeply rooted in grace, in his being in Christ.

In the body of Christ. Receiving the life of God and being incorporated into Christ are personal acts; we accept Christ by faith, and go out to Him in charity. Yet we receive and are united to Christ not in isolation, but as social beings. There is a sharing of Christ's life in the Church which is His body . . . grace is not the grace of Christ only, but the grace of Christ

---

[136] Cf. Acts 22:7 f.
[137] Gal 3:26 f.
[138] Rom 6:11; cf. 1 Cor 1:30.

[139] 1 Cor 6:11; Eph 4:30.
[140] Rom 8:29.

in His Church. All grace, as it is the grace *of* Christ and *in* Christ, is grace in the Church. There are not two ways of grace: personal and ecclesial, individual and social, but one. We live in Christ in the Church and are united in the Church to Christ.

The Church which is God's people, summoned and called by Him in Christ, is the source of grace. It is the setting for the life of grace. St. Paul stresses both the union of all peoples in the Church[141] and the fact that in Christ all men are called to salvation through grace. But Christ unites men to Himself by uniting them to His Church — the society of those who truly believe in Him. All of us, in our diversity and our differences, are united in the one body of Christ.[142] The Spirit is the principle of this unity of all in Christ, just as He is the principle of our incorporation into Christ.[143] The Church is the body of Christ[144] and the Christian's incorporation into Christ is at once an incorporation into the Church.

Conclusion. Our life of grace is a life in Christ in the Church. We live to Christ by a life in the society of the faithful people of God which is Christ's body. This of course does not mean that the individual and the personal is too obscured by the social. It does mean, however, that all our life as Christians is a life lived as members of the society which is Christ's body. Christ without the Church is "incomplete." Paul sees Christ as a "collective person" which is the fullness of the Church united as members of the body of which He is the head. The principle of union of all in Christ is the common sharing of the life of Christ (at least by faith). The Church is not the body of the Father but of Christ, in whom all things are created;[145] as head of the body Christ is distinct from it, though He is also united with it. The body is united in the Spirit, its soul and source of union and unity. The Church is the continuance of the incarnation; it is the body of all who love Christ and live in Him. We may recognize in the life of grace a divine force which unites us to the body of Christ existing here and now in the world as the Church. The Church is the *locus,* the setting, the mystical body, in which the Father vivifies us by uniting us to the life of His Son, in the vital efficacy of the Spirit. Our salvation, our life in the world, our final destiny is worked out by union with Christ, living in His body, His Church.

"One body and one Spirit, even as you were called in one hope of your calling: one Lord, one faith, one baptism; one God and Father of all, who is above all, and throughout all, and in us all."[146]

---

141 Rom 11:5, 17–24; Gal 6:15.
142 Rom 12:4–8; cf. 1 Cor 12:12–31.
143 1 Cor 12:13; cf. Eph 2:22; 4:4.
144 Eph 1:23.

145 Col 1:16.
146 Eph 4:4–6.

6. L. Cerfaux[147] studies Paul's notion of Christian life and his synthesis of justice, sanctification and life in the letter to the Romans, where he is consciously expressing one fundamental reality in various ways, namely, the manifold richness of the gift which a Christian receives.

The resurrection of Christ is the most important thing that ever happened, something so momentous that every world crisis becomes insignificant in comparison with it. Christ's resurrection is the first thing to happen in the realm of eschatology. It is a signal for the ultimate disposal of the world by God, and for every other resurrection to take place. A new world begins with Christ's resurrection, although it would be wrong to think of it and its eschatological consequences as an isolated unit. The first Christians had lived through Pentecost, and seen how those days were overlapped by certain realities that belong in fact to the end of time. The Spirit is part of the heavenly gifts, and is our inheritance. The *charismata* are the firstfruits of what belongs to us, and are given to us now. St. Paul's own personal intuition shows us how our present life is as if transformed by an anticipation of the resurrection. We have the pledge of the Spirit, and we are already in some way changed even

now by events that belong properly to the end of time.

Such a transformation can be nothing less than a new creation. God, who gave man his earthly nature, must come to him again, this time to bestow on him the perfection of spiritual being, or a life as of one raised from the dead. And so Christ's rising from the dead will be seen as the birth of the first and typical representative of a new line, which is the race of spiritual men who belong properly to the eschatological sphere.

Before we look more closely at Paul's notion of Christian life we will follow his own synthesis of justice, sanctification and life in the letter to the Romans. Here, as we shall see, he is consciously expressing one fundamental reality in various ways, namely, the manifold richness of the gift which a Christian receives.

Grace (justice), spirit (holiness), and life in Christ. In chapters 3 and 8 of Romans, Paul describes the supernatural reality which makes a Christian what he is. Sanctification can be considered under a twofold aspect. It implies a real, positive quality of our new being (justice is another name for it, suggesting the juridical aspect). At the same time it is closely connected with the supernatural life which we receive from the risen Christ, and with the power of the Holy Spirit. Justice,

[147] L. Cerfaux is an eminent Scripture scholar. This excerpt is from his book, *Christ in the Theology of St. Paul*, translated into English by Geoffrey Webb and Adrian Walker (New York: Herder and Herder, 1959), pp. 316–324. The original version of this work was published in 1951 by Editions Du Cerf, under the title *Le Christ dans la Théologie de S. Paul*.

holiness, life, and spiritualization all denote one and the same quality (from different viewpoints), and describe the new being of a Christian.

"Justice" is a helpful liaison between Christian life and Jewish theology. "Life" comes from faith in Christ's resurrection, and leads to the "mystiques" of Christ. Spirituality is a word for the Christian's experience of the Holy Spirit at work in the world.

Justice and grace in Romans 3:21– 4:25. The terms "to justify," "justice," and "justification" appear in the controversies in regard to the obligation of the Mosaic Law, and the "purity" of pagan converts to Christianity. St. Paul's teaching is that the profession of Christian faith produces justice and holiness through faith and baptism. A slight alteration is made in traditional Jewish terminology, so that henceforward man is justified not by the Law but by faith. Christian justice thus becomes the antithesis of Jewish justice, but because of the Christian experience, the idea goes deeper than that. There must be a real state of purity and holiness to go with the merely negative aspect of freedom from sin, and the more juridical aspect of friendship with God.

In the letters to the Thessalonians, Paul avoids speaking about justice. Here his message is summed up in a holiness turned toward the parousia which nonetheless allows of a *present* state. In the greater epistles, the emphasis changes, and Paul insists less on preparation for the parousia, and more on the divine reality now present in a Christian's life. Since he had to discuss the problems involved in justice with Jewish Christians, he chose the word "justice" to sum up the holiness that God brings about in us, and which gives us our specifically Christian being; see 1 Cor 6:11; 2 Cor 5:21; 6:14. Then comes a new widening of his thought, as not only Jewish justice but pagan wisdom also is condemned by God, and the pair are replaced by God's own justice and wisdom, brought down from heaven.

"Justice" is, then, God's gift *par excellence*. Its gratuitous quality is brought out first in Rom 3:24, 27 f. The basic contrast between Law and faith deepens into one between the works of the Law and the gratuitous quality of the divine gift. As Paul says: "by faith, so as to be by grace" (Rom 4:16; see 6:13). Thus it comes about that justice can be called grace (Rom 5:2, 15, 17, 20, 21, etc.; 6:14, 15, etc.). Catholic theology expresses both gratuity and the positive aspect of justice in the term "sanctifying grace."

Grace and life (Romans 5 and 6). In his second cycle of theological developments on justice, Paul introduces the word "life" into his description of the Christian state.

The Old Testament already offered a religious conception of life. It is the greatest of God's benefits to men here and now, and culminates in the resurrection of the body so that it is a future good as well. The idea of eternal life, developed by Greek philosophy and the teaching of the Rabbis in two different ways, is an additional feature.

Alexandrian Judaism had, moreover, combined the stoic idea of the virtuous and just life with the notion of the supernatural life that God gives to the soul by means of His presence in it. A distinction was made between *thnēte zōē* and *alēthinē zōē*, the true and divine life brought about by a *dynamis* of God.

Without necessarily influencing Paul's thought, these ideas may have been a help to him in making precise the notions involved in his own synthesis.

Christ's resurrection was the first communication of the divine life. It gives us the certitude of our own resurrection, and of our risen life with Christ (see 1 Thes 4:14; 5:9 f.). We are caught up in a movement which is begun by Christ. Our Christian being is a participation in Christ's risen life, so that the life which Christ communicates to us is only another facet of the Christian state of justice, holiness and grace.

In the letter to the Galatians, grace and life do not interpenetrate quite so completely, but Gal 2:19-20 at least introduces the life theme into a development on justice (see Rom 1:17). In the letter to the Romans, St. Paul establishes closer connections between the two themes. Having developed the double idea of justice and grace, he broaches the theme of life in 5:10.

His intention of tying the two themes together is clear enough in v. 18 when he speaks of the justice of one " . . . *eis dikaiosin zōēs*" (see v. 21). Chapter 6 contains the answers (which become exhortations) to two

objections coming from the doctrine of grace. In his answer to the first objection he uses the contrast of life and death (6:1-14) based on the symbolism of baptism. At the end, the terms justice and grace reappear (v. 13 f.). The second part of the chapter (v. 15-23), answering another objection, develops the contrast between the Law and grace. Again, the themes of justice, grace and life are closely interwoven as the basic antithesis develops. The Law means sin, slavery, and death. Grace is justice, holiness (v. 19) and freedom, or life. The ideas are all gathered together in the résumé of v. 22 f.: "Being made free now from sin, and become servants of God, your fruit is holiness, and your end is everlasting life. For the wages of sin is death, but the free gift [*charisma*] of God is eternal life."

Justice, life, and the Spirit. It is the Holy Spirit who brings the divine gifts promised to Christians into our present world (Rom 8:23; 2 Cor 1:22). In the epistles to the Thessalonians, the Spirit is connected with the extraordinary signs and miracles which accompany Christian preaching. . . .

To return to the letter to the Romans, there is a third cycle of development of the theme of justice in ch. 7, only this time it is equated to the Spirit. In his exhortation to "walk according to the Spirit," he shows that a Christian has something in the Spirit that replaces and surpasses the Law. The Spirit, like the Law, gives the basis of morality, but He gives also the strength to put precepts into practice. The Law is dead, and is replaced by the newness of the Spirit (7:6). The Spirit of God overcomes the flesh (7:25–8:11). The themes are quite deliberately involved with one another when Paul says: "The *Law* of the *Spirit of life in Christ Jesus* has delivered me from the Law of sin and death. There was something which the Law could not do, since because of the flesh it had no power; but this God has done, by sending us *his own Son* in a human nature like our own sinful nature. He did this to condemn sin in the flesh, so that the *justice of the law* might be fulfilled in us, who walk no longer according to the flesh, but *according to* the Spirit" (8:2–4). The three great themes are confused a little later, in v. 9–11, with a significant summing-up: the spirit is life through justice (v. 10).

In this third cycle, the word grace does not make an appearance, because the Spirit is equivalent to it, being the gift of God, *charis* and *charisma*, the divine reality given to us as a free gift.

The perspective broadens the more we follow the ascending movement of Paul's thought. The richness of a Christian's being must be expressed in many ways: as justice, holiness, and grace, as life in Christ, and as Spirit. Thus the whole new nature is described, and we can see what an impoverishment the Protestant error entailed, in isolating (and thus falsifying) the notion of justice.

All the various currents of Paul's thought converge into one reality, since each is a partial expression of it, so that

we have thus some projection of the divine unity into human life. There are three divine persons, and there is correspondingly a triple aspect in Christian life. First the Father gives us grace, and there is justice for all men in the redemption of Jesus Christ. Through the Spirit, Christ's risen life is a power at work in Christian lives, even constitutive of their new life. We participate in the Spirit who sanctifies our lives. We are sealed by the Trinity, with grace from the Father, life from Christ, and the presence of the Spirit. Their gift is one, and it is both mystic and real.

Christ as cause of the Christian life. The power which raised Christ from the dead does not confine itself to one resurrection but brings about in Christians a life which is of the same nature as that of the risen Christ. It is as if the new and divine life poured over from Christ into all Christians, so as to create them anew.

Thus the risen Christ is once more the centre or source from which there flows out a life which is a continuation of his own. . . . What is essential in the relationship between Christ's life and the life of Christians, can only be explained by causality. . . . Our dependence on Christ's life is connected with our resemblance to Him, which is so deep that it amounts to an identification of our life with His. The ideas of causality, influence and similarity are in the forefront of Paul's thought, and it is these which allow him to hold on to the moral demands of the Christian life.

V

GRACE IN THE EASTERN FATHERS

1. T. F. Torrance[1] finds grace in the Apostolic Fathers no longer the absolutely predominant factor that it is in the New Testament. The theology of the Apostolic Fathers represents a corrosion of the faith both from the side of Judaism and from the side of Hellenism, because the basic significance of grace was not grasped. The most astonishing feature was the failure to grasp the significance of the death of Christ. Grace was now regarded as pneumatic.

GRACE by its very nature, in the thought of the New Testament, must be the absolutely predominant factor in faith, else it is not grace. In the Apostolic Fathers grace did not have that radical character. The great presupposition of the Christian life, for them, was not a deed of decisive significance that cut across human life and set it on a wholly new basis

[1] T. F. Torrance: cf. Ch. I, n. 1. This excerpt is from *op. cit.*, pp. 133–141.

grounded upon the self-giving of God. What took absolute precedence was God's call to a new life in obedience to revealed truth. Grace, as far as it was grasped, was subsidiary to that. And so religion was thought of primarily in terms of man's acts toward God, in the striving toward justification, much less in terms of God's acts for man which put him in the right with God once and for all.

Two major factors contributed to that change. The first was the religion of Judaism with its insistence upon law by which the Church was enormously influenced in spite of St. Paul.[2] There can be little doubt about the fact that in this the Septuagint translation of the Old Testament played a decided role.[3] In it we have the break-up of some of the leading ideas of Hebrew revelation, and their replacement by much paler categories.[4] One major result was the break-up of the Old Testament doctrines of grace and righteousness and the separation thereby wrought between justice and mercy. With this version as their Bible the Christian Church was put directly in the way of interpreting the Gospel

in terms of Judaistic tenor. It is not to be wondered, therefore, that the thought that dominates Judaism: "By your works you will be judged," became its legacy to the post-apostolic Church. Throughout the whole of this period, almost without exception, this proved to be an ineradicable canon of thought. It was never dreamt that it might be otherwise, and whatever was understood of the Gospel came to be flung into the frame-work of this thought.

This is particularly clear in Barnabas and the *Didache*, where apparently, an old Judaistic thought-form was used to frame the way of the Christian life in opposition to the way of heathenism. The Gospel became erected into a New Law. . . . But by transforming the Gospel into a New Law the Apostolic Fathers returned to the impossible situation from which Christ came deliberately to redeem. The Gospel carries with it an eternal indicative, but post-apostolic Christianity laboured only under an imperative.

It is easy to see how this entailed a doctrine of salvation by works of righteousness, with grace introduced in an *ad hoc* fashion as enabling power. If the believer's activity was directed toward creating goodness in an attempt to bridge the gap between the actual and the ideal, the piety behind this could not but be essentially ego-centric. It was taken too much for granted in the early Church that the superiority of Christianity to paganism lay in its mode of life, in the call to follow in the sinless pattern of Christ. It failed to realise that the Christian ethic can

---

[2] It is to be remembered, however, that St. Paul's Epistles were not much in circulation, certainly as a collection, before about A.D. 110, though their collection and circulation about that time may account for the difference in emphasis between the *Didache*, for example, and the *Letters of Ignatius*.

[3] Justin Martyr rejected the Hebrew Old Testament because he thought it had been garbled and corrupted by the Jews. It was the LXX which he took for his supreme authority. See *Dial. Tryph.*, 71–74.

[4] See C. H. Dodd, *The Bible and the Greeks*, especially 25 f., 42 f., and 82 f.

be construed in such a way with the basic principles of the natural man as to evade the main issue of the Gospel of grace. The result is that the Fathers had all the formal characteristics of the Christian faith, but harnessed to the basic urge of man for self-justification. . . .

The second major factor which influenced the early Church in the second century was of course Hellenism. The Apostolic Fathers were Greeks, their language Greek, and their minds necessarily worked with Greek modes of thought. It is difficult for us to imagine all that the change from Hebrew to Greek meant, and to realise how strange it must have been for a Hellenistic mind to start thinking in terms of the Gospel whose roots went back into a long Hebrew tradition built up on the principles of divine revelation. Hellenism was intensely naturalistic, and it is not surprising that elements of thought which were part and parcel of the Hellenic mind are found to have broken their way through the newly acquired faith or to have modified it. Although there was no reason why a Greek should not apprehend the Gospel as well as a Jew, the latter had certain initial advantages, for his mind had been to a measured degree shaped by categories of thought from the Old Testament. The converted Greek faced a greater break with older modes of thought.

There can be no doubt therefore that in the early Church, as in the mission field today, the converts of the first few generations had great difficulty in apprehending the distinctive aspects of the Gospel, as for example the doctrine of grace. It was so astoundingly new to the natural man.[5] In our times, it often takes generations of careful doctrinal teaching before the implications of Christianity are fully realised,[6] and even then, there is always the temptation for old pagan ideas, such as the urge toward self-justification, to infiltrate into the faith. Under the mighty impact of the New Testament revelation the Greek language was used to convey the Gospel of grace, and in this Greek was transformed in accordance with the new content. But in the second century we find everywhere a serious relapse into natural Hellenic thought.

The position of second-century Christianity, however, is not to be understood as resulting from the direct influence of either Hellenistic or Judaistic types of thought, so much as in the coincidence of Hellenistic and Judaistic ethic under the wing of Christianity, consequent upon the failure to use the cardinal truths of the Gospel as articles of saving faith. . . . What facilitated the syncretism of Judaism and Hellenism was the idea, common in principle to both, of self-justification, but it was Christianity which provided the sphere in which the two could come together, for as

---

[5] Cf. 1 Cor 2:14.

[6] It was only after the circulation of Paul's epistles gave the churches an opportunity to study the New Testament Gospel that its real implications began to be grasped, as in Irenaeus. But meantime the whole Church had become thoroughly moralistic. Some of the implications of the Gospel, grace particularly, were never recovered until the Reformation.

opposed to Hellenism it brought the principle of revelation, and as opposed to Judaism it did away with the ceremonial law. As opposed to both, the Gospel of Christianity was so astounding just because it taught a doctrine of justification by grace alone. This was unpalatable to both sides. Judaism refused to accept it because of its revolutionary character and its attitude to the law. Hellenism simply failed to see the New Testament problems.

Both of these attitudes to grace are found in the Apostolic Fathers. Their theology represents a corrosion of the faith both from the side of Judaism and from the side of Hellenism, because the basic significance of grace was not grasped. That is seen very clearly in their attitude to all the main doctrines of the New Testament Gospel. It was not that they were opposed to them, but that they did not grasp them properly. They were willing to give lip service to them, but all unconsciously their preaching was shaped by the meagre and basically wrong categories of the natural mind, and their Christianity became in consequence greatly impoverished as a Gospel.

The most astonishing feature was the *failure to grasp the significance of the death of Christ*. That was where Judaism ought to have been a considerable help, for we know that in the New Testament itself, it was the Old Testament which first supplied the categories with which the death of the Messiah was understood. The idea no doubt was as totally foreign to the Greek mind as it was repulsive

to the Jew, but one would have thought that Greek and Jew alike who claimed to be Christian would have given far more attention to such a singular and outstanding fact in their faith, and that they would have wrestled with it until they had really grasped it. We find them, instead, passing over the matter in terms that are more or less traditional, and then proceeding to set forth the faith as though the death of Christ did not occupy a place of absolute importance. Salvation is wrought, they thought, certainly by divine pardon but on the ground of repentance, not apparently on the ground of the death of Christ alone. There is no doubt about the fact that the early Church felt it should take up the Cross and follow Christ, and it was willing to go all the way to martyrdom, but it felt that it was in that way the Christian made saving appropriation of the Cross, rather than by faith. That Ignatius, in many ways the most "Pauline" of all the Apostolic Fathers, should have laid so much stress on attaining to God through a martyrdom in imitation of Christ, and so failed to see that the death of Christ as an act of salvation can be appropriated by faith alone, is very significant indeed. It was not seen that the whole of salvation is centred in the person and the death of Christ, for there God has Himself come into the world and wrought a final act of redemption which undercuts all our own endeavours at self-justification, and places us in an entirely new situation in which faith alone saves a man, and through which alone is a man free to do righteousness spontaneously under the constraining love of Christ. That was not understood by the Apostolic Fathers, and it is the primary reason for the degeneration of their Christian faith into something so different from the New Testament. Failure to apprehend the meaning of the Cross and to make it a saving article of faith is surely the clearest indication that a genuine doctrine of grace is absent. . . .

As regards the bearing of all this upon the thought of grace itself in the Apostolic Fathers, three things may be said:

(1) Grace became related to the continuance of the Christian life, rather than to the decisive motion of God's love as the presupposition of the whole Christian life. Because the prime concern of the Christian was with the struggle of obedience in conformity to the New Law grace was related more to the receiving of divine aid, than to the objective act of salvation in Christ. That means that grace lost the primary eschatological character it had in the New Testament, the presence of the amazing love of God in Christ which unaccountably overtakes the believer and sets him in a completely new world. Instead grace became an *ad hoc* matter, an aid to the main work of sanctification, a *donum superadditum*. In other words, grace was something given by God to those who worthily strive after righteousness to enable them to attain their end. It was something to be acquired.

(2) Grace was now regarded as something *Pneumatic*. From the very earliest in this period grace was associated with the Spirit, and that soon became recognized everywhere. That might not have been so mischievous, were it not for a parallel change in the understanding of the Holy Spirit, which by this time had largely lost the inseparable attachment it has to Christ and His work in the New Testament, and came to be thought of in sub-personal fashion as pneumatic power (*dynamis*). . . . Grace was the gift of spiritual energy that ranged itself within the heart of the believer, and delivered him from evil by bringing him understanding of truth, power to resist evil and live a holy life. It was a phenomenon, a pneumatic energy implanted in the soul. Thus the relation of grace and man came to be thought of sub-personally, as cause and effect instead of as word and faith. It had to do with the heightening of the natural faculties in a semi-physical sense by the infusing of divine qualities into natural powers, even beauty and radiance. And it was granted to those who are worthy. This idea of grace as ghostly potency was not very different from the deifying *charis* of Greek mythology or the mystery religions. (The idea of deification was taken up even by such good theologians as Irenaeus and Athanasius. Nothing could be more characteristically Hellenistic.) There was one difference, however; it was the grace of the Holy Spirit. . . .

(3) Grace was taken under the wing of the Church in an official way. The Church was regarded as endowed in some way or other with this spirit-

ual power which made the believer godlike, and in fact united him to God. The Church as the body of Christ was looked on as the depository of pneumatic grace, which might be dispensed in sacramentalist fashion after the analogy of the mystery religions. The Church, in other words, possessed the means of grace. . . .

As regards the word *charis* there was a relapse to current Hellenistic usage. . . . More often *charis* fell into line with the current pneumatic tendencies in the Hellenistic world, and so lapsed altogether from its theological use in the New Testament into a psychological use. . . .

2. H. Rondet, S.J.,[7] sees the gift of the Holy Spirit commanding the whole theology of grace in the first centuries, and the doctrine of divinization standing out. But aside from Ignatius, the Apostolic Fathers treat this divinization quite soberly. With Irenaeus we find the first great synthesis of the Pauline and Johannine theology of grace. Clement of Alexandria first uses the term *theopoiein*, but the same doctrine of our divinization is found in other Greek Fathers.

Harnack has justly remarked that before beginning the history of the trinitarian and christological controversies, we must recall the soteriological presuppositions of the discussion.[8] For if there is discussion of the divinity of the Word or of the consubstantiality of the Holy Spirit, this will be in function of the traditional data about the dogma of the Redemption. "If the Holy Spirit is not God, if He has not the right to my adoration," Gregory of Nazianzen says more than once, "how can He divinize me?"[9] Harnack, it is true, has pretended to demonstrate that the trinitarian and christological dogmas are only a scandalous compromise between Hellenism and the

Gospel.[10] According to him, one of the essential factors in the "birth" of these dogmas was the triumph in the third century of the "physical" conception of the Redemption. For the Greek Fathers, he affirms, the Redemption is before all the gift of happy immortality, and as this immortality is an essentially divine privilege, one had to conclude to the necessity of the Incarnation. . . .

What is true in the affirmations of Harnack is that Christian dogmas, without ceasing to have a value of disinterested truth, have been proposed to us only in view of a "pragmatic" end. The trinitarian or christological dogmas have been revealed to us only in connection with the evangelical message of the providential economy

---

[7] H. Rondet, S.J. Cf. Ch. III, n. 1. This excerpt is from *op. cit.*, pp. 77–98.

[8] A. Harnack, *Lehrbuch der Dogmengeschicte* (4 ed., 1909), t. II, pp. 45, 129.

[9] *Or.*, 31, 4, P.G., 36, 137 B; *Or.*, 34, 12, P.G., 36, 252.

[10] Cf. A. D'Alès, "La tradition chrétienne dans l'histoire," in *Études*, 1907, t. 112, pp. 367–370.

of salvation.[11] Between Arius and St. Athanasius, as Harnack has seen well, there is already an abyss: the one needs the Logos as a cosmological intermediary between God and creation, the other proclaims a Savior, who while being God is a real historical personage.[12] It is the same with what concerns the Holy Spirit. . . .

When the developments of dogma will lead the Church to reflect on herself, on her intimate life or her sacraments, ecclesiology will enter into the symbol only as a prolongation of the assertions about the Holy Spirit.

It is precisely the gift of the Holy Spirit which, at the beginnings of Christianity, commands the whole theology of grace. The Christians of the first centuries are aware of living a new life unknown up till then.[13] For a long time they would say "receive the Holy Spirit, lose the Holy Spirit, have the Holy Spirit" where we today say: "to be justified, to be in the state of sin, to be in the state of grace." The rite of baptism, the imposition of hands, absolution, all these sacramental actions are in strict conjunction with the gift of the Holy Spirit.[14] The transformation operated in baptism is lived out by the first Christians. Doubtless there is a dif-

ference between Cyril of Jerusalem's long discourses on the marvelous effects of baptism[15] and the much simpler way in which St. Justin speaks of the remission of sins, of regeneration and illumination.[16] It is incontestable, too, that the Apostolic Fathers with the exception of Ignatius of Antioch are sober enough in their treatment of the divinization of the Christian.[17]. . . .

In Ignatius of Antioch St. John found a disciple worthy of him. For Ignatius the doctrine of Christ is a doctrine of immortality and His flesh a remedy for immorality: whoever is united to Him by faith or baptism and is nourished on the Eucharist and remains a member of the Church uni-

---

[11] Henri De Tourville, Lumière et vie, 1925, p p.47–48.

[12] Harnack, Precis, p. 181.

[13] H. Schumacher, Kraft der Urkirche; das neue Leben nach den Dokumenten der ersten zwei Jahrhunderten, 1934.

[14] P. Galtier ("Absolution ou confirmation," RSR, 1914, pp. 207–209) justly insists on the importance of these remarks for the history of theology and sacramentary practice.

[15] Catech., 3, P.G., 33, 425–449.

[16] I Apol., 61, 2–3.

[17] J. Gross, La divinisation du chrétien d'après les Pères grecs, 1938, pp. 116–122. The author of the Didache speaks of the immortality promised to Christians in quite vague terms (Did., X, 2–3) and it is evident that he is thinking especially of the glorious resurrection (Did., XVI, 6–8). In the epistle of pseudo-Barnabas one finds an allusion to the new man of St. Paul and to the presence of God in the faithful (Ep. Barn., XI, 11), but the author still mixes up divine life and charisms. The effect of baptism is a purification and sanctification that are left unanalyzed (Ep. Barn., XI, 11); the Christian is called Son of God but only in passing (Ep. Barn., IV, 9). Clement of Rome is hardly more fruitful. One feels that the idea of the glorious resurrection expresses for these souls [which have] come from Judaism inexpressible richness (I Clem., 24–27). The author of the homily known under the name of II Clement insists on this idea and connects the gift of the resurrection with the presence of the Spirit in souls (II Clem., XIV, 5; cf. V, 5; XX, 5). There is little in Pastor Hermas.

fied by charity, is assured of salvation. Ignatius, the martyr who is glorified by the name of Theophor, has also made his own the doctrine of St. Paul. It is Christ who lives in him.[18]

But it is in Irenaeus that we find the first great synthesis of the Pauline and Johannine theology of grace. He abounds in formulas that are destined to become dear to both the Greek and the Latin traditions such as: God is made man so man can share in the divine life and become a son of God.[19] Christ has come to recapitulate humanity in Himself,[20] repair the work of God destroyed by sin, give men the Holy Spirit in abundance so that He can be not only the guest of their souls and bodies but a principle of interior unity and a pledge of the incorruptible life which the risen Christ already enjoys.[21] This Spirit, life of each of the members, is also the life of the Church, the body of Christ.[22] In St. Irenaeus the theology of salvation is bound to the idea of an educative Providence that slowly puts man on his way to his last end, "the vision of God, the life of men." Man has not been made God from the beginning but he has however been made to become god.[23] This doctrine is the foundation of a Christian optimism which will thenceforth be a traditional doctrine,[24] even if it must combine later on with what is commonly called with great injustice to St. Augustine "Augustinian" pessimism.

Thenceforth each time they speak of the effects of baptism, of regeneration and of the gift of the Holy Spirit, the Fathers will be as if inexhaustible, and it is this question one must first put to them if one wishes to know the theology of grace. This remark applies very specially to Clement of Alexandria and above all to the great Origen. It is certain that one does injury to Origen by limiting oneself to the statement that he was not a Semipelagian.[25] The Church has rejected

---

[18] The mysticism of Ignatius is essentially a mysticism of union with Christ present in souls. Christians have Jesus in them (*Magn.*, 12), they are God-bearers, Christ-bearers (*Ephes.*, IX, 2), temples of Christ (*Ephes.*, XV, 3). The ideas of eternal life, immortality, divine presence, recur often but centered on this mysticism of union with Christ.

[19] *Adv. haer.*, IV, 28, 1 (Harvey, II, 245).

[20] *Adv. haer.*, III, 18, 1 (Harvey, II, 95). Cf. A. D'Alès, "La doctrine de la récapitulation dans saint Irénée," RSR, 1916, pp. 189–190; E. Mersch, *Le corps mystique du Christ* (2 ed., 1936), I, 318–328.

[21] *Adv. haer.*, V, 7, 1–2 (Harvey, II, 336–338).

[22] *Adv. haer.*, III, 24, 1 (Harvey, II, 132).

[23] *Adv. haer.*, IV, 38, 2–4 (Harvey, II, 294–297); IV, 20, 7 (Harvey, II, 219); IV, 38, 4 (Harvey, II, 297). A. Verriele, "Le plan du salut d'après saint Irénée," RSR, 1934, p. 493.

[24] D. Reynders, "Optimisme et théocentrisme chez saint Irénée," in *Recherches de théol. ancienne et mediévale*, 1936, pp. 225–252.

[25] Some lines of Tixéront (*Hist. des dogmas*, I, 316) are very meager and the author hardly completes them in speaking of baptism or of the Holy Spirit. In the *Dictionnaire de théologie catholique* (hereafter DTC) (t. XI, col. 1544–1545), M. Bardy also turns to the question of the relations between grace and liberty. Happily, he put in relief elsewhere some other aspects of Origen's thoughts on grace-theology (G. Bardy, *La vie spirituelle d'après les Pères des trois premiers siècles*, 1935, ch. XIV).

the Origenist system, but in spite of his errors Origen was a Christian who knew he was bound by the rule of faith.[26] Not only do we find in him the idea of the educative Providence,[27] but we are beginning more and more to perceive that back of a system that was only a transitory expression of his theological thought there was in Origen a spiritual experience of the first rank and that we can truly speak of the mysticism of Origen.[28] Historians of theology, too much preoccupied with Origenism, have unfortunately left in the shadow this aspect of his thought. It can be that in his Trinitarian theology Origen was a subordinationist[29] and that this error influenced his doctrine of prayer,[30] but when he speaks of the sanctifying role of the Spirit the Alexandrine master remains faithful to Tradition.[31]

Much more even than the heirs of his thought does he insist on the presence of Christ in souls[32] and the mystery of our union with Him. The interest we bring today to the doctrine of the Mystical Body has had as an unexpected result a rehabilitation of Origen. The restitutionist thesis, otherwise so regrettable, led him to stress more than others the idea that before the end of time the total Christ has not yet reached His perfect stature.[33] At most one can reproach him with an excess of intellectualism.[34]

Regeneration, adoption, gift of the Holy Spirit, active presence of the same Spirit in souls and in the Church, identification with Christ by communication or participation of divine life, these ideas, of which none is absent from the work of Origen, recur at every moment in the discussion St.

---

[26] De princ., I, P.G., 11, 115–121. Cf. Bardy, "La règle de foi d'Origène," RSR, 1919, pp. 162–196.

[27] H. Koch, Pronoia und Paideusis, Studien über Origenes und seinem Verhältnis zum Platonismus, 1932, with the remarks of J. Lebreton, RSR, 1933, pp. 374–376.

[28] The book of W. Völker, Das Volkommenheitsideal des Origenes, 1931, marks a date in the history of the studies on the thought of Origen. On this book see Ch.-H. Puech, "Un livre nouveau sur la mystique d'Origène," in Revue d'hist. et de phil. rel., 1933, pp. 508–536.

[29] G. Bardy, "Origène," DTC, t. XI, col. 1523–1527; J. Lebreton, in Fliche and Martin, Histoire de l'Eglise, t. II, pp. 259–260.

[30] Origène, De la priere, 15–16, P.G., 11, 464 D-468 C. Cf. J. Lebreton, "Le désaccord entre la foi populaire et la théologie savante dans l'Eglise chrétienne du III siècle," in Revue d'hist. eccles., 1924, pp. 19–26.

[31] In the Peri Archon, treating of the Holy Spirit, Origen recalls that He is the source of our regeneration at the same time as the Father and the Son, and no one can be partaker of the Father and the Son without the Holy Spirit (De princ., I, 3, 5, P.G., 11, 150A). . . . Cf. H. Rahner, "Taufe und geistliches Leben bei Origenes," in Zeitschrift für Aszese und Mystik, 1932. The work of M. Verfaillie, La doctrine de la justification dans Origène, leaves too much in the shadow this aspect of the doctrine of the great Alexandrine.

[32] In Rom, V, 8, P.G., 14, 1037–1039 A; In Rom, V, 9, P.G., 14, 1043 C, etc.

[33] In Levit, hom. VII, 2, P.G., 12, 478–482.

[34] P. Mersch (Le corps mystique du Christ, t. I, 2 ed., 1936, pp. 352–362), insists more than is reasonable on the "Gnosticism" of Origen. A serene study of the texts will probably show that the Alexandrine master wishes to underline especially the necessity of moral effort, which he unfortunately binds too much to intellectual effort. He is a "Greek"! For him, knowledge and virtue are still poorly distinguished.

Athanasius had with the Arians. If we are adoptive sons of God, he says for example, then there is a son by nature. If we are participants of the Word by the Holy Spirit, then the Word is God. If the Word is not God, how can we be divinized? Creation makes us creatures of God. By adoption we become sons, and this because the Word is in us. He cannot come without the Father and the Holy Spirit and so the sanctification effected at baptism is effected by the Son in the Spirit.[35] It has often been remarked that it is easy to disengage from the polemic work of the great champion of Nicene orthodoxy a beautiful synthesis of the theology of salvation.[36] We would add that in this synthesis the doctrine of the Mystical Body will have an important place.[37]. . .

We shall not delay to find the same doctrine in the works of other Greek Fathers.[38] The struggle against the Macedonians[39] that began while Athanasius was still living, led the Cappadocians to stress the sanctifying role of the Holy Spirit. It is from His supernatural action in us that St. Basil draws an argument in favor of His divinity.[40] St. Gregory of Nyssa does the same[41] and it is well known how dear this argument is to St. Gregory of Nazianzen.[42]. . . This doctrine of the divinization of the Christian is a traditional good and the heretics, whether called Arius, Eunomius or Macedonius, do not contest it, though an argument is drawn from it against them.[43]. . .

Cyril . . . of Alexandria gives us a magnificent doctrine on sanctification and the presence of the Holy Spirit in souls. . . . As his predecessors, he resorts to the idea of our divine filiation to establish the divinity of the Word or that of the Holy Spirit. We are sons of God by grace, so Jesus is son by nature. The Holy Spirit divinizes

---

[35] Contra Arian., II, 19, P.G., 26, 361 C; I, 9, P.G., 26, 28 D 29 A; I, 70, P.G., 26, 296 B; II, 59, P.G., 26, 272 C–273 AB; Epist. ad Serap., I, 19, P.G., 26, 573 CD–576 AD; I, 20, P.G., 26, 577 C.

[36] X.-M. Le Bachelet, "Athanase," in DTC, t. II, col. 2166–2174.

[37] E. Mersch, Le corps mystique du Christ, 2 ed., t. I, 1936, pp. 374–409; L. Bouyer, L'Incarnation et l'Eglise corps du Christ dans la théologie de saint Athanase, 1943.

[38] A. Lieske, "Zur Theologie des Christusmystik Gregors von Nyssa," Scholastik, 1939, pp. 485–514; H. Englerding, "Die Kirche als Braut in den Ostsyrischen Liturgie," Orientalia periodica, 1937, pp. 5–48; J. Daniélou, Platonisme et théologie mystique, Essai sur la doctrine spirituelle de saint Gregorie de Nysse, 1944.

[39] G. Bardy, "Macedonius," DTC, t. IX,

col. 1478–1478: J. Tixeront, Histoire des dogmes, t. II, pp. 57–58.

[40] Basil, Contra Eunom., III, 2, P.G., 29, 660 C; V, P.G., 29, 725 S; De Spiritu sancto, XIX, 48, P.G., 32, 264 D (the Holy Spirit sanctifies and is not sanctified); Epist., I, 8, 11, P.G., 32, 156 B (we are the temples of the Holy Spirit, so He is God); Epist., II, 105, P.G., 32, 513 B (the Holy Spirit, source of sanctification, brings us the grace of adoption and immortality).

[41] Greg. Nyss., Adv. Maced., 22, P.G., 45, 1328 D–1329 AB. Cf. J. B. Aufhauser, Die heilslehre des heilig. Gregor von Nyssa, pp. 178–200; L. Malevez, "L'Eglise dans le Christ," RSR, 1935, pp. 260–280.

[42] Orat., 34, 12, P.G., 36, 252; Orat., 31, 28, P.G., 36, 165 A; Orat., 37, 18, P.G., 36, 304 A.

[43] J. Gross, La divinisation du chrétien d'après les Pères grecs, pp. 201–202.

us, so He cannot be a creature.[44]. . .
Filled with the doctrine of St. John
and of St. Paul, heir of St. Irenaeus,
of St. Athanasius and the Cappadocians, Cyril shows us in Christ the
new Adam who reestablishes us in our
original dignity and restores in us the
divine image. The Word of God is
made man to divinize men. In assuming a flesh like ours He has as it were
filled up with His presence all humanity. The Holy Spirit descends on
Jesus at the baptism, not for Him but
for His brothers, not to make him God
but to make of us sons of God since
we are already in Him. At baptism
each Christian renews for his own
proper account the historic action of
Christ, appropriates its effects, dies
and rises with Christ. God comes to
dwell in him. He is made a temple of
God, a son of God, a participant of
the divine nature. The Holy Spirit,
who is given to him, forms in him
Christ. Christ lives in all the baptized
faithful at their baptism and the Christians in turn are in Christ, united
with one another and with Him as
are the Father and the Son. They
form one sole body, one sole temple,
waiting for the glorious resurrection
that will complete this work of sanctification and divinization.[45]

We can see how rich and new and
traditional at the same time this doctrine is. But it poses a problem. In
affirming that from the Incarnation
humanity in its entirety has been divinized, is Cyril not the victim of a
Platonic illusion that reifies the universe?[46] And even if we suppose that
he has not separated the Incarnation
from the Redemption, how are we to
understand this mysterious union of
Christians with one another and with
Christ?[47] Later on we will see Petau
and then Scheeben try to support by
the Cyrillan doctrine their idea of a
special union of the just with the Holy
Spirit.[48] Let us leave now these problems that do not yet appear clearly.
It is enough to have marked in this
history of the theology of grace the
place of an author of great rank
whom St. Augustine himself should
not make us forget. . . .

In Maximus as in Pseudo-Denis,
mystical theology, far from being cut
off from ecclesiology, is on the contrary in intimate conjunction with the
doctrine of baptism and of the Eucha-

Mahé, "L'eucharistie d'après saint Cyrille
d'Alexandrie" in Revue d'hist. eccles.,
1907, p. 684; E. Mersch, Le corps mystique du Christ, 2 ed., 1936, t. I, p. 497;
H. Du Manoir, Dogme et spiritualité chez
saint Cyrille d'Alexandrie, 1945, pp. 184–
195.

[46] Cf. L. Malevez, "L'Eglise dans le
Christ," RSR, 1935, pp. 280–291.

[47] E. Mersch, Le corps mystique du
Christ, 2 ed., 1936, t. II, pp. 519–523.

[48] Petau, Theologica dogmata, VIII, 5–6,
ed. Vivès, 1865, t. III, pp. 466–486; VIII,
7, pp. 486–495; A. Mahé, "La sanctification
d'après saint Cyrille d'Alexandrie" in Revue
d'hist. eccles., 1907, pp. 485–492.

[44] In Joan., I, 12, P.G., 73, 153 AC;
II, 5, P.G., 73, 348 D; Thesaurus de SS.
Trin., XIII, P.G., 75, 189 BC; XXXIV,
P.G., 75, 596 D–598 D.
[45] In Joan., I, 9, P.G., 73, 161 C; II,
1, P.G., 73, 204 D–205 A; XI, 11, P.G.,
74, 557 D; II, 1, P.G., 73, 208 B; V,
2, P.G., 73, 753 AC; VI, 3, P.G., 74,
792 D; I, 9, P.G., 73, 128 A; II, 1, P.G.,
73, 244 C–245 B; IV, 2, P.G., 73, 584 C;
X, 2, P.G., 74, 333 BC–341 B. Cf. A.

rist.[49] It is this theology which down the centuries is repeated and resumed by Byzantine theologians, from the eighth century to our days.[50]

For the Protestant historians of dogma this is a veritable scandal, and they have not enough scorn for a theology of grace which to them seems an unlikely synthesis of pantheism and magic.[51] But the Greco-Russian Church, however cramped it may be, is conscious of still living out the riches of this theology and today more than ever it means to defend and demonstrate that by it it is attached to the purest Christian tradition.[52]

We do not decide against them. We regret only that in being faithful to the tradition of the first four or five centuries the Greek Church has not comprehended that the deposit of rev-

elation can only remain alive in the measure that this tradition once again reflects on itself in the face of new problems. But the Greek Church seems satisfied with this sublime doctrine of divinisation and is not concerned to deepen the theology of grace properly so called.[53] More, it remains indifferent to the great controversy that began at the beginning of the fifth century, forty years before the council of Chal-

---

[49] However, among these authors the divinization is especially tied to the mystical life, and the mysticism of baptism marks a recoil.

[50] In his work on La vie en Jésus-Christ (P.G., 150, trad. Broussaleux), Nicolas Cabasilas, in the 14th century, shows that baptism makes us to be born to a new and properly divine life (cf. M. Lot-Borodine, "La grâce déifiante des sacrements d'après Nicolas Cabasilas" in Revue des sciences phil. et théol., 1936, pp. 299–300; S. Salaville, "Vues soteriologiques de Nicolas Cabasilas," in Etude byzantines, 1943, I, p. 21; M. Jugie, Palamas, XI, 1757–1758; W. Lossky, Essai sur la théologie mystique de l'Eglise d'Orient, 1945, pp. 74–75.

[51] A. Harnack, L'essence du Christianisme, 1907, pp. 272–291; Lehrbuch der Dogmengeschichte, 4 ed., 1909, t. 11, pp. 437–438; R. Seeberg, Lehrbuch der Dogmengeschichte, 3 ed., 1923, t. II, pp. 321–322, 347–348.

[52] Mme Lot-Borodine ("La doctrine de la déification dans l'Eglise grecque" in Revue de l'histoire des religions, 1932, pp. 31, 33, n. 1).

---

[53] Catholic theologians exert themselves to find in the Greek Fathers or in the Latins before Augustine the notion of created grace. The Holy Spirit, the divine seal, is distinct from the imprint He leaves in the soul, the image of God is not God Himself, etc. (see for example J.-B. Terrien, La grâce et la gloire, 1897, t. I, pp. 80–82). But the texts adduced are not always as clear as one says (v.g., Basil, Advers, Eunom., V, P.G., 29, 724 BC); sometimes they simply speak of the grandeur of the soul (Ambros., Hexahem., VII, 42–47, P.L., 13, 258BC–260 CD) or they seem on the contrary to affirm that the Holy Spirit is Himself this divine imprint (Cyril. Alex., Thesaurus, P.G., 75, 609 D–611 A). The Orthodox theologians in return tend here to oppose Greeks and Latins, and especially Greeks and Scholastics. M. Lossky (Essai sur la théologie mystique de l'Eglise d'Orient, 1945, p. 65–66) takes up the doctrine of the divinization of the Christian, but refuses to accept the idea of a created grace or of a supernatural order (p. 85). He bridges the abyss between God and the divinized creature by uncreated energies flowing eternally from the unique essence of the Trinity (p. 71), deifying energies that are communicated to us (p. 83). The following part of our study will show how the notion of sanctifying grace is born in the Occident and that the dogma is not identified with the theory of grace-quality. On the usage and the sense of the word charis in the Greek Fathers, see the study of N. Gloubokovsky, in Whitley, ed., The Doctrine of Grace (London: SCM Press, 1931), pp. 87–105. [Reprinted below, in Section 3 of this chapter.]

cedon, and opposed "Pelagians" and "Augustinians" and led the Church of the West through all sorts of vicissitudes to formulate an entire doctrine of grace, sin, justification, and predestination, a doctrine whose authentic expression at the Council of Trent provoked new reflections and new doctrinal discussions that manifested once again the truth that dogma, far from being the death of reason, is on the contrary the best stimulant of reflection.

3. Nicholas N. Gloubokowsky[54] says the Greek Fathers did not theorize on grace because they instinctively enjoyed it. Theory began in the West with the disorderly life of individuals. All God's acts in creation, providence, and redemption are grace. Each Person of the Trinity has His part in every act. Each man is free to choose and has at his core what is congenial to grace. "Original grace" does not enable a man to enter the Kingdom. For this, specific grace is needed and an enlarged capacity.

"The grace of God that brings salvation has appeared to all men"; "by grace are you saved"; "by the grace of God we have had our conversation in the world" and our very being as Christians, for everybody firmly believed about himself, with the Apostle St. Paul: "by the grace of God I am what I am"[55] — such was the dominating and universal conviction of primitive Christianity from the first times. It may seem therefore the more astonishing that in patristic and particularly in Eastern Greek literature, there are no special researches about this most essential element of Christianity. On the other hand, what partial declarations there are on this subject are

neither strictly dogmatic nor sufficiently definite. Evidently the Christians of that epoch did not feel the necessity of such discussions, and it was certainly so because they were permanently conscious of the grace of God existing in them directly and wholly; it was a vital fact of their personal experience common to all of them without exception. They breathed the ether of this grace, washed themselves in its streams, were completely embraced by it. . . . Believers lived, then, in grace according to the Holy Scriptures, without making a theoretical analysis of it, nor punctiliously quoting the Scriptures.

Reflection began under the influence of certain disorders in the harmony of the Christian society caused by the deviations and errors of individual members. It revealed itself in this way at first in the West (St. Cyprian and St. Augustine), and ac-

[54] Rev. Nicholas N. Gloubokowsky, D.D., was emeritus professor, Sofia, Bulgaria, in 1931. This excerpt is taken from his article, "Grace in the Greek Fathers" (*To St. John of Damascus*) and "Inter-Church Union," in *The Doctrine of Grace*, ed. W. T. Whitley (London: SCM Press, 1931), pp. 61–105.

[55] Ti 2:11; Eph 2:5, 8; 2 Cor 1:12; 1 Cor 15:10.

cordingly existing disagreement expressed itself in explicit doctrine. In the East during the whole of the patristic period, it was not so much speculation and teaching but rather appropriation and contemplation of the reality of grace that were predominant. Neither have we the right to apply to them the schemes of scholasticism, but may only describe the fundamental charitological tendencies of thought, with a view to the purpose of inter-church reconciliation.

It is quite natural that, under the described conditions, the whole Christian life was itself a matter of grace, as everything in it was a work of grace, from its origin, by transformation and accommodation under the action of this Divine power. In such a case we must admit in principle that there is everywhere grace, and all is the work of grace: without such an antecedent the gracious influence itself would be unnatural and impossible, because in that case it would have to be self-energised.

Upon this vital ground is based the following immovable and continuous conviction of the Eastern Church authorities: everything accomplished by the Triune God, through His goodwill, in creation, providence and redemption, is very grace, as St. John Chrysostom says: "For what belongs to the law (of Moses) was itself the work of grace, as well as our very creation out of non-existent things, since not for our preceding good deeds did we receive such an recompence . . . but because the beneficence of God is everywhere beforehand. . . ."[56]

[56] In Joan., hom. XIV, 2: P.G., 59, 94.

It means that to everybody and to everything the Divine grace is inherent. And this is really so, because the whole Holy Trinity takes part in it and because all their actions are fulfilled with grace. . . . It means that "where there is one hypostasis of the Holy Trinity there the whole Trinity is present," and — because of its indivisibility — "it is impossible that Christ should not be where the Spirit is present."[57] All "the dispensation respecting us is distributed among Father, Son and Holy Spirit,"[58] but the first source is always God the Father, as He has two "bodyless hands": the hand creative which is the Son, and the fashioning and renewing hand which is the Spirit.[59]

And so, in grace from the very beginning of mankind according to the will of God there acts invariably the unlimited goodness of the Father, the love of Christ that passes all understanding, and the inscrutable kindness of the Spirit.[60]. . . Therefore for the Eastern fathers it was dogmatically sure that the Divine grace is universal and but one, and that it is present in a certain way even with those who have sinned after having been baptised.[61] For this reason the grace of the Word doubtlessly can be found among

[57] St. John Chrysostom, in Epist. ad Rom., hom. XIII, 8.

[58] St. John Chrysostom, De s. Pentec., hom., I, 2.

[59] St. Basil the Great, Contra Eunom., V: P.G., 29, 713, 756, 760.

[60] Blessed Macarius of Egypt, Hom., XVIII, 6: P.G., 34, 640.

[61] St. Basil the Great, De Spirit. S., XVI, 40: P.G., 32, 141.

the Gentiles[62] and its saving seed was reserved for some of the Jews[63] and already in the time before Christ the best of the Gentiles (e.g., Socrates, Heraclitus) were as Christians in their lives.[64]. . . . The peculiarities and differences of the manifestations of grace mean only that it is "not the Spirit Himself who is divided, but the grace received through Him"[65] and this grace "its partakers enjoy in the measure of their receptivity, but not in the measure possible for the Holy Spirit."[66]. . . .

While so broadminded a view was taken, at the same time those differences were in no wise forgotten which exist in the manifestations of grace, and the necessity for everyone to proceed from lower degrees to higher ones. . . . So true is it that one cannot enter the Kingdom of God without strengthening by the Divine power,[67] which Kingdom is just the Holy Spirit.[68] Here the influence of the "original grace," equally spread over all mankind, is not by itself sufficient,[69] but the highest and exceeding grace is necessary, and this last in comparison with the insufficiency of the former seems even to be specifically separate — at least in its degree and qualitative intensiveness. . . . The difference is, consequently, not in the nature of the operating power, which is always and everywhere gracious, but in the superiority of the energy in its manifestation, and of its actual influence. Inasmuch, however, as the Holy Spirit is divinely abundant and inexhaustible, all the variations and gradations are conditioned only by the receptivity of the people, their preparation, adaptability and worthiness.

All this presupposes a previous securing of the human capacity, which was procured by the redemption of our Lord and Saviour, and can be received through fellowship with Him. This last is available through the institution of Christ's Church, and therefore it is absolutely obligatory for all people to join it by the sacrament of baptism. . . . .

According to the Western authorities it seems to be accepted that when the "ecclesiastic grace" appears, any other grace disappears or at least loses its activity. This was natural enough because of the excesses of the Western hamartiology, according to which man's liability to sin is treated almost as an evil in nature and hardly left ground for contact with the heavenly grace. The Eastern theologians always maintained broader tendencies and always safeguarded the idea that the whole world came into existence according to the grace of God and is fulfilled by this grace in its every part. Therefore for them the Fall into sin could result only in a reduction of the grace and diminution of its actual effect, but not in its cessation or deadness, be-

---

[62] St. Justin the Martyr, *Apol.*, II, 13.

[63] St. Justin the Martyr, *Dial. cum Tryph.*, c. 55.

[64] St. Justin the Martyr, *Apol.*, I, 2.

[65] St. Cyril of Jerusalem, *Catech.*, XVII, 12.

[66] St. Basil the Great, *De Spirit. S.*, IX, 22: P.G., 32, 109.

[67] *Epist. ad Diogn.*, C. IX.

[68] St. Gregory of Nyssa, *De orat. Dominica or.*, III: P.G., 44, 1157.

[69] St. Gregory of Nyssa, *De hominis opificio*, C. XVI.

cause in this last case existence itself would cease. The Eastern understanding admitted a certain swooning of the gracious energy along with the weakening in its previous function as to the appropriation. Inasmuch as this power acted from the beginning and was applied exclusively by the will of God, absolutely unconditioned externally, it is evident that even when the receptive apparatus was destroyed, God could not sacrifice His own gift, but was obliged Himself to save it through bringing it back to its initial purity. In the light of this, Christ's redemption, as well as the gracious serving ministry of the Church as its realisation and continuation, was understood in the ancient Greek East; there the idea of "regeneration" in the sense of a renovation of what was actual but temporarily stopped in its development is entirely dominant. . . .

In all these respects the supremacy of the regeneration by grace is evident as well as the exceptional significance of the Church, which is necessary for all regenerated people and for which nothing else can be substituted for anyone. It is however not quite new objectively as well as subjectively. If here "takes place the change of the form of the soul into the likeness of the prototype,"[70] then it is clear that the creative power in both cases remains the same, only in the second case it must be more intense in order to reform what was corrupted and to safeguard the restoration and to bring it to sublime perfect-

---

[70] St. Gregory of Nyssa, De perfectione ad Olympium monachum: P.G., 46, 253.

ness. Consequently it is the same grace, but in a peculiar manifestation through Christ and in a special application through the Spirit.

Neither does this involve any unnatural surprise for him who is regenerated. Being wholly a creation of God's grace, he was stimulated and disposed by his very God-created nature to the incessant growth in grace, otherwise he would betray his vital principle and would remain without any essential basis, thus preparing for himself complete annihilation. The weakening of the progress in grace was a result of sinful and morbid violence, and therefore the regeneration was a desirable and natural revival of the previous process, an especially efficient and more fruitful activity of the original gracious agency. This is why the Church, being the appointed depository of this abundant energy, and inviting all the people within its pale, asserts only the universal prevalence of this power and its essentially identical quality, though it be of reduced and even small intensity.

Thus on the whole we affirm that from the objective point of view the whole world and everything in the world participate in God's grace, and in the Church it finally attains its reasonable and saving purpose. But the same is true from the subjective point of view, with reference to the capacity and actual participation of those who have to be saved in the whole human complex of God's creation. As regards this subject, the whole Eastern theology was explicit in acknowledging the receptiveness of all men for grace, and the spirit of this theology is adequately expressed by the Russian authorities in safeguarding the "sanctuary of freedom."[71] . . .

All this makes clear that the supremacy of grace is very considerable, but still the participation of man is evident, who is not at all a passive member only mechanically or magically recepting the influences from above. On the contrary, he has natural inclinations, capacities and powers; he controls the impulse of his will, which at the beginning is indeed his own work.[72]. . .

Thus it is certain that the extremes of Augustinianism and Pelagianism which had their historical grounds in the West were quite strange to Eastern theology: in the East they had no basis to rest upon. In the problem of human salvation, Eastern theology, decisively and without exception, maintained the idea of the freedom of the will which although considerably damaged by sin is not destroyed entirely and not exchanged for slavery to an evil mind. At the same time, man still preserves the inborn tendency towards good, and hence possesses sufficient energy, being free, to manifest actively and to fulfill the possibilities of ethical choice very really if not perfectly.

From this point of view Divine grace meets in every man as such with readiness and organic capacity and, for this reason, in its functioning and application it is not bound by insurmountable natural barriers seated in the receiving subject. Or, to put it better, the ultimate factor in every member of the human family, is congenial to it — and grace in its action is not limited necessarily from the subjective point of view, just as it is free objectively. . . .

This principal thesis of Eastern charitology is exceedingly important for the problem of mutual approach of the Christian Churches, because it affords them a dogmatic guarantee of the available and actual realisation of this purpose. If we admit that grace abides exclusively in the Church and nowhere else — then all circles standing outside the Church would not be objects of its saving grace and would thus be deprived of brotherly fellowship with "church-people." But as it is, in view of the participation in grace of every man according to his very nature as created by God, and according to his inborn capacity for grace — there is secured to all mankind a common basis for spiritual approach and for everyone is open the way to that delightful end to which the grace of God calls the whole creation through Jesus Christ.[73]

---

[71] Bishop Theophanes Govorov.
[72] Blessed Macarius of Egypt, *Hom.*, XXXVII, 9: P.G., 34, 756.

[73] Origen, *De princ.*, I, 6, 1.

4. **Ch. Baumgartner, S.J.,[74] views the grace doctrine of the Greek Fathers from a triple point of view, sacramentary, christological, and trinitarian. From the first aspect he looks mainly to the baptismal grace that gives the Holy Spirit. From the second, to Incarnation and assimilation and adoptive filiation. From the third, to the sanctifying Spirit.**

We can distinguish — if we are careful not to oppose them — two currents in the patristic theology of grace. One current is "Johannine" and one is "Pauline." The Johannine current — of divinizing grace, or as the Scholastics will say later on of "elevating" grace — predominates with the Greek Fathers. The Pauline current — of liberating or "healing" grace — is especially represented by St. Augustine.

But it would be excessive to wish to discover in this difference of viewpoint or accent an opposition in doctrine. The Johannine grace divinizes man only in liberating him from the darkness of sin and death. The Pauline grace is not merely a force opposed to the sin that it destroys: it triumphs only because it is a life in Christ. The Greek Fathers, in speaking of the divinization of the Christian by the Incarnation of the Word, never separate this Incarnation from the redemptive act of Christ, and always keep in mind that divinized humanity is a fallen humanity which always needs to be pulled away from its state of fall. And so does Augustine. He is the doctor of the grace that heals the will and gives it the strength to accomplish good, but he is also the doctor of

the mystical body and of Christian divinization.

The Fathers first let us know their doctrine of grace in connection with the sacraments of initiation and of penance. The trinitarian and christological polemic, especially at the beginning of the fourth century, furnished the Fathers the occasion to explain the sense of the Incarnation and sanctification of the Christian, as consisting in a participation in the sanctity of the Father through the Son in the Spirit. We shall place ourselves successively at this triple point of view, sacramentary, christological and trinitarian.

I. Sacraments and Grace

1. Irenaeus. Except for the *Didache* the second-century authors see in the remission of sins and the gift of the Holy Spirit the two fundamental aspects of baptismal grace. They do not mention the Pauline theme of the death and the resurrection with Christ. Pseudo Barnabas alludes to the new creation. By baptism man is created anew.[75] *Pastor Hermas* says one goes down into the water dead and comes out alive. The gift of the Holy Spirit appears less as a force for moral

---

[74] Ch. Baumgartner, S.J., cf. Ch. I, n. 12. This excerpt is from *op. cit.*, pp. 40–57.

[75] One will find the texts and the development of this doctrine in A. Benoit, *Le Baptême chrétien au second siècle*, pp. 40–45.

life than as a treasure to be guarded. Lost by sin, one recovers it by penitence.[76] For Justin baptism is the bath of regeneration.[77]

According to Irenaeus[78] baptism gives the Spirit. He insists less on the remission of sins than on the regeneration (*lavacrum regenerationis*[79]), the second birth, the renovation of man by the gift of the Spirit.[80] The Christian possesses the Spirit, dwells in Him, is united to Him. This participation in the Spirit makes a man perfect and spiritual.[81] The Spirit who vivifies man makes of him a child of God, renders him spiritual, and like to the Son and the Father while waiting for the plenitude of all these graces in the eternal life of the vision of God which procures incorruptibility.[82] The union with the Spirit is inseparable from union with the Son and with the Father.[83] So the Spirit, the gift of the Father and of the Son unites and likens us to them.[84] The uncreated gift of the three divine Persons regenerates and renews man and spiritualizes him. This is already the equivalent of the distinction between the uncreated and the created gift, with the latter the effect and consequence of the former.

2. Origen. According to Origen baptismal grace is the foundation of the whole spiritual life from its beginning to its most elevated summits. And in all its degrees and all its stages the spiritual life is the development of this same grace. Origen's moral doctrine has its source in a mysticism, and in this essential point is only the echo of the Pauline and Johannine theology of grace. The Christian participates in the life of the Logos in the Spirit, by faith, knowledge and love so as to mount up to the Father. Baptism is the principle and source of these divine graces.[85] . . . Baptismal grace consists in liberation from the slavery of the demon, in the unique and total remission of sins. At baptism the Holy Spirit fills the one who is converted and a divine fire destroys all that is material and terrestrial.[86] He becomes a new man.[87]

In what do this newness of life and this regeneration consist more precisely? Baptismal grace is a death and a resurrection with Christ.[88] At baptism we become sons of God and brothers of Christ, members of Christ and temples of God.[89] So it is a participation of the divine nature in charity by the Spirit who has been diffused in our hearts.[90]

---

[76] *Ibid.*, pp. 115–138.
[77] *Ibid.*, pp. 143–148.
[78] *Ibid.*, pp. 186–221.
[79] *Adv. haer.*, P.G., 7, 1166.
[80] SCh., *Demonstration de la prédication apostolique*, 3, 5, 7.
[81] *Adv. haer.*, V, 6, 1; 8, 1, 2; 9, 2; P.G., 7, 1137, 1141–1142, 1144–1145.
[82] *Adv. haer.*, IV, 20, 5; P.G., 7, 1035.
[83] *Dem.*, 5; *Adv. haer.*, III, 19, 1; IV, 20, 5; 38, 3; V, 9, 4; 14, 2; 27, 2; P.G., 7, 938–939, 1035–1036, 1108, 1147, 1162; 1196.
[84] *Dem.*, 7, 97; *Adv. haer.*, III, 7, 2–3; V, 1, I; 6, 1; P.G., 7, 930, 1121, 1137 f.

[85] *Comm. Jo.*, VI, 33; GCS, IV, 142–143.
[86] *Comm. Jo.*, VI, 32; GCS, IV, 141.
[87] *In ex.*, hom. V, 5; GCS, VI, 190.
[88] *In ex.*, hom. V, 2; GCS, VI, 186.
[89] *Comm. Jo.*, XX, 37; GCS, IV, 377; *In lib. Jesu Nave*, V; GCS, VII, 313–321.
[90] *Comm. Rom.*, IV, 9; P.G., 14, 997.

Without the Father, the Son and the Holy Spirit there is no regeneration by God with a view to salvation. And it is impossible to become a participant of the Father or the Son without the Holy Spirit. At baptism one receives the grace of the Holy Spirit.[91] By the Holy Spirit one participates in the Son. As the Spirit so the Logos is the principle of divine life in us. The Word is the spouse of the soul.[92] This matrimonial union of the Church and individual souls in the Church is realized in baptism. . . . The coming of the Logos in the bosom of the Virgin and His birth are renewed in the mystical body. The inhabitation of the Logos, the image of God, in the soul, transforms it to its image.[93] . . . The soul transformed to the image of the celestial man at baptism becomes the temple of the Trinity dwelling in it. . . .

The life of the soul consists then in possessing God, that is in having in it the three divine Persons. All three unite themselves directly to it and sanctify it by themselves. The sanctity whence they sanctify is that of the divine nature itself with which the divine Persons are identical.[94] The participation of the divine nature is the communication of charity. Its source is the divinity of the Father and from this source proceed the Son and the Spirit. The gift of the Holy Spirit is the gift of divine charity itself. To receive the Holy Spirit is

[91] De princ., I, 3, 7; GCS, V, 54, 55, 56, 58: I, 8, 3; ibid., V, 100.
[92] In Num., hom. XX, 2; GCS, VII, 188.
[93] In Lc., hom. VIII; GCS, IX, 56, 57.
[94] Comm. Jo., XIII, 23–24, GCS, IV, 247.

to receive by the Son that which comes to Him from the Father, that is the presence and participation of the divine nature or charity.

II. The Incarnation, Principle of Divinization and Filial Adoption.

1. Incarnation and assimilation to God: image and resemblance.

The religious philosophy of the hellenist world at the epoch of the Fathers propagated the platonic doctrine of the assimilation to the divine. The initiates of the mystery cults aspired to divine resemblance by participation in the privilege of immortality. The Fathers utilized the theories and aspirations of their milieu to illustrate the biblical theme of the creation of man to the image and likeness of God, but christianized them. The participation in the divine nature, assimilation to God or deification is not a conquest of man who by his own proper efforts attempts to mount up to God. It is not the result of a rational dialectic, of a wholly human ascesis and purification, or of magic rites. It is a gift of God who comes down toward His creature to draw nearer to him and associate him more intimately than by creation with His own proper life. It is to elevate us to Him and make of us sons and gods and divinize us, as the Fathers repeat so often after Clement of Alexandria in translating the Christian mystery of filial adoption in terms borrowed from the hellenistic culture. The tripartite scheme on the soteriological base of Irenaeus: creation of man to the image and likeness of God, degradation of the image by the Fall, restoration of the image by the redemption, becomes a traditional theme of the Greek Fathers. . . .

Irenaeus takes up and deepens the idea of Theophilus of Antioch of a progressive assimilation to God whose term is incorruptibility. He is the first author to distinguish the image from the resemblance, though often enough he identifies them. The image as distinct from the resemblance is the natural being of man, body and soul. It cannot be lost. The resemblance, on the contrary, has been destroyed by sin. It is restored to us by the Word made man and by His Spirit. It consists especially in participation in the divine incorruptibility, the fruit of the vision of God. As Irenaeus, so Clement of Alexandria and Origen distinguish the image from the resemblance. But unlike Irenaeus they do not put the image in the body of man but only in the *nous* [mind]. . . .

Not all the Fathers maintain the distinction between image and resemblance. Athanasius and Gregory of Nyssa do not. The *eikon* [image] is then the divine seal impressed on the spirit, obscured by sin and restored to its splendor by the redemption. It is the concrete spirit, intelligent and free, capable of God, ontological ordination to the resemblance. The *homoiosis* [likeness] is a superior assimilation, more perfect and "supernatural" and almost specifically like properties reserved to God. It is due to man's effort to imitate God, but this effort is possible only in dependence on the initiative and action of God who by the Incarnation of His Son procures the virtual divinization of all humanity but

only by faith and the sacraments brings about the actual participation of the divine nature in individuals.

In what does the resemblance to God, the deification consist more precisely? Negatively: it does not make man consubstantial with God. Positively: one line of thought that traverses the entire Greek patristic doctrine puts the divinization in immortality and incorruptibility, properties that are reserved to God. Participation in the divine nature will attain its perfection in eternal life after the resurrection at the end of time. But here below the Christian really anticipates this immortality and incorruptibility. Even now he is assimilated to the eternal God by baptism and the Eucharist. However, according to the Fathers, to be divinized is not only to receive a created similitude of God, but to possess God Himself. The created resemblance is only the consequence or the effect of the real possession of God Himself. Divinization consists in an assimilative union or a unitive assimiliation to God, that is to the Father by the Son in the Spirit.

2. Incarnation and adoptive filiation. The divinization of the Christian is also identified more or less clearly with adoptive filiation. That the last sense of the mystery of the Incarnation is the communication of adoptive filiation, this idea is fundamental among the Greek Fathers. It particularly commands the thought of St. Athanasius and St. Cyril of Alexandria. One meets it also in Irenaeus, and it is implicit in Ignatius of Antioch.

The doctrine of Ignatius of Antioch

is centered on union with Christ. Unlike St. Paul his mysticism is more a mysticism of the Eucharist and of the martyr than a mysticism of baptism; but the union with Christ is evidently inaugurated by the sacrament of initiation. The Christians are in Christ; they are bearers of Christ; they are temples of Christ. The Eucharist is a medicine of immortality, an antidote so that one will not die but live in Jesus Christ forever. United to Christ, they are united to the Father. The Christians are God-bearers. The bodies of Christians are temples of God, they are filled with God and participate in God. Perfect union with Jesus Christ and with God will consist in incorruptibility and eternal life.

Ignatius underlines more the role of the Spirit in the hierarchy than in the Christian community. However he mentions His presence in the community but he does not call the Christians Spirit-bearers but Christ-bearers.

The center of the theology of Irenaeus is the mystery of the redemptive Incarnation, the source of salvation for men conquered by sin and death and the demon. The Word of God is made man so that men may become sons of God. Irenaeus often returns to this theme. The Incarnation is the necessary means for divine adoption, for likeness to God, for regeneration by the Spirit, for "deification." . . .

Athanasius. The divinization so much pondered by the Greeks can only be by grace and participation since created and corruptible human nature is infinitely distant from God. This gratuitous gift is offered to us. It is a participation of the Word who is the unique and perfect Image of the Father. In participating in Him man has not only been created but made to His image, *logikos*, and thus capable of participating in the knowledge that the Word has of the Father. It is "life according to God" in an endless beatitude. The Incarnation has for its end to restore the work that was compromised by sin. . . .

In his discourse against the Arians Athanasius takes up again the same idea and completes and develops it in more explicitly New Testament terms. He insists more on the point of departure: there is only one Son, perfect and unique Image, perfectly one and consubstantial, the only one to know the Father and participate in His eternity, the only one participable. Participating in Him by grace, we are made sons in the unique Son, all united together in Him as He is united to His Father, and united by Him to the Father whom He makes us know as His Father. It is by the whole process of the Incarnation that this filial assimilation is realised. Because the Son has taken a true human body, our grace, unlike that of Adam, is harmonised to the corporal human condition. The flesh "verbified" has the power to receive grace. Because He has deigned to assimilate Himself to our nature, by this physical resemblance we can assimilate ourselves to His filiation. We are sons by the presence in us of the Son who became incarnate to be present to us and to unite us to God. He sends us the Spirit, who is the Spirit of the Son, and who is in us as

Spirit of filiation and says "Father," and is the seal of the Son and conforms us to the Son.

Cyril of Alexandria. "Sons of God we are in some sort naturally in Him and by Him; by participation and according to grace, by Him, in the Spirit." "In Him and by Him we are sons of God naturally and by grace. Naturally we are sons in Him and in Him alone, by participation and by grace we are by Him in the Spirit."[95]

These texts sum up the Cyrillan doctrine of the grace of filiation. The divine filiation is attached to the redemptive Incarnation. From the fact of the Incarnation, the Christ who was consubstantial to His Father, became consubstantial to men. That which made Him consubstantial to us is the flesh, the body. . . . From the fact of the Incarnation too Christ has a relation of the ontological order with humanity in its entirety. This is in some real fashion included in Him. But this inclusion on the plane of "nature," being altogether essential, does not constitute the supernatural filiation properly so called. It is still only a sort of potential radical, fundamental filiation. To achieve the filiation of grace and adoption, there is need of the sanctifying action of the humanity of Christ by the sacraments and the free action of man by faith. Cyril distinguishes in effect a double relationship of humanity with the Son, a "physical" relationship and a relationship effected by grace and participa-

tion. This grace which makes us sons of God is twofold: the grace of baptism and that of the Eucharist. Christ sanctifies us corporally as man by the Eucharist, and spiritually as God by the communication of His Spirit in baptism.

The Word ought to be related to us according to the flesh before communicating to us His Spirit. We thus become the temples of the Holy Spirit by a union with the Spirit who is personal and substantial. But the union itself is not substantial, it is only "relative" and "accidental," but so real that it makes us truly participate in the divine nature. The participation of the Son in the Spirit involves an intimate relation with the Word; we are brothers of the Word, brothers of the Son, and at the same time sons of the Father. Our divine filiation is in the order of grace, an imitation of the real and substantial generation of the Son by the Father. The adoption is a conformity with the natural Son by participation in the Holy Spirit. It is a true generation, founding the union of the faithful with one another.

The Eucharist is a participation that is somehow "physical" in the flesh and blood of Christ and thereby an accidental participation in the divinity of the Son. The Word sanctifies us in Himself by using His eucharistic body. It is a completion of our supernatural relations with the divine Persons. Cyril puts in relief the idea of an instrumental causality of the humanity of Christ in the donation of the Spirit of adoption.

Thus our radical relationship with

[95] *De recta fide ad Theol.*, P.G., 76, 1177 A; *De Inc. Unig.: De recta fide ad Theol.*, P.G., 75, 1229 B.

God in Christ is realised at the moment of the Incarnation. Our supernatural relationship by Christ depends on the physical mediation of the Incarnate Word, that is, on His constitution as Man-God by the fact of the Incarnation. It is established only in the Spirit, concretely, after the resurrection, when Christ as the new principle of humanity communicated the Spirit of adoption to the apostles on that same Easter day and communicates Him to the faithful at the moment of their baptism. We are sons of God by Christ in the Spirit.

III. The Sanctifying Spirit.

"The Fathers who incarnate in the fourth century the doctrinal movement called the school of Alexandria, all witness to the existence and the vitality in the Greek Church of the idea that the Christian is deified. They equally have in common that they are interested in this idea less for itself than for its furnishing them arguments in favor of the divinity of the Logos and the Holy Spirit."[96] In what regards the Holy Spirit we must keep in mind P. Galtier's remark: "It is not their purpose [the Fathers] to expound what the Third Person properly possesses that distinguishes Him from the others; their unique end is to set forth what distinguishes Him from creatures and manifests His divinity."[97] The Holy Spirit is sanctity itself and sanctifies us directly by Himself; so He is God. . . . Athanasius, the Cappado-

cians, St. Cyril of Alexandria are especially the great witnesses of this doctrine in the course of the controversies over the Holy Spirit.

1. Athanasius. The Christian is divinized by participation in the Word and the Spirit. There is question of the participation in the Word in the discourses against the Arians. The letters to Serapion treat the participation in the Spirit.

"The Spirit makes us all participate in God . . . but if He were a creature we could not have in Him participation in God; we would be united to a creature and be strangers to the divine nature, having nothing in common with it.". . . In the Spirit we participate in the Word and by the Word in the Father. There exists only one sanctification, that of the Father by the Son and realized in the Holy Spirit.[98]

2. Basil. The doctrine of the Cappadocians on the role of the Holy Spirit in the sanctification or divinization of the Christian does not differ essentially from that of St. Athanasius. . . . In c. 26 of the treatise on the Holy Spirit St. Basil explains in what sense the Holy Spirit is in us. "One says that the form is in the matter, the power in him who receives it, the disposition in him who is affected by it and so on for the rest." Then in so far as the Holy Spirit perfects rational creatures in giving them their last completion, He shows Himself as a form. He has the character of a form. For He who no longer lives according to the

96 J. Gross, *La divinisation du chrétien d'après les Pères grecs*, p. 252.
97 P. Galtier, *Le Saint-Esprit en nous d'après les Pères grecs*, p. 8.
98 *Première léttre à Ser.*, 20, 28, 30; SCh., pp. 118–120, 133–135, 136–139.

flesh but is moved by the Spirit and bears the name of son of God and becomes conformed to the image of the Son of God, he is called "spiritual."

A little further on St. Basil remarks that "to be in" is said of the Holy Spirit only with regard to creatures; for the Father and the Son we say he is "with them." To speak of the presence of the Holy Spirit in us, is to speak of the effects of grace that He produces. But assuredly He is there too. St. Basil teaches two things: the personal presence of the Holy Spirit in the soul and the state which results from this. It is on the last point that he insists. In effect the particle "in" denotes in no way any inferiority of the Holy Spirit. St. Basil wants to stress the importance of created grace. It is by the effects of grace which are regularly attributed to Him that he proves the equality of the Spirit with the Son and the Father.[99] . . .

3. Cyril of Alexandria. He insists so much on the role of the Holy Spirit in the union of souls with God that he appears to refer to this union with the Holy Spirit all sanctification. In him uncreated grace stands out in such relief that created grace is rejected and remains in shadow.[100]

The Holy Spirit is holy not by participation but substantially. He is a "sanctifying nature." By that He is distinguished not from the Father and from the Son but from created beings. The sanctification lost in Adam and recovered in Christ consists in our recovery of our conformity with the Son

and the Father. This is obtained in us by the Spirit. We are regenerated spiritually (at baptism) in being rendered conformed to the Son and in being refashioned by the Spirit to the image of his divine and supernatural beauty. We recover communion with the divine nature by entering into participation of the Son in as much as He is God. The Spirit is given in view of conformity and union with the Son and the Father. . . .

Union with God, divine adoption, participation in the divine nature are realized only in union with the Holy Spirit. It is in and by the Spirit that the Father and the Son communicate themselves to us. He is the bond that attaches our souls to the Son and to the Father. . . .

As all the works of God, so sanctification will be "from the Father, by the Son and in the Holy Spirit." The Father is the first source of the power to sanctify, the Son receives it from Him and by the Son it comes to the Holy Spirit. When They sanctify us in or by the Spirit, the Father and Son sanctify us by Themselves. As the Son, so the Spirit is the bond that attaches us to the Father by reason of His consubstantiality and His origin in the Trinity.[101]

Does this mean that according to St. Cyril and the Greek Fathers generally, the three Persons of the Trinity are united to the just only according to what is common to them, according to the divine nature, and not according to the hypostasis or that which distinguishes one from another? . . .

---

[99] P. Galtier, *op. cit.*, pp. 162–165.
[100] *Ibid.*, pp. 217–218.
[101] *Ibid.*, pp. 221–263.

VI

GRACE IN THE LATIN FATHERS

1. E. W. Watson[1] thinks that the idea of grace was at first naïvely confident, and that it was only the subsequent experience of the power of sin and the fuller study of St. Paul's teaching that led to modifications which culminated in the Augustinian doctrine of grace not merited but freely given. Ambrosiaster gave consistency and its complete vocabulary to the scheme of thought which St. Augustine and Calvin were to impress with such cogency on the mind of Christians.

WE MAY regard the possibility and the honour of martyrdom as the dominant thought of the Western Christians when they turned their minds to the idea of grace. As to themselves personally, they were, no doubt, modest;

---

[1] Rev. Canon E. W. Watson, D.D., was regius professor of ecclesiastical history in the University of Oxford in 1931. This excerpt is taken from his article, "Grace in the Latin Fathers to St. Augustine," in *The Doctrine of Grace*, ed. W. T. Whitley (London: SCM Press, 1931), pp. 106–113.

they could not think that they merited the privilege that was within their reach; but they could indulge their capacity for admiration in regard to their brethren. They could readily think that these had deserved their high estate.

And so a theology sprang up among people who had not been disillusioned by a sense of the prevalence of sin nor by the haunting thought of the fall as a dominating fact in human life. If high favour was, on the one side, conferred by God, on the other it was earned or deserved by men. No hesitation was felt about the use of such language. . . . And so serious a thinker as St. Cyprian has no hesitation in using repeatedly the words, *promereri Deum* as descriptive of the relation of man at his best to God.

The justification for this confidence was the fact of Baptism. This had given to men who had received the Sacrament a new power for good in which they were to place an absolute trust. It would be their own fault if it failed them; they would have refused to cooperate. This power was not limited to adults: it had equal value when conferred on infants. A baptized child might be expected to receive inspiration; Cyprian in times of anxiety was wont to look for guidance to *puerorum innocens aetas*. Baptised children were the appropriate vehicles, and he had no thought of its validity being tarnished or limited by hereditary sin.

We may say, then, that the idea of grace was at first naïvely confident, and that it was only the subsequent experience of the power of sin and the fuller study of St. Paul's teaching that led to modifications that culminated in the Augustinian doctrine of a grace not merited but freely given. The reaction was inevitable, and may be compared with that of the eighteenth century in England, when the doctrine of salvation by faith and works broke down under the Evangelical assault.

The first systematic Christian writer to write in Latin was *Tertullian,* whose views on grace suffered no essential change when he became a Montanist. Baptism for him is the beginning of the new life, and is of equal value for all who receive it. He does not contemplate the possibility of necessary failure for any of them. Receiving Baptism, they receive sufficient grace to enable them to appropriate its blessings. God will not compel them to follow the path of true happiness, but He will incline them so to do, and it is their fault, not His, if they err from the way. No temptation is irresistible if there be the will, as there is the power, to withstand it. . . .

There was but one danger that had to be faced. What if the Christian fell into such sin as robbed his Baptism of its power? For Tertullian took sin very seriously, and there were sins which to his mind dechristianised the believer. Therefore the Christian must not be hasty in putting on the armour of Baptism, for sin into which he might fall would cancel it. It was a strange and formidable paradox. It was safer to abstain from this necessary means of grace than to run the risk of frustrating it by committing sin against which God would dissuade, though He would not enforce obedience to His desire for the soul's welfare. For man — and in this case we are concerned only with man when baptised — is free; otherwise he would not be made in the likeness of God, who is free. God, therefore, permits sin, but He punishes it, just as He rewards obedience, which He promotes by the offer of grace through the Holy Spirit. And the harder the struggle, especially that of persecution, the higher the honour of victory and the greater the reward. The whole Christian life is measured in terms of the struggle; a struggle in which every Christian, if he will use the opportunity when it comes, can with certainty be the victor. Free will, aided by grace, cannot be overcome by temptation unless the Christian voluntarily succumbs.

The teaching of St. Cyprian, though he was misguided by his expectation of an almost immediate end to the world, and therefore was induced to simplify the problem of grace to an undue extent, was practically identical with that of Tertullian. . . . Disobedience to the express revelation frustrated the Covenant; a new Covenant, that of Christ, had in due time displaced it. That Covenant was by Baptism. Those who accepted and were true to it were safe, for in Baptism all sins are abolished. But it depends on ourselves how far we profit; our power to become good is proportional to our faith as shown by our obedience. God's grace is given, but given in return for

loyalty. It is earned or deserved; such language is characteristic of St. Cyprian. In fact, his working theology is such as we find in the Offertory sentences of our communion service, collected from the Book of Tobit and elsewhere. In the one case suffering, in the other almsgiving, is represented as meritorious. The offer of grace is unconditional and universal; it is made to all who are baptised, and only they can frustrate it. . . .

It remains to mention that Cyprian, in contrast to Tertullian, insists on the Baptism of infants at the earliest possible moment, attaching more importance to the grace so obtained than to the danger of loss by its abuse. . . .

But if Hilary (of Poitiers) felt painfully the change (from the enthusiasm of martyrdom), his teaching on the subject of grace contained nothing new. Some time passed before the less confident frame of mind found expression in a modified doctrine. Dr. Tixeront in his *Histoire des Dogmes* actually says that on the subject of grace, "St. Hilary, St. Optatus and even St. Jerome have made statements which we can only describe as semipelagian." So, with the old conception of the potency of Baptism, Hilary writes: "This is the whole office of our nature that it should desire to incorporate itself into the family of God, and should make the beginning. It is the work of the Divine mercy to aid the desirous, to uphold the beginners. . . . But the start is from ourselves, that He may perfect the work." If our share be so great in the work, the thought of human merit cannot be excluded; man cannot be helpless under the load of sin, nor can that load be so crushing as St. Augustine was to find it.

But in contrast to this hopefulness the opposite mode of thought was, through the circumstances of the time, steadily gaining ground. The Roman Empire was visibly breaking down in the fourth century; this was as obvious to the pagan historian Ammianus Marcellinus as it was to St. Ambrose and St. Augustine. An explanation of this fact must be found, and Christians came more and more definitely to assign sin as the cause. If that were true, it would fall in with the philosophy of the age, which was that of evolution by way of degeneration, each generation being worse than its predecessor; so St. Cyprian had taught, seeing in the physical deterioration of mankind, of which he was convinced by observation, a proof of the approaching end of the world.

Man, according to this theory, is helpless and degenerate. He has no merit. On the contrary he has a hereditary tendency to sin, and even an inheritance of actual sin and a guilt deserving of punishment, which is common to him with all his ancestry. This dark conception, which was doubly fortified by pagan theories which seemed to be confirmed by the decay of the Roman Empire and by the Pauline doctrine, grew steadily more explicit till it found its classical expression in St. Augustine. For instance, St. Hilary of Poitiers shows signs of interest in the Fall and its consequences, though only in occasional passages and without allowing it to control his conception of the share of man in contributing to his own salvation after Baptism.

St. Ambrose, a convert in middle life, who had not only been trained in philosophy, but as a Christian composed a *De Officiis* closely modelled on Cicero's work of the same name, as a textbook of Christian ethics, was a moralist deeply concerned with sin and inspired by a sense of human helplessness. As Dr. Williams in his Bampton Lectures on "The Fall and Original Sin" has said, he was the first to introduce into Western theology that notion of an original perfection from which man fell which was being propagated in the East by his great Cappadocian contemporaries. This notion was decisive against the earlier ideas of an element of good in man which could approach God and work with Him towards salvation.

The preliminary stages towards the full Augustinian position were accomplished by the writer known as "Ambrosiaster," whose name was Hilary, and who obtained additional credit for his own able work from St. Augustine's mistake in identifying him with his namesake of Poitiers. Ambrosiaster, we may say, gave consistency and its complete vocabulary to the scheme of thought which St. Augustine and Calvin were to impress with such earnestness and cogency upon the mind of Christians.

2. J. Tixeront[2] says that not until St. Augustine will a teaching somewhat complete about actual grace be exposed: before him, the teaching of the Church consists merely in the general affirmation of the need in which we stand of God's help to do good, and also of the duty incumbent upon us to cooperate by our own deeds toward salvation. Tertullian has vigorously sketched the theory of merit and of satisfaction, and the West has made it its own. The problem of predestination was barely touched upon up to the time of St. Augustine.

Though Tertullian developed in none of his works his soteriological teaching, but only sketched it, yet it is manifest that he looked upon the Incarnation as the consequence of a substitution of Jesus Christ the innocent in the place of sinners, and of an expiation supplied by the same Jesus Christ dying for us. On the other hand, Jesus Christ is the new Adam in whom all souls were contained; and His Father had sent Him, who was sinless and holy, precisely that He might die for sinners. This the Saviour did, and thus He freed us from our faults and from the death we deserved for them.[3]

However, salvation is a personal work, and the merits and satisfactions of Jesus Christ do not exempt us from meriting by ourselves our happiness

and atoning for our sins. This theory of merit and satisfaction is perhaps the one which, in his whole work, betrays most his legal spirit. He framed for that theory a terminology which still survives and remains a characteristic of Latin theology.[4] Not that our author ignores the share of Jesus in the fulfilment of good works;[5] but, outside this consideration, the relations between God and man are, for him, nothing, strictly speaking, but the relations between lord and servant and involve their consequences. If we act well, we gain *merit* with God, nay we merit God.[6]. . . God becomes our debtor: *Bonum factum deum habet debitorem, sicuti et malum, quia iudex omnis remunerator est causae.* (A good deed has God as its debtor, just as an evil one, because the judge is the remunerator of every cause.)[7] The reward is a price: *eadem pretia quae et merces* (the same price which is also a reward).[8] On the contrary, through sin, we *offend* God and be-

[2] J. Tixeront was born in 1856 and died in 1925. He was a professor at the University of Lyons and later at that of Toulouse. He was the author of many works, such as *Apologetical Studies, Handbook of Patrology, Holy Orders and Ordination.* This excerpt is taken from his book, *History of Dogmas* (St. Louis: B. Herder, 1910), Vol. I, pp. 318–322, 354–362, 426–427; Vol. II, pp. 274–283.

[3] *De pudicitia,* 22; *De patientia,* 3; cf. *De resurrectione carnis,* 53; *De anima,* 40; *De baptismo,* 11.

[4] Harnack, *Lehrbuch der Dogmengeschichte,* III, pp. 16 ff., n. 1; *History of Dogma,* Vol. V, pp. 16 ff., 18, note.

[5] *Ad uxorem,* I, 8; *De anima,* 21.

[6] *De paenitentia,* 6.

[7] *De paenitentia,* 2; *De exhort, castit.,* 2.

[8] *Scorpiace,* 6.

come His debtors; but we can and we must give Him satisfaction.[9] We satisfy through penance, which is a *compensation* we offer to God.[10]. . .

Our author devoted a special treatise to Baptism. This Baptism, he says, is administered in the name of the three divine Persons, and the Christian, as the divine *ichthus* (fish), is born in water.[11] In the actual economy, Baptism is required for salvation, though it can be replaced by martyrdom. Its effect is to remit sins; it is imparted only once.[12]

St. Cyprian is not a speculator, nor a theologian properly so called: of all theological notions, that of the Church is about the only one he has somewhat deeply investigated: even in this, he is not altogether original. . . . Considered in her visible elements, the Church, St. Cyprian tells us, is the gathering of the bishop and his flock, the clergy and the faithful.[13] Considered in her mystical state, she is the spouse of Jesus Christ to whom she must give spiritual children.[14] Her function consists in being the depositary of the heavenly blessings, of the grace, of the treasures brought by Redemption, and at the same time of the sanctifying power of Jesus Christ, so that these can be found in none but in her.[15] Hence the

necessity to belong to that Church. Whosoever departs from her "does not have life and salvation" (*vitam non tenet et salutem*);[16] whosoever rejects her rejects Christ whose spouse she is.[17] "He cannot have God for his father who does not have the Church as his mother" (*Habere non potest Deum patrem qui ecclesiam non habet matrem*).[18] She is the ark in which alone we can be saved and purified.[19]. . .

In St. Cyprian's theory, the Church is the depositary of the power of Jesus Christ and the bestower of His graces. The Sacraments are therefore *her* Sacraments, and she alone can confer them validly. . . . Baptism is a second birth, the principle of salvation and faith: it remits sins, sanctifies man and makes him God's temple. It must be imparted to children and, unlike circumcision, may be administered before the eighth day. By this Baptism, children receive grace, just as well as adults, the more so that having not sinned and being afflicted through their birth from Adam only with the contagion of the former death, they obtain the forgiveness, not of their own sins, but of borrowed sins. However, the Baptism of water may be replaced by martyrdom which also confers grace, nay a more abundant and excellent grace.[20]. . .

---

[9] *De paenitentia*, 7; cf. 10, 11.
[10] *De paenitentia*, 5, 6; *De ieiunio*, 3; *De pudicitia*, 9, 13; *De patientia*, 13, 16.
[11] *De baptismo*, 13, 1; *Adv. Prax.*, 26.
[12] *De baptismo*, 12, 13, 16, 18, 1, 15; *Adv. Marc.*, I, 28.
[13] *Epp.*, LXVI, 8; XXXIII, 1.
[14] *De cathol. eccles. unit.*, 4–6; *Ep.*, LXXIV, 6.
[15] *Epp.*, LXXIII, 7, 10, 11; LXXI, 1.

[16] *De cathol. eccles. unit.*, 6; *Ep.*, LXIX, 4.
[17] *Ep.*, III, 1.
[18] *De cathol. eccles. unit.*, 6.
[19] *Epp.*, LXIX, 2; LXXIV, 11.
[20] *Ad Fortunatum*, praef., 4; *Epp.*, LXXIII, 22; LXIV, 5, 2; LXXIII, 12; *Ad Donatum*, 4.

The doctrine and theology of the Church on the eve of Arianism. . . . Jesus Christ came to save and redeem us: with His death they [the Latin Fathers] associate this work of redemption and salvation. The blood of Jesus Christ is regarded as the price of our ransom paid to God's justice; this is already a way of satisfying; but another theory, still deeper and developed out of St. Paul, emphasizes this last idea, by exhibiting Jesus Christ as the representative of the whole humanity, expiating in its name. That is the theory of our *recapitulation* in the Saviour and also of His death considered as a sacrifice. . . .

The theory of original sin is still to be framed; but its elements are mastered, and although nobody has a distinct and clear idea of what the hereditary fault is in itself, yet Christians are conscious at least of a physical and moral fall, consequent on our birth from Adam the sinner. Not until St. Augustine will a teaching somewhat complete about actual grace be exposed: before him, the teaching of the Church consists merely in the general affirmation of the need in which we stand of God's help to do good, and also of the duty incumbent upon us to cooperate by our own deeds towards our salvation. Tertullian has vigorously sketched the theory of merit and of satisfaction, and the West has made it its own: in the East, the progress has been slower, and the relations of God and man are determined in a way less juridical and precise. . . .

Latin theology in the fourth century. While they were little inclined to merely speculative problems, the Latin theologians of the 4th century took up more readily the study of man, of his condition and needs in the Christian economy. . . . What was the primitive condition of Adam and Eve? St. Hilary supposes that they were immortal, since death is the consequence of sin. St. Ambrose and Zeno go still further. They not only ascribe to our first parents wisdom, virtue and exemption from concupiscence; they seem to believe also that Adam and Eve were heavenly and similar to the angels and consequently needed no food.[21]

According to Zeno, their fall resulted from a sin of lust; according to St. Ambrose, it was due to a sin of which pride was the origin. They were condemned to die, and made subject to concupiscence and to the miseries of life. All agree that, like an inheritance, their chastisement falls upon us. Hilary declares that Adam has transmitted to us his sentence of death and the dismal condition of his existence; concupiscence with which we are assailed is a consequence of our nature, but also of our birth "under the origin of sin and under the law of sin" (*sub peccati origine et sub peccati lege*), owing to the sin of Adam, we are spiritually captive; sin is the father of our bodies, and infidelity, the mother of our souls. Similar statements are found in Zeno, St. Ambrose, St. Jerome and the Ambrosiaster.[22] But, while

---

[21] Hilary, *In psalm.*, LIX, 4; Zeno, *Tract.*, I, 12, 2; Ambrose, *De paradiso*, 24, 63, 42.

[22] *In psalm.*, CXVIII, sermo VII, 8; Hilary, Zeno, *Tract.*, I, 13, 5; I, 2, 8; Ambrose,

these authors admit our physical and moral fall in Adam, do they hold that there exists also in us real sin? Do they believe that the fact of being the children of Adam causes us to be born actually stained with guilt? This is, properly speaking, the problem of original sin. . . .

The primitive fall has not done away with our liberty, and sin is our own work. Yet we can hardly avoid it, and even though flesh is not the responsible source of a disorder which is willed by the soul, but only its organ, still it cooperates with iniquity. Without grace we cannot be saved. The writers now before us do not seem to demand this supernatural or *medicinal* grace for the fulfilment of all the works that are simply morally good; still less do they seem to look upon the works performed outside the Law as sinful. Thus St. Jerome thinks that, outside Christianity, one may live uprightly; he even thinks that this rectitude prepares one for the reception of faith. . . . St. Ambrose does not reject the natural virtues of the heathen; however, he declares that these virtues are useless, and that those who practise them are similar to the trees that are covered with leaves, and bear no fruit.

But when these Fathers come to treat of supernatural and meritorious works, then they speak quite differently. Hilary, Victorinus, Ambrose and Jerome agree in affirming that, without grace, we cannot perform any work conducive to salvation and pleasing to God. . . . Nay, Victorinus and Jerome observe that the act itself by which we will what is right, is the work of God and is wrought through the influence of grace. . . .

So far, so good; but, when they come to the subject of the necessity of grace for the beginning of good works and of faith, some of the writers of whom we are speaking seem to fall short of orthodoxy. This does not apply to St. Ambrose. . . . On the other hand, when treating of the same subject, St. Hilary, St. Optatus and even St. Jerome have made a certain number of statements which now would be looked upon as Semipelagian. . . .

While they do not agree on the necessity of grace for the beginning of faith and of good works, the Latin theologians of the 4th century affirm unanimously the need of our cooperation to render grace efficacious. . . . From this teaching to the theory of merit is but one step. As a matter of fact, the concept of merit and the word itself are often found in the texts which we are now considering. Faith has a great share in our justification, and, according to Victorinus especially[23] this share is very important; however, works must follow and support this faith. . . . Nevertheless it seems that, especially among those Latin theologians who studied the views of the Greeks, the rigorous justice of Tertullian's doctrine is tempered . . . so that, in fact, this reward

---

In psalm., LIX, 4; I, 4; Zeno, *Tract.*, I, 12, 2; Ambrose, *In Lucam*, VII, 234; Jerome, *In Ionam*, III, 5; Ambrosiaster, *In epist. ad Romanos*, V, 12.

[23] *In epist. ad Galat.*, III, 22, col. 1172 B; *ad Philipp.*, III, 8, 9, col. 1219 CD.

results more from God's mercy than from our merits. . . .

The problem of predestination was barely touched upon by Latin theologians up to the time of St. Augustine. . . .

3. J. Nörregaard[24] considers Augustine peculiarly the theologian of grace at a critical time. It molded all his theology: God is a personal Will, ever creative; man is designed for fellowship with Him. Grace is manifested in Christ, whose work is accounted by God as canceling man's sin. But to appropriate this benefit man is powerless apart from God's grace. It is God who initiates, both the extirpation of sin and the implantation of good, unitedly "justification." This occurs at baptism. Grace that is irresistible is conferred on a select number.

Augustine, the theologian of grace. In the early Church Augustine is peculiarly the theologian of the grace of God. In a critical moment, when a theology was taking shape which threatened to water down the New Testament message of salvation, in so far as (for the most part in the spirit of the age and with general approval) it was on the verge of substituting man's own efforts and self-improvement for forgiveness and grace, Augustine raised a fiery protest, which ever since has been recalled in the Western Church, when there were danger of forgetting it.

In one respect his theology is very simple and can be stated in a few words: Sin, the Grace of God incarnate in Christ, imparted by the Holy Spirit in the Catholic Church. When more closely observed it appears, how-

ever, as a wide-spreading complex composed of many elements, disparate in reality, but blended with such art that the leading thoughts can scarcely be isolated from one another, as they receive their full significance only when brought into relation with all the separate elements of Augustine's thought. . . .

In the first place we must observe somewhat more closely Augustine's thoughts about God. . . . There are scholars who assert that his conception of God is in reality neo-Platonic through and through. This, however, is certainly exaggerated. If we return to *Confessiones*, I, iv (and countless other texts could be quoted), there can be no doubt that God is to Augustine not an impersonal highest conception, but a personal Will, loving, merciful, full of grace, who only wishes to do good and to communicate Himself — though always in quiet, yet always working, creating, perfecting.

Man's destiny. That is why God created the world and man. Herein

24 J. Nörregaard, Th.D., was professor of Church history at the University of Copenhagen in 1931. This excerpt is taken from his article, "Grace in St. Augustine," in *The Doctrine of Grace*, ed. W. T. Whitley (London: SCM Press, 1931), pp. 114–132.

already He reveals His goodness. . . . Especially is this true of man. He was destined for personal fellowship with the personal God. Turned to God, obeying His will in everything, ruling over lower creation, he was to receive everything from God in undisturbed harmony and to enjoy eternal life through the blissful vision of God. Thus is God's ordaining. . . .

Man has turned his back on God and is only concerned with lower things.[25] In this perverse misdirection of the will, sin consists.[26] It has two chief forms: pride and lust. . . . Even the best actions of man are tarnished by pride, for he believes that he can himself, without God, accomplish good.[27] And all this is not something accidental, but a law ruling the whole of human life. The will is enthralled by evil and to such an extent as to make man unable to do good, even if he desire it. Indeed he does not want to do it. Augustine has depicted this most terrible affliction of human life with impressive earnestness.[28] He himself lived it through in all its depth. Wherever he looked he saw the same thing and the witness of experience was supplemented by the Scriptures.

But how had this come about? Augustine's answer to this question is the doctrine of original sin.[29]

Original sin. Adam was so created that there was no strife and no dis-

harmony between his higher and lower nature; the lower subordinated itself to the higher, and he subordinated himself to God, who on His part helped him with His assisting grace (*gratia adjutoria*). The relation to God was based on a cooperation of the Divine grace and Adam's free will. But with free will the possibility was given not only to remain in the right relationship to God, but likewise to fall. It would have been easy for Adam not to fall; thus he would from the state of being able not to sin or die or forsake God (*posse non peccare et mori et deum deserere*) have attained that of being unable to sin or die or forsake God (*non posse peccare et mori et deum deserere*).

The fall. But Adam did fall, deceived by delusion of the Devil. Love of God was changed into love of self. In the same moment he lost God's assisting grace (*gratia adjutoria*), harmony changed to anarchy. . . . Adam's destiny became an inability not to sin or die (*non posse non peccare et mori*). Death of the soul was immediate, followed later by death of the body. The whole human race was infected by Adam's sin, each single soul came under the curse of original sin. For all were in Adam when he sinned.[30]. . . Through this the human race has become a mass of perdition and a prey of perdition. And man constantly adds new sins to his original sin. Even the best deeds and thoughts spring from the love of self and are tainted with evil. . . . Of the original condition, only a certain faint recognition of

---

[25] *Conf.*, IV, xii (19).
[26] *De Genesi ad litteram imperf.*, 3.
[27] *De natura et gratia*, 36.
[28] *Conf.*, VIII, v–xi.
[29] *Enchiridion*, xxvi ff.; *De civitate Dei*, XIII, iv f., XIV, *passim; De correptione et gratia*, 33.

[30] Rom 5:12.

good and a restless longing for good has remained. But the free will really to accomplish it, which Adam possessed before the fall, is entirely lost.[31] . . . Yet Augustine stands strongly opposed to the metaphysical dualistic (Manichaean) conception of man. Man's nature is not essentially evil (*natura mala*). It has become tainted and deteriorated (*natura vitiata*). He is not necessarily given over to perdition, he can be saved. But in himself he has no strength for it, salvation can come exclusively from God.[32]

Grace of God. And here is the essential meaning of the grace of God, namely that though it is undeserved and there is no merit of man,[33] He works salvation in this mass of perdition which would otherwise absolutely perish because it has turned wilfully away from God. The saving grace of God is manifested in Christ.[34] God, supreme over all, has in Him come quite close to man.[35] In His person and in His deeds, the very Being of God in its entire fulness is recognised as grace.[36]. . . And so the essential innermost nature of God, His will for salvation, has been made manifest to the world through the humility and sacrifice of Christ. How then shall men avail themselves of this salvation? After some uncertainty in his first Christian period Augustine answers: only by the grace of God. It is not the case that God comes forth with His offer and that man either accepts it in faith or rejects it by his free will. For if this were so everything would really depend in the last resort on man himself and therefore not on grace. That man accepts the grace of God is based on the grace of God. The whole adoption of salvation is effected by the grace of God.[37]

Gratia praeveniens. The grace of God comes first (*gratia praeveniens*). It is always God who begins, and without being dependent on the initiative of man, begins in a way which equals a new creation (*gratia operans*) whereby the image of God is renewed in man. This happens through (first) the rooting out of sin, and (secondly) the planting of something new in the heart of man.[38] The conditions for this in man are Faith (which takes the place of the former delusion of reason) and the good will which takes up the battle with the concupiscence and drives it back.[39] But these two essential predispositions are themselves a gift of God, a grace.[40]

Justification. Both moments Augustine has united in the expression "justification." Justification springs from faith, in as much as the forgiveness of sins is effected entirely without consideration of past works; but in the same place it is a justification out of love inasmuch as man actually from unrighteous becomes righteous (*ex injusto justus fit*) and this happens by the Holy Spirit shedding the spirit of

---

[31] *Enchiridion*, xxx.
[32] *De gratia et peccato originali*, II, xxix.
[33] *Enchiridion*, cvii.
[34] *Ibid.*, xxxiii.
[35] *Sermo*, 81, 6.
[36] *De catechizandis rudibus*, 7.

[37] *Ep.*, 184, 4.
[38] *Opus imperfectum*, II, 227.
[39] *Enchiridion*, cxvii; *De spiritu et litera*, 5.
[40] *Ep.*, 184, 4.

love in our hearts. This justification (*ex charitate*) can likewise be called justification out of faith, because the full conception of faith in Augustine is a faith which is permeated by an inward love for its object — God,[41] and therefore manifests its activity in the love of one's neighbor.

Regarding the question where this justification takes place, Augustine answers on principle, in accordance with the ideas then traditional in the Church, in Christian baptism, which imparts forgiveness of sins as well as the Holy Spirit.

Gratia cooperans. God's grace, as initial grace, is conceived as a single act. But it is taken up and continued by God through concurrent grace (*gratia cooperans*). God's new creation is not finished once and for all.[42] The concupiscence is relegated into the background, but it always makes itself felt, and therefore renewed forgiveness of sin and new loving gifts of grace from God are necessary and will be so up to man's last hour, because sin is never quite overcome in this life.[43] In a continual struggle with the temptations of sin, often with backslidings, the new life must grow and develop and love must more and more permeate the heart.

If grace is now called concurrent, this is not to be understood as a co-operation of Divine and human activity — thought of as two independent factors — the liberated spirit now being able to work on the basis of its own initiative. In the scheme of salvation everything always depends upon God, and nothing on the human will. God's grace works with itself alone. It has begun and it continues. He, who has begun the good work, will also continue it. It is true that Augustine uses the term "to acquire merits." His real meaning, however, is that God alone accomplishes His work in the soul[44] and that the merits of man are in their true sense God's: "When God crowns our merits, He crowns nothing but His own gifts."[45]. . .

Predestination. But all this is not yet the grace of God in its highest sense. God may have done His work in a man for some time, and in spite of it man falls back into sin and is not saved. The reason is that vocation and election are not one and the same. Only those who are called according to His purpose keep steadfast to the end, because grace works in them as irresistible, which gives them a gift of perseverance.[46] The irresistible grace is by no means given to them because they have acquired merits. It is only given by the hidden decree of God, and it is impossible to resist it. Those who remain steadfast in this fashion God has predestinated from all eternity to salvation.[47]

It is a certain number which is neither increased nor diminished. Predestination is not based on the fact that God foresaw that they would act according to His will, but on an un-

---

[41] *Sermo*, 144, 2.
[42] *De gratia et libero arbitrio*, 33.
[43] *Enchiridion*, lxiv.
[44] *Ep.*, 186, 10.
[45] *Ep.*, 194, v (19).
[46] *De correptione et gratia*, 34.
[47] *De praedestinatione sanctorum*, 19.

fathomable decree.[48] It is vain to try to understand it, it is presumptuous to speak of injustice because some are predestined to salvation while some are given over to perdition. The latter have no right to complain, for it is only justice that is done to them, as they have rebelled against God; and the others receive in an immeasurable degree the loving-kindness of God which is beyond all understanding.

The above gives in the broadest outline Augustine's doctrine of the grace of God, which in its essentials was already complete before the Pelagian controversy, but which was put forth at the time of this controversy with evergrowing sureness and clarity. In itself is raises a number of questions which require an answer.

(1) How has Augustine reached this doctrine? . . . Without doubt it is based upon a thoroughly religious motive of great depth and permanent value. We owe God everything. . . . With this argument another goes hand-in-hand. Augustine thought to find the doctrine of predestination in the Scriptures. . . . Texts, which were of primary importance to him, are among others Rom 9:16; 1 Cor 4:7; Phil 2:13; Jn 15:6; 1 Cor 1:31; Eph 2:8–10. . . . Augustine's doctrine of grace cannot be dismissed as a compound of Manichaeism and neo-Platonism. On the contrary, one might say that the elements of Manichaeism and neo-Platonism which remained in his teaching as sediments here and there, really impair his innermost intentions.

48 Ibid., 34.

(2) But a new question arises: is not his whole doctrine magical? Is not the ethical character of sin destroyed by the doctrine of original sin, of sin becoming nature; and is not the ethical moment in salvation put on one side by the assertion that grace works as an irresistible force where it accomplishes its work? In any case it must be made clear that Augustine tried very hard to show that the ethical concept is maintained and that it is the will which is the subject of salvation. For sin is inverted direction of *will*. . . . Therefore Augustine was concerned to show in his later years that his doctrine did not render ethical admonitions superfluous, as was asserted by some who were near him, but were unable quite to follow his ideas. Whether Augustine or any other succeeded in bringing lucidity is naturally another matter. His assertions are such that they can be interpreted differently, even as half semi-Pelagian. The question, whether eventually the freedom of man did not retain a small place in Augustine's system, was especially and passionately discussed during the Jansenist controversy.

(3) A further important question concerns the relation which Augustine's doctrine of grace has to his doctrine of the Church and sacraments. Is grace subjected to the Church and sacraments or not? From the outset no doubt seems possible. In baptism man comes under the influence of God's initial grace, and baptism is the entrance into the Church. Augustine asserts with Cyprian "Outside the Church, no salvation." . . . The point

at once arises, whether the predestinated must always belong to the visible Church at death. Doubtless, this is, on the whole, the opinion of Augustine. But he has not carried it through without exception. . . . Consequently grace is not solely confined to the Church. . . . Therefore it is not at all certain that anything is received through the sacrament and it is by no means clear why God should not give His gift quite without any sacrament.

(4) In spite of all objections that can be raised against Augustine's doctrine of grace, it still has its abiding importance which, among other things, is demonstrated in its continual revival in ever different form. What it wanted to say, namely that God is always the First and the Last, that we entirely depend upon Him, owe everything to Him and that in relation to Him man has no merit whatever, is entirely correct and follows the Gospel teaching. The form in which it is expressed may be very questionable, as here thought moves at its utmost boundaries, where the best theology is confession, not clear comprehension.

4. H. Rondet, S.J.,[49] sees Augustine as the father of occidental theology, especially dominating it by his doctrine of sin and grace. He treats the traditional doctrine of the divinization of the Christian, but his special contribution lies in his development of liberating grace. If he owes much to Plotinus, he owes much more to St. Paul. Perhaps he surpassed the Greeks in his understanding of the mystery of divine inhabitation.

Augustine, the father of occidental theology. Augustine is the father of occidental theology.[50] With him trinitarian doctrine reached an expression that the Greek Fathers had not achieved.[51] His idea of creation, his metaphysical solution of the problem of evil are definitive. His theory of faith still dominates our researches.[52] His ecclesiology is the despair of liberal Protestants who cannot comprehend how the "first modern man" could be Catholic and accord such importance to the hierarchy and sacraments.[53] One

---

[49] H. Rondet, S.J.: cf. ch. III, n. 1. This excerpt is from *op. cit.*, pp. 99–111.

[50] E. Portalié, *Augustin*, DTC, t. I, col. 2317–2325. [Eng. tr.: *A Guide to the Thought of St. Augustine*, trans. by R. J. Bastian, S.J. Henry Regnery Co., Chicago, 1960.] L. Duchesne, *Histoire ancienne de l'Eglise*, t. III, p. viii. A. von Harnack, *Précis de l'histoire des dogmes*, trad. Choisy, 1893, livre II, ch. III, IV, and *Lehrbuch der Dogmengeschichte*, 4 ed., t. III, p. 65.

[51] E. Portalié, *art. cit.*, col. 2346–2347; J. Chevalier, *Saint Augustin et la pensée grecque*, 1940.

[52] In his articles on "Les yeux de la foi" (RSR, 1910) P. Rousselot is a debtor of St. Augustine even more than of St. Thomas or of Newman. Elsewhere he speaks of him in magnificent fashion ("La religion chrétienne" in *Christus*, pp. 1115–1119).

[53] A. von Harnack, *Das Wesen des Christentums*, 1907, pp. 310–311; *Lehrbuch der Dogmengeschichte*, 4 ed., t. III, pp. 98–99, 140–141.

could show that in eschatology Augustine is the term of the patristic tradition. But what especially dominates our theology is his doctrine of sin and grace. Too much so perhaps, in the estimate of some, who would willingly think that to become acceptable the theology of grace should shake off Augustinism. . . . These, and they are not always heterodox, would almost accuse Augustine of having been a Jansenist before Jansenius. Let us put aside for the moment these accusations and first put into relief the way in which Augustine approaches the theology of grace.

Divinization. Sometimes Augustine's theology is opposed to that of the Greek Fathers: for them divinizing grace, for him grace that is the remedy for sin. There is some truth in this opposition but we must be on our guard against systematization.[54]. . . For all, "Greeks or Latins," take as the point of departure of their theological reflection the doctrine of the divinization of the Christian and of our unity in Christ. This is manifest in St. Augustine.[55] In his letter on *the presence of God* he teaches with all tradition that the soul of the just is the temple of the Holy Spirit,[56] and that sanctity is measured by the intensity of this divine presence.[57] This sanctity is something ontological since it is anterior to every free act and the baptized infant is already the temple of God.[58]

But the sanctity of Christians is a sanctity of members and by a spontaneous movement Augustine passes from the presence of God in just souls to His presence in the Church, itself also a temple of the Holy Spirit. Christ has died to assemble in one same city, one same body, one same edifice, the children of God.[59] There is the same doctrine in the letter to Honoratus on the grace of the New Testament. By grace we become children of God and partakers of the divine nature.[60] More than once he returns to this doctrine in his admirable commentary on the First Epistle of St. John, where he shows that fraternal charity is the manifestation of the divine presence and deepens the notion of presence.[61]. . . Here perhaps he surpasses the Greeks in his understanding of the mystery of divine inhabitation, even though his concern to keep intact the divine unity and transcendence led him to the somewhat strict theory of appropriation.[62]

---

[54] Cf. P. Rousselot, "La grâce d'après Saint Jean et d'après saint Paul," RSR, 1928, pp. 87–104.

[55] On the opposition of the two Adams cf. *De peccato originali*, 28, P.L., 44, 398–399; *De nuptiis et concup.*, 46, P.L., 44, 462–463, etc. To prove the divinity of the Holy Spirit the Greek Fathers start from the divinization of the Christian. To establish the doctrine of original sin and of the necessity of grace, Augustine starts from baptism, the sacrament of incorporation in Christ. Christ saves us, assumes us, makes us pass from death to life. . . . Christ is the new Adam. . . .

[56] *Epist.*, 187, 35, P.L., 33, 845.
[57] *Epist.*, 187, 17, P.L., 33, 838.
[58] *Epist.*, 187, 26, P.L., 33, 841.
[59] *Epist.*, 187, 33, 37, P.L., 33, 845, 846.
[60] *Epist.*, 140, 10, P.L., 33, 542.
[61] *In Epist. Joan. ad Parthos*, VIII, 12; IX, 1; P.L., 35, 2043; 33, 2045.
[62] On the opposition between the Greek theory and the Latin theory of the Trinity in *ad extra* works, see Th. De Regnon, *Etudes sur la sainte Trinité*, Iᵉ serie, 1892,

On still another point he gave immense progress to the theology of the divinisation of the Christian. Augustine is, after St. Paul and St. John, the great doctor of the mystical body.[63] Exploiting marvelously one of the hermeneutic rules of the Donatist Ticonius[64] he seeks Christ everywhere in the sacred books: the Christ . . . the Word made flesh . . . and by an audacious formula, the total Christ.[65] It is Christ who speaks in us, prays in us, suffers in us, because He lives in us and because, as Augustine says audaciously, He is us: *quia et nos ipse sumus.*[66] The Church, the mystical body of Christ, is with its head as it were a unique man, *tanquam integer vir.*[67]. . . and when the figure of this world has passed away the body in its entirety will also be elevated to heaven after its head. . . . Then will be fully verified what, according to Augustine, ought to be the law of Christian charity: "There will be one Christ loving Himself" (*Erit unus Christus amans seipsunt*).[68]

Liberating grace. Augustine thus accepts all the data of tradition. It is important to return to this before manifesting his special and immense contribution to the development of the dogma and the theology of grace. If he appears to insist less than others on the doctrine of divinization, it is because he was led by his Pelagian polemic and by his religious experience to develop over and over another theme, that of liberating grace. Grace indeed is in us a principle of superior life, a participation of the divine nature, but it also heals us of our original misery. In man wounded by sin the grace of Christ appears as a principle of liberation from the servitude of the passions, just born or inveterate.

Augustine more than any other was here predestined to comprehend St. Paul. . . . He was better prepared to understand the thought of Paul than Origen or Chrysostom or even the Cappadocians, "those excellent young men who had known only the ways of the school or the church."[69] He set himself with predilection to describe the way grace draws us, delights us and acts on the diverse powers of our soul, doing sweet violence to our will to draw it to what it refused at first.[70]

In the 18th century Jansenius will abuse this and other texts like it, but the Jansenist doctrine of *delectatio victrix* is only a caricature of Augustine's thought.[71] Augustine does indeed

pp. 357–362, and 3e serie, 1898, Etude 27, pp. 501–574.

[63] E. Mersch, *Le corps mystique du Christ,* 2 ed., t. 11, pp. 35–138; M. Pontet, *L'exégèse de saint Augustin prédicateur,* 1946, pp. 311–418.

[64] *De doctrina christiana,* III, 44, P.L., 34, 82–83. Cf. E. Mersch, *op. cit.,* p. 96. You will find the rules of Ticonius in P.L., 18, 15–22, and in the critical edition of Burkitt, *Texts and Studies,* t. III, 1894.

[65] *In Epist. Joan.,* I, 2, P.L., 35, 1979; *In Joan.,* XXVIII, 1; P.L., 35, 1622.

[66] *In Joan.,* CIX, 6, P.L., 35, 1929.

[67] *En. in Psalm.,* 138, 2, P.L., 37, 1784.

[68] *In Epist. Joan. ad Parth.,* X, 3, P.L., 35, 2055.

[69] P. Rousselot, "La grâce dans saint Jean et dans saint Paul," RSR, 1928, p. 99.

[70] *In Joan.,* XXVI, 4–7, P.L., 35, 1608–1610.

[71] E. Gilson, *Introduction a l'étude de saint Augustin,* 1931, pp. 204–205 and note.

say: "It is necessary that we act according to what pleases us more" (*Quod amplius nos delectat, secundum id operemur necesse est*),[72] and he understands well that for the just good works become in some fashion spontaneous and connatural, but he maintains the necessity for man to cooperate for his salvation. The spiritual life for him is a combat . . . that demands a perpetual renunciation. . . . Liberating grace appears then as a principle of interior unification, capable of harmonizing the divergent tendencies in the sinner's soul. By grace and charity this soul will find its lost unity.[73]

Leaving aside philosophical definitions Augustine here loves to show how liberty is the fruit of a liberation, a liberation always imperfect; for only God is fully free, since only He is incapable of sin. Liberty starts where man already has some participation of this impeccability. In this sense Augustine refuses liberty to the sinner.[74]

Thus Augustine's doctrine of the relations between grace and liberty, as well as between charity and justification, is very dynamic. We will meet it again later, but how deformed, in Baius and Jansenius. The great Scholastics will have a more static conception from their preoccupation with the divine character of grace. Each epoch

will thus illumine an aspect of our divinisation and redemption by Christ, but nonetheless Augustine will remain the incomparable doctor of grace.

Formation of ideas. To comprehend the formation of his ideas, we must remember that in him two "mystiques" are reunited, that of Plotinus and that of St. Paul.[75] Not that he was first converted to Neo-platonism so as then to come to Christianity; but from reading the *Enneades* he got a very elevated idea of the transcendence of God, and all his life he remained impregnated by this idea that God is in us the source of all being, all truth, all goodness.[76] God, source of all good, moves us not only by drawing us as last end sovereignly desirable, but He acts more intimately on our liberty so that if man seeks what properly pertains to him, what he owes to no one, he will find only error and lie.[77] "Of himself no one has anything save lie and sin" (*Nemo habet de suo nisi mendacium atque peccatum*).

This radical formula, which the Council of Orange will adopt,[78] will

[72] *Exp. Epist. ad Galat.*, 49, P.L., 35, 2141.

[73] *Sermo*, 159, 6, P.L., 38, 870; *Confess.*, V, 18, P.L., 32, 714; VIII, 22, P.L., 32, 759.

[74] *Op. imperf, contra Jul.*, V, 38, P.L., 45, 1474; *In Joan.*, 41, 11, P.L., 35, 1698; *Enchiridion*, 30, P.L., 40, 246; *In Joan.*, 41, 10, P.L., 35, 1698.

[75] On the role of Neo-platonism in the conversion of St. Augustine see the classic book of P. Boyer, *Christianisme et Néoplatonisme dans la formation de saint Augustin*, 1920; F. Hoffmann, *Der Kirchenbegriff des heiligen Augustinus*, 1933, pp. 9–22; P. Henry, *La vision d'Ostie*, 1938; Grandgeorge, *Saint Augustin et le Néo-platonisme*, 1896; E. Portalié, "Augustin," in DTC, t. I, col. 2325–2331; P. Henry, *Plotin et l'Occident*, 1934, pp. 63–145.

[76] *De civitate Dei*, VIII, 10, P.L., 41, 235.

[77] *In Joan.*, V, 1, P.L., 35, 1414; *Retract.*, I, 9, 6, P.L., 32, 598.

[78] Can. 22, D. 392.

provoke many commentaries when abused by Baius and Jansenius. It will come to pass, too, that the Church, though continuing to see in Augustine the doctor of grace par excellence, will express orthodox doctrine in formulas that at first sight will seem to contradict primitive Augustinism.[79] However one seeks to reconcile these affirmations, one must remember that when Augustine was writing men did not have the idea of distinguishing between supernatural grace and God's concurrence with free acts. This distinction will only come with Scholastic theology, and will itself be still quite imprecise in the great Augustinians of the 13th century. It is an anachronism to put to Augustine or his Pelagian adversaries questions that are too subtle.[80] In reality Augustine resolves a philosophical problem by starting out from revealed data. Later and not without reason the two problems will be dissociated, and both Banezians and Molinists will invoke Augustine, but those who will try to pass by this quarrel will still have to make a study of the doctor of grace. For in him the philosophical problem of the relations between divine causality and human actions remains bound up with the developments on the question of the

relations between grace and human consent.

If Augustine owes much to Plotinus, he owes much more to St. Paul. Before him in their commentaries on Scripture, the Latin Fathers, St. Hilary, St. Ambrose, St. Jerome, had underlined man's essential dependence on God.[81] Marius Victorinus, an African orator, translator of the *Enneads* . . . had even found some beautiful formulas to show that man depends on God in what is most personal, the use of his free will.[82] But this theology remained compendious, and when it tried to translate its affirmations into psychological language it resulted in explanations which, viewed from the angle of history, allied with Semipelagianism.[83] Augustine himself is not beyond reproach in this matter. He had first believed one could leave to man the beginning of conversion and the march toward salvation. . . . But in 397, urged by his friend Simplician, he set himself to study St. Paul further and to wrestle with his text. In this combat, he tells us, grace won, and he understood that, to come to justification, preaching and good will were not sufficient, but an in-

---

[79] D. 1927.

[80] Theologians have asked if Pelagius, who denied the necessity of grace, did not also deny the necessity of natural concurrence. But the authors whom Portalié cites (col. 2382) and Portalié himself make an anachronism here. Neither Augustine nor his adversaries had precise ideas on the distinction between grace and natural concurrence.

[81] Hilar., *In Psalm.*, 118, lit. I, 12, P.L., 9, 509 B; Ambros., *In Luc.*, II, 84, P.L., 15, 1583 C; Jerome, *Epist.*, 133, 7, P.L., 22, 1155.

[82] *Epist. ad Phil.*, 2, 13, P.L., 8, 1212.

[83] Hilar., *In Psalm.*, 118, litt. 16, 10, P.L., 9, 610 B; for St. Jerome, cf. J. Fayey, *Doctrina Scti. Hieronymi de gratiae necessitate*, 1937; on the pelagianising tendencies of Ambrosiaster, cf. G. De Plinval, *Pélage*, 1943, pp. 88–89.

terior appeal was also necessary.[84] But how does Augustine understand this vocation? The Jansenists will claim later that Augustine remained Semipelagian till toward the year 412.[85] This affirmation is paradoxical and poses a historical and theological problem. To situate this problem, it is enough to remark here that up to this date at least Augustine seems to disjoin the interior appeal and the will's consent as if he wanted on the psychological plane to distinguish the call of God and the response of man, without ceasing to attribute to God all the good man does.[86]

There would be here then a bit of the Molinist theology, and theologians after Trent who seek to put in relief the role of liberty in the process of justification happily cite these texts. Congruists will invoke St. Augustine to show that God calls us interiorly by adapting the omnipotence of His

grace to our temperament and to our psychological reaction as foreseen by Him.[87] But we must avow that the writings of this latter period are far from favorable to this interpretation. Must we then admit a change of attitude in St. Augustine's thought? Impotent to express the mystery of the action of God in the very heart of the will, did he sometimes stress victorious grace, sometimes man's free response, as if the two elements could be dissociated in the consciousness of man? Or on the contrary must we admit that after having interiorized the divine call and thus refuted Semipelagianism in advance, he contented himself with showing how grace draws us by creating in us more liberty in our dependence on God?[88] This problem we leave in suspense, content to have shown how future theological discussions are germinally in the writings of St. Augustine.

5. Ch. Baumgartner, S.J.,[89] looks at many aspects of Augustine's doctrine: grace and liberty, works of sinners and infidels, salutary faith, the effects of baptism, the graces of justification and the aid needed by the justified, merit and final perseverance, predestination and the universal salvific will.

St. Augustine was providentially prepared to show in the grace of Christ

a principle of action, of liberty and of spiritual liberation. Neo-platonic

---

[84] De div. quaest. ad Simplicianum, I, 12, P.L., 40, 118; Retract., II, 1, P.L., 32, 629; De libero arb., II, 54, P.L., 32, 1270.

[85] This assertion of Portalié (col. 2378) needs to be verified. It is not in Jansenius himself, who supposes that Augustine was in possession of his system from 397 (Augustinus, t. III, De gratia Christi, lib. II, c. 30, ed. de Reims, 1643, pp. 90–92).

[86] De spiritu et littera, 60, P.L., 44, 240.

[87] E. Portalié, "Augustin," DTC, t. I, col. 2389–2392; Ch. Pesch, Praelectiones theol. dogmaticae, t. V, 2e ed., 1900, n. 276–279.

[88] X. Léon-Dufour, "Consentire vocationi Dei propriae voluntatis est," in RSR, 1946, pp. 129–163.

[89] Ch. Baumgartner, S.J.: cf. ch. I, n. 12. This excerpt is from op. cit., pp. 58–71.

metaphysics, the teaching of the Bible about God, his personal experience in the light of Pauline theology helped him elaborate his personal doctrine of grace.

To Neo-platonic influence St. Augustine owes a profound notion of participation. God is the transcendent source of all being, of all truth, of all goodness. All finite good comes from God. Our free acts are eminently finite goods and thus in us a participation of divine goodness. They exist in us only in dependence on Him. To the Old Testament and to Christian thought St. Augustine is indebted for a very lofty idea of the omnipotence of God and of His sovereign dominion over the life and will of men. He had the painful experience of an intellectual and moral conversion. In the light of Pauline soteriology he understood that his conversion was not the result of his own efforts, but the gratuitous work of God. Converted, Augustine found himself grappling with the anthropology of Pelagianism which exalted without measure the moral power of the human will. The personal history of Augustine, the Pelagian heresy which he had to face, led him to construct for the first time a theology of grace from the viewpoint of man who is fallen and a sinner, a theology of its necessity and gratuity and efficacity. The Augustinian anthropological perspective will be a characteristic trait of the history of dogma and of the theology of grace in the West down to our days.

The problem of liberty and grace was also posed in the Orient but in very different circumstances. From the beginning it was imposed on the thought of the Greek Fathers in their strife with Gnosticism and Manicheism. These doctrines denied liberty. Hence the Fathers' insistence on the value and necessity of moral effort. The *pneuma* is not, as the Gnostics pretended, something amoral and inamissible. Man can lose it by sin. Pastor Hermas and II Clement had underscored this before Irenaeus. It is well known how Clement of Alexandria and Origen had insisted on the moral effort demanded of the baptized. The Fathers knew and affirmed that salvation comes from God, that the good that is in our power is not accomplished without the aid of God, that man's effort toward the divine likeness depends on the initiative and action of God; but all, Alexandrines and Cappadocians and Antiochenes, did not weary of proclaiming the necessary contribution of liberty and human cooperation, in formulas which often have a "Semipelagian" appearance.

But this is not merely an appearance. The Greek Fathers envisage divinization rather in the line of being and of formal and exemplary causality. On the plane of action they insist more on liberty, that fundamental trait of the image of God in man. Yet for all that they do not ignore the initiative of God in the work of salvation.

1. Fallen man is slave of concupiscence and sin. He has lost *liberty* or the *power to love good* and *accomplish it*. To be free is to love good, to be pleased and delighted with jus-

tice, to order all actions to the pursuit of eternal life, or in other words it is to have the power to love God above all things in preference to perishable goods. It is this liberty that fallen man no longer possesses. . . . But St. Augustine has never called in question liberty of choice.

2. The grace of Christ in justifying fallen man gives him back liberty, that is, love or delight in good and in justice. The liberty to do good, the power to accomplish justice and to live well, to observe the commandments as required for eternal life, this is given back to fallen man by the grace of justification. Justification is the action of God who converts the sinner by stirring up good will and consent. The divine operation progressively frees man from carnal cupidity so as to restore in him the reign of charity. It gives him the *delectatio victrix* and by this the power to vanquish concupiscence. . . . The grace of justification is thus the delight of spiritual good or of charity. It makes of the will a good will, capable of doing truly good actions. Good will consists in loving the true good of man. . . . The truly and fully good act is that which is inspired by a motive of charity.

3. Are all the works of infidels sins? Fallen man is impotent to do good without the grace of Christ. St. Augustine concludes from this that free will captive under sin can only do evil. One day the Church will condemn similar propositions of Baius (D 1927, 1928). Would all the works of sinners and infidels be sins, according to St. Augustine?

Let us first consider the actions of Christian sinners or the actions accomplished without charity. It is certain that for St. Augustine only works animated by charity are truly good. But he does not conclude from this that all that the Christian sinner does is bad.[90] In the discussions with the Semipelagians he often speaks of the good initial actions of those who have not yet received the grace of justification. . . .

The case of infidels is different. They have not the faith. Without explicit knowledge of Christ they are in principle deprived of grace. Can they do good actions? First of all, it is certain that St. Augustine affirms among the infidels the existence of good actions and he does this even in his polemic with the Pelagians. A second fact that is certain is that St. Augustine, especially against Julian of Eclanum, held that all the works of infidels are sins.[91] . . . To understand St. Augustine's thought one must remember that his notion of sin is broader than that of the scholastic theologians.[92] Augustine regards as sin every human act deprived of the rectitude it ought to have, even if this defect is not here and now imputable to the subject.

Original sin in us is a veritable sin, formal and voluntary, although only by analogy with sin that is personally

---

[90] *De pecc. mer. et rem.,* 18, 31, P.L., 44, 169; *Ad Simpl.,* I, 2, P.L., 40, 111–112.

[91] *De spir. et lit.,* 28, 48, P.L., 44, 230; *C. Jul.,* IV, 3, 14 f., P.L., 44, 743 f.

[92] *De perf. just.,* 6, 15, P.L., 44, 298; *De lib. arb.,* III, 19, 54, P.L., 32, 1297.

committed. This state of sin extends and communicates itself in some way to the acts of the infidel which are not and cannot be ordained to eternal life. These acts are as it were informed by the culpability of the original sin and deprived of the salutary goodness they ought to have. And in this sense they are bad and can be styled formal sins because the subject who does these acts is in a state of sin. But their malice being identical with that of original sin, these "sins" do not constitute a new fault, worthy of a new chastisement distinct from that of original sin. These acts are bad because the men who do them are bad; they are in the state of original sin, they have not the faith, they do not and cannot accomplish their good works in view of eternal life. This defect or this disorder is a sin. It necessarily affects the works and the virtues of the infidels. But it does not follow, as St. Augustine tended too much to believe, that they are almost always positively referred to a bad end, and inspired by a disordered cupidity.

4. The salutary faith without which a man is not justified is itself a gift of God. Man is impotent to make an act of salutary faith in the message of the gospel without the prevenient grace of God, interior illumination and attraction of the will with its consent. On this point St. Augustine's thought has evolved. Before his episcopal consecration (396) he thought that only the exterior preaching of the gospel was a gratuitous gift of God. But at the moment he wrote De diversis quaestionibus ad

Simplicianum (397) his thought was fixed. Thenceforth his teaching will remain constant: the exterior preaching of the law or of the doctrine and even the accomplishment of miracles have no efficacy to produce faith in the auditor or witness, without an interior operation of God. Not only is faith a gift of God, a prevenient and interior grace of His mercy, but every beginning of good will, and every desire of faith and of conversion.[93]

5. It is by baptism that the believing sinner is regenerated, incorporated into Christ and the Church, and becomes son of God and temple of the Holy Spirit. The operation of God makes of the sinner a just man, a man in whom charity triumphs over carnal cupidity and celestial delight over terrestrial delight. This dynamic reality of justice and charity, permanent of itself and progressive, is the *grace of justification;* it is inaugurated by baptism, the sacrament of incorporation into the Church and Christ. If St. Augustine insists against the Pelagians on the medicinal and liberative aspect of grace, he does not ignore its divinizing aspect. The grace of Christ destroys sin and returns to fallen man his lost liberty only by renewing him interiorly; it re-creates him to the image of God, makes him an adoptive son and the temple of the Holy Spirit.[94]

St. Augustine is the great doctor of

[93] De praed. sanct., II, 5, P.L., 44, 963, 968; III, 7 f., P.L., 44, 964; Epist., 217, 2, 5, P.L., 33, 980.

[94] C. Faust., III, 3, P.L., 42, 216; Enarr. in ps., 49, 2, P.L., 36, 565–566; Tract., 110, P.L., 35, 1920 f.

the mystical body. "Every man is Adam, just as in those who have believed, every man is Christ, because all are members of Christ" (*Omnis autem homo Adam; sicut in his qui crediderunt, omnis homo Christus, quia membra sunt Christi*).[95] To express the union of Christians with Christ, he exploits the Johannine comparison of vine and branches and the Pauline image of the body and the members. He first and magnificently spoke of the total Christ. Not only does Christ live in us, but we are identified with Him.[96]

The doctrine of the inhabitation of the Holy Spirit is common to him and the Greek Fathers. In his *De praesentia Dei*[97] St. Augustine teaches with the whole Tradition that God dwells in the soul of the regenerated. The beginning of this inhabitation is baptismal regeneration. This inhabitation is not equal in all. It is already realized in the baptized infant, anteriorly to every free personal act. In the commentary on the First Epistle of St. John, Augustine attaches the inhabitation of God to charity. The soul in which God dwells, far from containing Him, is on the contrary contained by Him.[98]

6. Justification includes the uncreated gift of the Holy Spirit and the created gift of charity. Sometimes St. Augustine designates by the

word *grace* the Holy Spirit Himself.[99] More often, however, *grace* signifies rather the effect produced in our souls, the created gift and the absolute gratuity of this gift. It is in this sense that he interprets Rom. 5:5: "Indeed the love of God is said to be diffused in our hearts, not the love whereby He Himself loves us but that love whereby He makes us His lovers; just so the justice of God whereby we are made just by His gift. . . . For this justice of God which He teaches not only through the precept of the law but also gives through the gift of the Spirit" (*Caritas quippe Dei dicta est diffundi in cordibus nostris non qua nos ipse diligit, sed qua nos facit dilectores suos; sicut justitia Dei qua justi ejus munere efficimur. . . . Haec est justitia Dei quam non solum docet per legis praeceptum, verum etiam dat per Spiritus donum*).[100] The decree of the Council of Trent on justification will be inspired by this passage of St. Augustine. There is no gift more excellent than charity, he explains in *de Trinitate*. Other gifts are given us by the Holy Spirit, but without charity they avail nothing. The Holy Spirit is the gift of God "insofar as He is given to them who, through Him, love God" (*in quantum datur eis qui per eum diligunt Deum*).[101]

The grace of justification or charity makes man who is of himself a bad tree become a good tree, producing

---

[95] *Enarr. in ps.*, 70, 2, 1, P.L., 36, 891.

[96] *In Jo. ev.*, tract. 111, 6, P.L., 35, 1929, etc.

[97] *Epist.* 187, P.L., 33, 832–848.

[98] *In ep. Jo.*, I, tract. 8, P.L., 35, 2043–2045.

[99] *Serm.*, 144, 1, P.L., 38, 788.

[100] *De spir. et lit.*, 29, 32, 51, 56, P.L., 44, 233–237.

[101] *De Trinitate*, XV, 18, 32; XIX, 35; P.L., 42, 1082–1086.

fruit pleasing to God. It transforms his heart of stone into a heart of flesh, as God promised by the prophet Ezekiel. It frees free will from the servitude of sin and returns to it health.[102]

7. The justified man always needs the actual aid of God to accomplish salutary works and to persevere in justice. Grace restores to fallen man the power to do good, to dominate the attractions of the flesh. . . . Grace is necessary for the salutary act itself. It gives not only the power, but the act. Man, once converted by the operation of God, continues to have need of this divine operation to live in justice. Only in the future life will the grace of Christ render to man health or perfect liberty. In the meantime the grace of justification does not give man the liberty of the anterior state.[103]

Justified man is like a convalescent. He must always lean on the help of God so as not to fall. There remains in him a certain impotence to persevere in good. First of all, he cannot avoid all venial sins. Here below the grace of God never suppresses this infirmity totally for any saint, if one excepts the Blessed Virgin Mary. Further, the justified man remains subject to disordered inclinations of concupiscence,

source of grave temptations. He can surmount them only by the grace he must ask of God. Prayer is absolutely necessary, not only the prayer of adoration and praise, but the prayer of petition. This relative impotence of the justified man to persevere in good God remedies by giving him not only the power but the act of efficacious grace. God gives him in some way the power in the act itself. For St. Augustine grace habitually designates the actual efficacious aids by which God produces, with the consent of the will, the free and salutary acts. It includes exterior and interior aids. These last are of two kinds, those which produce indeliberate movements of the will and those which produce the free act. The first solicits the will to good by stirring up in the soul indeliberate thoughts and sentiments.[104]

This interior operation of God, preceding the consent of the will, is called by later theologians *gratia excitans,* a terminology that has its foundation in that of St. Augustine. Actual grace, according to Augustine, is especially *adjuvant.* This is the efficacious grace of later theology. Although the *auxilium sine quo non,* and the *auxilium quo* of which St. Augustine speaks, are not strictly synonymous with sufficient and efficacious grace (the *auxilium sine quo non* is the aid without which Adam could not persevere, while the *auxilium quo* is the ensemble of aids that assure the final perseverance of

---

[102] *De spir. et lit.,* 30, 32, P.L., 44, 233; *De praed. sanct.,* 8, 13, P.L., 44, 971; *De gratia Christi,* 18, 19–22, P.L., 44, 369–370.

[103] *Op. imp. c. Jul.,* VI, 11, P.L., 45, 1520; *De perf. just.,* 4, 9, P.L., 44, 296; *De natura et gratia,* XXX, 35, P.L., 44, 264; *Ad Simpl.,* I, 2, 3, P.L., 44, 113.

---

[104] *De praed. sanct.,* 2, 5, P.L., 44, 962; *Serm.,* 99, 6, P.L., 38, 598; *De natura et gratia,* 42, 49, P.L., 44, 271.

Christians), yet one can say to simplify things a bit that Augustine's actual grace is not only an *auxilium sine quo non* but an *auxilium quo*. For it gives not only the "ability to act salvifically" (*posse agere salutariter*) but the "salvific acting" (*agere salutariter*) itself, with the consent of the will.[105]

The Augustinian grace is excitant and adjuvant, it procures and assures infallibly the consent of the will and in this sense it determines it (without necessitating it). This doctrine is a consequence of the fact that fallen man, having lost liberty, has this only partially restored here below. This imperfect restitution explains why the just man needs, for each of his acts, a divine aid that makes him accomplish it.

Adjuvant grace (*gratia adjuvans*) is also a corollary of the Augustinian notion of predestination. As a result of the fall of Adam all men constitute a *massa damnata*. In this mass by a free decree of election (predestination) God choses a certain number of elect who will persevere till the end and will obtain eternal life. This predestination, being absolute, implies on God's part the irrevocable will to give to the elect graces that will aid them to act well, procure for them infallibly the good exercise of liberty and assure this exercise anteriorly to the consent of man. It must be noted that St. Augustine never explained the manner in which grace is efficacious while respecting liberty.

One sees that St. Augustine considers grace as the operation of God in man. It is an operation, a continuing motion that gives not only the power to do good and to act salutarily but the act itself. It is required for the beginning of good works as for their accomplishment, from the most humble beginning of *caritas imperfecta* up to the supreme act of perfect charity. It is necessary for all and each of our salutary acts and for the just to persevere.[106] The aid of God that confers the indeliberate act is called grace by St. Augustine only in so far as it leads man in fact to make a free and salutary act. To put it otherwise, excitant grace is grace inasmuch as it is united to adjuvant grace. It is this last which is for him the actual grace par excellence. The fundamental place of humility and prayer in Christian life is a consequence of this doctrine.[107]

8. **The justified man, cooperating with the grace of God, merits eternal life; however, final perseverance is a gift of God which he can obtain only by prayer ("suppliciter emereri").** As its name indicates, grace is essentially a gratuitous gift of God. If it is due to merit it is no longer grace. Before his elevation to the episcopate, St. Augustine did not have a clear consciousness of the absolute gratuity of grace. To safeguard the justice of the divine election, he believed he had to admit some human merit prior to grace. But from the "*div. quaest. ad Simplicianum*" he aban-

---

[105] *De pec. mer. et rem.*, II, 18, 31, P.L., 44, 169; *De cor. et grat.*, XII, 33–39, P.L., 44, 936 f.

[106] *Epist.*, 217, 5, 6, 16, 21, 32, P.L., 33, 984–986.

[107] *De cor. et grat.*, XII, 38, P.L., 44, 939.

doned this way of viewing it. There is absolutely no difference in the *massa damnata* to account for the divine election. This is the doctrine that St. Augustine will not stop defending against the Pelagians and the Massilians. If grace were the recompense of works, it would be no longer be grace. One cannot merit grace by works since one can do the works only by grace.[108]

St. Augustine will even defend this doctrine to excess in the sense that he will draw from it a rigorist conclusion that will be difficult to reconcile with the universal salvific will. Grace can be absolutely gratuitous, St. Augustine thinks, only if it is refused to certain ones, to all those who are left in the *massa peccati*. As much as St. Augustine denies to human works before grace all value of merit or impetration, so much does he ascribe this value to all works whose first source is grace. But there is no merit without liberty. Merit in the proper sense supposes in man justice or charity. The life of justice and charity should be a growth, a movement toward the perfection of charity. It is God who operates in us this growth with the consent and the cooperation of the will. By his good works, though these are a gift of God, the just man merits really the augmentation, the increase of justice up to its consummation in glory. Although the merits of the saints are unequal, they will all have the same recompense, eternal life. Though it be a recompense, eternal life is a grace, since our merits themselves are the fruit of grace and of the gifts of God. St. Augustine even thinks that faith can merit in some manner the grace of acting well; this is then merit that is equivalent to impetration.[109]

The justified man will receive eternal life as recompense for his merits, if he dies in justice or charity, or to put it otherwise, if he perseveres to the end. But this final perseverance he cannot merit; he must ask it of God by prayer. It is the object of predestination.[110]

9. Predestination and the universal salvific will. St. Augustine treats predestination especially in these three treatises: *De correptione et gratia, De praedestinatione sanctorum* and *De dono perseverantia.*[111]

Predestination is the act by which God knows and decrees *ab aeterno* the salvation of those who will effectively be saved. The notion of predestination implies that of divine prescience and purpose. Its object is not precisely faith or entry into the Church as in St. Paul (Rom 9–11), but final perseverance. In interpreting St. Paul, Augustine transposes texts from the historical plane to that of eternal life and passes from a collective perspective to an individual perspective. "Here is the predestination of saints, for it is nothing else: it is the prescience and the preparation of the divine graces by which

---

[108] *C. 2 epist. pel.*, IV, 12, P.L., 44, 617; 13–14, 618.

[109] *Epist.*, 186, 7, P.L., 33, 818; *Epist.*, 194, 19, 33, P.L., 33, 880.

[110] *De dono persev.*, 6, 10, 14, 35, P.L., 45, 999, 1014.

[111] P.L., 44, 915–946, 959–992; 45, 993–1034.

are most certainly liberated all who are liberated."[112]

Predestination is a choice that always achieves its end: the certitude of salvation. One predestined can momentarily not pertain to the Church; he can for a time lose his way. God will bring him back freely by grace. On the contrary some who are justified and in the Church do not persevere, certainly by their great fault. They have not received the gift of perseverance. The number of the predestined is fixed. The elect will be small in number compared to those who perish. All in fact ought to be condemned because of original sin, and this is why God saves only a smaller part.[113]

Predestination is absolutely gratuitous. The just man acts well and perseveres to the end because God, by a sovereignly free act, has chosen him to act well and persevere in preference to others. To the question: who has chosen you there is only one answer: the gratuitous mercy of God whose decree is the sole last reason of salvation and the good works that merit it. Predestination is then entirely independent of the prevision of future or futurible merits of men, it is rather the reason of these merits, that is, of grace.[114]

St. Augustine has hardly spoken of predestination to faith and to justification except where this is included in predestination to glory, to eternal life. In other terms, he speaks especially of predestination *adaequate sumpta*, as the scholastics will say, and so understood it is evidently the reason of the prevision of merits. In this sense one can say that St. Augustine teaches predestination *ante praevisa merita*. But he is neither for nor against the theory of predestination *ante* or *post praevisa merita* as this will be elaborated by post-tridentine scholastics, for the very simple reason that he never posed these questions.

St. Augustine would not understand a predestination to sin. God only predestines what He operates Himself, and consequently He only predestines good. Sin being evil, God cannot will and operate it. He foresees and permits it. But Augustine admits predestination of sinners to punishment or, as he also says, to eternal death.[115]

From the *"div. quaest. ad Simplicianum"* (397) on Augustine had spoken of the *massa damnata* and the vases of wrath in terms that appear hardly reconcilable with the universal salvific will of God. From about 418 he shows himself so exclusively preoccupied with predestination, with the absolute salvific will concerning the elect, that he proposes inadmissible interpretations of 1 Tim 2:3 ff. Certainly Augustine does not deny the universality of the redemption. But in his polemic against the Pelagians, he underlines so much the efficacy of grace and its absolute gratuity and consequent refusal to all who are left

[112] *De dono persev.*, 14, 35, P.L., 45, 1014.
[113] *De civ. Dei*, XXI, 12, P.L., 41, 727.
[114] *In Jo. ev.*, XV, 86, 2, P.L., 35, 1851; *De praed. sanct.*, 18, 36, 37, P.L., 44, 987–988.

[115] *De pecc. mer. et rem.*, II, 17, 26, P.L., 44, 167.

in the *massa damnata,* and he gives these doctrines such a stress that rigorism remains one of the undeniable aspects of his theology of grace.

Augustine had a profound sense of sin, of the misery of man without Christ, of his impotence and his repugnance to loving and doing good. It is by the divine operation in the depth of his spirit that man comes to liberty in being born to life and charity. Certainly man is only liberated if he consents to his liberation. But he can consent to it only under the motion of God. Of this divine motion (it is under this dynamic aspect that he especially envisages grace) Augustine has shown the necessity and gratuity and efficacy.

On the one hand his theory of predestination brought him to oppose the gratuity of grace to its universal diffusion in humanity, since in his eyes grace cannot be gratuitous if it is offered and given to all men. On the other hand he underlined in a too unilateral way the divine causality in the work of salvation. He did not deny man's liberty in consenting to grace, but in his doctrine liberty does not have the place it demands. If the free act is not the first cause of the efficacy of grace, it conditions this efficacy. Finally, Augustine does not seem to have been sufficiently aware of the redoubtable power created liberty has of resisting grace and giving God a definitive refusal.

6. **F. Cayré, A.A.,**[116] stresses Augustine's doctrine on the necessity, gratuity, nature, and efficacy of actual grace, and Augustine's special esteem for the mystical graces that enable man to unite himself perfectly to God by acts of pure charity, the graces of intelligence and wisdom.

Justification
Sanctifying grace. Augustine defended the *reality* of sanctifying grace against the Pelagians, who reduced justification to barely more than the destruction of sin.[117] He taught that baptism truly effaces sin and does not

merely "erase" it, as he was accused of saying: concupiscence remains, but strictly speaking it is not sin: and as for the "infirmity" of our fallen nature, it also is but an effect of sin and will gradually disappear.

Sin is therefore destroyed, but justification supposes in addition a positive element, some reality inherent in the soul. . . . Saint Augustine readily thought of it as a divine adoption or as a deification of the soul which is thus rendered an image of its Creator, more perfect than nature alone could make it, and, lastly, as a participation

[116] F. Cayré, A.A., is an honorary professor at the Institut Catholique of Paris and editor of *L'Année Theologique.* Among his publications we mention *Spiritual Writers of the Early Church.* This excerpt is taken from his two-volume *Manual of Patrology* (Paris, Tournai: Desclée & Co., 1936), v. I, pp. 680–688.

[117] J. Rivière, "Justification," in DTC, col. 2103–2105.

in the very justice and holiness of God. It is this image, lost by original sin, which is instantaneously restored to the soul at the moment of baptism, and which grows in perfection in the measure that the soul "is renewed in the knowledge of God, that is to say, in the justice and holiness of truth."[118]

In these latter texts, these effects are attributed to *wisdom:* elsewhere they are usually attributed to *charity.* The reason for this is that Saint Augustine makes little distinction between grace, which is the source of justice in the soul, and the virtues which flow from it, until complete perfection is obtained. He never forgets that man was perfect as he came from the hands of God, and that in so far as is possible he should become so again. This ideal is realised in great measure by charity, which achieves the union with God, especially when it is accompanied by wisdom in which Augustine seems to perceive some traces of those privileges of which man was despoiled by original sin. In order that this ideal may be realised Augustine exhorts man incessantly to renew himself interiorly by a veritable moral transformation. This explains why sanctifying grace, although it remain at the base of charity and wisdom, is kept in the background, and also why, even apart from the Pelagian controversy, *actual grace* is given such importance in Augustine's works.

Actual grace. 1. St. Augustine affirms, against the Pelagians, the existence of both *exterior* and *interior* graces. The latter are accorded either in the form of *illumination,* which reveals to us our duty, or in the form of *inspiration,* which affects the will and moves it to act. The Pelagians admitted chiefly the exterior graces, notably the Law and the Gospels, as well as the example of Jesus Christ. It is possible that they also recognized certain interior illuminative graces; but they categorically denied the latter [graces of inspiration], asserting that to do and to accomplish depend solely on free will.[119]

Necessity of grace. Saint Augustine considers that *grace is necessary* to man; first and foremost in the *supernatural* order, in order that he may *believe* revealed truths and give to his *acts* a supernatural goodness, and secondly, not only that these acts may be brought to their full perfection, but also that he may begin and persevere in good works. In his refutation of Semi-Pelagianism he particularly stressed the necessity of grace for the beginning of faith, and also the grace of final perseverance. Even in the *natural order* he insists —at least for the accomplishment of the majority of the precepts on account of the infirmity of fallen man — on some supernatural aid, which, moreover, is not refused to the heathen, since for Augustine, whatever may have been said to the contrary, *faith* is not the condition of all moral good; he admits and mentions good works accomplished by unbelievers, for instance, the mercy

---

[118] *De Trinit.,* Bk. XIV, c. xvi, xvii, n. 23; *De Serm. Dom. in monte,* I, xxiii, 78; *Sermo,* 109, 5; 342, 5.

[119] J. Tixeront, *Hist. Dogm.,* II, 443–445.

of Ahasuerus. Should he appear to deny this goodness in other passages, it must be taken as meaning that perfect and meritorious goodness which in the plan of God is always required of man. He had all the more reason for not making *charity* the condition of all moral good since for Augustine this word does not always strictly signify perfect love, but often enough all good love as opposed to concupiscence.[120]

Gratuity of grace. Augustine defended the *gratuity* of grace, or the divine *gift,* no less than its necessity. From the year 397 he affirmed the absolute gratuity of the *first graces* (desire of faith, conversion), and especially in his controversy with the Semi-Pelagians; they can be the object of no merit whatever. On the contrary, the *second graces* can be merited in a certain measure by those who have faith: here, he refers to the graces necessary for accomplishing good acts and persevering in virtue; but these are nevertheless obtained chiefly by prayer. *Final perseverance,* like the first graces, cannot be merited, but it can and should be prayed for. As for *salvation,* it is, strictly speaking, the reward merited by the just man; but although it is a reward, it does not cease to be a grace, since *our merits* themselves are gifts of God, according to that expression so dear to Saint Augustine: "When God crowns our merits, He does nothing but crown His own deeds" (*Cum Deus coronat merita nos-*

tra, nihil aliud coronat quam munera sua).[121]

2. *Nature of actual grace.* Man redeemed "has need of a more powerful grace" than innocent man. With his nature, Adam received the supernatural gift of grace and a righteous will. . . . In order to accomplish good actions he needed only "the help without which he would not be able to remain in it [grace] even if he wished" (*auxilium sine quo in ea non posset permanere, si vellet*): this grace, which gave him the *posse,* was enough; the *agere* and consequently perseverance remained in the power of his free will. Redeemed man, on account of his natural infirmity, has need of a more efficacious aid, which gives him: a) justice, righteousness and good; b) the *posse,* and what is more, the *velle* (*auxilium quo*) or the very act of willing; c) lastly, perseverance which can be obtained only by means of a similar aid (*auxilium quo*). This more powerful grace, moreover, is not refused to man, who finds it superabundantly in Christ, the Incarnate Son of God so that the saints, in spite of the many temptations to which they were exposed, remained faithful to God, whilst Adam fell in spite of all his advantages.[122]

This grace, which affects the act of will, was often described by Saint

---

[120] De gratia Christ. et pecc. orig., 1, 25; De gr. et lib. arbitrio, 33–39; J. Tixeront, op. cit., II, pp. 487–489.

[121] Epist 194 (Ad Sixtum), n. 19, P.L., 33, 880.

[122] De corrept. et grat., n. 30; modern theologians usually reduce these two conceptions, the *auxilium quo non,* and the *auxilium quo,* to the notions of sufficient and efficacious grace, which moreover they explain with certain divergences. But it would seem that Augustine's idea is not

Augustine. The classical text is that of the *De gratia et libero arbitrio*, which shows God first preparing the will to act (*ut velimus operatur incipiens*) and then *cooperating* with it in the very act of willing and guiding its operation to the perfect accomplishment of the perfect act.[123]

The *gratia operans* gives a beginning of charity (*aliquid dilectionis*) which enables the will to receive still more by its docile correspondence to these first graces. Here the word charity indicates all supernatural love of good, even in its lowest form. In the *gratia cooperans*, this same charity, together with the action of the will, is in a sense perfect in relation to the act in question, since this act is actually produced. There are here, therefore, two operations which are co-ordinated, or rather one of which is subordinated to the other; man indeed wills and acts, but is moved by the divine operation which penetrates his will, his heart and his free will; all the acts he accomplishes are properly his and are rightly attributed to him, but inasmuch as they are meritorious they are properly attributed to God, since they derive all their supernatural goodness wholly from grace.[124]

Moreover, it should be sedulously

noted that the *liberty of man*, far from being diminished by this cooperation, is on the contrary strengthened. Augustine never supposes that free will gives way before the divine action. In the *De gratia et libero arbitrio* he proves this continuously from Scriptural citations; the precepts contained in Holy Writ have no meaning if man is not free. Grace itself postulates rather than suppresses free will. But it may be wondered how these assertions can be made to agree with what has gone before. Saint Augustine did not develop a system which would immediately harmonize the action of grace and that of free will since complete harmony is to be found in those eminent principles which guide the two systems.[125]

Whence comes the *efficacy* of grace? Saint Augustine did not study this question from such a precise angle as modern theologians. But his ideas on the subject may be gleaned from the following principles: a) the *will of God* is all powerful and most efficacious; b) that *grace* which affectively determines the adherence of the will is *gratia congrua*, adapted, that is to say, to the dispositions of the subject as they are known to God; c) free will which has of itself a real power with regard to evil is able to place obstacles in the way of grace and hinder its action, although of itself it is not able to render grace efficacious by corresponding to it.[126]

directly represented by this point of view. He was more directly concerned with showing the differences which exist between the state of innocent man and that of redeemed man, and with showing that God has measured His grace in proportion to man's needs, but increases its intensity so that man may overcome his passions.

[123] *De grat. et lib. arb.*, n. 33; P.L., 44, 901.

[124] *De dono perseverantiae.*

[125] *De corrept. et grat.*, 4; *De grat. et lib arb.*, 33–34.

[126] *Enchiridion*, c. 95 f.; *Ad Simplic.*, I, q. 11, n. 13; *De corrept et grat.*, n. 31.

Jansenism reduced the whole of Augustine's teaching on the efficacy of grace to the influence of some *heavenly delectation* which imposed itself on the will, apart from any deliberate act of volition, in order to enable man to overcome all concupiscence or earthly delectation, for man is at the mercy of both these delectations: "For it is necessary that we act in accord with that which delights us the more" (*Quod enim amplius nos delectat, secumdum id operemur necesse est*).[127] This teaching in Saint Augustine has more of a moral bearing than a strictly theological value, and this and other similar texts should be taken as implying a relative necessity. Moreover, it is not exact to say that according to Augustine all the movements of grace take the form of delectation; but even should they all be reduced to such, either desired or already possessed, this delectation, far from suppressing deliberate volition, would on the contrary provoke it, since it would induce the will to incline towards the good presented to it. Lastly, this heavenly delectation is found in but a feeble measure in those souls which have made little progress in the practice of virtue, and who, says, Augustine, are the least free on account of the predominance of the passions. This delectation increases and becomes more powerful in the saints, who may be said to be truly free, with that spiritual liberty, which has its foundation in a veritable *libertas a necessitate interna* (freedom from internal necessity), the fruit of charity, and in those eminent

127 *In Gal.*, n. 49.

graces which form the subject of the following section.

Mystical graces. Among the graces vouchsafed to redeemed man, Saint Augustine holds in especial esteem those which enable man to unite himself perfectly to God by acts of pure charity. Their chief effect is *contemplation,* for they give a very eminent idea of God, which is spiritual, stripped of all rude imagery, and also animated, ravishing the soul with admiration and leading it to unite itself effectively to God. These graces which, while they *enlighten* the soul with regard to God, also permit Him to be *savoured,* are the graces of *intelligence* and *wisdom.* These are the graces which are especially termed the *mystical graces.* For Saint Augustine, as also for Saint Teresa, they constitute the conditions of perfect love or at least of the state in which this love predominates, and which Augustine always describes as being accompanied by intense graces. Saint Augustine often describes such graces, either in connection with Biblical figures, in whom he saw a representation of the contemplative life: Rachel, Leah's sister, Mary, Martha's sister and Saint John the Evangelist or in his commentary of the Beatitudes or that of the *seven gifts of the spirit,* mentioned in Isaiah, which he attributes to Christ and to the faithful.[128]

In these latter passages, *wisdom* and *intelligence* are given a special place: by them, as it were, man is introduced

128 *Contra Faustum,* Bk. XXIII, c. 52–57; Serm., 103, 104, 169, 179, 255; *De consensu Evangelistarum,* Bk. I, c. 5; *De sermone Domini,* Bk. I, c. 1–4.

to the state of perfection. The other gifts seem to be given only to produce these two, and themselves can only come to perfection, in and through the graces of intelligence and wisdom. But although they are not contemplative and mystical in the same degree, they serve a purpose in the perfecting of the soul, which they help to become wholly docile to the guidance of the Holy Spirit.

Saint Thomas followed in the traces of Augustine when he showed these graces as the consummation of the whole spiritual organization of the soul, destined to *subject the soul entirely to God*.[129] All graces tend to this submission of the creature to the Creator; perfection consists in total submission and it is that which characterizes the gifts which are meant to guide the soul in the life of perfection. They are preeminently *operating graces,* but not in the sense of provoking only indeliberate acts. They suppose on the contrary free cooperation, which increases in perfection in the measure that the obstacles to grace in purified souls decrease.

From another point of view, these mystical graces are also *ordinary aids.* Saint Augustine never considered them as the privilege of a few chosen ones, but thought of them as being meant for all, although in reality few souls receive them fully. That superior knowledge of God which is given by contemplative wisdom is certainly said to be a vision, but it is a vision which perfects faith without destroying it, and which always remain a vision in an image, in a mirror (*in speculo*), inferior to the beatific vision which is immediate.[130] *Mediate vision* which comes through the ordinary mystical grace of contemplation certainly throws light on all the objects of faith, but it does not bear directly on God, who is the primary object, and it is thus distinguished from *extraordinary visions* which God can produce supernaturally to the eyes of the body (corporeal vision), in the imagination (imaginative vision) or in the mind alone (intellectual vision). Saint Augustine distinguishes mystical graces in the strict sense from these latter effects which are accessory and exceptional. He also classes them apart from the *charismata,* which may sometimes exist in the absence of charity.[131]

The spiritual benefits especially stressed by Augustine as the *effects of mystical graces* are: a) spiritual *delectation,* vouchsafed to the soul which has "found" God in contemplation; b) perfect *liberty* or the *libertas* of the innocent man, partly attained through this perfect union with Truth and Goodness; c) a greater *understanding* of the divine mysteries in general, and notably that of the Blessed Trinity.[132]

---

[129] *Sum. theol.,* 1–2, q. 68, art. 1.

[130] *De Trinit.,* Bk. XV, c. viii, 14.
[131] *Ad Simplic.,* Bk. II, q. 1.
[132] *Confessions,* Bk. X, c. xxvi.

7. Eugene Portalié, S.J.,[133] offers different interpretations of Augustine's system, a brief historical development of his thought on grace, the fundamental idea of Pelagianism and three fundamental principles of the Augustinian system.

1. **Different Interpretations of St. Augustine's System.** The part of God and man in salvation and the harmony between grace and liberty indisputably form the central core of the teaching of the Bishop of Hippo. Here is where his thought was at the same time the most personal, the most powerful, and the most contested. It was the most personal because he was the first to synthesize the great theories of the fall, grace, and freedom of choice and still more because he has offered a profound explanation to reconcile them, truly his own since no trace of it is found in his predecessors. Thus the word *Augustinian* has commonly been reserved to designate Augustine's system of grace, not his entire teaching. His thought was the most powerful on this question, because, as everyone admits, he was chiefly responsible for the triumph of freedom of the will against the Manicheans and of grace against the Pelagians. His teaching in great part has been solemnly adopted by the Church, and the canons of the Council of Orange are borrowed word for word from his writings. But his doctrine is also the most contested. Just like St. Paul whose teaching he develops, he has been often quoted, and often misunderstood. Friends and enemies have exploited his teaching in the most diverse senses. Without making a detailed study here of the interpretations which have been put upon his teaching, we will mention three facts which merit attention.

At all times adversaries of freedom of the will — predestinarians, Wycliffites, Calvinists, and Jansenists — have availed themselves of the authority of Augustine.

Catholic theologians, it is true, have generally recognized that Augustine safeguarded the rights of freedom of the will, but they are strangely divided concerning the nature of this freedom and the explanation of the divine action in Augustine's writings.

In our time, we must admit, a good number of critics on all sides favor the strict interpretation which sees in Augustine a theory of divine determinism fatal to freedom of the will. . . . The learned Benedictine Dom Odilo Rottmanner concludes a penetrating analysis of Augustine's teaching on grace in this manner: In St. Augustine's teaching on predestination a disagreement between his theory and practice becomes manifest. The mild-

---

[133] Eugene Portalié, S.J., was born in 1852 and died in 1909. In 1899 he held the chair of positive theology at the Institut Catholique of Toulouse. Most of his writing was done for the Jesuit periodical, *Etudes*. This excerpt was taken from R. J. Bastian's translation of his DTC article on Augustine and entitled *A Guide to the Thought of St. Augustine* (Chicago: Henry Regnery Co., 1960), pp. 177–200, 223–229.

ness of his practice remained unchanged, as is shown by his sermons; his theory, at first inoffensive, continually developed in the direction of an excessive rigorism and an irresistible influence of God on freedom of the will. Moreover, this endless variation prevents him from developing a complete system whose parts are logically connected.[134]

Contemporary Protestant critics, even the most sincere admirers of Augustine, are unmerciful. Although the earlier reformers invoked his authority to deny freedom of choice, their successors set themselves up as the defenders of liberty against his teaching.[135] Loofs accuses him of holding an irresistible predestination and grace which are opposed to freedom of the will, to the teaching of St. Jerome, and to popular Catholicism. . . . Harnack sees "numerous contradictions and remnants of Manicheism" in the Augustinian theory of grace.[136] Like Loofs and many others, he was deceived by this false idea of an irresistible grace. . . .

Despite quite noticeable exaggerations on certain points, despite difficulties which explain disagreements without taking a position, we think that the texts are sufficiently clear and the critics sufficiently impartial to propose a revision of the stricter views. Therefore we unhesitatingly affirm first, that St. Augustine has formed

a true and perfectly logical system without contradictions, the basis of which did not vary since the time he became bishop if we judge by his later works; second, that in this system human liberty was affirmed until the day of his death so accurately that no trace of an irresistible and necessitating impulsion ever appears in it.

2. Historical Development of Augustine's Thought on Grace. . . . The problem of grace arose long before Augustine's first struggles with Pelagianism in 412 — that is a fact beyond doubt today. In proportion as Augustine condemned Manicheism and resolved the problem of evil by showing the part human freedom played in it, there arose for him the problem of good under a threefold aspect: philosophical, theological, and especially Pauline. (1) *Philosophical aspect.* The philosopher accustomed to look for the influence of God in everything must ask himself how the two sovereignties of divine government and human liberty can be reconciled. The divine foreknowledge, which the ancient philosophers had denied to safeguard liberty, did not disturb him. . . . The foreknowledge has no more influence on the future than memory has on the past. . . . The aspect on which Augustine riveted his attention was the special role God plays in moral life. Virtue, holiness — are these due only to human free will? Or, if their origin must be sought in God, what becomes of freedom of choice? (2) *Theological aspect.* The theologian's problem is further complicated by revelation which asserts Christ's mys-

---

[134] Dom Odilo Rottmanner, *Der Augustinismus* (Munich, 1892), p. 29.

[135] Cf. Haag, *Histoire des dogmes chrétians,* I, 207–213.

[136] Harnack, *History of Dogma,* V, 217, 219–220.

terious and continual influence on the Christian: "Without Me you can do nothing" (Jn 15:5). The problem of supernatural grace was added to that of providence. (3) *Pauline aspect.* The Pauline dogma of divine predestination, separating the elect from the reprobate as if vessels of honor and of shame were formed from the same potter's clay, adds this further question: Why was human liberty not destroyed by the fall of Adam and the gratuitous predestination of God? This is the state of the question which faced Augustine at the beginning of his apostolate. He had already attempted a rough answer to it in the *Explanation of Some Questions from Romans* (396–398).[137]. . .

System Complete in 397: Importance of "Various Questions for Simplicianus." Another exaggeration which must be dispelled is that Augustine's doubts continued indefinitely. According to proponents of this view, Augustine, pushed by the arguments of the Pelagians, continually restricted the scope of freedom of the will until toward the end of his life he taught an absolute predestination which annihilated freedom altogether. This is a mistake. If his teaching of predestination destroyed liberty, Augustine denied it already in 397, for at the very beginning of his episcopacy (fifteen years before the Pelagian controversy began) he formulated his system in a famous reply which has not been sufficiently studied or understood.

Simplicianus, Ambrose's successor to

the see of Milan, posed several questions to his old pupil. Among them, he asked Augustine about Chapter IX of the Epistle to the Romans. The reply, *On Various Questions for Simplicianus,*[138] constitutes a true key to the Augustinian system because of its accuracy, its fullness, its clarity, and especially because of the rational explanation which it gives to the dogma. It must be reread if one wishes to grasp the depth of its thought and the significance of the formulas which, though in constant use later, are rarely explained elsewhere. . . . In his later years Augustine refers his adversaries to this book with an insistence not often noticed. . . . In addition, some very competent critics have grasped the importance of this book although they do not seem to have understood all its doctrine. According to Loofs the whole of the specifically Augustinian teaching on grace as it was defended later against the Pelagians and Semipelagians can be reproduced by citations from this one book to Simplicianus.[139]. . .

3. The Pelagian System. The Pelagian system must be known if one wishes to understand the theory and terminology of Augustine.

a. *Dogmatic Errors of the Pelagians.* Their dogmatic errors were clearly enuntiated in the first condemnation pronounced at the Council of Carthage in 411.[140] Coelestius, a disciple

---

[137] ExR, 55, 60, 61, 62 (35, 2076–2080); DD, 83 66, 1 (40, 61).

[138] DD7 1, 2 (40, 110–128).

[139] Loofs, "Augustinus," *Realencylopädie für prot. Theol. und Kirche,* II, 279–280.

[140] See Mercator, *Commonitorium,* 1 (48, 69–70) and in *Liber subnotationum* (48, 114–115). Cf. Mansi, IV, 289–292.

of Pelagius bolder than his master, was accused of the following errors: (1) Adam was created mortal; whether he sinned or not, he had to die. This is a negation of the supernatural elevation of the first man. Therefore there existed neither original justice nor the preternatural privileges which flowed from it. (2) The sin of Adam injured himself alone, not the human race. This is a negation of original sin. (3) Infants today are born in the state in which Adam was before his fall. This is a combination of the first two errors. Death, concupiscence, and so forth are not the result of Adam's sin, but the original condition of humanity. (4) "Adam by his death (or by his sin) does not subject the whole human race to death; (because) Christ by His Resurrection does not give new life to the entire human race."[141]. . . Therefore, they conclude, Adam was the cause of bodily death for no one and of death of the soul only for those who imitate his sin, but not for all. . . . These errors are the consequences of a system. What is the guiding principle which has given rise to them?

b. *Fundamental Idea of Pelagianism.* (1) *Not solely a denial of the supernatural.* The underlying idea of Pelagianism is not solely its denial of the supernatural order. In great part, it is true, Pelagianism is a naturalism which excludes supernatural elevation, divine adoption, the fall, all merit of a higher

order, but which admits that the will depends on the divine government. . . . There is no doubt that Pelagius denied all supernatural grace — whatever the Jansenists might say — and admitted only the external gifts of revelation, the law and the example of Christ.[142] But Pelagius denied more than that. Even prescinding from the supernatural order, he exaggerated the powers of freedom of choice. . . .

(2) *Basic error: absolute independence of human liberty.* The foundation of the Pelagian system, then, is the absolute independence of human liberty in relationship to God and its unlimited power for good as well as for evil. . . . According to Pelagius, man owes existence and freedom of choice (which he calls the possibility of good) to God the Creator. This is the only gift of God and, since it is gratuitous, Pelagius calls it a grace, playing on the words. Any further influence of God on freedom of choice would destroy it. . . .

(4) *Omnipotence of free choice.* The omnipotence of freedom of choice for good was a result of its emancipation. . . . In reality, Pelagius affirmed that even in the Old Testament those who were called holy and just were really without sin and in a state of complete perfection which was acquired solely by their freedom of choice.[143]. . .

Consequent Rigorism. . . . Since perfection is possible for man, it is obligatory. For Pelagius, as for the Stoics,

---

[141] The words in brackets are variant readings borrowed from the edition of the *Commonitorium* by Baluze, Mansi, IV, 293, and from the *Liber subnotationum* of Mercator (48, 115). The sense is the same without them, but not so clear.

[142] Cf. DGrC, 7–10, 8–11 (44, 364–366) and the admissions of Julian in OJ, I, 94 (45, 1111).

[143] Cf. DPB, III, 1, 1 (44, 185).

every good act is obligatory; there are no counsels, only precepts. . . . The Pelagians therefore damned for all eternity every Christian guilty of the slightest venial sin, or, to put it another way, every sin was mortal for them. For a lie, an idle word, one ceases to be just and becomes reprobate and a sinner, worthy of hell.

Grace as Developed by Augustine. Augustine's theory of grace includes three sections. First, there are dogmatic elements (in direct opposition to Pelagius' conclusions rather than his principles) for which Augustine merited the official approval of the Church. Second, there are more general principles which constitute the very basis of the Augustinian system and which have not been, at least explicitly, the object of a definition. Third, there are applications of these principles to the special questions of the condition of Adam, original sin, and predestination — applications which for the most part have not been treated by the Church in her decisions.

Concerning the first category, an over-all view of the dogmas established by Augustine is provided in two important documents: the canons of the Council of Carthage (418) and the twelve truths of the Catholic faith which Augustine enumerates in his letter to Vitalis.

a. *Council of Carthage.* Three great truths are summarized in the eight (or nine) canons of the Council of Africa. (1) Original sin . . . immortality of Adam before the fall (canon 1), the transmission of sins to his descendants, the necessity for infants

to be baptized (c. 2). . . . (2) *Role of grace.* On the necessity and the role of grace, the Fathers assert that justifying grace is not only the pardon of past sins but also "an aid that sins be not committed" (c. 4). This help is not only a light which reveals the law, but the love of the good "that we may also love and be able to act" (c. 5). The necessity of this aid is absolute and not merely "that we may act more easily" (c. 6). (3) *Impeccability.* Against the impeccability and the perfection extolled by the Pelagians, the Fathers proclaim and demonstrate by the Scriptures that in reality Providence allows men, even the most just, to fall into sins. . . .

b. *Letter to Vitalis.* The letter to Vitalis develops a fourth truth, the gratuity of grace, in twelve rules of faith. It is an excellent résumé of Augustine's struggle against the Semipelagians. After the affirmation of original sin (article 1), he stresses the gratuity of grace and its universal necessity for all, even for infants (a. 2) and for every action of adults (a. 3). This gratuity is proved by the distribution of grace: God does not give it to all, but to those whom He wills (a. 4, 5, 6). . . .

Three Fundamental Principles of the Augustinian System. Father Wolfsgruber maintains that the key to the whole Augustinian system lies in Augustine's assertion of these two truths: Man is free; he can do nothing without grace.[144] These two statements are undoubtedly of great value; but they

---

[144] Wolfsgruber, *Augustinus* (Paderborn, 1898), p. 824.

only create a mystery, they do not explain it. The true key, therefore, is elsewhere in the Augustinian explanation of the divine government of wills. This is a theory which is as original and profound as it is absolutely unknown to the most intelligent Protestant critics such as Harnack, Loofs, and so forth. There are at the basis of the Augustinian system, not two, but three fundamental principles whose precise meaning must be determined. First, God, through His grace, is the absolute master of all the determinations of the will. Second, man remains just as free under the influence of grace as he is in its absence. Third, the reconciliation of these truths depends upon the method of the divine government.

a. *First Principle*. The absolute sovereignty of God over the will is opposed to the Pelagian principle of the emancipation of liberty. (1) *Affirmation of this sovereignty*. . . . God, the first cause, is the author of all good, of all moral perfection, of all salvation. No man is good or virtuous without the gift of God which is called grace because it is completely gratuitous. No one is saved without the special gift of final perseverance, prepared by a specially gracious predestination of God. . . . (2) *Exercise of this sovereignty*. Augustine has formulated three laws concerning the exercise of this sovereignty. The first is that every good and salutary act without exception is the fruit of a grace, of a gift from God. . . . The second law, a consequence of the first, is the priority of grace over good will. . . .

The third law states that not only is Pelagian inerrancy, the preservation from all, even the slightest faults, incapable of realization for weak human beings without a special grace, but that this gift itself is a privilege so rare that it has been granted only once or twice in the history of humanity. . . . (3) *Extent of this dependence*. Even in the natural order the dependence of every created will is so universal that no act of virtue is performed without a gift from God. . . .

b. *Second Principle*. Freedom of choice, even under the influence of efficacious grace was always safeguarded by St. Augustine. Everybody grants two important facts. First, St. Augustine had from the very beginning defended freedom of choice against the Manicheans so ardently that his works are an inexhaustible arsenal. . . . Some, however, have claimed that little by little, caught up in the logic of his ideas, he had sacrificed freedom of the will on the altar of divine determinism. But the texts are absolutely against this accusation. (1) Augustine never retracted his principal ideas on freedom of choice; he never modified his thought on the factor which is its essential condition, that is, its complete power of choosing or determining itself. . . . (2) On the contrary, there is not a single one of his later anti-Pelagian works in which Augustine does not positively proclaim the complete power of choice. . . . (3) Efficacious grace works infallibly, but never by an irresistible impulse, for even under its influence the will remains master of itself. . . .

c. *Third Principle.* The Augustinian theory on the divine influence reconciles both grace and freedom of the will. Is there a contradiction between the two principles just stated? Harnack, Loofs, and others thought so because, according to them, Augustinian grace is an irresistible impulse. Is this, however, the true thought of the great doctor? He thought, certainly, that he had reconciled the two dogmas and was astonished that the monks of Hadrumentum had not understood him. This solution has been pointed out by older theologians and in our days by Schwane and others, but in too summary a fashion.[145] An explanation of it will justify the system of the Doctor of Hippo.

Explanation of the Way Grace Operates. The solution rests on three Augustinian theories and gives an equally valid explanation of the divine influence on both natural and supernatural virtues. (a) *Theory of volitional psychology.* The will never determines itself without a motive, without the attraction of good perceived in the object. . . . Now, although the will remains free in the presence of any motive, in point of fact it often makes different resolutions according to the different motives which are presented to it. There is the whole secret of the influence exercised by eloquence (the orator does not but present motives), by meditation, or by good reading. What power would he not have over the will who would be able to present such or such a motive for action at his pleasure? Well, that is precisely the privilege of God in virtue of the first principle. (b) *Theory of intellectual psychology.* St. Augustine noted this truth of universal experience that man is not master of his first thought. He can influence the course of his reflections, but he himself cannot determine the objects, the images, and consequently the motives which are presented to his mind. "No one has power over what chances to come into his mind," he says, "but to give consent or to withhold it is in the power of one's own will."[146] But since *chance* is only a word, it is really God who determines these first perceptions of man as He pleases, either through the providential action of external causes or interiorly by the ministry of angels or men by a divine illumination sent to the soul.[147] . . . (c) *Theory of the divine knowledge.* Not only does God send at His pleasure the illuminations and enticements which are the will's inspiration in determining itself, but He knows, even before choosing among all the illuminations of the natural and supernatural order, the answer which the will will freely make to each one of them. . . .

This theory, most assuredly, need not be accepted, for the Church has never adopted it as her own; one can ask where and how God knows the result of these graces, for Augustine always affirmed the fact and never

---

[145] Schwane, *Dogmengeschichte,* II, 129; Hergenröther, *Kirchengeschichte,* II, n. 117; Wolfsgruber, *Augustinus,* pp. 825–830.

[146] DSL, 34, 60 (44, 240).
[147] Cf. the very characteristic passage in DGnL, IX, 14, 25 (34, 403).

inquired into the manner.[148] But can the thinker who created and defended this logical system until his dying day be accused of fatalism and Manicheism? This, then, was the solution which Augustine always laid down as the foundation of his system. . . .

Augustinian Theories in Apparent Opposition to the Above System. . . .

a. *First Theory: Freedom of Choice Lost Through the Fall.* Augustine teaches in his later works that "man lost freedom of choice through the Fall."[149] The answer to this is easy. Augustine explains most explictly that this liberty which was lost is not the power to choose between good and evil as one pleases (a power which we still have and without which, he says, man could not even sin). It is rather that original perfection of the will freeing it from concupiscence, which Adam had received and which, Augustine says, alone merits the beautiful name of freedom in its fullest meaning.[150]

b. *Second Theory: Necessity of Sin in Fallen Man.* Augustine maintains that in fallen man there are absolutely necessary sins, a necessity of sinning. He proves this by concupiscence, which is both an inevitable sin and a source of sin.[151]

Augustine, however, is careful to explain that in this passage he does not call the faults for which we are responsible and which God can punish necessary sins, but rather the unregulated desires of the senses which are a shameful, though inculpable, decadence in formerly innocent human nature. Pelagius and Julian exalted human nature and its power to arrive at absolute perfection, dispassionateness, and sinlessness. Augustine raises an objection based on the moral deformity of these involuntary rebellions of nature; only in heaven will our freedom of choice be liberated from these disorders which later Scholasticism was to entitle materials sins.[152]

Once these explanations are proposed, it becomes impossible to confuse Augustine's theory with that of Baius which is condemned by the Church.[153] The resemblance is merely verbal: Baius understands that the involuntary desires of concupiscence constitute so many personal sins, "a true disobedience to the law," for each of which unbelievers and sinners will be judged and punished in hell.[154] . . . Therefore . . . every personal sin is essentially free according to Augustine and presumes the complete power of not committing it. (2) The same thing applies to ignorance. . . . (3) Thus St. Augustine taught to the very end that no commandment of God is impossible. His celebrated formula in *On*

---

[148] Molinism, in trying to answer this question, is thus distinguished from Augustinism.

[149] Cf. DCG, 12, 37 (44, 939); OJ, I, 47 (45, 1067–1068); II, 17 (45, 1148); VI, 11 (45, 1520); etc.

[150] CD, I, 2, 5 (44, 552); cf. III, 8, 24 (44, 607).

[151] Cf. DPJ, 1–3 (44, 291–295).

[152] CD, I, 10, 19 (44, 560); 17, 35 (44, 566); II, 2, 2 (44, 572).

[153] Baius, propositions 46, 50, 51, 75, 76, Denzinger, *Enchiridion*, nn. 1946, 1950, 1951, 1975, 1976.

[154] Cf. Ernst, *Zeitschrift für katholische Theologie*, 1895, p. 191.

Nature and Grace remains the perfect expression of his thought to the very end: "Therefore God does not command impossibilities, but when He commands He counsels you to do what you can for yourself and to ask His aid in what you cannot do."[155]

c. *Third Theory: God's Grace Is Invincible.* An Augustinian maxim which is repeated under hundreds of forms is that the grace of God is invincible; one cannot resist the will of God; one cannot stay His omnipotence. "The weakness of the human will is helped by the fact that it is unavoidably and insuperably influenced by divine grace."[156]

Here again a comprehensive understanding of Augustinian vocabulary will explain everything. If *grace* means, as in our theological language, any divine inspiration, Augustine would be a Jansenist. But the *grace* which Augustine speaks of against the Pelagians is almost always and especially here[157] only efficacious grace, that which God gives knowing that it will surely meet with acceptance. Now this grace or this series of graces, although not irresistible, in fact will always be victorious. This is the infallibility of the divine success which Augustine consistently explains by remarkably accurate expressions: "No man's will resists God when He wills to give salvation. For to will or not to will is in the power of the one who

wills or does not will in such a way as not to impede the divine will."[158] With this grace man does not resist, he does not hinder, he does not overcome; but he can resist, he can hinder, he can overcome because he can will not to do it. If Augustine sometimes says that man cannot resist the will of God[159] he means that freedom of choice cannot hinder God from choosing among His graces that one which will in fact meet with acceptance.

d. *Fourth Theory: Salvation Effected Entirely by God.* At the end of his life Augustine attributes everything in the work of salvation to God. He seems to retract, therefore, all his earlier teaching on the role of freedom of choice.[160]. . .

Again the difficulty lies in a misunderstanding of Augustinian language. "To ascribe all to God" does not deny man's action, but rather the fact that this action can accomplish nothing without grace, not even a good desire or a very short prayer. The meaning of this expression in the Augustinian theory (which is the same as Catholic teaching here) is that each of the elect in heaven must say: "There is not a single good act in my life for which I do not owe thanks to God." In reality this theory is opposed to Augustine's early error which attributed the beginning of faith to free will. In 397 he received an understanding of the text: "What do you have that you have not received?"

---

[155] DNG, 43, 50 (44, 271).

[156] DCG, 12, 38 (44, 940).

[157] In *On Punishment and Grace,* which treats solely of final perseverance and of the celebrated *auxilium quo.*

[158] DCG, 14, 43 (44, 942).

[159] *Ibid.,* 45 (44, 943).

[160] DPS, 7, 12 (44, 970); En, 32, 9 (40, 248).

From then on there was no further variation in his teaching. He saw that everything comes from God. But far from denying the part of man and his merits, he asserted their importance to the very end of his life in even his most rigorous works.[161]

e. *Fifth Theory: Grace Not Given to All Men.* Augustine did not only assert that grace was gratuitous, but also that God, at His pleasure and without injustice, absolutely refuses it to many men.[162]

That is true, but what, according to Augustine, is the kind of grace which God refuses? It is only efficacious grace (of faith for adults, of baptism for infants). But who doubts that God does not give efficacious grace to all? . . . As for those who have received this special gift, Augustine, far from depriving them of other sufficient graces, explicitly presumes the presence of these gifts when he distinguishes the different types of divine calling or appeals and when he attributes damnation to the will's resistance.

f. *Sixth Theory: God Wills to Save Only the Elect.* The divine will to save all men (according to 1 Tim 2:4), first asserted by Augustine in 412,[163] was later modified and progressively confined to very narrow limits. He no longer admits that God wishes to save all men, but only the elect.[164]

This objection has been answered, and very learnedly, by the great theologians.[165] Basically, this problem too is a matter of vocabulary. The meaning given to the word *divine will* changed as Augustine grew older, entailing at the same time some changes in his formulas and in his exaggerated interpretations of the saying of the Apostle: "He wishes that all men be saved." The will of God can be sufficiently sincere to bestow the gift of sufficient graces without being absolute and efficacious. Having this view of the divine will in his earlier works, therefore, Augustine stated that God wishes to save all men. However, as the Pelagian controversy pressed him, he turned his attention more and more to efficacious grace which alone distinguishes the elect and, as a consequence, he came to consider God's absolute will of saving men. Now it is evident that God does not have the absolute will to save all souls. . . . Therefore, in the very text which is used as an objection against us, Augustine preaches the doctrine of two wills in God: one a conditional will which is not realized since freedom of choice resists it; the other an efficacious will which is realized but which does not extend to all men.

---

[161] For example, DDoP, 2, 4 (45, 996); E, 194, 3, 6 (33, 876); especially RI, 23, 2–3 (32, 621).

[162] E, 217, 5, 16 (33, 984).

[163] DSL, 33, 58 (44, 238).

[164] See, in 421, CJ, IV, 7, 42 (44, 759); En, 103 (40, 280); in 426, DCG, 15, 47 (44, 945); in 428, DPS, 8, 14 (44, 971).

[165] St. Thomas, *Summa theologica*, I, q. 19, a. 6 ad 1; *In I ad Timotheum, II*, lect. 1; Alticozzi, *Summa augustiniana*, I, q. 1, a. 5; Faure, notes on the *Enchiridion*, Chap. 103, p. 195.

VII

GRACE IN THE COUNCIL OF ORANGE

1. J. Tixeront[1] sets forth the development of Semipelagianism. He touches briefly on Cassian, St. Prosper, Faustus and St. Fulgentius, St. Caesarius and the Second Council of Orange. He sketches briefly three "Semipelagian" propositions that were prevalent in Southern Gaul in 429.

. . . as early as the year 427, when Augustine's CXCIVth letter to Sixtus was read in the monastery of Hadrumentum, in Byzacene, quarrels and disturbances arose among the inmates. . . . But this was only the beginning.

The real fight was preparing in Southern Gaul. There, theologians received indeed the decisions of the African councils and the Popes, but nothing more. They looked upon several of St. Augustine's theories, if not as manifest errors, at least as dangerous exaggerations. Unfortunately they failed to

---

[1] J. Tixeront, cf. Chap. VI, n. 2. This excerpt is from *op. cit.*, III, p. 264–301.

distinguish between what was unquestionable truth and disputable theory, and to draw from previous decisions the conclusions that ought to have been drawn. Rejecting Pelagianism as a whole, they upheld some of its more subtle errors, and when confronted with the abstruse questions that were then being agitated, some remained or became heretics for fear of falling into the opposite extreme. These were called Semipelagians.[2]

John Cassian. The first author of that time in whose works we find Semipelagian ideas expressed is the abbot of St. Victor of Marseilles, John Cassian.[3] Cassian had sojourned in Egypt, in Palestine, and at Constantinople, where he had been raised to the diaconate by St. John Chrysostom. The deep impression which the latter had made on his mind accounts for the very slender liking he conceived for St. Augustine's teaching. Cassian, who never forgot St. Chrysostom's continual exhortations to personal effort and action, and who, besides, had daily to encourage his monks on the way of self-renunciation and sacrifice, could not understand the passivity to which the Bishop of Hippo seemed to reduce the human will under the influence of grace. If God really does everything in us, where does merit

come in? And if we can do nothing without grace, what becomes of our liberty?

It is mainly in the XIIIth conference, *De protectione Dei*, written between 420 and 426, that Cassian has laid down his principles. . . . A freedom that would not enable a man to will and do what is good of himself (*a semetipso*), would not be genuine liberty.[4] Hence, before dispensing His grace, God demands and expects of us previous efforts.[5] . . . Once he is called by God and illuminated by His light, man can of himself believe and have the faith,[6] for he can freely either reject or follow divine grace.[7] . . . Hence, Cassian concludes, let us not say that grace is not gratuitous, nor that there is parity between our efforts and the future reward, for those efforts amount to nothing if compared to the action of grace and the greatness of the reward.[8] Nor let us say with the Pelagians that grace is bestowed on man because he has merited it, and in proportion to his merit; unlike them, we must not ascribe the whole work of salvation to free will, which can claim only the least share in that work, or, at times, no share whatever.[9]

Yet, no matter what Cassian said to the contrary, to his mind the last word in the problem of salvation ultimately depended on free will. To deny that God wills to save all men was regarded by him as an awful blasphemy;

---

[2] We may observe that the word Semipelagianism is unknown to antiquity. St. Prosper styles Semi-Pelagians *"pelagianae pravitatis reliquiae"* (*Inter epist. August.*, epist. CCXXV, 7). The term is, however, quite appropriate.

[3] Cassian is quoted here from the P.L., vols. 49 and 50. The *Conferences* are found in the forty-ninth volume.

[4] Col. 925, 927.
[5] Col. 932.
[6] Col. 936.
[7] Col. 929, 933.
[8] Col. 934.
[9] Col. 942.

he absolutely rejected predestination *ante praevisa merita,* and held that grace is given to all indifferently, and that the use or abuse which we make of it determines our salvation or condemnation.[10]. . .

Three "Semipelagian" Propositions. This is a brief sketch of the opinions that were prevalent in the monasteries of Southern Gaul in 429, according to Prosper and Hilary.[11] At a much later date these views were qualified by theologians as Semipelagianism. They may be summed up in the three following propositions: (1) Man is able, without grace, to desire and will, but not to perform, supernaturally good deeds; he can begin to believe, but he cannot impart to himself complete faith. (2) God wills all men to be saved, and offers to all the grace of salvation. All can cooperate with His grace and persevere in it, if they will. (3) There is no absolute predestination; predestination and reprobation, considered in God, are consequent upon His foreknowledge of the merits and demerits of each individual; considered in man, they are merely the consequences of his conduct. Of these three propositions the first alone seems at first blush reprehensible and tainted by Pelagianism; the other two, whilst calling for further explanation, on the whole fairly express the constant belief of the faithful. This mixture of truth and false-

hood was apt to make the task of refuting them rather difficult. . . .

The quarrel between Augustinians and Semipelagians went on in Southern Gaul. The Bishop of Hippo did not live to see its sequel; he died on August 28, 430. The task of upholding his cause and continuing his work devolved on Prosper.

St. Prosper's Opposition.[12] Prosper was a layman, and must have been about forty years old when St. Augustine died. An Augustinian through and through, he had identified himself as it were with his master and claimed but to reecho his teaching.[13] . . . This is true of the *Letter to Rufinus,* the poem *De ingratis,* and the *Answer to the Genoese.* But in his other works Prosper, under the pressure of controversy, adopts the theory of predestination to hell *post praevisa merita,* and expresses himself so ambiguously and with so much hesitancy on other points, that some critics have been led to mistake his true sentiments. On the whole, however, he was a faithful pupil of his great master and staunchly supported his teaching. . . . Notwithstanding the vigor of his argumentation and his literary ability, he did not succeed in converting his adversaries. Cassian, whom he had directly attacked, did not condescend to answer; Pope Xystus III, whom he had indirectly entreated to intervene, did not intervene; and in the year 434, Vincent of Lerins pub-

---

[10] Collat. XIII, 7, 17, 18; XVII, 25.

[11] Cf. two letters written in 429 by St. Prosper and Hilary to St. Augustine. They are printed among the letters of St. Augustine, CCXXV and CCXXVI.

[12] The works of St. Prosper are found in P.L., 51.

[13] *Respons. ad capita Gallorum,* col. 156, 157.

lished his *Commonitorium,* in which, under the mask of ancient heretics, fond of novelties, St. Augustine seems to be aimed at. The weakness of Prosper's defense came from the fact that he represented the particular views of the Bishop of Hippo as the teaching of the Church. Rome refused to admit this identification. . . . St. Prosper had failed to obtain a solemn condemnation of his opponents; and the latter saw in the blame that Rome inflicted on a part of their teaching, at most a reason to tone down its expression and moderate their language. This they seem to have done. There followed a sort of truce, and the controversy abated for a while. . . .

Faustus and St. Fulgentius. The truce between the Augustinians and the Semipelagians lasted about forty years. Then an incident occurred that again stirred up the discussion. About 452, Faustus, former abbot of Lerins, had been made bishop of Riez.[14] He was a versatile and cultivated man, of austere morals, a zealous bishop of excellent repute, who had, however, brought from Lerins the views that prevailed there on the subject of grace. One of his priests, Lucidus, espoused Predestinarianism — the error that regards men as predestined to heaven or hell, and irresistibly pushed to the one or the other, whatever they may do. Faustus tried to bring him back to a safer teaching. When he saw that his entreaties were useless, he threatened,

unless he recanted, to have him condemned by a council about to meet at Arles, probably in 473. . . . Lucidus finally yielded to Faustus' request. . . .

So far everything went smoothly, and the Augustinians themselves could not but be gratified at what had taken place. But the trouble was not yet over. Faustus was commissioned to condense into a systematic treatise the points of doctrine that had been decided at Arles and Lyons in connection with Predestinarianism. He set himself to the task and wrote the treatise *De gratia libri duo,*[15] which started the dispute anew. The views of Faustus have received various interpretations. Some critics have looked upon his Semipelagian formulas as mere verbal exaggerations against Predestinarianism;[16] others have found in them a distinctly Semipelagian bias, very close indeed to strict Pelagianism.[17] Whether this last estimate is correct or not, the Semipelagian attitude of Faustus can hardly be denied. . . .

Faustus' writings do not seem to have given offense, at first, and during the last years of the 5th and the first years of the 6th century, the theologians of Provence held their views without being molested. . . . But when Faustus' treatise fell into the hands of the Scythian monks at Constantin-

---

[14] Faustus is quoted after the edition of A. Engelbrecht, *Fausti Reiensis . . . opera* Vindobonae, 1891 (Corpus script. ecclesiastic. latin., tom. XXI). Cf. also P.L., Vols. 53 and 58.

[15] Engelbr., 3 f.; P.L., 58, 783 f. It will be noticed that the divisions of the P.L. do not agree entirely with those of Engelbrecht.

[16] For instance, J. Heller, *Fausti Regiensis fides in exponenda gratia Christi* (Monachii, 1854).

[17] This view is held especially by R. Seeberg, *Lehrbuch der Dogmen-Geschichte,* II, 516.

ople[18] it gave serious offense. . . . To ascertain Faustus' standing, they applied to the African bishop, Possessor, who was then in exile at Constantinople. He in turn applied to Hormisdas.[19] The Pope's answer, dated August 13, 520 . . . whilst not forbidding the reading of Faustus' books, did not regard them as authoritative, and advised any one who was anxious to know the authentic teaching of the Church on grace, to consult the works of St. Augustine, particularly his two treatises, De praedestinatione sanctorum, and De dono perseverantiae, or, still more safely, the ecclesiastical decisions, i.e., probably the auctoritates gathered at the end of Celestine's XXIst letter.

This somewhat indefinite answer did not satisfy the Scythian monks. . . . The legates sent to Rome . . . lost patience at Hormisdas' delay in approving their Christological formulas and applied to the African bishops who had fled to Sardinia, one of whom was St. Fulgentius.[20] Their communication referred not only to the Incarnation, but also to the question of grace, which they set forth as they understood it.[21]. . . The answer of the bishops came from St. Fulgentius. This is the Epistula XVII, better known as the Liber de incarnatione et gratia Domini nostri Iesu Christi.[22]. . . .

These documents enable us to form an idea of the teaching which St. Fulgentius and the African bishops opposed to that of Faustus.[23] Their doctrine is strict Augustinianism set forth more plainly even than in the works of St. Augustine himself, and shorn of all attenuations introduced by St. Prosper. . . .

St. Caesarius and the Second Council of Orange. While St. Fulgentius was thus bending all his energies to crush the system of Faustus, the Bishop of Riez had been dead for many years.[24] But his ideas were still championed by a certain number of theologians, and the struggle between Augustinians and Semipelagians in Gaul might have continued indefinitely, had there not arisen a man who succeeded in having both parties accept a solution which, whilst on the whole favoring the Augustinians, refrained from sanctioning their harshest assertions and ascribed to human liberty a legitimate share in the work of salvation. This man was St. Caesarius, bishop of Arles.

Caesarius had received his theological training partly at Lerins, and therefore knew the strong dislike there entertained for the ideas of St. Augustine. . . . Recent discoveries make it certain that, whilst he did not countenance the extreme assertions of Augustinianism, Caesarius did accept

---

[18] Cf. Tixeront, op. cit., p. 124.

[19] Relatio Possessoris afri, in P.L., 63, 489.

[20] Liber Petri diaconi et aliorum . . . de incarnatione et gratia Domini nostri Iesu Christi ad Fulgentium (P.L., 65, 442). This treatise must have been composed in 519 or 520.

[21] Ibid.

[22] P.L., 65, 451 f.

[23] Cf. on this subject: F. Woerter, Zur Dogmengeschichte des Semipelagianismus, 3, Die Lehre des Fulgentius von Ruspe.

[24] He died after 485, but several years before 500.

its spirit and main teachings. These teachings were still opposed in Southern Gaul. In 527 or 528, there met at Valence a council chiefly of Burgundian bishops dependent on Vienne . . . there were some opponents of the Bishop of Arles there, who determined to secure the triumph of their views.[25]. . . The danger was averted, at least for the time being. In order to forestall its recurrence, Caesarius turned to the Pope — then Felix IV — whose vicar he was in the transalpine territories, and sent him for approval the nineteen *Capitula Sancti Augustini in urbe Romae transmissa*.[26] The Pope returned this document, after having altered it considerably. Of the nineteen *capitula* eight only were left; the others, and particularly numbers XI–XIV, referring to predestination and reprobation, had been set aside. On the other hand, sixteen new propositions, taken from the *Sententiae* extracted from St. Augustine's writings by St. Prosper, had been added.[27] Caesarius introduced still another,[28] revised those which he had received back from Rome, drew up a sort of conclusion in the shape of a profession of faith, and submitted the whole thing to the bishops gathered at Orange, July 3, 529. Including Caesarius, there were but fourteen of these bishops, who had come for the consecration of a basilica; but, as a result of the papal confirmation, their decisions soon obtained almost as great an authority as that of the most important councils. The substance of these decisions is as follows:[29]

1. Through the sin of Adam, man has been "changed for the worse in both body and soul" (*secundum corpus et animam in deterius commutatus*). 2. By sinning Adam injured not only himself, but all his posterity, to which he transmitted both the death of the body, which is the punishment of sin, and also sin "which is the death of the soul" (*quod mors est animae*). 3. Grace is not granted to prayer; but it is by grace that we are led to pray.[30] 4. God does not wait until we wish to be cleansed from sin; it is the Holy Spirit who produces this desire in us. 5. As the growth of faith, so also the *initium fidei* and the *ipse credulitatis affectus* do not come from nature, but are the work of grace. 6. Mercy is not granted by God to those who, without grace, believe, will, desire, strive, work, watch, apply themselves, ask, seek, and knock; but it is the Holy Spirit who makes us believe, will, etc.,

---

[25] This is the common explanation. Some critics place the Council of Valence after that of Orange.

[26] Mansi, VIII, 722–724. I follow M. Lejay, "Le rôle théologique de Césaire d'Arles, II, Le péché originel et la grâce," in the *Revue d'hist. et de littér. religieuses*, X (1905), p. 250 f. A Namur MS. has ten other *capitula* (Pitra, *Analecta sacra*, V, 161, 162), but Dom Morin thinks these were subsequently added by Caesarius to develop his ideas.

[27] P.L., 45, 1861 or 51, 427. They are sentences 22, 54, 56, 152, 212, 226, 260, 297, 299, 310, 314, 317, 325, 340, 368, 372.

[28] It is number X in the definitions of the Council of Orange.

[29] Cf. the text in P.L., 45, 1785: Mansi, VIII, 712; Hefele-Leclercq, *History of the Councils*, Vol. IV, p. 155 f.

[30] In other words, prayer does not precede grace, but there is a first grace that precedes prayer.

in the right way. Likewise, the *adiutorium gratiae* does not come as an addition to man's humility and obedience, but obedience and humility are themselves a grace of God. 7. "If anyone affirms that he is able by the power of nature, without the illumination and inspiration of the Holy Spirit, to think or choose as is expedient any good pertaining to the salvation of eternal life, or assent to salutary, that is, evangelical preaching . . . he is deceived by a heretical spirit" (*Si quis per naturae vigorem bonum aliquid quod ad salutem pertinet vitae aeternae cogitare ut expedit, aut eligere, sive salutari, id est evangelicae praedicationi consentire posse confirmat absque illustratione et inspiratione Spiritus sancti . . . haeretico fallitur spiritu*). 8. It is false to say that some come to baptism "through mercy" (*misericordia*) and others "through free choice" (*per liberum arbitrium*); for this is tantamount to affirming that free will has not been depraved in all, or at least has not been wounded to such a degree that some can, *sine revelatione* and *per seipsos*, seek the mystery of salvation. (In other words, free will has been wounded in all men to such a degree that not even some can, *sine revelatione Dei* and *per seipsos*, seek the mystery of salvation. . . . 16. Let no one glory in what he has, as though he had not received it, or believe that he has received it because he has read or heard externally the divine word; what we have, we have received from the grace of Jesus Christ. . . . 18. "Since no merits precede grace, a reward is owed to good works if they

are to be done; but grace, which is not owed, precedes them in order that they may be done" (*Nullis meritis gratiam praevenientibus, debetur merces bonis operibus si fiant; sed gratia, quae non debetur, praecedit ut fiant*). 19. Even though human nature were in the state of integrity, in which it was created, it could not preserve itself without divine help; much less, can it, without that help, regain what it has lost. 20. "God does many good things in man which man does not do; but man does no good things which God does not provide in order that man might do them" (*Multa Deus facit in homine bona quae non facit homo: nulla vero facit homo bona quae non Deus praestat ut faciat homo*). . . . 22. "No one has of himself anything except lie and sin" (*Nemo habet de suo nisi mendacium et peccatum*). What man possesses of truth and righteousness, he has from God. . . . 24. The faithful live in Christ like the branch in the vine; hence it is of advantage to them that they abide in Christ, and He in them. 25. "The best gift is to love God. He who though not loved yet loves has Himself already given in order that He might be loved. Having been loved we are still displeasing in order that there might be in us something whereby we might please" (*Prorsus donum est diligere Deum. Ipse ut diligeretur dedit qui non dilectus diligit. Displicentes amati sumus, ut fieret in nobis unde placeremus*).

The profession of faith that followed these *capitula* emphasized their main points, especially the necessity of grace for the beginning of every good work, and added that all those who are baptized "with Christ helping and cooperating" (*Christo auxiliante et cooperante*) can and must "if they would want to work faithfully [fulfil] those things which relate to salvation" (*si fideliter laborare volueruint, quae ad salutem pertinent adimplere*). Then "Not only do we believe that some have been predestined to evil by the divine power, but we also utter an anathema with every detestation on those, if there are any, who wish to believe so great an evil" (*Aliquos vero ad malum divina potestate predestinatos esse non solum non credimus, sed etiam si sunt, qui tantum malum credere velint, cum omni detestatione illis anathema dicimus*).

After the signatures had been obtained, Caesarius applied himself to obtaining the papal confirmation of all that had been done and decreed at Arles, and turned again to Rome. Meanwhile Felix IV had died, and it was his successor, Boniface II, who, on January 25, 531, answered the Bishop of Arles.[31] In his reply, the Pope approves the decisions of the synod and declares its profession of faith "as in agreement with the catholic norms of the Fathers" (*consentanea catholicis Patrum regulis*).[32] He expresses the hope that, through his learning and zeal, Caesarius may succeed in bringing back to truth those who had been led into error.

This hope was not frustrated and,

gradually, peace prevailed in Gaul as regards these vexatious questions. The theologians accepted the teaching of Caesarius and his council. Whilst sanctioning the doctrine of the inability of the unaided will to do good[33] and of the necessity of prevenient grace even for the beginning of faith and the work of salvation, these teachings make no reference to those Augustinian assertions that were the most vulnerable and the most fiercely contested on both sides. Nothing was said on the intrinsic malice of concupiscence; on its agency in the transmission of original sin; on the *massa damnata*; on the lot of unbaptized children; on the nature of grace and its irresistibility; on the twofold delectation and the way in which we are carried away by the one or the other; on the small number of the elect and God's will to save all men. Nothing is said of predestination, except to condemn those who assert that God predestines men to sin and evil. On the other hand, the Council affirms that, by joining their efforts to God's grace, all those who are baptized can and must fulfil their duties. This was equivalent to declaring that grace is never wanting to Christians, and that it does not accomplish everything in them.

Thus, whilst adopting the substance of St. Augustine's views regarding the divine action in man and the economy

---

[31] *Epist.*, I, P.L., 45, 1790 and 65, 31.
[32] The Pope's approval seems to refer particularly to the profession of faith.

[33] This is the most specifically Augustinian feature of the declarations of the Council. Cf. *capitula* 9, 17, 20, and especially 22, which repeat sentences 22, 297, 314, and 325 of St. Prosper. *Capitulum* 22 has given rise to many discussions.

of salvation, the Church did not sanction all his speculations. No doubt, at the end of those protracted controversies, which had lasted more than a century, St. Augustine remained the victor. Pelagius had taught that man, through the energy of his will and the exertions of his nature, is the cause of his own salvation and that God intervened merely to make it easier for him to reach heaven. This meant the confusion of two distinct orders, the natural and the supernatural. Against this error St. Augustine had proclaimed God as the real and the chief cause of our salvation. By original sin, he said, man has been reduced to such a state of helplessness that he cannot by himself accomplish anything good; God must then predestine him gratuitously, prevent, raise and sustain him, and carry him, as it were, into heaven. According to Pelagius supernatural works were wrought by nature; according to St. Augustine, there were no merely natural good works; nature indeed supplied one of the conditions for salvation, i.e., the effort of the will under the action of grace, but grace worked with nature and permeated all its actions.

Now, some thought that the Bishop of Hippo had overrated man's disability, and that his theory of absolute predestination made God responsible for the lot of the reprobates. But these critics also confused the natural and the supernatural orders[34] in teaching, as they did, that free will, which has been wounded but not destroyed, can, without grace, accomplish some good, not only in the moral order, but even in the supernatural and divine order. This was a revival of Pelagianism, and the name of Semipelagianism, although comparatively recent, accurately describes the views of Cassian and Faustus. Their error was correctly sized up and justly condemned by Prosper, Fulgentius, Caesarius, and the Council of Orange. These taught that nature and free will, left to themselves, are incapable of accomplishing and even of beginning the supernatural work of salvation, and that God is the primary and necessary agent who creates in us the first desire of good and brings about its effective accomplishment. Unquestionably, St. Augustine on the whole came out victorious. He is the doctor of grace, and the substance of his teaching has become the Church's. However, the efforts of his opponents have not been useless. By upholding the claims of nature, they forestalled the official adoption of his too rigorous conclusions and thereby aided in preserving the humane character of the Church's teaching.

---

[34] This confusion is clearly noted by Pope Boniface II, *Epist.*, I, 3.

2. Ch. Baumgartner, S.J.,[35] considers Semipelagianism as a necessary but excessive reaction against strict Augustinism, provoked by Augustine's too rigid doctrine of predestination and efficacious grace. He sees the Council of Orange as the consecration of moderate Augustinism, variously repeating two ideas: the initiative of salvation comes from God, and no salutary good is had without grace.

The doctrine of Semipelagianism. Semipelagianism is a reaction that is necessary, on one hand, but excessive, against strict Augustinism. It was provoked by Augustine's too rigid doctrine of predestination and efficacious grace.

In his polemic with the Pelagians he was careful above all to safeguard the absolute gratuity of grace as well as its efficacy, and he stressed only the restricted salvific will of God at the expense of the universal salvific will and sufficient grace. The Semipelagians . . . admitted the necessity of grace for salutary acts and the existence of original sin. They were not wrong in affirming the universal salvific will. But they went too far in their opposition to St. Augustine, especially to his doctrine of predestination in which they saw a source of quietism and discouragement. They thought they could eliminate or neutralize the Augustinian theory by confusing predestination with divine prescience. It is no longer God who predestines men, but ultimately men predestine themselves. God is not, they say, a *personarum acceptor*. He loves all men equally and offers indifferently and equally His graces to all. If, in fact,

He portions out His gifts unequally, this depends uniquely on the different ways in which men desire them, demand them, etc. God waits, in general at least, on the will of men who, by their own powers, realize the *initium fidei* (the desire of salvation, the call for the physician, the prayer to obtain grace, etc.). If men make good use of this good of nature ("initial grace") they receive "salvific grace." In the same way, final perseverance is an affair of man, it is not a special gift of God.

The "initium fidei." The expression comes from the Canticle of Canticles, 4:8, according to the version of the LXX and the Itala. Of this expression Augustine has made a technical term in the theology of grace. Among the Semipelagians the *initium fidei* did not designate only the ensemble of acts that prepared faith, but it was also faith itself, as it existed in its initial state in one newly converted. The *augmentum fidei* or *fides integra* is the completion of faith by the grace and charity that justify. The error of the Semipelagians turned them not only on the preparation for faith but on faith itself. For them the complex ensemble of acts that prepares for justification is in the power of na-

---

[35] Ch. Baumgartner, S.J.: cf. ch. I, n. 12. This excerpt is from *op. cit.*, pp. 79–82.

ture. They admitted that the charity that justifies is impossible without an interior grace.[36]

The Council of Orange. It is the consecration of moderate Augustinism. Two ideas are repeated under all forms: the initiative of salvation comes from God, and no salutary good is had without grace. The council enumerates:

1) the causes of the necessity of grace, original sin, the weakening of the will by original sin (can. 1 and 2, cf. D 378, 396) and the very condition of creature (can. 19);

2) the role of grace before justification. It precedes every effort. From grace come prayer (can. 3), the good will and desire (can. 4), the *initium salutis* (can. 5), every effort toward faith (can. 6), every salutary act (can. 7), every preparation (can. 8 and 12), all merit (can. 18);

3) the role of grace in justification: it repairs (can. 13), it liberates (can. 14), it changes for the better (can. 15), it gives the justice of Christ (can. 21);

4) the role of grace after justification in the just; it is necessary to do good for God (can. 9), to persevere (can. 10), for vows (can. 11), for the great Christian virtues (can. 17), for the life of Christ in us (can. 24), for the love of God (can. 25);

5) the universal role of grace and the extent of its necessity for avoiding evil and for doing all good (can. 9, 20, 22).

Moderation is affirmed for 1) predestination is formally rejected (D 397); there is no predestination to evil; 2) all the baptized have the full and entire power to save themselves, if they will (D 397), thus affirming at the same time their liberty and the grant of sufficient grace to all the baptized.

3. G. C. Berkouwer[37] sees a difference between Augustine and Orange. At Orange Rome rejected so-called Semipelagianism and again honored God's grace. But the council did not accept Augustine's doctrine of predestination and it is silent about the irresistibility of grace and about election. Thus the Church has not accepted the whole of Augustinianism. But what was accepted may rightly be called a great inheritance.

The conflict of grace. Our discussion of some aspects of the conflict concerning grace touches a most essential point in the struggle between Rome and the Reformation. This central issue took its historical form in the Reformation preaching of justification by faith alone. For in this

---

[36] J. Chéné, "Que signifiaient 'initium fidei,' et 'affectus credulitatis' pour les semi-pélagiens?" in RSR, 1948, pp. 566–588.

[37] C. C. Berkouwer is an outstanding present-day Reformed theologian. Some of his publications are *Barthianisme en Katholicisme, Conflict With Rome, General Revelation, The Person of Christ, The Providence of God, Faith and Sanctification.* This excerpt is taken from his book, *The Conflict with Rome* (Philadelphia: The Presbyterian and Reformed Publishing Co., 1958), pp. 76–80.

proclamation the pure understanding of the divine grace in Jesus Christ was at stake. The church and theology did not struggle about a few purely theoretical distinctions as a superficial spectator might think when an abundance of such distinctions are encountered as early as the sixteenth century. But as insight deepens, the religious conflict behind the theological debate appears on many fronts because the issue is the grace of God. Our view of grace is a reflection of our faith seizing hold of this grace and receiving it in gratitude and profound joy. But such reflection is not useless, for on the basis of the Scriptures it may be said that the gospel is *not* after man,[38] and also that in the history of the church the resistance to the gospel of God's sovereign grace has been strong.

Such resistance may appear in the rejection of grace as being too humiliating for the striving, self-sufficient and autonomous man. But there is also a resistance which, while explicitly recognizing God's grace, in actual fact derogates from its sovereign character.

When studying the Roman Catholic doctrine of grace, pride and pharisaism ought to be guarded against. Even though the Reformation correctly interpreted the Biblical message of grace, a Protestant is not thereby exempt from danger. "God resisteth the proud and giveth grace to the humble."[39] Pharisaism, judaism, and the seeking of our own justification have always been a menace to "glorying in the Lord." . . .

The Reformation reproached Rome for having obscured the religious antithesis between sin and grace. Since then Rome has tried to prove that such a reproach was based on ignorance and misunderstanding. The Roman church, too, claims that it wishes to honor God's grace absolutely. It is understandable that — in the church — people are extremely sensitive to such a reproach. For when reflecting on God's grace and mercy we are concerned with the very heart of religion. And who would be ready to admit that he is derogating from the sovereign and all-sufficient character of divine grace? It is largely owing to this fact that the struggle for grace has been so sharp and urgent. It has been asked, "When will this clamor about the Catholics being Pelagians cease"?[40]

Not only the charge of Pelagianism, but that of semi-Pelagianism is characterized by Rome as an "old Protestant grievance founded in ignorance and misconception." Rome still endorses the condemnation of Pelagianism at the synod of Carthage in 418.[41] In contrast to the Pelagian view, God's sovereignty seems to be perfectly safe with Rome. The more so as at Orange in 529 Rome also rejected so-called semi-Pelagianism and again honoured God's grace. Naturally this condemnation of semi-Pelagianism plays an important part in Roman Catholic polemics and defense. To the frequent charge that Rome went astray into

---

[38] Gal 1:11.
[39] 1 Pt 5:5.

[40] G. Brom, *Gesprek,* p. 273.
[41] Denz. 227.

semi-Pelagianism, Piket, e.g., observes that the church solemnly condemned all semi-Pelagianism at the Council of Trent.[42]

These dogma-historical notes really contain the whole problem of grace.

How is it possible that in spite of all this the accusation crops up again and again? Bavinck held that although semi-Pelagianism had been condemned by Rome, it reappeared in "a round-about way."[43] In such reproaches the Council of Orange in 529 is not overlooked. This council is even a constantly recurring subject in the discussion. Bavinck points out that through the canons of Orange — sanctioned by Boniface II — it became the doctrine of the church that "the entire man has been depraved by Adam's sin, and that both *initium* and *augmentum fidei*[44] are not due to ourselves but to the grace of God."[45] He adds: "Since then the *gratia interna praeveniens*[46] was taught by all." Bavinck asks whether by this *gratia praeveniens* Rome understands something more than the outward call of the gospel, for the description of this grace is sometimes very weak. But Bavinck admits that Rome acknowl-

edges that it includes an influence on the understanding and the will.[47] His final conclusion is that "Orange" shows some "indecision," which becomes manifest later on in the struggle of Gottschalk.[48]

Some "indecision" in the canons of Orange is frequently evidenced by the fact that this council did not accept and profess Augustine's doctrine of predestination. This difference between Augustine and Orange is acknowledged by Rome. Sometimes Orange is even honored for having avoided and for having protected the the church against the onesidedness and specific peculiarities of the church-father.[49]

A century after Augustine's death, Orange was almost completely silent about election, and the "doctrine" that anybody could be predestinated by God to do evil was anathematized.[50]

The Scriptural doctrine of election cannot be more seriously mutilated than by reducing it to a deterministic and fatalistic doctrine. Yet the restriction to the above-mentioned antithetical pronouncement of Orange is typical after Augustine. The council mentions the *help* and *cooperation* given by Christ to the baptized in order that

---

[42] Dr. Piket, in *Het Schild*, February, 1941, in a remark on my *Barthianisme en Katholicisme* in which I had written that Rome continued in the way of semi-Pelagianism.

[43] H. Bavinck, *Geref. Dogmatiek*, III, p. 509; cf. A. G. Honig, *Handboek Dogmatiek* (1938) who says that in the church "semi-Pelagianism gradually triumphed" (p. 530).

[44] The beginning and the increase of faith.

[45] Bavinck, *Dogmatiek*, III, p. 507.

[46] "Preceding internal grace."

[47] Bavinck, *Dogmatiek*, III, p. 508: "The synod of Orange spoke of a *Sancti Spiritus infusio et operatio in nobis*."

[48] *Ibid.*, II, p. 313.

[49] J. van Ginneken, *De Ziel van Augustinus en haar God* (1930), p. 65. Cf. Dr. A. Bruining, *Verz. Stud.*, I, p. 260 ff.

[50] "*Aliquos vero ad malum divina potestate praedestinatos esse, non solum non credimus, sed etiam si sunt, qui tantum mali credere velint, cum omni detestatione illis anathema dicimus*" (Denz. 397).

they shall attain to salvation, if they are willing to work.[51] In connection with the admitted "correction" of Augustine[52] there is sufficient reason to ask if Rome has really honored God's sovereign grace. The question cannot be fully decided by referring to the resolutions of the Council of Orange.

The canons of Orange quote a number of texts which had a considerable influence on the thought of Rome's most radical opponents, especially with respect to the doctrine of grace.[53] . . . These quotations serve to lay strong stress on the work of God in the salvation of man. Any view is rejected that wishes to explain the initial stage or the increase of faith as something in us *naturaliter*.[54] Nothing can be done without the grace of God. . . . Everything circles around the grace and mercy of God. . . . The free will has been weakened[55] and depraved. It needs recovery, and such recovery is brought about by a divine act in baptism.[56] And if anyone should point out that the word "weakened" also played an important part in semi-Pelagian-

ism,[57] Rome answers that such a weakening means that nobody can love God as he should, or believe in God, or do good, without the previous grace of God's mercy.[58]

For all these reasons Rome feels entitled to state that full justice is done to the absolute priority of God's grace in the Roman church, that the divine grace has been confirmed by Paul and John, and that therefore the Reformers' criticism of the Roman doctrine is nothing but "beating the air."

In his discussion of the resolutions of Orange, Seeberg points out that they are silent about the irresistibility of grace as well as about election. So the church has not accepted the whole of Augustinianism. But what was accepted may rightly be called a great inheritance. All kinds of emphases found in Augustine re-appear in Orange, although not "all tendencies to rely on justification by works that were present in the Western system were suppressed." But it is of decisive importance to know whether those many Biblical quotations from John and Paul could really *function*, or whether they have lost a great part of their *evangelical* force. There is a close connection between this loss and the

---

[51] *"Christo auxiliante et cooperante"* and *"si fideliter laborare voluerint"* (Denz. 397).

[52] Cf. Kardinal de Jong, *Handboek der Kerkgeschiedenis*, I (1947), p. 280, on Orange: "Thus the essential part of the doctrine of grace defended by Augustine against the Pelagians is definitively approved of; no pronouncement is made concerning the above-mentioned private aspects of his speculation and the church has, therefore, never taken over the latter."

[53] Denz. 373, 374, 375.

[54] *"Naturaliter nobis inesse"* (Denz. 375).

[55] *"Infirmatum"* (Denz. 378, 383).

[56] Denz. 383.

[57] The semi-Pelagians rejected the Pelagian construction but refused to go any further than an *infirmitas liberi arbitrii* (R. Seeberg, *Dogmengeschichte*, II, p. 571 ff.). By the weakening of free will grace becomes *cooperans* (cooperating grace).

[58] *"Ut nullus postea diligere Deum sicut oportuit, aut credere in Deum aut operari propter Deum quod bonum est, possit, nisi eum gratia misericordiae praevenerit"* (Denz. 396).

indecision that Bavinck thought he noticed in Orange.

In the midst of the splendid words quoted from the Bible rises the problem of Orange: the relation between God's sovereign grace and the weakened freedom of the will. This problem is posited as a relation between "causes" and "effects." But grace as a divine favor, as justification and acquittal, is not dealt with. The result is that a vacuum arose which in the course of doctrinal development was to assume a special significance, and Biblical expressions were to acquire a new sound in the Reformation.

4. **H. Rondet, S.J.,[59] considers the council a document of extreme importance for the history of dogma and the theology of grace, but one that still poses some historical problems. With it Augustinism has taken a great step, but with a certain reserve in the question of predestination.**

The Semipelagian controversy ended six or seven years later, thanks to a man who had the opportunity of being both a student of the monks of Lerins and a great reader of Augustine, Caesarius of Arles.[60] At the council of Orange in 529 he reduced the Semipelagian opposition by bringing about the consecration of a moderate Augustinism that he thought was Augustine's own. The essential dependence of man on grace, even for the beginning of salvation, became a dogma of faith.[61] Against the Semipelagians it was affirmed that there are not two classes of men, of whom one comes to salvation by the efficacy of an irresistible grace and the other by the will alone; but whoever is saved, is saved by grace.[62] Grace precedes liberty and accompanies it without ceasing, operating both the willing and the doing.[63] Without its perpetual action, no perseverance is possible.[64]

All this is an aspect of St. Paul's doctrine which, thanks to St. Augustine, is now made manifest. But the council, more clearly than the Indiculus, rejects a predestinarian interpretation of Augustinism and anathematizes all who teach that certain men are predestined to evil. In advance it condemns Jansenius by affirming that the just always have the grace necessary to persevere (D 397).

The second council of Orange is then a document of extreme importance for the history of dogma and the theology of grace. This was, however, only a small provincial council of 14 bishops, including Caesarius. But thanks to him its decisions received the approbation of Rome.

Still the interpretation of this capital document remains delicate. For it

[59] H. Rondet, S.J.: cf. ch. III, n. 1. This excerpt is from *op. cit.*, pp. 156–160.
[60] P. LeJay, "Le rôle théologique de Césaire d'Arles," in *Revue d'hist. et de littér. religieuse*, 1905 pp. 217–266. — Id., "Césaire d'Arles," DTC, t. II, col. 2168–2185.
[61] Can. 3 (Denz., *Enchirid.*, n. 373 f.).
[62] Can. 8 (Denz. n. 378).
[63] Can. 9 (Denz. n. 379).
[64] Can. 10 (Denz. n. 380).

poses some historical problems on which depend the value accorded to the anathemas which the text contains. . . . However, we see that what is put in relief is above all the necessity of prevenient grace for the beginning of salvation.[65] Augustinism has taken a great step. Doubtless this progress is accompanied by a certain reserve in the question of predestination[66] but more and more occidental theology will accept as its own the doctrine of De praedestinatione sanctorum. If Augustine is corrected, this will be done in another way.

5. F. Cayré, A.A.,[67] sees Augustinism triumphant at Orange. The points that were affirmed constitute the essence of Augustinian teaching in this matter, but fairly numerous elements of the Augustinian system were left in the shade.

Augustinism was triumphant at Orange: the existence of original sin, the moral weakening of fallen man, the necessity of grace for all supernatural good were strongly affirmed, and these points constitute the essence of Augustinian teaching in this matter. By the very fact, Semipelagianism was definitely rejected in Catholic instruction. Nevertheless fairly numerous elements of the Augustinian system were left in the shade.[68] Thus with regard to original sin, no reference was made either to the evil of concupiscence, or its role in the transmission of the first fault, or the *massa damnata*, or the damnation of unbaptized children. Similarly nothing was said of the infallible efficacy of grace, or double delectation, or the number of the elect and God's will to save all men. Predestination to evil was rejected but nothing positive was affirmed. But these omissions were after all only secondary and may be deduced from the points stated above, which contain all the essentials.

It would be a mistake to think however that the matters neglected at Orange have been eliminated in Catholic theology. Two points alone are probably rejected by all at the present time; the part played by concupiscence as such in the transmission of original sin, and the damnation of children on account of this sin. Some points indeed were adopted by a later council: St. Augustine was echoed at Trent when it was declared that concupiscence may be called "sin," if reference is made only to its historical cause or its effects.[69] The *massa damnata* represents the Catholic doc-

---

[65] The letter of approbation of Boniface II applies here formally.

[66] DB, n. 397.

[67] F. Cayré, A.A.: cf. ch. VI, n. 116. This excerpt is from *op. cit.*, II, pp. 206–207.

[68] See J. Tixeront, *Hist. Dogm.*, III, pp. 310–312.

[69] "Peccatum vocatur, non utique quia peccatum est, sed quia ex peccato facta est," says St. Augustine, *Cont. 2 Ep. Pelag.*, Bk. 1, ch. xiii, 27. It is therefore exaggerated to say that he teaches the intrinsic evil of concupiscence.

trine of the universality of original sin. The efficacy of grace is also conceived in the same sense as in St. Augustine by several schools of theology, which reject the theory of double delectation, though only in the Jansenist sense. As regards God's will to save all, there has been merely a change of viewpoint: recent theologians insist less on God's will as manifested in its ultimate effects, as St. Augustine preferred to do, than on the will of God considered in its effects as a whole. Since nothing at all positive is known about the number of the saved, opinion has freely covered a wide field. Although the doctrine of predestination had never been explicitly defined, it is everywhere admitted by Catholic theologians in the very meaning defended by St. Augustine, i.e.,

the absolute gratuity of predestination to grace and of total predestination (to grace and glory).

These observations should suffice to show how subjective and groundless is Loof's strange assertion: "This history of Roman Catholicism is the history of the gradual elimination of Augustinism."[70] What has really been eliminated is Pelagianism and Semipelagianism. Moreover, there was another doctrine which wholly perverted the Augustinian teaching on grace and predestination; that of salvation by faith without works; and this was speedily rejected by St. Augustine himself. It appeared again only in the sixteenth century, sponsored by the self-styled disciples of Augustine.

[70] Loofs, *Leitfaden zum Studium der Dogmengeschichte*, 3 ed., p. 196.

VIII

GRACE IN CATHOLIC THEOLOGY BEFORE TRENT

1. Frank Gavin[1] sees the conception of grace in the Middle Ages not as a creation but as an inheritance from Tertullian via St. Augustine, with its essential notes much further back in primitive Christianity. Albert the Great is a fair example of the nexus between the doctrine of grace and all the other elements of the general outlook of medieval Catholicism. The assimilation of Aristotelianism entailed a more metaphysical and philosophical discussion of grace. St. Thomas had received much from Albert when he carried on the systematization of theology in his *Summa*.

---

[1] Rev. Frank Gavin, Ph.D., Th.D., was professor of ecclesiastical history, General Theological Seminary, New York, in 1931. This excerpt is taken from his article, "The Medieval and Modern Roman Conceptions of Grace," in *The Doctrine of Grace*, ed. W. T. Whitley (London: SCM Press, 1931), pp. 134–136, 144–149.

THE conception of grace in the Latin thought of the Middle Ages is an inheritance, not a creation. If it is ultimately derivable from Tertullian via St. Augustine, its essential notes lie much farther back in primitive Christianity.

It might be well at the outset to see what alternative meanings might be comprised within the term itself:[2] (1) favour, elicited by man from God, and (2) favours as gifts (i.e., the divine disposition manwards, goodwill towards men), therefore showered by God upon man; (3) the love of God in action manwards; (4) God in Christ imparting Himself to man; (5) a certain secret and mysterious quality, often conceived quite apart from personal relationships; (6) love; (7) supernatural knowledge; (8) the Holy Spirit. None of these is necessarily exclusive, and some involve aspects of others. From varying points of view grace may be the actual infusion of the Holy Spirit Himself into the soul (a kind of Real Presence), or it may mean the sharing of a power of God — whether as wisdom, illumination, dynamic force, or the like.[3]

At every point in any attempted discussion of the subject, it must not be overlooked that the discussion of grace — as of any separate element of Catholic theology — is, as it were, a text apart from its context. The nexus of Catholic doctrine is an organic whole, and each part has its bonds integrally connecting it with all the rest. In short, the conception of grace is essentially bound up with the idea of God, His nature and attributes; the Incarnation, Person and work of Christ; the Atonement; the Doctrine of the Church and the Sacraments; and the Doctrine of the Last Things. On its subjective, as distinguished from its objective side, the doctrine of grace bears directly upon the nature, destiny, fall, and rehabilitation of man, and upon ethics, moral theology, and eternal life. . . . In general, one might say of the scholastic outlook — especially as it came to be developed in the great master — that the doctrine of grace interrelated itself at every point with philosophy (as metaphysics and cosmology), with theology (dogmatic, ascetical and mystical), and with practice (both devotional and ascetic, corporate and individual, as worship and ethics). As a fair example of the nexus between the doctrine of grace and all the other elements of the general outlook of Medieval Catholicism. Doms' acute study of *Die Gnadenlehre des seligen Albertus Magnus*[4] may be drawn upon to illuminate the ramifications of the subject as treated by developed scholastic thought.

Albert the Great. The basic groundwork of the whole outlook of

---

[2] "The new life by which the Christian becomes a son of God; in other words, sanctifying grace" (cf. 1 Pt., v. 12), in G. H. Joyce, *The Catholic Doctrine of Grace* (London, 1920), p. 21.

[3] Cf. Van der Meersch, "Grâce," in *Dictionnaire de théologie catholique*, VI (Paris, 1920), col. 1557: "The theologians define grace considered in general: a supernatural gift (or the ensemble of supernatural gifts) given by God to a creature endowed with intelligence in view of eternal salvation."

[4] Breslau, 1929.

Albert is in his doctrine of Creation: all creaturedom strives for such fellowship with God as it, by the nature of each individual creature, is capable of attaining. Creaturedom strives to surmount the temporal and changing and ever to secure its permanent self-realization in the Infinite Creator.[5] Albert's sources are, in this respect, St. Augustine and Neo-platonism (possibly Boethian).

Since all natural things tend to strive toward that by which their several natures realise fulfilment, man's nature demands the full enjoyment of God. With less than God man cannot be content, but to attain Him he stands in need of special assistance. While God stands in the same relation to all things whatever, all things do not so stand in relation to Him (*Deus aequaliter se habet ad omnia sed non omnia aequaliter ad ipsum*). Perfection and conservation are achievable in the case of man only through a God-manward relationship which is grace: "The will of a rational creature is not perfectly turned toward God save by grace."[6]

So grace may be considered as a super-added "accident" seen as movement Godward (stimulated by Him); but viewed as to its form (the integrity of the human self), as imitation of God, life, light, perfection, cleansing, beauty, etc. . . . Commenting on the famous phrase of St. Augustine, Albert says: "He has not made us such as to be able to ascend to Him of ourselves, but only by the help of His grace. Hence it is needed that grace be in us as something received from God."[7]

The philosophical-theological basis of his whole doctrine of grace rests in the fact of the relationship between a finite personal creature and the infinite and personal Creator. Such a relationship — of person to Person — can only be brought about by some alteration in the essential relations between man and God: no mere empowering of the natural faculties would suffice by reinforcing them to achieve fellowship with God. "That mysterious spiritual 'something' which accomplished this change is grace, and the original factor is none other than God Himself. Hence we arrive at the conception of *gratia creata* as the medium between God and the human spirit for the end of personal intercourse of man as personal with God as Person, i.e., insofar as He is a self-contained Being . . . entirely other than the world." This perfection of human personality through grace gives man the capacity for that participation in God's own life which God vouchsafes Him in His loving self-sharing with man.[8]

The assimilation of Aristotelianism by the later Scholastics entailed a more metaphysical and philosophical discussion of grace. St. Thomas had received much from Albert when he carried on

---

[5] "*Inclinatio uniuscujusque rei naturalis in id quod debetur ei secundum naturam*" (S. de creat., II, quest. 68a, 1 sol; cf. Schneider, "Die Psychologie Alberts d. Gr.," in *Beiträge zur Geschichte der Philosophie des Mittelalters*, Bd. II, 1913, p. 278 ff.).

[6] *Sum. Theol.*, I, q. 70, m. 4 ad 5.

[7] *Ibid.*, II, q. 98, m. 1 ad 4.

[8] Cf. Doms, *op. cit.*, pp. 285–286 ff.

the systematisation of theology in his *Summa*. Grace is both the effect of, and itself is, God's eternal love for man: there are two personal factors — the omnipotent and all-loving Creator as giver, and the yearning and striving human creature as co-operating recipient.[9] Grace is a gift from God to man, a "somewhat" coming from His love, "infused" (for lack of better symbolic language to describe its advent) and stimulative of the faculties of the human spirit which as means both constitute and strive for kinship with God.[10] The characteristic Thomist conception of grace is frequently apparent: "The gift of grace is naught else than a kind of participation in the Divine Nature."[11] This effluence is operative also in the realm of that pre-eminent activity of God and man which is so central in the Thomist outlook — the intellect. For the knowledge of any truth man stands in need of God's aid; the communication of supernatural knowledge is by "the light of grace superadded to nature."[12]

But what should be said of this root conception of grace whether as dynamic illumination or as "participation in the Divine Nature"? Harnack, in his criticism of the point of view of Scholasticism, writes as follows: "These theologians, when they think of God, look not to the heart of the Father Almighty but to an inscrutable Being which, since it created the world out of nothing, is also the source whence emanate inexhaustible forces for knowledge, betterment, and essential transformation. And when they think of themselves it is not of the central focus of human selfhood, the spirit, which is so free and lofty that it cannot content itself with even the most magnificent gifts but must needs hold converse with a Divine Person. They taught *God and Grace* instead of: Confident faith in God and thereupon fellowship with Him who is Love."[13]

As this passage (and many others are like it) expresses a criticism of the medieval doctrine which has become a conviction in many hearts, attention may here be drawn to the discussion which Harnack's *Lehrbuch* and his *Dogmengeschichte* elicited.[14]

---

[9] "But on last analysis it is God who moves the creature both to its natural and supernatural destinies"; cf. J. E. O'Mahony, *The Desire of God in the Philosophy of Thomas Aquinas* (Cork, 1930).

[10] Cf. "*quiddam supernaturale in homine a Deo proveniens . . . gratia (dicitur) ipsa aeterna Dei dilectio . . . infundit aliquas . . . qualitates supernaturales secundum quas suaviter et prompte ab ipso moveatur ad bonum aeternum consequendum,*" *Sum. theol.*, I–II, q. 110, art. 1 and 2.

[11] "*Donum gratiae nihil aliud est quam quaedam participatio divinae naturae*" (cf. 2 Pt 1:4), in the context: "*solus Deus deificet, communicando consortium divinae naturae per quandam similitudinis participationem,*" in *Sum. theol.*, I–II, q. 112, a. 1; q. 110, 3, 4; q. 113, 9; q. 114, 3; II–II, q. 19, 7; III, q. 2, 10 ad 1, q. 3, 4 ad 5.

[12] "*Lumen gratiae est naturae superadditum,*" *Sum. theol.*, I–II, q. 109, art. 1.

[13] *Dogmengeschichte*, pp. 415–416.

[14] Cf. M. Notton, *Harnack und Thomas von Aquin* (Paderborn, 1906). The essay of Karl Heim, *Das Wesen der Gnade und ihr Verhältnis zu den natürlichen Funktionen des Menschen bei Alexander Halesius* (Leipzig, 1907), brings the criticism of the fundamental ideas to the his-

Roughly speaking, the answer of the defenders of the scholastic position today [1931] may be found in such expositions as those of Doms.[15] Divergent outlooks on God, man, their relationships, on sin, salvation, and the created universe are ultimately responsible for the difficulties experienced by Protestants in understanding the Catholic tradition with sympathy and even with insight. That this is the case is most evident in the repeatedly-urged indictment of "magic" brought against Catholic sacramentalism, as, e.g., by Harnack (D.G., p. 416). Until presuppositions shall have been brought out clearly into conscious recognition, and hidden preconceptions and premises, as well of thought as of feelings, discerned and lucidly objectified by analysis and exposition, it will be impossible to reach that measure of mutual understanding by which alone progress can be achieved. . . .

2. **F. Cayré, A.A.,[16] sees in St. Bonaventure a true disciple of St. Augustine, a mystic, who in his doctrinal explanations has recourse to the nobler enlightenment of the gifts of the Holy Spirit. Bonaventure's work was the term of two centuries of intense Christian thought and furnishes a complete, powerful, and homogeneous synthesis and a magnificent interpretation of Augustine's teaching.**

Of all the doctors who lived after the period of the Fathers, St. Bonaventure and St. Thomas undoubtedly occupy the first rank. Both were outstanding as theologians. St. Bonaventure, unlike St. Thomas, did not compose a *Summa theologica,* but he commented on the *Book of the Sentences,* and the depth and penetration of this work makes it a model of its kind. Though the method he adopted constrained him to build upon the accepted framework of the time, Bonaventure's genius is revealed in many admirable and personal opinions, while his kindly and affectionate nature is reflected in the moving passages he wrote as a worthy son of St. Francis. . . .

The Seraphic doctor . . . codified, as it were, though not in its final form,[17] *Franciscan Augustinism.* There is no doubt that his school, though not the sole exponent of the Augustinian spirit, embodied it in a very eminent degree. The doctrinal corpus of St.

torical field, and is dealt with most recently by Doms, *Gnadenlehre des seligen Albertus Magnus* (Breslau, 1929), p. 130 ff. R. Seeberg, *Die Theologie des Johannes Duns Scotus* (1900), represents another appreciative critique, from the Protestant side, of a typical scholastic Father of the non-Thomist tradition. Perhaps the best answer to the criticism of the scholastic point of view can be obtained by a searching restatement of its chief premises. Dr. J. E. O'Mahony's study (*The Desire of God in the Philosophy of St. Thomas Aquinas,* Cork, 1930) is an example of this badly needed treatment.

[15] Cf. *op. cit.,* p. 285 ff.

[16] Cf. ch. VI, n. 116. This excerpt from *op. cit.,* II, pp. 506, 509, 519–520.

[17] St. Bonaventure's synthesis was fairly radically revised by Duns Scotus.

Bonaventure does no more than reproduce the master's teaching on many points, while in a number of others it transcends it. His clarification and completion of the profound though summary data of the Bishop of Hippo are mainly found in philosophy. He introduces a methodical classification that is occasionally astoundingly subtle. Whatever he found to serve his purpose in Aristotle he borrowed without scruple;[18] he was influenced by Jewish and Arabian philosophers[19] and still more by Dionysius the Areopagite. He reaped the harvest of two centuries of intense and abundant Christian thought, and his work, which represents its term, furnishes a complete, powerful, and homogeneous synthesis. Though it may not, perhaps, be entirely identified with St. Augustine's teaching, in spite of the spirit that wholly imbues it, it nevertheless constitutes a magnificent interpretation. Others may be found equally satisfying, but none so fine.[20] . . .

The *grace* that is given to us by Christ in the sacraments, is the Holy Spirit Himself, the Gift pre-eminent, and also a created reality that takes form in the soul[21] and which derives from the Holy Spirit as the light comes from the sun. St. Bonaventure is fond of comparing with light the grace that makes us like to God. He considers that it is inherent not in the substance of the soul alone, but in the substance together with its faculties.[22] Grace is a likeness of God, for the purpose of a greater and supernatural assimilation to God, and finally, for union with Him.

Its first effect is to justify man and make him pleasing to God; hence the name *gratia gratum faciens* usually given to sanctifying grace.[23] Its function is to restore to man in this world, at least some measure of the perfect righteousness he has lost through sin and which was characterized by the easy accomplishment of the noblest activities of the soul; and on the other effectively submit him to God. A true ordination of the faculties should thus be established in order to produce actions that will become more and more perfect: these may be termed, first, intermediary, and final. On this basis, in the order of supernatural knowledge we may distinguish *credere, intelligere, videre intellecta.* In order

---

[18] I.e., theory of the two intellects, very current at this period.

[19] For instance, the teaching of the hylomorphic composition of spiritual substances is due to Avicebron, though Bonaventure attempts to ascribe it to Augustine.

[20] The very complexity of Augustine's work renders it refractory of inclusion in a single synthesis.

[21] *In II Sent.,* D. xxxi, a. 1, q. 1–3. St. Bonaventure thus differs from Lombard on this point.

[22] The soul's faculties, in his teaching, are not so clearly distinguished from the soul's essence as in St. Thomas. The same is to be said of sanctifying grace and the virtues.

[23] St. Bonaventure gives to *actual grace* the name of *gratia gratis data* (in *II Sent.,* D. xxviii, a. 2, q. 1), an expression that also means an exceptional grace given for the benefit of others. The expression "actual grace" is current mainly from the time of the Council of Trent, and was little used by the scholastics; they paid more attention to sanctifying grace, unlike St. Augustine. St. Thomas prefers the expressions *"motio," "auxilium."*

to set up this hierarchy both in the faculties and their actions, grace must be diversified in *virtues* that rectify, *gifts* that excite and *beatitudes* that make perfect.[24]

Mystical graces. St. Bonaventure connects the mystical graces with the gifts, especially with that of wisdom, with regard to what is essential in them, particularly that "experimental knowledge of God"[25] or contemplation. "The gift of wisdom concerns the knowledge of supernatural truths according to eternal reasons, but inasmuch as these reasons lead to the taste and experience of the divine suavity."[26] The last chapter of the *Itinerarium* magnificently describes this contemplation considered in its most perfect expression. It is, of course, inferior to the beatific vision[27] since the divine essence cannot be perceived in this life.[28] But it is superior to the most profound knowledge of God that may be obtained in the ordinary human way; not only that which proceeds from the transcendent ideas of truth and goodness[29] for in all these modes human activity preponderates. Though it is not denied that God in contemplation (*contuitus*) is *seen with* the first ideas that constitute the light of

the mind, He is seen independently of our reflective operations, by means of the activity of the Holy Spirit who arrests all human operation; raising man in an ineffable manner above himself, the Holy Spirit brings him into contact with God.

Here we must speak of taste, of experience and touch rather than of vision in the true meaning of the term. Knowledge certainly plays some little part[30] for at the outset the act of wisdom is intellectual before achieving its end in feeling and a certain savouring. This is the essence of contemplation.[31] That which St. Bonaventure describes is wholly passive and infused. He terms it *excessus*, a kind of ecstasy, which, however, he regards in no way as extraordinary.[32] He describes only the essential act, not perhaps in its highest but certainly in its most absorbing manifestation;[33] he was nevertheless aware that wisdom may act

---

[24] See *Breviloq.*, V, c. iv. Gifts and beatitudes thus characterize perfection, produced by the former and constituted or manifested by the latter.

[25] In *III Sent.*, D. xxxv, a. 1, q. 1, concl.

[26] *Ibid.*, q. 3, ad 1.

[27] Although these acts are termed "beatitudes."

[28] With the exception of a most extraordinary favor, vouchsafed perhaps to St. Paul.

[29] Cf. Chaps. i–iv of the *Itinerarium*.

[30] A relative light, not without its obscurity from other standpoints. *Itiner.*, vii.

[31] In *II Sent.*, D. xxxv, a. 1, q. 1, concl. St. Thomas says, on the contrary, that the act of the gift of wisdom "*causam quidem habet in voluntate, scilicet caritatem, sed essentiam habet in intellectu.*" *Sum. theol.*, II–II, q. 45, a. 2. St. Thomas apparently speaks from a philosophical standpoint, while St. Bonaventure bases himself on experimental data.

[32] Not only does he not consider it rash to aspire thereto, but as a true son of St. Francis he encourages fervent souls to achieve it. See E. Gilson, *La philosophie de S. Bonaventure* (Paris, 1924) (Etud. phil. med. iv), pp. 69–98. [English trans. *The Philosophy of St. Bonaventure* (New York: Sheed & Ward, 1946).]

[33] For St. Theresa, the highest manifestation of wisdom, in the viith Mansion, does not usually occur with such vehemence.

within the soul in a less superhuman manner, first in the saints, apart from these moments of intense grace, and also in virtuous souls who prepare themselves for it, according to the counsel of the blessed doctor who imposes on them this preparation. It will be obvious that all his ascetic teaching and even his moral theology find their justification in his mysticism.

3. H. Rondet, S.J.,[34] treats St. Anselm and Abelard, Peter Lombard and St. Thomas, as well as the introduction of Aristotelian ideas into Latin theology and the synthesis and systematization that resulted. He sees St. Thomas as more attentive to the ontology of justification than to the psychology of its preparation. He regards the Thomist synthesis as the Augustinian synthesis rethought in function of a doctrine of the absolute supernatural and the presence of the Holy Spirit in souls. It would be a long time before this eminently catholic synthesis, in which so many traditional elements are assembled, unified and assimilated, would be fully comprehended.

When we pass from St. Augustine we find ourselves apparently in an altogether new world. Not only the method of exposition, but even the spirit in which questions are treated, seems to be different. . . . But we must not rely on appearances. Augustine remains the uncontested master of these learned constructions. From the 5th to the 13th century he remains the great spiritual educator of the Occident. . . . Whether one deals with the Trinity, or creation, or the angels, or the Church, or the sacraments or the last end, everywhere everyone invokes Augustine. This is particularly true in the questions of sin, of grace and of predestination.[35]

St. Anselm. A better Augustinian than the most fervent disciples of Augustine who preceded him, St. Anselm studies the question of the relations between grace and liberty and seeks to define liberty: "freedom of choice is the power of serving right will for the sake of right will itself" (*libertas arbitrii est potestas servandi rectitudinem voluntatis propter ipsam rectitudinem*).[36] He takes up the problem of perseverance and the redoubtable question of predestination, and recalls that for God there is neither past nor future but only an eternal present.[37] In his *Meditations* Anselm speaks admirably of the necessity of grace, and Augustinian theses permeate his thought. But he insists strongly on free

[34] Cf. ch. III, n. 1. This excerpt is taken from *op. cit.*, pp. 180–199, 200–234.

[35] M. Gilson remarks somewhere that when one studies an author of the middle age and he seems to bring up a new idea one must always verify if it be not in Augustine.

[36] *De libero arbitrio*, 3, P.L., 158, 494 A.

[37] *De casu diaboli*, 2, P.L., 158, 329 C; *De concordia praescientiae, praedestinationis et gratiae cum libero arbitrio*, II, 2, P.L., 158, 520 B.

will, and in speaking of it is closer to
the Augustine of the anti-Manichean
writings than to the author of *De Correptione et gratia.* However he still remains in the spirit of Augustine when
he attributes to grace all that he comes
to lay open by his reflections.[38] The
Augustinism of Anselm is then a new
theology which at first finds only an
audience of elite spirits. The others are
content, as was Fulgentius . . . to repeat the bishop of Hippo. . . .

But we must make an exception
for two great spirits that confront each
other in the 12th century, Abelard
and St. Bernard. Bernard hardly gets a
mention in theological manuals, but
Protestant historians of dogma give him
an important place. And they are right.
But in spite of their secret desire to
show in Bernard a precursor of Luther,
they must recognize that the great
monk was authentically Catholic.[39]
Bernard is as it were the religious
conscience of his epoch, he is a new
Augustine. Augustine in his *Confessions* speaks of Christ in unforgettable
terms, but his theology was not Christocentric.[40] Bernard's work however, as

his entire life, is wholly impregnated
with devotion to the Incarnate Word.[41]
Beyond Augustine, it is rather Origen
and Ignatius of Antioch that we find
in the monk of the 12th century. His
voice will resound down the centuries
even if his influence on strict theology
is apparently only mediocre.

Abelard. Abelard is the living antithesis of Bernard. Whatever they may
say of him, he is not a rationalist. He
looks to Christ and to St. Paul and
proclaims himself a son of the
Church.[42] But in his enthusiasm for
dialectic he went too far. . . . Between
him and Bernard conflict was inevitable. Abelard was condemned in 1140
but the council of Sens was concerned
less with a system than with a dangerous tendency.[43]

in him there is a religious attitude that
implies a revolution or if you prefer a
deepening of the Augustinian theology.
This Christocentric piety will be that of
Luther, but also of the modern age and
today it still looks for its theologians. . . .

[38] *Meditationes,* 18, P.L., 158, 800 B;
De concordia, 14, P.L., 158, 540–542.

[39] A. von Harnack, *Lehrbuch der Dogmengeschichte,* t. III, pp. 342–344; R.
Seeberg, *Lehrbuch der Dogmengeschichte,*
t. III, 1930, pp. 132–140.

[40] *Confess.,* VII, 9, P.L., 32, 741. Augustine sees in Christ especially the mediator,
the man Christ Jesus (1 Tim 2:5) who
brings fallen man back toward his principle. Devotion to Christ, indispensable for
a Christian, remains so to speak secondary,
a consequence of sin. M. Gilson (*La théologie mystique de saint Bernard,* 1934,
pp. 102–103) takes up the same trait in
St. Bernard. However it seems to me that

[41] *In Cant.,* XV, 6, P.L., 183, 847A.
Cf. P. Pourrat, *La spiritualité chrétienne,*
t. II, 1921, pp. 60–76; L. De Grandmaison,
Jésus-Christ, t. II, pp. 643–645.

[42] *Epist.,* 17, P.L., 178, 375. Cf. E. Portalié, "Abélard," DTC, t. I, col. 41; J.
De Ghellinck, *Le mouvement théologique
du XIIᵉ siècle,* 1913, p. 103. E contra, A.
von Harnack, *Précis de l'histoire des
dogmes,* p. 328.

[43] On the Roman approbation and the
number of *capitula,* cf. J. Rivière, *Recherches de théologie ancienne et mediévale,*
1933, pp. 5–22; E. Vacandard, *Saint Bernard,* 1927, t. II, pp. 118–180; P. Lasserre,
"Un conflit religieux au XII siècle, Abélard
et Saint Bernard"; G. Delagneau, "Le
concile de Sens de 1140, Abélard et Saint
Bernard," in *Revue apologetique,* 1931,
pp. 385–408; E. Gilson, *La philosophie au
moyen âge,* 2 ed., 1944, pp. 278–296; J. E.
Sikes, *Peter Abaelard,* 1932.

Abelard was condemned . . . for maintaining that free will, by itself and without grace, can do some good (D 725). This can seem astonishing if we note that later on the Church in condemning Baius seems to return to Abelard's thesis (D 1927). But there is only an apparent contradiction. In the 12th century they did not yet distinguish the natural concurrence of God and grace properly so called, but stuck to Augustinian formulae. Abelard himself thought that original sin had not taken away man's free will and sought to show that pagan philosophers had true virtues.[44] He goes too far and . . . simply seems to return to the ideas of Pelagius and Pelagians.[45] But these are explicable deviations. If a heretic is one who prefers his own judgment to that of the Church, Abelard is not a heretic,[46] and Baius basically will be less Catholic than he. But we are not here to judge the secret sentiments of Abelard. What interests us more is his influence on the progress of theology. And as with Origen of old, it seems that he gave to research and teaching an entirely new impetus.[47] . . .

Peter Lombard. In his work (*Books of Sentences*), that was soon to become the breviary of theologians, the Italian master gave grace a greater place than did his predecessors. He treats predestination in connection with divine knowledge,[48] grace and liberty in connection with the probation of the angels,[49] and he returns to the subject in connection with the creation of Adam.[50] It is at this point in his work that he puts a whole treatise on grace and merit.[51] Further on, in connection with the Incarnation, he studies faith, hope and charity.[52]

But Lombard is only a compiler who accumulates authorities pro and con.[53] Augustine and his disciples are brought back to bear witness but without any assessment of the coherence and suppleness of their thought.[54] It is difficult for us today to understand the success of such a book. But it served as a point of departure and a textbook for a St. Bonaventure and a St.

---

[44] Cf. L. Caperan, *Le problème du salut des infidèls*, 1934, t. I, pp. 175–176.

[45] Cf. *I apol.* (*Opera*, ed. Cousin, II, 731), 721, P.L., 178, 707. See also A. Landgraf, *Zeitschrift für Katholische Theologie*, 1931, pp. 220–224.

[46] Cf. J. Cottiaux, "La conception de la théologie chez Abélard," in *Revue d'hist. ecclés.*, 1932, pp. 247–250, 822–828.

[47] See E. Portalié, "Abélard," DTC, I, 50–51; J. De Ghellinck, *op. cit.*, pp. 99–102; G. Robert, A. Paré, et P. Tremblay, *La renaissance du XII siècle, les écoles et l'enseignement*, 1933, pp. 275–313. However M. Bliemtzrieder, the editor of An-

selm of Laon, takes it ill that one makes Abelard the initiator of scholastic theology (*Recherches de théol. ancienne et médiévale*, 1935, p. 48, note). It is true for Abelard as for Origen that it is difficult to speak dispassionately. . . .

[48] *I Sent.*, dist. 40–41, ed. Quaracchi, t. I, 249–259 (recall that the detail of actual division is not that of Peter Lombard); cf. J. De Ghellinck, DTC, t. XII, col. 1967).

[49] *II Sent.*, dist. 5 (I, 327).

[50] *II Sent.*, dist. 25–26 (I, 428–444).

[51] *II Sent.*, dist. 27–29 (I, 444–460).

[52] *III Sent.*, dist. 23–32 (II, 655–696).

[53] J. De Ghellinck, DTC, XII, 1986.

[54] The index of the edition of Quaracchi shows that in the citations made by Lombard Augustine has the lion's share. Then

Thomas, for a Duns Scotus and a multitude of theologians of lesser stature.[55]

From a doctrinal point of view Lombard has hardly left a trace. Our manuals of theology recall one opinion of the Italian master, but only to condemn it. In speaking of the Trinity Peter Lombard studied the relations between the Holy Spirit and charity and concluded very simply that the two must be identified.[56] It was a paradoxical thesis, impossible to accept as it stands, in spite of the authorities invoked.[57] But Peter Lombard had touched on a deep problem which Occidental theology with rare exceptions has misunderstood.[58] God is charity[59]

and loves Himself in us,[60] and our participation in the divine nature seems explicable only if we admit that the three persons of the Trinity, present in our souls, there renew their mystery. Some mystics of incontestable orthodoxy insist on this aspect of the theology of grace.[61] In the 16th century John of the Cross will go so far as to say that the just participate in the active spiration of the Holy Spirit.[62] There is then a great problem for theology and for spiritual life, but Peter Lombard touches it lightly without suspecting its depths. His thesis, momentarily discussed in the schools, ended by being unanimously rejected.[63]

The great scholastics out of respect for his memory were content to save his intentions. St. Thomas explains that the Italian master meant to magnify charity. He did not dream, he says, of identifying the Holy Spirit with the movement of the will by which we love God and neighbor; he only claimed that in us the Holy Spirit

come St. Ambrose, St. Gregory the Great, St. Jerome, Isidore of Seville, St. Hilary, St. Fulgence, Prosper of Aquitaine. St. Anselm appears only twice. Of the Greek Fathers there are two citations of St. Athanasius and St. Cyril, 15 each for Origen, Chrysostom and St. John Damascene, only one of Didymus or Pseudo-Denys. According to the custom of the time contemporaries are not named, but there are very large borrowings from Abelard, Hugh of St. Victor, the *Summa Sententiarum,* Yves of Chartres and Gratian.

[55] On the success of the book, see J. De Ghellinck, DTC, t. XII, col. 2003–2014, and P. Glorieux, "Sentences," DTC, XIV, 1860–1884.

[56] *I Sent.* dist. 17, c. 1 (Quaracchi, t. I, p. 106).

[57] These authorities finally reduce to some Augustinian texts that are summarized in this formula: *"caritas usque adeo est donum Dei ut Deus vocetur"* (*Serm.,* 156, 5, P.L., 38, 852. Cf. *De Trin.,* VIII, 12, P.L., 42, 958. See A. Cavallera, "Augustin et le Maître des Sentences," in *Archives de philosophie,* 1930, pp. 186–199.

[58] See, for example, Otto De S. Emmeran, P.L., 146, 63D: *"caritas est Deus, gratia autem Dei est caritas, Dei gratia ergo Deus est."* Paschase Radbert, *De fide, spe et*

caritate, III, 2, P.L., 120, 1460; Guillaume De Saint-Thierry, *De natura et dignitate amoris,* 5, P.L., 184, 387. See A. Landgraf, "Anfänge einer Lehre vom concursus simultaneus im XIIIten Jahrhundert," in *Recherches de théol. anc. et med.,* 1929, pp. 202–212.

[59] J Jn 4:16.

[60] Guillaume De Saint-Thierry, *Liber de contemplando Deo,* c. 7, P.L., 184, 375A.

[61] Cf. Ruysbroeck, *Le miroir du salut éternal,* ch. 17, trd. des Benedictins de Wisques, 1919, t. I, pp. 127–128.

[62] *Cantique spirituel,* 38th strophe, éd. Chevallier, 1930, pp. 308–309. Cf. Ph. Chevallier, *Vie spirituelle,* t. 28, 1931, supplement, pp. (47)–(49), and *L'Ami du clergé,* 1932, pp. 294–300.

[63] Cf. A. Landgraf, art. cit., in *Rech. de théol. anc. et med.,* 1928, pp. 212, 228.

is the proximate principle of this act. But this thesis, the Angelic Doctor says, ultimately leads to the detriment of charity. It is precisely because the act of charity in us is something divine, that we must put in man a proximate created principle, a virtue of charity that is the effect of the presence of the Holy Spirit in us.[64]

To grasp this page of St. Thomas we must see it in the historical dimensions which somewhat escaped its author. It is the fruit of a long labor of deepening investigation that brought into theology the Aristotelian notion of *habitus*. We are so accustomed to speak of infused theological and moral virtues that we forget this systematization came relatively late. It was the fruit of an otherwise happy encounter between Christian tradition and Greek thought. Augustine and his disciples spoke of charity and also of the moral virtues, but they did not dream of connecting these two points of view.[65] The treatise on the virtues appears only in the 12th century.[66] Hugh of St. Victor begins to distinguish natural and supernatural virtues but he makes them principles of movements of the soul, not principles of action.[67] Peter Lom-

bard identifies grace and virtue. Both the one and the other are good movements of the soul that God put in us. He refuses to see virtues in the natural good use of the will.[68] Among the virtues he puts faith, hope and even charity, though less explicitly, and then the four cardinal virtues of justice, fortitude, prudence and temperance.[69] But he does not try to produce any general theory. Peter of Poitiers takes up the ideas of his master[70] and tries to give a classification of virtues.[71]

Aristotelian idea of virtue. Paralleling these attempts that stay in the Augustinian line another current is visible that will end up in victory. Abelard introduces into theology the Aristotelian idea of virtue, *qualitas difficile mobilis,* but as one might expect he puts the accent on the acquired virtue and on the cardinal virtues.[72] Theologians formed in his school indicate that although virtue is above all acquired, it can also be an innate disposition and soon they come to the idea of infused virtue. What nature gives to man grace can also give. Faith is not only an act. It is also a reality anterior to the exercise of liberty. The baptized infant can have faith *in habitu* before having it *in usu.*[73] How-

---

[64] II–II, q. 23, art. 1; cf. *De caritate,* qu. unic, art. 1; cf. Landgraf, *art. cit.*

[65] Cf. *Epist.,* 155, 6, P.L., 33, 669 (no virtues without grace); *Epist.,* 167, 8, P.L., 33, 736 (connection of virtues among themselves).

[66] O. Lottin, "Les premières définitions et classifications des vertus au moyen âge," in *Revue des sciences philos. et théol.,* 1929, pp. 369–407.

[67] *De sacramentis,* I, 6, 17, P.L., 176, 273–274: "*virtus nihil aliud est quam affectus mentis secundum rationem ordinatus.*"

[68] *II Sent.,* dist. 27, c. 5, t. II, 446.

[69] *III Sent.,* dist. 23, c. 2, t. II, 655; dist. 26, c. 1, t. II, 670; dist. 27, c. 2, t. II, 673; dist. 33, c. 1, t. II, 697.

[70] *III Sent.,* c. 1, P.L., 211, 1041 C.

[71] *III Sent.,* c. 17, P.L., 211, 1078–1080.

[72] *Dialog. inter philosophum judaeum et christianum,* P.L., 178, 1651 C (*Opera,* Cousin, t. III, pp. 684–685).

[73] On this evolution, besides the study already cited of Dom Lottin and the unpublished texts in the appendix (*Revue des sciences phil. et théol.,* 1929, pp. 389–

ever in this work of deepening theology other problems arise, stirred up by the introduction of Aristotelianism into theological speculation. What are the relations between grace and the virtues, grace and charity, grace and nature? Finally we come to the systemization we know: grace is a new nature, in which the infused virtues and in first place, faith, hope and charity are rooted as proximate principles of our supernatural acts.[74]

Of some discussions of . . . these problems . . . we have some witness in the documents of the Magisterium. In 1201 a letter of Pope Innocent III is content to report the opinions.[75] But a century later in 1311 the Council of Vienne will side with the Aristotelian theology and affirm that infants receive in baptism grace and the infused virtues.[76] But the debate is not closed and the existence of supernatural virtues other than faith, hope and charity, is left in question.[77]

At the same time that they discussed the virtues the theologians also discussed the nature of grace and justification. Is grace a movement of the soul, an *affectus*? Or on the contrary is it a *habitus*, a form, a quality? These questions were virtually posed by Augustinian texts in which grace appeared sometimes as a psychological reality, sometimes as a permanent principle of spiritual life.[78] In classical Augustinism the accent was put on what is later called actual grace. In the 13th century, on the contrary, St. Thomas will say explicitly that the name of grace is reserved to habitual grace.[79] At a stroke justification ceases to be a psychological process and becomes a metaphysical reality. "Incipient charity is incipient justice, mature

---

407), see: G. Engelhardt, "Die Entwickelung der dogmatischen Glaubenspsychologie in der mittelalterlichen Scholastik," in *Beiträge zur Gesch. der Phil. des M. A.*, t. XXX, 1930, pp. 124–137, and A. Landgraf, "Die Erkenntnis der heiligmachenden Gnade in der Frühscholastick," *Scholastick*, 1928, pp. 28–64; "Kindertaufe und Glaube in der Frühscholastik," *Gregorianum*, 1928, pp. 337–372, 497–543.

[74] A. Landgraf, "Studien zur Erkenntnis des Uebernaturlichen in der Frühscholastik," *Scholastik*, 1929, pp. 1–37, 189–220, 352–389; id., "Die Erkenntnis der helfenden Gnade in der Frühscholastik," in *Zeitschrift für katholische Theologie*, 1931, pp. 177–238, 403–437, 562–591; O. Lottin, "Les dons du Saint Esprit chez les théologiens depuis Pierre Lombard jusqu'à saint Thomas d'Aquin" in *Recherches de théol. anc. et med.*, 1929, pp. 41–97.

[75] *Epist.* "Majores Ecclesiae," D 780.

[76] Conc. Vienn., D. 904.

[77] Theologians even today discuss the way in which grace and the virtues increase. . . . We will see further on that Scotus and the Nominalists refuse to admit infused moral virtues.

[78] *Epist.*, 175, 2, P.L., 33, 760; *De gratia et libero arbitrio*, I, 26, P.L., 44, 896–897.

[79] *De veritate*, q. 24, art. 14. On the terminology of the 12th century, see A. Landgraf, *Zeitschrift für katholische Theol.*, 1931, p. 179. The vocabulary of Albert the Great is quite imprecise; he ignores actual grace and when he speaks of grace without qualification he ordinarily means habitual grace (H. Doms, *Die Gnadenlehre des Albertus magnus*, 1929, p. 163). The *gratia gratis data* which St. Bonaventure opposes to *gratia gratum faciens* is not yet the actual grace of modern theologians (H. Bouillard, *Conversion et grâce chez saint Thomas d'Aquin*, 1944, p. 61). After St. Thomas, actual grace will be designated under the name of *auxilium speciale* in opposition to *auxilium generale* (H. Bouillard, *ibid.*, pp. 190, 219).

charity is mature justice, perfect charity is perfect justice" (*Caritas inchoata, inchoata justitia est, caritas provecta provecta justitia, caritas perfecta perfecta justitia*), Augustine said,[80] but St. Thomas and his contemporaries teach that justification is instantaneous.[81] Two attitudes, two epochs. Yet the theologians of the 13th century cannot deny that one must be prepared for justification. To be so prepared is there need of a supernatural *habitus,* an anterior *habitus?* Some do not hesitate to affirm this, but they are then forced to admit an indefinite series of *habitus.*[82] To escape these conclusions others think that the general influence of God as finalized toward habitual grace is enough to assure this preparation for justification. The psychological point of view and the theological point of view are badly combined and not always well distinguished from one another. St. Thomas, who discusses the opinions of his predecessors, is much less interested in the remote preparation than in conversion properly so called.[83] The council of Trent will try to make a synthesis of St. Augustine and his great medieval disciples.

But this labor of deepening theology would have been impossible if there had not been an effort to make more precise the relations between the natural and supernatural orders. In classical Augustinism the distinction between the two orders was very imprecise. Augustine opposed nature and grace but by remaining in the concrete order. The word "nature" is for him polyvalent. Nature is the integral part of innocent man; it has been vitiated by sin to such an extent that in fallen man nature can do absolutely nothing without grace.[84] The spirit if not the letter of Augustinism supposes that nature is, in us, both desire for and refusal of the supernatural. Though Augustine does not speak formally of the supernatural he does not confuse *in re* the supernatural and the miraculous.[85]

Aristotelianism on the contrary brings a very firm notion of nature and thereby one was led to comprehend that in the primitive state itself one must distinguish natural gifts and supernatural gifts.[86] This permitted many precisions in speaking of the grace of Adam. In Lombard's time three opinions about the grace of Adam were in dispute. Some thought innocent man never had grace, others that he had it from the first instant of his creation, still others that he had grace but was created *in naturalibus.*

---

[80] *De natura et gratia,* n. 84, P.L., 44, 290.

[81] I–II, q. 113, art. 7.

[82] *De veritate,* q. 24, art. 15. Cf. H. Bouillard, *op. cit.,* p. 62.

[83] Guillaume d'Auxerre, *Summa aurea,* II, tract. 26, cap. 1 (H. Bouillard, *op. cit.,* p. 64, pp. 66–67); cf. *Recherches de science religieuse,* 1946, pp. 92–114.

[84] *De natura et gratia,* 3, P.L., 44, 249; *Epist.,* 175, 6, P.L., 33, 762.

[85] H. de Lubac, "Remarques sur l'histoire du mot surnaturel," in *Nouvelle revue théologique,* 1934, p. 353.

[86] The supernatural appears first as that which has been superadded to nature (cf. H. De Lubac, *op. cit.,* pp. 388–394), but the consideration of the last end led them to speak of the supernatural properly so called. According to P. De Lubac (*op. cit.,* pp. 398–402) the preponderant influence here was that of St. Thomas.

In the 12th century grace and virtue are still poorly distinguished, but in the 13th century this tripartite division makes the data of the problem precise. There is even a tendency to eliminate the first opinion. According to St. Thomas innocent man had grace (habitual grace) from the first instant of his creation.[87] St. Bonaventure, more in love with psychology, thinks there was a preparation for justification in the first man.[88] But the two theologians are agreed that the question of the necessity of grace is not bound to that of original sin. If man has need of grace, this is first of all because he has been ordered to a supernatural end, the face-to-face vision of God: "Man," writes Aquinas, "needed grace after sin for more things than he did prior to sin, but he did not need more grace, because even before sin he needed grace to attain eternal life, which is the chief necessity for grace" (Homo post peccatum ad plura indiget gratia quam ante peccatum, sed non magis, quia homo ante peccatum indigebat gratia ad vitam aeternam consequendam, quae est principalis necessitas gratiae).[89]

The great scholastics remain Augustinians but, under many influences including that of Pseudo-Denys, they renew relations with the Greek tradi-

tion.[90] God has been made man so that man can become God, says St. Thomas.[91] And in some audacious pages which will give headaches to commentators after the condemnation of Baius, he seeks to prove that the natural desire of man and of every rational creature can only be satisfied in the face-to-face vision of God.[92] He teaches also that the light of glory, of which grace here below is an anticipation, makes angels and men like God, deiform, godlike.[93]

Thus the synthesis is achieved and the ideas about the desire of God that were dear to Augustine now meet the Greek tradition head on. In the 12th

---

[87] I P., q. 95, art. 1, 2; II–II, q. 5, art. 1; II Sent., dist. 29, q. 1, art. 2. Cf. A. Landgraf, "Die Erkenntnis der helfenden Gnade," in Zeitschrift für katholische Theologie, 1931, pp. 403–422; J. B. Kors, La justice primitive et l'état primitif de l'homme d'après saint Thomas, 1922, 1 p.

[88] II Sent., dist. 29, art. 2, q. 2 (Opera, Quaracchi, II, 703).

[89] I P., q. 95, art. 4, ad 1.

[90] St. Thomas has commented on Pseudo-Denys, whom Scotus Erigena and some others had known in the West (cf. G. Thery, Etudes dionysiennes, 1932), and citations from Pseudo-Denys abound in his work (J. Durantel, Saint Thomas et le pseudo-Denys, 1919). Of the Greek Fathers, except for some commentaries of Origen and Chrysostom, he only knew what the florilegia presented (G. Bardy, "Sur les sources patristiques grecques de saint Thomas," in Revue des sciences philos. et théol., 1923, pp. 493–502), but he used this marvelously (I. Backes, Die Christologie des heiligen Thomas und die grieschischen Väter, 1931).

[91] III P., q. 1, art. 2.

[92] Recall the classical texts of Contra Gentiles, III, c. 25–50, of the Compendium Theol., c. 104 (Opera, Vives, XXVII, 41–42) and the beginning of I–II. On the interpretation of these texts and recent discussions, cf. P. Rousselot, L'intellectualisme de saint Thomas, 3e éd., 1936, pp. 182–183; G. De Broglie, De la place du surnaturel dans la philosophie de saint Thomas, in Recherches de science religieuse, 1924, p. 193 f.; J. E. O'Mahony, The Desire of God in the Philosophy of Saint Thomas, 1931, and the abundant bibliography in the Bulletin thomiste, t. III, pp. 651–676.

[93] I P., q. 12, art. 5.

century the ensemble of theologians was still hesitant and afraid to take the data of Scripture literally.[94] . . . St. Thomas himself does not have this hesitation. The word deification did not frighten him and he always speaks of it with full awareness, *semper formalissime loquitur*. Grace, he teaches, really makes us partakers of the divine nature.[95] If he sometimes seems to attenuate his expressions,[96] this is because he wants to reserve for the beyond the full participation of divine life.[97] At other times he speaks without reservation[98] and does not hesitate to say that divinised men are gods by participation.[99]

Now all the questions about the necessity of grace or predestination are situated in a great synthesis where the fundamental idea is no longer, as it was with Augustine, that of the original fall, but that of ordination to the supernatural end. . . .

The Thomist synthesis. In the *Summa Theologica* . . . St. Thomas' theology of grace is somewhat dispersed. To the questions of the *Prima*

Secundae which treat it ex professo,[100] must be added the questions in which he speaks of predestination,[101] of the divine missions,[102] of the grace of the angels,[103] of the first man,[104] of the infused virtues,[105] of the new Law,[106] of charity,[107] of the grace of Christ,[108] and of His predestination,[109] and finally of the effect of the sacraments.[110] And before putting them into the *Summa Theologica* St. Thomas had already expounded his ideas in various works, and especially in the *Quaestiones Disputatae*, where we find long developments of predestination,[111] faith,[112] free will,[113] grace and justification,[114] the infused virtues,[115] and charity.[116] . . . Let us begin by putting into a few words the idea the Angelic Doctor has of man enroute to God.[117]

Every being here below possesses an end toward which it tends and which it can procure thanks to means that have been given to it with its nature. But man is an exception to this rule.

---

[94] In the 12th century when the Greek renaissance had miscarried, William of Saint-Thierry speaks very prudently. He does not name explicitly any of the Greek sources and he avoids as much as possible the use of words or expressions that carry a too oriental savor (e.g., *deificari*). Cf. J. Dechanet, *Œuvres choisies de Guillaume de Saint-Thierry*, 1945, introduction, p. 17.

[95] I–II, q. 112, art. 1.

[96] I–II, q. 62, art. 1, ad 1; II–II, q. 19, art. 7.

[97] III P., q. 1, art. 2.

[98] I–II, q. 110, art. 3.

[99] I–II, q. 3, art. 1, ad 1.

[100] I–II, q. 109–114.
[101] I P., q. 23–24.
[102] I P., q. 43.
[103] I P., q. 62.
[104] I P., p. 95.
[105] I–II, q. 62–65.
[106] I–II, q. 106.
[107] II–II, q. 23.
[108] III P., q. 8.
[109] III P., q. 24.
[110] III P., q. 62, 69, 79.
[111] *De ver.*, q. 6.
[112] *De ver.*, q. 14.
[113] *De ver.*, q. 24.
[114] *De ver.*, q. 27–29.
[115] *De virtutibus*, q. unica.
[116] *De caritate*, q. unica.
[117] I repeat here freely some pages of an article on "Nature et surnaturel dans la théologie de saint Thomas d'Aquin," in RSR, 1946, pp. 56–91.

The end for which he has been created is absolutely out of proportion to his nature.[118] Like the angel, man is spirit and by that ordered not to such a being or such a particular good, but to all being and all good,[119] that is to say that by his nature he is capable of God.[120] And because of this grandeur he is called the image of God, while other creatures are only simple vestiges of their Creator.[121] But this very grandeur makes for misery. Created for a less high end, man could have reached it by his own proper powers, like other creatures. To attain to this God who alone can beatify him fully, he needs the divine help, freely offered by God, freely accepted or refused by the creature. . . .

Why has God not given to man an interior virtue which would orientate him invincibly toward his end?[122] That, says the Angelic Doctor, was impossible. Beatitude, that is beatifying vision, can be natural to no being

but God Himself.[123] The Creator, wishing man to participate in it, has made him a present of free will, a means of turning to God who gives beatitude,[124] and our author adds magnificently: this is a great thing for it is better to be destined to a sublime end, free to receive it from another, than to pursue alone a miserable end.[125] The God who created us is then a veritable friend.[126] He puts His grace at our disposition, asking only one thing, that we accept it with humility and gratitude.[127] To refuse this grace is, as far as its own nature goes, to desire to remain in the natural order, to desire in fact the privation of the vision, that is to say damnation.[128]

Despite its borrowings from Aristotle this synthesis is none other than the traditional Augustinian datum. We find its equivalent in St. Thomas' contemporaries, Alexander of Hales[129] or St. Bonaventure[130] for example. But more than St. Augustine, the Angelic

---

[118] In Boeth. de Trin., q. 6, art. 4, ad 5 (Opera, Vives, t. 28, p. 550); De veritate, q. 10, art. 11, ad 7; I P., q. 62, art. 2.
[119] I–II, q. 2, art. 8; II–II, q. 2, art. 3.
[120] I–II, q. 113, art. 10; III P., q. 9, art. 2, ad 3.
[121] I P., q. 45, art. 7; I P., q. 93, art. 3, art. 4; De veritate, q. 10, art. 1, ad 5. The Son is the perfect image of the Father, but man is only ad imaginem (I P., q. 35, art. 2, ad 3) in the manner in which a piece of money bears the imprint of the visage of the king (I P., q. 93, art. 1, ad 2). The difference between the image and the vestige founds a distinction between the manner in which we love irrational creatures and that in which we love rational creatures (II–II, q. 25, art. 3, ad 2); it explains why only a rational creature can be assumed by the Word (III P., q. 4, art. 1, ad 2).
[122] I–II, q. 5, art. 5, obj. 1.

[123] I–II, q. 5, art. 7; cf. De veritate, q. 27, art. 2.
[124] I–II, q. 5, art. 5, ad 1; cf. De veritate, q. 22, art. 7.
[125] I–II, q. 5, art. 5, ad 2; cf. II Sent., dist. 26, art. 1, ad 3; De virtut., q. un., art. 8, ad 9.
[126] I–II, q. 5, art. 5, ad 1; I–II, q. 109, art. 4, ad 2.
[127] Contra Gentiles, III, c. 159; cf. I–II, q. 79, art. 3.
[128] Quodlibet., 5, art. 2; cf. De malo, q. 6, art. 16, ad 3.
[129] Sum. theol., Opera, Quaracchi, t. I, 1924, col. 602; on the image of God cf. Opera, t. II, col. 408–415; on the relations between nature and grace cf. ibid., col. 741.
[130] II Sent., dist. 38, art. 1, q. 4, sed contra 2, Opera, t. II, col. 888; on the image of God in man cf. In II Sent., dist. 16, art. 1, q. 1 (Opera, t. II, col. 395).

Doctor insists on the transcendence of the last end. Aristotelianism brought him a very firm notion of nature which Augustinism lacked. . . . Without yet dreaming of pure nature. St. Thomas here unites philosophy and the theological tradition and shows how the supernatural finality of the rational creature gives to the natural order its veritable consistency.

Natural end and supernatural end. This supposes a distinction between the natural end and the supernatural end to which St. Thomas returns indefinitely,[131] but which must be well understood under penalty of misconstruing his thought. This distinction is one thing in the posterior Thomist tradition, another thing in its origin. If there is question of the angel, the distinction properly speaking is without object. For an angel to have a natural end it must be in potency relative to this end. But the angel has by its nature all the perfection of which it is naturally capable. Natural happiness does not present itself to the angel as an end to be pursued, for it flows spontaneously from the powers of its being.[132] Only supernatural beatitude has for it the character of an end.[133] This offers it the term of an option.[134] For an angel no sin is possible in the order of nature, but only with relation to the supernatural end.[135] Man on the contrary pursues

simultaneously two last ends. One is proportioned to his natural powers: it is the terrestrial beatitude of which the philosophers speak, the human wisdom which one reaches by long effort, thanks to science and virtue.[136]. . . The true last end, that which satisfies man's desire, is none other than God possessed in the face-to-face vision.[137] The philosophers have not been able to discover it,[138] because it is the object of a revelation. But their analyses are precious to the theologian. The Aristotelian ethic, with its doctrine of beatitude and virtue, is easily transposable into Christian terms. . . .

Adam's grace. Adam possessed habitual grace.[139] Was this grace already the grace of Christ? St. Thomas does not say expressly, even though he admits that our first father had faith in Christ.[140] . . . Ordained to a supernatural end, the angels first, then innocent man, had need of grace, that is habitual grace.[141] If the end is supernatural, the means will also be; the creature can only tend to it efficaciously by placing acts proportioned to this end. Only the gift of grace, par-

---

131 I P., q. 62, art. 1; q. 23, art. 7, ad 3; *De veritate*, q. 14, art. 2; q. 27, art. 2.

132 I P., q. 62, art. 1; cf. q. 63, art, 3, obj. 2.

133 I P., q. 62, art. 3, ad 3.

134 I P., q. 62, art. 2.

135 Cf. Ch. V. Heris, "L'amour naturel de Dieu," in *Mélanges thomistes*, 1923, p. 304; cf. also our article on "Nature et surnaturel dans la théol. de S. Thomas," RSR, 1946, p. 59.

136 *In Boeth. de Trinitate*, q. 6, art. 4, ad 5; in *I Sent.*, prol., q. 1, art. 1; I–II, q. 5, art. 5; *De veritate*, q. 14, art. 2.

137 I P., q. 12, art. 1; I–II, q. 3, art. 8; *Contra Gentiles*, III, c. 50.

138 *Contra Gentiles*, III, c. 48.

139 I P., q. 95, art. 1, art. 3.

140 II–II, q. 2, art. 7; cf. III P., q. 1, art. 3, ad 5. St. Thomas at first conceded to Adam only an implicit faith in Christ (*IV Sent.*, dist. 25, q. 2, art. 2).

141 I P., q. 62, art. 1.

ticipation of the divine nature, surmounts an abyss that otherwise would be insurmountable.[142] By grace man becomes pleasing to God, God takes pleasure in him,[143] dwells in him,[144] is present in his soul by a different presence than that of Creator in his creature, one which permits man in all truth to possess God.[145] and enjoy Him.[146] By grace man enters into the divine family. Charity is in fact a love of friendship which involves reciprocity and gives birth to a kind of fellowship between God and man, beginning a life of intimacy that will be perfect in heaven.[147] Grace makes man an adoptive son of God, in fact a god.[148]

Nature and grace. Grace is the principle of merit and the germ of glory. It is fitting that God recompense acts that proceed from our free will, but only the presence of the Holy Spirit can give these acts a divine value.[149] The notion of merit implies, certainly, the idea of a right to recompense, and thus one remains in Augustinian perspectives. It is God Himself who gives us the wherewithal to reach and love Him, as a father gives his son the wherewithal to merit a new gift.[150] So one also remains in Pauline and Johannine perspectives: grace is a germ of life that grows and

fructifies for eternity.[151] A marvelous synergy is realised between God and man which human categories, borrowed from a juridical world or a biological world, cannot express.[152]

Aristotelian that he is, St. Thomas tells us that grace is a quality since it is the splendor of the soul.[153] But he does not insist on this and seems to prefer the idea of new nature.[154] The infused virtues root themselves in grace as faculties in the substance of the soul.[155] The distinction between the two last ends commands natural virtues and supernatural virtues.[156] Man, ordained to multiple terrestrial ends is predisposed to them by natural virtues, in part innate, in part acquired.[157] But this whole ensemble is assumed into the supernatural order and finalised by charity.[158]

Ensemble of supernatural virtues. At baptism, the time of the first justification, man receives at one stroke this whole ensemble of supernatural virtues,[159] which express man's spiritual demeanor toward the last end inasmuch as this prolongs the proximate

---

142 I P., q. 62, art. 4; I–II, q. 114, art. 2.
143 I–II, q. 110, art. 1; *Comp. theol.*, c. 222.
144 *De verit.*, q. 28, art. 2.
145 I P., q. 43, art. 3, art. 5.
146 I P., q. 43, art. 3, ad 1; q. 38, art. 1.
147 I–II, q. 65, art. 5.
148 III P., q. 23, art. 1; I–II, q. 3, art. 1, ad 1.
149 I–II, q. 114, art. 3.
150 I–II, q. 114, art. 1.

151 I–II, q. 114, art. 3, ad 3.
152 II–II, q. 24, art. 6.
153 I–II, q. 110, art. 2.
154 I–II, q. 110, art. 4, art. 2, ad 3.
155 I–II, q. 110, art. 4, ad 1. This systematization supposes a real distinction between grace and charity (*De verit.*, q. 27, art. 2; I–II, q. 110, art. 3). On St. Bonaventure's position see *Opera*, Quaracchi, t. II, col. 656–657.
156 I–II, q. 62, art. 1; *De virtutibus*, q. un., art. 10.
157 *De veritate*, q. 27, art. 2; *De virtutibus*, q. un., art. 8, art. 9; I–II, q. 63, art. 1, art. 2.
158 II–II, q. 23, art. 7; I–II, q. 65, art. 2.
159 III P., q. 69, art. 4, art. 6.

ends of human activity.[160] Prudence, fortitude, justice and temperance, with their multiple ramifications, form an ensemble of moral virtues[161] which crown the three theological virtues of faith, hope and charity.[162] And there must be added the gifts which make the justified soul supple and render it docile to the inspirations of the Holy Spirit.[163]

At first sight this whole ensemble appears a bit complicated and later Scholasticism will sometimes try to throw away the ballast, by sacrificing for example the infused moral virtues. It will try in that way to unite directly the human order and the supernatural order, the natural virtues and the theological virtues. . . . Others will faithfully conserve the Thomist edifice. But they will not always see its coherence and will be more embarrassed than they will admit by the objections of their adversaries. One might even be tempted to think this coherence is only apparent.[164] But a profound study

will probably show that in Thomist thought nature and grace combine harmoniously.[165] But here above all abstractions must not be reified and oppositions must not be solidified, which are before all diverse aspects of one same activity.

---

[165] I say *probably*. The word will perhaps astonish. However, in spite of all the efforts made thus far, we are still too little habituated to studying St. Thomas historically. Dom Lottin, who has done much to attach him to his predecessors while underlining his profound originality, avows that he has not yet begun the supernatural moral doctrine of St. Thomas (Lottin, "Pour un commentaire historique de la morale de saint Thomas d'Aquin," in *Rech. de théol. anc. et med.*, 1939, p. 270, note; this article gives the bibliography of the anterior works of the same author). It has already been noted that St. Thomas, in utilizing the Moral of Aristotle, made it break apart. He is not content to lay the supernatural on a preexistent natural morality. But in introducing a supernatural finality into the Aristotelian cadres and orienting each detail toward a view of the ensemble wherein nature and grace combine somewhat as potency and act, matter and form, body and soul, has he fully succeeded in explicitating a magnificent intuition that constitutes the foundation of his thought? I would not dare to decide. Of all the great philosophical systems one can show that they hide a profound ambiguity and that the system and the intuition which gave birth to it are much less in accord than the author thought. It is probable that without irreverence one can extend this remark to St. Thomas, with this difference that on arriving at the term of his career and feeling the formidable disproportion between what he had realized and what needed to be said he declared with that great loyalty that characterized him: *omnia paleal* A magnificent word which ought to be extended evidently and especially to the relationship between the work and the supernatural realities which it had sought to translate into human terms.

---

[160] Cf. G. De Broglie, "De la place du surnaturel dans la philosophie de saint Thomas," in RSR, 1925, p. 25.

[161] I–II, q. 63, art. 3.

[162] I–II, q. 62, art. 1, art. 3.

[163] I–II, q. 68, art. 3. For the historical context see O. Lottin, "Les dons du Saint-Esprit depuis Pierre Lombard jusqu'à saint Thomas d'Aquin," in *Recherches de théol. anc. et medievale*, 1929, pp. 41–61; J. Bonnefoy, *Les dons du Saint-Esprit d'après saint Bonaventure*, 1929.

[164] Certain texts would seem to give assurance to the partisans of the supernatural *quoad modum*, e.g., *De veritate*, q. 24, art. 1, ad 2, but of this act made without charity St. Thomas neither says that it is fully good nor that it is made by the forces of nature alone in the modern sense of the term.

For St. Thomas man is one. When he has said that intelligence and will are really distinct from one another and from the substance of the soul, the Angelic Doctor adds that it is the same man who is and who thinks and who wills. It is the same in the supernatural order. The systematisation of the virtues expresses a unique man's spiritual comportment relative to the multiple ends that solicit him.[166] Between the infused moral virtues and the corresponding acquired moral virtue there is a perpetual interference: man is moved and he acts, grace constructs him and he constructs himself.[167] Prudence and temperance are gifts of God, but they are also acquisitions of man.[168]

One sees then that between the natural order and the supernatural order there is a perfect correspondence. But the systematisation adopted is not without danger. If grace is a new nature, can there be before justification veritable *habitus* of faith or hope? If every mortal sin simultaneously takes away grace and charity, why don't faith and hope also disappear? And if they remain, why are the moral virtues expelled? These problems will be still more difficult for the theologians of the future to resolve when the council of Trent, while accepting a number of Thomist ideas, will formulate a doctrine of justification that is more supple and disengaged from the theses of the school. It is not easy to see how St. Thomas himself would reply to the questions thus posed.[169]

Necessity of grace. The same difficulty of interpretation is encountered in connection with the consequences of original sin. St. Thomas studies the question of the necessity of grace in a series of questions, whose statements later theology will accept without taking full account of the evolution of terminology. His study is based first of all on the opposition between the integral nature of Adam before his sin and the fallen nature which is ours.[170]

---

[166] I–II, q. 60, art. 1, ad 3.

[167] De malo, q. 2, art. 11; cf. II–II, q. 24, art. 6.

[168] To speak truly, I am aware that I am interpreting a bit texts that are less clear. St. Thomas does not treat this question explicitly. In the *Summa* he is content to oppose the finality of the acquired virtues and that of the corresponding infused virtues (I–II, q. 63, art. 4). *De virt.*, q. un., art. 11, seems to envisage only the virtues acquired anterior to justification. . . . Cf. Th. Demen et D. de Lanversin, "Accroissement des vertus," in *Dict. de spiritualité*, t. I, col. 137–166.

[169] St. Thomas teaches that every mortal sin takes away charity (II–II, q. 24, art. 12); faith and hope however do not disappear (*ibid.*, ad 5) or rather *fides formata* becomes *fides informis* (*De verit.*, q. 14, art. 7; II–II, q. 4, art. 4). The reasoning would seem to demand that it be the same for the infused moral virtues. St. Thomas says they cannot exist without charity (I–II, q. 65, art. 2). Elsewhere he affirms that in the sinner there can be some good "secundum quod habet aliquod aliud donum Dei, vel fidem, vel spem, vel etiam bonum naturae quod non totaliter per peccatum tollitur" (II–II, q. 23, art. 7, ad 1). The theologian who reads this text concludes that for St. Thomas acquired natural virtues remain in the sinner, but this word *natural* is full of equivocations. It is a different problem to know what St. Thomas thinks and to know what the theologian ought to think today to remain faithful to the spirit of St. Thomas.

[170] I–II, q. 109, art. 2, art. 3, art. 4, art. 8, etc.

For innocent man grace (the habitual gift) was only elevating; for fallen man and in general for man wounded by sin it is elevating and medicinal.[171] It is elevating in the sense that without grace he can have no supernatural merit . . . and medicinal in the sense that it permits man to observe the Law and to love God above all things.[172]. . .

Is it necessary for every morally good act? At first glimpse St. Thomas here seems to be more of an optimist than St. Augustine his master, for he tells us that not all the acts of the sinner are necessarily sins. Without grace the sinner can avoid evil at least for a certain time; but with his own powers alone he cannot go on for a long time without committing a new mortal sin.[173] This thesis will be taken up by the majority of theologians after the council of Trent in reaction against the pessimism of Calvin or Baius. And manuals of theology even today invoke the patronage of the Angelic Doctor in this matter.[174]

But we must look at the matter more closely. Modern theologians who possess a very clear distinction between actual and habitual grace do not put the question as it was put in the 13th century. The grace of which St. Thomas is speaking here is habitual grace, we repeat. And what is more, he tells us expressly that without this grace fallen man is at most capable of doing acts in which true morality seems to be only remotely involved, such as "building houses, planting vineyards and things of this kind." (*aedificare domos, plantare vineas et alia hujusmodi*).[175] In what concerns the consequences of original sin it seems then that St. Thomas is as radical as St. Augustine his master. The historians of medieval thought are not mistaken.[176]

Would St. Thomas then be a precursor of Baius? No, for there is an immense abyss between the two theologies. The one ignores elevating grace, the other puts it at the center of its synthesis. The one denies that man can truly cooperate in his justification, the other insists that he can and the council of Trent makes this truth its own. But in the impotence of the free will of fallen man as such it seems that St. Thomas remains faithful to the Augustinian tradition. He understands the fundamental axiom *sine me nihil* in the way of St. Augustine but without indicating clearly enough the nature of the divine aid that man needs to come out of his sin and place truly good acts.[177]. . .

Protestant historians of dogma have accused St. Thomas, and especially his

---

[171] St. Thomas does not employ the words *gratia elevans* but he speaks of elevating grace as a *virtus altior* (I–II, q. 109, art. 5). Grace without qualification is this grace which first puts us into the supernatural world in the strongest sense of the word; cf. I–II, q. 109, art. 2; q. 111, art. 1, art. 2, art. 3; q. 109, art. 2 and 3; II–II, q. 6, art. 1.

[172] I–II, q. 109, art. 5; q. 114, art. 2; q. 109, art. 4, art. 3.

[173] I–II, q. 109, art. 8; cf. q. 63, art. 2, ad 2; *De veritate*, q. 22, art. 5, ad 7.

[174] H. Lange, *De Gratia*, 1929, n. 151, p. 91.

[175] I–II, q. 109, art. 2, art. 5.

[176] Cf. E. Gilson, *L'esprit de la philosophie médiévale*, t. I, 1932, pp. 126–129.

[177] I–II, q. 109, art. 6, ad 2.

contemporaries, of a more or less hidden Semipelagianism.[178] Recent studies have shown that we must here distinguish between the first teaching of the Angelic Doctor and the *Summa Theologica* or the *Summa contra Gentiles*. For it was when he wrote these that he discovered the Semipelagian error and the question of the *initium fidei*; and he discovered them in the writings of Augustine and not in the council of Orange of which, paradoxically, the 13th century was unaware.[179] At the same time he discovered some very important texts of Aristotle[180] and realised that the preparation for grace demands not only a supernatural Providence but also an interior aid for the will.[181]

There are then, from the historical point of view, some very subtle questions that are still difficult to resolve. It would probably be too hasty to identify his *auxilium Dei moventis* with our actual grace.[182] It would be even more anachronistic to accuse St. Thomas of not having admitted *gratia actualis entitative supernaturalis*.[183] Theologians are often too obsessed by the problems of post-tridentine scholasticism, even when they are being historical. St. Thomas is not a contemporary of Suarez. We will be content to stress here that the Angelic Doctor, whose moral theology reveals a great psychological finesse, gave too little attention to the problems posed by the psychology of justification. In deepening Augustinism he paralysed it a bit, and the spiritual edifice he presents us remains a static construction even in its grandeur. It lacks the movement, the interior tension that characterised Augustinian thought.

We are going to find the same qualities and the same defects in what concerns the supernatural life of the justified man. This man acts conformably to his new nature, St. Thomas tells us, drawn as he is to do supernatural good by the Spirit who dwells in him and the grace that is diffused in his heart.[184] The justified man is under

---

[178] Harnack (*Lehrbuch der Dogmengeschichte*, 4 ed., t. III, 1906, pp. 650–654) is very radical here. Cf. F. Loofs (*Leitfaden zur D.G.*, 1906, pp. 548–553); R. Seeburg (*Lehrbuch der Dogmengeschichte*, 4 ed., t. III, 1930, pp. 480–484). . . .

[179] H. Bouillard, *Conversion et grâce*, pp. 92–123.

[180] J. Stufler, "Die entfernte Vorbereitung auf die Rechtfertigung nach dem hlg. Thomas," in *Zeitschrift für katholische Theologie*, 1923, pp. 161–184; Th. Deman, "Le liber, 'De bona fortuna' dans la théologie de saint Thomas d'Aquin," in *Revue des sciences phil. et théol.*, 1928, pp. 38–58; Bouillard, *op. cit.*, pp. 123–125.

[181] *Quodlib.*, 1, art. 7; cf. I–II, q. 109, art. 6; J. Rivière, "Justification," DTC, t. VIII, col. 2120. . . .

[182] H. Bouillard, *Conversion et grâce*, p. 176. P. Portalié studied this question ("Augustinisme," DTC, t. I, col. 2534–2535)

but he was too quick to identify *auxilium Dei moventis* with the actual grace of later theologians. The question is more complex. P. Bouillard's analyses themselves provoked criticisms and an explanation from him (RSR, 1946, pp. 106–111).

[183] J. Stufler (*Zeitschrift für kathol. Theol.*, 1923, p. 183) finds that the position St. Thomas came to is not yet in perfect accord with the council of Trent. To which one can reply: (1) the Fathers of the Church themselves said inexact things at times when the Church had not yet pronounced on them; (2) modern theology itself identifies a bit quickly certain common positions with catholic orthodoxy.

[184] I–II, q. 108, art. 1, ad. 2.

the new law, and this is a law of love and charity[185] before being an exterior law. Even though justified, however, man needs beside habitual grace a perpetual help of God, as well because of his ordination to the last end as because he is not completely healed of the wound of original sin.[186]

Augustine had strongly shown that even though justified, even though aided by divine grace, man cannot hope to avoid all venial sin. The Church had ratified this doctrine at the council of Carthage[187] and St. Thomas can but repeat it. But he shows it is well founded. Man, he tells us, cannot be so master of himself that he represses all the movements of the inferior part of the soul.[188] Impeccability is an essentially divine privilege. God alone has by nature a will that is fixed in good, while every created will is by nature a deficient will.[189] The liberty of the elect is one thing, that of pilgrims another.[190] The degree of union with God is the measure of participated impeccability. Confirmation in good here below is only an exception.[191] This exception was

made in favor of the Apostles,[192] but without taking away from them the possibility of venial sin. The Mother of God had the unprecedented privilege of avoiding every sin, even the slightest.[193] As for Christ, He was God, and from the first instant of His terrestrial existence He enjoyed the liberty of the elect.[194]

This hierarchy of wills takes up again . . . the Augustinian theme of liberating grace. But we must admit that the disciple [Thomas] is content with a static representation. He does not show how grace comes to the aid of liberty in the life of the sinner, working to free him more and more and enabling him to do today what he could not do yesterday. He prefers to the Augustinian analyses a study that is basically Aristotelian. The relations between intelligence and will, grace and nature are examined much less from the phenomenological point of view than from the heights of metaphysics. Thus there is an effort to rationalize what of itself is essentially irrational, and an appearance of determinism which will leave to his successors a heavy heritage.[195]

---

185 I–II, q. 106, art. 1.

186 I–II, q. 109, art. 9. Here still the relations between actual grace and habitual grace are badly defined. Some later theologians will demand an actual grace properly so called *ad singulos actus hominis justificati* while others will be content with habitual grace and a providential aid.

187 Denz., 222 ff.

188 I–II, q. 109, art. 8.

189 *De veritate*, q. 24, art. 7; cf. P. De Lubac, "Esprit et liberté" in *Surnaturel*, pp. 231–260.

190 I P., q. 62, art. 8, ad 3.

191 I–II, q. 106, art. 2, ad 2; *De veritate*, q. 24, art. 9.

192 *De verit.*, q. 24, art. 9, ad 2.

193 III P., q. 27, art. 4.

194 III P., q. 18, art. 4, ad 3.

195 The very probing analyses that St. Thomas makes of the free act, especially in connection with faith, are finally deceptive. He decomposes admirably the free act into its elements but he does not sufficiently indicate that their synthesis escapes us. Cf. A.-D. Sertillanges, *La philosophie de saint Thomas d'Aquin*, t. II, 3 ed., 1922, pp. 206–289; J. Laporte, "Le libre arbitre et l'attention selon saint Thomas," in *Revue de métaphysique et de morale*, 1931, pp. 61–73; 1932, pp. 199–223; 1934,

But one must not exaggerate. No more than Augustine is St. Thomas disposed to admit an irresistible grace.[196] Grace does no violence to liberty, it supposes it. God would not justify man without his cooperation in his justification.[197] In good philosophy it is necessary to admit that the first mover moves each of the second causes according to its particular nature. God is the source of all being and all determination. He reaches the free act in its very existence, but the will cannot be determined *ad unum* without ceasing to be itself.[198] Perseverance in good does not escape these rules.[199] The priority of grace is a priority of nature, not of time. Most of the questions urged here vanish when one makes manifest this principle formulated by Augustine and repeated by St. Anselm, that there is in God neither past nor future but an eternal present. God is not in time and one cannot even say that He adapts means to ends. But, transcendent and dominating duration, He wills an order of things in which there are objectively means and ends. This profound doctrine is gathered up in an axiom of incalculable import: "Not because of this does God will this, but rather He wills this to be because of this" (*Non propter hoc vult hoc Deus, sed vult hoc esse propter hoc*).[200] This magnificent

metaphysics dominates the whole question of predestination. Grace and glory are temporal effects of an eternal act of God which is, properly speaking, predestination, and which puts into being and into supernatural life not isolated individuals but the immense multitude of the redeemed grouped around their head, Jesus Christ.[201]

St. Thomas does not treat by itself the problem of the relations between grace and liberty, but only the more general problem of necessary causes and contingent causes. But necessity and contingency are understood *ex parte creaturae*, never *ex parte Creatoris*. The first Cause is neither necessary nor contingent, it is transcendent.[202] From this metaphysical point of view the Thomist position is impregnable, and it is regrettable that we had to wait for the 20th century to comprehend its profundity and serenity. In spite of their declarations Banezians and Molinists will often agitate false problems.[203] At the bottom of their discussions and often without their knowledge subtle questions will be involved of which we must admit St. Thomas never dreamed. But let us not demand that

---

pp. 25–57; J. Maréchal, *Le point de départ de la métaphysique*, 5e cahier, 1926, pp. 274–305, etc.

[196] I–II, q. 21, art. 4, ad 2.
[197] I–II, q. 113, art. 3.
[198] I–II, q. 10, art. 4.
[199] I–II, q. 114, art. 9.
[200] I P., q. 19, art. 5.

[201] I P., q. 23, art. 5; III P., q. 24, art. 4.
[202] *In Perihermeneias*, lib. I, lect. 14 (*Opera*, Vivès, t. 22, p. 50).
[203] See the strong pages of P. Sertillanges, *La philosophie de saint Thomas d'Aquin*, t. I, pp. 257–258, and our study: "Prédestination, grâce et liberté," in *Nouvelle revue théologique*, 1947, pp. 449–474. On the question of vocabulary see M. J. Congar, "Praedeterminare et Praedeterminatio chez saint Thomas," in *Revue des sciences phil. et theol.*, 1934, pp. 363–371.

such a great man have foreseen everything. . . .

So the Thomist synthesis is none
other than the Augustinian synthesis,
one can see, but rethought in function
of a doctrine of the absolute supernatural and of the presence of the
Holy Spirit in souls. This last point
of view, which Augustine had not
disregarded but of which he had not
spoken in his polemic with the Manicheans, Donatists or Pelagians, has
now become dominant. The Latin tradition rejoins the Greek tradition perfectly, but it jealously guards all the
progress that Augustinism has made,
for medicinal grace holds a considerable place in the theology of the supernatural as St. Thomas and his contemporaries understand it. Does this
mean that the synthesis thus realised is
perfect in all points?

It has been said that the greatest
authors remain victims of an unconscious verbalism. St. Augustine had
profound ideas on time and eternity
and yet did not succeed in escaping
all anthropomorphism in his discussions with Pelagius and Julian of
Eclanum. We are coming to see that
St. Thomas also . . . is open to criticism. . . . Sin and resistance to grace
are not studied sufficiently in their
concrete reality as revealed by psychology and history. To achieve full
satisfaction we must construct a synthesis wherein metaphysics is combined with the temporal unfolding of
the spiritual history of man and humanity in its entirety, in such a way
that the development of grace in souls

and in the Church does not compromise the transcendence of the first
cause. The Angelic Doctor has not
attempted this synthesis.

Not that he is unaware of the philosophical and theological value of history. . . . In the *Summa Theologica* he
has taken up the great Pauline themes
on the theology of history. . . . But
only in passing. Just as St. Thomas is
more attentive to the ontology of justification than to its psychological
preparation so, if we may say so, he
prefers the metaphysics of the Church
to its history. He is nearer to the
Epistles of the Captivity than to Second Corinthians or Romans. . . .

But let us remember that the doctrine of the mystical body holds as
considerable a place in his theological
thought as it did in Augustine's, even
though in a different way. A time
will come when this doctrine will be
misunderstood. Modern individualism
will no longer comprehend how there
can be a communication of grace and
merit between the members of Christianity. Protestants will be indignant
that we are taking away from Christ
some absolutely unique privileges. St.
Thomas has answered them in advance, and when the agony is over
we come back to his profound affirmations: "head and members are as it
were one mystical person, and therefore the satisfaction rendered by Christ
pertains to all the faithful, as to His
members, much as when two men who
are one in love, one can render satisfaction for the other" (*caput et membra
sunt quasi una persona mystica, et ideo*

satisfactio Christi ad omnes fideles pertinet, sicut ad sua membra, in quantum etiam duo homines sunt unum in caritate, unus pro alio satisfacere potest).[204]. . .

It will be necessary to wait a long time before this eminently catholic synthesis in which so many traditional elements have been assembled, unified and assimilated will be fully comprehended. One will first see the defects. How could it be otherwise? . . .

4. Ch. Baumgartner, S.J.,[205] touches briefly a number of points of St. Thomas' doctrine, the last end of man, fallen nature, created and uncreated grace, the mission of the Son and of the Holy Spirit, adoptive filiation, and sanctifying grace as participation in the capital grace of Christ.

(1) The last end of man. The last end of human life is that to which Our Lord Jesus Christ showed the way in His person: it leads us by the resurrection to eternal beatitude; the way "by which we can by rising attain the happiness of eternal life" (*per quam ad beatitudinem immortalis vitae resurgendo pervenire possimus*).[206]

It is the beatitude of God Himself. It consists in the vision of the divine essence. In a sense this vocation is natural to man, for being spirit he is by nature capable of God. Made to the image of God the soul has an aptitude to receive perfect beatitude.[207] This thesis is not peculiar to St. Thomas. It is that of the Fathers of the Church, of St. Augustine in particular, and of the medieval theologians. "Nature" is envisaged essentially in the perspective of a creation that regards an end for which the rational creature has a natural inclination but which it is impotent to attain by its own proper powers. To put it another way, for St. Thomas who in this point is a faithful echo of traditional thought, "nature" is nothing else but the ontological presupposition of the vision for which it has been created. This vision in which perfect beatitude consists, only God possesses by nature. Man can receive it only as a gift. It is God Himself who makes man happy, if he is converted to Him.[208]

St. Thomas will insist on the transcendence of the last end more than St. Augustine or rather otherwise than St. Augustine. St. Augustine envisaged uniquely the historical nature of man as God in fact had created it from the beginning. The adoption of the Aristotelian idea of nature in a metaphysical sense, with its content only what is

---

[204] III P., q. 48, art. 2, ad 1; q. 19, art. 4.

[205] This excerpt is from *op. cit.*, pp. 84–104.

[206] III P., prol.

[207] I P., q. 93, a. 4; cf. I–II, q. 113, a. 10; *In II Sent.*, d. 26, q. 1, a. 1, ad 2.

[208] I–II, q. 5, a. 5, ad 1; cf. *In Boeth., de Trin.*, q. 6, a. 4, ad 5; I–II, q. 5, a. 7.

essential to man as such independently of the diverse concrete states in which human nature can be realized, will permit St. Thomas to establish a firm distinction between the natural end and the supernatural end. The natural end is that which is proportioned to the powers of man. It is the terrestrial, imperfect beatitude of which the philosopher speaks. Perfect beatitude is supernatural and surpasses the natural powers not only of man but of every creation.[209] . . . The only perfect beatitude of which St. Thomas speaks is the vision of God. Though not at all intrinsic to nature it is however ordained to it. God elevates the rational creature above its natural condition to the participation in the divine good.[210]

(2) **Fallen nature.** Original sin has changed nothing in the supernatural vocation of man. The only last end to which he remains ordained is the perfect beatitude consisting in the vision of God. But as a consequence of original sin human nature has been deprived of grace and integrity, the means which permitted it to tend to this end efficaciously and in harmonious fullness of free activity. Fallen man is a wounded being whom the grace of Christ must heal and elevate. To live well man needs a double help of God, the habitual gift of grace and the *auxilium Dei moventis*.

What is the end of the *donum habituale?* Twofold. To return to God fallen man needs grace for two reasons. Corrupted human nature must be healed, and in addition it must be elevated in view of works that surpass the proportion of nature and merit eternal life.[211]

Healing grace. The doctrine of healing, curing or medicinal grace takes up and makes more precise Augustine's doctrine of the impotence of fallen man to do good without the *gratia justificationis*. It rests above all on the opposition between the integral nature of Adam before sin and the fallen nature that is ours.[212] In the two states man's situation is identical in two points. First he always needs the *auxilium Dei moventis* which moves him to the good action. Then to accomplish the good that surpasses the powers of nature and is supernatural and meritorious he needs to receive from God a gratuitous superadded virtue, a habitual gift that permits him to do actions proportioned to the supernatural end to which he must tend efficaciously.

In what concerns natural moral good on the contrary, the situation of innocent man and that of fallen man differ profoundly. In the state of integrity Adam could accomplish all the moral good proportioned to his nature. Doubtless he needed for that the *auxilium Dei moventis* but he did not need *gratia gratum faciens*. This grace's unique purpose was to make his moral activity merit the supernatural end but not to make this moral activity possible by giving to his nature powers that it lacked. Without habitual grace Adam was able not to

---

[209] *In Boeth., de Trin.*, q. 6, a. 4, ad 5; I–II, q. 5, a. 5; I P, q. 62, a. 1; q. 12, a. 4.
[210] I–II, q. 110, a. 1; cf. I P., q. 62, a. 1.

[211] I–II, q. 109, a. 9.
[212] I–II, q. 109, a. 2.

sin either mortally or venially.

Did the privation of the gift of integrity, which consisted in the perfect submission of the spontaneous appetites to reason and liberty, leave intact in fallen man the power to do all the moral good proportioned to his nature? St. Thomas does not think so. Without the *gratia gratum faciens* which heals his weakened powers fallen man is impotent to realise a fully moral attitude and conduct. The Angelic Doctor does not go so far as to refuse him the power to do particular morally good actions. Contrary to the last thought of St. Augustine or at least to certain of his formulas, he admits that the infidel can do some good actions. Since nature is not totally corrupted by sin man has enough power to do "some particular good, such as to build houses, plant vineyards and other things of this kind" (*aliquod bonum particulare, sicut aedificare domos, plantare vineas et alia huiusmodi*). He can do works "leading to some particular good connected to man, such as to work in the field, to drink, to eat, to have a friend and other things of this kind" (*perducentia ad bonum aliquod homini connaturale sicut laborare in agro, bibere, manducare, et habere amicum et alia huiusmodi*). He can work for the conservation of the city. He can help his parents, pay his debts, etc.[213]

These actions are not necessarily vitiated by *cupiditas* even if they are still not ordered by faith or charity to the last supernatural end. They are

orderable to it.[214] By repetition of these acts man can acquire the virtues of patience, courage, prudence, incomplete natural virtues indeed but virtues which are not necessarily corrupted by a vicious intention. What fallen man is incapable of doing without *gratia sanans* (i.e., sanctifying grace) is all the moral good proportioned to his nature. In particular and especially the act of natural love of God above all things is absolutely impossible for him. He cannot love God above all things "insofar as He is the object of happiness" (*secundum quod est objectum beatitudinis*); that is obvious. But no more can he love Him above all things "insofar as He is the beginning and end of natural good" (*prout est principium et finis naturalis boni*).[215]

This is the profound reason why man is impotent without *gratia gratum faciens* to observe all the precepts of the moral law and to resist grave temptations for a long time. According to St. Thomas then, there is no truly consistent natural morality without the *gratia habitualis sanans naturam*.[216] On these points St. Thomas' thought has evolved. To see this it is enough to compare the teaching of the *Summa* with that of the *Sentences*.[217]

Elevating grace. Grace is a principle of moral health for fallen man. But this is not the first and fundamental reason of its necessity. The end of the

---

[213] I–II, q. 109, a. 2, a. 5; II–II, q. 23, a. 7.

[214] II–II, q. 23, a. 7 et ad 1.

[215] I–II, q. 109, a. 3.

[216] I–II, q. 109, a. 4, a. 8.

[217] In *II Sent.*, d. 28, q. 1, a. 2 et 3; cf. *Quaest. disp. de Veritate*, q. 24, a. 12 and C.G., III, 160.

nature is eternal life. Though ordained to divine life nature of itself is radically incapable of achieving it; it can only receive it. This impotence is absolute and physical. It originates not solely from the fact that man is a fallen being but first of all from the fact that he is a creature. If the distance that separates the creature from his Creator is to be surmounted, this can only be done by the action of God communicating to angel and man a superior power inhering in grace.[218]

Eternal life is an end that surpasses human nature and is not proportioned to it. That is why man with only natural means cannot produce meritorious works proportioned to eternal life. To be able to do this he necessarily needs a superior power, the power of grace. Under this aspect the condition of fallen man is identical with that of innocent man.[219]. . .

The gift of grace has then for its first purpose to establish a proportion between the activity of the creature and the supernatural last end toward which he must tend efficaciously. It is a created, supernatural, superadded principle which transforms the natural being and activity by divinising them.

(3) **Created grace and uncreated grace.** In St. Thomas grace ordinarily means the created gift and not the love of God. He has constructed a theology of created grace. If he thus puts the stress on the anthropological aspect of grace we should not conclude that he has lost sight of the more theocentric Pauline notion of *charis*

that signifies the love and benevolence of God for man. On the contrary. Because he has a full awareness of the creative transcendence of this love he very insistently underlines the good that flows from it for the creature. The love of God is essentially creative of value (*infundens et creans bonitatem in rebus*) and has as its consequence the production of an effect in us.[220]. . .

It will be noted how the uncreated gift of the love of God and the created gift are strictly joined in the theology of St. Thomas. The love of God tends to give itself to the creature and from this it follows that there is in the creature a supernatural created reality. In the *Disputed Question on Truth* (*De Veritate*) St. Thomas puts in still greater relief the efficacy or realism of the "acceptation" of God, or what is the same thing, His love. . . . Having grasped that the love of God is creative St. Thomas gives his attention to the ontological transformation of the soul. He interprets participation in the divine nature in terms of exemplary and efficient causality. In his theology of the beatific vision he brings in the notion of quasi-formal causality to explain the immediate union of the spirit with the divine essence, but in his theology of grace on the contrary, at least in the *Truth* and in the *Summa*, he does not appeal to this. He even seems to exclude it explicitly. God does not vivify the soul *as a formal cause but as an efficient cause*. The soul is the formal cause of corporal life and vivifies the body without any form inter-

[218] I II, q. 109, a. 5.
[219] I–II, q. 109, a. 2.

[220] I P., q. 20, a. 2.

mediate between the body and it. It is not so with divine life. Here there is a form intermediate between God and the soul: "just as a painter effectively makes a wall white through the means of whiteness, but the whiteness does so by no mediating form, because it formally makes the wall white" (*sicut pictor album facit parietem effective albedine mediante, albedo vero nulla forma mediante, quia facit album formaliter*).[221]

God is like an agent transforming a subject "not by its substance but by the form it causes in matter." However between the spirit and God there is no intermediary: "neither by way of efficient cause because it is immediately created and justified by God, nor by way of beatifying object because the soul is beatified by the very fruition of God." To this immediacy the "formal medium by which the soul is assimilated to God" is not opposed.[222] This immediacy is not even possible except by the mediation of the created form. St. Augustine also affirms the transformation of the soul by God, but he sees this transformation especially in the act of charity which God makes us make.[223]

Peter Lombard had held that charity is not an infused virtue as faith and hope. The Holy Spirit Himself, present in the soul, makes us make the act of charity without the mediation of a created form.[224] Scholasticism has

not followed Peter Lombard. As St. Augustine so St. Thomas teaches that justification of an adult is accomplished in and by an act of conversion. God operates in us that we may love Him freely. But precisely so that this act of conversion which is stirred up by God may truly emanate from us and be fully and truly ours and be actively placed by the subject and not just received in him as in a simple instrument, it is necessary that we be transformed in the depths of our being, in our essence itself and not only in our spiritual faculties.[225]

This transformation in the essence of the soul is nothing else than *gratia gratum faciens*.[226] This *gratia gratum faciens* that informs a subject is not a substance, it is an accidental form, a supernatural quality, a new manner of being, an *esse divinum*, an *esse supernaturale*.[227] . . .

The *gratum faciens* grace expands into the faculties of the soul in the infused virtues of faith, hope and charity. This is habitual grace properly speaking. Charity is really distinct from the *gratia gratum faciens*, as the essence of the soul is from its powers. With sanctifying grace and charity are the infused moral virtues, distinct from the acquired natural moral virtues not only by their principle, which is grace, but also by their formal object. St. Thomas also admits that the gifts of

---

[221] *Quaest. disp. de Veritate*, q. 27, a. 1, ad 1.

[222] *Ibid.*, ad 10.

[223] *De spir. et lit.*, 32, 56, P.L., 10, 44, 237.

[224] II–II, q. 23, a. 2.

[225] *Ibid.*

[226] In II *Sent.*, d. 26, q. 1, a. 3; *Quaest. disp. de Veritate*, q. 27, a. 6.

[227] In II *Sent.*, d. 26, q. 1, a. 3, a. 4, ad 2 et 3; a. 5, ad 17; a. 6 et ad 3 et 4; *Quaest. disp. de Veritate*, q. 27, a. 6; a. 3; I–II, q. 110, a. 3 ad 3; a. 2; a. 4.

the Holy Spirit, as traditionally explained, are habits distinct from the infused virtues.[228]

(4) The mission of the Son and of the Holy Spirit. The created gift of *gratia gratum faciens* is the effect in man of the love of God. This effect is peculiar and unique in that in it and by it the Holy Spirit proceeds temporally to sanctify the rational creature, and the Son and Holy Spirit are sent invisibly into the soul where they are present according to a new mode of being, and the three divine Persons give themselves to the soul and are possessed by it, and the whole Trinity comes and dwells in the just.

The temporal procession of the divine Persons. Creatures go out from God to return to Him. The procession of the divine Persons is the "reason for the making of creatures by the first principle" (*ratio productionis creaturarum a primo principio*). It will also be the "reason for returning to the end" (*ratio redeundi in finem*).

Just as the Father has created us by the Son and in the Spirit, so by the Son and the Holy Spirit are we united to the Father, the last end. We can envisage the procession of the divine Persons in creatures in two ways. First as the *ratio exeundi a principio*, i.e., of the creation of the "nature." Second as the *ratio redeundi in finem*, and then there is question only of *gratia gratum faciens* and glory, the gifts that unite us immediately to the last end. . . .

The temporal procession of the Holy Spirit which occurs according to *gratia gratum faciens* includes in it the donation of the Holy Spirit Himself. There is a new relation of the creature to the Holy Spirit as to a Person whom it possesses. How can we possess a divine Person? In only two ways is this possible: *vel ad fructum perfectum*, and this is the possession of the divine Person by the gift of glory; *vel ad fructum imperfectum*, and this is the possession of the divine Person by the gift of *gratia gratum faciens*. Or rather, St. Thomas adds, the divine Person is possessed as the principle of conjunction to the end and object of fruition. This procession is had, as he explains it, "insofar as these divine persons by a kind of personal seal leave in our souls some gifts which we formally enjoy, namely, love and wisdom" (*in quantum ipsae personae divinae quadam sui sigillatione in animabus nostris relinquunt quaedam dona quibus formaliter fruimur, scilicet amore et sapientia*).[229] . . . It follows that in the reception of these gifts, the divine Persons are possessed in a new manner, "as it were leading us from the end or joining us to the end" (*quasi ductrices in finem vel conjugentes*). . . .

The temporal procession of the divine Persons is thus the *ratio redeundi in finem*. It occurs only according to grace and glory, the gifts that unite us immediately to the last end. It includes the donation of these Persons in glory and grace, in the gifts of love and of wisdom of which grace is the source.

---

[228] *In II Sent.*, d. 26, q. 1, a. 4; I–II, q. 110, a. 4 et ad 1; q. 68; cf. Is 11:1–3.

[229] *In I Sent.*, d. 14, q. 2, a. 2; d. 15, q. 4, a. 1.

The mission of the divine Persons. The temporal procession of the divine Persons is identical with their mission. The first is envisaged rather as the *ratio redeundi in finem,* the second as the peculiar trait of involving for the person sent a new manner of being present in the one to whom he is sent. Just as the donation was included in the temporal procession of the divine Persons, so it is also included in their mission. But this differs from donation, for the idea of donation does not imply distinction between the donor and the gift. One person can give himself. Donation only demands that the gift be distinct from the donee. Mission on the contrary implies the distinction of the person sent from the sender. Mission supposes *auctoritas,* i.e., in God, eternal origin. So only the Son and Spirit are sent, not the Father or the Trinity. . . .

The invisible mission of the divine Persons occurs only according to the *donum gratiae gratum facientis,* just as the donation which it includes. The divine Person is sent in that He exists in someone in a new manner. He is given in that He is possessed by someone. Let us first view the new presence of God, then the donation of the Persons.

The presence of God. There is a common mode according to which God is present in all things as the cause in its effects. There is in addition a special mode befitting the rational creature, in which God is present as known in the knower and loved in the lover. When the rational creature attains to God Himself by knowledge and love according to this special mode, God is not only present in it but dwells in it as in His temple.[230] For a divine Person to be sent then is *novo modo existere in aliquo,* to exist in a new way, to dwell in a rational creature. This is possible only by a created gift, habitual knowledge and love of which *gratia gratum faciens* is the principle.[231] . . .

Priority of the created or the uncreated gift. If we receive a created gift and an uncreated gift, we can ask in what order we receive them. It is not a question of temporal succession but of a priority of nature. On the one hand it seems that the priority belongs to the Holy Spirit, for by Him the other gifts come to us and He is the first Gift. On the other hand the created gifts dispose us for the possession of the Holy Spirit, and a disposition is anterior to that which it disposes. In reality there is a mutual priority in a different line of causality. From the viewpoint of the subject who receives the Holy Spirit, the disposition precedes that for which it disposes: in this sense we receive the gifts of the Holy Spirit before we receive Him, for by the gifts received we are assimilated to the Holy Spirit. From the viewpoint of the efficient cause and end it is the other way round, for what is nearest the agent or end will be called first: in this sense we receive the Holy Spirit before His

---

[230] I P., q. 43, a. 3; cf. q. 43, a. 4, ad 1; *In I Sent.,* d. 15, a. 2, ad 4.
[231] I P., q. 43, a. 2, ad 2 et 3; cf. *In I Sent.,* d. 37, q. 1, a. 2.

gifts because the Son has given us all the rest by His love. And this is what is *prius simpliciter*.[232]. . .

The distinction of the invisible missions of the Son and of the Spirit. Just as there is an invisible mission of the Holy Spirit so there is an invisible mission of the Son. In the *Summa* St. Thomas establishes this in dealing with the notion of inhabitation. The entire Trinity dwells in the soul by *gratum faciens* grace. For a divine Person to be sent to someone by invisible grace signifies a "new mode for that person to dwell within [men] and [it likewise signifies] His origin from another [divine] person" (*novum modum inhabitandi illius personae et originem ejus ab alia*). As the Son and the Holy Spirit dwell in the soul by grace, and as they are both *ab alio*, they are also both sent invisibly. The Father dwells in the soul by grace but as He is not *ab alio*, He is not sent.[233]

In the return of the rational creature to God there is a temporal procession of the divine Person in that the proper relation of the divine Person Himself is represented in the soul by a certain similitude received in it, a similitude whose exemplar and origin is the very property of the eternal relation. The proper mode according to which the Holy Spirit is referred to the Father is love; the proper mode according to which the Son is referred to the Father is to be His Word or manifestation. Just as the Holy Spirit then proceeds invisibly in the soul by

the gift of love, so the Son proceeds by the gift of wisdom. This gift manifests the Father "who is the ultimate to which we return" (*qui est ultimum ad quod recurrimus*).

The gifts of love and of wisdom make the divine Persons be in us by a new mode of being and be possessed by us in a new way. . . . The similitude of the Word is wisdom; the similitude of the Holy Spirit is love.[234] The two missions are then distinct. . . .

(5) Adoptive filiation. Father Mersch believes we must distinguish in St. Thomas two series of texts. "In the first adoption appears as a certain grandeur that God gives the soul, by which it receives through a second birth the likeness of the divine nature and the right to the eternal inheritance. This likeness and this right constitute the characteristics of filiation and give the quality of adoptive sons. This donation is made by the whole Trinity. One can call it . . . the juridical conception of adoption. . . . In the second series of texts adoption appears in special relation to the Person of the Son, and it is a participation in the Son. This is . . . the theological or mystical or trinitarian conception of adoption. Thus on the one hand there is filiation by appropriation and on the other by "a very strict relation to the strict Filiation.". . . "Filiatio adoptiva est quaedam participata similitudo filiationis naturalis."[235]

In spite of appearances this inter-

---

[232] *In I Sent.*, d. 14, q. 2, a. 1, sol. 2.
[233] I P., q. 43, a. 5, a. 3, ad 2.

[234] *In I Sent.*, d. 15, q. 4, a. 1.

[235] III P., q. 3, a. 5, ad 2. Cf. E. Mersch, *La théologie du corps mystique*, II, Desclée De Brouwer, 1944, pp. 44–49,

pretation of texts does not seem very solid. St. Thomas' thought stays constant: the Father who is the term of the adoptive filiation is not the first Person of the Trinity but the entire Trinity. To be convinced of this it is enough to read in III, P., article 2 of question 23: "does adoption belong to the whole Trinity?"

There is a difference between the adoptive son of God and the Son by nature. The Son of God by nature is generated, He is not made. The adoptive son is made. We also say he is generated because of the spiritual regeneration which is gratuitous and not natural. But although to generate in God is proper to the Person of the Father, yet to produce any effect in creatures is common to the whole Trinity because of the unity of nature. For where there is unity of nature there also must be unity of virtue and operation. That is why it belongs to the whole Trinity to adopt men as sons of God.

We can see that supernatural generation is interpreted exclusively in terms of efficient causality for when there is question of adoptive filiation to generate is to produce in men an effect of grace, and not to communicate to them formally the paternal nature as far as this is possible to rational creatures. The reply to the second objection is perfectly clear. By adoption we become the brothers of Christ, we have in effect the same Father as He, but in a different way. The Father is the Father of Christ *naturaliter generando*, so that natural generation is proper to Christ. The Father is our Father

voluntarie aliquid faciendo, but this production or effection is common to the Father and the Son and the Holy Spirit. That is why Christ is not the Son of the entire Trinity as we are. Adoptive filiation applies to the Father by appropriation. . . . Although adoption is common to the whole Trinity, it is appropriated to the Father as to its author, to the Son as to its exemplar, to the Holy Spirit as to the one who imprints in us the likeness of the exemplar.

This position is common to scholastic theologians, and it is explained by the fact that they wish to interpret adoptive filiation too exclusively by the aid of the categories of efficient and exemplary causality, or what comes to the same thing by the fact that they attach adoptive filiation too exclusively to created grace alone. They refer it to the Trinity as *Deus unus*. Only the notion of quasi-formal causality will permit us to comprehend that the relations of the just to each divine Person are concretely different. This objective difference is expressed by the fact that we reserve the name of Father to the first Person of the Trinity. He is the Principle without Principle and to Him are related the Son and the Spirit. We receive them by uncreated grace and we receive them inasmuch as they proceed from the Father. If these two Persons communicate themselves to us with their nature identical with that of the Father and formally inasmuch as they proceed from the Father, this communication cannot be called paternal. In what regards the Son it is a filiation in the

Son. In what regards the Holy Spirit it is the gift of love of the Father and Son.

(6) **Sanctifying grace as participation in the capital grace of Christ.** Every grace derives from the glorified humanity of Christ. Christ has received the plenitude of grace. He possesses it in its perfection and in its totality, whether under the aspect of intensive grandeur or under that of "virtue" or universal influence. This means that grace by reason of the hypostatic union has been conferred on Christ "as to a certain universal principle in the class of those having grace" (*tamquam cuidam universali principio in genere habentium gratiam*).[236] His grace, finite though it be, is infinite *secundum propriam rationem gratiae*; it is not susceptible of increase.[237] The infinite excellence of the grace of Christ makes it the source of all grace. His personal grace is a *gratia capitis*. All of us have received from His plenitude. It is a plenitude of "efficiency and effluence which belongs to the man Christ alone as author of grace." The plenitude of the grace of Christ is the source of every grace found in intellectual creatures.[238]

"To give the Holy Spirit belongs to Christ as God authoritatively, but it also belongs to Him as man instrumentally, inasmuch as His humanity was the instrument of His divinity." "And so His actions in virtue of the divinity were salutary for us, as causing grace in us both by way of merit and by a certain efficiency.[239] . . .

Christian grace considered essentially is that which makes natural human activity proportioned to salvation and the supernatural end. In St. Thomas the general treatise of grace is the means of return to God, considered existentially as such. It is not concerned with a hypothetical supernatural order that is not Christian, or with a *gratia Dei* that would not be the *gratia Christi*. St. Thomas knows only one kind of grace, the *consortium divinae naturae* of the humanity that was redeemed by Christ.[240]

---

236 III P., q. 7, a. 9.
237 III P., q. 7, a. 12, a. 11.
238 *Super ev. s. Jo.*, lect. 10.
239 III P., q. 8, a. 1, ad 1; a. 5 et 6.
240 I–II, q. 62, a. 1.

IX

GRACE IN THE REFORMERS

1. **T. P. Neill and R. H. Schmandt[1] give a brief sketch of Luther's role in the Reformation, the development of his doctrine of grace, and some of his propositions that were condemned by Pope Leo X in the bull *Exsurge Domine*.**

ON HALLOWEEN of 1517 an Augustinian monk, Martin Luther by name, posted ninety-five theses on the church door at Wittenberg in Saxony. In them he attacked the Church's handling of indulgences and the exactions levied

[1] T. P. Neill was born in 1915. Among his many published works are *Weapons for Peace* and *Makers of the Modern Mind*. He is a member of the History Department of St. Louis University. R. H. Schmandt was born in 1925. He was formerly a member of the History Department of De Paul University and now is an Associate Professor of History at Loyola University, Chicago. This excerpt was taken from their combined work, *History of the Catholic Church* (Milwaukee: The Bruce Publishing Company, 1957), pp. 303–304, 306–308, 310–312, 320–321.

by the Italian Curia on the Church in Germany. A child born in this year might have lived to see half of Europe lost to the Catholic faith. Most of the northern German states and the Scandinavian countries adopted Lutheranism within a generation. Calvin's reformed religion was established in Holland, Scotland, and a large part of Switzerland, and it made considerable headway in certain parts of almost all other European countries. The Anglican religion was established in England, and various minor sects, such as the Anabaptists and Zwinglians, were scattered in various places throughout Europe. . . .

On the surface there was reason for not taking Luther's protests seriously at first. Such protests had frequently been made in the past. Such heretical doctrine as Luther was soon to preach publicly had been held by men like Wycliff and Hus — and the Church had weathered each storm apparently without serious damage. . . .

What Pope Leo X and other leaders in the Church did not realize is that there existed in Europe a concatenation of political, social, economic, cultural, and religious factors which, combined with serious abuses in the Church, furnished the combustible material for spreading and perpetuating this incendiary movement sparked by Luther's protest. This, indeed, is what happened. It is impossible to account for either the rapid spread of the Protestant Revolt or its permanent success on religious grounds alone. We must remember that the early sixteenth century was an age of revolution in

Europe. A geographic revolution had swung the center of trade westward, had sent ships around Africa to the Orient, and had resulted in the discovery of the new world twenty-five years before Luther posted his theses on the church door at Wittenberg. . . .

The non-religious causes of the Protestant Revolt, then, cannot be ignored if we are to account for its success. But neither can the serious abuses in the Church be overlooked. . . . Attempts at reform had been made, but no effective, permanent reform could be accomplished except through the papacy itself. Popes faced the problem of reform, but they shied away from it when cardinals and bishops having a vested interest in the abuses threatened to revive the conciliar movement. . . .

Ecclesiastical abuses were more serious in Germany than elsewhere in Europe. . . . Under the control of a frequently unfit hierarchy was a host of lesser ecclesiastics, some of whom were exemplary men while others were ignorant, irresponsible and in no wise fit for the religious life.

The rapid expansion of the Lutheran heresy cannot be adequately accounted for without adversion to this factor of ignorance on the part of ecclesiastics and laymen throughout the Christian world in 1517. We must remember that Luther's teaching dealt with the difficult problem of nature and grace, a problem not clearly defined until the Council of Trent. Moreover, many of the universities were in a state of confusion on unsettled theological points such as this, and thus it was possible for theologians in large numbers to believe that Luther was right. Wordly bishops and lower clergy — both diocesan priests and friars — were not well educated, and it was possible for them to look upon Luther as a "reformer" rather than a "heretic" at least until 1541 when the new religion was consolidated. . . .

To understand the development of Lutheran doctrine one must remember that Luther was a heretic before the indulgence controversy occurred and that the force of argument against Catholic defenders of the faith pushed him into holding further heretical propositions. As a young novice Luther had been abnormally worried about his salvation. At length he had arrived at the consoling theory that man is justified solely by trust in God. Good works are unnecessary. Thus Luther shifted the burden of salvation from the individual's shoulders to Christ's alone. He had taught this doctrine in the seminary at Wittenberg before the indulgence controversy, and it was in its defense that he denied papal authority and within a few months the authority of a general council in matters of faith and morals and the interpretation of Scripture. The Bible came to be the sole authority in those matters, and each individual was to interpret the Bible himself. Logically, then, there was no need for a mediatory priesthood in the Lutheran system. Five of the seven sacraments were denied — baptism and the Holy Eucha-

rist alone being considered valid — and the Catholic doctrine of transubstantiation was replaced by Luther's theory of consubstantiation. . . .

Meanwhile the Roman Curia moved toward Luther's excommunication, many long consistory meetings being held before the bull of excommunication was finally formulated. Dated June 15, 1520, the bull *Exsurge Domine* listed forty-one Lutheran errors on free will, original sin, the sacraments, faith, grace, sin, penance, confession, good works, purgatory, communion under both kinds, papal primacy, the authority of general councils, and the power of excommunication. Luther was given sixty days from the publication of the bull in which to recant. John Eck arrived in Germany in August with the bull and officially published it in the following month. In December Luther, more of a national hero than ever, publicly burned the bull of excommunication, together with books on canon law and some of his adversaries' works; and on January 3, 1521, the papal bull *Decet Romanum Pontificem* pronounced him excommunicated from the Catholic fold. . . .

Some of the Propositions condemned by Pope Leo X in the Bull "Exsurge Domine":

1. It is a heretical, although common, opinion that the Sacraments of the New Covenant confer sanctifying grace upon those who do not place any obstacle in their way.

2. To deny that sin remains in an infant after Baptism is to tread underfoot St. Paul and Jesus Christ.

3. Even though there is no actual sin, concupiscence prevents the soul from immediately entering heaven when it leaves the body.

15. Persons who approach the Sacrament of the Eucharist confident that they have confessed their sins, have not committed any mortal sin, and have made their preparation and recited their prayers, are in profound error. Such persons, indeed, eat and drink their own damnation. But if they believe and are confident that they will receive grace, they will be rendered pure and worthy by this faith alone.

25. The Roman Pontiff, the successor of St. Peter, is not the vicar of Jesus Christ, established by Jesus Christ Himself in the person of the blessed Peter over the churches of the entire world.

31. The just man sins in every good work.

32. A good work, even though well performed, is a venial sin.

35. No one is certain that he is not constantly committing mortal sin, because of the hidden vice of pride.

36. After sin, free will is a term without meaning; and when it does what is in its power, it sins mortally.

2. J. Lortz[2] gives an interesting sketch of Luther as man, as reformer, as theologian. He looks at his rich and complex personality, his capacity for personal involvement, his theological development in which the word of God became the only norm, his tendency to see justification as the sole content of revelation. He sees the Reformation as an historical necessity.

Two characteristics strike us immediately: Luther was an amazingly rich and complex personality, and an extremely original one. He is a mine of

[2] Father Joseph Lortz was born in 1887. He is an eminent Catholic historian. Among his works are *Die Reformation in Deutschland* (now being translated into English) and *How the Reformation Came*. This excerpt was taken from his book, *The Reformation: A Problem for Today* (The Newman Press, 1964), pp. 104–106, 126–129, 132–137, 147–148, 151–152.

inexhaustible wealth, amazingly productive in his writings and sermons . . . in the ultimate sense of the word, an individual. It is true that all of his vast work is based on a small number of basic principles to which he recurs again and again. . . . He is always the master of his basic principles, expanding and deepening their field of application. . . .

Luther was also a highly original

man, but here we must distinguish between the theologian and the reformer. The practical demands of Luther the reformer reflect not only the needs of the sixteenth century; he simply takes many of them directly from the writings of the earlier reformers. His true originality was as a theologian.

It is true that Luther was also dependent on the theology of his own day, as he learned it from his professors — in other words, on a form of Ockhamist theology. This is so true that, unless the intellectual seed had been planted in his course of theology, it can be shown that Luther would never have become a reformer. This can be proved by a simple experiment. Take a good, modern preferably Protestant study of Luther's development and subtract the ideas which are Ockhamist in origin. Immediately all the elements which caused the friction, sparked the struggle, and ultimately led to the open break, vanish. The "reformation" elements in Luther are so closely connected with the traditional theses of Ockhamist theology that without the latter it is simply impossible to explain Luther's revolt rationally.

And yet it is true that Luther was essentially independent of his Ockhamist background and that the latter had no influence on Luther's most distinctive characteristics. The real sources of Luther's development are all within him, in the dynamic factors at the very core of his personality. His struggle was a lonely one, inaccessible to others, and it is impossible to follow the course of his development step by step. In spite of Luther's dependence on the tradition in which he was educated, it is true in a deeper sense that absolutely no one had a part in Luther's formation.

Moreover, from his earliest days, he manifests great independence of the authorities of tradition to a dangerous degree — he rejects Aristotle, as he had been taught by his Ockhamist teachers, but also extends this attitude to Thomas Aquinas and even Augustine. One can easily see what an advantage this independence in regard to the tradition was for the professor who was later to organize the new University of Wittenberg. He was quite unrestricted and free to indulge his penchant for innovation. However, there is an obvious danger here in the intellectual as well as the religious sphere that became acute in the case of a man like Luther, with his absolutely unique character, his lack of balance, and his tendency to see only one side of any question; all of this made calm and balanced judgment so difficult. . . .

It is extremely important that we should know the extent to which Luther's point of departure was Catholic. Luther himself thought that his point of departure was Catholic and that in leaving it behind he was abandoning Catholic doctrine. He was wrong. In starting the Reformation Luther was struggling against a Catholicism that was no longer Catholic in the full sense of the word. . . . For one thing, Luther did not have a truly Catholic understanding of sin and its forgiveness. From the theology of his day he had imbibed the notion that sinful tendencies were already sins. Then he demands that at every confession and absolution he be able to feel, here and now, that the burden of sin has been removed. . . . A third consideration . . . The Church was not a vital element in Luther's thought (and this was true of much of the theology of the day). Luther was essentially a lone worker, even in the cloister. . . .

We can sum up everything that we have said about Luther by saying that he was not attentive to the voice of the Church. We may now ask a further question: Was Luther attentive to the voice of the Bible?

Luther's theological and religious development is bound most closely to the word of God found in the New Testament. For him, the word of God became the only norm. From it he drew all his justification for denying that the pope and the Roman Church deserved the name of Christian. . . . Was Luther thoroughly attentive to the word of God? . . .

There is no doubt that Luther wanted to be attentive to the divine word and nothing more, ready at all times to submit himself to the judgment of Scripture. Here we are not concerned with intentions but with facts. What does it mean to be fully attentive to the word of Scripture? . . . We are not going to assert that everything in Holy Scripture is of equal value. Christians are again and again brought face to face with the vital problem of finding out what the es-

sence of Revelation is. But this essence, or the formula which expresses this essence, must be broad enough to include everything significant in the Bible. Nothing essential can be left out. . . .

Luther, as is abundantly clear by now, did not see the Gospel as the good news of the fact that God is our Father. This was evident from the experiences he had at the time of his First Mass. All of his struggles in religious life came from the same source. . . .

He was also a victim of his subjective tendency to see only one side of the question; practically he could see God only as a judge, and therefore as a source of punishment and anxiety. . . . Luther never really understood the parable of the unprofitable servant; he had eyes only for the Pauline theology of sin as it is presented in the famous Chapter Seven of the Epistle to the Romans. In this chapter the doctrine is presented in as strong a language as possible in order that the thought may receive the emphasis it deserves. In addition, not all of Paul's doctrine is contained in the Epistle and not all of the doctrine of the Epistle is given in Chapter Seven. In Luther's case, Paul's theology of sin was emphasized to the point of exaggeration because of the intensity of his own internal struggles and of his experience of sin. . . . Luther did not have a high opinion of the Epistle of St. James or the Apocalypse of St. John. . . .

If we consider all the elements of the New Testament that are left out of Luther's doctrine . . . we would have reason to say that Luther's claim to be guided entirely and solely by Scripture was utterly unfounded. We are thus forced to the conclusion that Luther was not receptive to the full message of Scripture. . . .

By reducing all of revelation to the question of justification, Luther did indeed hit on a central point, from which the most important elements of the message of the New Testament proceed in logical order and from which they derive their efficacy. If this is the meaning of receptivity to the whole Scripture, then we agree that Luther was receptive. However, this type of strict unity is nothing but an inadmissible tendency to a one-sided view which we must reject as contrary to the spirit of Scripture.

The weakest aspect of Luther's doctrine was his exaggerated tendency to see justification as the sole content of revelation. Christianity is salvation, but it contains a number of elements beyond an anthropocentrically conceived process of justification: adoration of the Father; the prayer, "Thy Kingdom come"; the revelation of the divine life which our Lord shares with His elect — all of these are essential elements of Christianity.

What were the discoveries made by Luther? Luther discovered the essence of Catholicism for himself but oversimplified it in such a way as to be led into heresy. We will have to be satisfied with a few indications of this, omitting much of the development and further precisions which could be made.

Luther's first point was that justification comes through faith alone. The Gospel message is realized in a personal, absolutely free encounter with God by sinful man whom He raised to Himself. On the side of man, his will as the result of original sin is utterly powerless to aid him in the process. God's approach is due entirely to the faith which He freely grants, and does not depend either on works or on the mediacy of a sacramental priesthood. Not only is the man who is justified also a sinner, but his sin is his justification.

Second: the Gospel, as its name suggests, is the proclamation of the good news of God, not the news of the divine wrath. In accordance with this conviction, Luther taught his distinctive doctrine of trust in God and a subjective conviction of salvation.

Because of this, the charge was made that he preached a superficial and ill-founded type of confidence, but such an interpretation is unjust to Luther. It is true that in his doctrine there are aspects of quietism that are dangerous. His paradoxical form of expression offers many difficulties and a tendency to offer rash solutions for every problem is perhaps the greatest source of danger. But there is an important fact on the other side of the ledger: at the time the Reformation began, Luther's first thesis on indulgences read as follows: "When our Lord Jesus Christ said 'Do Penance,' he intended that the entire life of the Christian should be an act of penance." This does not sound like the advice of a pietist or quietist to "rest in the wounds of Christ," and this remained a prime concern of Luther his whole life long. In addition to his theology of confidence and inseparable from it, Luther has a profound theology of the Cross. Concerning his confidence in salvation, Luther rejects confidence entirely if it is superficial; confidence in one's own salvation is guaranteed only by one's doubts.

Third: justification is realized not through an interior transformation by means of infused grace; rather it is conceived in a purely ethical framework and the sacraments are definitely pushed into the background.

Fourth: dogmatic traditions and the living magisterium are neglected in ever-increasing measure and finally are utterly rejected. For Luther there is only one source of the faith — the word of God in Holy Scripture.

In making this bare enumeration, we must realize that though all of Luther's doctrine rests on a small number of basic conceptions, it is not capable of being derived from them. Different elements are always being developed by Luther, with infinite variety. The further evolution of Luther's doctrine and his open battle with the Church were strongly, even essentially, dependent on the rich variety of religious experience and the tremendous earnestness with which Luther took the question of religion. . . .

Perhaps I should say a word about Luther's famous statement: *"pecca fortiter."* In this statement as in his other, "It is of no great significance that we commit serious sin," we have an example of a dangerous rashness that marks not only Luther's formulation of a view, but his position itself. He thought and spoke in an undisciplined way. Ideas so formulated create great danger that those who do not share Luther's religious concern will find in them an excuse for letting themselves go in religious and moral matters. Without doubt, Luther's words often had this effect. The same thing happened when Luther preached so strongly his doctrine of faith alone without good works. Luther did not leave the slightest doubt that a Christian life which does not express itself in good works would be nothing but a hollow lie. Yet he cannot be exonerated of the charge that a number of people without any ill will interpreted his doctrine in a very lax sense. He was too careless in his manner of speaking and his point of departure was too negative. This is quite evident when we compare Luther's phrase, *"pecca fortiter"* with St. Augustine's "love and do what you will"! Augustine presupposed the close connection of the moral order with faith; this was his starting point. The lack of this connection was one of the greatest deficiencies of Luther's work. . . .

We conclude with a brief summary. During the period preceding the Reformation, the Church, particularly the higher clergy, and much of the contemporary theology, were in dire need of radical criticism; this made the Reformation a historical necessity. . . . Thus the Reformation becomes a Catholic concern insofar as Catholics must share responsibility and guilt for bringing it about.

Martin Luther, the immediate cause of the Reformation, in the process of resolving his profound struggles of conscience, left the Church although he had not previously intended to do so. For this action the Catholic theology of the day must bear a great deal of the blame. Throughout these events Luther appears as a thoroughly religious man who drew great inspiration from the Bible and shared this with others.

Luther's theology of confidence in God and of man's certitude of salvation, has, in the sense in which Luther intended them, nothing to do with superficial indifference. Luther's whole doctrine on this point is characterized by an absolute seriousness proper to the Christian in such matters.

Luther's whole disposition tended toward subjectivism and made him see all in a rather one-sided way.

Luther's separation from the Church was a gradual rejection of those elements in his thinking and his point of view that were not thoroughly Catholic.

Luther's interpretation of the Bible was profoundly conditioned by his own personality, likes, and dislikes.

Luther justified his struggle against the Church by giving an essentially erroneous picture of Catholic doctrine which was passed on by tradition to later generations of Protestants.

The conclusion that must be drawn is extremely serious. If Luther left the Church because he misunderstood the true Catholic doctrine, and if he gave his followers an essentially false picture of what Catholic doctrine was, then first of all, we must deny that he had any real justification for leaving the Church, and secondly, the false picture must be replaced by a true one.

Thus it means that it was wrong for Catholics and Protestants to divide, to separate, in the first place. At the same time our true positions are seen to be incomparably closer to one another than we had suspected. . . .

If we truly deserve the name of Christians, there is no time for hesitation or delay. As Christians, all of us have a serious obligation to consider anew the task of the Reformation. It is clear that in our own day this is not only possible but offers much hope of success. Here again we must emphasize even more strongly that the most powerful means at our disposal is prayer. . . . We can do nothing better than invoke the aid of God Himself by prayer.

What I have said before, I must repeat: this prayer of union in faith is not something that we may make or omit as we please; it is our *duty*. We must make a firm resolution to do everything in our power to spread an understanding of this fact among those with whom we come into contact.

3. H. Hermelink[3] thinks that in their conception of the grace of God the continental Reformers, Luther, Melanchthon, Zwingli, and Calvin are thoroughly at one and in like measure determined by the fundamental experience of the faith that justifies sinners. He touches on the salient points of Luther's doctrine — rejection of the scholastic concept of grace as an infused quality — affirmation of gospel grace, of grace as favor of God, of grace alone, of faith alone, of justifying faith as the final end of the divine institution of grace. He feels that the fundamental thoughts of Luther remain on the whole the same during the long period of his reforming activity.

The Conflict With the Scholastic Conception of Grace as "Habit" and "Quality"

The first thing that strikes us is the circumspection with which Luther and Melanchthon handle the idea of Grace, because this term appears hampered by the tradition of Scholastic Catholicism. The Reformers use the Latin word only with certain precautions against the association of *gratia infusa* (infused Grace), which all too easily insinuated itself in their day. All ideas of a new *quality* poured into man are rejected. The conflict with the Aristotelian and Scholastic doctrine of a "habit of Grace" is taken up on a wide front.

(a) **Gratia evangelica (gospel grace) in the youthful Luther.** In his first lectures on the Psalms and the Epistle to the Romans, as well as on the Epistle to the Hebrews (in the years 1513/1518), Luther has not yet stripped off the ideas of "infused Grace" or the "infusion of Grace," but from the outset he seeks to divest the idea of its materiality and of the "habit" character, by underlaying it with new contents. Grace is described as the epitome of the *personal* activity of God in revelation and salvation, and in each case is identified with its individual acts.

Here already begins the replacement of the word "Grace" by "God's favor"[4] or "kindness,"[5] "free kindness,"[6] "the gracious power of God that helps the elect."[7] As to its content, Grace is stressed as "the Grace of the Gospel," which is identical with the "righteousness of faith."[8] This "Gospel" Grace, in its several acts, is

---

[3] Rev. Heinrich Hermelink, D.D., was professor of Church history at the University of Marburg in 1931. This excerpt is taken from his article, "Grace in the Theology of the Reformers: Luther and Melanchthon," in *The Doctrine of Grace*, ed. W. T. Whitley (London: SCM Press, 1931), pp. 176–208.

[4] III, 481, 25. The words of Luther are cited according to the Weimar edition (Roman numbers refer to number of volume; the two Arabic numbers to number of page and line).
[5] III, 311, 1.
[6] III, 42, 20.
[7] III, 111, 30.
[8] III, 560, 20 f.

the mercy[9] and the truth of God, which give effect to the promises.[10] As mercy and faithful fulfilment of all the promises "Grace is *identical with Christ,* who is Grace, the way, life and salvation."[11] "Christ's righteousness is also your completion, given you by the Grace of a merciful God."[12] . . . Thus Grace is God Himself working in us, or His Spirit, a "living, moving, and active spirit";[13]. . . "God cannot accept a man unless God's grace justifies him,"[14] just because Grace is nothing but the friendly condescension of God to man.

All these expositions came, as has been said, from Luther's early period before 1518. Even where Luther takes over from Scholasticism the figure of the "infusion" of Grace, he makes use of the possibility, involved in the terminology of infusion ("Grace infused by love"), of putting, by an emphasis on *love,* the personal psychological operation of Grace most strongly in the foreground, in opposition to all magically sacramental ideas: "Grace infuses love, whereby it becomes more confident."[15] In a contemporary letter Luther describes this Grace and infusion of love in the following way, which characteristically avoids all assertions of quality: "Grace causes the Word to please and be believed, but this means to love";[16] " it wonderfully rejoices the conscience; for this is infusion of Grace."[17]

(b) "Grace alone"; "faith alone" (Grace as the complete turning of God to the sinner). It was only after he came forward in the public arena that, in defending his faith about justification against the scholastic theologians of Louvain and Cologne,[18] Luther defined his doctrine of Grace still more sharply, as against the scholastic formulation, and at the same time stressed its inward working on the peace of the heart: "I take Grace here strictly for the favour of God, as it should be taken — not for a quality of the soul, as is taught by the more recent of our doctors" (Duns Scotus and Ockham). And finally this Grace truly brings about peace of heart, so that a man, cured of his own corruption, feels that he has also a gracious God. Here Luther sets forth the parallel nature of the ideas of "Grace" and "faith." "Faith has to complete inwardly in man his healing from corruption"; "Grace" comes to him from without as forgiveness of sins, a gift of peace ("faith is a gift and an eternal good opposed to sin — to cleanse it away; and God's Grace is a good from without, God's favour, as opposed to wrath"). . . .

The whole of the relation of Grace is set forth, from the nature of God, in the following propositions most

---

[9] III, 226, 10.

[10] III, 351, 17; 226, 15.

[11] III, 269, 17.

[12] *Gloss on Romans,* VI, 14, ed. Ficker, I, 56, 12.

[13] I, 227; cf. Thesis 55 (directed against late Scholasticism) of the "Disputation against scholastic theology," 1517.

[14] Thesis 56, I, 227, 4 ff.

[15] I, 115, 2 ff.

[16] Enders: *Correspondence,* I, 408, 36 ff.; cf. also *Epistle to Hebrews,* gloss 65, 15 (ed. Ficker).

[17] *Romans* V:4 f.

[18] *Confutation of Latomus's Argument,* 1521.

characteristic of Luther: "It follows now that these two things, wrath and Grace, are such . . . that they are poured out without reserve: he who is under wrath is wholly under the whole wrath, he *who is under Grace* is wholly under the whole Grace, because wrath and Grace are concerned with persons. For the man whom God thus receives into Grace, He receives wholly, and him whom He favours, He favours wholly. Again, He is wholly wroth with the man with whom He is wroth. For He does not allot this Grace as He allots gifts, nor does He love the head and hate the feet, nor favour the soul and hate the body."[19] Hence there is no gradual process of Grace, no inpouring of partial installments of Grace, but *Grace is the complete turning once for all of the angered God toward the sinner*, who first hereby receives into his heart peace and reconciliation by faith. In contradistinction from the dismemberment of the gifts of Grace in the scholastic doctrine of "unformed Grace," "formed Grace," "Grace of perfection," etc., the complete turning to us of Divine Grace is described as the unitary operation of the word of reconciliation (the "word of promise") with a personal application: "thy sins are forgiven *thee*." . . . Hence Luther prefers the term "favour" or "promise of God" for the expression of God's friendly attitude of heart and its personal appropriation. . . .

Summing up now, we affirm that Luther and Melanchthon oppose the qualitative idea of grace found in "the

[19] VIII, 106, 37–107, 5.

scholastic doctrine of habit" and infusion: (a) in their description of the content of the several acts of God's Grace (forgiveness, mercy, revelation of truth, faithfulness and fulfilment of the promises) the livingness and completeness of the Divine mode of operation is stressed; (b) Grace is accordingly the operation of God Himself, i.e., Christ, in so far as He is given to men as the revelation of God, or the Spirit of God working in man; (c) this operation of God in man is nothing but forgiveness (instead of anger), revelation of the Gospel (instead of the Law), goodness and love (instead of judgment). It is summed up as the "word of the promise"; (d) the word of promise of the personal God is personally appropriated: "to thee," "for you." In the individual case it can be grasped only by faith. *Sola gratia* and *sola fide* are correlative terms.

The Conflict With the Work-Righteousness and Doctrine of Merit in Scholasticism

In the Reformation idea of Grace, *sola gratia*, to which corresponds subjectively the parallel *sola fide* in the human sphere, the Reformers' opposition to every kind of *work-righteousness* and *doctrine of merit* in Scholasticism and the theology of contemporary Catholicism finds expression. *Gratia* is not only favour or *charis*, i.e., gracious, glad and joyful condescension on God's part; there is contained in it also the *gratis* in the sense of opposition to any consideration of reward and every claim of merit in the sphere of religion. Luther's association with Paul and Jesus is at no point so clear as in this rejection and contemptuous flagellation of all Pharisaic righteousness and its claims. The merit of man and his self-willing was not excluded in the Catholic-scholastic schematising of Grace from Augustine onward, in spite of its emphasis on the preponderance of Grace. On the contrary, after the Aristotelian ideas were taken over into the scholastic doctrine of Grace by Alexander of Hales (the distinction of material and form, "quality," "habit"), the merit and self-capacity of man were actually incorporated with the circumstantial process of God's bestowment of Grace on man.

a) **Passivity in the youthful Luther.** Thus . . . the opposition even of the youthful Luther to these ideas still held by him is determinal on the one hand by the intent of transcribing the operation of God as a *spiritual power of will in the soul that can be psychologically experienced.* Grace produces the extirpation of a man's own egoistic will of concupiscence (concupiscent affection is not eradicated save by a superabundant infusion of Grace or by the severest resignation), so that we must be prepared, should it be God's will, for "resignation to hell and damnation."[20] Grace works emancipation of the will to inward freedom, to a voluntary, glad doing of the will of God; the Holy Spirit makes men of free-will, who do not serve God in painful fear or erratic love.[21] . . . Accordingly Luther is

concerned to eliminate the natural powers. The breaking through of Grace is a *creative act of God,* in which the creature keeps entirely passive: "their bearing toward remission is one of complete passivity."[22]

For Luther this passivity is associated with the figure, so frequently used by him, of the *marriage of the soul with Christ,* which (like the thought of passivity itself) come from mysticism: "Towards initial Grace and towards glory also our attitude is always passive, like a woman's towards conception. For we too are the bride of Christ. Therefore, though before reception of Grace we pray and seek, yet when Grace comes and the soul is to be impregnated by the Spirit, it behooves us neither to pray nor work, but only undergo. And this indeed is hard to do and greatly distresses us, because for a soul to be without activity of reason or will is for it to go into darkness and as it were into 'perdition and annihilation' — a thing from which it strongly recoils. Hence the noblest man frequently deprives himself of the activities of Grace."[23]

(b) **The question of quietism in the Luther of later days.** . . . Luther maintained the thought of the soul's passivity in face of the decisive action of God's Grace so often, even down to his latest days, that even in his lifetime as well as later he often drew the reproach of *quietism* upon his doctrine of Grace and conception of religion in general. And yet, it is any-

[20] *Romans*, II, 218, 10 ff.
[21] I, 191, 27 ff.

[22] IV, 487, 19 ff.
[23] *Romans*, II, 206, 10 ff.

thing but a quietistic element that lies at the basis of Luther's genuine reforming conception of Grace, rightly understood. Side by side with the principle, already adduced, that human, creaturely contribution, however correctly accomplished, and Divine working are mutually exclusive, the apparently quietist demand of the reception of Divine Grace aims at hinting a profound psychological truth — that precisely our decisive thoughts and moral resolutions well up from the inner silence of the unconscious life (*ex corde*) as something new, as a wonder.

Again in the figure of the bride-relation of Christ and the soul Luther explains, in reply to the oft repeated objections based on 1 Cor 13:2 (as though love were more important than faith): "faith is idle and useless and love alone justifies":[24] "We must shun that false interpretation as a hellish person, and conclude with Paul that we are justified by faith alone, not by faith formed by love. Therefore the power of justifying is not to be ascribed to that benevolent form, but to the faith that grasps the Saviour Christ Himself, and possesses Him in the heart. This faith justifies without and prior to love. . . . By faith we are in Him and He in us (Jn 6). This bridegroom Christ must be alone with His bride in their rest, apart from all servants and the whole household. But afterwards, when the Bridegroom has opened the door and come forth, let the servants run to Him and the

maids minister, let them bring Him food and drink. This then is where works and love begin."[25]

Luther indeed does not shrink from saying right out that the miracle of Divine Grace takes place in an incomprehensible darkness ("Therefore faith justifies, because it has that treasure, because Christ is here; though in what way, surpasses our thought. . . . Faith is a certain knowledge or darkness which sees nothing, and yet in that darkness Christ sits, apprehended by faith, just as God sat on Sinai and in the temple in the midst of darkness. Therefore our formal justification is not love informing faith, but faith itself and the darkness of the heart, i.e., trust in something that we do not see, i.e., in Christ, Who is present precisely on the terms that He is not seen."[26]

(c) **"Faith alone."** Accordingly the operation of Grace in man, "faith alone," is by no means merely passive, but like every living work of God it is a fertile union of God and man, and one full of fruitful decisions; faith is as living as Christ Himself; it is the movement of the heart that holds Christ fast. It is with faith as with the miracle of the incarnation of God in Christ: faith has Christ and the Holy Spirit present in itself: "Faith is not some idle quality or empty seed-vessel in the heart, which could exist in a state of mortal sin, till love comes in and gives it life; but if it is true faith, it is a kind of

---

[24] XL, i., p. 239, 20.

[25] XL, i., p. 240–241.
[26] XL, i., p. 229.

certain trust of the heart and firm assent whereby Christ is grasped, in such a way that Christ is the object of faith, nay, not object, but Christ is present, so to speak, in faith itself."[27]

"We therefore conclude with Paul that we are justified by faith in Christ alone, apart from law and works. But after a man is justified by faith and now possesses Christ by faith and knows that He is his righteousness and life, he will certainly *not be idle,* but as a good tree he will bring forth good fruits. For the believer has the Holy Spirit; where He is, He does not allow a man to be idle, but incites him to all the exercises of piety, to love of God, to patience in afflictions, to prayer, thanksgiving, and the showing of love toward all."[28] "Faith constantly vivifies, justifies, does not remain idle, but is incarnated and becomes man." — "I say, humanity is not divinity, and yet man is God. . . . They come together in a concrete and composite entity."[29]

This faith, the relation of the Grace-endowed man, which is wrought in the Grace of Christ and the Holy Spirit and inseparably associated therewith, participates in all the wonders of Grace. It is thus active and living, because it not only has God Himself as its presupposition, but sets itself as it were in a reciprocal relation: "faith is creative of divinity." .. . And here Paul out of faith in God makes the highest worship, the highest deference, the highest obedience and sacrifice out

of faith in God. Let an orator exalt this passage (Rom 3:16; Jn 15:6) and he will see that faith is an omnipotent thing and that its power is incalculable and infinite. For it ascribes the glory to God, than which nothing greater can be ascribed to Him. But to ascribe glory to God, is to believe Him, to reckon that He is true, wise, just, merciful, omnipotent, in short, to acknowledge Him the author and giver of every good gift. It is not reason but faith that does this. It completes divinity and, if I may so, is creative of divinity, not in the substance of God but in us. For apart from faith God misses in us His glory, wisdom, righteousness, truth, mercy, etc. . . .

The activity of this faith has to be put to the test daily. For the believing Christian lives in a twofold attitude; on the one hand he remains in sin and has daily to experience it, and on the other hand he lives by Grace, i.e., has everything in Christ. Since Grace does *not* bring about any "momentary infusion of a new quality,"[30] he is at *once sinner and righteous.* The title of righteous is given not to him who is so, but to him who is becoming so;[31] "the man is ever in a state not of being, but becoming . . . i.e., always sinner, always penitent, always righteous. Thus a Christian remains in pure humility and pride. It behooves him sometimes to be conscious of sin — and as deserving of wrath — of the hate and wrath of God, that he may be humbled and not puffed up in this life. And yet he is conscious of being loved in

[27] XL, i., p. 228.
[28] XL, i., p. 265, 8 f., 29 ff.
[29] XL, i., 426, ii., 42 f., 6.

[30] I, 43, 5 ff.   [31] I, 42, 33.

spite of this wrath, not for his own sake, but the beloved Christ's. Thus wrath is overcome by faith in Christ. Sophists laugh at these things, because they do not understand Christian righteousness. It is not mere reputing, but involves faith itself and the apprehension of Christ's suffering for us, which is not an easy thing."

To this train of thought belongs also the celebrated, not to say notorious, letter of Luther to Melanchthon of August 1, 1521, in which Luther, writing from the Wartburg, at the close of long explanations and anxieties about his work, could write to his anxious friend at Wittenberg: "If you are a preacher of Grace, preach not feigned but real Grace; if Grace is real, bring real not feigned sin. God does not love sham sinners. Be a sinner and sin boldly, but more boldly also rejoice by faith in Christ, Who is the conqueror of sin, death and the world. We cannot but sin, as long as we are thus: this life is not the dwelling place of righteousness, but we await, says Peter,[32] new heavens and a new earth, wherein dwelleth righteousness. It is enough to recognize, through the riches of God's glory, the Lamb Who takes away the sin of the world; from Him sin will not tear us away, even though we commit fornication or murder, 1,000 times, 1,000 times in one day. Do you count so small the price and redemption made for our sins in so great and pure a Lamb? Pray boldly, for you are a very bold sinner."[33]

Luther can strike such unwonted notes, because for him Grace was really *forgiveness through Christ* and for *Christ's sake,* and nothing else. The strongest reproach that can be raised against work-righteousness and the advocates of a legal piety is that they take from Christ the glory of His work and at the same time their surest and only comfort from men. Even in Christ's life we must take seriously the reality of sin; according to the words of Scripture "He was made a curse for us,"[34] "the Lamb of God, Who takes away the sin of the world,"[35] "He laid on Him the iniquity of us all."[36]

(d) "For Christ's sake." ... "This is our supreme comfort, thus to put on Christ and involve Him in the sins of me and you and the whole world, and to see him bearing all our sins. And thus seen He easily does away with the fanatical opinions of our opponents about justification by works."[37]

The Papacy is Anti-Christ, because its theologians deprive Christ of His central significance by their doctrine of "faith informed by love." These statements are all Satanic and blasphemies against God, whereby they call us right away from Christian

---

[32] 2 Pt 3:13.
[33] Enders, 3, 208 f.; cf. with this F. Kattenbusch in *Studies and Systematic Theology,* presented to The. von Häring (Tübingen, 1918), p. 50 ff.; K. Holl, *Luther,* 2nd and 3rd edition, p. 236. For Luther's whole train of thought cf. Rud. Hermann, *Luther's Thesis, at Once Righteous and Sinful* (Gütersloh, 1930).
[34] 2 Cor 5:21.
[35] Jn 1:29.
[36] Is 53:6.
[37] XL, i., p. 436.

teaching, from Christ the Mediator, and from a faith that grasps Christ. If love is the form of faith, then it is the greatest thing in the Christian religion, and I lose Christ, His wounds, works, and all His benefits, and I stick fast in love, that I should love, and I come into moral doing, like the Pope. In place of this Luther will hold to the verse: "The just lives by faith" (Rom 1:17). "Then I abide safe under cover of Christ and keep in view the Mediator Himself, His blood; those things are not snatched from my sight, but faith continually sets forth the invisible Christ. Therefore, "by faith alone.' "[38]. . .

Accordingly the man who demands the works of the law as a condition of Grace denies Christ and robs God of His glory. *By doing the law I reject Grace.* The law is good and holy, but not for righteousness. He who performs the law with a view to righteousness rejects Grace, refuses Christ, does not want to be saved by His sacrifice, but to make satisfaction by himself and the law, by his own righteousness; he tramples on the glory of God. This is a horrible thing to say — that man should be so evil as to reject the Grace and mercy of God; yet the whole world does it, even though it does not want to seem to do it, but says that it renders God the greatest honour."[39]

(e) In the last resort, it is impossible to separate off a single idea like that of Grace in Luther's sense of the word, from the other processes of salvation. Each of the ideas of Grace, faith, righteousness, spirit, promise, gospel, etc., describes as it were the whole of the Christian experience of salvation. This is most clearly attested by the celebrated *preface to the epistle to the Romans in Luther's "September Bible."*[40] . . . "Grace and gift are thus distinguished — that Grace means properly God's goodwill and favour, which He bears toward us in Himself, by which He is disposed to pour into us Christ and the Spirit with His gifts. Now although the gifts and the Spirit increase in us daily and are not yet perfect, so that evil desires and sin, which strive against the Spirit, still survive in us, yet Grace does so much that we are counted whole and fully righteous before God. For His Grace does not divide and dismember itself, as do the gifts, but takes us completely into favour, for the sake of Christ our intercessor and mediator, and because the gifts have begun in us. We are still sinners on account of our unmortified flesh; but because we believe in Christ and have the beginning of the Spirit, God is so favourable and gracious to us that He will not heed nor judge such sin, but deal with us according to our faith in Christ, until the sin is slain." . . .

The Word as means of grace. . . . In his conflict with the "heavenly prophets" (Karlstadt, Münzer, the Anabaptists, Schwenckfeld, and others),

[38] XL, i., p. 422 f.
[39] XL, i., p. 301 f.

[40] I.e., the translation of the New Testament made at the Wartburg, which was published in September, 1522.

Luther sees the essence of spiritualism in the self-wrought work of the "goddess (Hulda) Reason." Thus here also the conflict for "Grace alone" demands the recognition of the glory of Christ in opposition to the imaginary claims of the fantasies of human reason. And the decisive weight must be laid on the *hearing of the personal word of Grace.* It was not by a voice from heaven ("immediately from God, without agency") that Abraham once heard the call to emigration from his fatherland,[41] but, as Luther holds, through the patriarch Shem, and other men inspired by God's Spirit,[42] who brought him the message. The hearing of the Word and faith in the Word is the decisive point in the operation of Grace from Abraham onward. . . .

"We deal with the forgiveness of sins in two ways — firstly as to the way in which it is attained and acquired, secondly as to the way in which it is distributed and given to us. It is true that Christ has acquired it on the cross, but He did not distribute or give it on the cross. He did not acquire it in the Lord's Supper or Sacrament, but therein He *distributed and gave it through the Word,* as also in the Gospel, where it is preached." . . . Our sophistical opponents do not perceive "that the whole business is with the distribution, and that Christ wrought the acquirement for the sake of the distribution and put it into the distribution."[43] "The incarnation of Christ would have profited no one, if no 'gospel' had come out of it, whereby all the world might know Him and be informed why He became man, that the promised blessing might be distributed to all who believe in Christ through the Gospel. . . . His business was with the Gospel and our faith, therefore He let His Son become man, in order that the Gospel might be preached by Him, and that His salvation might thus approach and come to the whole world through the published Word. . . . *What is the use of Christ, if He is not possessed by faith? But how can He be possessed by faith, where the Gospel is not preached?*[44] . . . But our doctrine is that bread and wine are of no assistance, nay, even the body and blood in the bread and wine are of no assistance — I will go yet further: Christ on the cross, with all His suffering and death, is of no assistance, although it is the object of the most fervent, glowing, hearty recognition and reflection; there must be still something else: what then? *The Word, the Word, the Word!* For though Christ were given and crucified for us a thousand times, it would all be in vain, *unless the word of God came and distributed it and gave to me and thee:* this shall be thine, take and have it for thyself."[45]

Word and Sacrament. . . . *The Word has the decisive place also in the Sacraments* as means of Grace. . . . The explanation given by Luther in the celebrated controversial writing of

---

[41] Gn 12:1 ff.
[42] XLII, 437, 37 ff.; 439, 15 ff. and 28.
[43] XVIII, 203, 27 ff.; 205, 18 ff.

[44] X, i, 2, p. 7, 4 ff.; cf. also X, 1, 1, 353, 6 ff.
[45] XVIII, 202, 22 f.

1520, "On the Babylonian Captivity of the Church," holds good of the Sacraments quite generally. "Sacraments are not fulfilled by being performed, but by being believed" — "Let us therefore open our eyes and learn to note the Word rather than the sign, the faith rather than the work or use of the sign, knowing, wherever there is a Divine promise, that there faith is required, and that both are so necessary that neither can be efficacious without the other."[46] . . .

Word and Holy Scripture. The Word of Grace is further also the content of Holy Scripture. . . . Their collective content is "Christ" and so far as the individual books "deal in Christ," they are of authoritative significance for faith. . . . "I preach the Gospel of Christ, and with the living voice I bring Christ into thy heart, that thou mayest form Him in thyself. If now thou believest rightly so that thy heart grasps the Word and the voice sticks in it, tell me, what hast thou in thy heart? Then thou must say, thou hast the genuine Christ."[47] "The Scripture has nothing in it besides Christ and Christian faith."[48]. . .

Word and Church. Luther defended the Church too as the gracious institution of the Word and Sacrament against the Baptist spiritualists, after he had previously exalted its purely spiritual, invisible character as against the Catholic papal Church. . . . It is the business of all the signs of the Church to show that "the holy Christian people of God," which according to Luther would be a much better name than the foreign word *ecclesia* or Church, is above all and only where the justifying Word is heard and is received by justifying faith. . . . "God's Word cannot be without God's people. And again, God's people cannot be without God's Word."[49]. . .

On this account Luther can call the *Word of justifying faith* actually the *dogma of his Church*. It is the "article of a standing or falling Church." "I believe that this dogma of mine stands firmly — faith alone justifies; but that this does not oblige us to deny that Word, Sacrament, Christ, preacher, Spirit and God our Father, justify. For God does all things toward our justification, Christ merited our justification. The Word is the agent whereby the Spirit follows up Christ's merit, and likewise the Sacrament and the preacher. But *formal justification is left to faith alone,* since without faith neither God nor Christ nor anything else avails for righteousness."[50]

---

4. **G. C. Berkouwer**[51] **looks at the conflict between Erasmus and Luther over Luther's rejection of free will and at the deepest religious motive of Luther's thought about the servile will. He sees Calvin's struggle for**

---

[46] VI, 533, 12 f.
[47] XIX, 489, 9 ff.
[48] VIII, 236, 19.
[49] L, 629, 28 ff.

[50] XI, 302, 23 ff.
[51] Cf. ch. VII, n. 37. This excerpt is from *op. cit.,* pp. 104–110, 120–122, 146–148.

the assurance of salvation against the synergism of Rome's doctrine of grace as a fight against justification through works in its most refined form.

Luther and Eramus. In connection with the character of the struggle for grace, the conflict between Erasmus and Luther was very important in the history of the Church, as well as in a dogmatic sense. . . . We are concerned with the point where Erasmus and Luther knew they held fundamentally different views with respect to free will. It is clear that in a critical phase of the Reformation Erasmus thought it his duty to defend the cause of free will against Luther. Immediately Luther saw the importance of the conflict and answered Erasmus' diatribe with an elaborate treatise.[52] . . .

Erasmus took occasion for his opposition in Luther's positive and radical rejection of free will in the latter's *Assertio*.[53] Erasmus understood perfectly that this was not merely an isolated theological opinion of Luther's, but that the whole of Luther's revolt against Rome was involved in it.[54] How does Erasmus react to Luther's protest?

After pointing to the clear testimony of tradition and to "the entire choir of the Saints who firmly believe in free will,"[55] in opposition to the new individual opinion of Luther, he reminds his readers of the countless passages in the Scriptures which evidently teach free will.[56] It is true, there are other texts "which seem to destroy it entirely," but the Holy Spirit does not contradict Himself. It must, therefore, be possible to come to a harmonious synthesis. In order to find the latter Erasmus gives a definition of free will: "By free will we understand in this context the power of the human will by which man can turn towards or away from that which leads to eternal salvation."[57] For this free will Erasmus prepares to adduce the relevant texts, showing clearly that man is given a choice. . . .

To Erasmus there is no doubt "that it is in our power to turn our hearts away from the grace given to us."[58] There is no dualism in the process of salvation according to Erasmus' description, but "cooperation" between grace and freedom. The one indivisible work has two causes: the grace of God and the will of man,[59] although grace remains the *principal* cause and the will

---

[52] Luther has always realized the importance of this writing, as late even as 1537 when he says of this work: *"nullum agnosco meum justum librum nisi forte de servo arbitrio et catechismum"* (F. Loofs, *Leitfaden*, p. 761). Martin Luther, *Vom unfreien Willen*. Herausg. von Friedrich Wilhelm Schmidt (1934), p. IX.

[53] *"Liberum arbitrium post peccatum res est de solo titulo et dum facit quod in se est, peccat mortaliter."*

[54] Cf. Karl Zickendraht, *Der Streit Zwischen Erasmus und Luther* (1909), p. 8.

[55] Erasmus van Rottendam, *Vom freien Willen* (Otto Schumacher, 1940). The quotations from Erasmus have been borrowed from this translation (p. 21).

[56] *Ibid.,* p. 23.

[57] *Ibid.,* p. 24.

[58] Erasmus, p. 80.

[59] *Ibid.,* p. 80.

is the *subsidiary cause*. This is why, according to Erasmus, it is possible to say that man owes all of his salvation to the grace of God, "for it is very little that is added by free will, and even that which it can do is a work of the grace of God who first created free will and then redeemed and healed it."[60] . . .

This is the kernel of Erasmus' anthropology, of his analysis of human existence, which forms the system co-ordinate to his doctrine of grace. From this Erasmus starts his fight against Luther and the Reformation. . . . For he considers this freedom and this humanity to be threatened and the higher and better part of man ignored in Luther's "determinism." In this controversy we hear Erasmus pleading the cause of free will, and — remarkably in agreement with the whole of Roman dogmatics — at the same time he argues that this doctrine does not in any way detract from the objectionable character of any trust in man's own merit.[61] Yet in the whole reasoning the conflict between Erasmus and the doctrine of sovereign grace is as clear as daylight.

This is not saying that Luther always made it easy for Erasmus to see the depth of his religious conviction. . . . It cannot be denied that in this attempt he used materials that more than once made a deterministic impression. For this reason it is emphatically asserted that there is reason for gratitude because after Luther, Calvin dealt with the problem of freedom

again without lapsing into Luther's error. . . .

But we emphatically deny that Luther arrived at his conception of free will starting from some philosophical concept of God via the concept of *necessitas*. It is true that Erasmus understood Luther in this way and after him the whole of Roman dogmatics. . . . But this fact clearly shows that Erasmus had not discovered the deepest religious motive of Luther's thought about the servile will . . . the primary religious motive hidden in Luther's fight against the natural freedom of the will of fallen man, namely the motive of sovereign grace. He was not concerned with a doctrinaire view of free will, with an analysis of human existence from a particular deterministic concept of God, but with justification by grace or — what was the same thing to him — by faith alone. . . .

There is no denying that Luther had an insight into grace different from that of Erasmus. With Luther grace is correlated with being a sinner, with the incapacity, blindness and limitations of human nature. There is no possibility here of cooperation, of synthesis in the sense of Erasmus, not on account of a deterministic view of the relation between God and man, but because of the nature of divine grace.[62] Here the circle of Luther's thought is always closed: *sola gratia*

---

[60] *Ibid.*, p. 80.
[61] *Ibid.*, p. 89.

[62] Cf. Luther: *"die wir Jesum Christum und nicht die Kraft des freien Willens predigen"* (*De servo arbitio*, ed. by Schmidt, p. 59). . . . In countless cases Luther speaks like this. But Erasmus and Roman dogmatics saw only Luther's "determinism." Cf. also pp. 62, 84.

Christi — sola fide. . . . Protestant writers admitted that in the expression of his basic religious thought Luther more than once moved in a climate which was not entirely free from determinism. But in spite of all this his real and most profound concept of sin and grace is simply undeniable. . . .

At the end of his work he gave the following summary of his basic tenets: "Therefore, when we believe that satan is a prince of the world opposing the Kingdom of Christ with all his powers, always armed for the struggle and the storm against it, that he will never release the people he has caught unless he is beaten off and vanquished through the power of the Holy Ghost and God's finger, it is once more manifest that there is no free will."[63]

We do not contest that in the elaboration of his view of grace, Luther incorporated elements that were really superfluous for his defense and which are no longer found in Calvin. They were the elements he had derived from the nominalism of the late Middle Ages (Ockham and Biel) and which belonged to the theological apparatus he employed. . . . We admit that Luther's conception was influenced by a view of predestination which here and there darkened the perspective of the full riches of his view of grace. . . .

The relation to God rules Luther's thought and determines his action. From this motive he fought against Erasmus in a highly emotional controversy which had one focus, namely, the sovereign character of grace as the omnipotent justifying acquittal by God, placing the sinner on the unshakable foundation laid by Jesus Christ. Only in this light can we understand his struggle against Erasmus about free will. "The central point in Luther's polemics does not concern the question whether man is capable of doing what he wants to do, but it concerns the entirely different question whether he can do what he should."[64] The Roman misconception of Luther's struggle cannot be more clearly seized upon in its kernel. Luther's opposition was not directed against human responsibility[65] but against such an "ethos" that pushed to the background the biblical preaching of grace, of justification for Christ's sake.[66]

---

[63] *De servo arbitrio* (Schmidt, p. 283). Cf. in this connection especially Theodosius Harnack, *Luthers Theologie*, Neue Ausgabe (1927), I, p. 137 ff.

[64] Werner Elert, *Morphologie des Luthertums*, 1931, I, p. 22.

[65] *Ibid.*, I, p. 21: *"Luther leugnete ja gar nicht die Verantwordlichkeit des Menschen. Von seinen Ablaszthesen an war sein gesamter Appell an die Kirche ein einziger Busruf gewesen."*

[66] Cf. also Calvin (*Acta synodi Tridentinae cum Antidoto, Corpus Reform.*, VII, p. 477): "Hoc semper lectoribus testatum esse volo, quoties in hac quaestione nominamus solam fidem, non mortuam a nobis fingi et quae per caritatem non operatur: sed ipsam statui unicam justificationis causam. Fides ergo sola est quae justificet: fides tamen quae justificat, non est sola. Quemadmodum solis calor solus est qui terram calefaciat: non tamen idem in sole est solus, quia perpetuo conjunctus est cum splendore." When Trent denounced the *sola fide* . . . "neque vero tam nos, quam Paulum anathematizant patres Tridenticolae cuius est definitio: justitiam hominis constare peccatorum remissio" (p. 477).

Calvin: assurance of salvation. . . . The antithesis between grace and works was posited in a radical way, not for the purpose of devaluating good works as such, but to emphasize the validity of Paul's conception which excludes the meritoriousness of all good works in our salvation. The struggle of the Reformation for the assurance of salvation may be called the counterpart to its protest against the meritoriousness of good works! That struggle was a fight against *justification through works* in its most refined form. Indignantly Calvin rejected the charge that he did not regard the numerous admonitions in Holy Scripture, the appeal to man, and the Biblical doctrine of the reward given by God. He made ample room for them in the elaboration of his thought, but he absolutely refused to base the assurance of salvation on them. He opposes synergism which coordinates the grace of God and human volition as two dynamic forces. In this Calvin is absolutely on the side of Luther against Erasmus. This is not a mere war of words. The interests of the pure religion of grace are at stake. The synergism of Rome's doctrine of grace was bound to lead to the denial of the assurance of salvation. Such a denial may be traced back to the humble avowal of man's own weakness and to the imperfect character of the present dispensation, but this does not derogate from the fact that here human activity is accorded an independent role and ultimately determines the effect of grace.

Calvin saw that Rome also wanted to speak of grace, and even held grace to be the principal cause of salvation. But it cannot be denied that Rome robbed God of part of His praise for our good works in order to transfer it to man.[67] . . . To Calvin it is impossible to deny the assurance of salvation because of the weakness of man. For faith is directed to the mercy of Christ who is truly merciful in and with respect to this weakness. In this weakness Christ is appealed to. For this reason Calvin thinks it impossible to recommend the way of attaining to certainty about one's own election outside of the divine Word and the promise. To him the certainty of one's election is not something *apart* from the assurance of faith. But *in* the assurance of faith and in his trust in God's mercy man is assured of God's election, resting in the word of the gospel. Here Calvin transcends the Roman "conjecture." . . .

Away with the dream — says Calvin[68] of those who indulge in the fancy that justification by faith and good works are *merged into each other*. There is indeed an indissoluble connection between justification and sanctification. And sanctification may be called a sign of justification and election. But such sanctification has no *foundational* meaning. Also on account of their imperfection our good works, if we wished to rely on them, would continually cause us to fall into doubting and uncertainty. . . . With unmistakable clarity Calvin repeated in all

[67] *Instit.* III, XV, 7.
[68] *Ibid.*, XI, 13.

kinds of connections, "that with respect to God's judgment not any support must be found in works and nobody should glory in any fantasy about works. This then is the agreement, namely, that the saints as regards the foundation and the establishing of their salvation exclusively direct their eyes to God's goodness without paying any attention to works."[69]

But Calvin is not a theologian of reaction and does not lose sight of the relation between justification and sanctification because of a rigid one-sidedness. To his clear words he is, therefore, able to add: "When thus our conscience is founded, lifted up, and confirmed, it is also confirmed by considering works, that is to say insofar as they are testimonies that God dwells in our hearts and rules us." Such an utterance should not be called contradictory. Calvin emphatically precludes any trust in works and says that our hearts must perfectly rely on the promise of unmerited righteousness. He adds: "but we do not forbid him to support and strengthen this

faith through the signs of God's loving-kindness towards him," and of the grace of good works he says: "it shows that we have received the Spirit of adoption."[70] Thus — in the communion of faith with Christ — the saints strengthen their faith with the innocence of their conscience and "derive reasons for joy from it." . . .

Calvin fully recognized the deep coherence between faith and good works, but this recognition implied that justification is by faith.[71] The coherence is founded in the fact that the righteousness of Christ cannot be embraced without striving for sanctification.[72] That is why living in *this sanctifica*tion results in strengthening our faith in the whole texture of our life.[73] But if anybody should try to infer from all these considerations that consequently also in Reformed theology works are given a function with respect to certainty, he should consider that here the fundamental difference between Rome and Calvin is laid bare: Calvin accepted the assurance of salvation and Rome did not.

5. E. Choisy[74] gives Calvin's definition of grace and his doctrine of general and special grace. Grace is the sovereignty of God manifesting itself in the world. General grace is a general revelation to all men. Special grace

---

[69] *Ibid.*, XIV, 18.
[70] *Ibid.*
[71] *Ibid.*, XVI, 1.
[72] *Ibid.*
[73] Cf. Dr. J. Ridderbos, "Versterking van het geloof uit de goede werken," *Geref. Theol. Tijdschr.* (1939), pp. 163, 168.
[74] Rev. J. Eugene Choisy, D.D. (Edin-burgh) was professor of ecclesiastical history at the Divinity Faculty, University of Geneva, and president of the Federation of Swiss Protestant Churches in 1931. This excerpt is taken from his article, "Calvin's Conception of Grace," in *The Doctrine of Grace*, ed. W. T. Whitley (London: SCM Press, 1931), pp. 228–234.

is a particular revelation, recorded in Scripture, which makes known the way of salvation, that is wholly wrought by God. Such a doctrine does not account for responsibility, which Calvin nevertheless urges.

Grace. It seems to me that with Calvin Grace may be defined in these terms: — The Sovereignty of God manifesting itself in the World, or: — The Sovereignty of God in the Service of His Love. God's sovereign Grace manifests itself in two ways: general Grace, or general revelation; special Grace or particular revelation.

General Grace. Calvin teaches that mankind, corrupted by the fall, would have been destined fatally to a total ruin, to a definitive degeneracy, had not God partially arrested, shackled, the action of sin, and hindered the annihilation of the work of His creation, by the action of His general Grace. In virtue of this general Grace, there is a general revelation, made to all men, including pagans; and experience shows that there really is *une semence de religion* implanted in all by a secret inspiration of God; that is natural religion.

By general Grace God confers, even on the wicked, virtues, which are by no means "natural." By this Grace man is not deprived of the light of reason; he has, "imprinted on his understanding," an instinct which prompts him to uphold society, civil order, government, policy. It is certain, says Calvin, that by now all honesty would be effaced between men, were there no admirable providence of God.[75]

The general Grace of God acts then

[75] *Opera*, xxviii, 10.

on the soul and on the heart of *all* men. It does not, indeed, destroy in them the germ of sin, nor does it save them unto life eternal; but it does restrain the power of sin in them. The maladies from which it frees, from which it *cleanses* the elect, it only represses with the reprobate: it hinders them, as by a bridle, from getting out of hand, according as God knows to be expedient, for the preservation of the whole world. That is why Dr. Kuyper could say that if Cain and Judas are the products of the corruption of mankind, Plato and Cicero are the products of general Grace.

Therefore although the whole world has been corrupted by sin, yet the whole world remains the object of the Grace of God. There is not on one side, part of the world experiencing Divine Grace, and on the other side, part of the world wholly beyond Divine Grace, a realm of thorough evil. God's Grace is among pagans, even as among Jews and Christians. Indeed, God's Grace is not only in the religious life, but in the *ordinary life*. All is the gift of God; philosophy, art, science, politics, like revelation and election (Bavinck).

Thus Calvin is absolutely opposed to a complete separation between religion and the world. In Calvinism no convents, no cloister, but a great moral seriousness, sometimes even rigorism.

Thus, in virtue of general Grace,

Calvin establishes firmly the independence of civil and political society. The state, society, politics, science, are not independent of God, since they are the gifts of His general Grace; but they are independent of the Church, which is another gift, another institution of God. The spiritual government is not a master and the political government is not its subject servant; both are equal before God, they ought to help one another in common work for the glory of God.

Finally, the last consequence of general Grace . . . is the encouragement given to activity outside the Church. A Christian should not neglect the gifts of God: to despise them would be despising God Himself. Hence His activity in every field: family life, social life, political life, scientific and artistic life. Whatever is good in civil society, whatever is good in Christian society, all this proves the same love of the same God.

This conception of general Grace is so large that it can be almost charged with denying the total corruption of human nature, or at least with reaching the same practical result as those doctrines which do deny it. But here there is only a specious resemblance; really the truth is that good is everywhere, evil is everywhere. Evil is everywhere, because even among the faithful, the corruption of nature persists; good is everywhere, because even the unbelieving are the object of God's Grace. But everywhere, good comes from God and His Grace (Kuyper).

Special grace. While there is general Grace and hence a *general revelation* made to all men, pagans included, there is on the other hand a *particular revelation* and a special Grace. To the general revelation of God in nature and conscience, is added the particular revelation whose document is the Bible, the Holy Scriptures of the Old and the New Testaments.

Because of sin, natural religion finds itself powerless. The knowledge of God that nature gives is "confused and scanty." But Scripture allows us to read clearly as in a deed what the true God is. Then by the same inner witness of the Holy Spirit the certainty of Bible truth is impressed on us. Now this Bible truth is essentially the Way of Salvation. By His Grace God accomplishes our whole salvation from beginning to end. By that same Grace He gives to the elect, and to the elect only, the spirit of regeneration. Grace is the counterpart of the Fall. In turning us to Himself God creates in us a new spirit, a new heart. All that springs from our own will is abolished, and all that follows is from God. It is a new birth.

God wishing to convince us of our impotence to do good by ourselves has given His Law and has bidden us do what is beyond our powers. Now if He bids what we cannot do, it is in order that, when we recognize ourselves incapable by ourselves of doing His will, we may know what we should ask from Him so as to seek in Him alone salvation and Grace. Thus the Law is a pedagogue that leads us to Christ the Saviour Who is the pledge of our election. With those who are the object of the prevenient and efficacious Grace of God, Grace is also the gift of perseverance. Instead of their corrupted nature God has given them a regenerated nature. And without being constrained but in virtue of the inevitable consequences of their state of Grace, they spontaneously do good. They persevere in good. They possess the liberty of good.

The election of Grace in nowise depends on the works nor the merits of the man. God saves whom He will, whom He has elected in His mercy. He gives them faith in Jesus Christ. And if He has elected them, it is that by a decree of His sovereign will, mysterious, unfathomable, He has foreordained them to be His children and heirs of His heavenly kingdom.

Since salvation by faith in Jesus Christ is the gift of the particular Grace of God, it follows that those who do not believe, those who are obstinate in their unfaith, do not share salvation. God has not elected them. God does not grant them His Grace. There is no injustice here. It is their perversity which is the cause of their perdition, and since the whole of mankind is corrupt it would without exception deserve condemnation and eternal death.

It is then by pure Grace that in the mass devoted to perdition, God chooses a small number of elect whom He foreordains to salvation. It is by pure Grace that He calls them by the preaching of His word, teaches them effectively by the illumination of the Holy Spirit and introduces them into His family, adopting them in Jesus Christ as His children.

By the doctrine of the foreordination of the great majority to perdition, Calvin explains logically and intellectually the fact of the disbelief or non-perseverance of the great majority of men. By the doctrine of the election of grace, of the foreordination to salvation of the small number of the elect, Calvin makes God and God alone the Author of the salvation of believers. If they believe and are saved, that is not of themselves nor from any merit or good work of their own. It is wholly because God has called them and bestowed on them faith.

By the doctrine of election and foreordination to salvation, the faithful know themselves to be in God's hands. They are freed from all sacramental magic and from all clerical or sacerdotal tyranny. Led by the effect of the particular Grace of God to faith on Jesus Christ, the unique and perfect Mediator and Redeemer, they have the assurance that despite their insignificance, their unworthiness, their sins, no human power, were it that of pope or emperor, can rob them of the salvation which God has given them in Christ, for whom He has elected them and foreordained them in virtue of His sovereign goodness.

Calvin protests against those who would infer from the doctrine of particular Grace leading on to double foreordination, the conclusion that the responsibility of the sinner is suppressed. At the risk of bearing the reproach of lacking logic, he affirms vigorously that while everything is foreordained, yet the sinner is responsible for his destiny. It is the "labyrinth" whence logic cannot emerge.[76]

The doctrine of particular Grace thus has a double aspect: a terrible aspect, since there is but a small number of elect, and the mass of mankind is devoted to perdition; a reasonable, consolatory aspect, since God has manifested Himself in Jesus Christ, Redeemer, and makes the elect participate in that redemption which is in Jesus Christ. And as we really do not know *who* will be saved, we ought to long for the salvation of *all*.[77] There are sheep outside the fold, and wolves within. Do we know that such vicious people are not of the elect, and that they may end by believing? This fact should inspire us with sentiments of breadth and tolerance. Let us then be patient, let us not cease appealing to all men.

"Since our salvation only proceeds from the pure goodness and gratuitousness of our God, why is it that He does not the like to those who are now going to perdition, as we have been?"[78] God certainly has good reasons to do so, but we have no right to ask what they are, since He has not revealed them. This is an inscrutable mystery.

Thus God acts differently towards those who are and those who are not the object of His particular Grace. But nothing, nobody, not even the wicked and the reprobate, is beyond the effect of His general Grace.

It is said justly that the thought of Calvin is like an ellipse with two focuses; intelligence and sensibility, external facts and internal experiences. So is it also with his doctrine of Grace: it is an ellipse whose two focuses are general Grace and particular Grace.

6. **H. Rondet, S.J.,[79] touches on Luther's life, his sudden illumination, his theology and the influences that shaped it, his doctrines of the radical corruption of fallen man, of the imputation of Christ's merits, of justification by faith and faith alone. In Calvin's doctrine he finds a theological system of capital importance, which maintains the Lutheran theses on justification but manifests its originality especially in its theses on predestination.**

In the history of the theology of grace Luther and the Reformation occupy an immense place. Against them the Church formulated her doctrine in a document of unusual amplitude. But it is difficult for a Catholic theologian to set forth Luther's thought objectively. . . . For we often know him only through the refutations of controversialists to whom the father of the Reformation was a species of anti-Christ. Protestant theologians and his-

---

[76] E. Doumergue, *Calvin*, iv, 377.

[77] *Institutio*, 1559, iii, 23, 14.

[78] *Opera*, LIII, pp. 125, 129, 135.

[79] Cf. ch. III, n. 1. This excerpt is from *op. cit.*, pp. 257–272.

torians in turn are hard put to speak without prejudice of Luther and the Counter-Reformation. Since the reactions stirred up by Denifle's[80] vigorous attacks, Catholics and Protestants have been trying to revise the summary judgments of their respective traditions, and in time history will disengage itself little by little from the legend.[81]

Luther's theology is difficult to expound. The father of the Reformation has nothing systematic about him. He is an intuitive type, a "prophet," a tumultuous torrent. He loves brutal images and pushes his thought all the way to paradox, so that one would be very wrong if he always took him literally.[82] . . . It is very important to remember that he lived in an epoch of extraordinary ferment. The West was in full effervescence, scholastic theology was in extreme decadence and the Church was far from stainless. Everywhere, in Italy, in France, in England, in Germany men were going back to antiquity and rediscovering the poets and philosophers, the Fathers of the Church and the Gospel itself.[83] Formed in a dessicated and soulless school of

scholasticism, obsessed by anguish over his salvation, tortured perhaps by an obscure desire to play a great role in the brewing commotions, Luther reacted against his masters in the light of a religious experience that was certainly far from ordinary.

To understand him we need not suppose with Denifle that he was obsessed by carnal temptations.[84] From the beginning Luther seems to have been a good monk who tried to observe his rule and multiplied ascetical practices, fasts, prayers. He was eager for union with God but he found no peace. Biel, Peter d'Ailly, Occam, the authors he had to read, passed lightly over the surface of his soul and left only the idea of the divine omnipotence and arbitrariness. But grace came to him, at first an exterior grace in the benevolent friendship of Staupitz, one of his superiors, who tranquilized him by saying: "Why do you torture yourself with predestination? Turn your gaze to the wounds of Jesus Christ and the blood He poured out for you. . . . No, God is not angry at you, it is you who are angry with yourself."[85] For a time this friendship consoled the unquiet monk. . . .

But anxieties took hold of him again. It was then, about 1513, that the famous event occured which, if we believe Luther, upset his whole life and

[80] H. Denifle, *Luther and Luthertum*, 1904–1906, 2 ed., 1904–1909; *Luther et le luthéranisme* (trad. J. Paquier), 4 vols., 1912–1913.

[81] The bibliography of the subject will be found in the remarkable little book of L. Febvre, *Un destin, Martin Luther*, 1928, 2 ed., 1945.

[82] J. Paquier, "Luther," DTC, t. IX, col. 1168–1175. R. Will, *La liberté chrétienne*, a study on the principle of Luther's piety, 1922, pp. xiv, 16.

[83] P. Imbart De La Tour, *Les origines de la Réforme*, t. I, 1905.

[84] H. Denifle et Paquier, *Luther et le luthéranisme*, t. II, pp. 402–405, and in the opposite sense, L. Febvre, *op. cit.*, pp. 44–46, in agreement with H. Grisar, *Luther*, t. I, 1911, p. 86 note.

[85] H. Grisar, *Martin Luther, sa vie et son oeuvre*, 1931, p. 32; J. Paquier, "Luther," DTC, t. IX, col. 1152.

would upset Germany and Europe.[86] The passionate man had a sudden illumination. Grace of God? Work of man? Who shall say? He must stop running away from sin, it said, abandon himself to God, stop being preoccupied with self, look on himself as incapable of being cured and cast himself on the divine mercy. God cannot change the heart of man. But he can close His eyes and act as if the heart were changed. He can regard as just one who remains a sinner and cover him with the merits of Christ as with a mantle. Sin will not be destroyed. It will remain but it will no longer be imputed. Works: it is futile to be preoccupied with them. Exterior works and unquiet care for one's perfection: this is Pharisaism. . . . Man cannot merit before God! But grace! The certainty of a God who regards a sinful man as if he were just and holy because of the merits of the Redeemer! Theologians speak of a *habitus*, a created reality in man that changes him miraculously. But this theology does not correspond to experience. Experience proves that as long as man remains on earth he remains a scion of the old sinful Adam, rotten to the marrow. Original sin which is identified with concupiscence poisons his whole life. Grace brings peace, suppresses all inquietude and removes all anguish on the subject of reprobation. To be saved, it is enough to have confidence in God and believe that one will be saved. Sinful man is justified by faith.

For Luther justification by faith is not a formula of the schools but a truth of experience. Faith is not first an intellectual assent. It is a spiritual attitude, a transport of the soul made up of joyous confidence and abandon and invincible assurance. Luther has the conviction that God is with him, the terrible God who damns whom He will, but who saves those who consent to abandon themselves to His infinite mercy. We cannot disregard the richness and depth of this theology. . . .

The famous illumination of Luther coordinates elements of diverse origin. Imputed justice is really an inheritance of Nominalism[87] which conceives the relations between God and man in an entirely exterior fashion. . . . To the influence of Nominalism we must add that of Augustinism.[88] From the day he discovered him Luther saw in Augustine the doctor par excellence whom he could never praise enough.[89] He opposed him to the moderns and to

---

[86] J. Paquier, DTC, t. IX, col. 1206–1209. — H. Grisar, *Luther*, t. I, pp. 319–326.

[87] J. Paquier, "Luther," DTC, t. IX, col. 1184–1188. Luther says of himself: "I am a disciple of Occam" (*Sum occamicae factionis*) (O. Scheel, *Dokumente*, p. 17).

[88] J. Paquier, DTC, t. IX, col. 1189. — A. Hamel, *Der junge Luther und Augustinus*, I, 1931; II, 1936.

[89] In the commentary on the *Sentences*, Luther praises Peter Lombard for holding to the eyes of the Church "*maxime illustrissimo jubari et nunquam satis laudato Augustino*" (W., IX, 29; Clemen, t. V, p. 4) but at the beginning he did not know the writings on grace. Reading *De spirtu et littera* seems to have impressed him very much. It introduced him to St. Paul.

Aristotle, the fabulator who perverted the Christian faith.[90] . . .

Augustine, who also spoke from experience, had underlined the misery of man even when redeemed and justified, and had seen in justification less a state than a becoming.[91] Luther goes still further and assures us that man, whatever he may do, will never be justified as long as life continues here below. For original sin has corrupted his whole being,[92] and where it reigns there can be no good. The virtues of

the pagans are only splendid vices.[93] Even the Christian is justified only by a juridical fiction. If he were not covered by the merits of Christ, the disorder of concupiscence would be enough to constitute him a sinner. Even when covered by them a man can only sin mortally in his own proper actions, but a divine decree renders these faults of the justified venial.[94] The great scholastics had put an ontological distinction between venial and mortal sin, but there is nothing of the sort here. The Nominalism which Luther had tried to exorcise reappears ceaselessly. It commands his interpretation of Augustine and it commands still more his interpretation of the Apostle.

The true master of Luther is St. Paul, the Paul of the Epistle to the Galatians and of the Epistle to the Romans.[95] The disturbed monk finds himself in those famous chapters where the Apostle describes the conflict between concupiscence and the law. To him the Pauline thesis of justification by faith appears more profound than the speculations of the theologians.[96] Paul set himself against the legalism

[90] Apropos the celebrated opinion of Lombard on charity Luther writes: "videtur magister non penitus absurdissime loqui; in eo quod habitum dicit esse Spiritum sanctum, quia commentum illud de habitibus opinionem habet ex verbis Aristotelis rancidi philosophi" (*In Sent.*, I, 17; W., IX, 43; Clemen, V, 7), and elsewhere: "melius hic Augustinus et verius de felicitate disputat quam fabulator Aristoteles cum suis frivolis defensoribus" (W., IX, 23; Scheel, *Dokumente*, p. 219).

[91] Luther, as St. Augustine, understands Chapter 7 of the Epistle to the Romans of the justified man and accuses the scholastics of infidelity to the thought of the doctor of Hippo. Denifle shows here with passion that Luther did not know the history of the question and was a mediocre exegete (Denifle et Paquier, *Luther et le luthéranisme*, t. VII, pp. 104–109).

[92] *In Rom.*, 5 (ed. Ficker, II, 144): "quid ergo nunc est peccatum originale. . . . Secundum subtilitates theologorum est privatio seu carentia justitiae originalis; secundum Apostolum et simplicitatem sensus in Christo Jesu est non tantum privatio qualitatis in voluntate, immo nec tantum privatio lucis in intellectu, virtutis in memoria, sed prorsus privatio universae rectitudinis et potentiae omnium virium tam corporis quam animae ac totius hominis interioris et exterioris. Insuper est pronitas ipsa ad malum, nausea ad bonum, fastidium lucis et sapientiae, dilectio autem erroris ac tenebrarum, fuga et abominatio bonorum operum, cursus autem ad malum. . . ."

[93] Luther attributes this formula to Augustine and Denifle is indignant over this (Denifle et Paquier, *Luther et luthéranisme*, t. I, pp. lviii–lix). Others note that if the formula is not Augustine's it still expresses a frequent thought of his (Lange, *De gratia*, 1929, p. 66, note).

[94] *Scholien in Rom.* 7 (Ficker, II, 179–180).

[95] Cf. J. Ficker, *Luthers Vorlesungen über den Römerbrief*, 4 ed., 1930: I, *die Glosse*, II, *die Scholien*. On the radical corruption and imputed justice cf. Paquier, DTC, IX, col. 1212–1229.

[96] On Lutheran faith cf. Paquier, "Lu-

of the Pharisees and the sufficiency of works. Luther believes that he is a new Paul and scornful of fifteen centuries of Christian reflection goes straight back to Paul. How could one of our greatest geniuses make such a clean sweep of his spiritual inheritance? Whatever one may say of him, Luther reads St. Paul through the prejudices of an Augustinian nominalist.

He will thus be the prisoner of a system or rather of a religious experience erected into a universal truth that will lead him to all sorts of negations. The true unity of Luther's thought is this powerful but wild individualism which will bring him to overthrow the established order, institutions and doctrines instead of trying only to reform them. . . . Luther becomes the prophet of a new Gospel and makes himself the defender of Christian liberty. . . . And in the meantime he has pushed the consequences of his thought and of his interpretation of the doctor of Hippo to their extremity. He continues to say that man in his entirety is vitiated by sin and that only faith justifies him by an extrinsic imputation of the merits of Christ,[97] but two theses stand out in sharper relief: the impotence of free will and the subjective certitude of justification.

On the first point he came into conflict with Erasmus in a resounding debate.[98] The De libero arbitrio of Erasmus represents the reaction of reason, of a reason emancipated from the tutelage of the Church. To defend free will Erasmus starts from considerations drawn from the social order. Luther refuses to do battle on this terrain, and in De servo arbitrio (1525) he will speak only of Scripture and of the sovereign dominion of a God who makes of His creatures what He pleases. In the hands of his Creator man is only an instrument. God alone acts and man is passive, or rather he is like a mount ridden by a horseman. If the horseman is God man will do well, but if it is the devil he will necessarily do evil.[99] An audacious

---

ther," DTC, t. IX, col. 1231; L. Cristiani, "Luther au couvent," in Revue des questions historiques, 1914, t. I, pp. 336–370. We have noted that in St. Paul faith is a very complex notion, and the best exegetes recognize that it implies besides intellectual adhesion an element of confidence, an act of obedience and finally charity (F. Prat, La théologie de saint Paul, t. I, 25 ed., pp. 203–205). But between the Catholic thought and the Protestant thought there is much more than a difference of vocabulary. The intellectual element is not absent from the Lutheran notion but it is not in the foreground and it gives way more and more to a blind confidence in Jesus the Savior of the world. . . .

[97] This thesis is expressed in the famous words that Catholic apologists so willingly cite, without remembering sufficiently that Luther loved paradox: "si gratiae praedicator es, gratiam non fictam, sed veram praedica, si vera gratia est, verum non fictum peccatum ferto. Deus non facit salvos fictos peccatores. Esto peccator et pecca fortiter, sed fortius fide et gaude in Christo, qui est victor peccati, mortis et mundi" (letter to Melanchthon, August 1, 1521, Werke, Clemen, t. VI, p. 53).
[98] Erasmus of Rotterdam, Essai sur le libre arbitre, trad. P. Mesnard, 1946. — J. Paquier, "Luther," DTC, t. IX, col. 1283–1295. — H. Humbetclaude, Erasme et Luther, 1909.
[99] De servo arbitrio (W., XVIII, 635; Clemen, t. III, p. 126).

image that expresses violently in Luther's manner a theological thesis against which not only the Church but Lutherans themselves are going to react. . . .

Luther is thus the enemy of free will, but he is also the enemy of every juridico-ontological conception of justification. In classical Augustinism sacramental theology was the indispensable complement of the theology of grace. One is justified by entry into the Church or by the imposition of hands that marks the completion of the penitential process. This communal aspect of the supernatural life Luther calls into question and later one of his most illustrious disciples will say: "The entire difference between Catholicism and Protestantism lies in this that the Protestant goes directly to Christ, while the Catholic demands the mediation of a visible Church."[100] Luther wants to recognize no supernatural efficacy in the sacraments. His individualist mystique fears magic here and he wants to see in the rites only simple excitants of the faith which alone justifies.[101] How will the Christian know if he is at peace with God? If he is truly united to Christ and covered with his merits? Only by an incommunicable subjective experience.[102] The contemporaries of Christ had the consolation of hearing it said by a man of flesh and bone: "Go, your sins are remitted!" The Catholic thinks that the priest who absolves is truly the mandatory of Christ. The Lutheran can only turn to an interior witness that is subject to all sorts of illusions. Between the point of view of the person and that of the community founded by Christ no synthesis is achieved. But the Catholic Church will only have to reflect on its proper life to discover this interiority toward which the Luther of the early years aspired. . . .

There are then three essential theses against which the Catholic Church will have to define its proper position: radical corruption of man wounded by original sin, extrinsic imputation of the merits of Christ, justification by faith and by faith alone. . . .

We will not stop at Zwingli whose doctrines had only a momentary glow. . . . Calvin will hold us longer. For the French Reformer gives us a theological system of capital importance, and refutations will take better hold on him than on the unseizable Luther.[103] Luther was especially devoted to St. Paul. Calvin is more specifically Augustinian, with the radical Augustinism of a legist who has also read Bradwardine. With Luther he speaks of Christian liberty but he knows well this should not be abused, and so he brings back into honor the observ-

---

[100] F. Schleiermacher, *Der Christliche Glaube*, 1 ed., 1821, pp. 137–138.

[101] L. Cristiani, "Réforme," DTC, t. XIII, col. 2062.

[102] J. Paquier, "Luther," DTC, t. IX, col. 1232–1237.

[103] On the theology of Calvin see the articles of A. Jundt (*Encyclopédie des sciences religieuses* de Lichtenberger, t. II, col. 545–557) and A. Baudrillart (DTC, t. II, col. 1398–1402) and tome IV of *Origines de la Réforme* of P. Imbart De La Tour. See also the articles of Cristiani in DTC (*Réforme*, t. XIII, col. 2050–2051, 2059–2061) and DAF (*Réforme*, t. IV, col. 644–645).

ance of the Law. Where Luther put an abyss between the Law and the Gospel, Calvin reconciles them.[104] One must live, one of his interpreters will say, as if there were no Gospel, and die as if there were no Law.[105]. . .

Calvin's originality manifests itself especially in his theses on predestination. On the first plane he puts the glory of God.[106] God is the sovereign master of the universe and holds in His hand the being and life of everything that is. He can have no other motive for His action than His own proper glory. So before the beginning of time he decreed immutably that men would be predestined to manifest this glory, some by their gratuitous election, many more others by their damnation.[107] In interpreting Augustinism Calvin goes further than Jansenius will go for he has reprobation and predestination precede all consideration of the sin of Adam. Adam himself fell because he was predestined to sin.[108] Man's liberty yields before the sovereign dominion of God. The relations between creature and Creator are conceived in a very anthropomorphic fashion. There is a theological determinism of the most rigorous sort.

But does not Scripture speak of the universal salvific will? Calvin answers by a distinction. First, the text of the first Epistle of Paul to Timothy must be interpreted in the manner of Augustine: there is no class of men, no "state" in which God does not recruit His elect.[109] Secondly we must distinguish between the *vocatio generalis* and the *vocatio specialis*. God calls all men to salvation by exterior preaching, but he moves efficaciously and definitively the heart of the predestined alone. There is a universal vocation "by which the Lord calls to Himself all men indifferently" and a special vocation which is proper to the faithful or rather to the predestined alone, since some are called to the faith only for a time.[110]. . .

Augustine had spoken roughly of fallen man . . . going so far sometimes as to say that he had lost liberty. Calvin expands even more complacently on the ravages caused in us by original sin.[111] He bluntly refuses to distinguish between the will of God and His permission.[112] He supposes that God willed the sin of Adam with all its consequences[113] and hardens the heart of those who must serve to manifest His justice.[114] In the heart of those

---

[104] F. Loofs, *Leitfaden zur D.G.*, p. 883. P. Imbart De La Tour, *op. cit.*, t. IV, p. 85–89, 93–97.

[105] R. Will, *La liberté chrétienne*, p. 72.

[106] *Christian. religionis institut.*, ed. de 1539 (*Opera in Corpus reform.*, t. I, col. 27).

[107] *Institution chrétienne*, III, 21 (*Opera*, t. IV, p. 454).

[108] *Inst. chrét.*, III, 23, 4 (*Opera*, t. IV, p. 490). This is supra-lapsarian predestination.

[109] *Inst. chrét.*, III, 24, 15 (*Opera*, t. IV, p. 526).

[110] *Inst. chrét.*, III, 24, 8 (*Opera*, t. IV, p. 516).

[111] *Inst. chrét.*, II, 2 (*Opera*, t. III, p. 297).

[112] *Inst. chrét.*, III, 23, 8 (*Opera*, t. IV, p. 495).

[113] H. Bois, "La prédestination d'après Calvin" in *Revue de métaphysique et de morale*, 1918, pp. 670–671.

[114] *Inst. chrét.*, I, 18 (*Opera*, t. III, p. 269). This is voluntarism pushed to its extreme consequences.

whom He leads to salvation God acts by an irresistible grace. So liberty is identified with spontaneity, and Calvin in turn takes up the image of the charger whom God or the devil rides and attributes it to St. Augustine.[115]

Calvin maintains the Lutheran theses on justification by faith but he bends them in the sense of his theories on predestination. He is justified who firmly believes that he is of the number of the elect. Where Luther taught that only the sin of infidelity could make one lose the state of grace, Calvin goes further: the state of grace is absolutely unlosable.[116]

But do not take these words, the state of grace, in a Catholic sense. No more than Luther does Calvin want to be understood as speaking of a created grace. For the fathers of the Reformation the scholastic precisions on actual and habitual grace and on grace and charity no longer have any meaning. They content themselves with juxtaposing juridical categories and the data of religious experience.

For Calvin as for Luther the certitude of justification is a purely subjective assurance that is subject to illusion. But nonetheless it is capable of stirring souls to enthusiasm. Cromwell's soldiers, good Puritans, will draw an incomparable force from the certitude that their cause is that of God and that they are predestined.[117] And Cromwell himself when dying will console himself by thinking that he is sure to have been in the state of grace.[118]

But differently from Luther Calvin made much of works. He understands that man is incapable of any merit[119] and he is certain that the observance of the Law is impossible for man[120] but he thinks rightly that Christian life is communitarian. The Christian community for him is not an unseizable reality, a metempiric church. For him as for the Catholic it is a well-defined church which defends its faith, excommunicates heretics and chastises the perverse.[121] There is nothing astonishing then in the fact that he puts stress on the Law and its prescriptions, for the Law is the expression of the divine will. To obey the heads of the Church is to obey God Himself. Thus Calvinism is a species of neo-Catholicism but more intransigent since its dogmas are less tested by a living tradition. . . .

---

[115] Inst. chrét., II, 4, 1 (Opera, t. III, p. 354).

[116] Inst. chrét., III, 24 (Opera, t. IV, p. 504).

[117] A. Maurois, Histoire d'Angleterre, 1937, p. 464.

[118] J. Paquier, "Luther," D.T.C., t. IX, col. 1237, citing D. Hume's History of England.

[119] Inst. chrét., III, 15 (Opera, t. IV, p. 294).

[120] Inst. chrét., II, 5, 6 (Opera, t. III, p. 369).

[121] P. Imbart De La Tour, Les origines de la Réforme, t. IV, pp. 98–111.

7. T. P. Neill and R. H. Schmandt[122] give a brief outline of John Calvin, his *Institutes of the Christian Religion*, his theological system, and his contribution to the Reformation.

The divisive nature of the Protestant Revolt soon threatened to weaken the movement and make it possible for the Church to win back the people who had left the faith. . . . The man who saved the Protestant movement from this disintegrating tendency was a French layman, John Calvin, who gave the movement a systematic theology when he published his *Institutes of the Christian Religion* (1536) and infused into it a missionary zeal with his doctrine of the Elect. The success of Calvinism consolidated the Protestant Revolt from the Church and ensured its permanence. Moreover, the followers of Calvin were a more aggressive group than Lutherans and they played a large part in giving the Western world a new attitude toward life, a new ethic, and a new economic order. . . .

Among the French reformers of these days who left the Church during one of the brief periods of "persecution" was John Calvin. Born at Noyon, in Picardy, of a solid, middle-class family, young Calvin studied among the humanists and then went to Orleans to take a law degree. Calvin's first writing, a commentary on Seneca's *De Clementia*, shows him to be a thorough humanist in 1532. By the end of the following year, however, he seems to have adopted a posi-

tion that was essentially Lutheran. Calvin went into hiding when the government took action against Nicholas Cop, rector of the University of Paris, for an address which Calvin helped him prepare.

In the next three years Calvin traveled from place to place, eventually settled at Basel in 1535, where he wrote the first edition of his *Institutes of the Christian Religion*. By this time he had broken off from the humanist reformers and had adopted a purely evangelical form of religion. The first edition of the *Institutes* contains the main outlines of Calvin's mature thought, but his ideas are not well developed until later editions, especially those of 1541 and 1559. Calvin addressed his work to the French king, whom he hoped to convert to his evangelical religion. Although he failed to accomplish his immediate purpose with the *Institutes,* he produced the greatest work on systematic theology by any Protestant and one of the most influential books of modern times. . . .

Calvin's theological system is the first complete and systematic body of thought to be worked out by any Protestant. There was little original thought in Calvin's *Institutes,* but the work is distinctive for weaving the various strands of Protestant thought together and drawing them to logical conclusions. The cornerstone of Calvin's thought is the absolute sover-

---

[122] Ch. IX, n. 1. This excerpt is from op. cit., pp. 323, 326–327, 332–333.

eignty of God and the complete depravity of man. Fallen man cannot earn his justification but some are predestined by God to salvation. Man's sole function — whether he is one of the Elect or one of the damned — is to glorify God. Calvin held that God's plan for salvation and for the conduct of the world is set forth in Holy Scripture.

Calvin's religion was more extreme and barren than Luther's. He denied all but two sacraments, Baptism and the Eucharist, and taught that neither of them is necessary for salvation. For Calvin baptism is only a rite whereby a person is admitted to the Church. In the Holy Eucharist, he claimed, Christ is only dynamically present. Religious service in the new religion was cold and severe, consisting mainly of preaching, hymn singing, and a "memorial service" to commemorate the Last Supper. All "superstitious" practices were ruthlessly eliminated, and the church of the new religion was a plain, unadorned structure. . . .

We miss the chief importance of the Calvinist revolt from the church if we confine our attention only to those Churches which came directly from Geneva. For Calvinism influenced the other Protestant religions and even to some extent Catholic peoples who lived in close contact with reformed Protestants. Calvin's theology and morality appealed along class rather than national lines. His doctrine fitted in nicely with the aspirations and ambitions of the rising middle class, and it is therefore natural

that Calvinism should spread along the trade routes, center in the cities, and win large numbers of adherents in the commercial areas of Europe.

Calvin's doctrine of the Elect worked out curiously, but logically, to promote wealth seeking for its own sake. Calvin's followers came to believe that prosperity in this life was the best possible objective indication of election for salvation, for certainly God would favor in this life the few He has marked out for salvation in the next. Moreover, the virtues on which Calvin laid great stress were all virtues that made for economic success: hard, unremitting labor, frugality, and industriousness. These virtues make for large income and small spending, in other words for the accumulation of capital. Calvin insisted upon restless activity, and since man is already predestined to salvation or damnation, this activity is naturally to be directed to worldly concerns. That is why R. H. Tawney writes of Calvinism:[123]

"It is perhaps the first systematic body of religious teaching which can be said to recognize and applaud the economic virtues. . . . Such teaching, whatever its theological merits or defects, was admirably designed to liberate economic energies, and to weld into a disciplined social force the rising *bourgeoisie*, conscious of the contrast between its own standards and those of a laxer world, proud of its vocation as the standard-bearer of

[123] *Religion and the Rise of Capitalism* (New York: 1926), 111.

the economic virtues, and determined to vindicate an open road for its own way of life by the use of every weapon, including political revolution and war, because the issue which was at stake was not merely convenience or self-interest, but the will of God."

Thus the followers of Calvin glorified work as it had never been glorified before. . . . From Geneva, Calvin sent out a class of men who were to be important not only the field of religion but also in creating modern European and American society and in making the world the sort of place it is today.

X

GRACE IN THE COUNCIL OF TRENT

1. **J. F. Clarkson, S.J., J. H. Edwards, S.J., W. J. Kelly, S.J., and J. J. Welch, S.J.,[1] give us an excellent translation of Trent's decree of January 13, 1547, on justification — as found in Denzinger.**

Decree on Justification[2]

Preface. Since at this time a certain erroneous teaching about justification is being broadcast with the con-

sequent loss of many souls and serious damage to Church unity, this holy,

[1] John F. Clarkson, S.J., John H. Edwards, S.J., William J. Kelly, S.J., John J. Welch, S.J., of St. Mary's College, St. Marys, Kansas, translated and prepared for publication this selection, which is taken from pp. 229–241 of their book, *The*

Church Teaches. This book was published by B. Herder Book Co., St. Louis, Mo., 1955.

[2] One of the most important sessions of the Council of Trent was the sixth, which lasted from June 21, 1546, until January 13, 1547. After long debate, much discussion, drafting, and redrafting, the decree on justification was finally published.

ecumenical, and general Council of Trent[3] . . . intends to set forth for all the faithful of Christ the true, sound doctrine of justification, which the "Sun of justice" (Mal 4:2) Jesus Christ, the author and finisher of our faith (see Heb 12:2), has taught, which the apostles have handed down, and which the Catholic Church, under the inspiration of the Holy Spirit, has always preserved. The council gives strict orders that hereafter no one is to presume to believe, preach, or teach anything contrary to what is defined and declared in this decree.

Ch. 1. The Insufficiency of Nature and the Law to Justify Man.

First, the holy council declares that, for an honest, unprejudiced understanding of the doctrine of justification, it is necessary to admit that all men had lost innocence in the sin of Adam (see Rom 5:12; 1 Cor 15:22). . . . So completely were they slaves of sin (see Rom 6:20) and under the power of the devil and of death, that neither the power of nature for the Gentiles nor the very letter of the Law of Moses for the Jews could bring liberation from that condition. And yet their free will, though weakened and unsteady, was by no means destroyed.

---

[3] Presiding over the council in the name of our most holy father and lord in Christ, Paul III by divine providence pope, are the very reverend lords, John Mary Monte, bishop of Praeneste; Marcellus, titular priest of Santa Croce in Jerusalem; cardinals of the holy Roman Church, and apostolic legates *de latere.* . . .

Ch. 2. God's Dispensation and the Mystery of Christ's Coming.

And so it came about that, when the glorious fullness of time had come (see Eph 1:4; Gal 4:4), the heavenly Father . . . sent Jesus Christ His Son to men . . . that the Jews who were under the Law, might be redeemed, and that the Gentiles, who were not pursuing justice, might secure justice (see Rom 9:30), and that all might receive the adoption of sons (see Gal 4:5). . . .

Ch. 3. Who are Justified through Christ.

But even though Christ did die for all (see 2 Cor 5:15), still all do not receive the benefit of His death, but only those with whom the merit of His Passion is shared. Truly, men would not have been born without justice except that they were born children of Adam's seed. For it is because of their descent from him that in their conception they contract injustice as their own. So likewise they would never have been justified except through rebirth in Christ, for this rebirth bestows on them through the merit of His Passion the grace by which they are justified. . . .

Ch. 4. A Summary Description of the Justification of a Sinner. . . .

In the preceding words a description is given of the justification of the unjust. Justification is a passing from the state in which man is born a son of the first Adam, to the state of grace and adoption as sons of God (see Rom 8:15) through the second Adam, Jesus

Christ our Savior. Since the gospel was promulgated, this passing cannot take place without the water of regeneration or the desire for it, as it is written: "Unless a man be born again of water and the Holy Spirit, he cannot enter into the kingdom of God" (Jn 3:5).

Ch. 5. The Necessity for Adults to Prepare Themselves for Justification. . . .

Moreover, the holy council declares that in the case of adults justification must begin with God's prevenient grace through Jesus Christ. That is, it must begin with God's call, a call which they do not merit. The purpose of this call is that they who are turned away from God by sin may, awakened and assisted by His grace, be disposed to turn to their own justification by freely assenting to and cooperating with that grace. The result is that, when God touches the heart of man with the illumination of the Holy Spirit, the man who accepts that inspiration certainly does something, since he could reject it; on the other hand, by his own free will, without God's grace, he could not take one step towards justice in God's sight. . . .

Ch. 6. The Manner of Preparation.

Adults are disposed for justification in this way: Awakened and assisted by divine grace, they conceive faith from hearing (see Rom 10:17), and they are freely led to God. They believe that the divine revelation and promises are true, especially that the unjustified man is justified by God's grace "through the redemption which is in Christ Jesus" (Rom 3:24). Next, they know that they are sinners; and, by turning from a salutary fear of divine justice to a consideration of God's mercy, they are encouraged to hope, confident that God will be propitious to them for Christ's sake. They begin to love God as the source of all justice and are thereby moved by a sort of hatred and detestation for sin, that is, by the penance that must be done before baptism. Finally, they determine to receive baptism, begin a new life, and keep the divine commandments. . . .[4]

Ch. 7. The Nature and the Causes of the Justification of a Sinner.

Justification itself follows upon this disposition or preparation, and justification is not only the remission of sins, but sanctification and renovation of the interior man through the voluntary reception of grace and gifts, whereby a man becomes just instead of unjust and a friend instead of an enemy, that he may be an heir in the hope of life everlasting (see Ti 3:7).

[4] This disposition is described in Holy Scripture: "He who comes to God must believe that God exists and is a rewarder to those who seek him" (Heb 11:6); and: "Take courage, son, thy sins are forgiven thee" (Mt 9:2; Mk 2:5); and: "The fear of the Lord driveth out sin" (Sir 1:27); "Repent and be baptized every one of you in the name of Jesus Christ for the forgiveness of your sins; and you will receive the gift of the Holy Spirit" (Acts 2:38); and: "Go, therefore, and make disciples of all nations, baptizing them in the name of the Father, and of the Son, and of the Holy Spirit, teaching them to observe all that I have commanded you" (Mt 28:19); finally, "Prepare your hearts unto the Lord" (1 Sam 7:3).

The causes of this justification are the following: The final cause is the glory of God and of Christ, and life everlasting. The efficient cause is the merciful God, who freely washes and sanctifies (see 1 Cor 6:11) sealing and anointing with the Holy Spirit of the promise, who is the pledge of our inheritance (see Eph 1:13 f.). The meritorious cause is the beloved only-begotten Son of God, our Lord Jesus Christ, who, when we were enemies (see Rom 5:10), by reason of His very great love wherewith He has loved us (see Eph 2:4), merited justification for us by His own most holy Passion on the wood of the cross, and made satisfaction for us to God the Father. The instrumental cause is the sacrament of baptism, which is the "sacrament of faith," without which no one has ever been justified. Finally, the only formal cause is "the justice of God, not the justice by which He is Himself just, but the justice by which He makes us just," namely, the justice which we have as a gift from Him and by which we are renewed in the spirit of our mind. And not only are we considered just, but we are truly said to be just, and we are just, each one of us receiving within himself his own justice, according to the measure the Holy Spirit imparts to each one as He wishes (see 1 Cor 12:11), and according to the disposition and cooperation of each one.

For although no one can be just unless he is granted a share in the merits of the Passion of our Lord Jesus Christ; still, in the justification of the unjustified that is precisely what happens when, by the merit of the same most holy Passion, the charity of God is poured forth by the Holy Spirit into the hearts (see Rom 5:5) of those who are justified and remains in them. Whence in the very act of being justified, at the same time that his sins are remitted, a man receives through Jesus Christ, to whom he is joined, the infused gifts of faith, hope, and charity. For faith without hope and charity neither perfectly unites a man with Christ nor makes him a living member of His body. . . .[5]

Ch. 8. The Correct Meaning of the Statement: The Sinner is Gratuitously Justified by Faith.

But when the Apostle says that man is justified "through faith" and "freely" (Rom 3:22, 24), those words must be understood in the sense that the Catholic Church has always continuously held and declared. We may then be said to be justified through faith, in the sense that "faith is the beginning of man's salvation," the foundation and source of all justification, "without which it is impossible to please God" (see Heb 11:6), and to be counted as His sons. We may be said to be justified freely, in the sense that nothing that precedes justification, neither faith nor works, merits the grace of justification; for "if out of grace, then not in virtue of works; otherwise (as the same Apostle says) grace is no longer grace" (Rom 11:6).

---

[5] Therefore it is said most truly that faith without works is dead (see Jas 2:17 ff.). . . .

Ch. 9. Against the Heretical Teaching of Presumptuous Trust.

It is necessary to believe that sins are not remitted and have never been remitted except freely by the divine mercy for Christ's sake. Nevertheless, it must not be said that sins are forgiven or have ever been forgiven to anyone who boasts a confidence and a certain knowledge of the forgiveness of his sins and who relies upon this confidence alone. This empty, ungodly confidence may exist among heretics and schismatics and actually does exist in our times and is preached against the Catholic Church with bitter arguments. Furthermore, it should not be asserted that they who are truly justified must unhesitatingly determine within themselves that they are justified; and that no one is absolved from his sins and justified except one who believes with certainty that he is absolved and justified. Moreover, it should not be asserted that absolution and justification are brought about by this faith alone, as if to say that whoever lacks this faith doubts God's promises and the efficacy of Christ's death and resurrection. For no devout man should entertain doubts about God's mercy, Christ's merits, and the power and efficacy of the sacraments. Similarly, whoever reflects upon himself, his personal weakness, and his defective disposition may fear and tremble about his own grace, since no one can know with the certitude of faith, which cannot admit any error, that he has obtained God's grace.

Ch. 10. The Increase of Justification in One Who Has Been Justified.

Therefore, in this way the justified become both friends of God and members of His household (see Jn 15:15; Eph 2:19), advancing from virtue to virtue (see Ps 83:8), renewed (as the Apostle says) day by day (see 2 Cor 4:16), that is, by mortifying the members of their flesh (see Col 3:5) and showing them as weapons of justice (see Rom 6:13, 19) unto sanctification by observing the commandments of God and of the Church. When faith works along with their works (see Jas 2:22), the justified increase in the very justice which they have received through the grace of Christ and are justified the more. . . .[6]

Ch. 11. The Observance of the Commandments: Its Necessity and Possibility.

No one, even though he is justified, should consider himself exempt from keeping the commandments. And no one should say that it is impossible for the just man to keep the commandments of God, for that is a rash statement censured with anathema by the Fathers. "For God does not command the impossible; but when He commands, He cautions you to do what you can, and also to pray for what you cannot do," and He helps you so that you can do it. . . . For granted that

[6] as it is written: "He who is just, let him be just still" (Apoc 22:11), and again: "Fear not to be justified even to death" (Sir 18:22), and again: "You see that by works a man is justified, and not by faith only" (Jas 2:24) . . .

in this mortal life, however just and holy men be, they sometimes commit at least slight daily sins, which are also called venial sins; still, they do not on that account cease to be just.[7] . . . Hence, it is clear that they are against the correct doctrine of religion when they say that the just man commits a venial sin in everything he does, or (what is more intolerable) say that he merits eternal punishment. They also are incorrect who state that the just sin in all their works if . . . they look for an everlasting reward in addition to their primary intention of glorifying God. . . .

Ch. 12. Rash Presumption of One's Predestination Must Be Avoided.

And no one, so long as he lives in this mortal life, ought to be so presumptuous about the deep mystery of divine predestination as to decide with certainty that he is definitely among the number of the predestined, as though it were true that, because he is justified, either he cannot sin again, or, if he does sin, he should promise himself certain repentance. For it is impossible, without a special revelation, to know whom God has chosen as His own.

Ch. 13. The Gift of Perseverance.

The same is to be said of the gift of perseverance, about which it is written, "He who has persevered to the end will be saved" (Mt 10:22; 24:13). . . . Let no one feel assured of this gift with an absolute certitude,

---

[7] For the just say truthfully and humbly, "Forgive us our debts" (Mt 6:12). . . .

although all ought to have most secure hope in the help of God. For unless men are unfaithful to his grace, God will bring the good work to perfection, just as He began it, working both the will and the performance (see Phil 2:13). Yet, let them who think they stand take heed lest they fall (see 1 Cor 10:12), and let them work out their salvation with fear and trembling (see Phil 2:12) in labors, in sleepless nights, in almsgiving, in prayers and offerings, in fastings, and in charity (see 2 Cor 6:3 ff.). Knowing that they are reborn unto the hope of glory (see 1 Pt 1:3) and not yet unto glory itself, they should be in dread about the battle they must wage with the flesh, the world, and the devil. For in this battle they cannot be the victors unless, with God's grace, they obey the Apostle who says: " . . . For if you live according to the flesh you will die; but if by the spirit you put to death the deeds of the flesh, you will live" (Rom 8:12 f.).

Ch. 14. Those Who Sin after Justification and Their Restoration to Grace.

Those who have received the grace of justification but have lost it through sin can be justified again when, awakened by God, they make the effort to regain through the sacrament of penance and by the merit of Christ the grace they have lost. For this is the manner of justification by which those who have fallen into sin are restored. . . . For it was for those who had fallen into sin after baptism that Jesus Christ instituted the sacrament of penance with the words: "Receive the Holy Spirit; whose sins you shall forgive, they are forgiven them; and whose sins you shall retain, they are retained" (Jn 20:22 f.). . .

Ch. 15. Grace, but Not Faith, Is Lost by Every Mortal Sin.

We must also assert, in opposition to some clever men who "by smooth words and flattery deceive the hearts of the simple" (Rom 16:18), that the grace of justification, once received, is lost not only by unbelief, which causes the loss of faith, but also by any other mortal sin, even though faith is not lost. The assertion defends the teaching of divine law that excludes from the kingdom of God not only those without faith, but also those with faith who are fornicators, adulterers, effeminate, sodomites, thieves, covetous, drunkards, evil-tongued, greedy (see 1 Cor 6:9), and all others who commit mortal sins. These sins separate men from the grace of Christ, and they can be avoided with the help of divine grace.

Ch. 16. The Merit of Good Works as a Result of Justification. . . .

Therefore, with this in mind, justified men, whether they have continuously kept grace once they have received it, or whether they have lost it and recovered it again, should consider these words of the Apostle: "Abound in every good work, knowing that your labor is not in vain in the Lord" (see 1 Cor 15:58); "for God is not unjust, that he should forget your work and the love that you have shown in his name" (Heb 6:10); and: "Do not lose your confidence, which has a great reward" (see Heb 10:35). And eternal life should therefore be set before those who persevere in good works to the end (see Mt 10:22) and who hope in God. It should be set before them as being the grace that God, through Jesus Christ, has mercifully promised His sons, and "as the reward" which, according to the promise of God Himself, must assuredly be given them for their good works and merits. For this is that crown of justice which the Apostle says is laid up for him after the fight and the race; the crown that will be given him by the just Judge, and not to him alone but to all who love His coming (see 2 Tim 4:7). Indeed, Christ Jesus Himself always gives strength to the justified, just as the head gives strength to the members (see Eph 4:15) and the vine gives strength to the branches (see Jn 15:5). This strength always precedes, accompanies, and follows the good works of the justified and without it the good works cannot be at all pleasing to God or meritorious. . . . And they may be regarded as having likewise truly merited the eternal life they will certainly attain in due time (if they but die in the state of grace) (see Apoc 14:13). . . .

2. **G. C. Berkouwer**[8] **sees Rome's problem complicated at Trent where she had to ward off the Reformers' attack without derogating from the decrees of Orange. Grace and freedom: in Roman dogmatics this was the burning problem. Augustine is repudiated in his "exaggeration" of the effects of original sin and the whole Roman Catholic doctrine of freedom is concerned with an ontological conception which is the basis of a relative optimism.**

The Reformation had accused Rome of legalism and the denial of sovereign grace. Between Orange and Trent lies a long process of development, namely, scholasticism, with its elaboration of the doctrine of the meritoriousness of good works, and the Roman system of penitence. And it was the Reformation that made an appeal to Augustine in connection with the confession of grace.[9] Luther as well as Calvin strongly emphasized the doctrine of election precisely in connection with the confession of God's sovereign grace.

Hence the situation became much more complicated for Rome in Trent than when, in 529, semi-Pelagianism had to be condemned for its "weakening" of grace. For it was the Reformation which with great seriousness appealed to the very words quoted at Orange. Could the work of the Reformers not be characterized by these words: "If righteousness comes by the law, then Christ is dead in vain"? And was the *sola fide* anything else but the counterpart of the confession of

sovereign grace? And did not the Pauline words about grace and works again start to function in the Reformed confession?

In the face of the renewed clarity of the fundamental words of the gospel, Trent had to ward off the Reformers' attack without derogating from the decrees of Orange. The texts quoted at Orange appeared again and again in the words and the testimony of the Reformation and had to be maintained. The *gratia praeveniens* had to be taught without relapsing into the *sola fide* of the Reformers.[10] That is why the Orange texts are repeated in Trent,[11] especially in the decree on justification. However, Orange dealt with free will in opposition to those views that were a threat to grace because of too great a liking for "nature." The terms "depraved" and "weakened"

---

[8] Cf. ch. VII, n. 37. This excerpt is from *op. cit.*, pp. 80–104.

[9] E.g., to Augustine, *De gratia et libero arbitrio*, of which Lekkerkerker says that this writing is "a defense of grace from beginning to end" (*Studiën over de rechtvaardiging bij Augustinus* [1947], p. 146.)

[10] Cf. Roger Aubert, *Le problème de l'acte de foi* (1945), p. 76: "The catholic doctrine which, while maintaining the pre-eminence and necessity of grace, to which belongs the initiative, at the same time affirms the free cooperation of man with the divine action."

[11] Christ is professed to be "the author and finisher of our faith" (*fidei nostrae auctor et consummator*) (D. 1520). Grace does not stem from works; "otherwise grace is not grace" (*alioquin gratia non est gratia*) (D. 1532).

were intended in an antithetical sense to any overestimation of free will. The priority of grace was strongly emphasized in opposition to the devaluation of grace.

But at Trent, Rome was confronted with a religious confession which laid every possible stress on sovereign grace, on the justification of the ungodly. For this reason Trent became much more representative of the Roman doctrine of grace than Orange. . . .

The opponent at Trent is different from the one at Orange. . . . In opposition to the adversary at Orange the human will had to be limited in its power: the will has been *weakened*, and is not in a position to perform that which Pelagians and semi-Pelagians deem it able to do.[12] The church rejected the "too naturalistic trait given to grace, if the latter was identified with nature."[13] Even before Orange the church had maintained that grace does *not* cancel or exclude free will.[14] But the emphasis on the "influence of grace" was of first importance.[15] But at the time of the Reformation grace was

sharply put in the foreground by the Reformers as "the sole necessity," and the total depravity of human nature was confessed.

In opposition to this doctrine the Roman church was called upon to "shed a clear light on the other part of the fulness of truth" because the Reformers were accused of denying the freedom of the will. Rome became the "guardian" of nature and freedom in the performance of its vocation. . . . Although Rome is prepared to act as the guardian of nature and freedom, the priority of grace will not be wiped out, nor the great "influence" of grace denied. . . . We might then ask: what is the meaning of Rome's passionate defense of the "physical" freedom of the will? Is this freedom of the will only an anthropological problem, or has it *some* direct relation to the question of grace? And has it any significance for the supernatural order? . . .

Grace and freedom: in Roman dogmatics this has remained a burning problem. One thing has been unassailably established, viz., the "natural freedom of the will" is not merely concerned with natural strivings of the will in one direction or another as a psychological fact. But the natural freedom of the will is somehow also important in connection with grace. . . . The view was taken that in fact this problem existed only for the Roman church and theology. For only they compose salvation out of two factors, or at least in them the realization of

---

[12] K. Steur, *De vrije wil* (1935), p. 12.

[13] *Ibid.*, p. 15.

[14] In this connection Steur first refers to the word "weakened" in the Orange canons: "weakened always presupposes the existence of a matter that has been weakened" (p. 12). Cf. also Leo IX's pronouncement in 1053, coordinating the *praevenire* with the *liberum arbitrium* (D. 685).

[15] Cf. Trent contra: "Without divine grace through Jesus Christ, man can be justified before God by his own works, whether they were done by his natural powers or the doctrine of the Law" (*Hominem suis operibus quae vel per humanae naturae vires vel per Legis doctrinam*

fiant absque divina per Christum Jesum gratia posse justificari coram Deo) (D. 1551).

salvation depends on two factors: grace and freedom. The heresies of Pelagianism as well as the Reformation knew only one factor. Pelagians retained only liberty, and the Reformers only grace. Opposed to this is the complex character of the problem with Rome: grace *and* freedom.[16]

The composition of these two factors is *the* problem of the Roman doctrine of grace. For here the question arises whether or not one factor is limited by the other and thereby relativized. This is the case especially if grace is quietly paralleled with freedom and mention is made of the "influence" of grace. . . .

Here we are confronted with the Roman doctrine that "human nature was not corrupted by the fall into sin by Adam."[17] At this point Rome is sharply opposed to the Reformation and Jansenism, and to all who hold that fallen man is necessarily directed to evil, if he is not set free by grace. "If anyone should say that after Adam's sin the free will of man has been lost and extinguished, or that it is a title without any corresponding reality, a fiction introduced into the church by Satan, he is condemned."[18] . . . With Conrad Martius, we might in this case speak of "cosmological optimism," or clearer still, of "anthropological optimism" forming an element of the background of the Roman doctrine of grace. . . .

Whatever Rome may mean by "the death of the soul," in any case it does *not* mean the radical corruption of human nature. This is not only clear from the entire context of the Trentine decrees, but it is even more apparent when we see Rome involved in a permanent struggle against . . . the "exaggeration" of the effects of original sins. There is no hesitation to repudiate Augustine on *this point*.[19] He, too, is alleged to have exaggerated the effects of sin when he considered human nature as totally corrupt[20] and called the virtues of the pagans shining sins. The Reformers agreed with Augustine in their opposition to the optimism of the humanists. But Rome is of the opinion that Augustine had lost sight of the exact proportions and that his example should not be followed.[21] . . .

With Rome it is a question of a relatively independent basis of grace, of an independent view of humanity, making it conceivable that man can accept grace. But in the Reformed conception the issue in connection with sinful humanity is a much greater discontinuity, breach and distance. This religious aspect is the obviously dominant factor in Reformed theology,

---

[16] Cf. M. van Wagenberg, *Inherente Gerechtigheid. Het Schild* (1947), p. 34.

[17] H. van Rooyen, *De genade*, p. 24.

[18] Trent, Sess. V, can. 5 (D. 1555).

[19] Kardinaal De Long, *Handboek der Kerkgeschiedenis* (1947), Deel I, pp. 276, 277; cf. F. Hofmann, *Der Kirchenbegriff des H. Augustinus* (1933), p. 455 ff.

[20] F. v. d. Meer, *Catechismus*, 81. Jansen is supposed to have reverted to the "most gloomy utterances" of Augustine in the struggle against the Pelagians. L. H. Cornelissen, *Geloof zonder prediking* (1946), pp. 84, 110.

[21] F. v. d. Meer, *op. cit.*, pp. 82, 83. Cf. Kardinaal De Long, *Handboek*, I (1947), p. 280: "a milder view."

whereas, in the Roman conception the anthropological foundation becomes significant — the structure of the *humanitas* — in connection with the effect and the power of grace. For with Rome a particular ontological view comes to the fore with far-reaching consequences. And it is perfectly clear that at this point Rome and the Reformation part company. The cardinal difference has often, and not unjustly, been denoted as the difference with regard to nature and grace. And the whole of the development of the Roman doctrine of grace proves that we are not mistaken.

This fact explains the Roman reproach of pessimism directed to Augustine. It was a pessimism with respect to human nature which — as was sometimes thought — could be traced back to reminiscences of his Manichaean past. . . . This issue is not a nuance in anthropology, or the acknowledgment or rejection of psychological facts, but it is concerned with a central religious antithesis of the first order. For the analysis of human nature acquires a dominant significance for the problem of the relation between nature and grace. . . . It may at any rate be stated with certainty that Rome consciously tries to accomplish an analysis of existence, but denies that this analysis is construed in such a way that it is a threat to the sovereignty of grace.[22] . . .

In the Reformed view the issue was

not an analysis of existence, but the religious aspect of all of preserved human existence. In this the Reformation kept close to Holy Scripture, which describes man in his lost state and in his perdition. Anyone who keeps this religious aspect in view will never again find a reason to limit this pessimism and to make room for "a certain optimism" on account of the fact that human nature and its powers and faculties have been preserved. For the question is how this human nature with all that belongs to it is related to God. . . .

We can now understand why, e.g., Conrad-Maritius speaks of "the entire, strictly ontological, and, as it seems to us, unshakably founded doctrine of the will of Thomas." For the whole Roman Catholic doctrine of freedom is concerned with an ontological conception which is the basis of a relative optimism. . . . This ontological conception culminates in the thesis that all "being" is good because it *is* and thereby participates in God as the source of all "being." . . .

At the parting of the ways[23] Rome evidently turns into the other direc-

---

[22] Cf. J. C. Groot, *Karl Barth en het theologisch kenprobleem* (1945), on the *potentia oboedientialis:* "That is why Catholic theologians always strongly emphasize

that the *potentia oboedientialis* is not directly related to some action, to which the creature is summoned from above, but that it is directly and exclusively related to the Creator of such higher perfections" (p. 300). This emphasis is meant to prevent the "naturalization of grace."

[23] Kuyper also speaks of "a parting of the ways": "In this sinful world there was, also outside of the church, so much beauty, so much that is worthy of respect, so much that roused our jealousy. This fact leaves us the choice between denying all these good things against our better knowledge and thus falling into the error of the

tion, where the freedom of the human will is the subject of discussion, on account of which a certain optimism is justified. In this way ontology as-

sumes decisive importance and Rome's passionate defense of free will can be explained only by taking account of Rome's choice of direction. . . .

3. Ch. Baumgartner, S.J.,[24] briefly sets forth the three states of justification which the council distinguishes in its decree. The first consists in the passage from infidelity to faith; the second in the conservation and development of the grace received; the third in the recovery of the grace that was lost. A chapter is added on merit, the fruit of justification.

The council distinguishes in its de-cree three states of justification. The first consists in the passage from in-fidelity to faith (c. 1–9); the second in the conservation and development of the grace received (c. 10–13); the third in the recovery of the grace that was lost (c. 14 and 15). The council adds a chapter on the fruit of justifi-cation or merit (c. 16).

The first fundamental idea, accord-ing to the council, is that justification is a divine work. This divine work, that of the Son of God dying for all men, is clearly affirmed at the very beginning of the decree as the princi-ple on which all the rest is going to rest. Then are affirmed the impotence of nature and of the law to free man from the servitude of sin, of the devil and of death (c. 1), the mission of

the Redeemer (c. 2), the communica-tion of the merits of the passion by rebirth in Christ (c. 3). After giving a general notion of the justification of the impious: "translation from that state in which man is born a son of the first Adam into the state of grace and of adoption of sons of God" (trans-latio ab eo statu in quo homo nascitur filius primi Adae in statum gratiae et adoptionis filiorum Dei), the council affirms man's cooperation in justifica-tion (or salvation) in c. 5 and 6 and makes precise the nature of justification.

Cooperation of man in justifica-tion. This cooperation is necessary. Adults must prepare themselves by means of grace and with grace. The intention of the Fathers of the council is twofold: to oppose to all forms of Semipelagianism the initiative of di-vine grace and to affirm against the Protestants the possibility and the nec-essity of free cooperation. Chapter 6 describes the manner of this prepara-tion. It enumerates a series of acts that succeed one another in the following order: dogmatic faith, fear, hope,

Baptists, or representing fallen man as not so very much apostate and thereby losing ourselves in the Arminian heresy. And when placed before this parting of the ways the Reformed Confession has refused to turn in either of these two roads." Kuyper then takes another route, namely, that of common grace.

[24] Cf., ch. I, n. 12. This excerpt is from op. cit., pp. 112–120.

initial love, penitence before baptism, resolve to receive baptism and keep God's commandments. Thus the adult must dispose himself for justification by salutary acts. Dogmatic faith is one of these acts, but the faith-confidence of the Protestants if understood in an exclusive sense is not one of them. Further while faith is necessary it is not sufficient for other acts are required.

The council is concerned with the acts that temporally precede justification and are its remote preparation. This preparation for sanctifying grace designates a series of supernatural acts by which a man makes his way progressively to justification. (St. Thomas treats this in I–II, q. 112.) In outlining this abstract psychological scheme of conversion the council does not wish to teach that it must be applied just so, in this chronological order, in every conversion or that the preparatory acts necessarily precede the conversion in time.[25]

The nature of justification. At the termination of this preparation justification itself follows. After giving a more precise definition of justification the council indicates the cause and essence and properties of justification. Chapter 7 is the culminating point of the decree.

Definition. "After this disposition or preparation comes justification itself. This is not merely the remission of sins, but a sanctification and renovation of the interior man by a voluntary

reception of grace and gifts, whereby a man becomes just instead of unjust and a friend instead of an enemy, that he may be an heir in the hope of life everlasting."

Causes of justification. The final cause is the glory of God and of Christ and eternal life. The efficient cause is the God of mercy. The passion of Christ is the meritorious cause. Baptism, the sacrament of faith, is the instrumental cause. Finally, the only formal cause of justification is the justice received, the justice that is interior to man and not the justice of God.

Essence of justification. It is under the title of formal cause that the council teaches the essence of justification. First it affirms its intrinsic character and then it discards the theory of double justification.

Man is truly renewed and justified. We receive justice in us and in this sense it is a justice proper to each one and it inheres in us with its accompaniment of supernatural gifts of faith and hope and charity. The grace we receive is not a pure imputation nor only the remission of sins nor only the favor of God, but an internal reality which the Holy Spirit diffuses in the just soul and which remains attached to it.

The magisterium of the Church discards the theory of double justice of the school of Cologne. This school affirmed two formal causes, so that we are formally just by the external imputation of the justice of Christ as the complement of our imperfect jus-

[25] J. Riviére, art. "Justification," DTC, t. 8, col. 2180.

tice. The council rejects this doctrine by saying that the formal cause of our justification is one (*unica*). The form by which we are just is a justice inhering in the soul, but it is still true that our justice depends on the justice of Christ as on an efficient and exemplary cause which is ceaselessly active. At every instant our justice is suspended from the influx of Christ (D 1530 and 1546). It is a life in Christ.

The properties of justification. Its gratuity. How is man justified by faith and gratuitously? This must be understood according to the *perpetuus consensus* of the Catholic Church. We are justified by faith because faith is the beginning of salvation, the root and foundation of all justification. We are justified gratuitously because the faith and works that precede justification do not (condignly) merit justification (ch. 8).

Its incertitude. The Christian cannot and need not be assured of his own proper justification. This assurance of salvation is not sufficient, it is not necessary, it is not possible. Not that we should doubt God, but we always have in our persistent misery grave reasons for doubting ourselves. The Christian has motives for a legitimate confidence, but he must not ever forget those that impose on him the duty of salutary fear. The legitimate confidence of the Christian cannot be an infallible certitude of faith (ch. 9). The same principles apply to the problem of predestination (ch. 12 and 13).

Its inequality and perfectibility. Since the grace of justification is an interior reality and conditioned by our personal preparation it will not be the same for all. Each of us receives justice according to the measure that the Holy Spirit portions out conformably to His free will and according to our personal dispositions and cooperation (ch. 7). Justice thus is susceptible of progress and normally is called to develop itself (ch. 10). And so there is affirmed the supernatural value of our moral works which are under the action of grace the agents of this progress. While diverse in detail these works all fall into the general category of observance of the commandments of God and of the Church. Luther had maintained the impossibility, the uselessness and the harmfulness of the law, including even the Christian law. This doctrine is rejected in chapter 11, which affirms that the practice of the Christian law is possible and necessary and fruitful.

Its amisibility. Just as the origination so the preservation of justification does not depend solely on faith but on works. There are two ways of losing the grace of God. One is total (on which the council does not insist), when one loses the faith that is at its base. The other is less complete, when faith survives the ruin of charity destroyed by mortal sin (ch. 15).

Merit. In chapter 16 the council sets forth the Scriptural and Augustinian doctrine of recompense and merit.

"Vere mereri" (condign merit). The council of Trent presents merit as "the fruit of justification." ". . . To justified men, whether they have always kept the grace they received, or whether they have recovered it after losing it, must be proposed the words of the apostle: 'abound in every good work knowing that your labor is not in vain in the Lord' (1 Cor 15:58); 'for God is not unjust, that he should forget what you have done and the charity that you have shown for his name' (Heb 6:10). And again: 'do not lose your confidence, it has a great and just recompense' (Heb 10:35)." To those then who work up to the end (Mt 10:27) and put their hope in God "eternal life is to be presented both as a grace mercifully promised through Jesus Christ to the sons of God, and as a reward which is to be faithfully rendered to them according to the promise of God Himself" (*proponenda est vita aeterna et tanquam gratia filiis Dei per Christum Jesum misericorditer promissa, et tanquam merces ex ipsius Dei promissione bonis ipsorum operibus et meritis fideliter reddenda*).

Eternal life is then both a grace and a recompense, a gift of God and a remuneration of the efforts of man. The grace that is the principle of merit is the grace of Christ the Head. Thus the gift of God does not exclude the merit of man but founds it. And in addition merit is a principle of increase of grace or of filial life. . . .

Such are the essential ideas on merit formulated by the council of Trent. It is a gift of God, an effect in us of the grace of Christ, and a free ac-

tion of man. Grace is a divine life that develops. It is in real continuity with eternal life and merit is an essential principle of this continuity.

Merit "de congruo." The distinction between condign and congruous merit goes back to the 13th century.[26] . . . According to the doctrine of the *Summa* it seems that there is congruous merit only in a man in the state of grace. . . . After St. Thomas, Soto and some other theologians seem to reject all congruous merit. At the time of the council of Trent the opinion that the sinner who disposes himself for justification acquires a congruous merit is defended by some theologians. It is rejected by others who limit themselves to the idea of disposition or impetration. The council of Trent did not pronounce on this point, but it did not exclude congruous merit (D 1532). After the council of Trent and by reason of it the majority of theologians seem to admit that the sinner who prepares himself for justification with the aid of grace merits congruously not only the ulterior graces that dispose him for it but justification itself. They add that in this case there is even a merit *de congruo infallibili*. But it is certain that these acts have an infallible impetratory value before God.[27]

Conclusion. The council of Trent has put strongly in relief the two fundamental Catholic theses. First, jus-

[26] R. C. Dhont, *Le problème de la préparation à la grâce*, 1946, p. 124.
[27] J. Riviére, art. "Mérite," in DTC, t. 10, 754, 755.

tification is not something extrinsic but a radical transformation of man, an ontological change that situates the divine friendship in an order altogether other than that of simple moral or juridical categories. Then, in this transformation man is not a passive, inert instrument but truly cooperates in his justification and his sanctification.

4. H. Rondet, S.J.,[28] considers Trent's decree on justification one of the most beautiful pages in the history of dogmas. Equally removed from the neo-Pelagianism of the Humanists and from the pessimism of the Reformers it presents both the psychology of justification and its ontology. It avoided pronouncements on points controverted among Catholics but it bluntly condemned the subjectivist thesis of justification by faith which concealed the most fundamental principle of the Reformation: man alone face to face with God alone.

The Fathers of Trent formulated the Catholic doctrine of justification in a document that is one of the most beautiful pages in the history of dogmas. . . .

Equally removed from the neo-Pelagianism of the Humanists and from the pessimism of the Reformers, the Council first recalled the consequences of original sin and the necessity of Redemption.[29] To have a part in this a man must be born again from on high.[30] Son of old sinful Adam he must become a son of God, by Christ our Saviour.[31] This he becomes by baptism but not without his personal cooperation. Luther and his followers had insisted on the impotence of free will. The council condemns their errors[32] and shows forcefully that, if man can do nothing without grace in the order of salvation, he can however and must respond to the invitation given him. Without any merit on his part he has been called but it does not follow that his will must remain inert and passive.[33] The efforts a man makes when "prevented" by grace to get out of his sins in no way render him hateful in the eyes of God, as the Reformers maintain.

Then in a magnificent page that is inspired more by Augustine than by scholastic theology the council describes the manner in which a man disposes himself for justification.[34] It is God who has the initiative both through exterior preaching and through the interior call of grace, but man responds freely by realizing the misery of being a sinner and slowly passing from salutary fear to hope and to the initial love that makes him

---

[28] Cf., ch. III, n. 1. This excerpt is from *op. cit.*, pp. 274–285.
[29] Ch. 1–2 (D. 1521–1522); can. 1, 2, 3 (D. 1551, 1552, 1553).
[30] Ch. 3 (D. 1523).
[31] Ch. 4 (D. 1524).

[32] Can. 5 (D. 1555); can. 6 (D. 1556).
[33] Ch. 5 (D. 1525); can. 9 (D. 1559) and especially can. 4 (D. 1554).
[34] Ch. 6 (D. 1526).

detest his sins and resolve on the new life demanded of one baptized.[35]

After giving the psychology of justification the council now gives its ontology, drawing its inspiration from scholastic theology but apart from every systematization.[36] Justification, as the seventh chapter tells us (one of the masterpieces of the decree), is not a simple remission of sins but a profound transformation by which a man, enriched by a gift of God and a free acceptance of grace and its accompanying gifts, becomes just and a friend of God and an heir of eternal life.[37] He is justified not by an extrinsic imputation of the merits of Christ,[38] but by a justice that is proper to him and which the Holy Spirit pours out in hearts according to His good pleasure and each one's free cooperation.[39] This justice remains in

him as a permanent principle,[40] and it implies the presence of the three supernatural virtues of faith and hope and charity.[41] Without hope and charity faith alone cannot justify a man nor make him a living member of Christ.[42]

If faith justifies, the eighth chapter says, it is because it is the beginning and the foundation and the root of justification.[43] The council expressly refuses to identify faith and confidence,[44] and it refuses still more to accept the religious individualism that the Protestant thesis supposes. To found the certitude of justification on a subjective experience is an aberration that has led a number of men to schism and to heresy.[45] Certainly we must believe in the efficacy of the Passion of Christ and of the sacraments, but no one can know with a certitude of faith that excludes all doubt whether he is in the grace of God.[46] Here the

---

[35] The words *diligere incipiunt* are to be noted, which the council designedly leaves vague (Riviére, "Justification," DTC, t. 8, col. 2180).

[36] Ch. 7 (D. 1528–1531). This chapter is one of the most important of the decree, and it was also one of the most discussed (J. Riviére, DTC, t. 8, col. 2180–2185).

[37] D. 1528. The word *voluntariam* was added to recall once again the Catholic thesis of the necessary cooperation of the subject (cf. J. Riviére, DTC, t. 8, col. 2181).

[38] Can. 11 (D. 1561).

[39] Ch. 7 (D. 1529). On the interpretation of Rom 1:17 in Occidental theology before Luther see Denifle's dissertation, *Die abendländischen Schriftauslegung bei Luther über Justitia Dei und Justificatio* (1905). For the Pauline exegesis properly so called, see the commentary of P. Lagrange and the very documented pages of H. Lange, *De gratia,* 1929, pp. 221–230, and especially the study of P. Lyonnet, *De justitia Dei in Epistula ad Romanos* (*Verbum Domini,* 1947).

[40] Ch. 7 (D. 1530); can. 11 (D. 1561).

[41] Ch. 7 (D. 1530). All these formulas evoke scholastic theology but without canonizing it. See J. Riviére, "Justification," DTC, t. VIII, col. 2185, and A. Prumbs, *Die Stellung des tridentinischen Konzils in der Frage nach dem Wesen der heiligmachendem Gnade,* 1909.

[42] Ch. 7 (D. 1531).

[43] Ch. 8 (D. 1532).

[44] Can. 12 (D. 1562).

[45] Ch. 9 (D. 1533–1534): *"quamvis autem . . .* up to *Nam sicut nemo . . .";* can. 13, can. 14 (D. 1563, 1564).

[46] Ch. 9 (D. 1534). This text is the result of a long discussion (H. Hutmacher, "La certitude de la justification au concile de Trente," in *Nouv. revue théol.,* 1933, pp. 263–340). The council practically ranged itself with St. Thomas' view (I–II, q. 112, art. 5) against the position attributed to Scotus, as Biel comprehended it (cf. J. Riviére, "Justification," DTC, t. 8, col.

decree on justification implicitly prepares the decree on Penance and the
value of absolution.

Once justified the Christian can increase in justice. Justification admits
degrees that are measured by the grace
of God and the free cooperation of
man.[47] And here the council opposes
to the new errors the true notion of
Christian liberty. Grace does not suppress the Law.[48] Christ the Redeemer
remains the legislator to whom we owe
obedience.[49] And contrary to what Calvin teaches[50] He does not command
us anything that is impossible but,
according to the beautiful words of
St. Augustine, He invites a man to
do what he can and to ask of God
His aid to accomplish what is beyond
his strength today.[51] Once again the
council reaffirms against the Reformers
the traditional distinction between mortal and venial sin and declares that
the just man himself is not without

sin,[52] and that without an extraordinary privilege no man can be exempt
from all fault.[53] But the just man
remains the friend of God in spite of
his faults and, to use the words of
Augustine again, God never abandons
him first.[54] It is man's task then to be
faithful! To reach salvation it is necessary not only to have believed but
also to have suffered with Christ so
as to be glorified with Him.[55] This
supposes always that man cooperates
in the work of his salvation. One must
reject the insensate thesis that would
make every effort of man and every
hope of recompense a disorder and
a sin.[56]

Here the council links in two
chapters predestination and final perseverance. The subjective certitude of
predestination is no less intolerable
than that of justification.[57] It is a delusion to believe with Calvin that once
justified a man cannot sin or that if
he sins this means that he never was

2187). Catharin (De certitudine gratiae)
will try to show that one can found the
certitude of his justification on a theological
conclusion, but his thesis will appear little
in accord with the council. Theologians
will attempt to dissipate the anxieties the
council's doctrine can beget in souls by
showing that one can have a practical certitude of the state of grace founded on diverse
personal and social considerations (Suarez,
De gratia, lib. IX, cap. 9–11, Opera, Vives,
t. IX, pp. 524–553; Billuart, De gratia,
diss. 6, art. 4; Summa sancti Thomae, ed.
nova, 1769, t. 6, pp. 421 428).

[47] Ch. 10 (D. 1535). Can. 24 (D.
1574).

[48] Ch. 11 (D. 1536). Can. 20 (D.
1570).

[49] Can. 21 (D. 1571).

[50] Can. 18 (D. 1568).

[51] Ch. 11 (D. 1536). Cf. Aug., De natura et gratia, 50, P.L., 44, 271.

[52] Ch. 11 (D. 1537). This is a resump-
tion of the affirmations of Carthage (D.
228–229) and of the Augustinian doctrine.
The distinction between mortal and venial
sin will be affirmed more clearly apropos
of Penance (D. 1680).

[53] Can. 23 (D. 1573).

[54] Ch. 11 (D. 1537). (Cf. Aug., De
natura et gratia, n. 29, P.L., 44, 261). This
text is very liberal but it still remains rugged
enough, for it deals only with the just and
in the measure that they are faithful. Much
progress is still to be made in the question
of the distribution of grace to rejoin the
Gospel. This will be achieved in the discussions with Jansenism.

[55] Ch. 11 (D. 1538).

[56] Ch. 11 (D. 1539). Can. 25 (D.
1575).

[57] Ch. 12 (D. 1540).

justified.[58] Final perseverance is a gift. A man can never flatter himself that he has received it from God,[59] but he can count on Him to attain it. Here too the entirely gratuitous gift and the free cooperation of man are inseparable,[60] and one of the leitmotifs of the decree reappears once again.

If man has the unhappiness of falling into sin he can regain grace by the sacrament of Penance wherein the acts of the penitent, confession, contrition and satisfaction have a large part.[61] The council will return to this question in connection with the sacraments. Here it is content to recall against certain innovations of Luther that every mortal sin, and not only that of infidelity, makes one lose the grace of justification.[62] But the sinner is not excluded from the Church. He remains a faithful member of the Church,[63] for if he no longer has living faith he still has an authentic faith.[64] The return to grace will be by a process analogous to that described above, with the sacrament of Penance replacing baptism, but with this difference that Penance remits the guilt but does not in the same way remit the punishment.[65] Here the doctrine of justification is joined to belief in purgatory which Luther's negations had equally affected.

The 15 chapters we have touched on suppose a fundamental doctrine that the council is now going to put in relief: the doctrine of merit. To the Reformers the word and the reality were a horror. But in a chapter of great extent the council shows that our merits are at the same time a gift of God and the result of a free effort of man.[66] It is a magnificent decree in which the purest Augustinian doctrine lives again but now strengthened by the profound reflection of two or three centuries of scholasticism. Luther is condemned and Calvin is condemned and with them the excesses of Nominalism are discarded. We return to the doctrine of the great Augustinians of the 13th century, after it has been softened and nuanced and put back into the concrete data of experience and of spiritual life.

Many questions remain in suspense which the council did not intend to resolve. It avoided pronouncements on points controverted among Catholics. . . . It was enough for it to have condemned the subjectivist thesis of justification by faith, which concealed the most fundamental principle of the Reformation: man alone face to face with God alone. It was enough for it to have placed in strong relief the two fundamental Catholic theses: 1. justification is not something extrinsic but a radical transformation of man, an ontological change that situates the divine friendship in an order altogether other than that of moral or juridical categories; 2. in this progres-

---

[58] Can. 23 (D. 1573).
[59] Can. 16 (D. 1566).
[60] Ch. 13 (D. 1541).
[61] Ch. 14 (D. 1542–1543).
[62] Ch. 15 (D. 1544).
[63] *Ibid.*
[64] Can. 28 (D. 1578).
[65] Can. 30 (D. 1580). Cf. Can. 39 (D. 1579).

[66] Cf. J. Riviére, "Mérite," DTC, t. 10, col. 738–761, on the history of these texts.

sive transformation man is not a passive, inert instrument but he truly cooperates in his justification. God will not save him without him.

These two aspects of the doctrine defined at the council of Trent are going to become the point of departure for theological reflection. For . . . the formulation of a dogma is not the arrest but the life of religious thought. If a lazy theologian is often content to see there a limit imposed on free discussion by authority, the true theologian will always see there a light that guides him in the dark night of research. . . .

5. T. P. Neill and R. H. Schmandt[67] give a brief outline of the council of Trent, its work and its significance.

The most noteworthy Council in the history of the Church was held under difficult conditions, in the face of innumerable obstacles, in the imperial city of Trent. The sessions took place in three different meetings between 1545 and 1563. The Council of Trent was the cornerstone of Catholic reform. Its provisions on the conduct and education of the clergy, its regulations on monastic life, its arrangements for episcopal authority are still in effect. Its definitions of doctrine provided an admirable statement of Catholic truth on original sin, justification, the Mass, and the sacraments which cleared the air of doctrinal haziness and made it clear to any thinking person what was Catholic doctrine and what was heretical. . . .

After the Council's organization was settled in the first sessions, the legates turned to the fundamental points of difference between Catholics and Protestants. The first subject considered was the rule of faith. The Nicene Creed with the *filioque* clause was accepted in its entirety. Against the Protestants Scripture and Tradition were set down as having equal authority. . . .

In defiance of the emperor's demands, the legates next introduced the question of original sin and its effects on human nature. The traditional Catholic doctrine was set down against Protestant teaching of human depravity in the fifth public session on June 17, 1546. Discussion of original sin led to the most important doctrinal consideration of the Council of Trent, the question of justification. This was the fundamental point of doctrinal difference between Lutherans and Catholics. Although the emperor tried to prevent discussion of the subject, the pope insisted that a definition of Catholic teaching be formulated. The decree was finally published in the sixth public session, on January 13, 1547, after six months of work. Only one bishop had argued for the Lutheran view of justification by faith alone, but the precise role of free will and

[67] Cf. ch. IX, n. 1. This excerpt is from *op. cit.*, pp. 370–373, 379–380.

of grace led to much discussion, to drafts, redrafts, and alterations of the statement, until finally a formulation satisfactory to the entire Council was enacted. Its importance lies in that it safeguards the efficacy of good works and the role of free will, while at the same time it states that justification is through Christ alone and that His freely given grace is necessary for salvation. Thus God's omnipotence and man's freedom to co-operate with grace are both safeguarded in the Catholic definition.

The Significance of the Council of Trent. . . . The quality of work done at Trent was due in large measure to the unusually capable theologians and canonists who were present. Prominent among these were three companions of St. Ignatius, early members of the Society of Jesus, two of whom served as the pope's theologians — Alphonse Salmeron, James Lainez, and Claude le Jay. Prominent Dominicans included Dominic Soto and Melchior Cano, and among the famous Franciscans of the day were Louis Carvajal, André de Vega, and Bernardine d'Asti, while the Augustinians were represented by their capable theologian, Girolamo Seripando. These men kept discussions on the highest possible theological plane. The generality of the assembly represented the best of Christian humanism, and their conclusions were clearly those of men in the Catholic tradition handling modern problems as Christian humanists could be expected to handle them — with due reverence for God's exalted position and due respect for the human person's individual worth.

The Council of Trent successfully accomplished its two main objectives. In the first place, it clearly defined Catholic teaching on (1) the sources of religious truth, (2) original sin and justification, (3) the nature of Mass and the sacraments, and (4) such contested other points as Purgatory and Indulgences. The importance of these definitions is apt to be lost on the student who benefits from them in the twentieth century. But in the sixteenth century sincere religious thinkers could not know what was true Catholic doctrine. There were all sorts of teachings, and one never knew whether he was a heretic on some of these points until it was too late. Now for the first time Catholic teaching on many of these points was set forth clearly. Now there were definitions against which to check some enthusiastic preacher's sermons. . . .

XI

GRACE IN THE
SIXTEENTH THROUGH EIGHTEENTH CENTURIES

1. N. Abercrombie[1] treats Baius, Molina, and Jansen. Baius represents the most advanced school of "positive" theologians, with a contempt for Scholastics and with Augustine the final authority in all matters of grace. It would be difficult to name a single treatise of dogmatic theology which has more profoundly affected the history of dogma than Molina's *Concordia*. Its doctrine of grace was the irritant which determined Jansen to compose his *Augustinus*, which was built on St. Augustine's authority and directed against the neo-Scholastic theologians of his time.

THE theologians of the sixteenth century fall roughly into three groups. The first, which includes Baius and the Reformers, deliberately and more

---

[1] Nigel Abercrombie, M.A., D.Phil. (Oxon.), was lecturer in French, Magdalen College, Oxford in 1936. This excerpt is from his book, *The Origins of Jansenism*, pp. 87–94, 112–115, 118–126, 153–158. The book was published in 1936 at Oxford by the Clarendon Press.

or less completely, broke with the traditional scholasticism of the Middle Ages. The second, which is represented by the Order of Preachers, deliberately and more or less faithfully, held to that tradition, and attacked the new theology solely from the standpoint of the old. The third group was the Society of Jesus, with the theologians who openly allied themselves therewith: this was the "left wing" of the intellectual counter-Reformation. These men, no less than their Protestant opponents, were sons of the Renascence, in that they were not content with the conclusions and methods of the medieval schools; they differed from the first group in the degree of their tenacity to that corpus of belief and opinion, which, in their time, constituted Catholic thought. The most interesting representative of this third group is Luis de Molina. . . .

Baius. . . . Baius[2] represented the most advanced school of "positive" theologians who were attempting to do for theology what the scholars of the Renascence were doing for other branches of learning; that is, to dispense with all intellectual equipment other than the indispensable minimum of basic principles, and the scholar's own wits, and so, by ignoring the accomplishments of the Middle Ages, to surpass them. In philology, this desire led to a contempt of glosses, and the publication of "critical" editions; in the natural sciences, to a contempt of Aristotle, and the religion of "observation and experiment"; and in theology,

[2] Baius: Michael du Bay, 1513–1589. Cf. Denziger 1900.

to a contempt of the scholastics, and a servile attachment to the letter of revelation (wherever the particular "positivist" might find it). Accordingly, Baius, relying on the testimony of many Popes, and the best-informed early opinion, fastened upon Augustine as the final authority in all matters of grace, and determined to have no other master.

One of the concepts with which the scholastics had enriched theology was that of the "state of pure nature." If the state of our first parents in the Garden was one of supernatural elevation, and if the state in which men are now born differs from it, not only by the absence of grace, but also by the presence of guilt, then it would seem that neither can be described as the state of *pure* nature. Without apparently violating the laws of reason, we may assume the possibility (but not the positive existence at any time) of human nature existing without any of the supernatural prerogatives which were enjoyed in the state of innocence, and equally without the stain of original sin. The importance of such a postulate for the philosopher, and for the scholastic theologian, is obvious.

If we wish to form a mental picture of man as he would be in the state of pure nature, we have only to look at the man as he now is, and think away everything about him which flows from original sin, as guilt, or from the gifts of grace, as supernatural. He would have the same powers of mind and body as we have, the same incapacity to attain, of himself, to supernatural beatitude, the same difficulty in remaining true to his best self, the same more or less effectual natural desires: but he would not possess the revelation of divine truth, nor feel any supernatural desires; his temptations would be only those of the world and the flesh; and any assistance he might receive from God to combat these temptations would be restricted to the natural order — its effect would terminate with the positing of a purely moral action. In short, he would exhibit exactly those characteristics which arise from the union of an intellectual soul with a corruptible body, and no more.

This concept has no place in the thought of Augustine, for two good reasons. First, Augustine was ever concerned with facts, and had little use for hypotheses which did not immediately serve to explain facts. And secondly, it was a fundamental principle with him that man's goodness must always and only be the gift of God's good pleasure: he could not think of man "left to himself" — either man enjoys the favour of God, and so is good, or he does not, and so is bad. The possible middle way, wherein man, like the rest of creation, should pursue his own natural good, without the special favour or enmity of God, could not enter the field of Augustine's vision.

Baius simply denied the possibility of the "state of pure nature"[3] and thus went farther than his master, who simply did not invent this possibility. He declared that the state of innocence

was the "natural"[4] state of man; but in this assertion he was guilty of a serious confusion. There are three ways in which a thing may be called "natural" to man: first, when the thing does not conflict with the exigencies of human nature, or when it "sorts with" human nature; and in this sense, nobody denies that the privileges of the state of innocence were "natural" to man. Secondly, a thing which arises out of the specific principles of human nature is "natural" to man; and in this sense even Baius denies that Adam's exalted state was "natural."[5] Finally, a thing is "natural" to man when his nature demands it as its own necessary complement, so that without it his nature suffers privative evil; and there is no doubt that Baius argued directly from the fact that the privileges of Adam were natural in the first sense, to his position that they were natural in the third sense.

These privileges consisted essentially in the subjection of man's lower nature to his mind, and of the whole man to God; and this "adhesion to God," which is as natural to men as hearing to the ear, is immediately dependent, *ex natura rei,* upon the inhabitation of the Holy Spirit in man.[6] Such is Baius' position and he states it without ambiguity or qualification. For him the concept of human nature necessarily implies a form of union with God which all scholastic theologians had agreed was supernatural. He saw, with Augustine, that the goodness

---

[3] Prop. 55. D. 1955.

[4] *De Pr. Hom. Jus.,* 4.
[5] *Ibid.,* 11.
[6] *Ibid.,* 1.

of man and the favour of God are in fact convertible terms; but as he saw this relation of identity, it implied an imperative demand on the part of man, and a corresponding obligation on the part of God, that man should receive the favour of God. For Augustine, Adam's rectitude was a free gift from God; for Baius, Adam had an inalienable right to this gift of rectitude.

As the holiness of Adam was natural, so, if he had persevered, he would have received beatitude as *a merces*, but his desert would not have been "merit" in the theological sense — the reward of cooperation with grace. The holy angels received their reward upon the same conditions.[7] This view limits the notion of grace to the divine mercy as extended to sinners, and denies the name to the supernatural exercise of divine liberality towards innocent creatures: it establishes a purely commercial relationship between the latter and their creator. For this reason Baius has rightly been described as "the Pelagius of Paradise." His system exhibits precisely the same "optimism" and "naturalism" as that of Pelagius; but he thought to escape Pelagianism by applying its principles only to innocent nature.

Adam had nothing, before the Fall, of which he could be deprived, without his nature being radically vitiated. Accordingly, "original sin" is not a mere privation, coupled with guilt, but a "vicious" act — the act of desiring, or "coveting" creatures for their own sake. This is "concupiscence," which

is identical with original sin. In children this sin is latent; but it grows, as it were, organically, with the psychological growth of the man. It becomes apparent with the use of reason, and progresses in strength *pari passu* with the power of human desires.[8] The definition of sin is "disobedience to the law of God": original sin is disobedience to the law *non concupisces*, and this sin is imputable as guilt wherever it is found, whether actually, as in actual sin, or habitually as in young children. Voluntary action is not part of the definition of sin, but only the cause and origin of sin: therefore there is no need to seek for the "voluntary" element in original sin in order to explain its guilt.[9]

Nothing more deplorable than the moral condition of fallen man, in the Baianist system, can be imagined. Even his indeliberate and inoperative desires, being infringements of the law "do not covet" (*non concupisces*), are actual sins.[10] Each sin merits an eternity of pain, for all sins are by their nature mortal sins.[11] There is no certainty that God will "give what He commands"; the opinion that God commands nothing impossible finds no support in Augustine, but derives from Pelagius.[12]

The general conclusion, so well summed up in the words of the condemned proposition: "all the works of

[7] *De Mer. Op.,* i. 2, 3.

[8] *De Pecc. Or.,* 2.
[9] *Ibid.,* 7.
[10] *Ibid.,* 11.
[11] Prop. 20. D. 1920. Cf. *De Mer. Op.,* ii. 8.
[12] *De Pecc. Or.,* 12.

unbelievers are sins,"[13] is established and defended by Baius in the *de Virtutibus impiorum*. There is, he says, only one end of man, which is supernatural beatitude, and only one way of loving God, which is charity. Therefore there is no such thing as natural virtue, but without charity (which presupposes faith) there is only sin.[14] The argument of this book receives a strongly Augustinian colour from the use of the terms *officium* and *finis*, and the reproduction of the passage in the *De Civitate Dei* concerning "pagan virtues." But the whole work is highly characteristic of its author, and centres about one of his most important axioms: namely, that man has two loves, charity and concupiscence, good and evil, and that outside these two loves he has nothing. The absence of half-lights and penumbrae was a great part of Baianist technique in theological statement.[15]

Christ came to restore to fallen man the spiritual state which was his due in the Creation, but which, owing to the fact of sin, is now "grace." Just as man is wholly characterized and determined, before redemption, by evil concupiscence, so that his every movement is a sin, so redeemed man lives and merits heaven by charity. Charity is "that motion of the soul whereby we love God and our neighbour"[16] and proceeds immediately from the touch of God, who is charity.[17] Justi-

fication, in the sense of "fulfilling all justice," means no more than "having charity": this proceeds from "actual grace" and may come before the remission of sins; it bears no intrinsic relation to formal or juridical "justification" in the sense in which the scholastics used the term.[18]

No doubt but that God can infuse a "habit" of charity; but the scholastic insistence upon the importance of "habitual grace" was quite mistaken. The origin of charity in man is an *animi motus*, and this is all that matters, because this enables us to live in perfect justice.[19] If we are to distinguish between imperfect and perfect charity, this can only be as between the inchoative and the complete — the beginning to will aright is imperfect charity; perfect charity consists in doing well, and overcoming natural (evil) desires. Perfect charity is not to be defined by reference to any sacrament or juridical "state."[20] In the same way "justification" is really a continual process, wherein man performs more and more good works under actual grace, and overcomes more and more sinful desires — that is, "makes progress in the remission of sins."[21]

This circumstantial denial of the importance, if not of the existence, of habitual or "sanctifying" grace, has an important bearing upon the notion of merit. For Baius, man's work, of itself and alone, merits heaven or hell:

---

[13] Prop. 25. D. 1925.
[14] *De Vir. Imp.*, 5, 8.
[15] Cf. *De Char.*, 6 (Prop. 38. D. 1938).
[16] *De Char.*, 2.
[17] *Ibid.*, 3.

[18] *Ibid.*, 7.
[19] *Ibid.*, 2.
[20] *Ibid.*, 9; cf. Prop. 31–33. D. 1931–1933.
[21] *De Just.*, 1,

heaven, if it proceeds from charity; hell, if from concupiscence. The scholastic belief that it is our adoption as sons of God and members of Christ which enables us to "merit" supernatural beatitude, seemed to him entirely erroneous.[22] Consequently, there is no need for a man to be "in a state of grace" in order that his work may be meritorious.[23] And by a not less rigorous logic it follows that the dignity of Christ's person in no way increased the merit of His good works — except in so far as it modified the substance of those works, as, for example, His performance of a work of humility showed more humility than ours.[24]

The Pharisaism of Baius' doctrine of merit corresponds to the Pelagianism which we observed in his description of innocent man, and reveals well enough that extraordinary singularity which makes it impossible to call his system by any other name than his own. In endeavoring to set aside all "tradition," in order to find the pure spirit of Augustine, he fell into a disastrous, but deeply interesting eclecticism. . . .

We have only to bear in mind the following considerations about Baius. First, that he set up the anti-Pelagian treatises of Augustine, against the whole body of post-Augustinian thought, as the sole repository of orthodox teaching upon grace. Secondly, that he professed to mistrust any attempt to interpret, de-

velop or modify the doctrine of Augustine by the use of philosophical or psychological reasoning. Thirdly, that he was not afraid, but rather glad, to arrive at conclusions, in matters of faith and morals, which were in open contradiction with all contemporary Catholic opinion. Finally, that he taught the following doctrines: that the "state of pure nature" is not only a useless fiction, but a chimera, in that it involves an insoluble contradiction; that the justice and merits of man in the state of original innocence, and of the holy angels, are "natural," that is, not of grace; that fallen man is determined to evil, simply because he is not drawn by "charity" into holiness; that God may command man to do the impossible without injustice; and that the motion of actual grace, which is charity, is the only, and infallible source of good works. . . .

Molina. Molina[25] published at Lisbon, in 1588, as the result of a lifetime of thought and study, his *Concordia liberi arbitrii cum gratiae donis, divina praescientia, providentia, praedestinatione, et reprobatione, ad nonnullos primae partis D. Thomae articulos.* The brilliance and originality of this work are certainly not surpassed by the *Opuscula* of Baius, to which it is, in some sort, a reply; while its in-

---

[22] *De Mer. Op.,* ii. 2.
[23] *Ibid.,* ii. 1.
[24] *Ibid.,* ii. 7.

[25] Luis de Molina (1563–1600) was born at Cuenca and joined the Society of Jesus at Alcala. For nearly twenty years he taught theology at Evora. His writings are the *Concordia* (1588), the commentaries on the *Prima Pars of the Summa* (1592), and *De justitia et jure* (1593, 1596, and posthumously). Cf. Denziger 1997.

fluence upon Catholic thought has been incomparably greater. It would, indeed, be difficult to name a single treatise of dogmatic theology which has more profoundly affected the history of dogma. For these reasons, and because a slightly modified form of the doctrine of Molina provoked Jansenius to erect his system, it seems desirable to give here some analysis of the justly celebrated, but too little known, *Concordia*.

The passages from the *Pars Prima* of the *Summa Theologica*, to which the argument of Molina serves as a commentary, have little importance for the understanding of that argument. It is not so much Aquinas, as scholastic theology as a whole, that Molina comments and develops.

The *Concordia* falls easily into five divisions. In the first, Molina investigates the nature, value, extent, and limitations of human liberty, especially the liberty of fallen man. In the second, he discusses in general the relation between the activity of the first cause and the activity of second causes; that is, the nature of the *concursus divinae potestatis*, in virtue of which all secondary causality is operative. In the third part of his work he treats of "actual grace." In the fourth, he propounds and defends the notion of *scientia media*. In the last, he gives an account of Predestination and Reprobation — which is, in some ways, the least valuable part of the *Concordia*. . . .

The system of Molina marks the point in the development of the Au-

gustinian doctrine of grace, beyond which the term "development" ceases to have any appropriateness. In two important points this system retains the mark of its origin; but for the rest it is partly the result of a millenium of Catholic intellectual effort, and partly an original contribution to theology.

Molina's account of the necessity of grace is substantially the same as Augustine's, in spite of the apparently infinite gulf which separates the two modes of expression. In the *Concordia*, one limitation which is constantly set to the fullness of liberty in fallen nature, and in human nature however constituted, is that without the aid of grace man cannot do a single action "as he ought to" (*sicut oportet*), that is, ordered to his supernatural end. Another limitation which is found in fallen nature, and in the state of pure nature, is that man cannot long survive temptation, or persevere in even moral action, without a special *auxilium*, which, in the order of things as they are, must be supernatural. There is, then, a double necessity of grace, based first on the sublimity of the end to which man is called, and secondly on the intrinsic deficiency of human nature. These two grounds were precisely those upon which Augustine had established the necessity of grace.[26]

Again, Molina described prevenient grace as an "illumination of the intellect" (*illustratio intellectus*) and a "motion and affection of the will" (*mo-

---

[26] Cf. *supra*, pp. 6–8.

tio et affectio voluntatis). In this his language faithfully echoes that of Augustine; and there is hardly any part of the treatise of grace to which Augustine devoted more attention than to this.[27]

Molina is content to codify the conclusions of the later scholastics in his doctrine concerning the state of innocent man — that the state of "original justice," consisting in the interior harmony of man and his subjection to God, is separable from the gifts of grace and supernatural elevation, and depends upon them only in virtue of the positive law of God. He appears to have taken for granted the rationalization of the fall of man which Aquinas first propounded.[28] It was a commonplace of later scholasticism to identify the state of fallen nature with the state of pure nature, except that the guilt which stains the former would have been absent in the latter; and from this identification to argue the possibility of performing morally good actions in the state of fallen nature, as well as the impossibility of persevering in moral goodness in the state of pure nature. Molina takes over from the scholastic tradition all that he has to say of habitual grace and the infused virtues; and his interpretation of the maxim "God does not deny grace to the one who does what he can" (*facienti quod in se est, Deus non denegat gratiam*) is no less traditional, although it never held undisputed sway in the Schools.

27 Cf. *supra,* pp. 34–39.
28 Cf. *supra,* pp. 69–72.

His attempt to reconcile the infallible efficacy of divine grace with complete human freedom was almost wholly original; and his doctrine of predestination was necessarily modified by his attribution to God of the so-called *scientia media,* in which this originality principally consisted. His system, as a system, would have been more satisfactory if he had devoted more attention to working out the extent of these necessary modifications; but . . . his treatment of predestination and reprobation is less finished than any other part of his work. He was equally original in isolating the *concursus generalis* from every other form of divine action in creation, and in his balanced and orderly philosophical discussion of this *concursus.*

In spite of the stylistic and dialectical unevenness of the *Concordia,* it was at once realized that the "system of Molina" was a coherent whole, and a thing of the highest theological importance. Some part of its influence must, no doubt, be attributed to the controversies which it aroused; but it is no less true that the range and ferocity of these controversies gives some measure of the power of Molina's book. A better indication of this is found in the fact that the system of Molina became, within a decade or two, the norm of the treatise of grace, as expounded by the theologians of the whole Society of Jesus. The modifications of detail which this wide diffusion of Molinism necessarily brought about within that system are unimportant by comparison with the fidelity of the Society to the fundamental principles of the *Concordia*. . . .

Suarez — himself a far greater figure than Molina — wrote his *de Divina Gratia* after the disputes concerning grace between the Jesuits and the Dominicans had been officially brought to a close. His work exhibits a unity and polish which is lacking in the *Concordia;* and his extraordinarily acute mind enabled him to find in the texts of Augustine, Aquinas, and other weighty authorities a far greater wealth and variety of doctrine and opinion than the normal student would ever discover. His interpretations are rarely forced, even when they are most original, and his reverence for indisputable authority, whether Scriptural, Patristic, or Scholastic, is almost excessive. The "Doctor Eximius" was, perhaps, the greatest theologian of the Society of Jesus. Yet his debt to Molina, in the treatise of grace, is more important than his contribution to Molinism. This contribution is reducible to four points. . . . Apart from these four points — the *medium quo* of the "conditioned" knowledge of God, the description of actual grace as received, the scope and *munus* of sufficient grace, and the subdivision of Molina's *concursus generalis* — the doctrine of Suarez is precisely that of the *Concordia*.

Molina, Vasquez, and Suarez represent the limits within which the Jesuit doctrine of grace, at least for the first century of the Society's existence, was wholly contained. This doctrine was not inelastic; but it exhibited, wherever it was found, certain obvious distinguishing characteristics: as, for example, a preoccupation with human liberty, and a determination to allow no obscuration of this term of the problems of grace; and a firm belief in the existence and importance of *scientia media*. The Jesuit doctrine of grace, as we shall see, was the irritant which determined Jansenius to compose his *Augustinus*. . . .

The Dominicans. . . . The first Dominican to challenge publicly the conclusions which Molina and other Jesuit theologians had reached in the treatise of grace was the Spaniard Dominic Bañez.[29] The fact that a Dominican was among the approbators of the *Concordia* is evidence that, before the activities of Bañez began, there was no recognized formal opposition between the "new" doctrines and the teaching of the Order of Preachers. Bañez, however, whose devotion to the authority of Aquinas was such that he proudly claimed never to have swerved a hair's breadth from the strictest adhesion to the whole doctrine of Aquinas, attacked the *Concordia* in particular, and the nascent Jesuit theology in general, as heretical novelties. His influence was enough to bring about a fierce antagonism between the Spanish Inquisition and the Spanish Jesuits from

---

[29] Dominic Bañez (1528–1604) became a Dominican at Salamanca in 1546. He taught theology most of his life. He was St. Teresa's confessor (1562–1566). He was gifted with a very forceful personality, logical vigor and metaphysical profundity. He became the spokesman of the rigorous interpretation of Thomism and was followed by the majority of Dominican theologians.

which the only possible issue lay in the appeal to Rome. The dissension was so sharp that a special Roman Congregation was appointed to deal with the whole question *de Auxiliis* in 1598. This Congregation heard an infinity of arguments upon both sides; but even the great power and authority of a Bellarmine was insufficient to bring it to a definite and conclusive decision. In 1607 the deliberations were ended; their positive result being formulated by Pope Paul V in a prohibition to both parties of the use of injurious language, and of mutual accusations of error or heresy.

For all practical purposes such was the historical origin of the so-called "Thomist" theory of grace. It suffers from two essential defects: the first, that it is characterized only by opposition to the Jesuit system; the second, that it contributes nothing to the problems in question, but a somewhat narrow — some would say "superstitious" — devotion to the letter of Aquinas' text, embellished by an exclusively Dominican gloss. This negative and parochial character is not seriously denied by the adherents of the system, who form a closed corporation and claim, with varying degrees of force, a monopoly of orthodoxy.

For our present inquiry we are concerned only with the three chief points of the system: the negation of *scientia media;* the statement of the doctrine of predestination; and the belief in "physical premotion."

In regard to the first point, the Dominicans claim that Aquinas knew of only two kinds of divine knowledge. The first, *scientia simplicis intelligentiae,* has for its object all that is absolutely necessary, and all that is simply possible. The second, *scientia visionis,* has for its object all things that were, are, and ever will be. The source of this second kind of knowledge is the eternal presence with God of all things, in their proper existence; and the root of this presence is solely the eternal Decree, or Decrees, both positive and negative, whereby God constitutes this universe and no other. . . .

The Dominican theory of the distribution of graces is closely connected with their denial of *scientia media.* In this theory there are two acts *per modum imperii* of the divine intellect, which include corresponding acts of will: by the one, God elects some to share His beatitude in glory, and prepares graces which shall be efficacious, so that, by their help, the elect shall be saved; by the other, He "permits" all other rational creatures to fall into sin, and so render themselves liable to damnation, and prepares, for all these, "graces" which shall be "sufficient," in the sense that the responsibility for their inefficacity shall rest upon the recipient. These two acts take place "before" the divine prevision of any human actions whatsoever, and out of all relation to such prevision. The act of reprobation, on the other hand, is consequent upon the divine prevision of human sin, and includes the positive will to punish men for their sins. . . .

The third, and the most characteristic, of the chief features of the Dominican system, is the theory of "physical premotion.". . . It is regarded as absolutely necessary for any and every operation of any and every created cause, since it alone can make their operation possible and real; even the transition from one action to another, however closely connected the two actions may be, is not possible without a new "premotion," any more than it would be possible, in the Jesuit system, without the *concursus*. The "premotion" is an immediate influx of the divine causality into the created agent, enabling and causing it to operate. In time it is simultaneous with the operation of the second cause, but in the order of reason it takes precedence; wherefore it is called *praemotio*.

The human will stands in need of it, no less than any other created cause; and, since it is not a moral suasion, but is rather in the order of efficient than of final cause, it is called *praemotio physica*. Because it is held to correspond to Aquinas' "motion and application to acting" (*motio et applicatio ad agendum*), and is yet necessary for any and every act of human will, it cannot be supposed to receive its specification from the recipient, but is defined as a "predetermination to one" (*praedeterminatio ad unum*), by which alone the will can emerge from total indetermination; and because it is divine it is infallibly efficacious. "Efficacious grace" is simply a subdivision of *praemotio physica*; by this particular "premotion" the powers of

the soul are raised to the supernatural level, as well as being applied to the performance of a morally good work. It follows that grace is either "efficacious or inefficacious of itself" (*per se efficax* or *per se inefficax*).

It is not impossible to imagine that a final solution of this dispute (between Dominicans and Jesuits), now more than three centuries old, may be found in a closer and more exact analysis of the notion of "instrumentality.". . .

Jansen (Jansenius).[30]. . . It has not been sufficiently realized by the Catholic historians of Jansenism that there is no need to seek for special causes of Jansen's attitude towards the Jesuits. The mere fact that he was educated in the University of Louvain gave him the choice between the two opposed intellectual camps, of which one was organized for the defense of the late Michael du Bay and his principles, while the other accepted the condemnation of Baianism, and acquiesced, or even co-operated, in the great revival of scholasticism which accompanied the disputes *de Auxiliis*. It may have been the influence of Jansson, or it may equally well have been some other, that determined the young Jansen to enter the Baianist camp. Once this choice was made — and his temperament did not admit of vacillation

---

[30] Cornelius Jansen (1585–1638) was promoted to the episcopal see of Ypres in 1634 and died shortly after in 1638. His great work, *Augustinus, seu doctrina s. Augustini de humanae naturae sanitate, aegritudine, medicina adv. Pelagianos et Massilienses*, was first published after his death in 1640. Cf. Denziger 2001–2007.

— he was committed to an absolute opposition to the theology of the Society of Jesus, and indeed to neo-scholasticism as a whole; while his subsequent career as a member of the University afforded him frequent opportunities for attacking the Society as an educational body.

His *Augustinus*[31] makes no pretense to be a disinterested study of Augustine, but is undisguisedly polemical in intention. On the other hand, it was not primarily an attack upon contemporary Jesuit theologians. First and foremost it was an "Apology for Baius," and, as a necessary consequence, a counter-attack upon the recent revival of Scholasticism, which, more than any papal Bulls, was annihilating the effect of Baius' work by causing a general rejection of his characteristic method. Only because the Jesuits were the principal exponents of the new scholasticism were they the chief object of Jansen's attack, and the most determined opponents of his system. . . .

The genesis of the *Augustinus* appears to have been in a sincere conviction of Jansen, that all the unedifying and unprofitable disputes *de Auxiliis*, and the unsatisfactory nature of their conclusion, were due to the complete neglect in which the profoundest lesson of Baius had been swallowed up — the lesson that the authority of Augustine must be supreme in matters of grace. That this lesson was in fact ignored by certain of the neo-scholastic theologians is certain; and Lessius, of

[31] Cf. Abercrombie, *op. cit.*, pp. 126–153 for a summary of this work.

whose doctrine and influence Jansen must have had more personal experience than he had of that of the Spanish or Italian writers, seemed so intolerant of Augustine's authority that some of his own Society — notably Bellarmine — saw fit to rebuke him on this score. Jansen had therefore ample justification for his attempt to set before theologians a true account of the doctrine of this holy teacher.

Two elements of this doctrine seemed to Jansen at once of the greatest importance in themselves, and in the estimation of St. Augustine, and also particularly liable to escape the notice of his scholastic contemporaries: the "slavery of sin" (*servitus peccati*), and the description of grace as *delectatio* or *suavitas*. The root cause of the *servitus peccati* was clearly "concupiscence"; the *servitus* itself must be the foundation of the necessity of grace — so much follows from the mere fact of regarding this phenomenon as of fundamental importance. The notion of a *servitus peccati* will receive clearer definition from an understanding of the nature of the "liberating" power, which is grace: to emphasize the aspect of grace which is expressed in the word *delectatio* is to make the *servitus peccati* a matter of "desires." In some such fashion Jansen appears to have arrived at his dominating conception of the "strife of desires" (*lucta delectationum*).

Once the nature and importance of this strife have been determined, the Jansenist account of the state of fallen nature is essentially complete. A passage from the *de Correptione et Gratia* furnished Jansen with an apparently Augustinian method of arguing from the state of fallen nature to that of innocent nature: Jansen's account of the latter derives from the opposition, which he found in Augustine's account of the *adiutoria quo* and *sine quo non,* between supra-lapsarian self-sufficiency and infra-lapsarian dependence.

These seem to be the fundamental conceptions and guiding principles of Jansen's system. The rest of that system follows from these premises in two ways: either by retracing the arguments of Augustine — as, for instance, those which concern the universal salvific will — without reference to later interpretations or developments of Augustine; or by the simplest inference from what has been established as the doctrine of Augustine. Such an inference from the supposedly Augustinian theory that the "victorious delight" (*victrix delectatio*) is the sole immediate cause of human action in the state of fallen nature leads Jansen to his emphatic and circumstantial denial of the universality of grace — in view of the fact of human sin, the presupposed theory points directly to the conclusion that grace is often absent.

We have already suggested that Jansen's method involved him in the gravest danger of error. Jansen was too much the typical representative of a fundamentally scholastic age, and his intellectual training had been too profoundly influenced by scholasticism,

for him to be able to approach the treatises of a fifth-century writer with neo-platonist affinities in that purely "positive" spirit which alone could give value to his treatise. Augustine was simply unaware of that rigid and logical demarcation of the sphere of the "supernatural" which was to become an essential element of all theological thought in the West; to look for it, or for any of the ideas which depend upon it, within Augustine's universe of discourse is to commit a heinous anachronism. Jansen was unable to conceive a system of thought from which this series of ideas should be completely absent; he therefore concluded that Augustine must have neglected the distinction between nature and supernature (as that distinction was taught in the Schools) of deliberate purpose, and because that distinction was unreal. From this capital error of interpretation there arises a wholly mistaken view of the *servitus peccati,* since the category of "natural moral good works," for which there was no place in the system of Augustine, is unjustifiably introduced, as a precisely defined order of human activity, into the Augustinian notion of "sin."

A second misinterpretation of which Jansen was guilty, though less important in itself, had momentous consequences. Augustine found his Pelagian opponents ready enough to admit the notion of "grace," but disposed to define it as an intellectual assistance. He answered that "illumination" was not peculiarly the effect of "grace," and that grace was not only intellectual assistance but also volitional, so that a spiritual "sweetness," begetting holy desires, differentiates grace from other interior and exterior sources of "enlightenment." There is little doubt that Augustine was influenced in his expression of this doctrine by his peculiar theory of knowledge — he was so familiar with a conception of "natural" divine illumination that he laid, perhaps, disproportionate emphasis upon the volitional element which characterizes grace. Jansen was not in a position to appreciate this point; he understood Augustine to mean that no intellectual assistance can be more than a "half-grace," whereas Augustine's thought is better expressed by saying that "intellectual assistance is but the half of grace." He took the differentiating aspect of grace for its whole definition.

The parallelism between this description of grace and "concupiscence" considered as the characteristic feature of the *servitus peccati* was so plain as to focus Jansen's attention upon the "strife of desires" (*lucta delectationum*) of which Augustine had incidentally written; in this way Jansen came to see in this "strife" the whole economy of the Christian life, and so rejoined the system of Baius. But he followed up the consequences of this position farther than his predecessor, and did not shrink from an extreme form of determinism, which is, perhaps, his most original and important contribution to modern heterodoxy.

A third misunderstanding of Augustine, and less important than either of the two we have just discussed, is evident in Jansen's treatment of the *adiutorium sine quo non*. As we have seen, Jansen found in the eleventh and twelfth chapters of the *De Correptione et Gratia* the account of an opposition between the state of innocent nature and that of fallen nature, which he regarded as of capital importance and very wide application. It did not, in fact, deserve the attention which he paid it, for it is intended only to explain the problem of perseverance in the state of fallen nature by contrast with the fall of man from innocence. But Jansen's fault would have been of little consequence if it had consisted only in this exaggeration. Unfortunately, he was led by his own idea of the importance of Augustine's distinction to identify it with another distinction with which he was familiar — that between "sufficient" and "efficacious" grace. This identification must have been due to a desire to find in Augustine a thing which could not possibly be there — an account of *gratia sufficiens* as contrasted with *gratia efficax*. Jansen could not have arrived at his identification by reasoning from the Augustinian or from the scholastic positions: for Augustine is silent as to the scholastic distinction; and while the Jesuits taught that all grace was "resistible," and operative only with the consent of the human will, the Dominican definition of "sufficient grace" includes the notion of inefficacity, which must be absent from any interpretation of the *adiutorium sine quo non*. Jansen was thus distorting equally the notions of *gratia sufficiens* and *adiutorium sine quo non* by identifying the two, and satisfying only his own wish to find an authoritative account of *gratia sufficiens*. From this double distortion there follow two erroneous consequences: the first, that *gratia sufficiens*, being identical with the assistance which Augustine attributes only to Adam, is not given to fallen man; the second, that man in the state of innocence, being in such a condition that he needed, for his final perfection, only *adiutorium sine quo non* — a thing of little moment, since it is identical with *gratia mere sufficiens* — must have enjoyed powers of mind and spirit considerably greater than the scholastic theologians allow. Thus arises a certain supra-lapsarian optimism, which complements the infra-lapsarian pessimism, of the Jansenist *servitus peccati* and gives coherence to the whole system.

In spite of this coherence, and of the plainly heretical nature of certain fundamental postulates of the system, the *Augustinus* was never condemned as a whole, but only censured and prohibited. Two of the doctrines which it contains were formally and repeatedly condemned by the Holy See: namely, the "double determinism" of concupiscence and grace, and the denial of any kind of universality in the bestowal of grace upon men.

As regards the first of these points, Jansen's deterministic account of the

servitus peccati was condemned in the first proposition, which, as we have seen, is taken textually from his work. . . . The other aspect of Jansen's "determinism" was condemned in the second, third, and fourth propositions. The second proposition, like the first, is a transcription of one of the opinions attributed by Jansen to Augustine. . . . The third proposition is not to be found textually in the *Augustinus* but is a scrupulously fair and convenient summation of the sixth and eighth books *de Gratia Christi*. The fourth proposition is collected from the seventh book of the first volume. . . . The fifth proposition, in which Jansen's denial of the universality of grace is condemned, is an attribution to the Semi-Pelagians, as heretics, of the belief that Christ died for all men. . . . The correct inference is that Jansen rejected the doctrine. The fifth proposition, therefore, does him little injustice; but it is not, perhaps, perfectly representative of his exact expression.

In addition to the formal condemnation of Jansen's determinism, and of his limitation of the field of Christ's redemptive work, severe censure was passed upon his book, as containing certain of the condemned propositions of Baius.[32] The most cursory examination of the doctrines of Baius and Jansen will serve to convince the student of the close affinities between the two systems; many of the condemned propositions of Baius are to be detected in *Augustinus,* at least so far as the sense of these propositions is

[32] In the Bull *In eminenti.* Cf. Denziger 2000.

concerned. In particular, the following points of Jansen's doctrine are identical with condemned Baianist opinions: that "natural morality" is a mere philosophoumenon, without reality; that every action of an unbeliever is a sin; that grace is due to new-created man, by the essential postulates of his nature; that the rational creature has only two kinds of voluntary action, namely concupiscence and charity; that true liberty is always compatible with natural necessity; that the precepts of God are sometimes impossible to just men of good will; and that the "state of pure nature" involves a contradiction, and is therefore absolutely impossible.[33]

2. H. Rondet, S.J.,[34] studies Baianism and Jansenism and the *de Auxiliis* controversies that came between them. Baius admits for the primitive state of man a neo-Pelagianism with some Renaissance ideas, while for the fallen state he resorts to somewhat attenuated Protestant theses. Jansen's *Augustinus* is built on the idea that the true theology of grace is to be found in the strictest Augustinism.

Baius. Baius is not a great theologian but rather a constricted spirit in love with little syntheses which he expresses in elegant language.[35] But his doctrine has a certain coherence that needs to be underlined.

It can be characterised rather briefly. For the primitive state of man Baius admits a neo-Pelagianism that aims to incorporate Renaissance ideas. But for fallen humanity he resorts to Protestant theses, though with some attenua-tions.[36] . . . Manuals of theology in speaking of Baianism give special attention to the precisions that his condemnation produced in the question of the relations between nature and the supernatural. But they do not stress sufficiently his opposition to St. Thomas regarding the state of grace and merit.

St. Thomas centred all his theology of grace on the idea of a created gift that makes us participants in the divine nature. Baius ignores elevating grace. St. Thomas labored to coordinate the juridical and the ontological points of view in the question of merit. Baius knows only categories that are borrowed from a banal moralism. He is a jurist theologian for whom innocent man has rights before God.[37] In the

---

[33] Prop. Baii: 16, 25–27, 38–39, 54–55; cf. *ibid.*, 3, 5, 7, 21, 23, 34, 40–41, 66–68, 74, 78–79. Cf. Denzinger 1901–1980.

[34] Cf. Ch. III, n. 1. This excerpt is from *op. cit.*, pp. 287–297, 309–316.

[35] On Baius and his work, see F.-X. Jansen, *Baius et le baianisme*, 1931; X.-M. Le Bachelet, "Baius," DTC, t. II, col. 38–57; H. De Lubac, "Deux augustiniens fourvoyés, Baius et Jansenius, in *Recherches de science religieuse*, 1931, p. 442–443. Baius is cited here according to the edition of Dom Gerberon, *Michaelis Baii Opera* (Cologne, 1696).

[36] Cf. X.-M. Le Bachelet, "Baius," DTC, t. II, col. 46–47.

[37] H. De Lubac, *Surnaturel*, p. 16.

strength of the divine ordination by which God had decided to recompense his good works, Adam could demand his due. Eternal life for him is a veritable recompense.[38] That the Holy Spirit's presence is required for authentic merit Baius thinks is altogether incidental.[39] In his notion of merit the accent is solely on the proportion between work and recompense, between work and punishment.[40] Here we see the heritage of Nominalism.

But we see too an extreme Augustinism. Apart from the gift of creation only justice regulates man's relations with God in the terrestrial paradise. After the fall we are incapable of doing the least good by ourselves and can no longer count on anything but His mercy. It is by grace that we are saved. But we must understand this properly. For contrary to what the Reformers think, mercy reopens the ways to justice. So Baius tells us. Without the grace of the Redeemer we can accomplish no good work. But once this grace has been accorded us we reencounter the primitive economy. The grace of Christ makes us again

capable of doing good works[41] and in virtue of the first ordination these works necessarily demand their recompense. Eternal life in paradise was only a recompense, but for us it is both grace and recompense.[42] That our works should be meritorious derives solely from their proportion to the promised recompense.[43] Grace enters in only to give us anew the natural forces that sin had destroyed in man.

In this Baius thinks he is a faithful Augustinian. But in reality he is antipodally removed from the spirit of Augustinism, which makes a rational creature at every instant dependent on God[44] in whatever state he is found.

His theory of justification suffers from the same basic vices. From an assiduous reading of the works of the doctor of Hippo Baius made his own the thesis of progressive justification.[45] Justice is rectitude of the will. But since the original fall man remains disordered, turned back on himself. Grace could straighten out this will, but God gives the grace to whom He wishes and as He intends. So some never reach faith. Others believe but do not preserve chastity. A St. Peter

---

[38] De meritis operum, I, 4, Opera, pp. 27–28. One should cite here this treatise in its entirety, for it gives the key of Baianism. Baius divides it into two books, distinguishing that which Christian faith imposes and that which is matter of free opinion. . . . But he slips into this first treatise all his personal ideas. It is from this work that the first 19 propositions condemned by Pius V were extracted (D. 1901–1919). See the commentary of M. LeBachelet, DTC, t. II, col. 74–79.

[39] De meritis operum, II, 1, Opera, p. 35–36.

[40] De meritis operum, II, c. 2, Opera, p. 36.

[41] De meritis operum, I, c. 5, Opera, p. 29.

[42] De meritis operum, I, c. 6, Opera, p. 31.

[43] De meritis operum, I, c. 2, Opera, p. 33.

[44] See the text of the council of Orange (c. 19) and the excursus of H. De Lubac on the prayer of Adam in Surnaturel (1946), pp. 87–100.

[45] De justificatione, c. 1, Opera, p. 147: "nihil aliud est justificatio quam continua quaedam et indesinens ad justitiam progressio . . . tam in operatione virtutum quam in remissione peccatorum."

receives the gift of an immense love.[46] Justice remains for man an ideal out of his reach. He must be content with an imperfect justice which God in His mercy consents to regard as a true justice.[47] A sinuous line that mimics a straight line, that concretely is justification,[47a] an uninterrupted succession of remissions of sins and of virtuous acts that are always deficient. So Baius ignores the state of grace[48] and retains from Augustine only the dynamic notion of charity and justification.

But the council of Trent has decided certain questions and spoken clearly of the efficacy of baptism or absolution. So it is necessary to be conformed to dogma. This our jurist theologian thinks he can achieve by dissociating the social and sacramental point of view from the personal point of view. A catechumen who has faith and is able to be moved by grace is capable of doing good acts, acts that in Baius' sense are strictly meritorious. But so long as he has not been baptised, his sins will not be forgiven him.[49] So a man can be in the state of mortal sin and yet have charity. . . .

It is necessary to stress two very important points of his doctrine which connect him with Luther and Calvin: the radical impotence of the fallen will and the negation of liberty of choice. To innocent man Baius gives the power to make his destiny for himself. But he thinks fallen man is incapable of any good whatever without the grace of Christ; and only a Pelagian, he assures us, can affirm the contrary.[50] All the works of pagans are sins and the virtues of the philosophers are disguised vices.[51] The sinner enslaved by sin can only entangle himself further.[52] The grace of

---

[46] De libero arbitrio, c. 12, Opera, pp. 87–88.

[47] De justitia, c. 5, Opera, p. 106. This is not Luther's position, for Baius puts the stress on works, but it is in Nominalist perspectives.

[47a] De justitia, c. 8, Opera, p. 109.

[48] The bull of Pius V condemns this proposition: "Justitia, qua justificatur per fidem impius, consistit formaliter in obedientia mandatorum, quae est operum justitia; non autem in gratia aliqua animae infusa, qua adoptatur homo in filium Dei et secundum interiorem hominem renovatur ac divinae naturae consors efficitur, ut sic per Spiritum sanctum renovatus, deinceps beate vivere et Dei mandatis oboedire possit" (Prop. 42, D. 1942). This proposition is not drawn word for word from the works of Baius and he has protested that this is a caricature of his doctrine (Apologie à Pie V, Baiana, p. 102). But it is quite certain that Baius made little of the habit of charity, and consequently of grace as permanent gift. Here is the way he writes in De caritate (c. 2, Opera, p. 91): "an vero praeter hunc animi motum qui caritas dicitur, aliqua quaedam habitualis atque accidentalis qualitas in voluntate ponenda sit quae etiam caritas nuncupatur, non magnopere contendendum existimo."

[49] De justitia, c. 7, Opera, p. 107. See the condemned proposition, n. 43, D. 1943, and the commentary of P. Le Bachelet, DTC, t. II, col. 102–103.

[50] De virtutibus impiorum, c. 8, Opera, p. 70.

[51] De virtutibus impiorum, c. 5, Opera, pp. 66–67. Cf. L. Caperan, Le problème du salut das infidèles, 1934, 2 ed., p. 276.

[52] The Bull condemns proposition 40: "In omnibus suis actibus peccator servit cupiditati dominanti" (D. 1940). This formula is not as such in Baius and he protested in his Apologie à Pie V (Baiana, p. 101). But it well represents his thought (cf. X.-M. Le Bachelet, "Baius," DTC, II, col. 87).

Christ can free him from this servitude, but in turn this grace necessitates him. So attached to Augustine's formulas is Baius, and so opposed to all philosophical analysis that he practically identifies spiritual liberty and spontaneity. Thus he prepares the way for Jansen.[53]

The system evidently is only a narrow Augustinism, that makes a *tabula rasa* of the past and refuses to integrate into itself the progress made by medieval theology.[54] The divinisation of the Christian is ignored and medicinal grace outweighs elevating grace. The notion of merit that he pretends to defend against the Reformers is emptied of all that formerly gave it grandeur. Justification is not a renovation of the whole being, but a compromise between juridical extrinsicism and psychological moralism. In spite of his desire to renew theology Baius remains imprisoned by the rigidity of his first formation. And if he sometimes

reads Augustine with the eyes of Augustine, more often he reads him with the eyes of Luther and Calvin.

The Church could not fail to react. . . . In 1567 Pius V pronounced the condemnation of Baius that marks an important date in the history of Catholic theology.[55]

De Auxiliis. Between the condemnation of Baius and that of Jansen are situated the famous Congregations *de Auxiliis* . . . the controversies over grace. . . . For some time a new current of theology has been visible. To give a better answer to Protestantism it insisted on the role of the subject and liberty of indifference.[56] To be free, isn't this to have the power to choose between the two terms of an alternative, without being constrained by anything exterior? Of two men who receive the same grace, cannot one consent and the other not? In reality Molina and his followers posed the problem in a more subtle fashion. But to their doctrine in its simplified form the Thomist theologians of Salamanca were vigorously opposed and urged with St. Augustine and St. Thomas that even if a man can do evil of himself, to do good he must have

---

[53] *De libero arbitrio* analyzes the notions of will, of appetite, but very quickly leaves the scholastic precisions to show that the true notion of liberty is in scripture and in St. Augustine (*De lib. arb.*, c. 5, *Opera*, p. 77). He shows then that this liberty remains where man has not the power to choose: *"huic libertatis modo impertinens est, utrum id quod libere fieri dicitur etiam possit non fieri"* (*ibid.*, c. 7, *Opera*, p. 79). Cf. D. 1939, 1941, 1966 and Le Bachelet's commentary in DTC, II, col. 81–83.

[54] Baius defends well the idea that the Holy Spirit was given to Adam (*De prima hominis justitia*, I, c. 1. *Opera*, pp. 49–52): it is an essential part of his thesis on the exigence of the supernatural, but he bypasses completely the spiritual riches contained in the texts he brings to support his affirmation.

[55] Oct. 1, 1567. Cf. Denzinger 1901–1980.

[56] E. Gilson, *La liberté chez Descartes et la théologie*, 1913, p. 290–294. It is very difficult to set forth objectively the history of the *De Auxiliis* controversies. Cf. E. Vansteenberghe, "Molinisme," DTC, t. X, col. 2098; P. G. Schneemann, S.J., *Controversiarum de divinae gratiae liberique arbitrii concordia initia et progressus*, 1881; P. De Scorraille, *Francois Suarez*, t. I, 1912, pp. 349–467; F. Stegmuller, "Geschichte des Molinismus," in *Beiträge zur Geschichte der Phil. des M.A.*, t. 32, 1935.

divine aid. In 1584 Bañez edits his course and Molina publishes extracts from his. But it is Molina's *Concordia* that sets fire to the powder. In Spain the two religious families had already had occasion to quarrel. Now they took up the cause of their respective champions. The Inquisition and Philip II also took a hand. Rome finally had to intervene but soon it left to the parties their entire liberty.[57] Molina then published at Antwerp the second edition of his *Concordia*.[58]

In the Low Countries the Jesuits were battling against Calvinism and Baianism. They read Molina eagerly and found in the *Concordia* a theology of divine knowledge that appeared to them most suited to refute Predestinationism, whether infralapsarian or supralapsarian.[59] Lessius, who had a luminous spirit but was something of a simplifier, turned Molina's obscure and nuanced thought into a serviceable scheme that would be successful. God predestines the just to glory only on prevision of their merits. He decides from all eternity to offer to Peter and to Judas the same grace, but He knows by His knowledge of conditional futures what use each will make of it. Sufficient grace becomes efficacious by the free concurrence of man but not without God having foreseen and

willed this. In 1587 this doctrine of Lessius was censured by the Faculty of Louvain which had continued to be very close to the Augustinian tradition.[60] It was also suspect to the greater theologians of the Society of Jesus.

Neither Bellarmine, who had solidly refuted Baius, nor Suarez, who was teaching in Spain after having been a professor at the Roman College, were fully satisfied with it. For each was a determined Augustinian and taught predestination *ante praevisa merita*.[61] For the Bañezian thesis of grace that is efficacious of itself they substituted a thesis inspired both by St. Augustine and by Molina. From all eternity God knows by His *"scientia media"* what Peter and Judas would do if they were offered a particular grace. If then Judas damns himself he can only blame himself. But because God loves Peter with a love of predilection He decides to give him a grace so powerful that, in the light of his character and tendencies and profound psychology, he cannot refuse it. Thus the gratuity of predestination and final perseverance is fully saved, while the mystery of the relations between grace and liberty is carried into the domain of the possi-

---

[57] E. Vansteenberghe, DTC, t. X, col. 2141–2145.

[58] Molina, *Concordia liberi arbitrii cum gratiae donis, divina praescientia, providentia, praedestinatione et reprobatione ad nonnullos primae partis divi Thomae articulos* (Lisbon, 1588; Antwerp, 1595).

[59] Letter of Lessius to Bellarmine (1587) in X.-M. Le Bachelet, *Bellarmin avant son cardinalat,* 1912, pp. 148–149.

[60] E. VanSteenberghe, "Molinisme," DTC, t. X, col. 2099–2100; Ch. Van Sull, *Leonard Lessius,* 1930, ch. 10.

[61] In his *Autobiographie* Bellarmine recounts that while he was a student at Padua P. Pharao Siculus taught him predestination *post praevisa merita*, but "N." (i.e. the young Bellarmine) *"in scriptis suis ponebat doctrinam sancti Augustini de gratuita praedestinatione"* (X.-M. Le Bachelet, *Bellarmin avant son cardinalat,* 1912, p. 449).

bles and of conditional free futures.[62]

Bañez and his followers on their part put into relief the priority of the divine will. . . . He wishes to go back to St. Thomas and with him affirm the transcendence of God. But unaware that he is influenced by Nominalist theology, he goes back to a Scotist principle that he who wills the end wills the means.[63] Thus to save some God gives them efficacious aids, while the others are lost by their own powers. God is no more the cause of their sin than the one who presides over the destiny of a city is responsible for the disorders that follow on the opening of a brothel.[64] We should not judge the value of Bañez' theology by this simple comparison. For he is a profound theologian and he has read St. Thomas closely. But some still far off day a better understanding of the thought of the Angelic Doctor will bring one to reject as injurious to the majesty of pure act all this succession of hypothetical decrees meant to represent the relations between divine thought and will.

The conflicts are renewed and finally they are called to Rome. Intent on putting an end to this irritating question Pope Clement VIII decides to hear the two parties. And so the famous Congregations *de Auxiliis* begin at Rome in 1598. They are marked by all sorts of incidents and filled with interminable discussions in which Scripture texts and Patristic authorities are invoked pell-mell without any effort to situate them in their remote or proximate context.[65] . . . The famous congregations lasted nine years and ended in an admission of impotence. Paul V was content to impose silence on the two parties without settling what was what. As Bossuet will say later, the Church holds the two ends of the chain: man is free and the grace of God is all-powerful. To go further and to scrutinize the mystery is not forbidden, but the two parties must stop villifying one another.[66]

Jansen. Jansen is connected with Baius through Jacques Jansson, one of Lessius' adversaries at Louvain.[67] Raised in an atmosphere of passionate struggles against Molina and Molinism Cornelius Jansen decided that the true theology of grace was found only in St. Augustine. For a long time he worked in silence, first at Louvain and then in France with his friend Duvergier de Hauranne, the future

---

[62] See the texts of Bellarmine in X.-M. Le Bachelet, *Auctarium Bellarminianum*, 1913, pp. 86–93.

[63] Bañez, In *I part.* q. 23, art. 2 (p. 758) (edit. Venise, 1587). In his article in DTC, P. Mandonnet judges it useless to present the doctrine of Bañez, since it is none other than that of St. Thomas (Bañez, DTC, t. II, col. 145). That is a little hasty, especially for a great historian of ideas. M. Vansteenberghe (DTC, t. X, col. 2097–2098) is content to indicate the tendency. We need a disinterested study.

[64] *Ibid.*, q. 23, art. 3, dub. 2 (p. 784).

[65] E. Vansteenberghe, DTC, t. X, col. 2154–2165. R. De Scorraille, *Francois Suarez*, t. I, p. 402–460.

[66] Denzinger 1997. Cf. E. Vansteenberghe, DTC, t. X, col. 2165.

[67] E. Amann, "Janson," DTC, t. X, col. 529–531. On the theologians of Louvain see R. Guelluy, "L'evolution des méthodes théologiques à Louvain, d'Erasme à Jansenius," in *Revue d'hist. eccles.*, 1941, pp. 105–117.

abbé Saint-Cyran. He composed a great work that would ignore all the scholastic quarrels and carry the Church to the study of sources and thus cast definitive light on the question of grace and predestination. . . . He read and reread St. Augustine and went over his writings on grace thirty times, regretting that he had to give time to other tasks. He was promoted to the episcopal see of Ypres (1634) but soon died (1638) in great sentiments of piety, while submitting the work of his life, it is said, to the judgment of the Church.[68]

The *Augustinus* saw the light of day at Louvain in 1640, with a second edition at Paris in 1641.[69] It is a mounmental work and well ordered.[70] After a first tome on the history of the "Pelagian" controversies (Pelagianism and Semipelagianism) Jansen treats the grace of Christ and shows successively what was the condition of innocent man, what is the condition of fallen man today, and what the grace of the Redeemer has brought him.[71] He rejects in passing as absurd and alien to St. Augustine's thought the scholastic thesis on the possibility of pure nature.[72] The most important tome is evidently the third, *De gratia Christi Salvatoris.* There we find set forth the Jansenist notion of victorious

delectation. Between the two poles of love of self and love of God the will of fallen man oscillates, sometimes vanquished by concupiscence (identified with original sin), sometimes subjugated by the all-powerful grace of Christ.[73] Man is not free, at least not with the liberty of choice maintained by Molinists and Thomists. He is free only from all foreign influence but remains subject to an interior determinism, either that of sin or that of grace.[74]

The sinner sins freely but necessarily because he loves his sin.[75] The just man does the works of the Law with a spontaneity caused by the celestial delectation. "Each one's desire draws him on" (*Trahit sua quemque voluptas*). If a man issues from his sin it is because the always efficacious grace of Christ has been given to him and has drawn him in spite of himself from the abyss in which he was. Augustine had described the progressive liberation of the sinner. One could have tried to rethink his theses in the light of scholastic analyses, but Jansen does not want to hear any talk of philosophy and shuts himself up in the strictest Augustinism. He is obsessed with original sin. It is because man is a sinner that he is a slave of sin. It is because he is redeemed that the just man orients himself spontaneously toward the possession of God. The

---

[68] Cf. M. J. Carreyre in DTC, t. X, 1924, col. 319–330, 448–474, 500–522.

[69] J. Carreyre, "Jansenisme," DTC, t. X, col. 329–330.

[70] I cite the edition of Rouen, 1643.

[71] J. Carreyre (DTC, t. X, col. 331–448), analyzes the *Augustinus* at length.

[72] *Augustinus*, t. II, De statu purae naturae (J. Carreyre, DTC, col. 367–376). Cf. P. De Lubac, *Surnaturel* (1946).

[73] *Augustinus*, t. III, lib. IV, 4, c. 6 (col. 175–176). Cf. J. Carreyre, DTC, t. X, col. 400–402.

[74] *Augustinus*, t. III, lib. VI, c. 2, col. 256; c. 3, col. 258.

[75] *Augustinus*, t. II, De statu nat. lapsae, lib. IV, c. 21 (col. 260–264).

problem of conciliation between grace and liberty applies only to fallen man. Jansen wants to leave aside all philosophy and treat problems posed by Scripture and by Tradition as far as this evokes Augustine and his disciples.[76]

But consciously or not, our author narrows his horizon still more. He is unwilling to add anything to Augustine but he takes his distinction between the grace of Adam and our grace, the *adjutorium sine quo non* and the *adjutorium quo,* and makes it one of the foundations of his own theology of grace.[77] And so as with Baius the opposition between the primitive state and the state of fallen and redeemed nature is absolutely radical. In the latter absolute Predestinationism is the law but in the former the human will is granted everything. . . .

This opposition recurs again in the question of predestination. For angels or innocent man predestination must be understood as Lessius wishes, i.e., as a predestination *ex praevisis meritis* and thus perseverance is not a special gift.[78] . . . But if there is question of fallen man, his "Augustinism" is pitiless. He repeats Augustine's expressions but without having Augustine's genial views of time and history. Apparently he is only repeating Augustine's thought but in reality he deforms it, especially when he wishes to express it in the vocabulary of contemporary theology. For Jansen all humanity by its solidarity in the sin of Adam ought logically to be damned. Justly then God lets a part and the most considerable part of the *massa damnata* go to the abyss of hell. And infants dying without baptism are condemned to the pain of sense no less than to the pain of loss.[79] Sinful by nature and deprived of all grace that could help it out of its sin, the immense majority of all infidels is on the road to hell.[80] Since grace is gratuitous it cannot be given to all men. Infidels do not have it. It has not been given to Jews.[81] It is not given to all sinners.[82] What is more it is not even given to all the just, and on this point the debate will soon center.[83]

Theologians distinguish sufficient and efficacious grace but Jansen shuns this distinction. Sufficient grace as the "new theologians" understand it is a "monster." In the economy of fallen and restored nature which is ours, there is no true grace but the grace of Christ and this is always efficacious.[84] If a man cannot observe the law it is because grace is lacking to

---

[76] *Augustinus,* t. III, De gratia Christi, lib. VIII, c. 2 (col. 344); t. II, Prooemium, c. 7 (col. 7); c. 9 (col. 10).

[77] *Augustinus,* t. II, De gratia primi hominis, c. 10 (col. 51–52); t. III, De gratia Christi, lib. II, c. 4 (col. 40–43).

[78] *Augustinus,* t. III, De gratia Christi, lib. IX, c. 10 (col. 384).

[79] *Augustinus,* t. II, De statu nat. lapsae, II, 25 (col. 175).

[80] *Augustinus,* t. II, De statu nat, lapsae, IV (c. 237).

[81] *Augustinus,* t. III, De gratia Christi, III, 11 (col. 126), 9 (col. 122).

[82] *Augustinus,* t. III, De gratia Christi, III, 10 (col. 124).

[83] J. Carreyre, "Jansenisme," DTC, t. X, col. 392–394.

[84] *Augustinus,* t. III, De gratia Christi, II, 25 (col. 83).

him.[85] But he is nonetheless culpable because after original sin he sins freely by a natural spontaneity. This applies first of all to infidels but also to the faithful whom God lets fall back into their sin and to whom He refuses to give the gift of perseverance.[86] Only the predestined are saved, those whom God has predestined before all time. Christ has not died for all men. To hold the contrary would be Semipelagianism.[87] . . .

The Church could not fail to condemn Jansen. In 1641 Rome interdicted the reading of the *Augustinus* and had the work examined. The Jesuits of Belgium, the theologians of the Sorbonne, the historians of dogma, Sirmond and Petau, attacked him. . . . In 1653, 13 years after the appearance of the *Augustinus* (15 years after the death of the author), Innocent X solemnly anathematised the doctrine of Jansen.

Compared with that of Baius this condemnation is of an imperial brevity. Only five propositions are rejected but these reach the essential points of the system. . . . 1. There are some commandments of God which just men cannot observe with the powers they have at their disposal, even if they wish and strive to observe them and they lack the grace that would make this observance possible. 2. In the state of fallen nature internal grace is never resisted. 3. For merit or demerit in the state of fallen nature it is not necessary for a man to have freedom from necessity but only freedom from constraint. 4. The Semipelagians admitted the necessity of internal, preparatory grace for each individual act, even for the beginning of faith; they were heretics in that they wished this grace to be such that the human will could resist it or obey it. 5. It is Semipelagian to say that Jesus Christ died or shed His blood for all men without exception. . . .

Rome intervened several times to condemn on one occasion the lax moral doctrine, on another irresistible grace and the system that supported it.[88] But these new decisions added nothing essential to the condemnation of 1653. . . . With time Jansenists came to admit the existence of a sufficient grace . . . but sufficient only theoretically. And so they could say to God: *a gratia sufficienti libera nos, Domine.*[89]

3. F. Cayré, A.A.,[90] looks through Augustinian eyes at three Augustinian schools of theology, common Thomism, Augustinian congruism and Augustinianism. The efficacy of grace *ab intrinseco* is a doctrinal point they have in common, and by which they are differentiated from Molin-

---

[85] *Augustinus*, t. III, De gratia Christi, III, 13 (col. 134).

[86] *Augustinus*, t. III, De gratia Christi, III, 19 (col. 155).

[87] *Augustinus*, t. III, De gratia Christi, III, 20 (col. 157); III, 21 (col. 162).

[88] See the propositions condemned by Alexander VII (D. 2021–2025), Innocent XI (D. 2101–2165) and Alexander VIII (D. 2290–2331).

[89] Denzinger 2306.

[90] Cf. ch. VI, n. 116. This except is from *op. cit.*, II, pp. 752–763.

ism. Supernatural optimism he considers a more general characteristic common to them all.

The *Augustinian* theological schools of teaching on grace were somewhat numerous. All Catholic theologians invoke St. Augustine and even the Molinists were able to find in his works a number of texts in favour of liberty which they could legitimately use. They differed, however, from the Augustinians in the true sense of the word, by their tendency to modify the more characteristic Augustinian expressions on the efficacy of grace. The Bishop of Hippo explains this efficacy by always considering it from the divine angle, whilst the Molinists deliberately make it conditional on man's consent: no doubt this consent is forestalled and accompanied by grace, but Molinists hold that it is due to this consent that grace ceases to be purely sufficient and becomes efficacious. Efficacy is thus given to grace *ab extrinseco:* such is the specific element of Molinism, the rejection of which characterises the truly Augustinian schools: the latter affirm the efficacy of grace *ab intrinseco* due to the quality proper to this grace.

We shall mention no more than three Augustinian schools. Two of them are associated with St. Thomas: first, *common Thomism* which is currently explained in the majority of commentaries on the Summa from the 16th century; and secondly, a modified form of Thomism which we shall call *Augustinian congruism.* The latter must not be confused with a special interpretation of St. Augustine's texts

on grace made in the 17th and 18th century by a few theologians of the Augustinian Order: hence the name of *Augustinianism* as we propose to call it.

The efficacy of grace *ab intrinseco* is one of the doctrinal points admitted by these diverse Augustinian schools. A more general characteristic common to them all is a *supernatural optimism.*[91] In these schools it is not usual to stress to such an extent as in other theological circles, the goodness, even the relative goodness, of human nature. St. Augustine indeed, may perhaps have fallen into the opposite excess, the better to combat the naturalism of Julian of Eclanum. Yet these schools teach an unshakable faith and confidence in the divine goodness and mercy, and count on the abundance and efficacy of the succour that God vouchsafes for the salvation of men. . . .

All the Augustinians are also agreed in ascribing a twofold activity of grace on the will with regard to the way in which the latter is moved. First there is an objective action which is carried out by means of a presentation of the good, whose attractions determine the will to seek it.[92] Secondly [there is] a subjective action "consist-

[91] Better than all systems, this frank optimism appears calculated to dissipate fears in these matters and leaves the mind entirely free in face of the great and impenetrable mystery of grace.

[92] Also called, less precisely, *moral action,* in contrast to physical action. See H. Guillermin, "La grâce suffisante," *Revue thomiste* (1902), pp. 383–384.

ing in a modification directly produced in the will, changing its intrinsic disposition." To this is also given the name of *physical* influence, since it is carried out by a kind of entitative contact of God's active power with the activity of the human will which it bends in this or that direction.[93]

These two influences do not exclude but rather complement each other. Yet one aspect may be stressed more than the other according to the end in view. St. Augustine threw the objective influence into relief by his frequent use of the word *delectatio:* yet this delectation or delight which has its source in the object, is made complete by means of an interior attraction which contains the subjective movement itself.[94] St. Thomas, adopting a more metaphysical terminology, prefers to stress the idea of movement, and draws attention to the subjective influence (*motio ad exercitium*) of grace, though not forgetting the other (*motio ad specificationem*) which prepares and accompanies it. When his disciples speak of *physical premotion* they interpret his meaning correctly.

The majority of Augustinians also accepted the distinction between sufficient and efficacious grace, which was proposed in the 16th century. They even intensified it, the better to militate against the theory of the efficacy of grace due to consent *ab extrinseco.* They saw in efficacious grace a special assistance which is lacking in the other,

and which is not the effect but the source (intrinsic) of consent. The nature of this internal specific element of grace is variously explained in the Augustinian schools . . . all, however, admit it in principle[95] and in this again they differ from the Molinists. . . .

Common Thomism. That Thomism which is mainly represented by Bañez and followed by the majority of Dominican theologians insists before all on efficacious grace and underlines the physical nature of its activity. Molinism attributes the efficacy of grace to human consent and thus distinguishes sufficient from efficacious grace by a principle that is alien to both. The better to offset this theory common Thomism shows how they differ internally. Sufficient grace disposes the faculty and makes it capable of performing the act; but the act itself, effective activity, is due solely to efficacious grace which sweeps on the will by means of a real physical impulse and rides roughshod over all obstacles. This subjective influence, of course, must not be separated from the objective influence, in the absence of which "there could be no moral activity"; but, were the former lacking "no act would be effectively produced."[96]

---

[93] *Ibid.*, p. 378.

[94] Delectation may be considered either in the object which causes it, or in the faculty in which it is found.

[95] They all admit similarly that the expressions *infallibiliter, inimpedibiliter, insuperabiliter, indeclinabiliter,* as used by early authors do not prejudice liberty.

[96] H. F. Guillermin, *art. cit., Revue thomiste,* 1902, pp. 654–675; 1903, p. 20–31; 1901, p. 505–519; 1902, p. 383–384: "The moral agent, no less than others needs moving to action; but the moral agent,

Efficacious grace implies *sufficient grace,* or at least contains all the latter's virtualities in an eminent manner; but it goes farther still. Sufficient grace finds its necessary complement in efficacious grace, for of itself it can give only the capacity for action and is essentially and entitatively inferior. All the distance that lies between potentiality and actuality separates these two graces. As often as an act is produced and volition elicited, efficacious grace has added its complement to sufficient grace. The definition of the latter is obtained by contrasting it, as it were, with the former, the better to observe its essential nature; care must be taken however not to confuse sufficient grace in general with *purely sufficient grace.*[97] Neither of these produces an act; the difference is that although purely sufficient grace attains its immediate end, the real capacity for action, it is nevertheless deprived of its extrinsic end, for the attainment of which the complementary action of efficacious grace is needed.

In reality, the more the difference between sufficient and efficacious grace is stressed, the more clearly must be marked the *relations that unite them.*[98] Failure to do so would constitute a betrayal of Thomist thought. These relations do not enter into their definition, being no more than properties. Yet these properties are *essential.* These two graces, indeed, must not

be imagined as belonging to two different and dissimilar orders. They both "make part of a single plan of Divine Providence and both tend to the same end, the production of the same salutary free act. Sufficient grace must ordinarily precede efficacious grace in order to prepare and adapt the potentiality to the act which efficacious grace will cause it to produce. In the plan of divine mercy efficacious grace is, as it were, the natural complement of sufficient grace and will always follow it, provided the creature does not deliberately place obstacles in the way of their mutual concatenation."[99]

To sum up, every good and salutary act is due entirely both to God as first cause and entirely to man as second cause, depending absolutely on God. This dependency is the result of a physical and moral determination more physical than moral according to St. Thomas; but moral rather than physical in the language of St. Augustine, whose viewpoint seems to be that of the internal congruism as set out by various Thomists. . . .

Augustinian Congruism.[100] The theological system to which we give this name is fundamentally Thomist, for it maintains in this matter the essential Thomist principle, i.e., the intrinsic efficacy of grace. It has been

---

in addition, requires a previous knowledge of the object and motives of the act it is to accomplish and which is to be accepted by the will."
[97] *Ibid.,* p. 396
[98] *Ibid.,* p. 395 f.

[99] *Ibid.,* p. 396.
[100] Fr. Guillermin, O.P., dean of the faculty of theology at Toulouse has set out with a learning equalled by his moderation in the above mentioned article of the *Revue thomiste,* this attenuated form of Thomism which he has adopted. We give an outline of his explanation, stressing various special points.

elaborated, moreover, by convinced Thomists ever since the time of the controversies on grace, and its first official representative, Gonzalez de Albelda[101] who died in 1622, judged it to be more in conformity with the ideas of the early theologians than that of the disciples of Bañez himself, for he calls these *juniores thomistae.* This teaching, moreover, is "more than any other in perfect harmony with the language and thought of the Angelic Doctor."[102] It also corresponds excellently to those passages in which St. Augustine speaks of the adaptation of grace to the soul: *"Sic eum vocat, quomodo scit ei congruere, ut vocantem non respuat."*[103]

This system differs first from that which precedes as regards the question of *sufficient grace,* and in that undoubtedly lies its chief advantage. It "does not only bring to the free-will a complement which, in the purely potential order, makes it proportionate to the salutary act, but brings with it in addition a real impulse, by means of which the will is capable of really passing from potentiality to actuality and proceeding effectively to its operation." It is "a true physical premotion possessing everything, from the point of view of God, which enables the faculty to be the integral active prin-

ciple of the salutary act." It is really sufficient, for although it is not really and actually efficacious, it is so virtually, on account of its "intrinsic quality" to such an extent that if, concomitantly with it alone, the good acts is not produced, the whole fault lies with free will which culpably and freely places an obstacle in the way of the effective activity of grace."[104]

Of the three functions of grace mentioned above, sufficient grace here fulfils two: efficacious grace in addition, brings to pass the third condition: the suppression of voluntary resistance. It obtains this effect by its intrinsic quality, but not by a fresh movement in the true sense of the word. . . .

This conception possesses great advantages. On the one hand it shows that all grace, even sufficient grace is *movement* in the true sense of the word.[105] On the other hand it throws into relief, even more successfully than Molinism, the *responsibility* of the will in opposition to grace. . . . We may add that the congruist system furnishes a better explanation of the complex elements found in the production of the good act. The need of a determining movement even as regards individual good, of course remains, as it does in any grace; but in this theory less stress is given to this property of movement than to its adaptation to the actual dispositions peculiar to

---

[101] *Commentaria in Sum. theol.,* I, q. 19, Disp. 58; Vol. II, p. 80 f. See Guillermin, *art. cit.,* pp. 658–660. The other protagonists of internal congruism mentioned by Guillermin are: Gonzalez de Leon, J. Nicolai, and A. Massoulie.

[102] H. Guillermin, *art. cit.,* 1902, pp. 665–669.

[103] St. Augustine, *Ad Simplicianum,* III, q. 11, 13.

[104] H. Guillermin, *art. cit.,* p. 655.

[105] "The blessed Doctor invariably speaks of actual grace as a transitory movement, as an impulse to act, tending of itself to put the operative faculty into motion" — H. Guillermin, *art. cit.,* pp. 665–666.

each soul, and the victories and triumphant delight that accompanies it.[106] . . .

As may be seen, this system is truly Thomist and provides a felicitous complement to common Thomism. Both combine in revealing in a greater measure the abundance of St. Thomas and St. Augustine. The latter's viewpoint appears to us to be more in line with the congruist system, which, however, must never be confused with the "Augustinianism" of Noris and Berti.

Augustinianism.[107] This name is given particularly to a doctrine of grace evolved in the 17th century by Cardinal Noris (1631–1704) and maintained later by the theologian Laurent Berti (1696–1766). Both were Augustinians. Though accused of Jansenism and delated to Rome, they were never condemned; on the contrary. The first was created a cardinal by Clement X (1695) while the second obtained from Benedict XIV the famous brief of July 13th, 1748, which placed the teaching of his system on the same footing as that of the Thomists and the Molinists. In reality, though it appears so akin to Jansenism, it differs essentially by its sincere affirmation of free-will. It must also be classed apart from the foregoing

---

[106] In congruism, grace triumphs over an obstacle that derives from free will itself. The expression has quite a different meaning in Jansenism which suppresses free will. Cf. Guillermin, *art. cit.,* 1903, pp. 21–23.

[107] Though this system evolved at a later date, we discuss it here in order to distinguish it from the foregoing. See E. Portalié, "Augustinianisme," in DTC, col. 2485–2492.

system, though certain elements are similar, such for instance as concern the efficacy of grace, though, even as regards this, they cannot be regarded as identical.

According to Noris, grace acts on the soul by means of *delectation*. Man in his present state is determined to act, either by an evil delectation (concupiscence) or a good and spiritual delectation (charity). The latter is a sufficient grace when it gives the power of overcoming concupiscence; it is an efficacious grace when in fact it is victorious, not by necessity but infallibly and irresistibly. Physical determination is thus replaced by a kind of moral determination, but in such a way as appearing to suppress all active self-determination of the soul, which lies at the mercy of one or other of these determinations.

Furthermore this teaching is bound up with other traits in which the true feebleness of the system is found. 1. Grace and the other privileges of our first parents were due to them not in justice but *ex decentia creatoris,* since God must act by Goodness and Wisdom. 2. Fallen man has thus not only lost the gratuitous gifts, but has suffered in his very nature. 3. Hence the absolute necessity of a grace which overcomes without physical movement by means of a victorious delectation far superior to that required in Adam. 4. God wills the salvation of all men yet does not grant truly sufficient graces to all. 5. Lastly, the law of charity is more rigorous and more general than in other theological schools.

4. T. P. Neill and R. H. Schmandt[108] give a brief sketch of the origin and spread of Jansenism, its doctrine, its relation to Baianism and some of the propositions of Baius that were condemned by Pope St. Pius V.

Jansenism. The Gallican crisis interrupted a pernicious movement in the French Church known as Jansenism. This movement was an insidious and complicated affair that involved some of the high-placed persons in France, involved the Church in a bitter factional quarrel, and injected a Protestant element into Catholic circles in France. . . . Its proponents were, to use the phrase applied to the nuns of Port Royal, angelic in appearance but moved with the pride of Lucifer. Jansenists were ultra-Catholics, men and women holier than the Church. They were Protestant reformers who stayed in the Church because in France there was nowhere else to go.

Jansenism was based on a certain doctrine of justification that proposed rigorous views of human nature and the role of grace in man's salvation. It centered in practice around conditions for any frequency of reception of the sacraments. Jansenists were austere in their morality, and they considered anyone opposed to them as corrupted enemies of God. Their aim was to purify the Church of all accretions since the time of the primitive Fathers. They therefore rejected Scholastic philosophy and theology in favor of Scripture itself and the commentaries of the early Fathers. Jansenistic

teaching was condemned many times by the Holy See, but the Jansenists always managed to evade papal condemnation by various subterfuges and, although opposed by both the pope and the French king, they continued to exist in France down till the Revolution of 1789. . . .

Jansenism can be said to have had its origins in the sixteenth century. The Council of Trent had stated that good works meritorious for salvation are the result of both grace and the free will of man, but it did not define the precise role of each factor. Within Catholic circles two general schools of thought developed on this subject. The Jesuits stressed the role of man's free will; the Dominicans stressed the role of supernatural grace. In 1606 Pope Paul V ended the discussion by allowing each side to keep its opinions and forbidding them to accuse the other of heresy.

Meanwhile, a professor of Scripture at the University of Louvain, Michael Baius, had turned to St. Augustine to find what he thought was the true theory of grace and justification. Overstressing one aspect of St. Augustine's thought and neglecting other aspects of it entirely, Baius asserted that the preternatural and supernatural gifts with which Adam was endowed at creation were natural to him and therefore that original sin was more than a

---

[108] Cf. ch. IX, n. 1. The excerpt is from *op. cit.*, pp. 435–437, 444.

deprivation, as taught by the Church — it was a disorderly act which corrupts human nature and renders it incapable of doing good. In other words, Baius took an unduly optimistic view of man before the fall and an unduly pessimistic view of man after the fall. Free will, for Baius, is nothing but concupiscence. In his fallen state man can do nothing but sin. These teachings were condemned by Rome in 1567 and again in 1679, and Baius accepted the decisions. His teachings lingered on in the Low Countries, however, as the answer to the puzzle of grace and free will, and fifty years after his death they were given classic expression in a book called *Augustinus*.

Augustinus was the posthumously published work of Cornelius Jansen, former professor at the University of Louvain and later bishop of Ypres. Jansen had worked closely for a number of years with Jean Duvergier de Hauranne, abbot of St. Cyran, and the organizer of Jansenism in France. The two of them planned a thorough "reform" of the Church, especially in France. Jansen was to furnish the doctrine; St. Cyran was to build an organization for putting the program into effect. This he did through the influential Arnaulds. This large and wealthy family was connected with some of the most important people in France — and it was hostile to Jesuits. One of the daughters, Mother Angelique, was abbess of Port Royal Convent. It was here that St. Cyran established the headquarters of the movement.

As the name of Jansen's book suggests, the new doctrine was supposed to be obtained from the teaching of the great Bishop of Hippo. It was a systematic restatement of Baius' teaching on grace and free will. The Jansenists maintained that Christ did not die for all mankind but only for a few He has predestined for salvation. These cannot resist grace, any more than the reprobate can save themselves. Such a doctrine naturally killed prayer to the saints or to the Blessed Virgin for intercession with God. It also killed the practice of frequent Confession and Communion which the Council of Trent encouraged and which the Jesuits preached everywhere. Jansenists held that the sacrament of Penance is valid only with perfect contrition. They taught that absolution must be withheld until the penance is performed, and they tried to revive the old forms of penance in terms of days, weeks, and years. Holy Communion should be received, they believed, only a few times in a lifetime. No one is worthy to receive Christ. Respectful abstention from Communion honors Christ more than frequent reception. St. Cyran wrote to a nun who was saddened by not receiving that sacrament during her illness: "You will soon understand that you do more for yourself by not going to Holy Communion than by going."

Cardinal Richelieu ordered an investigation into the teachings and practices of the Port Royal group in 1638. As a result of these investigations, Abbot St. Cyran was imprisoned at Vincennes, where he remained until Richelieu's death late in 1642. Meanwhile, *Augustinus* had been published. It was actively opposed by Jesuits, Sulpicians, and Vincentians, and it was formally condemned by the Holy See in June 19, 1643. Meanwhile, the theological faculty of the Sorbonne and the French bishops took official French action against Jansenism. The Sorbonne summed up the fundamental errors of Jansenism in five propositions. Eighty-eight French bishops then signed a petition requesting the Holy See to examine these propositions and pass judgment on them. After lengthy study by a commission of cardinals, Innocent I condemned these propositions in 1653.

The Jansenists accepted the papal condemnation, but they insisted the five propositions could not be found in Jansen's writing. In other words, they agreed that the propositions as condemned by the Holy See, were heretical, but in the *Augustinus* these statements had a different meaning which was not condemned. To condemn Jansen's writing, they held, was to condemn St. Augustine as a heretic. The French clergy therefore assembled to find a formula to pin the Jansenists down to their heresy. They declared that the five propositions were truly to be found in Jansen in the sense in which they had been condemned by the pope. Then they drew up a declaration which the king enjoined upon all the clergy: "I condemn both in thought and by word of mouth the doctrine of the five propositions of Cornelius Jansen contained in his book *Augustinus,* which the pope and bishops have condemned; this doc-

trine is not that of St. Augustine, whose true meaning Jansen has distorted." . . .

Some propositions of Baius condemned by Pope St. Pius V:

The elevation of human nature and its exaltation to participation in the divine nature were due to the integrity of its primitive state and hence must be called natural and not supernatural.

The integrity of the first creation was not an elevation gratuitously bestowed upon human nature, but its own natural condition.

The immortality of the first man was not a gift of grace, but his natural condition.

All the acts of infidels are sins, and the virtues of philosophers are vices.

Without the help of God our free will can do nothing else but sin.

It is a Pelagian error to say that free will can make us avoid sin.

Everything the sinner does is sin.

Whoever acknowledges the existence of any natural good, i.e., a good founded on the forces of nature alone, is a follower of Pelagius.

Whatever is done voluntarily, even though it be done necessarily, is done freely.

In all his actions the sinner is obedient to concupiscence, which rules him.

No sin is venial by its nature, but every sin is deserving of eternal punishment.

The bad desires to which reason does not consent, and which man experiences despite his efforts, are forbidden by the Commandment: Thou shalt not covet.

Concupiscence or the law of the members, and its bad desires, which men experience in spite of themselves, are a real disobedience of the law.

In those who have fallen into mortal sin after the reception of the Sacrament of Baptism, concupiscence regains the ascendency, and is a sin just like all other bad habits.

XII

GRACE IN PROTESTANT THEOLOGY IN
THE NINETEENTH AND TWENTIETH CENTURIES

1. H. D. Gray[1] sees the eighteenth-century Rationalist movement as a pathway of promise for the Christian doctrine of grace by its complete dissociation of grace and infused supernatural power. The Reformation in the theology of grace might be said to have begun with Schleiermacher. German theologians divided into three schools, liberal, orthodox, mediating. In contemporary thought Kierkegaard has been very influential.

A pathway of promise. The eighteenth-century Rationalist movement, stressing reliance upon reason, did not appear to be the entrance to a pathway

---

[1] Henry David Gray, Ph.D., presents this historical sketch in his book, *The Christian Doctrine of Grace* (London: Independent Press Ltd., 1949). This excerpt is from pp. 91–102; 117–118.

of promise for the Christian doctrine of grace. Yet such it proved to be.

The beginnings were *not* promising. To the Rationalists grace was no more than man's natural endowments, the scriptures were books of morality and religious history, the miracles were myths, and Jesus was a great teacher whose character and work were shrouded in legend. The Rationalist interpretation of grace is Pelagian, affirming, as in Wolff and Lessing, that man can win his way to immortality, which is regarded as the true end of real religion. However many its deficiencies it had the great virtue of completely dissociating grace and infused supernatural power, and thereby it opened the pathway of promise.

Friedrich Schleiermacher.[2] First to place his feet firmly on the new pathway was Friedrich Schleiermacher at the cross-roads of the eighteenth and nineteenth centuries. He was a scholar, preacher, statesman, and Berliners flocked to hear his stirring *Speeches on Religion*. Originality and insight made his book, *The Christian Faith*, the initiator of a new era in theology. It might even be said that the Reformation in the theology of grace began with Schleiermacher.

In *The Christian Faith* Schleiermacher defined religion as the consciousness of being absolutely dependent on God, and Christianity as the religion in which everything is related to the redemption from sin ac-

complished in Jesus Christ. Men, he said, cannot achieve God-consciousness without help, and God-consciousness is the goal of a perfect man. In Christianity that help comes through faith in Jesus as Redeemer from a wrong way of life. Men were originally perfect, but that original perfection was deranged and confused by sin which has its source partly in ourselves and partly outside ourselves. The part outside ourselves is derived from original sin which, as a corporate act, has since then really become the sin of every man. In all men the original disposition to sin produces actual sin. Sin, alienation from God, always originates in man, and cannot be attributed to God. Opposed to sin is grace. Whatever fellowship man has with God rests on God's grace or creative influence in Christ.

The Church is the medium of grace, not as a Rome-centred organization, but as the fellowship of believers, fostering God's influence by contagion. Therefore, such fellowship is the sphere in which the Holy Spirit works. Christ gives the Church its grace-conveying character by His spiritual presence. He brings men into its fellowship, but only when there is living receptivity on the part of men. To live in fellowship with Christ is to be in a state of grace. If we continue in this state impulses flow from Him to us until we find that he has become the source of our activity. Consciousness of sin brings us into the sphere of Christ's influence, in which our redemption is wrought by Him in living relationship to us. He is the active

---

[2] F. Schleiermacher, *The Christian Faith* (English translation) is the source of all quotations.

giver; we are the passive receivers.

In Christian self-consciousness Schleiermacher distinguished two aspects of the life of grace, namely regeneration and sanctification.

In the former, conversion is held to be a changed form of life re-oriented around God by the acts of repentance and faith. This is likely to result from a slowly increasing God-consciousness rather than from sudden change by sacramental purification. Once received into fellowship with Christ, man's passiveness changes into spontaneous activity.

In *The Christian Faith* justification or acceptance by God concerns man's changed relation to God, whereby unworthy men are forgiven for their sins, released from their consciousness of guilt, and accepted as His true children. It dawns upon man with his act of faith. Civil righteousness, acceptance by men, is possible for the unregenerate, but only those in fellowship with Christ can produce good works which give God pleasure because they are in harmony with Him. Neither civil righteousness nor Christian good works merit reward in the sense of deserving credit.

The idea that the Holy Spirit is the common spirit of the Church is one of the most provocative thoughts of Schleiermacher. The Holy Spirit is the divine spark within the Church which continues from generation to generation. It is communicated to men through the Scriptures, the Word (God speaking to us through others or inwardly), Baptism, the Lord's Supper, the Power of the Keys (God's discipline of us in the Christian fellowship) and prayer, but none of these have magical potency which can be infused into men regardless of their attitude. The influence of God operates through the fellowship of spirit-inspired men.

As a result of his strong emphasis on dependence on God, Schleiermacher retained the idea of election to salvation, saying that God's power to foresee our faith was the real basis for it. Of the fate of those outside the state of grace he said, "They cannot so affect us as to give us reasonable cause to make any statement about them in this connexion," and therefore he set forth no doctrine of election to damnation.

The Christian Faith opened a new day in the theology of grace. Schleiermacher often rings true to the personal, ethical idea of God's dealing with men as free moral personalities. His writings mark a real break with the infused power idea of grace, the organizational concept of the Church, and all non-personal, merely intellectual, dogmas. . . .

The teaching of the German schools. While Coleridge and Campbell moved forward in Britain, German theologians, divided into Liberal, Orthodox and Mediating Schools, all claimed some degree of relationship to Schleiermacher, and all contributed something to systematic theological thinking. The Liberals, of whom Baur, Strauss, Biedermann, Pfleiderer and Lipsius are representative, held, in general, that God is not personal, that the world, including all evil, is merely an emanation of God, and that sin is simply a necessary step of making mistakes and overcoming them in human experience. On this purely naturalistic basis Christianity loses its distinctive emphasis on grace. The Orthodox School, of which Hengstenberg, Hofmann and Frank were members, was strictly Lutheran and adhered to the creeds. To these Confessionals the experience of conversion and re-birth was central and personal; and grace must be conveyed by the channels of Word, Church and Sacrament. They recognize that the assurance of salvation is not given once-and-for-all in conversion or turning one's life in a God-ward direction, but rather, is attained gradually by the gracious and dynamic working of God with men after they had turned to Him, but neither of these Schools contributed greatly to the emergence of the modern evangelical conception of grace.

The Mediating School, largely influenced by Schleiermacher, may be represented by Dorner,[3] as perhaps its most significant contributor to the development of the conception of grace. His volumes on systematic theology present as detailed a study of grace as is found in most Roman Catholic theologies. Dorner held that sin, as opposition to God and His holy precepts, embraced both individual and race. It is an inherited consequence of the original fall. Guilt, however, is not imputed to the individual until he has become conscious of what he

[3] I. A. Dorner, *System of Christian Doctrine*, 4 vols., is the source of all quotations in this section.

is doing, and is able to resist evil. By grace or the power of God's Spirit men are saved. This is a gift of God inspiring even our disposition to faith in Him. God's invitation to fellowship is universal, just as is the need and capacity for redemption, but there is no election which gives absolute assurance of eternal salvation. Such assurance would exclude freedom of acceptance or rejection and replace it by an almighty volition which would make mere puppets of men. He thought that to those who do not come face to face with the gospel in this life that opportunity will be presented hereafter.

By repentance man becomes acceptable before God and prepared for new life. This new life comes about through faith, both active and receptive, wherein man appropriates the clean, unguilty position provided through God's forgiveness, mercy and love. This is justification. Sanctification relates to the new life of fellowship with Christ in the Church, in which man's whole personality grows in the relation of sonship to God and service to others. Such conversion and renewal is the work of the Holy Spirit. This effect Dorner also ascribes to the influence of the Word of God, the Holy Spirit being the agent working through that Word, spoken or written, but especially through Holy Scripture, which has faith as its object. The sacraments are sacred actions, personal acts of Christ to persons, in which, under outward signs, invisible grace is dispensed. "The benefit of this offered grace is personally appropriated by faith." Grace in all its aspects is entirely the free gift of God's Spirit in Christ, and its end is holiness begun here, and completed hereafter.

The Mediating School consolidated the gains of Schleiermacher, retained much that is valuable in the credal position, accepted and used the results of liberal thinking, and combined the whole in a system which, if not invariably consistent, was always suggestive. Dorner's attempt to present man's freedom and God's sovereignty as different aspects of one personally unified whole is a significant stride forward.

Ritschl. Ritschl, a younger contemporary of Dorner, published in 1870–1874 a work which left its mark deeply upon theological thought throughout the world. In this great treatise on *Justification and Reconciliation* grace is ever regarded as fundamental.

Ritschl thought of grace chiefly as the disposition of God as Father to cleanse and reconcile sinners to Himself by love. Christ is the supreme gift of grace, the appeal of the Father's love to men; for Christ incarnates the very heart of God. The Kingdom of God, the state wherein reconcilation is completed is a state of grace, which is dependent for its character and continuance upon God's loving will toward men; but men must act as well as God, and the influence of the Holy Spirit is always free and personal. Reconciliation is not operative outside the Christian Church because only in the Christian community is God's Spirit received, yet the conviction of faith, though mediated by the community, has as its end "the individual's reconciliation and Divine sonship." Blessedness, here and hereafter, is freedom of fellowship with God; and this is accomplished by the personal influence of God on free persons.

The disciples of Ritschl have adhered to the conception of grace as a relation of persons. Harnack voiced the general opinion of the group when he characterized and condemned the Scholastic view of grace as "the desire to have, not God, but divine forces that can become human virtues."[4] The Schoolmen failed to conceive grace aright, because "there was no recognition of *personality,* neither of the personality of God, nor of man as a *person.*" To Ritschl and his followers, grace is a fellowship of persons; specifically it is the communion of man with God as a child in the Father's house.

The Comparative Religion School, with Troeltsch as its leading exponent, was a retreat from the significant advances of Ritschl and his followers. Pursuing one line of Schleiermacher's thought, Troeltsch attempted to interpret Christianity in terms of universal religious consciousness found in all religions. This, as our first chapter maintained, cannot do justice to the Christian conception of grace.

Contemporary thought. The great Danish thinker Kierkegaard belongs to the twentieth century even more than to the nineteenth century in which he lived. His influence is prob-

---

[4] A. Harnack, *History of Dogma,* Vol. VI, p. 278.

ably much greater now than it was in the days of his flesh. Kierkegaard[5] had no patience with churchly pomp and splendour. Grace was God in action, speaking pointedly to the soul of the sinner wherever he is, and ever seeking to win that soul for His own. God is the ever seeking lover of men, inexorable in justice, boundless in mercy, glorious in self-givingness. What God wants is not Christ-admirers but Christ-followers. To be a Christian is to apply God's way of grace seen in Christ to each and every facet of life. It is to let Christ live in you, so that your life becomes a channel for His life in the world.

Karl Barth, Emil Brunner, and Karl Heim, present-day German-speaking theologians, all have learned from the teaching of Kierkegaard. But they are by no means imitators. The strong Augustinianism of Barth is countered by the ethical awareness of Heim. Brunner's place is betwixt the two, as he takes his stand on the fact that Christ is the mediator between God and man. All these are Lutheran biblical theologians rather than followers of Augustine or Kierkegaard. Grace means that men are made right in the sight of God once they have been reconciled to Him in Christ. Grace means that men are enabled to live as Christ-followers, by the power of Christ living in them.

In England three noteworthy attempts to formulate the Christian doctrine of grace have appeared in the twentieth century. Each has developed along the lines indicated by Schleiermacher and more especially by Ritschl. The thesis of John Oman's masterly work on *Grace* and *Personality* is "absolute moral independence and absolute religious dependence are not opposites but necessarily one and indivisible,"[6] each being essential to the full experience of grace as a personal relation of God and man. N. P. Williams contends that grace as the personally operative healing power of God is the same as the Third Person of the Holy Trinity, the Holy Spirit.

The World Conference on Faith and Order held at Lausanne in 1927 gave rise, through the work of a distinguished international committee of theologians, to a symposium on *The Doctrine of Grace*. The conclusions therein set forth recognize the personal nature of God's grace and stress the personal manner of man's acceptance by faith of that free out-going love.

We are faced once more with the paradox of Paul; in the Barthian stress on the sovereignty of God, and at the same time the prominence of men's freedom in modern English interpretations of grace. This is the paradox with which our New Testament closes. The conflict is more apparent than actual. The task of the twentieth century is not to push God's sovereignty to one side and man's freedom to the other, but rather, recognizing the intrinsic difficulties of the problem, to bring both together in our thinking as actually as they are wedded in Christian experience. . . .

---

[5] See especially *Training in Christianity* and *For Self-Examination* and *Judge for Yourselves*.

[6] *Grace and Personality*, p. 26.

Summary. The Christian doctrine of grace centres in our conception of the nature of God as He is revealed to us in Jesus Christ, and in Christian thought and experience. Grace is God's fatherliness, manifested: — 1. In His spontaneous, free, undeserved love to sinners as His wayward children. 2. In His gift of forgiveness and blessedness by His personal revelation in Jesus Christ, so intrinsically attractive as to enlist our response in penitence and faith, and, 3. In His nurture of our personalities in His Kingdom, so immediately and constantly present in the personal fellowship of that realm of love, that His fatherliness is reflected in us.

Moreover, the first manifestation may fairly be described as in the Father Himself, the second as in the Son, and the third as in the Holy Spirit. Although thus manifested in three distinguishing ways grace is always one and the same for the "God and Father of Our Lord Jesus Christ" is the Giver of the gift and the Sustainer of the state. Nothing whatever is gained by glossing over the corruption of the doctrines of grace as crystallized in Roman Catholic dogma, and as is done by certain recent Anglican writers. Progress in Christian understanding will be promoted much more surely by forthright facing of the basic differences, and by a determined effort to recapture the viewpoint of the New Testament. . . .

2. **Robert McAfee Brown[7] sees Protestantism as the religion of grace. And grace is the grace of our Lord Jesus Christ. It is not a "thing," an object, an impersonal something or other. It is the way God gives us Himself. Grace is mercy or forgiveness and also power. It is the gift of new life. Our response to grace is faith — an utter trust in God and reliance on His steadfast love.**

The centrality of grace. Where do we start, if we wish to describe the "central Protestant affirmations"? We start with God. We start with a description of what God has done and is doing.

Where do we start, if we wish to describe "what God has done and is doing"? We start with Jesus Christ.

When we start with him we find that God is "a gracious God" and that Protestantism is the religion of grace.

The meaning of grace. "Grace" is therefore the most important word in the Protestant vocabulary. It is also the most abused. We have difficulty in answering why the rallying cry of the Reformers should have been *salvatio sola gratia* ("salvation by grace alone").

[7] Robert McAfee Brown was born in 1920. He was ordained a minister in the Presbyterian Church. From 1953–1962 he was on the faculty of Union Theological Seminary in New York. In 1962 he became professor of religion at Stanford. This excerpt is abridged from his book, *The Spirit of Protestantism* (New York: Oxford University Press, 1961), pp. 53–61. Also available in a Galaxy paperback.

And yet the destiny of Protestantism is bound up with that affirmation. Grace cannot really be described, it can only be experienced. All we can do is try to describe what is experienced.[8]

We miss the point if we talk in abstract terms. For grace, in Christian terms, is not the least bit abstract: it is very specific. It is the grace of our Lord Jesus Christ. We cannot talk about grace apart from him. The prologue to the Fourth Gospel reminds us that "the law was given through Moses, but grace and truth came through Jesus Christ" (Jn 1:17). Paul stresses this even more than the author of the Fourth Gospel, and it is not surprising that the Reformers leaned heavily upon him. For Paul, the heart of the gospel is "the grace of God which was given you in Christ Jesus" (1 Cor 1:4). . . . Grace is defined by who Jesus Christ is, or better, by what Jesus Christ does. He is the one who transforms grace from an idea into a reality. . . .

We cannot talk very long about the grace of God without talking about the love of God. And here again we have a problem, for love, in ordinary English, can mean a variety of things. . . . To learn about God's love we have to turn to the New Testament again and see that love in action. The New Testament words love (*agapē*) and grace (*charis*) are very close to one another in meaning. It would not be fair to make them identical. But it is fair to say that if God's love (*agapē*) is his love toward the loveless, love toward those who really do not deserve his love, then this is very close to what we mean by "the grace" (*charis*) of our Lord Jesus Christ. . . .

"The grace of our Lord Jesus Christ" is not a "thing," an object, an impersonal something or other. It can only be described in personal terms. Grace is not something God himself gives us, it is the way God gives us himself. Grace is *God's personal relationship to us*. But his relationship to us is unlike most of the human relationships we experience, and we must distinguish carefully between them. . . .

The relationship based on grace is unlike the relationship based on merit or need or appeal. God does not enter into personal relationship with his children because they are "good." They are not. Nor does he do so because he "needs" them. He does not. He is not gracious to them because they are "appealing." They are not. Quite the contrary. The Bible is emphatic in asserting that God's relationship to man is not based on the fact that man offers something to God, but on the fact that God offers everything to man. . . . "God does not love Israel because Israel is a great or a good nation. Israel, as a matter of fact, is an insignificant nation and by all nor-

---

[8] The most helpful over-all work on the doctrine of grace is Whitley, ed., *The Doctrine of Grace*, S.C.M. Press, a symposium of historical and systematic studies. On the biblical materials see Snaith, *The Distinctive Ideas of the Old Testament*, Westminster, and Moffat, *Grace in the New Testament*, Hodder & Stoughton. See also Torrance, *The Doctrine of Grace in the Apostolic Fathers*, Oliver and Boyd, and Watson, *The Concept of Grace*, Epworth.

mally accepted standards of judgment, a bad nation" And yet God loves Israel . . . simply because he loves Israel. That is the kind of God he is. . . .

We can discover two further things about "the grace of our Lord Jesus Christ" but they must always be mentioned together.

First of all, we learn that grace is *mercy* or *forgiveness*. . . . We have wilfully "hurt" God, and thus destroyed our relationship with him. We have spurned him, sinned against his children, answered his love by our hate. And what can overcome love answered by hate? Grace, and grace alone: grace as mercy, grace as forgiveness, grace that bears the hurt in suffering love, grace, in short, made real upon a cross.

Because it is mercy and forgiveness, grace is also *power*. It is the gift of new life. The one who has been forgiven lives in a new situation . . . "I am crucified with Christ, nevertheless I live, yet not I, but Christ liveth in me" (Gal 2:20). . . . As I die to self, I am raised up to a new life by the power of God. I *live, yet not I*, but *Christ liveth in me*: this new life is not something I have achieved. It is Christ himself who is at work within me. . . .

"All the great Reformation watchwords," Albert Outler writes, "*sola Scriptura, sola fide, sola gratia* — have one essential meaning: *solus Christus*. This is the source and center of Christian faith — and it is only when this faith is hardened into disparate doctrinal systems, and the systems substi-tuted for living faith, that community disintegrates."[9]. . .

The meaning of faith. Our response to grace is faith. We speak of faith more frequently than we speak of grace. But faith means many things on different lips, and we must disentangle some of these if we are to capture the distinctively Protestant flavor of the word. . . .

A Christian may assent to the notion that all the words of the Bible are true; he may assent to the Westminster Confession of Faith as containing the system of doctrine taught in Holy Scripture; he may assent to whatever the Roman Catholic church pronounces to be irreformable dogma without believing which he cannot be saved. In each case faith is *assent* to statements. This seems to have been the dominant understanding of faith among the late medieval schoolmen, and a rejection of it was one of the reasons for the Reformation.

In contrast to this, Luther and the other Reformers understood faith primarily as *trust*. To have faith in something is to commit oneself to it confidently. . . . When we talk about faith in God in this framework we mean primarily not that we assent to certain statements about him, but that we have utter trust in him and rely upon his "steadfast love."

This does not mean, of course, that there is no "assent" or that there is nothing to be "believed." A faith without content (a "faith in faith") would

---

[9] Outler, *The Christian Tradition and the Unity We Seek*, Oxford Univ. Press, pp. 128–129.

be the most dangerous thing of all, for we could change the object of belief at a moment's whim. But this does mean that the depths of faith have not been plumbed until assent is encompassed by trust. Luther makes the contrast with characteristic gusto:

"There are two kinds of believing: first a believing about God which means that I believe that what is said of God is true. This faith is rather a form of knowledge than a faith. . . . Men possessing it can say, repeating what others have said: I believe that there is a God. I believe that Christ was born, died, rose again for me. But what the real faith is, and how powerful

a thing it is, of this they know nothing. . . .

"There is secondly, a believing in God which means that I put my trust in Him, give myself up to thinking that I can have dealings with Him, and believe without any doubt that He will be and do to me according to the things said of Him. Such faith which throws itself upon God, whether in life or in death, alone makes a Christian man."[10]

As Luther said elsewhere, "Faith is a lively, reckless confidence in the grace of God." We can be content to leave it at that. . . .

3. L. Hodgson[11] aims to show that beneath their words both Catholicism and Protestantism are at one in the central doctrine of Christian theology, justification by faith. How then did they come into conflict? By emphasizing different elements in their common intellectual problem of reconciling the ethical and personal character of the Christian religion with the truth of man's utter dependence on God's free gift of salvation.

It is possible to distinguish three main uses of the phrase "the Grace of God" in Christian theology: (a) It is sometimes used in a very wide sense to cover all God's activity towards, upon or in His universe, whether in creating, maintaining, redeeming or perfecting, whether as transcendent or immanent, whether through "laws of nature" or in personal relationships. . . . (b) It is sometimes used in a narrower sense to cover only that activity of God which is

exercised in personal relations towards those of His creatures whom He has endowed in some measure with per-

---

[10] Cited in Lindsay, *History of the Reformation*, Scribners, Vol. 1, pp. 429–445. The full context can be found in the Erlangen edition of *Luther's Works*, xxii, 15, and xv, 540.

[11] The Rev. Leonard Hodgson, M.A., Hon. D.D., D.C.L., Canon of Winchester, and regius professor of divinity in the University of Oxford. This excerpt is from his book, *The Grace of God in Faith and Philosophy* (London: Longmans, Green and Co., 1936), pp. 23–34; 166–176.

sonality and freedom. . . . (c) It is used in a still narrower sense to denote one specific activity of God, that which is exercised in the forgiveness of sinners through Jesus Christ. . . .

We cannot say: "One school of theologians uses the word 'grace' to mean the single divine activity of forgiveness, while another uses it to cover other divine activities as well.". . . We cannot say this . . . because those who object to the extension of the use of the word grace to mean anything other than the divine activity of the forgiveness of sins in Jesus Christ, do so on the ground that this leads to false teaching about things. In their view it involves (i) a "materialisation" of the conception of grace, and (ii) a Pelagian view of the activity of man. Let us, therefore, dismiss for the present the question of language, and consider the Lutheran insistence on the centrality of the doctrine of justification and the importance of safeguarding it against any corruption which would introduce either materialisation or Pelagianism.

At this point there seems to be a confusion in Lutheran theology which it will be worth while to examine. It seems to be assumed that there is a logical connection between the materialisation and the Pelagianism, that the materialisation of God's grace implies a Pelagian denial of the essential character of grace, that it is God's free gift. . . . Let us for a moment forget the Lutheran theology and consider this medieval Catholicism against which Lutheranism was in revolt. What I wish to urge is that in so far

as it is both materialist and Pelagian, this is not because these are different facets of one error. On the contrary, the Catholic doctrine of *ex opere operato* is intended to safeguard the initiative of God and thus to combat Pelagianism, and the presence of each is due to an attempt to escape from the other. If the medieval Church had committed itself wholly *either* to an *ex opere operato* sacramentalism *or* to a Pelagian conception of man, it would indeed have lost hold on the truth. Instead of that, it strove to hold fast the truth by holding the two opposed tendencies in balance, in the hope that each would cancel out the other's error. . . .

Revolting against the Pelagian "materialisation" by which Catholicism was perverted in popular practice, the Reformation attempted to recall Christians to the two truths: (1) that true religion is a matter of personal communion between God and man, and (2) that man's salvation is God's free gift, which cannot be earned but only received. . . . It was on this latter truth that the reformers began constructively to rebuild, when they had wielded the axe of their destructive criticism against prevalent popular perversions of Christianity. Pelagianism was the enemy, and the foundation stone of the new building was the doctrine of Justification as God's forgiveness given to sinners, given freely to undeserving sinners who could not do anything to earn it, or claim it as a reward for merit. But the character of true religion as a personal, ethical relationship between man and God was safeguarded by regarding as the condition of reception on the human side the presence of faith, that faith which expresses itself in acknowledged dependence on Christ's saving work, and involves renunciation of and repentance for sin.

But here the old difficulty turned up again, the difficulty which had driven Catholicism into the doctrine of *ex opere operato*. If man had to provide faith in order to receive the saving grace, it could no longer be said that man could make no contribution towards his own salvation. He had to make the contribution of faith. Here again the cloven foot of Pelagianism was making its appearance. How was this dealt with? It was met by the doctrine that the faith which receives the saving grace is itself a free gift of God, just as much as the grace which it receives. And those who pressed this doctrine to its logical conclusion were led to formulate a doctrine of divine election according to which the ultimate ground for this man being saved and that man lost was the predestinating will of God, a will uninfluenced by any difference between the moral worth of the response of different men.

On this point no one could wish to criticize the reformers harshly. They were faced by a dilemma which no theologians as yet have been able to resolve. Any Christian thinker wrestling with it must deserve sympathy rather than hostility. But nevertheless, in the interests of truth and of fair play, it must be pointed out that, in passing on to this doctrine

of faith as divinely given, the reformers introduced (so subtly as to escape their own notice) a change in the meaning of the word "faith" so that in their teaching 'faith' became a *something*, as "mystical," "magical" or "quasi-physical" as any *ex opere operato* sacrament had ever been in Catholicism. For if "faith" be not the free expression of a man's personality, but something predisposing him to act in a certain manner, it matters not how completely it is the expression of God's free personal activity, as a factor in human life it is a non-ethical "something," working *ex opere operato*.

I have not used the epithets "mystical," "magical" and "quasi-physical" from any desire to import into the discussion a vocabulary of abuse, but because they are terms which are still used in all good faith to describe Catholic doctrine by those who maintain the Protestant doctrine of justification by faith. Nor is it my intention to come forward as a champion of Catholicism and a critic of Protestantism. I hope I have made it clear that my aim is simply to show that in respect of this central doctrine of Christian theology, when one looks beneath words to what they signify, both Catholicism and Protestantism are at one. If Protestants can justly use these epithets to describe the Catholic conception of sacramental grace, Catholics can use them with equal justice of the Protestant conception of faith.

What I would urge is that both Catholics and Protestants should eliminate such terms from their vocabularies when thinking and speaking of each other. . . . If we will do this, we shall find that both types of Christianity are facing the same problem, and in order to deal with it are adopting expedients essentially similar. It may be well to set this out in tabular form.

1. Both Catholicism and Protestantism wish to bear witness to three positive truths:

(i) Man's salvation is God's gift, freely given through the crucified and risen Christ.

(ii) Man's relation to God is a personal and ethical relation. This truth would be corrupted by any view which thought of man being "mechanically" or "physically" saved irrespective of his own personal character.

(iii) Being God's free gift, salvation is not in any sense earned by man or received as a reward of merit.

2. In Catholicism:

(i) This truth is accepted. The sacramental system is regarded as a divinely appointed mode for God's communication of His gifts to man.

(ii) This truth is safeguarded by the requirement of "penitence and faith" on the part of those who approach God either sacramentally or otherwise.

(iii) This truth is accepted, and in sacramental doctrine is safeguarded by the doctrine *ex opere operato*.

3. In Protestantism:

(i) This truth is accepted and forms the essence of the doctrine of justification.

(ii) This doctrine is witnessed to by the criticism of the Catholic doctrine of *ex opere operato*, and by the emphasis on "preaching the Word" as the right method of conversion.

(iii) This truth is safeguarded by the doctrine that the faith by which man receives God's gift of salvation is itself a gift of God freely given irrespective of the recipient's personal character.

It is clear that in both types of doctrine there is a contradiction between the second and third of these points, and that this is due to the apparent contradictions of the two truths to which they attempt to bear witness. The result is that both types are liable to perversion in popular practice, if one or other of these two truths is emphasized at the expense of the other. It is only by holding both together in tension that this danger can be avoided, and Christian charity requires exponents of each type to recognize that both are inspired by this common aim.

There remains, then, for all Christians, Catholic and Protestant, an intellectual problem which is common to all, the problem of reconciling the ethical and personal character of the Christian religion with the truth of man's utter dependence on God's free gift of salvation. . . .

We defined the problem as that of reconciling the ethical and personal character of the Christian religion with the truth of man's utter dependence on God's free gift of salvation. Just how it is possible for God to create free beings remains a mystery, as mysterious as the ultimate constitution of matter, the origin of life, and the beginning of evil. Our experience bears witness to this mystery: when we pray, for example, we are conscious of the truth that the more we remember our utter dependence on God for our very existence and power to pray, the more we find ourselves free from distractions and able to express our true selves in prayer. There remains an element of mystery, of paradox, the paradox which drove Catholicism to develop both a doctrine of merit and an *ex opere operato* doctrine of sacraments, the paradox which drove Protestantism to treat faith both as an exercise of human personality and as an *ex opere operato* activity of God. . . .

Let us now look back again on the controversies of the past and see what light can be thrown on them by these results of our inquiry. If it be true that Catholicism and Protestantism were both seeking to maintain the same paradox, how was it that they came into conflict with one another?

We saw that on the one side Catholicism sought to avoid Pelagianism by its *ex opere operato* sacramental doctrine, while on the other it developed a doctrine of merit to safeguard personal moral responsibility. On the other side Protestantism emphasised the need of personal faith in opposition to the alleged materialism of Catholic sacramental doctrine, and then depersonalized the faith to avoid Pelagianism. I suggest that in returning to the question after our excursion into the realms of secular thought, we can now see that the strength of Catholicism lay in its understanding of the needs of man arising out of the sub-personal elements in his being; the strength of Protestantism in its clear grasp of the importance and the nature of personal faith. The weakness of Catholicism was its doctrine of merit; the weakness of Protestantism its inadequate development of the truth that faith itself is God's gift. The attempt to safeguard personal moral responsibility by a doctrine of merit is the first step towards the degradation of Catholicism; the better way is by the doctrine of justification by faith. The doctrine of justification by faith needs safeguarding against Pelagianism, and Catholic sacramentalism rightly understood will here give Protestantism help where it needs it most.

Let us take first the doctrine of justification by faith. It is by faith that man lays hold on the forgiveness offered by God in Christ and is restored to his true life of growth in communion with God. This faith expresses itself in acknowledgement of sinfulness and impotence, in personal loyalty to Christ and reliance upon Him for strength to serve Him. This faith is both the expression of the man's own free response to the love of God shown forth in Christ, and also God's gift through which the man responds. How can this be so? Because it is exercised at that stage of development at which man can enter into relations with God as fully personal on both sides as those in which he stands to his fellow-men. The activity of God is always fully personal, and man is personal enough to be able to receive from God that kind of help which does not negate but confirms his own free personal growth. . . . Here, in this personal redemptive activity of God, whereby forgiveness is personally offered in order that by faith it may be personally received, we have the supreme manifestation of the grace of God.

But the same God who thus approaches man personally to win his personal response is also the Creator who has given its existence to that spatio-temporal process which we call the universe, sustains it in being, and promotes its development. . . . Is the Church, which exists to kindle the personal response of faith by preaching the Word, to bear no witness also to this creative and sustaining activity of God? That, to my mind, is the question which is posed by the teaching on grace characteristic of Catholicism and Orthodoxy.

For in Catholicism and Orthodoxy the sacraments express a more comprehensive activity of God than that which is directly related to man's personal response. When I come in penitence and faith to receive the sacrament of Holy Communion, I cannot limit the divine activity in me to that of which I am consciously aware. He bids me to do this in remembrance of Him, and I come in obedience to His command. So far all is mutually personal. But when I come, my personal response at its best is poor and meagre; and only too often it is not at its best but is the response of one who is sleepy, or wandering in thought, or even conscious of hardly being a real individual self at all. Then my faith has to be shown in trusting God through Christ to give me all the sub-personal growth I need to constitute me a person and enable me to make the personal response of faith. Through the practice of the sacramental life I learn for myself the evangelical truth that I need the grace of God in order to have the faith which can respond to the divine calling. . . .

It is this that enables me to appreciate and accept the Catholic doctrine of baptismal regeneration as applied to infants. Though the minister may pour the water and speak the words of administration, what gives its whole significance to the service is the fact that the true Agent is Christ Himself, in whose name His Church is baptising the children. It is Christ who is taking them up in His arms, laying His hands on them and blessing them.[12] What limits can we set to the divine activity in the life of children, nourishing their unconscious, sub-personal life with all that they need to become capable of conscious personal faith when they come to years of discretion? . . .

But, as we saw . . . this Catholic belief is liable to a degradation which involves both superstition and Pelagianism. How is this? We need not pause over the possible degradation due to forgetting that God's activity is always personal and therefore thinking of grace as a something. . . . The source of error against which we need to guard ourselves today is that which springs from failing to distinguish between the different stages of human development and the different treatment required by each.

The strength of the position characteristic of Catholicism and Ortho-

doxy is that it makes provision for the religious nurture of all sorts and conditions of men. Whatever the stage of their development in physical age or spiritual sensitiveness, there is a place for them in the sacramental life of the Church which there would not be if the only offer made to them were the demand for the response of fully personal faith, all or nothing. Its danger is the danger of forgetting that the only purpose of the sacramental system is to engender and nourish this fully personal faith, thus allowing men to be content with a good which is the enemy of the best. . . . Catholicism without the emphasis on justification by faith may degenerate into worldliness; Protestantism without the doctrine of baptismal regeneration may follow the Montanists and Donatists into a catharistic sectarianism. . . .

4. **F. J. Taylor[13] looks at the Reformation Doctrine and the present Anglican situation. Anglican theologians of the last two centuries have not spoken with the same unanimity on justification by faith alone as the majority of their predecessors. Theological developments and current criticisms thus require a critical reexamination of the older formulation of doctrine of justification by faith.**

Justification by faith alone: the reformation doctrine and the present situation. It has long been a commonplace of Church history that the theological basis of the sixteenth-century reformation in the West was

---

[12] Cf. Mk 10:16.

[13] F. J. Taylor, M.A., Vicar of St. Andrew's Oxford, tutor and lecturer of Wycliffe Hall, Oxford. This excerpt is from his article, "Justification by Faith Alone: the Reformation Doctrine and the Present Situation," in the book, *The Doctrine of Justification by Faith*, ed. G. W. H. Lampe (London: A. R. Mowbray & Co., 1954), pp. 9–30.

the doctrine of justification by faith alone, expressed in the battle cry *sola fide,* which once had an unrivalled power to stir the pulses of men. "Luther in Wittenberg wrestled with the exposition of the Epistle to the Romans, and in so wrestling found the word that set the world on fire."[14] Luther himself had no doubt that this affirmation was the *articulus aut stantis aut cadentis ecclesiae,* the unshakable foundation from which the work of reformation as well in theology as in ecclesiastical life should proceed. "It was one of those classical moments of intense theological perception, when one word, one dogma, one cry of repentance, one assurance of reconciliation appear to contain in themselves the whole truth of God and the whole duty of man."[15] For this reason, all the Continental Reformers, despite great differences in temperament and personal experience, were at one in teaching the doctrine of justification by faith alone as the heart of the gospel, if not in itself the whole content of the gospel.

The official Anglican declaration on the subject in the eleventh of the Thirty-Nine Articles, though cautious in tone and restrained in language, yet found it possible to employ the contentious phrase *sola fide* in asserting: "wherefore that we are justified by faith alone is a most wholesome doctrine and very full of comfort as more largely expressed in the homily

of Justification.". . . The writings of Anglican theologians of the classical period manifest an awareness of the significance of this doctrine, both in its consequences for the pattern of Christian life and in the fact that it presented the grand difference between the sons of Rome and the sons of the reformation.[16] In the essentials of this doctrine there was little to divide Wittenberg, Geneva and Canterbury from each other.[17]. . .

The widespread agreement on the formulation of this doctrine in the later sixteenth and early seventeenth centuries was undoubtedly responsible for the notion widely, though by no means universally, held, that it had acquired for non-Roman Christians of the West the status of an irreversible doctrinal decision. Nevertheless, despite the importance it seemed to possess both as the crux of the controversy between Roman and non-Roman theologians and as in itself the vivifying principle of Christian belief and practice, justification by faith, the material principle of the reformation, seems to occupy a singularly small place in the modern theological debate. From the later part of the seventeenth century, probably as a consequence of the theological anarchy which accompanied the Puritan

---

[14] E. C. Hoskyns and F. N. Davey, *The Fourth Gospel* (London, 1940), Vol. I, p. ix.

[15] *Loc. cit.*

[16] See the works of Latimer, Cranmer, Coverdale, Becon, Whitaker, Jewell, Grindal, and Sandys. Cf. also the expositions of Rogers and Nowell, and in the seventeenth century, Bishops Hall and Davenant.

[17] Augsburg Conf. IV; Belgic Conf. XXII–XXIV; Westminster Conf. XI, 1–3; Calvin, *Institutes of the Christian Religion,* iii, 13.3.

revolution, there has been an Anglican tradition of exposition of its meaning and importance which has revealed no inconsiderable embarrassment at the terms of the official Anglican formularies. . . . These facts oblige responsible theologians to consider whether the old formulation of justification by faith may not be more misleading than helpful; whether it does not seek to express an important truth in categories which are no longer meaningful; whether it can now be named, as popular protestantism still supposes, "as the grand question which hangeth yet in controversy between us and the Church of Rome"? . . .

Anglican theologians of the last two centuries have not spoken with the same unanimity on the subject of justification by faith alone as the majority of their predecessors in the earlier period appeared to do; nor have they declared their conviction in controversial writings that it is the most important subject in dispute with Rome. Theologians in the Church of England who have stood outside the evangelical tradition have indicated three directions in which reconsideration of the terms of the sixteenth-century debate has seemed to them to be desirable. In the first place the fear that justification by faith alone would promote a neglect of duty and other charitable works has not for long been absent from the minds of considering churchmen. . . . Secondly, it has been suggested that both Romanists and the Reformed have modified the severity of the theological language employed by their predecessors of the sixteenth and seventeenth centuries and the inference has been drawn that the gap between the two protagonists is in reality much narrower than either of them supposed in the heat of the controversy. The language of justification and the imagery of the law-courts which it summons before the imagination, is not in this age felt to be so eloquent of the relation between God and man as an earlier age liked to think, nor is it accepted as the only category in which Christian thought about the atonement can be adequately contained. . . . A third difficulty which the traditional doctrine of justification by faith has to meet in the minds of many modern writers is in its relation to the sacraments and the corporate life of the Church. Newman seems to have thought that the Lutheran doctrine of justification was grounded in subjective conviction or feeling upon the part of the believer and to have proposed instead what he believed was the true, Catholic doctrine of justification which rested upon an objective reality.[18] Christ is the justification of men by His indwelling in them, through the Spirit. This indwelling is mediated and maintained by sacramental means.[19] Justification by faith alone, at least logically if not in practice, can on this interpre-

---

[18] *Lectures on Justification,* J. H. Newman (Oxford, 1840), pp. 64–67, 164–166.

[19] *Op. cit.,* pp. 168–171. The more awful presence of God in Holy Communion will be the instrument of a higher justification (*ibid.,* p. 169).

tation dispense with such sacramental means.

Dr. J. P. Whitney, an historical scholar of standing, allowed himself to write that: "Luther enlarged St. Paul's 'justification by faith' into 'justification by faith alone'; taken along with the dangerous assertion that man's salvation depended upon his own conviction of its truth this expression became mischievous . . . it made man's feelings the central point, hence in the end it shut out the conception of God and His grace which it was originally meant to emphasize; this result was hastened by disregard of life with the Church; united to individualism the phrase became licentious."[20] A more formidable attack on justification by faith was launched by Dom Gregory Dix,[21] in his discussion of Anglican orders. He allowed that justification by faith was the fundamental question at issue in the reformation, but then proceeded to an account of it which was a complete travesty of the doctrine as formulated by the sixteenth-century theologians. The language used by Dom Gregory only touches reality in respect of some eighteenth-century pietists and latter-day sectarians. . . .

Changes in the theological climate, differences of emphasis consequent upon the passage of time, theological divisions within the Church of England which mirror the Catholic-Protestant debate in Christendom at large, all these circumstances combine to make necessary a careful re-examination of the doctrine of justification, to see whether the cardinal importance hitherto attached to it in the Anglican formularies and in more than one stream of Anglican tradition, can be reaffirmed or must now be modified. Biblical, linguistic, historical and dogmatic studies must all play a part in this struggle for fresh theological understanding, this willingness "to rethink all attainments.". . .

Official Roman theology did not and does not teach justification by works. But much depends upon the way in which official language is interpreted in the day-to-day activity of the Church. The category of merit dominated the interpretation of the doctrines of salvation in the later medieval centuries and a vast superstructure of pious practices which gained the sanction of the highest ecclesiastical authorities only confirmed this impression. The language of Trent, though designed to eliminate some of the worst scandals consequent upon the manipulation of the means of grace on the part of large numbers of priests, did not close the door against the idea of human merit, so that the conflict between Rome and reformed Christendom has been a real fight and not shadow boxing.

It must be emphasized that *sola fide* strives to give glory to God and not to flatter the sinner. It asserts that salvation is due only to the loving initiative of God and not to anything that the sinner has done or can do. The

---

[20] *The History of the Reformation*, J. P. Whitney (London, 2nd ed., 1940), p. 507.

[21] *The Question of Anglican Orders*, G. Dix (London, 1944), pp. 20 ff.

object of the doctrine is to eliminate human pride and to exalt the saviour. It follows, therefore, that it is a vulgar error to suppose that *sola fide* exhausts the content of the Christian message and renders superfluous the ordered life of the Church expressed in ministry and sacraments. . . . It must be allowed that in some Anglican circles deeply influenced by certain elements of pietistic theology, justification has virtually been equated with a conversion experience which has sometimes in practice been erected into the sole object of Christian life and faith and treated as though it were a good work. This is a perversion where it occurs, to be repented of. . . . Indeed, so profound has been the emphasis upon the sinfulness of man, that there has been very little evangelical writing on moral theology or on sociology, though it should never be forgotten that evangelicals have in practice been very active in both these fields. . . .

In the older text-books it was commonly assumed that linguistic and exegetical studies had confirmed the accuracy of the reformation interpretation of justification in the New Testament. The views of the editors of the Epistle to the Romans in the *International Critical Commentary* were clearly and emphatically expressed on this point.[22] Nevertheless it has to be recognized that this is not quite so settled an issue as was once supposed. Modern theological study has suggested that the biblical interpretation of the concept of justification is richer in content than the narrowly forensic terms in which it was usually presented in the past. The justified person is accepted with God in Christ (this term now requires a corporate rather than an individual interpretation) or put right with God through Christ (always to be thought of as Christ in His Body) and the word of God which justifies is a word effective to inaugurate a God-given relationship in which transformation of character is implicit.

Nevertheless, if interpretation is confined within the categories with which the Reformers had to work, modern critical exegesis confirms the substance of their interpretation. What is at issue now is the doubt whether these old categories are adequate for the exposition which contemporary biblical work demands. Theological developments and current criticisms thus require a critical re-examination of the older formulation of the doctrine of justification by faith, for it is an aspect of that Catholic-Protestant division which Amsterdam recognized as "our deepest difference."[23] If the Amsterdam report was right to add, "the essence of our situation is that, from each side of the division, we see the Christian faith and life as a self-consistent whole, but our two conceptions of the whole are inconsistent with one another,"[24] then it will not be true that justification by

---

[22] W. Sanday and A. C. Headlam (Edinburgh, 5th ed., 1902), pp. 28–31, 36–39, 118–124, 151–152.

[23] *The First Assembly of the World Council of Churches*, ed. W. A. Visser't Hooft (London, 1949), p. 51.

[24] *Op. cit.*, p. 52.

faith in evangelical Christendom is to be set over against justification by works in Catholic Christendom, but that justification by faith is held on both sides of the division, though on each side it plays a different part in relation to the "whole of Christian faith and life." To struggle for mutual understanding across this division becomes a matter of obligation for the heirs of both traditions.

5. T. F. Torrance[25] looks at justification, its nature and place in Reformed doctrine and life, through the eyes of Scottish theology. Justification thus is by Christ alone and this means the rejection of all forms of self-justification and the exclusion of all natural goodness, all natural knowledge, and all tradition. It calls in question all systems and orders.

The nature of justification. . . . Justification always involves a fulfilling of the righteousness, or the enacting of the truth. The Gospel teaches "the justification of the ungodly," and the astounding thing about it is that it means such a putting of the ungodly man in the right that through fulfillment of his condemnation he is justified, justified in both senses: judged and acquitted, condemned and vindicated, exposed as guilty and made righteous — but that is truth, *aletheia*, concrete reality only in Jesus Christ. . . .

Objective justification takes place in Christ, before the Father. The *Scots Confession* expounds it in this way. There was "enmity betwixt the justice of God and our sins,"[26] and therefore the Son of God descended to take to Himself a body of our body, flesh

of our flesh, and bone of our bones, and so to become *Mediator* between God and man. . . .

Subjective justification. It is illuminating to recognize that subjective justification, as well as objective justification, has already taken place in Jesus Christ. Not only was the great divine act of righteousness fulfilled in the flesh of Jesus, in His Life and Death, but throughout His Life and Death Jesus stood in our place as our Substitute and Representative who appropriated the divine Act of saving Righteousness for us. He responded to it, yielded to it, accepted it and actively made it His own, for what He was and did in His human nature was not for His own sake but for our sakes. . . . He stood in our place, taking our cause upon Him, also as Believer, as the Obedient One who was Himself justified before God as His beloved Son in whom He was well pleased. He offered to God a perfect confidence and trust, a perfect faith

---

[25] Cf. ch. I, n. 1. This excerpt is from his article, "Justification: Its Radical Nature and Place in Reformed Doctrine and Life," which appeared in the *Scottish Journal of Theology*, 13 (1960), pp. 225–246.

[26] *Scots Confession*, Art. VIII.

and response which we are unable to offer, and He appropriated all God's blessings which we are unable to appropriate. Through union with Him we share in His faith, in His obedience, in His trust and His appropriation of the Father's blessing; we share in His justification before God. Therefore when we are justified by faith, this does not mean that it is *our* faith that justifies us, far from it — it is the faith of Christ alone that justifies us, but we in faith flee from our own acts even of repentance, confession, trust and response, and take refuge in the obedience and faithfulness of Christ — "Lord I believe, help thou mine unbelief." That is what is meant to be justified by faith. . . .

When we look at it like this, we understand why John Knox hesitated to use the expression "justification by faith" and preferred instead concrete expressions which made it clear that we are justified only in Christ, by what He has done alone, and not by any act of ours, even if that act be an act of believing. We believe in Christ in such a way that we flee from ourselves and take refuge in Him alone — and therefore we can hardly speak about "justifying faith" without transferring the emphasis away from Christ and His faithful act to ourselves and our act of trust or believing. At this point Calvin and Knox stood in contrast to Luther, who approached the whole question from a point that tended to be anthropocentric: "How can I get a gracious God"? Luther made it indubitably clear that justification does not derive from the act of the self, but from a righteousness outside of us in Christ, from an *aliena justitia,* as he called it. But his basic question demanded an answer to the self, and inevitably gave the whole question of assurance undue prominence. With Calvin and Knox it was different — assurance had little place, because it was not needed. The very act of faith was pivoted upon Christ and His faith, not upon my faith or my need for this or that answer, and hence the assurance was unshakable, because it was grounded in the solid faithfulness of Christ.

It was only later in Scottish theology when the anthropocentric questions emerged, questions of conscience and soul-searching, when the eyes of the believer were turned inward upon his own heart rather than outward upon his Lord and Savior, that the demand for assurance became clamant. Whenever there is talk of "justifying faith" then uncertainty creeps in, for all our acts, even of repentance and faith, are unworthy before God. If it is upon our repentance and our faith that we have ultimately to rely, who can be saved, not to speak of being sure of his salvation? . . . If we are to use the expression "justification by faith alone," and there is no reason why we should not, then let it be crystal clear that "by faith alone" is meant "by the Grace of Christ alone," that faith is but an empty vessel to be filled by the Covenant Mercies and faithfulness of God in Christ.

The radical consequences of justification. Justification means justification by Christ alone — that is the reference of the expressions *sola fide, sola gratia, sola scriptura,* used in Reformed theology. Justification means that we look exclusively to Christ, and therefore that we look away from ourselves altogether in order to live out of Him alone. That radical nature of justification is expressed and its radical consequences drawn by the *Scots Confession* in the words we cited earlier: "We willingly spoil ourselves of all honor and glory of our own salvation and redemption, as we also do of our regeneration and sanctification."

This is something that very badly needs to be reiterated today within the Churches of the Reformation. Justification by Christ alone means the rejection of *all* forms of self-justification and all forms of justification by anything or out of any source other than Jesus Christ. Let us consider what this means in several areas of doctrine and life.

(a) At the Reformation justification by the Grace of Christ alone was seen to set aside all *natural goodness,* and all works-righteousness; but this applies to all goodness, Christian goodness as well, that is, to "sanctification" as it came to be called. . . .

(b) Justification by the Grace of Christ alone calls in question not only all natural goodness but all *natural knowledge.* Natural knowledge is as much the work of the flesh as natural goodness; it is a work of the natural man. It is at this point that Karl Barth has made such an immense contribution to the Reformation. We cannot separate knowing and being for

they belong to the same man, and it is the whole man, with his knowing and his acting, with the whole of his being, who is called in question by justification. Justification puts us in the right and truth of God and therefore tells us that we are in untruth. . . .

(c) Justification by the grace of Christ alone calls in question all *tradition.* . . . In other words, sheer attachment to the Word of God as the real object of knowledge meant detachment from all other sources and norms of knowledge, and the demand that all traditional ideas and notions had to be tested at the bar of the Word. That did not mean that tradition was to be despised, but that it was to be subjected to the criticism of the Word and the Spirit, and corrected through conformity to Jesus Christ. . . . There can be no doubt that every one of the great Churches of the Reformation — the Lutheran, the Anglican and the Reformed — has developed its own masterful tradition, and that that tradition today exercises massive influence not only over its way of interpreting the Bible and formulating its doctrine but over the whole shape and direction of its life. Those who shut their eyes to this fact are precisely those who are most enslaved to the dominant power of tradition just because it has become an unconscious canon and norm of their thinking. It is high time we asked again whether the Word of God really does have free course among us and whether it is not after all bound and fettered by the tradition of men. . . .

(d) Justification by Christ alone calls in question all *systems* and *orders* and calls them in question because Jesus Christ alone is central and supreme in the one Church of God. . . . Our quarrel with the Church of Rome in doctrinal matters concerns the centrality of Jesus Christ, the primacy and supremacy of Christology which is so obscured and compromised by Roman doctrines of merit and tradition, and above all by Mariology. In our debate with the Church of England over questions of order, we are also concerned with the centrality of Christ, and the primacy of Christology — and therefore the doctrine of the Church as the Body of *Christ* is in the forefront. . . . Justification by Christ alone means that we renounce the way of the flesh in seeking honor from men, or justification from one another; and therefore justification by Christ alone means that in any movement for reconciliation between Churches, the question of the recognition of orders cannot have priority without radical betrayal of the Reformation, nay, without radical betrayal

of Christ for He is thereby ousted from His place of centrality. . . .

(e) Nowhere does justification by Christ alone have more radical consequences than in regard to the pastoral ministry. Justification by Christ is grounded upon His mighty Act in which He took our place, substituting Himself for us under the divine judgment, and substituting Himself for us in the obedient response He rendered to God in worship and thanksgiving and praise. . . . Thus the whole of our worship and ministry reposes upon the substitutionary work of Christ. . . . At the Reformation this doctrine had immediate effect in the overthrow of Roman sacerdotalism — Jesus Christ is our sole priest. . . . But what has happened in Protestant worship and ministry? Is it not too often the case that the whole life and worship of the congregation revolves round the personality of the minister? . . . What is that but *Protestant* sacerdotalism, sacerdotalism which involves the displacement of the Humanity of Christ by the humanity of the minister?

6. K. Barth[27] says there can be only one grace, the grace of the one God and the one Christ. But here unfortunately the paths of Evangelical and Roman Catholic understanding have diverged widely. For while Romanist doctrine holds that in the last resort there is only one grace, yet it merely says this but insists much more on the division of grace than on its unity.

[27] Karl Barth was born in Basle, Switzerland, May 10, 1886. He became professor of theology successively at the Universities of Göttingen, Münster, Bonn, and finally of Basle. His best known works are *Der Römerbrief* and *Die kirchliche Dogmatik.* The exhaustive list of his writings until the end of 1955 was composed by Charlotte von Kirschbaum, *Antwort, Festschrift, Karl Barth* (Zollikon-Zürich, 1956), pp. 945–960. This excerpt is from his *Church Dogmatics,* Vol. IV, 1, *The Doctrine of Reconciliation* (Edinburgh: T. & T. Clark, 1956), pp. 83–88.

The grace of God in Jesus Christ.
. . . Christian obedience consists in
this, and its joy and certainty rest
and renew themselves on this: that
by the grace of God this is the relationship of God with man. For what
the Christian community can have
specially as knowledge and experience
of the atonement made in Jesus Christ,
for the power, therefore, of its witness
to the world, everything depends on
the simplicity of heart which is ready
to let the grace of God be exclusively
His grace, His sovereign act, His free
turning to man as new and strange
every morning, so that it does not
know anything higher or better or
more intimate or real than the fact
that quite apart from anything that
he can contribute to God or become
and be in contrast to Him, unreser-
vedly therefore and undeservedly, man
can hold fast to God and live by and
in this holding fast to Him.

In this introductory survey we must
also state that unfortunately the paths
of Evangelical and Roman Catholic
understanding have diverged widely
at this point. In the light of the latest
doctrine in relation to the Virgin
Mary (1950), the proclamation of
which has shed a new and garish light
on the situation, we can only say that,
humanly speaking, they have diverged
hopelessly. The heart and guiding
principle of the Romanist doctrine of
grace is the negation of the unity of
grace as always God's grace to man, as
His sovereign act which is everywhere
new and strange and free. It is the
negation of the unity of grace as His
grace in Jesus Christ. It is the division
of grace by which it is first of all His,
but then — and this is where the emphasis falls — effected and empowered
by His grace, it is also our grace.
Against this view we must at once
and quite definitely set our face.

In the Romanist teaching a distinction is made between *gratia increata*,
which is God Himself, who is the
divine will of love and therefore the
ground of all grace, and *gratia creata*,
which is the "finite product" of the
former, "but which is essentially different from God Himself."[28]. . . How
can it be essentially different from
God and yet be His grace which
reconciles us with Himself?

In the Romanist teaching there is
a *gratia externa* which works on us
only from without in the form of
teaching and example. "We have to
do here with the life and death of
Christ, His Gospel, His miracles,
providence, personal experiences. . . .
This influence is moral." For the most
part it is, of course, connected with
the *gratia interna*. It aims ultimately
at inward effects. But it does not produce them of itself. It simply prepares
the way. It makes the soul receptive.
In contrast, the inward grace "effects
the soul and its basic faculties, raising
it to a new order of being. Its influ-

---

[28] Cf. B. Bartmann, *Dogm. Handb.*, Vol.
2, 1929, 113.

ence is physical." It adheres to the soul as a new form. We ask: How can the life and death of Christ and the Gospel . . . be described as "only" an external grace and as such obviously impotent and defective? What is this "physical" influence compared with which that of the Gospel is "only" moral? — as though the outward moral grace were not the most inward and physical. And what is this form of the soul in a higher order of being in which we are not referred absolutely and exclusively to that *gratia externa* which has only moral significance but can find comfort and be reconciled with God physically, in and by ourselves?

Within the decisive *gratia interna* there is a personal grace of sanctification (*gratia gratum faciens*) and a grace of office (*gratia gratis data*), the charismatic endowment.". . . A further distinction then made between *gratia actualis* and *gratia habitualis* . . . between *gratia medicinalis* and *gratia elevans* . . . between *gratia praeveniens* and *gratia concomitans* . . . between *gratia operans* and *gratia cooperans* . . . between *gratia sufficiens* and *gratia efficax*. . . . Finally, there is a distinction (the most remarkable of all) between *gratia Christi* and *gratia Dei*, or *gratia supernaturalis* and *gratia naturalis*. . . .

If there is one God, and one Mediator between God and man, and therefore one grace — what place is there for all these abstractions? These are the questions which crowd in upon us as we face the final Roman Catholic distinction.

But the Romanist doctrine of grace insists on these abstractions. Naturally it also maintains — rather more emphatically on the Thomist side and rather less emphatically on the Jesuit — that in the last resort there is only one grace. But it merely says this: it does not make any use of it. . . . For, if it did, the fact would be revealed which is plainly enough proclaimed by all these characterisations and emphases, that it is definitely much more interested in the *gratia interna* than the *gratia externa*, in habitual grace than actual, in the grace which uplifts than the grace which heals, in *gratia cooperans* than *gratia operans*, in other words in the state and life and activity of grace in man than in Christ as the One who accomplishes the sovereign act of God and what man is in and by Him, in Mary than the Son of Mary, in the sacraments as the supposed means of grace than the Word and Spirit of God who reveals and attests and in that way really mediates it, in the Church as the form of grace, in the priesthood and its authority than the Lord of the community which lives by the Word and Spirit of God and therefore in His service. This is the system of fatal preferences which would be revealed if the theology of Rome were to speak of the unity of grace instead of its division, and it is to be feared that the unity which it would choose would necessarily be that of man in grace, of Mary, of the sacraments, of the Church ruled and directed by the priesthood.

Alternatively, the revelation of this

strange preference might cause it to take fright and to abandon it. It would then have to decide to become a real doctrine of the grace of Christ. It would have to notice that the subjective side to which it has everywhere addressed itself in the sphere of those twofold concepts is utterly dependent upon and can be known and determined only by the objective, which it has commemorated but then abandoned as though it were only a *conditio sine qua non*. It would have to learn to trust that the genuinely subjective is already included in the true objective, and will be found in it and not elsewhere. But in this case the Romanist theology would have to become Evangelical. And in view of its authoritative pronouncements it seems less likely to happen today than at any time.

What is certain is that we have to take warning at this point. If it is a matter of the grace of the one God and the one Christ, there can be only one grace. We cannot, therefore, split it up into an objective grace which is not as such strong and effective for man but simply comes before him as a possibility, and a subjective grace which, occasioned and prepared by the former, is the corresponding reality as it actually comes to men. But the grace of the one God and the one Christ, and therefore the objective grace which never comes to man except from God, must always be understood as the one complete grace, which is subjectively strong and effective in its divine objectivity, the grace which

does actually reconcile man with God. And the test of this understanding of grace must be that the state of man in relation to it — apart from what we can positively say concerning him in the light of it — is clearly and unequivocally described as one of absolute need: a state in which — with all that this involves — he is and remains always a recipient, a state in which he not only does not cease but can never do more than begin (and he will always be a beginner) to beg and to reach out for it in his poverty, in order that in that poverty he may be rich. The Romanist doctrine of grace cannot survive this test. It ascribes to man in grace an *exousia* in which he can look back to the grace of Christ as such as to an indispensable but preliminary stage which he has already passed. It furnishes him with a wealth in which he is no longer poor and needy and hungry and sick, in which, therefore, he cannot be the recipient of the one complete grace of God and of Christ. At the point where its true interest emerges, it definitely does not describe him as the being which has known and experienced and acknowledged the atonement as the sovereign act of God. As reflected in its description of man in grace, God has ceased to be the free subject of the atonement, the grace of the atonement has ceased to be His grace. And since this is so, there can be no peace between this and the Evangelical doctrine of grace.

But we must not omit an irenical

and ecumenical word at the conclusion of this confessional polemic. There is a very deep peace (beyond understanding) between us Evangelical Christians and our Catholic fellow-Christians who are badly instructed in this doctrine. We cannot believe that they do in fact live by the grace which is so dreadfully divided in their dogmatics. Rather, we have to believe, and it is comforting to believe, that they as well as we — if only we did it better — do live by the one undivided grace of Jesus Christ. . . . We wish that they would abandon both their teaching and many — very many — things in their practice which correspond so closely to it. . . .

7. C. Van Til[29] sees Barth as arguing insistently that we must think of grace Christologically. Thus we speak along the lines of the Reformation theology and escape the Romanist approach to grace and the free will of man. Only thus can the sovereignty of grace in relation to man be maintained.

In discussing the doctrine of grace, Barth argues again and again, we must do so Christologically. Speaking Christologically of grace is, in effect, speaking of Christ. It is not to speak of the *principle* of grace; it is rather to speak of "the living person of Jesus Christ himself."[30] Christology must *per definitionem* be that which grounds all our theological thinking. It must therefore also, and in particular, control us in our view of the relation of sin to grace.[31] We cannot first establish views concerning God and sin, and grace and afterward shore them up with Christological considerations.[32]

Thinking Christologically of grace is to keep the two aspects of grace in proper balance. On the one hand grace is inherently *free* grace. It is *sovereign* grace. It *produces* works in man which are new, takes sin seriously, and is incomprehensible. When man is saved by grace, there is a genuine turning-about in his life. On the other hand, grace is inherently universal grace. The primordial and unchangeable relation of God to man is that of grace in Christ, and the primordial and unchangeable relation of man to God is that of the receiver

---

[29] Cornelius Van Til was born in the Netherlands in 1895 and was ordained a minister of the Christian Reformed Church in 1927. In 1929 he was professor of apologetics at Westminster Theological Seminary. Among his published works are *The Defense of the Faith; The New Modernism: An Appraisal of the Theology of Barth and Brunner.* This excerpt is from his work, *Christianity and Barthianism* (Grand Rapids, Mich.: Baker Book House, 1962), pp. 30–53.

[30] *Kirchliche Dogmatik*, IV: 3; 1, p. 198.

[31] *Ibid.*, pp. 198 ff. In this section Barth rejects G. C. Berkouwer's charge that his theology is speculative in that for him grace makes it a foregone conclusion that sin will be defeated. Barth says that this charge is without foundation because he deals with the Person of Christ, not with the principle of grace.

[32] *Ibid.*, p. 200.

of grace in Christ. Sin is an "ontological impossibility" for man. The real man is the sinner who participates in God's grace."[33]

Thinking Christologically of grace enables us, says Barth, to speak along the lines of Reformation theology. Thinking Christologically enables us to escape the Romanist approach to grace and the free will of man. Romanism thinks along the lines of the analogy of being, and in doing so, is largely controlled by philosophical speculation. It is this philosophical speculation that accounts for its use of natural theology. In Romanist theology Christ comes into the picture too late; he comes in *afterwards,* and a Christ coming in *afterwards* is, in effect, Christ not coming in at all.

Against this the Reformers, thinking Christologically gave God the true priority over man and grace the true priority over man's participation in it.

But the Reformers did not consistently work out the relation of grace to sin along Christological lines. They were unable to fathom the full implication of their own idea of the sovereignty of grace. They did not realize that the full freedom and glory of God's grace to man in Christ is expressed in the very idea of his being the one who suffers the wrath of God for man.

Again, the Reformers, and notably Calvin, had no full appreciation for the biblical universalism involved in the true idea of grace. We must therefore go beyond the Reformers in stress-

ing both the full sovereignty and the full universality of the nature of grace.

Instead of thus going beyond the Reformers, later orthodox theologians all too often fell back on natural theology and on the idea of direct revelation in history. Thus they tended once more to make the consciousness of man think of itself as autonomous. And thus they became, all too often, the forerunners of the consciousness-theology of Schleiermacher and his followers.

This in turn prepared the way for a theology which was, in effect, as Feuerbach maintained, nothing more than an undercover anthropology.

If then we are to work out the true Reformation principle of theology, and therewith escape the synergistic views of Romanism, we must think of grace Christologically. And if we are to escape the narrowness of an evil orthodoxy and the subjectivism of the consciousness theologians, we must think of grace Christologically. And finally if we are really to enjoy the full certainty of the gift of the grace of God in Christ for all men, and in doing so laugh in Feuerbach's face, then we must think of grace Christologically.

Reconciliation as "Geschichte." Speaking of grace Christologically is to speak of grace as Geschichte. For Christ is *Geschichte.* In Christ as *Geschichte* Christ is identical with his work, and his work is that of the salvation of all men. Barth stresses this "biblical universalism," as he calls it, over and over. As *biblical* uni-

---

[33] III: 2, p. 36.

versalism it differs from philosophical universalism. Biblical universalism is, says Barth, not based upon man's inherent goodness. It in no way resembles the philosophical optimism of Leibniz and others. Biblical universalism wants to take sin seriously.

Man in himself and as such is utterly undeserving. He is under the wrath of God. He is blind.[34] His time is "problematic and unauthentic."[35] He is sinful and fallen. As such he is boastful of his own power.[36] He will not admit that he is lost and must live by the mercy of God[37] As a religious being he speaks but will not listen to the revelation of God. Moreover, his speaking and thinking is grasping and as such is contradictory of the revelation of God.[38] He is a fabricator of idols,[39] and is such because he thinks that he can possess the truth, failing to see that "no religion is true."[40] He seeks for a God beyond and apart from Christ, failing to realize that God can be known by God only.[41] He seeks for an analogy of God's knowledge in his own knowledge, not realizing that not he but only God is an authentic person.[42] When he thinks of God, he thinks of abstractions. He thinks of freedom rather than of God as free.[43] In all

this man as he is in himself is and thinks as an unbeliever, as a sinner, thinking and acting against the grace of God in Christ. . . .

The sin of man is therefore the act of rebellion against Christ as the electing God and the elected man. Christ as the electing God and elected man is the *Geschichte* of God saving all men. To understand the sin of man we must, accordingly, note that it is against God and his grace as expressed in the incarnation.

Jesus Christ as the electing God. The nature of sin can be understood only in terms of the cross of Christ where it was defeated by Christ as the victor over chaos. And Christ is victor over chaos because he is true God and true man. He is the electing God and the elected man. . . .

Jesus Christ as the elected man. The doctrine of the grace of God must also be studied by considering the fact that Jesus Christ is the elected man as well as the electing God. Failing to think of Christ as the electing God has made men fail to see both the freedom and the universality of grace. They then looked into the dreadful face of a God, beyond Christ, who arbitrarily might elect or might not elect them. Such arbitrariness is not true freedom. Such arbitrariness caused men to live in dread. And such arbitrariness excluded the universality as well as the freedom of grace.

Similarly failing to think of Christ as the elected man leads to the idea of grace as neither free nor universal. Let us then think with Barth of Christ

---

[34] I: 2, p. 33.
[35] *Ibid.*, p. 61.
[36] *Ibid.*, p. 67.
[37] *Ibid.*, p. 172.
[38] *Ibid.*, p. 330.
[39] *Ibid.*, p. 355.
[40] *Ibid.*, p. 356.
[41] II:1, pp. 47, 200.
[42] *Ibid.*, p. 305.
[43] *Ibid.*, p. 360.

as the elected man. This, as noted above, means first that Christ, and he alone, is *the* rejected man. As noted above, God's wrath must be appeased. Sin is real. Sin must be punished. But the wrath of God is a mode of His grace. Hence the punishment for the sin of man must be placed upon Jesus Christ as the God-man. Upon him the wrath of God expends itself completely. Thus other men must first of all be regarded as those whose sins are forgiven in Christ as their substitute. . . .

We see then that the freedom and the universality of grace are involved in Christ as the elected man. For as such He is, from eternity, the one who has borne the wrath of God for all men. Thus we have the objective completion of the work of redemption for all men once for all, because from eternity it was accomplished in Christ. . . .

Barth calls his position on election one of purified supralapsarianism. He calls it this in order to bring out the fact that grace is both sovereign and universal. Purified supralapsarianism hinges on the idea that Christ is both the electing God and the elected man. Having a proper view of grace, we know of no men and of no class of men who are permanently rejected of God. The form of the reprobate is a fleeing and disappearing one.[44] . . . It was Jesus Christ, alone true man, who alone was rejected of God.[45] Therefore the rejection of all other

men is inherently rejected by God. . . .

Beyond Romanism. At the time when Barth began the publication of the *Church Dogmatics* (1932), he said: "My whole work is concerned with the desperate question of achieving an evangelical theology which can stand worthily over against Roman Catholicism which I hold to be *the* great heresy."[46] And in the introduction to the first volume of that work, he thinks of the Romanist idea of *analogia entis* as a discovery of the Antichrist.

How then are we to meet this spirit of the Antichrist? Certainly not by setting over against the philosophy of Romanism another, a more Christian philosophy. We must have done with all philosophy. . . . We must start with Christ. In Him, and in Him alone, is the identity of being and knowing. Our whole approach must be Christological.

Of course, Roman Catholic theology is also Christological. Does it not subscribe to the Chalcedon creed? . . . Is there then anything lacking in Rome's Christology? Yes, there is! A true Christology must be one that speaks of Christ as Act, as *Geschichte*, "God is, who He is, in His works."[47] We may indeed concern ourselves with the being of God. But we must not think of being as prior to act. . . . Christ as *Geschichte* involves His contemporaneity with us. God in the fulness of His being is both wholly revealed and wholly hidden in the act

---

[44] II:2, p. 507.
[45] *Ibid.*, p. 506.

[46] *Theologische Blätter*, 1932, pp. 221–222.
[47] II:1, p. 291.

of His decision which is Jesus Christ. "There is not a moment in God's being outside of this act and decision."[48]

It is in terms of this Christ as the act and decision of God that Barth opposes Romanism. It is in terms of this Christ alone that the character of grace appears in its sovereign universality. It is in terms of this Christ that man is interpreted from above.

For here precisely, says Barth, the basic error of Rome is to be found. Romanism interprets man largely in terms of himself. Romanism claims to know to some extent what God is apart from Christ. That is to say, it has a natural theology. Romanism also claims to know to some extent what man is apart from Christ. It starts from man as a given intelligible something. The grace of God is not therefore given its rightful place of priority in the interpretations of man. Hence its claim that man is able to cooperate with the grace of God. Hence, in short, its synergism. Hence its claim that man knows the nature of sin before he knows grace. Hence also its claim to *possess* the truth about God and man and even about Christ. Hence, in short, its pride. Hence also its claim that the Church alone knows the truth. Hence its claim that there is no salvation outside the church as it understands the church. Hence, in short, its exclusiveness.

All of these objections of Barth against Romanism may, however, be said to have their center in the idea of *analogia entis*. He speaks of it as "the cardinal doctrine" of Romanism.[49] The Mariolatry of Rome is but an expression of it. In the *analogia entis* idea we have a misrepresentation of the whole God-man relation.

It is not that Barth wishes to reject every form of the analogy idea.[50] He does not wish to do this any more than he wishes to forbid us to speak of the being of God. But as he wishes us to speak of God as he is revealed in Christ, so he wishes us to speak of man primarily as the one who has faith in Christ. He wishes therefore to replace the analogy of being with the analogy of faith. He also calls this analogy of faith the analogy of relation. Man is to be interpreted from above through the relation that he sustains to Christ. Man can come to a true knowledge of God only if he has this knowledge in Christ.[51] Man is "taken up by the grace of God and determined to participation in the veracity of the revelation of God."[52] It is only when man is conquered by the grace of God that he truly knows God. It is only in Christ as his substitute that man can know God. But in Christ it is certain in advance that all men know God. It is thus from the point of view of Christ as *Geschichte* that Barth analyzes all Romanist theology and in particular the analogy of being idea.

The analogy of faith. The idea of analogy of being means primarily that man may start with an objective

---

[48] *Ibid.,* p. 305.

[49] *Ibid.,* p. 275.
[50] *Ibid.,* p. 256.
[51] *Ibid.,* p. 230.
[52] *Ibid.,* p. 239. Eng. tr., p. 213.

state of affairs.[53] Faith is . . . not a possibility inherent in man. "Faith takes its absolute or unconditioned rise in the Word of God, independently of inborn or inherited characteristics and possibilities in man. . . ."[54] It is only when in Christ we actually hear the Word that the possibility of hearing it is fixed. Our faith in Christ "arises and consists purely in the object of real knowledge."[55] Our faith as experience is at most a hint of the object to which it is attached. Where God is present in his revelation, he is always hidden in it. The moment we should wish to regard faith as in any way belonging to us, we should lose it.[56]

At this point we draw near to the precise distinction Barth makes between the analogy of being and the analogy of faith. . . . Speaking of man and his faith, Barth says: "By really apprehending the Word of God in faith he is actually made fit to apprehend it. . . . Apprehension of the Word of God could not take place, were there not in and along with this event something in common between God who speaks and man who hears, an analogy, a similarity, for all the dissimilarity involved in the difference between God and man, a 'point of contact' — now we may use this concept too — between God and man."[57]

How then, asks Barth, are we to distinguish our "conformity with God" from the Romanist idea of analogy of being? "Conformity with God" was the name we gave to the possibility of apprehending the Word of God. That is also expressed by the concept of the *imago Dei*. We must be quite clear that that puts us into hairbreadth proximity to the Catholic doctrine of the *analogia entis*. But even in and because of this proximity our doctrine will have to be quite a different one from that.[58]

In our analogy of faith we, therefore, stress the idea that it is man's *decision* that is similar to the decision of God. Only thus can we avoid the idea of the deification of man. The decision of man always depends on a prior decision of God. . . .

Barth rejects the *analogia entis* idea because it has no proper place for the priority of God in relation to man. It has no proper place for the sovereign freedom of God in his grace toward man. . . . The meaning of man's faith, of his freedom, of his will and of his knowledge, must all be interpreted from above. Man's faith, will and knowledge are what they are because their object is Christ.

Only thus can the sovereignty of grace in relation to man be maintained. . . . "It must be wholly and from the very first, and not merely occasionally or subsequently, a theology of revelation and grace, a Christological theology, if it is to speak at this point conclusively and effectively. If it is not this, or not this absolutely,

---

[53] Cf. Berkouwer, *The Triumph of Grace in the Theology of Karl Barth*, p. 181.

[54] I:1, p. 249.

[55] *Ibid.*, p. 250.

[56] *Idem.*

[57] I:1, p. 251.

[58] I:1, p. 252.

then the protest against the inversion will come too late and can never be effective."[59] "Thus our own opposition to the doctrine of the *scientia media* must have as its starting-point the simple recognition that the relation between God and the creature is grace, a free act of the divine mercy. This is true generally, and it is therefore true of the relation between His omnipotent knowledge and the free creaturely actions."[60]

Thus the basic fault of the Roman Catholic doctrine of grace is that it is not Christologically conceived. For this reason Romanism cannot do justice to grace as inherently given from above and as inherently universal. "The heart and guiding principle of the Romanist doctrine of grace is the negation of the unity of grace as always God's grace to man, as His sovereign act which is everywhere new and strange and free."[61]

8. J. Macquarrie[62] expounds Rudolf Bultmann's[63] concept of grace. For Bultmann grace is not a special quality of God but an event, which corresponds to the other event which we call the wrath of God. Grace is the event in which God restores to me and places within my grasp my lost possibility of authentic being, that is to say, the being which God intended in creation and from which man has fallen away into sin. Such grace is an act of forgiveness. . . .

Rudolf Bultmann's concept of grace. If conscience is one of the most obscure and confused concepts in the realm of ethics, the same might be said of grace in the realm of theology. On some theories it appears as a mysterious power — which comes near to being hypostatized — that enters men in some undefined way and takes control of them. As such it can be

"conveyed" in the sacraments, it can be "latent" or "active," it can be "stirred up," it can "infuse" righteousness. These all look like animistic ways of speaking, and while no doubt they point to realities of Christian experience, they can hardly be said to bring conceptual clarity to the understanding of what the experience of

---

[59] II:1, p. 658.
[60] *Ibid.*, p. 660.
[61] IV:1, p. 89.
[62] John Macquarrie of the University of Glasgow recently published a book on Bultmann, *The Scope of Demythologizing: Bultmann and His Critics* (Harper & Brothers, 1961). This excerpt is from a prior work of his, *An Existentialist Theology, A Comparison of Heidegger and Bultmann* (London: SCM Press Ltd., 1955), pp. 153–158, 181–192.

[63] Rudolf Bultmann was born on August 20, 1884, in Oldenburg in northern Germany. He is an outstanding contemporary existentialist theologian. Among his many published works are *Theology of the New Testament, Essays: Philosophical and Theological, Jesus and the Word, Jesus Christ and Mythology.* John Macquarrie seems to lean heavily on his *Theologie des Neuen Testaments* (hereafter *Th. des NT*), Tübingen, I, 1948, II, 1951, III, 1953 (E.T., *Theology of the New Testament*), S.C.M. Press, I, 1952, II, 1955.

grace is. Or again, grace may be said to be a quality of God, and may be contrasted with his wrath. But to speak of grace as a bare quality does not explain the experience of it in Christian living. A quality is perceived, but experience of divine grace is more than the perception of a certain quality in God.

Bultmann says that grace is not a special quality of God, and the New Testament does not suggest that we are to think of Him as gracious rather than wrathful.[64] But wrath is not a quality of God either — it is an event, namely, His judgment. God has created man responsible, with the possibility of gaining His true being or losing it. . . . In Saint Paul's words, "Everyone of us shall give account of himself to God."[65] My existence is not purely my own affair. When I lose myself, at the same time I lose God and am cast off from Him, I undergo His judgment and experience His wrath.

To believe in the grace of God, in Bultmann's view, is to believe in the possibility of being saved from his wrath. Grace also, then, is an event, which corresponds to that other event which we call the wrath of God. Grace is the event in which God restores to me and places within my grasp my lost possibility of authentic being, that is to say, the being which God intended in creation and from which man has fallen away into sin. Such grace is an act of forgiveness which delivers from past guilt and

breaks the power of sin over human life. For it was because of past sins that man was fallen into a situation in which to choose his authentic being was no longer an *existentiell* possibility for him. But into that situation came the event of God's grace, restoring the possibility and therefore blotting out the past, in the sense that man was delivered from that alienation from himself and from God into which his past had brought him. The event of grace, therefore, means both a deliverance from the past — forgiveness — and a new possibility for the future, from which, because of his past, man was hitherto cut off, so that it could only be restored to him from outside himself.

With the concept of grace (*charis*) we see how the New Testament — and with it, of course Christian thought in general — understands the possibility of a transition from fallen to authentic existence, and the irreducible difference which here separates Christian theology from atheistic existentialism. For the Christian it is God who gives to man the *existentiell* possibility of authentic being, though admittedly the gift can only be given because man in his fallen existence retains the existential possibility — if not, he would have ceased to be man. And with that existential possibility goes the possibility of having conscience, and the possibility of understanding and appropriating the gift of grace. . . .

Closely connected with the concept of grace is the other New Testament

---

[64] *Th. des NT*, p. 283.
[65] Rom 14:12.

concept of justification, the making just (*dikaios*) or righteous of someone who was in the opposite condition, which also implies a notion of transition. It is in connection with this concept that the contrast of the Christian view of man's attaining his true being through grace with all other possible views comes out most clearly. The Jews sought a legal righteousness, based on fulfilling the demands of the law. The non-theistic existentialist seeks a righteousness or authenticity based on effort of will and stern resolve. Both depend upon human striving, yet both are impossible of attainment because of human fallenness. Saint Paul on the other hands says, "We conclude that a man is justified by faith without the deeds of the law."[66] The kind of righteousness visualized here is neither legal nor ethical, but, in Bultmann's phrase, forensic. It implies a new relation to God, who is his Judge. And the new relation consists precisely in this, that man counts for nothing all his own striving and achievement, and recognizes that his true life is God's gift to him. He ceases to live by his own power, and surrenders himself to God. And this understanding of the Christian life is one on which Bultmann lays great emphasis.

Grace, on Bultmann's interpretation, is to be understood as an event. But what event? It is the event constituted by the mighty acts, the saving events (*Heilsgeschehen*) which God wrought in Jesus Christ. These mighty acts,

[66] Rom 3:28.

coming into the human situation from outside, that is to say, from God Himself, made possible forgiveness in so far as man was delivered from enslavement to his own past, from which he could never have freed himself, and at the same time made possible a new life in so far as Christ brought back to man his lost possibility of authentic existence as the child of God. For Bultmann, therefore, the work of God in Jesus Christ, or in other words, the grace of God given in Christ, is unique and decisive for human existence, and constitutes the only way to man's salvation.

This is worth pointing out, because Bultmann's radical criticism of some traditional elements in the Christian faith may cause the careless student of his thought to lose sight of the fact that on this central issue Bultmann stands firmly on the ground of historic conviction. Bultmann — and here again we point out that he has much in common with Barth — is actually far more orthodox, in the best sense of the term, than much of the liberal theology of last century which tended to think of the coming of Christ as simply the highest manifestation of God, continuous with and not differing in kind from the manifestations of God in conscience, in nature, and in non-Christian religions. But for Bultmann it is an event on a different plane altogether. It may be called supernatural in the sense that it is a true intervention from outside into man's situation — and in no other way can man be saved, if the preceding analysis of his being is anywhere near the truth at all. Bultmann is influenced by existentialism and he makes no secret of it, as we know, but that does not prevent him from seeing perfectly plainly the place where Christianity and existentialism part company, and the distinctive indispensable element in Christianity as a supernatural religion which no philosophy can supply.

To return to the argument, grace is an event, namely, the act of God in Christ. But is not that a past event, whereas grace is surely present? Can we accept this simple identification of grace with the saving event which occurred once for all nearly two thousand years ago? Bultmann's reply to that would be that grace — and, of course, that means the saving event itself — is present whenever the Word is proclaimed and authentically heard, so that to the hearer of the Word is restored his lost possibility of gaining his true being. That possibility is placed before him as something for which he can decide — and for which he may, in fact, decide in the act of faith. It is in this way that the mighty acts touch his existence now, and so grace is present.

Here we have evidence of the strong evangelical and Protestant influence in Bultmann's thought. His concern is with the proclamation of the gospel to the world. It follows that he attaches great importance to preaching, and the sacraments also he regards as ways of proclaiming the Word. No doubt the Word can be proclaimed and heard in other ways also — for instance, simply in the reading of the New Testament. But in whatever way the Word may be proclaimed and heard, the point is that, in such proclaiming and hearing, grace is present to me, the saving events are significant to my existence now.

To say that anything is significant for my existence means that it presents me with a possibility — and that is precisely what the divine grace does, as we have seen. It presents to man the possibility of attaining his true being. . . . We noted at the very outset that Bultmann goes to the New Testament with the question of human existence in mind. The question is, What does this mean for my existence? or alternatively, What possibility is presented to me here? . . . In the case of the mighty acts, in order that a possibility may be presented to me now, or — which is the same thing — in order that the event may be significant for my existence, it is necessary, as Bultmann contends, that grace, which is itself the saving event, should be present to me in the proclaiming and hearing of the Word. But if that is so, then the saving events are not merely past historical happenings — not just facts of history, as we commonly understand that expression. Thus, of the resurrection of our Lord, Bultmann claims that belief in the resurrection is identical with the belief that the Risen One is present in the Word now proclaimed.[67] The past event is at the same time present event, and it is the present event that is significant for my existence — it is

[67] *Th. des NT*, p. 301.

the grace by which I can experience forgiveness and have the possibility of new life.

But is this not the abandonment of the position stated earlier, when it was said that Bultmann identified grace with the saving events wrought by God in Jesus Christ? These events had a once-for-all character (*Einmaligkeit*) and can be assigned to a definite period of history. But now it appears that grace is a whole series of events, and repeats itself every time the Word is proclaimed and heard. But Bultmann would deny that there is any contradiction here. We have not a series of different events, but one event — albeit an event of a peculiar kind. Bultmann calls it an eschatological event. It is past, in the sense that some nineteen centuries ago God acted in a decisive way and intervened in man's situation. It is present, not merely in the sense that there remain with us the abiding consequences of what happened in the past, but more importantly in the sense that God acts now in a decisive way and intervenes in my situation, and only for that reason can the event be called a saving event, significant for my existence and relevant to men today. . . .

The mighty acts. . . . We generally speak of the mighty acts in the plural. Bultmann prefers to think of one unitary act centred in the cross, to which both the resurrection and the incarnation must be related for them to have significance. This concept of a unitary act in which the cross is pre-eminent seems at first sight acceptable enough. Clearly the mighty acts are a unity in that they all belong to Christ. And further, as Bultmann shows, their unity is explicitly stated in the New Testament. Saint Paul frequently brings cross and resurrection together in a unity, and nowhere more significantly than in his remarks on baptism.[68] Cross and incarnation are likewise brought together.[69] Thus it would seem legitimate to consider the mighty acts as a unity centred in the cross. . . .

However, having once criticized Bultmann for what we consider to be his reckless and arbitrary denial of an objective-historical element in the resurrection, we now turn to the appreciation of his positive teaching on the subject. Briefly that teaching is that for Christian faith and for theology as the exposition of Christian faith the primary understanding of the resurrection is the understanding of an existential-historical or eschatological event. Just as faith in the cross was said to be not simply the belief that Jesus was once crucified but rather that in the cross God offers me a possibility of existence now, so belief in the resurrection is not simply belief that a miracle once happened but a belief that a miracle of new life can happen now for me. . . .

For faith, the resurrection is present. It is understood not as past objective happening, but as the present possibility of new life which God offers in Christ and for which man may decide. This is the existential-

[68] Rom 6:2–5; cf. also Rom 4:25; 1 Cor 15:3–4.
[69] Cf. 2 Cor 8:9; Phil 2:6 ff.

historical understanding of the resurrection which is an eschatological event, an event containing authentic repeatable possibility. "The belief in the resurrection of Christ," says Bultmann, "and the belief that in the proclamation of the Word Christ himself — yes, God himself, — speaks, are identical."[70] Bearing in mind the reservation that we have made earlier, we may say that this statement sets out the essential significance of the resurrection for Christian faith. We do not prove or accept without proof — that something once happened, and go on to deduce what that happening now means for us. We begin with the present possibility which Christ offers in the proclaiming and hearing of the Word, and from that we infer that something did once happen, but precisely what that something was is a matter for academic speculation only and of no particular relevance to faith. . . .

But this view of the idealists is poles apart from Bultmann's position.

[70] *Th. des NT*, p. 301.

The idealist identifies the essence of Christianity with a high philosophy of the universe, but for Bultmann Christianity is a religion with saving power. For the idealist the mighty acts become mere optional symbols of suprarational truth, but for Bultmann they constitute God's unique act of grace. For the idealist the significance of these acts for the individual is a purely intellectual one, but for Bultmann they summon to a decision, in so far as they present a possibility of existence. Thus when his view is compared with that of idealist theologizing, it will be seen that it is not Bultmann who destroys the historical. His aim is not to destroy the historical foundation of our religion, but to exhibit it in its cosmic dimensions as authentic repeatable possibility, significant for the existence of men today. In his own words, it is the case "of a historical Person and his Destiny being raised to eschatological rank."[71]

[71] *Ibid.*

XIII

GRACE IN NINETEENTH- AND
TWENTIETH-CENTURY ORTHODOX THEOLOGY

1. Frank Gavin[1] sees the development of the theology of grace in the Eastern Church as largely a modern achievement. The doctrine of grace is bound up with the doctrine of God and of man and of redemption. Grace is necessary, it is free, and it is universal but not irresistible. In general, Roman and Orthodox teaching agree as to the conditions and terms of justification, against the Protestant theory of justification by faith alone.

The sources of modern Orthodox teaching. In the first place the de-

[1] Frank Gavin: ch. VIII, n. 1, p. 35. This excerpt is taken from his book, *Some Aspects of Contemporary Greek Orthodox Thought* (London: S.P.C.K., 1923 [1936]), pp. 206–223, 226–236.

velopment of the theology of Grace, so far as concerns the Eastern Church, is in the largest degree a modern achievement. For practically all the explicit teaching we are dependent upon the work of synods and councils subsequent to the Ecumenical Councils for the basis of the material of this and the following lectures. This brings up the question, Of what weight are the dogmatic formulations of Orthodoxy since the time of the Ecumenical Councils? As we saw[2] the full tradition of the Church includes more than the decrees of the Ecumenical Councils, since important doctrines of the Church — the Sacraments, Justification, and the like — were not enunciated until after the Schism.[3]

Rhôsse holds that the decrees and definitions of the Councils and Synods of the 16th century and on, have binding force upon every true member of the Orthodox Church;[4] Mesolora says that they have not the obligatory character of the Creed and of the Seven Ecumenical Councils, but are only of illustrative and secondary value;[5] Androutsos calls them "secondary authorities." . . .

It is apparent then, that the subsequent ratification of the acts of a local synod by other assemblies or councils accords to such acts a real, definite and *binding* authority; and that the reason prompting such ratification and validation, in the case of dogmatic pronouncements, is their consistency in doctrine and its formulation with what had been defined[6]

before by the chief authorities of the Orthodox Church — the Bible, and Sacred Tradition, that is, the Ecumenical Councils and the teaching of the Fathers. There is then a genuine and actual development of doctrine in the Orthodox Church, and an adequate organ for its formulation, Palmieri to the contrary notwithstanding.[7] The Orthodox Church claims that she "has never added to nor changed what had been decreed by the Ecumenical Councils. . . . Her dogmas are those of the early Church. . . . Her teaching is primitive Christianity. . . . She holds unaltered and immutable the primitive and genuine Christianity of the first eight centuries, which was first preached by the Apostles in the Greek countries and in the Greek language."[8] The Vincentian canon, according to Rhôsse, is "in harmony with the local and sectional councils of the Eastern Church and with them only" — that is, in contrast to Roman development — "for they have neither added to, nor taken away from the dogmas of the ancient Catholic Church of the time before the Schism, but remain faithful to them, thus by their unanimity of teaching and true orthodoxy forming the continuation, truly and canonically, of the ancient Catholic Church."[9] What is taught then by the synods of the sixteenth century and on, being only the amplification and formulation in explicit language of the teaching of

[2] In Lecture I, pp. 27–30.
[3] Rhôsse, *Dogmatike*, pp. 59–60 and n.
[4] *Ibid.*
[5] I. E. Mesolora, *Sumbolike tes orthodoxou anatolikes Ekklesias* (Athens, 1883), Vol. I, pp. 12–13.
[6] Cf. Sakellaropoulos, *Ekklesiastikon dikaion tes anatolikes orthodoxou Ekklesias* (Athens, 1898), p. 37.
[7] Cf. *Theologia Dogm. Orth.*, Vol. 1, Ch. 3, particularly p. 63 ff.
[8] *Antipapika*, Diomede Kyriakos (Athens, 1893), pp. 28, 46.
[9] *Dogmatike*, pp. 103–104.

the Catholic Church, has for all practical purposes the authority of dogma for the Orthodox Church.

The explicit formulation of the doctrine of Grace, Justification, the Church[10] and the Sacraments is due chiefly to the local synods and councils subsequent to the Reformation. . . . The effect of the Reformation on the Orthodox Church is seen in the work of the seventeenth-century Synods. It is not my purpose here to discuss the history of the times in which the various "Symbolic Books" and *Confessions* had their origin, nor to enter upon the various questions as to authorship, sources, causes, and occasions which provoked them. Our interest in them is solely because they are sources for the dogmatic teaching of the Orthodox Church. With the exception of the *Confession of Gennadius Scholarius*,[11] written sometime between 1453 and 1468, all the remaining Symbolic Books were the result entirely of the Reformation, directly or indirectly. These texts include: (a) The *Answers* of the Patriarch Jeremiah II to the Tübingen theologians, of the years 1576, 1579, and 1581, which while they were written against the Lutherans, yet have little polemic coloring, and do not show a controversial spirit.[12] They deal practically with the whole range of the Orthodox Faith, with special emphasis on matters of difference between Orthodoxy and Lutheranism. (b) The *Confession* of Metrophanes Kritopoulos, Patriarch of Alexandria, written at Lemstadt in 1625 at the request of Lutheran friends. It is so sympathetic with Protestant thought and so conversant with Protestant terminology as to lend color to the accusation of being heretical and not truly Orthodox.[13] (c) The *Orthodox Confession* of Peter Mogila, Metropolitan of Kiev,[14] which appeared in Greek for the first time in its present form probably about 1667.[15] The *Con-*

---

arch of Constantinople (1555–1565), relations between the Orthodox and the Lutherans were initiated, which developed in 1573 in a mission of the Lutherans to Constantinople. . . . In the year 1576 Jeremiah II (Tranos, Patriarch 1572–1579, 1580–1584, 1588–1595) whom Meletios calls "a man endowed with every virtue" . . . wrote his first "Answer," discussing the Confession of Augsburg (text in Mesolora, I, pp. 124–194, preceded by historical notes and introduction, pp. 78–123 *ibid.*). . . . Palmieri says of the *Answers* that they expound Orthodox doctrine by appealing to tradition, are without either the style or color of polemic, and are rightly included among the Symbolic Books (*op. cit.*, p. 458).

[13] Born in 1599, Kritopoulos became a monk of Mt. Athos and was singled out for distinction by Cyril Lucar, who sent him to England, in 1616, where he studied at Oxford. He went to the Continent in 1623, traveled extensively, and in 1625 wrote his *Confession*.

[14] Born 1596, died 1646.

[15] Following Legrand, *Bibliographie hellénique* (XVII siècle), Vol. IV (Paris, 1896), and Vol. II, *ibid.*, p. 204. . . . Mogila had two practical difficulties with which to deal: (a) the Roman Church, with its strong hold on Poland, the policy

---

[10] "The doctrine of the Church, from the (time of the) Reformation, became particularly the 'sign spoken against' about which all other dogmatic differences center." Androutsos, *Sumbolike*, p. 56.

[11] Introduction and text in Mesolora, *op. cit.*, I, pp. 66–67; on him cf. Palmieri, *op. cit.*, pp. 434–441.

[12] During the reign of Joasaph II. Patri-

fession is divided into three sections, on *Faith, Hope,* and *Love,* and in a popular and brief style treats of the fundamentals of Orthodoxy. (d) The *Acts* of the Synods of Constantinople (1638), Jassy (1641–1642), Jerusalem (1672)[16] and Constantinople (1672). Of these Synods, by far the most significant is that of Jerusalem. All of them dealt with practical problems arising out of the *Confession* of Cyril Lucar, which was strongly Calvinistic in tone. The difficulties of the Orthodox Church were many — pressure from Continental Protestantism, from Roman proselytism under French protection, and the normal difficulties of the Church under Turkish domination. *The Confession of Faith* of Dositheus, appended to the *Acts* of the Synod of Jerusalem, contains mat-

ter of fundamental value for the student of modern Orthodox theology. The last Synod (Constantinople, 1672)[17] did little of import. Its acts are mostly of a practical character, and concern discipline and practice rather than dogma and theology.

Despite the fact that Orthodoxy and Protestantism have in common as essential characteristics a strongly anti-Roman and anti-Papal bias, despite the fact also that they both appeal to primitive Christianity, the upshot of all the negotiations between Continental Protestantism and the Orthodox Church was the discovery that there really was nothing fundamental in theology or spirit upon the basis of which Orthodoxy and Protestantism could unite. It is significant that with the exception of the abortive attempt of the Non-Jurors, no Anglican advances have yet met Orthodox repudiation. All of the later synods direct their fulminations against Calvinistic and Lutheran doctrines. It is also significant that in the main the development of Greek theology has paralleled that of the Western Church. The doctrine of Grace, the Church, and the Sacraments is indigenous, legitimate, and inevitable in both East and West. In both East and West the formulation of doctrine has taken place subsequent to the Schism between the Eastern and Western Churches.

---

of the Uniat movement, and the presence of the Jesuits; and (b) Protestantism, which had no inconsiderable influence at this juncture on Orthodoxy, disrupted by the defection of Cyril Lucar, and unable to cope with Western scholarship and learning. The first sentence of the *Confession* comes into sharp conflict with Protestantism on the subject of faith and works . . . while the treatment of the *Filioque* leaves no room for the suspicion of a pro-Roman tendency. Its final endorsement by Nectarius of Constantinople, Joannicius of Alexandria, Macarius of Antioch, Paisius of Jerusalem, nine metropolitans, and others, in 1662, set the seal of Orthodox official approval on the *Confession*.

[16] These *Acts* are all in Mesolora, *op. cit.,* vol. II. On pp. 7–24 he gives a history of Cyril Lucar leading up to an introduction to the Synod of Constantinople (pp. 24–28), acts af the same (pp. 28–32); introduction to the Synod of Jassy (pp. 32–37), the two *Epistles* (pp. 37–42); introduction to the Council of Jerusalem (pp. 43–54) and texts of the *Acts* (pp. 55–87).

---

[17] It was convened by Dionysius IV, five times Patriarch of Constantinople (1671–1673; 1676–1679; 1683–1684; 1686–1687; 1693–1694), as an answer to difficulties propounded to the Orthodox Church, many of which reflect Protestant stimulation. . . .

The Doctrine of Grace.

1. The nature of grace. During the sixteenth and seventeenth centuries the minds of men in the West were occupied with questions concerning the doctrine of grace, faith, free will, predestination, and the efficacy of the sacraments. To this movement of thought in the West, with its parallel effect in Orthodox circles, we are indebted for the explicit definition of Orthodox teaching on these matters.

The doctrine of Grace has a very wide range of contact in any Christian dogmatic system. In Orthodox doctrine this is particularly true. (a) It is bound up with the doctrine of God, since God who is preeminently good, and acts freely in all He does, freely created man of His own goodness and benevolence. So it is of His nature as Christians know it, that He give to man, beyond man's deserts and without the consideration of expediency or of a covenant obligation, what is so essential to man's needs. In this sense Rhôsse speaks of the Grace of the Holy Spirit of God cooperating with man's natural endowment, the cooperation of man with it constituting his pristine state of righteousness and innocence.[18] (b) The doctrine of Grace is closely knit up with the teaching about man, who being created by God with relative free will, endowed by Him with all he needed to lead a life of happiness in obedience to God, was yet to be sustained by God's constant protection and empowering oversight. Still more did man after his Fall stand in need of that without which he could never hope for recovery, the gift of which is so entirely consistent with God's Nature and Essence. (c) The doctrine of Grace is intimately connected with the problem of man's free will and God's Providence, His Foreknowledge and Foreordination. (d) Preeminently is the doctrine of Grace involved in the dogma of Redemption, for by Grace only can man appropriate the fruits of the redemptive and atoning work of the Saviour and make them effective in his own individual life. As Christian dogma forms a unified whole, so the whole nexus of doctrine, especially in its practical religious and moral bearings, is permeated with the teaching about Grace. It is obvious also that this doctrine constitutes the starting point and basis for all of the rest of Orthodox dogmatic.

Definition of Grace. Androutsos' definition of Grace involves its relation to the doctrine of the Church and of the Sacraments. "Grace is," he says,[19] "the divine power by which we appropriate the redemptive work of Our Lord. Since it works the justification and salvation of man it depends upon certain subjective conditions in him. It is stored up in the Church, and administered through the Sacra-

---

[18] Rhôsse, *Dogmatike,* p. 434.

[19] Androutsos, *Dogmatike,* pp. 218–219. He takes occasion to note the various distinctions and definitions, such as a "prevenient and concomitant," "external and internal," etc. of scholastic terminology, but says that they are "without actual content or significance" (*ibid.*).

ments. . . . In general, it is the manifestation of the love and benevolence of God towards man; in particular, it means the saving power of God by which He brings home to each individual the Redemption consummated for all by our Lord, regenerating and cultivating the life in Christ and preparing (man) for eternal life." "By the death of our Lord on the Cross, who was the Mediator between God and Man, mankind was reconciled with its God and Father, thereby was reestablished the relation of fellowship with God, sundered because of original sin, and God's saving Grace made known to man. This Grace we need to lay hold of through faith in Christ generated by love, by which we become God's children. . . . The redeeming work of the Saviour is called divine Grace because by it salvation is bestowed from God on us. . . . The continuous operation and energy of the Holy Spirit is also (called) divine Grace. . . . In this sense, then, it may be defined as that supernatural power of the Holy Spirit by which the appropriation of the redeeming work of the Saviour is achieved."[20] In the divine economy the ministry of Grace is the work of the Holy Spirit, while our Lord is the cause of our receiving it. This is testified in Holy Scripture, and is the reason for calling the Holy Ghost, "the Spirit of Christ."[21] The term is applied not to natural helps towards righteousness, nor to the example of

Our Lord's life, nor to God's law, but to that "power which regenerates and nourishes the spiritual life, given freely by God and not by reason of our merit."[22]

Three characteristic notes of grace. We may distinguish three characteristic notes of Grace, all of which are essential to the true conception of it. It is (a) absolutely necessary, (b) it is free, and (c) it is universal. It is absolutely *necessary* "since man cannot be justified and saved by his own works, nor could he even believe unless Christ first draw him, and unless . . . his will be aroused by some higher energy."[23] . . . Grace is, in short, as necessary as was Redemption: if the work of Christ was an unnecessary work on God's part, then so is Grace unnecessary, as the Pelagians held."[24]

Grace is, secondly, *free,* as the very word implies. This means that it is based upon no human covenant, whereby it is given by God as the fulfilment of a promise or an obligation. It is not a return for human merit or deserving, but a free gift of God's love.[25]

Thirdly, grace is *universal,* but not *irresistible.* "The Grace of Redemption is offered to all men, calling them to salvation and assisting them to every good work. If some accept the call, many on the other hand approach . . .

---

[20] Mesolora, *op. cit.,* III, pp. 243–244.
[21] Rom 5:5; 8:9; Gal 4:6; Acts 1:8; 2:33; 10:44; Jn 6:44; Eph 3:5.
[22] Androutsos, *op. cit.*
[23] Mesolora, *op. cit.,* p. 247, and cf. Jn 3:5.
[24] Androutsos, *op. cit.,* p. 221, and cf. Mesolora, *op. cit.,* p. 246. The Pelagians were condemned by the Council of Carthage.
[25] Rom 9:11, 18; 11:6; 2 Tm 1:9; Ti 3:5.

but fall away from it, which phenomenon is to be attributed to the free will of man who may accept or reject the call and fall from Grace. Since all that happens in time and in the world is constituted by the eternal will and design of God, and the Redemption in a very special sense is, as we have seen, the carrying out of God's eternal will, it is clear that the election of some to life in Christ and the rejection of others are things determined and decreed before the world by God. Before the foundation of the world He chose them, foreordaining some to eternal life, and others to eternal condemnation."[26] . . . Nor does it contravene either the goodness or righteousness of God, who wills that all be saved and all come to the knowledge of the truth. . . . The foreordination which St. Paul speaks of[27] is founded upon the foreknowledge of God, which takes for granted the existence of the rational use by man of his natural light, or the innate law of God in him . . . together with his free will. God knows in advance those who are to be worthy of His Grace, which prevents, helps, and calls all men, of whom some by the right use of their reason, will and knowledge of the good, lay hold of it and are thereby justified, and others, making no use of these faculties . . . stand apart from God, and are thus self-ordained to condemnation; while God foresaw what they would do. . . . He did not foreordain them to it, inasmuch as He simply knew in advance what would happen. . . .

2. The operation of Grace. The operation of Grace in the concrete is regarded properly as a process — a progress and development of the individual in the Christian life, beginning with conversion and regeneration and ending in the glory to which man is called. Six states of this progress have been enumerated by different Orthodox theologians: the *call, conversion, regeneration, justification, sanctification,* and *mystical union.* Thus Antonius[28] and Mesolora.[29] Androutsos does not see the necessity of this division and on the basis of Rom 8:29–30 distinguishes: (a) "the *call, or conversion or preparation for justification,* (b) *justification or sanctification,* and (c) *glory* — in which justification holds the middle place following the *call* and preceding *glory.*"[30]

(a) The *call* is comprised of two elements — the external, the preaching of the word, and the internal, the receptive attitude of man by which he through Grace accepts the invitation of God. This action of Grace on the inner man creates the *fidem informem* by which he is disposed to accept God's revelation, and directly affects his whole spiritual nature, bringing into him the graces of faith, hope and love.[31] "This preparation is the *sine quo non* and condition of justification . . . not the efficient cause of it. Man cannot merit the gift of justify-

---

[26] Androutsos, *loc. cit.*
[27] Rom 8:29–30.

[28] *Dogmatike theologia,* p. 275 ff.
[29] *Op. cit.,* III, pp. 254–269.
[30] *Op. cit.,* pp. 229–230.
[31] Cf. Dositheus in Mesolora, *op. cit.,* II, p. 104.

ing Grace in the sense that God is bound to give it to him in return for his meritorious acts.

(b) "Justification as an actual change in man is both the doing away with sin and guilt, and the implanting of a new life; . . . negatively, the remission of sins, and positively, sanctification. So justification and salvation are often used interchangeably, and it may be said either that man is *justified* or that he is *saved*, by faith and works. If men died immediately after justification they are saved, just as much as, if they live thence forward without falling from Grace, they are potentially inheritors of eternal life which is dependent on justification. The two elements, forgiveness of sins and sanctification, are not separate from each other in time as if sanctification followed upon cleansing from sin, but they are two aspects of one and the same thing. . . . This remission of sins is no mere imputation of freedom from sin . . . but an actual effacement of it. The judge in pronouncing an accused man innocent does not make him so, but only publicly proclaims him what he already is. But God in judging a sinner does not regard him as righteous while he is a sinner, but makes him actually righteous. . . . The state of sin is removed entirely by God's power in the act of justification. We say 'entirely' because while the impulse to sin yet remains in the justified, it is not accounted to him as sin, since his will does not follow the tendency of this impulse to sin."[32]

[32] *Dogmatike*, pp. 231–233.

"Inasmuch as sanctification constitutes . . . the essence of justification, it is obvious that justification, according to both Orthodox and Roman teaching, is different in individual believers, and capable of greater development and progress."[33] . . . We may fall from Grace any time: "he that thinketh he standeth must take heed lest he fall."[34] Consequently "no one may be sure of his own salvation nor may be predict with certainty that he will be able to keep himself from grievous sins in the future and remain in (the state of) justification."[35]

3. Faith and good works. The one and only way by which we may appropriate the merit of our Saviour and come to apprehend it by sanctification, is *faith*, which means obedience to the voice of God. "Faith is not a mere acceptance of the truths of the Faith, but a cleaving to the Saviour and an adherence to His work bound up with acceptance of Gospel Truth. It is not only a work of the intellect, but is above all moral . . . since giving up this world and cleaving to the Saviour means to love Him, which love takes for granted the action of the will."[36] "Whether one say that faith or love or good works or the carrying out of God's commandments justify and save, it is all one, because of the intimate connection between faith and love. . . . The full statement . . . which includes both the

[33] *Ibid.*, pp. 237–238.
[34] 1 Cor 10:12, and cf. Rom 11:20; 1 Cor 9:27.
[35] Androutsos, *Dogmatike*, p. 241, and cf. pp. 238–240.
[36] *Ibid.*, pp. 241–242.

theoretical and practical element . . . is the proposition that man is justified through faith that worketh by love."[37]

Androutsos, while admitting two senses of the word in St. Paul's and St. James' usage, does not regard them as necessarily different and mutually exclusive, and so does not solve the problem of justification by this method. "Both[38] are talking about different aspects of the one process. St. James, consistently with his practical aim, ranges works over against faith, as something standing by itself and establishing a proper equilibrium, but elsewhere[39] frequently postulates the organic union of both, discussing faith as the foundation of works and works as the complement of faith. . . . St. Paul lays down the terms of justification according to their internal organic connection.". . .

The Protestant objection to the doctrine of faith and works as taught by the Orthodox Church, is that "works" bring about a certain sense of merit and pride in the believer, and hence the view that they are essential may not be accepted. As Mesolora says: "The Christian may not boast about his good works nor believe that he can be justified through them alone, for . . . our justification depends in the first place upon divine Grace and the merits of the Saviour from whom we have our faith as a free gift. . . . Our Church teaches that faith only cannot justify or sanctify a man, nor can good works of themselves per-

fectly fulfil the divine will, since they are not sufficient for salvation without faith . . . but are well pleasing to God and necessary to salvation . . . demonstrating the life and power of God's Grace in us, and our appropriation of the redeeming work of Christ."[40] Protestantism is wrong in refusing any merit to good works. . . . Furthermore . . . the merit of our works may not exceed the measure of our duty."[41] . . . Consequently the Roman doctrine of "works of supererogation" and "the treasury of merits" is a teaching which is both unjustified and unreasonable."[42]. . . The Roman doctrine of the superabundant merits of the Saints, which may be applied to those yet in debt, has no foundation in Holy Scripture, for "the Saints may be helped by the prayers of the faithful."[43]

In general, Roman and Orthodox teaching agree[44] as to the conditions

[37] Ibid., p. 242.
[38] Cf. Jas 2:24; Gal 5:6.
[39] E.g., 1:3, 4; 2:17, 18, 20, 24–26.

[40] Mesolora, op. cit., III, pp. 275, 279.
[41] Androutsos, Dogmatike, p. 249.
[42] For a full discussion of the Roman doctrine and of the Orthodox position against it, cf. Androutsos' Sumbolike, p. 235 ff.
[43] Androutsos, Dogmatike, pp. 249–250.
[44] Androutsos, op. cit., p. 251. With this statement many Orthodox theologians disagree, e.g., Mesolora, op. cit., II, p. 263; Damalas, Peri arxon, p. 151; Balanos, Krisis tes Dogmatikes . . . pp. 41, 58, and Dyobouniotes, Opheil. apantesis, pp. 96–99. The latter says: "There is no possibility of doubt that the basis of the doctrine of justification is the teaching about the original state of man, and the doctrine of the Fall. Since Roman and Orthodox doctrine differ widely on this point, it follows that their doctrine of justification must be different. . . . Not only do they differ as to infused Grace but also as to the merit of good works . . . as Philaret of Moscow observes,

and terms of justification, against the Protestant theory of justification by faith only. "While Orthodox teaching regards justifying faith as naturally manifesting itself in good works, the Protestants regard it as a passive and receptive organ only and think that God justifies a man as he believes (that is, 'accepts'), not as he loves, thus forcibly sundering faith and works; they are worlds apart from the teaching of Orthodoxy."[45]

2. Metropolite Seraphim[46] considers the redemption not the entirely exterior act of pardon of sins on the part of God but also the real renovation, the rebirth of human nature by the aid of a divine force, the grace of the Holy Spirit. The Holy Spirit operates the new birth, gives the true spiritual life and appropriates to the faithful the work of salvation realized by Jesus.

The work of redemption. . . . It goes without saying that among all these gifts of Christ bringing salvation to men, there is comprised the pardon of sins that reconciles men with God and reestablishes communion with Him. Man participates in this salvation because Christ has become the new chief (head) of humanity, who has recapitulated humanity. As such He is also called the "second Adam" as head of the humanity redeemed by Him. This forms in its ensemble a unique spiritual organism, a unity in a multiplicity of persons. This is why the redemption accomplished by Christ extends to the totality of the human race. . . .

The work of salvation accomplished by Christ comprises also a re-established union between men and the Holy Spirit. For the redemption is not the entirely exterior act of pardon of sins on the part of God; it is also the real renovation, the rebirth of human nature. This can be accomplished only by the aid of a divine force, the grace of the Holy Spirit.

even if the distinction be a delicate one" (pp. 97–98, *Opheil. apant.*). Androutsos denies that this deduction follows from the premises (*Dogm. Meletai*, A, p. 105). "Justification, both according to our own and the Roman teaching, is not only the removal of sin but an actual change and renewal of the inner man, as teach Damalas and Mesolora. . . . The Roman phrase, *virtus infusa* . . . is a technical term . . . to mean the steadfast turning of the man towards God . . . which is a common doctrine of all who hold justification to be a moral matter." "If there be any difference between us and the Latins as to the terms of justification, these are in respect to practice not theory," and to the deductions made by Rome from legitimate doctrine. (Androutsos, *Dogmatike*, pp. 251–252, n., and his *Sumbolike*, p. 215 ff.)

[45] Androutsos, *Dogmatike*, pp. 251–252.

[46] Metropolite Seraphim, spiritual head of the vast ecclesiastical Orthodox province comprising all of central Europe, and at the same time archbishop of Berlin and of Germany, is the author of the first part and redactor of the entire book entitled *L'Eglise Orthodoxe*, Les dogmes, la liturgie, la vie spirituelle (Traduction Francaise de Jacques Marty Docteur en Theologie) published by Payot, Paris. This excerpt is selected from pp. 36–43.

There is question of the Spirit of Pentecost, promised and then sent by Christ to His disciples. The Holy Spirit operates the new birth, gives the true spiritual life and appropriates to the faithful the work of salvation realised by Jesus. Every man redeemed by Christ is then a bearer of the Spirit. Without the Holy Spirit, human nature would remain in its anterior state, and man would not have part in the power of the grace without which he cannot conquer sin and put on again justice and sanctity. Without the Holy Spirit he would not have any hope of immortality, since the Holy Spirit is the unique dispenser of life.

Orthodox soteriology also comprehends the idea of deification. "God has become man so that man may become God," expresses the fundamental principle of the orthodox doctrine of salvation. This deification is expounded not only in the works of the fathers and doctors of the Church but also in the liturgical books. But naturally it does not mean that man becomes God according to essence but only according to grace. . . .

The incarnation of the Word of God is evidently the principle of this deification, or to put it more precisely the divinisation of those redeemed by Christ is the consequence of the incarnation of the divine Logos. By the hypostatic union of the two natures, the divine and the human, in Jesus Christ the God-man, his human nature was divinised, deified. But by His human nature the Word made flesh is organically united to all humanity and thus our human nature too is divinised. Since the effect of deifying grace depends on the degree of union between the human individual and Christ, deification for most men is not yet a real fact but it is given to all of them as a real possibility in *potentia*. . . .

From this it follows that the salvation and redemption of man is absolutely a work of God, a work of the love of the heavenly Father and of the incarnate Son of God and of the grace of the Holy Spirit. The new birth and renovation and sanctification and deification of man are the gifts of God and at the same time consequences of the work of salvation accomplished by Christ and effects of the power of the grace of the Holy Spirit.

Participation of man in his salvation. This does not mean that the redemption and pardon of sins, the justification and sanctification produced by the work of salvation due to Christ are only applied to man from without, mechanically or magically. No. According to orthodox doctrine man himself must collaborate and appropriate actively what Christ accomplished objectively, and to penetrate into the new life that appeared in this world with Christ he must follow the prescription of St. Paul: "Work out your salvation with fear and trembling."[47]

In what does man's active participation in his salvation consist? The orthodox Church's reply is only the expression of its ascetical ideal of life:

[47] Phil 2:12.

"But from the days of John the Baptist until now the kingdom of heaven has been enduring violent assault and the violent have been seizing it by force (Mt 11:12), Christ has said. In other words active participation consists in battling against passion and sinful nature and in repentance and detachment from the powers of evil. It is purification from sin, establishment of the will in good, accomplishment of the will of God and of the divine commandments, increase in virtuous life and the love of God and neighbor, renunciation of self, offering of self and bearing the cross of Christ. And for all this naturally the support of divine grace is wholly necessary. The salvation of man is a divine-human process.

To the question: what justifies man? the reply of Roman Catholics and of Protestant Christians are not in agreement. What the theologians of the Roman Church say is that what justifies man is faith and good works. But the Protestants hold that it is faith alone and they blame the Roman practice for a contemptible sanctity of works. Yet most of the time the opposition is found in words rather than in things. And on one side and the other there is essential agreement with the orthodox Church when it answers with the apostle Paul that it is "faith which works through charity."[48]. . .

Sanctification by the grace of the Holy Spirit. The objective redemption accomplished by Christ is appropriated to man by the grace of the Holy Spirit, provided that man is or makes himself worthy of this appropriation. This is sanctification by the Holy Spirit. Certainly the orthodox Church also teaches that the three hypostases of the Holy Trinity participate in this sanctification, but it is preferably attributed to the Holy Spirit because He accomplishes it. . . .

3. H. S. Alivisatos[49] studies the Orthodox conception of sacramental grace: its nature and necessity and effectiveness. This grace is not a special grace, nor anything magical; it is the Holy Spirit Himself and His power which comes to us through the Sacraments.

Examining the subject of Sacramental Grace, it is necessary to point out that the attempt to define the orthodox conception of Sacramental Grace is attended with considerable difficulty, since neither the Greek Fathers, nor the Orthodox Church by an official decision of an Oecumenical Synod, has yet fixed the doctrine of the Sacraments in all its details.

A more systematic examination of the question from the orthodox side

[48] Gal 5:6.
[49] Hamilcar S. Alivisatos, D.D., was professor of Canon Law in the theological faculty of the University of Athens in 1931 and formerly procurator of the state on the Holy Synod of Greece. This excerpt is from his article, "The Orthodox Church and Sacramental Grace," in *The Doctrine of Grace*, ed. W. T. Whitley (London: SCM Press, 1931), pp. 247–265.

was not made before the thirteenth century[50] and with more exactitude not before the seventeenth century. For this reason even the term Sacramental Grace is entirely unknown to the orthodox terminology, since the Grace received through the Sacraments is nothing special, but simply the ordinary Grace of God received through the Sacraments. This late development of the Sacramental doctrine, although mostly based on the holy Scriptures and the holy Tradition, is not uninfluenced in some of its details both by the Roman Catholic Theology, as is surely the case with the orthodox confessions of the Russian Moghila (1642), and the Greek Dositheus (1672), and also the Protestant Theology, as the Confession of Lucaris (1629, 1633), clearly shows.

It is true that with slight exceptions the Greek Fathers and writers, being chiefly busy with other very important dogmatic problems, speak only occasionally about the Sacraments, but the relative parts of their writings, mostly disregarded by contemporary orthodox theologians, would give sufficient material for sketching a pretty full scheme of the Sacramental doctrine of the Greek Orthodox Church more or less independently of the later orthodox confessions and later or contemporary theological writings.[51]

The Orthodox Church having not yet defined its doctrine about Sacraments by the decision of an Oecumenical Synod, as the Roman Catholic Church did by the Tridentinum as well as other Synods, contents herself merely with the later dated orthodox confessions mentioned above, and many of the contemporary orthodox theologians do regard them as the official confessions of the Orthodox Church, while many others would not recognize them entirely or in all their details as such.

It is therefore evident that in the subsequent development more attention should be given to the patristic point of view about Sacramental Grace, without ignoring those points of the later orthodox confessions, which are in full accordance with the first. But points of these confessions, as well as of contemporary theological development, that are evidently influenced either by the Roman Catholic (Scholastic) or by the Protestant theology, are not regarded at all.

Surely it is not out of the question that several points of the doctrine of Sacramental Grace now under discussion among theologians may later be accepted and fixed, officially, by the Church, if at the same time theology shall clearly show them to be in full accordance with the Holy Scripture and the holy Tradition.

Outoward signs and Sacramental

---

[50] The Monk Job (1270), and Michael Palaeolog's *Confession* to the Synod of Lyon (1274).

[51] Rev. Dr. Frank Gavin in his excellent book *Some Aspects of Contemporary Greek Orthodox Thought*, 1923, gives, in pp. 269–393, a perfect idea of what contemporary Greek theologians do teach and accept about the Sacraments, without, however, perceiving entirely its accordance with the older orthodox spirit of the Fathers.

Grace. The Church has always had several means of conveying and transmitting Christ's Grace to the faithful, because she continues through her organs the salvation-work of Christ, her Founder. But the most effective means of communicating Grace are of course the Sacraments, which, consisting of external and tangible signs and acts do mediate through themselves a participation in the regenerating, justifying and sanctifying Grace of God.[52]

Naturally it is not the outward and tangible signs and acts themselves which mysteriously convey the Grace, but the presence of the Holy Spirit and His power, acting through these signs. St. Basil speaking about the Grace transmitted through the water in baptism says: "If there be any Grace in the water, it is not from the nature of the water, but from the presence of the Spirit."[53]

Necessity and quality of . . . the Sacraments in connection with Sacramental Grace. Of course this conception of the Greek Fathers, surely shared also by the later and the contemporary orthodox theology[54] as to the secondary role, so to say, which the outward and tangible signs of the Sacraments play, brings to the front the quite natural question about the absolute necessity of the same, since they do not themselves confer the Grace. The same Fathers themselves, however, give the explanation, insisting upon the absolute necessity of the outward signs, just because they have been so introduced, ordered, and even used by our Lord Himself; and, then, in regard to their quality, because these outward signs are by prayer and invocation purified and sanctified . . . and given in some way a peculiar character that makes them somewhat different from what they were before the sanctification and enables them to be transmitters of the Grace. Some of the Fathers go so far, as to speak clearly, many centuries before the development of the scholastic theology, about some kind of transformation or "transelementation" of the outward signs and elements of the Sacraments. . . . The above quotations make it evident that, according to the orthodox doctrine, although in Sacraments the power of the Holy Spirit is that which effects and communicates Christ's Grace, together with its consequences, and not the tangible signs and outward acts, it is through these only, after their sanctification and purification through the presence and energy of the Holy Spirit that Grace is communicated and transmitted.

Definition of the Sacrament. . . . Moghila in his *Confessio Orthodoxa* says: "The sacrament is a ceremony such that under some visible form it is a (true) cause, and brings into the believer's soul the invisible Grace of God, it having been ordained by our Lord, through whom each of the faith-

---

[52] K. Dyobouniotes, *Ta musteria tes anatolikes orthodoxou Ekklesias* (Athens, 1913), p. 3.

[53] *De Sanct. Spirito,* 15; Migne, 2, col. 132.

[54] *Confessio Orthodoxa*, Questio XCIX apud Kimmel, p. 170; Dyobouniotes, *op. cit.*, p. 15, etc.

ful receives the divine Grace,"[55] and Gabriel of Philadelphia defines the Sacraments as: "Certain sacred matters liable to sense-perception having in themselves a hidden divine power, whereby they supply to men salvation and the things that pertain to salvation;[56] not otherwise Macarius of Moskaw,[57] Dyobouniotes,[58] Androutsos[59] and others.

The Grace conferred. . . . Greek Fathers do not define of course the close relation between the outward elements and the Grace conferred or its precise degree. They are satisfied to express the firm belief in the fact that Grace is surely conferred through the Sacramental elements, but they are not concerned at all to define a doctrine or even a theory as to the way in which Grace is conferred through the elements. The Grace conferred through the Sacraments is the supernatural power of the Holy Spirit by which the appropriation of the redeeming work of our Lord is achieved through the Church's means of sanctification (Word and Sacrament) provided that the individual's faith answers to God's benevolent attitude. It is therefore not a special Grace, nor anything magical; it is the Holy Spirit Himself and His power, which comes to us through the Sacraments.[60] Dositheus in his *Confession* believes that Grace: ". . . cooperating and em-

powering and also establishing in the love of God, that is to say, in the good things which God wills us to do (which also the initial Grace enjoined), justifies and makes us predestinate."[61] This is an explanation of what the Greek Fathers teach about Grace proceeding directly from the gracious kindness of God to men, enabling them to do every good action and work and effecting finally their salvation. . . . The Grace conferred through the Sacraments is of a different form corresponding to the several spiritual needs of human nature; thus in baptism and Chrism the Grace is regenerating and justifying, in the Holy Eucharist, feeding and quickening and so on.[62]

Necessity and effectiveness of Sacramental Grace. It is generally recognized that the Grace conferred through and by the Sacraments is absolutely necessary, since its effect is sanctification and finally salvation. This does not mean that the Sacraments are the only means of salvation, because the Omnipotent God can use other means also; and again not all Sacraments are absolutely necessary, because each one must use only those necessary for him. But the necessity of the Sacraments and the Grace conferred through them is in many respects shown by its effects both subjective and objective, both positive

---

[55] Questio XCIX apud Kimmel, I, p. 170.

[56] *Syntagma de s. sacram.*, 4.

[57] *Dogmatic Theology.* Greek translation by Pagidas (Athens, 1883), p. 384.

[58] *Op. cit.*, p. 8 f.

[59] *Dogmatic* (Athens, 1907), p. 292.

[60] Hence the term "sacramental grace," quite unknown in Greek theology, is not used here in the sense of the Western Scholastic theology.

[61] *Decretum,* III, apud Kimmel, I, p. 428.

[62] See Dyobouniotes, *op. cit.*, p. 23; Androutsos, *op. cit.*, pp. 297–298.

and negative. The Grace conferred and its power affect firstly the outward and tangible signs, which after the sanctification become instruments of Holy Grace and its means of sanctification. . . . Further, the Sacramental Grace conferred effects positively for the worthy and reverend partaker of the Sacraments sanctification and salvation, but also negatively for the unworthy and in certain cases for the scoffing partaker of the Sacraments, sin and condemnation. . . .

Of course such a conception of the effect of Grace, does not mean that the effect of Sacramental Grace is magical; not only because it is the act and the work of God and the Holy Spirit, but because, in spite of the presence of Grace through participation in the Sacraments, the sinful disposition is not extinct just because of the great power of sin and the strong persistence and opposition of the sinful free will of men. . . . It results from this that the effect against sin and sinful disposition must be constant and continuous in spite of the presence of Grace. . . .

4. M.-J. Congar, O.P.,[63] reflecting on a study of deification in the spiritual tradition of the Orient, sees the differences between the oriental and occidental spiritualities determined by two different anthropologies, resting on two different conceptions of causality or participation.

A study of Mme. Lot-Borodine that appeared in the *Revue de l'Histoire des Religions*[64] can help us grasp the spiritual tradition of the Orient. It is an extremely penetrating study bearing on the doctrine of deification. . . .

The Orient distinguishes in God the unknowable essence (a superessence surpassing all intellectual knowledge) — and the divine actions or energies (essential uncreated energies). It is the divine energies that are manifested to us in theophanies, in inspiration, in supernatural experience of God. But the essence is hidden in the "cloud," in the "darkness," and remains absolutely inaccessible to every created spirit even though divinized by grace.[65] This knowledge of the divine nature hidden in the darkness that is only the fringe of its inaccessible light is apophatic knowledge. By it we attain only to what

[63] Yves Congar, O.P., is a very eminent theologian and author and a "peritus" at the Second Vatican Council. This excerpt is from his article, "La deification dans la tradition spirituelle de l'Orient" . . . in *La Vie Spirituelle*, v. 43, Avril-Juin, 1935, pp. 93–106, Editions Du Cerf, Paris VII, France.

[64] M. Lot-Borodine, "La doctrine de la 'deification' dans l'Eglise grecque jusqu'au XI siècle," in *Revue de l'Histoire des Religions*, TCV (1932), pp. 5–43; CVI (1932), pp. 525–574; and CVII (1933), pp. 8–55.

[65] Cf. the very remarkable article of M. V. Lossky, "La notion des 'Analogies' chez Denis le Pseudo-areopagite" in *Arch. Hist. litt. doctr. du m. age*, 1930, pp. 279–309, especially p. 282 and n. 1.

God is not, to His actions, while the mystery of the three hyopstases remains obscure. In Latin theology, on the contrary, the intuitive vision of God is the term of supernatural life and the beatifying act of the divinized soul, while for Moses and St. Paul there is even admitted a transitory vision of the divine essence.[66] Not that the great theologians of the Occident sacrifice the divine transcendence. They simply do not conceive it in function of the distinction between "superessence" and "energies," for they are unaware of this.

This difference would be of relatively little importance, however, if the respective orientations of the two spiritualities were not determined by two different anthropologies, reposing on two different conceptions of causality or participation. . . .

The Christian Orient is principally inspired by the Platonic tradition. It seeks to conceive and explain beings by a *participation of God* (or of a divine world of Ideas) in the order of formal cause. Things are participated *similitudes* and the world is an *expression* of God. If we apply this point of view to grace, we will conceive it especially as an impression, a more perfect image of God. If there is question of the relation of nature and grace, their distinction is less marked than their continuity. Nature appears as an imperfect image of God and grace perfcctly realises this likeness — in the same line so to speak.[67]

The Occident, even when Platonised, is not entirely Platonic.[68] Its instinct accords more with the genius of Aristotle. In things it envisages *the existing being* rather than the likeness of God. For it the world is more a world of natures and causes, of powers and influences, than a symbolic world or an epiphany of the beyond. Cosmic and religious points of view are mixed in the Occident. The explanation of reality is sought less in the line of formal cause and the order of likeness-participation than in the line of *efficient causality* and the order of genesis or coming into existence. Things thus have their own proper consistency.

If we apply this point of view to grace, grace will be conceived as a new power added to nature, a principle of new activities distinct from the activities of nature. In short, it will be a *habit* (entitative) in the Thomist sense of the word, and the distinction between nature and supernature will be more clearly marked.[69]

---

[66] St. Thomas admits it, but only on the authority of St. Augustine.

[67] This point of view is always found to some degree in Occidental theologians when they have a Platonizing notion of participation. So Albert the Great. Cf. our article: "Albert le Grand, theologien de la grâce sanctifiante," in *La Vie Spirituelle*, janv., 1933, pp. 109–140.

[68] So St. Augustine, Albert the Great, and his disciples. In the West there are some representatives of the specifically Oriental point of view: Scotus Erigena and to an extent, Eckhart. . . .

[69] In the political order . . . the Occidental middle age knows of theocratic realizations. But the logic of its genius pushed the Occident to a distinction of the orders and one can hardly see how any other conception would be possible for it than laicism or subordination in the sense

We can also say that the Orient is more intent on the *ontology* of things and the order of being (the line of formal cause), while the Occident is more intent on activity and the order of operation (the line of efficient cause).

The Orient speaks of "deification." It is concerned with realising the likeness to God, with becoming "consubstantial" with God, and thus the reality of grace represents a completion of the ontology of man. . . . It deals with an elevation of human ontology, with an illumination that transforms the being and even the nature of man.[70]

The Occident speaks of "beatitude." It is concerned to see God as He sees Himself. Here the term is not merely the completion in us of the likeness to God and the realisation in us of His clarity, but an operation of which grace and glory are conceived as subjective principles of action. Grace is a radical principle of supernatural operations. It is conceived as a participation in the divine nature, i.e., in that which in God is the principle of acts properly divine. Glory or the *lumen gloriae* is the efficacious prin-

ciple of a beatifying act of vision by which we see God as He sees Himself: here there is no longer question of an unknowable essence, of a "super-essence" distinct from "energies." Certainly a participation in the very being of God is impossible. But grace and glory are conceived as a participation in the principle of divine operation by which God apprehends Himself as object. By this participation we operate as God and see divinely.

To this double conception of term (as deification-similitude and as beatitude-operation) there corresponds a double conception of man. On the one hand there is an anthropology conceived in an ontological manner, an essentially religious and mystical conception of human nature as god-bearing, as the image of God ontologically. On the other hand there is an anthropology conceived from the operational point of view, in the order of psychological, ascetical, and mystical experience. In brief there is a *moral* anthropology with an ethical point of view. Nature is considered as a power of action oriented toward an end. We stress end and beatitude and are concerned to win by good action this beatitude which is God. We are restless till we rest in Him.

The itinerary of the soul toward God is materially and really very much alike in the two spiritualities. But theologically it is conceived in quite diverse manners. Here (in the Occident) as movement toward a beatitude (God the supreme Good) to be won by holy actions. There (in

---

of St. Thomas (Church and State being conceived as two distinct "powers," something strange to the Orient).

[70] For St. Thomas also grace is the elevation of our potential of life and the perfection of nature. But unfortunately since Baius less stress is put on St. Thomas' admirable doctrine about the vitality of our supernatural acts and of the beatific vision, and more on his theses on "the distinction of the natural and the supernatural." Cf. P. Festugiere, *L'idéal religieux des Grecs et l'Evangile* (Coll. *Etudes bibliques*) (Paris: Gabalda, 1932).

the Orient) as deification, as realisation of the "consubstantiality" of the soul with God through a progressive illumination of the being.

Here with the same real elements and often the same practices we find two different "asceses" marked by the eternal opposition of Aristotle and Plato. We also find two quite different manners of envisaging the cosmos. In the one the stress is on utilizing and dominating the cosmos. In the other the solitary soul progressively illumined begins the regeneration of entire nature and thus preludes the creation of a "new earth."[71]

If we look at knowledge and especially religious knowledge, the consequences of the different points of view are quickly manifest. For the Orient, knowledge is an affair of the whole being, and religious knowledge is a charismatic transfiguration of the whole being, in continuity with natural knowledge just as grace is

with nature. Philosophy finds its fulfilment in pneumatic wisdom (cf. Vl. Soloviev). For the Occident knowledge is an affair of a particular power and of special "virtues" of this power. The "powers" of reason are carefully distinguished from those of the soul elevated to the state of grace, and they are considered to have validity and autonomy in their order. There is a consistency proper to philosophy.

If we speak more specially of the "self-knowledge" that spiritual authors recommend to the soul seeking God, we find the same difference: the life of union with God rests on the twofold "knowledge" of God and of self. On the one hand there is an entirely negative mystical knowledge of the divine nature hidden in the darkness of its inaccessible light, and of a knowledge of human nature scrutinized in the depths of its divine resemblance. On the other hand, to "know" God is especially to know His merciful omnipotence, and to "know self" is to know one's own impotence and misery: cf. St. Catherine of Siena.[72]

If there is question of Christ and His work, in both traditions Christ is the Savior, the Mediator, the Lord, the incarnate, crucified, resurrected and glorified Word. But here . . . His work is a work of reconciliation, and it is conceived not on the cosmic

---

[71] On the one hand a monastic ascetism, primitive in character; on the other hand, a realizing and conquering asceticism: conquest of self, conquest of the world rather than its spiritualization, by fasting, etc. If there is spiritualization, it is in ordering the material to the spiritual in the order of operation. From two sides matter is for spirit and the world finally serves the contemplative life of the elect. But in the Platonic Orient the body is subordinate to the soul less in the sense that it serves the soul than in the sense that it must be spiritualized by the soul, swept into its life of purity and light. In the Occident the subordination of body to soul is rather conceived in the sense that it serves for its perfection, for the operations by which it perfects itself and exercises its higher life; for the soul gets in touch with ideas not directly but through the body.

[72] To this is added a concept of miracle and its role in the life of saints. This appears less as an intervention of the First Cause derogating from the laws of nature than as a return to the spiritual power of innocent man and an annunciation of the future restoration of his spiritual royalty.

plane and in the ontological order but rather on the moral plane. There . . . His work is one of regeneration, of re-creation, of respiritualisation of human nature and consequently of all things. The cosmic and ontological value of the Incarnation and the Eucharist stand out. . . .

Finally, if we consider the Church and sacraments . . . for the Orient the Church will be a milieu of deifying operation through sacraments and cult. . . . "The essence of the Church is the divine life unveiling itself in the life of creatures. It is the deification of the creature by the power of the Incarnation and of Pentecost."[73] All the stress is on the priesthood, sacra-

ments and liturgy, and there is a tendency to forget the militant character of the Church.

For the Occident the Church is certainly a loving and contemplative Church, but very strongly also a militant Church and a milieu of moral action organized so as to help us as much as possible to win the Sovereign Good and the reality of Beatitude. The governing hierarchy, the magisterium, the public organs that direct Christian activity — these hold a very great place. And the preponderance given to action that is oriented toward the supernatural end will put into particular relief the notion of "merit."

---

[73] It is a question of accent — or perhaps of epoch. To be convinced that knowledge of self as image of God was alive in the Occident cf. E. Gilson, L'esprit de la phi-

losophie médiévale (Paris: Vrin, 1932), t. II, p. 1 ff. [Eng. tr., New York, 1936]. S. Boulgakov, L'Orthodoxie (Paris: Alcan, 1932), p. 5.

XIV

GRACE IN NINETEENTH- AND
TWENTIETH-CENTURY CATHOLIC THEOLOGY

1. **H. Rondet, S.J.,**[1] notes that for post-Tridentine theology the gift of grace was primary while the divine presence was only one of the numerous effects of this gift. The mystery of the divinization of the Christian was barely mentioned in passing. Then came a return to the Greek Fathers and a strong emphasis on the divinization of the Christian on the part of Petau, Scheeben, and De Regnon, an emphasis that continues in grace-theology today.

Return to the Greek Fathers. Looking back over the history of theology we are forced to state that for a long time Western thought was as

---

[1] H. Rondet, S.J., cf. ch. III, n. 1. This excerpt is from *op. cit.*, pp. 329–339.

if obscured by the problems posed by the genius of Augustine. Grace and liberty, grace and merit, justification and predestination, all these themes long occupied the theologians. . . . When we reread the beautiful decree of the council of Trent on justification we note with regret that the mystery of the divinization of the Christian is barely mentioned in passing.[2] A quite unilateral development of theological thought and even more the needs of controversy put in the shadow a doctrine that was at the heart of Catholic thought and whose importance neither Augustine nor the great scholastics had misconstrued.[3]

But from the end of the middle ages there came a break between the treatise on the Trinity that dealt with the mission of the Holy Spirit, and the treatise on grace. Created grace comes into the foreground while the gift of the Holy Spirit is still affirmed but with less prominence. As we noted, the Greek Fathers had spoken only incidentally and rather imprecisely about created grace.[4] But for post-Tridentine theology on the contrary what is primary is the gift of grace, while the divine presence is only one of the numerous effects of this gift. There are lengthy discussions of the distinction between grace and charity, of the relations between mortal sin and the loss of grace, of the infusion of virtues before justification or their increase in the soul of

the just. But the treatise on grace is so encumbered with disputes with Protestants and Baianists or Jansenists that the divinization of the Christian, adoptive filiation, the mystery of union with Christ and the inhabitation of the Holy Spirit occupy only a minimal place.

It is as a protest against this error of perspective that we must view Petau's famous attempt.[5] Petau as we know is the father of the history of dogma. He wrote at the height of the Jansenist controversy and took up the defence of St. Augustine against the innovators. Though he himself adopted Lessius's theses he declared unambiguously that only the theory of predestination *ante praevisa merita* could claim to be St. Augustine's.[6] But he was less interested in those questions than in the affirmations of Scripture and the Fathers on God's presence in us.

In Book VIII of his treatise on the Trinity he studies at length the mission of the Holy Spirit and cites the beautiful texts of the Fathers that call Him the gift of God or speak of His coming into us. Among the Fathers of the Church it is Cyril of Alexandria who especially holds his attention. This great doctor shows how the Holy Spirit acts in us by Himself, sanctifies us, unites us to Himself and makes

[2] Cf. D. 1524, 1545.

[3] Cf. I P., q. 43, aa. 2–5.

[4] Cf. J.-B. Terrien, *La grâce et la gloire*, 1897, t. I, pp. 80–82.

[5] Cf. P. Galtier, "Petau," DTC, t. XII, col. 1334–1335. — Th. De Régnon, *Etudes de théologie positive sur la sainte Trinité*, III serie, t. II, pp. 524–535.

[6] Petau, *Dogmata theologica*, t. II, De praedestinatione, lib. IX, cap. 6–9, ed. Vivès, 1865, t. II, pp. 28–53.

us participants in the divine nature.[7] Petau comments on these texts at length and shows that in the soul of the just there is not only a created grace but the Holy Spirit Himself. We are His temple, He dwells in us, He is in us, He makes us like Himself and makes us gods in giving Himself to us.[8] And all this Petau says ought to fill us with joy and gratitude to God.[9] Without renouncing created grace he finds that what is primary is the gift of God Himself, and to prove the divinity of the Holy Spirit[10] he justly invokes the texts of the Fathers which start from the divinization of the Christian.

By such strokes Petau gradually paves the way for his personal theory. The great historian is aware that he is moving on difficult terrain here[11] for his theory is opposed to the accepted opinions of the School. Theologians commonly teach, he says, that the presence of God and the union that results from this are the work of the three Persons, and are only attributed to the Holy Spirit by a kind of accommodation. But to do this is to minimize the affirmations of the Fathers of the Church.[12] We can no more be content to attribute the sanctification of our souls to the Holy Spirit, Petau thinks, than to attribute the Incarnation to the Son. Though the three divine Persons operate the Incarnation every Christian must agree that only the Word is Incarnate. And in the same way, Petau says, there is something in our sanctification that is personal to the Holy Spirit and pertains only to Him.[13] The Holy Spirit is in us in the manner in which the Word is in the holy humanity of Christ. In the humanity of Christ the Father, the Son and the Spirit are present, but the Son is there in a manner that pertains only to Him, as a principle, a substantial form that makes this man be God. So it is with the Holy Spirit in us.[14]

But Petau knows well that it is not just the same for the union of the Word to the holy humanity and for the union of the just with the Holy Spirit. This latter is not a physical union, not a hypostatic union, and we are not gods by nature but only by grace. Christ is God and not only divine. Although the Holy Spirit exercises in us the role of form He does not make us spirits but only spiritual.[15] Here Petau is at a loss in his explanation for he is not a great speculative intellect. But he is content to have drawn attention to truths too often disregarded and to leave to others the task of explaining them.

The doctrine of appropriation which he opposed had its roots in the Greek tradition,[16] but it derived especially

---

[7] *Dogmata theol.*, VIII, c. 4, col. 459.

[8] *Ibid.*, col. 459 A.

[9] *Ibid.*

[10] *Ibid.*, c. 5, n. 8 (col. 471 A).

[11] Petau repeats indefinitely the same things, with visible satisfaction, but he especially tries to impress the scholastics by an accumulation of texts. . . .

[12] *Ibid.*, c. 6, n. 5–6 (col. 484 A).

[13] *Ibid.*, c. 6, n. 6 (col. 484 B–485 A).

[14] *Ibid.*, c. 6, n. 8 (col. 486 A).

[15] *Ibid.*, c. 7, n. 13 (col. 494 A).

[16] Cyril of Alexandria, *In John*, XX, c. 3, P.G., 35, 1557–1558, cited in F. Galtier, *L'habitation en nous des trois personnes*, 1928, p. 12–13.

from Augustinism. Where Augustine, fearful of anything that would imperil the divine unity, had strongly affirmed that everything in *ad extra* works was common to the three divine Persons,[17] the Greeks on the contrary had emphatically underlined the distinct role each of the three Persons played in our sanctification.[18] St. Thomas is the heir of the two traditions. So he strongly affirms the Augustinian principle but at the same time insinuates that the divinization of the Christian is not uniquely an *ad extra* work. For the Holy Spirit is the gift of God[19] and by sanctifying grace we are made friends of God and the divine Persons themselves are given to us so that we can enjoy their presence.[20]

But unfortunately St. Thomas does not insist much on this latter aspect and so comes to speak of our adoption in a manner that is certainly little conformed to Scripture. For in whatever way you consider the Incarnate Word He is the Son of the Father and not of the Trinity, and yet, says the Angelic Doctor, we are sons of the Trinity.[21] This affirmation is not without danger and first of all in Christology. For the incarnate Word as man possesses sanctifying grace. Why then should not He too as such be son of the entire Trinity? St.

Thomas rejects this conclusion but Durandus of St. Pourcain draws it boldly and so goes back to the Adoptionist error.[22] And in the XVIth century Suarez denounces the illusion of Durandus of St. Pourcain but himself falls into another error. . . .

Petau's opinion was almost unanimously rejected and the more so because he claimed that the privilege of this special union with the Holy Spirit was reserved to the just of the New Law.[23] But his thesis is thriving nonetheless. For it was not enough to condemn it. An answer had to be given to the problem he posed.

Toward the end of the XIXth century it was taken up again by a German theologian, Matthias Joseph Scheeben. While Petau was familiar with Cyrillan thought, Scheeben is also a scholastic and a fervent disciple of St. Thomas, and so by resuming relations with the great scholastic tradition he joins together the mysteries of Christianity. His theology of the Trinity effectively commands his theology of grace. With St. Thomas he shows how the invisible mission of the Holy Spirit operates. The Holy Spirit is in us and there enkindles a flame, a love analogous to the substantial love that He is. But by grace we possess not only the Holy Spirit. The Word Himself is given to us, is engendered in us, and we become living images of the Father, reflecting His splendor. The three Persons are in us

---

[17] E. Portalié, "Augustin," D.T.C., t. I, col. 2348–2349.

[18] Th. De Regnon, *Etudes de théologie positive sur la sainte Trinité*, III serie, t. II, Etude 25, pp. 385–386.

[19] Iᵃ Part, q. 38, art. 2.

[20] I Part, q. 43, art. 3, ad 1.

[21] III Part, q. 23, art. 2, ad 2.

[22] Durandus, *In IV Sent.*, lib. III, dist. 4, q. 1.

[23] Petau, *Theologica dogmata*, lib. VIII, cap. 7, n. 1 (col. 487 B).

substantially and personally, and this not only in the sense that God is present in every creature but because the Three impress on us their imprint as a seal does on wax. But while the imprint of the seal remains when the seal is removed, the imprint of the three Persons remains only as long as they are present. The three Persons are given us as an earnest of eternal life, Scheeben tells us according to St. Thomas, so that down here we can enjoy their presence. God does not show Himself at a distance but is very near.[24]

The presence of God is then an ontological presence. But is it personal? hypostatic? Do the persons come into us with their personal character, each in the manner that is proper to Him? As the Son proceeds from the Father and the Spirit unites them by love? Unhesitatingly Scheeben says yes. The Holy Spirit is in us formally by what constitutes Him a person, as the emanation and proof of the love of the Father, by which the Father loves us in His Son as His adoptive sons. The Holy Spirit comes into us as the flower of divine tenderness and amiability, in a word, as the Kiss of the Father and the Son that we receive in the intimacy of the soul. But on our side in the measure that we are aware of this presence of the Holy Spirit or rejoice in its possession, we send back to the Father His Kiss and ourselves enjoy its inexpressible sweetness. In Him and by Him we reach the Father and the Son, in Him and by Him we lift ourselves by knowledge and love to the enjoyment of the other two persons from whom the Spirit comes to us.

As long as we remain on earth these ineffable realities are wrapped in mystery but they will be revealed in heaven. If the presence of the Spirit is more manifest to us here below, Scheeben adds, it is because here below love outweighs knowledge.[25]. . .

As Petau did formerly so Scheeben now proceeds to give a personal theory, and without much more success. Scripture tells us the Holy Spirit is in us as in His temple. This temple consecrated by the divine presence is a *possession* of the Holy Spirit. Is this just a manner of speech? . . . Possession of the Holy Spirit only by appropriation? Scheeben does not believe so and enunciates his thesis that the Holy Spirit possesses us in a special fashion, after the manner in which the Word possesses His holy humanity. By Him and in Him the other two Persons possess our souls as their temple and their dwelling. The possession is not exclusive but it is truly personal. And this is why the liturgy in its echo of Tradition and Scripture designates the Holy Spirit under the words: *dulcis hospes animae.*[26]

From this doctrine are derived two consequences, one concerning sanctification, the other adoptive filiation.

[24] M. J. Scheeben, *Die Mysterien des Christentums,* #26, 1865, p. 147–151.

[25] *Ibid.*, p. 152, 153. Cf. also *Dogmatique,* trad. Belet, t. III, pp. 624, 646–647 (*Handbuch der kathol. Dogm.,* t. II, p. 363).

[26] *Die Mysterien,* p. 158.

The Holy Spirit is not only the efficient cause of our sanctification together with the other divine Persons, but He is its formal cause. He does not replace created grace. This is at the same time an effect of His presence and a disposition to receive it. But it is the gift of the Holy Spirit that is primary.[27] Secondly, if we are adoptive sons this is first due to the Spirit who is given to us and is in us the principle of unity and the bond of love that unites us to the Father and to the Son as He unites the Father and the Son. The soul that is sanctified by the Spirit is daughter of the Father and spouse of the Holy Spirit and thus by the gift and the presence of the Holy Spirit there is consummated between God and His creature the union of love of which St. John speaks.[28]

A theology so new could at first only arouse criticism. The Jesuit Granderath . . . urged objections from the council of Trent on the formal cause of justification, but Scheeben explained himself and the controversy died down quickly enough.[29] Some notable authors as Franzelin, Hurter, Christian Pesch without siding with Scheeben showed a certain sympathy for his thesis and said that the Holy Spirit is the analogical formal cause of our justification. . . .

Though P. De Regnon in his beautiful studies on the Holy Trinity sets up a somewhat exaggerated opposition between the theology of the Latins and that of the Greeks, he does not conceal his sympathies for the Greek theology. He aims to complete the theories of Petau and Scheeben while renouncing the exclusiveness of their special union with the Holy Spirit.[30] So the three Persons come into us and act in us simultaneously but they come under a particular title: the Father comes as Father, the Son as engendered by the Father, the Holy Spirit as the bond of love that unites the Father and the Son. We are not adoptive sons of the Trinity but sons of the Father and brothers of Christ and it is the Holy Spirit who spiritualizes us.[31] If it is objected that sanctification of souls is an *ad extra* work and that all works God does outside Himself are common to the three Persons, P. De Regnon replies that the divinization of the Christian is not uniquely an *ad extra work*. In the natural order the Persons act only through the common nature, but in the supernatural order they act inasmuch as they are persons.[32] Between the eternal life of God and our sanctification there is a mysterious correspondence. That which goes on in eternity is reproduced in time.[33]

So we rejoin the Greek Fathers and through them the data of Scripture. This old and new doctrine awakens profound resonances in the souls of today, and the beautiful prayers of a

[27] *Ibid.*, pp. 160–161.
[28] *Ibid.*, p. 164.
[29] A. Bellamy, "Adoption surnaturelle," DTC, t. I, col. 429–430.

[30] Th. De Regnon, *Etudes de théologie positive sur la sainte Trinité*, III serie, t. II, Etude 27.
[31] Th. De Regnon, *op. cit.*, pp. 551–552.
[32] *Ibid.*, pp. 535, 546.
[33] *Ibid.*, pp. 573.

Sister Elisabeth of the Trinity addressed to the three divine Persons ... have become more and more familiar to those who have comprehended that God is in us and lives in us.[34]

2. P. De Letter, S.J.,[35] surveys contemporary theology of grace and finds that it benefits by the three main trends which mark present-day theological and ecclesiastical studies in general: (1) return to the sources, Scripture and Tradition, (2) historical perspective or awareness of the growth and development of the doctrines; and (3) close contact with spiritual and pastoral doctrine. Its prominent themes are sanctifying grace, divine indwelling, in Christ and in the Church.

Contemporary theology of grace benefits by the three main trends which mark present-day theological and ecclesiastical studies in general: (1) return to the sources, Scripture and Tradition, or stress on positive theology, (2) historical perspective or awareness of the growth and development of the doctrines, and (3) close contact with spiritual and pastoral doctrine. After first pointing to some of the recent writings on grace in these fields, we wish to indicate the themes which, as a consequence of this doc-

trinal renewal, stand out in the theology of grace today.

Present-Day Trends

1. **Return to the sources.** In a recent sketch of the manner of constructing our theological treatise on grace, Canon G. Philips, professor at the Louvain University, states in the first place the need of renewing our documentation from the sources, Scripture and Tradition. In fact, though a considerable amount of research has been done on points of biblical and patristic theology, the results of these studies have not yet been sufficiently integrated in our theology of grace. Considering the state of flux and progress in which much of this positive theology is still found, and the scarcity of synthetic studies in that field, this is not surprising.

Grace in Holy Scripture. Since the long and comprehensive, not to say over-comprehensive, article on grace in the *Dictionnaire de la Bible*, Supplement (1938)[36] relatively few synthetic studies on grace in Scripture

---

[34] R. Plus, *Dieu en nous*, 1920. This volume has known a significant success. ... The little book of P. A. Dorsaz, *Notre parente avec les personnes divines* (1921) contains some excellent things, but his fundamental idea is very debatable (if Adam had not sinned, we would have known only the *gratia Dei* which would have divinized us without putting us in relation to the three persons). ...

[35] P. De Letter, S.J., professor of theology at St. Mary's College, Kurseong, India, has published a great deal on matters theological and spiritual. This excerpt is from his article, "Contemporary Theology of Grace" in *The Clergy Monthly*, India (Ranchi, India: The Catholic Press, 1957), Vol. 21, pp. 288 ff.

[36] Bonnetain, art. "Grâce," *Dictionnaire de la Bible*, supplement 3 (1938), 701–1319.

have appeared. We may mention two of them. First, the three chapters on the subject in H. Rondet, *Outline of a History of the Theology of Grace:* on the Old Testament, the Gospel message, and the theology of St. Paul.[37] These brief chapters, for all their unavoidable simplification and systematization, develop the characteristic of each of the three stages in the biblical doctrine on grace, as hinted in the subtitles: grace as an expression of God's providence for His chosen people, grace as filial spirit revealed and given by Christ in the Gospel, and grace as forgiveness of sin in St. Paul's theology.

More detailed and more sensitive to different shades of meaning, despite its briefness, is the article on grace in the Dutch *Biblical Dictionary* by P. van Imschoot.[38] After noting the Old Testament imperfect equivalents of our notion of grace (*ḥēn* and *ḥesed*), the author studies first the meaning of the word *charis* . . . then the teaching on grace (a) in the synoptics: God shows His fatherly love by the first grace He grants to men: Christ Himself who comes to inaugurate the kingdom of God, in which men are admitted by grace and guided by God's help; (b) in St. Paul: grace as justification from sin through faith in Christ the Redeemer, in whom we

acquire a new relationship with God by receiving His Spirit; (c) in St. Peter, who speaks of the divine gifts Christians receive: a seed of immortality, the spirit of glory, the promise of sharing in the divine nature; (d) in St. John who describes the life of grace as the eternal or divine life begun now through faith in Christ by a new birth from above which plants in us the seed of God, incompatible with sin. . . .

A sketch of the mystery of grace as proposed in the New Testament is given by P. De Haes, in an article on the "personalistic concept and presentation of the doctrine of grace."[39] He draws the picture of God's self-gift to men[40] around three key phrases: "in and through Jesus Christ": grace is essentially christological, involving a relationship to Christ; "in the Spirit," who prepares and completes Christ's work for our salvation; "in the Church": grace incorporates into the Church, the Body of Christ animated by the one Spirit, and creates a relationship of social union with all the members of the Church. . . . L. Cerfaux's outline of St. Paul's theology of grace[41] is one more sample of this

---

[37] H. Rondet, *Gratia Christi, Essai d'histoire de dogme et de theologie dogmatique.* Tome I. Esquisse d'une histoire de la théologie de la grâce (Paris, 1948), 31–74.

[38] A. Van den Born, J. Coppens, *Biijbels Woordenboek,* 2 ed., Roermond-Masseik (1955), 564–569. [Eng. tr. *Encyclopedic Dictionary of the Bible* (New York: McGraw-Hill, 1964).]

[39] P. De Haes, "Personalistische opvatting en voorstelling van de genadeleer," *Collectanea Mechliniensia* (1953), pp. 301–330.

[40] Cf. 1 Jn 4:8–10; Ti 3:3–7; Gal 4:4–6.

[41] L. Cerfaux, "La théologie de la grâce selon saint Paul," *Vie spirituelle* 83 (1950), pp. 5–19. Of permanent value is the excellent article of P. Rousselot, "La grâce d'après saint Jean et saint Paul," *Recherches de science religieuse,* 1928, pp. 87–104. Its main idea is that St. John stresses the elevating aspect of grace, St. Paul, the healing aspect; the former is continued in the idea of divinization of the

personalistic presentation of the life of grace. Men, he says, are remade by a new creation and placed in special relationships with the Father, the Son and the Holy Spirit, without however renouncing their human tasks in the world; but their commitment to these is no longer unconditional, because they already live in a higher world. . . . J. Bonsirven in his *Theology of the New Testament*[42] expounds the theology of grace from different approaches. In the gospels, grace is the life in the kingdom of the Son, presupposing forgiveness of sin, entailing within the living Church a sharing in the life of the Holy Trinity and possession of the Holy Spirit. In St. Paul we see how grace, communicated through Christ in the Church, involves identification with Christ, guidance of the indwelling Spirit, and sonship of the Father who is the principle and term of the life in Christ.[43]

These few samples of present-day biblical theology of grace may suffice to show the trend. We are witnessing an intense effort to discover the full meaning and riches of the scriptural doctrine which is the foundation and starting-point of our theology of grace.

Grace in Tradition. Among the Fathers of the Church St. Augustine is traditionally known as the doctor of grace. . . . And his teaching has imprinted its mark on the whole his-

tory of the doctrine of grace. It may well be that this title was misunderstood at times in the sense of a sort of monopoly for St. Augustine in the doctrine of grace; it did at any rate unduly blind theologians to the teaching of other Fathers. The present-day renewal of patristic studies, marked by re-editions and translations of their texts and studies of their teachings[44] has done away with this danger.

There may not be many monographs on the theology of grace of one particular Father. Such studies as do exist rather deal with some particular aspect of the life of grace, as that of rebirth from God or our divine adoption.[45] Nor is there any synthetic study on the theology of grace in the Fathers of the Church, except that of Book Two in Fr. Rondet's *Gratia Christi*,[46] unless we say . . . as well we might, that the historical study of the doctrine of the Mystical Body by Fr. E. Mersch contains what is practically a theology of grace in the Fathers seen under the particular aspect of its re-

---

Greek Fathers, the second in that of liberation from sin of St. Augustine.

[42] J. Bonsirven, *Théologie du Nouveau Testament* (Paris, 1951).

[43] Cf. also Bonsirven's earlier works: *Les enseignements de Jesus-Christ* (Paris, 1944), and *L'evangile de Paul* (Paris, 1948).

[44] One or other example: *Corpus Christianorum* (the "new Migne"), cf. *Clergy Monthly* (1953), pp. 194–196; Latin series in course of publication, and Greek series projected; French translations, *Sources chrétiennes* (Paris, 1941); English, *Ancient Christian Writers* (Westminster, Md., 1946).

[45] H. Rahner, "Die Gottesgeburt. Die Lehre der Kirchenväter von der Geburt Christi in Herzen der Glaübigen, in *Zeitschrift für katholische Theologie* 1953, p. 35 ff.; E. Janssens, "Notre filiation divine d'après saint Cyrille d'Alexandrie," in *Ephem. théol. lovan.* (1938), pp. 233–278.

[46] H. Rondet, *op. cit.*, pp. 77–161

lationship with Christ and with the Church.[47]

One result of the contemporary interest in the writings and teachings of the Fathers is to have drawn into relief the contribution of the Greek Fathers to the theology of grace. That contribution is a complex of ideas about the nature of the Christian life which centre in that of our divinization or deification, of which J. Gross wrote a history.[48] The mission of the Holy Spirit who inhabits and sanctifies us, with the stress on the positive aspect of sanctification rather than on the remission of sin; imparting of the divine life, seed of immortality and resurrection; rebirth through baptism to the adoptive sonship of God; union and identification with Christ by sharing His life and His sentiments; new relationships with the Trinity — these are so many aspects of our deification or *theopoiesis*.[49] The consequence of this re-discovery of the Greek theology of grace for the place in our treatises of sanctifying grace and of Uncreated Grace will be pointed out later.

By a rather natural reaction the study of the Greek Fathers also led

to a more thorough investigation of the teaching of the Latin Fathers, particularly of St. Augustine. Their teaching on the "elevating" role of the grace of Christ, perhaps put in the shadow by their stress on its healing effects; on the permanent state of sanctifying grace, overlooked somewhat in the defence of the gratuitous divine help needed for every good action; also on the permanent divine presence in the members of Christ,[50] all this was a partial re-discovery. And so the schematic opposition of the Greek and Latin theology of grace, proposed by Fr. Rousselot[51] — elevating, sanctifying, uncreated grace on the one hand, and healing, actual, created grace on the other — for all its being correct and enlightening as far as it expresses a difference of emphasis, is given a more balanced evaluation.

In connection with the present-day stress on positive theology we may recall the warning which *Humani generis* sounded against an injudicious concept of the return to the sources, such namely as would involve an undue depreciation of scholastic theology and of the ecclesiastical magisterium.[52] A healthy Catholic attitude realizes a happy marriage of both positive and speculative theology under the vigilant eye of the magisterium.

2. Historical perspective. The return to the sources of the revelation,

---

[47] E. Mersch, *Le Corps Mystique du Christ, Etude de théologie historique*, 2 vols. (Paris, 1936); English, *The Whole Christ. The Historical Development of the Doctrine of the Mystical Body in Scripture and Tradition* (Milwaukee, 1938).

[48] J. Gross, *La divinisation du Chrétien d'après les Pères grecs* (Paris, 1938); cf. also M. Lot-Borodine, "La doctrine de la deification dans l'Eglise grecque," in *Revue de l'histoire des religions*, 105, 1932, 5 ff., 106, 1933, 525 ff., 107, 8 ff.

[49] Cf. H. Rondet, *op. cit.*, pp. 77–98.

[50] *Ibid.*, pp. 99–103; G. Philips, "De ratione instituendi tractatum de gratia nostrae sanctificationis," in *Ephemerides théologicae lovanienses* (1953), p. 356 f.

[51] Rousselot, *art. cit.*, above.

[52] Pius XII, *Humani generis*, Denzinger 3881; cf. 3886.

giving positive theology its rightful place in our theology of grace, is one aspect of the historical perspective which is typical of our day and marks the very study of the sources. Without in any way falling victim to the historicism or dogmatic relativism denounced and condemned by *Humani generis*[53] it is proper to have a sense of the development and growth of dogmatic and theological doctrines. This can and does give a more realistic understanding of them and this is all to the benefit of Christian life and doctrine.

Fr. H. Rondet, in his already quoted *Gratia Christi*[54] has given the first over-all sketch of the history of the dogma and theology of Christian grace. That history, at any rate in the Latin Church and making due allowance for the contribution of the Greeks, almost coincides with the history of Augustinism, both in its dogmatic and its theological vicissitudes.

The history of the *dogma* of grace is, in its negative aspect, that of the heresies which Augustine fought or which have arisen in opposition to or from a misunderstanding of Augustine's teaching: Pelagianism and Semi-Pelagianism during and shortly after St. Augustine's lifetime, in connexion especially with the dogma of actual grace, its necessity and gratuity; predestinationism, a misinterpretation of Augustine's teaching on predestination and reprobation; the Protestant doctrine of forensic justification, a mis-

understanding both of St. Paul and St. Augustine; the errors of Baius and Jansenius, two straying Augustinians, mainly concerning the necessity and efficacy of grace.[55] On its positive side, the history of the dogma of grace centres round the dogmatic definitions of the Church of which the two main ones are those against Pelagianism and Semi-Pelagianism in the 5th and 6th centuries[56] and the Tridentine teaching on justification, a fairly complete though rather one-sided (anti-Protestant) exposition of the Catholic faith on grace, especially sanctifying grace.[57] To these solemn definitions must be added the teaching of the ordinary magisterium, of which a [relatively] recent example is [Pope Pius XII's] encyclical *Mystici Corporis.*[58]

The history of the *theology* of grace also bears the mark of the development and vicissitudes of the Augustinian ideas. We mention two main points of that history. First, the transition from the patristic to the scholastic expression of the dogma of grace. Here the history of pre- and early Scholasticism traces the rise of the scholastic concepts and their application to the

---

[53] *Ibid.*, Denzinger, 3878, 3883.

[54] H. Rondet, *op. cit.*, Book II to IV.

[55] H. Rondet, *op. cit.*, pp. 112 ff., 144 ff., 165 ff., 257 ff., 287 ff., 309 ff.

[56] Cf. the canons of the Council of Carthage, the Indiculus on grace, and the canons of the Council of Orange, Denzinger 222 ff., 238 ff., 370 ff. H. Rondet, *op. cit.*, pp. 246–260, gives a French translation of these documents.

[57] Cf. Denzinger 1520–1583; Rondet, *op. cit.*, pp. 361–375.

[58] Pius XII, *Mystici Corporis*, Denzinger 3800–3822.

doctrine of grace.[59]. . . A central place in that history must be given to the elaboration of the theology of habitual grace according to Aristotelian terminology. This development led up to the synthesis made by St. Thomas of Augustinism and Aristotelianism in which the traditional idea of our divinization through grace and our relationships with the Blessed Trinity find their due place.[60] The historical studies on Scholasticism and on Thomism in particular enable us to follow the growth of the various conceptions of grace and to realize their time-conditioned character. We may mention here in particular the study of Z. Alszeghy, *Nova Creatura*[61] on the notion of grace in the medieval commentaries on St. Paul, in which he discovers two forms of thought or currents of doctrine, one dynamic and Augustinian, the other more static and Aristotelian — two complementary rather than opposed ways of expressing the doctrine of grace.[62]

Another point in the history of the theology of grace which deserves mention is the gradual neglect and the recent 're-discovery' of the essentially relative character of created grace and of the complex of relationships which grace entails. . . . So many influences . . . gradually led one to overlook the relation of created with Uncreated Grace; the stress was laid on actual rather than on habitual grace, and in the study of the latter, more on the inherent perfection it gives than on the divine Reality to which it links.[63] It is only in the latter part of the last century that the connexion with patristic theology, barely kept alive by a few positive theologians like Petau and Thomassin, was revived in the theology of grace of Scheeben, with his insistence on the divine indwelling that goes with grace.[64] Contemporary theology of grace lays full emphasis on the Uncreated Grace and the relationships with the divine Persons that spring from the life of grace.[65]

3. Contact with spiritual and pastoral doctrine. A third feature of present-day theological trends is the close contact of speculative theology with the theoretical and practical doctrine of the spiritual life and with the doctrine of the pastoral care of souls. *Spiritual theology.* The times are past or fast fading away when one could speak of a divorce between the-

---

[59] Cf. A. Landgraf, *Dogmengeschichte der Frühscholastik*, I, 1–2, *Die Gnadenlehre*, Regensburg, 1952–1953; O. Lottin, *Psychologie et Morale aux XII et XIII siècles*, 4 tomes in 6 vols; Louvain, 1942–1954; e.g. on infused virtues, III, 99–150, 153–194, 197–252, 459–515; on the gifts of the Holy Spirit, III, 329–456, IV, 667–736.

[60] Cf. H. Rondet, *op. cit.*, 200 ff.; Philips, *art. cit.*, 357.

[61] Z. Alszeghy, *Nova creatura. La nozione della grazia nei commentari di S. Paolo*, Analecta Gregoriana 81 (Rome, 1956).

[62] For the development of the doctrine of grace in high Scholasticism, cf. J. Auer, *Entwicklung der Gnadenlehre in der Hochscholastik*, 2 vols. (Freiburg, 1942, 1952).

[63] Cf. H. Rondet, *op. cit.*, 235 ff., 285 ff.

[64] *Ibid.*, 329 ff.

[65] Cf. De Letter's article "Sanctifying Grace and the Divine Indwelling" in *Theological Studies* (1953), 243–272.

ology and mysticism[66] And the efflorescence of ascetical and mystical studies typical of our century[67] could not but react favourably on the theology of grace. Spiritual theology being the study of the actual living of grace, of its requirements and laws, its development and results, cannot fail to take into account the dogmatic and theological teachings on grace. Nor can these ignore, except to their own detriment, what the science of the Saints teaches from experience. Speculative theology, by taking into account the study of the history and theology of the spiritual life especially in its higher stages, has been helped to emphasize mainly three aspects of the life of grace: (1) the dynamic and vital character of the created gifts of grace — by what spiritual theology teaches on the role of the gifts of the Holy Ghost as being in a way characteristic of the mystical life[68]; (2) the relationships with the Blessed Trinity which go with the state of sanctifying grace — the mystical graces which follow in many if not most cases a trinitarian pattern[69]; (3) the christo-logical and ecclesiological aspects of the life of grace or its necessary location within the Mystical Body of Christ — the gifts of the contemplative life require as a guarantee of their genuineness submission to and conformity with the Church of Christ, and whatever their contemplative character, are oriented to the apostolate, every contemplative being an apostle.[70]

Pastoral theology. The demand for a pastoral orientation of theology is in a way as old as the Church. . . . Today's stress on the pastoral purpose of theology, recalled recently by Pope Pius XII himself, in his Apostolic Constitution *Sedes sapientiae* on the training of religious priests[71] seems to be commanded mainly by two new factors: the special needs of the modern apostolate including the participation of the laity (which calls for a "theology for the layman"), and the present-day missionary task of the Church. . . .

For the theology of grace this contact with the needs of the apostolic ministry goes to strengthen the influence of spiritual on dogmatic theology . . . with the additional stress on our

---

[66] Cf. Fr. Vandebroucke, "Le divorce entre la théologie et la mystique," in *Nouvelle revue théologique* (1950), 372–389.

[67] Cf. "Problems of Mysticism," in *Clergy Monthly* (1952), 19 ff.

[68] Cf. *ibid.*, 22 and 24.

[69] Two examples of Trinitarian mysticism: Bl. John Ruusbroec, cf. P. Henry, "La mystique trinitaire du bienheureux Jean Ruusbroec," in *Rech. sc. rel.*, 1952, 335–368; 1953, 51–75; St. Ignatius of Loyola, cf. J. de Guibert, "Mystique ignatienne" A propos du journal spirituel de Saint Ignace de Loyola," in *Revue d'ascetique et de mystique* (1938), 3–22, 113–140.

[70] An example of both orthodoxy and of apostolic orientation of genuine mysticism: St. Teresa of Avila, cf. Fr. Marie-Eugene, *A Practical Synthesis of Carmelite spirituality,* esp. Vol. 2, *I am a Daughter of the Church* (Cork, 1956); cf. *Clergy Monthly,* 1956, 148 ff. On the apostolic orientation of the contemplative life; cf. Pius XII, allocution to the first international congress of the states of perfection, Rome, 1950; cf. *Clergy Monthly,* 1951, 371 f.

[71] *Clergy Monthly* (1957), 81–88, esp. 87 f.

Christian dignity[72] and on the all-importance for Christians to live in grace.[73] In particular, the social aspect of the life of grace, the grace of Christians being the grace of the members of Christ[74] naturally comes into prominence in a teaching directed towards the ministry. So does the need of prayer and of reliance on God's help as the practical expression of the dogma of actual grace, of its necessity and gratuity. While the dogma of merit at the same time states the need of personal effort in living the life of God's adopted children. . . .

Prominent themes. The prominent themes in the contemporary theology of grace are less a matter of new ideas and doctrines than of perspective and emphasis in presenting the traditional teaching on grace and its organic connections.

Sanctifying grace. A first feature is the stress on sanctifying grace rather than on actual grace.[75] It is not so long ago that our manuals *De gratia* gave the first place and the bulk of their theses, proofs and discussions to actual grace, habitual grace coming in a second, not to say secondary

place.[76]. . . The perspective has now been reversed. Grace now means first of all sanctifying grace, and pride of place is given to the study of the state of grace and of all that it implies, of what leads to it (the process of justification) and what follows on it (growth in grace by merit).[77] This . . . required a return to the sources beyond St. Augustine, to the teaching of Scripture on the state of those who enter the kingdom, are sons of God, members of Christ, temples of the Spirit, made just and holy. . . . That reversal was helped by the rise of spiritual theology which centred its research on the mystery of our union with God in Christ through sanctifying grace rather than on the help of grace required for the vital activity of the life of grace. The shift from the prominence of actual grace to that of habitual grace was pregnant with further developments one of which, perhaps the most important, and at any rate the most striking today, is the growing awareness of the essentially relative character of sanctifying grace.

Divine indwelling. For Catholic dogma and theology, sanctifying grace is a reality in the soul whose presence or absence makes all the difference between the state of sin and the state of grace. It is a quality, a per-

[72] Cf. L. Sempe, *Our Christian Dignity,* adapted from the French by C. A. Vrithoff (Ranchi, 1945).

[73] Cf. P. M. Corti-Gardenal, *Vivere in Grazia,* 2 ed. (Milano, 1955). English adaptation, *That They May Have Life.* The Apostolate of bringing men to live in God's grace through the help of lay people (Anand, 1950).

[74] E. Mersch, *Morality and the Mystical Body.* Translated by D. F. Ryan (New York, 1939), Ch. 5.

[75] Cf. G. Philips, *art. cit.,* 357 ff.; striking is the very limited place assigned to actual grace, *ibid.,* 364.

[76] An example is the manual of C. Pesch, *De Gratia,* 2 ed. (Freiburg, 1900): Part I, De gratia actuali, 6–172; Part II, De gratia habituali, 173–209; Part III, De fructu gratiae seu merito, 210–237.

[77] Cf. Philips, *art. cit.,* 357 ff., 363 ff. Few manuals approach the ideal proposed by Philips. Hervé is perhaps one of those that go in the right direction.

fection, a habitus, an entitative habitus which affects the very being of the soul and not only its activity.[78] But it is more than that. It is also a link uniting us with the Uncreated Grace, God inhabiting us and making us His temple. And it is so of necessity and of its very nature, in such a manner that created grace and Uncreated Grace are correlatives involving one another in their concept and in reality.[79] They are two sides of one reality — our sanctification or 'divinization' — created grace being a quality which assimilates and unites to the indwelling Trinity.

This idea of sanctifying grace as a link uniting us to God is not new. It is found in St. Thomas' doctrine of grace, even though it does not take a prominent place there and he insists more on created grace than on Uncreated Grace — the reason being that he leaves the study of the divine indwelling for the treatise of the Trinity and the missions of the divine Persons.[80] It was proposed by post-Tridentine theologians such as Lessius, who called grace a "link of the Holy Spirit"; or Petau for whom grace is a "link or nexus by which the substance of the Holy Spirit is united to our souls"; or Thomassin who considered grace as "an inchoate con-

nexion and union with God."[81] Today the idea is widely accepted. Grace is said to be the dispositive cause for our having the Uncreated Grace or the inhabiting Holy Spirit (Waffelaert); it is the foundation of a new relationship between God and the soul (Dumont); it is an "adaptation, perfection, divinization which exists only in actual union with God and cannot be conceived alone apart from God: it is an entity of union" (Mersch); it is "a transcendental relation to God as actuating us" (G. de Broglie) — this is an application of de la Taille's idea of grace as created actuation by the Uncreated Act, that is, as a created and finite reality which of its essence is a link with the Infinite; it is a created gift which is inseparable from the Uncreated Gift of which it is both the effect and the preparation (Rondet).[82] The result of the acceptance of this idea is, in the words of Fr. Galtier, that "the opinion is growing ever more common which holds that the special indwelling of God in the soul belongs to the very

---

[78] Cf. the Thomistic theology of grace, S. Th. I, II, q. 110.

[79] It may be well to note that this relation is unilateral; the relation of union between the just soul and the indwelling God is real in man but of reason only or rational in God, every relation from God to the creatures being of reason only.

[80] S. Th. I, q. 43, a. 3; I, II, q. 114, a. 3 ad 3.

[81] Lessius, De perfectionibus divinis, 12, 11, 76, "vinculum Spiritus Sancti"; Petavius, De Trinitate, 8, 6, 4 "vinculum quoddam sive nexus quo cum animis nostris illa Spiritus Sancti substantia copulatur"; Thomassinus, De Incarnatione Verbi, 6, 19, 5 "exordialis quaedam connexio copulaque cum Deo."

[82] Waffelaert, "gratia sanctificans . . . est causa dispositiva ad habendam gratiam increatam seu Spiritum Sanctum inhabitantem," Collationes Brugenses (1910), 626; P. Dumont, Revue des sciences religieuses (1934), 92; Mersch, in Nouvelle revue théologique (1938), 816; G. de Broglie, De gratia, 139, "relatio transcendentalis ad Deum ut actuantem"; Rondet, in Nouv. rev. théol. (1949), 579.

idea of formal cause of our justification,"[83] that is, created sanctifying grace is inconceivable without the Uncreated Grace.

The foundation of this idea of grace is the very teaching of Holy Scripture and of the patristic, particularly, Greek tradition. There the indwelling of God in the souls of the just appears as inseparable from the state of grace, even more so than created grace. It is the inhabitation of the Word, or the Spirit, or the Trinity, that makes us just, saints, divinized.[84]. . .

The consequences of this concept of sanctifying grace are many. One regards the manner of constructing the doctrine of grace rather than the doctrine itself. If created grace and Uncreated Grace are correlative realities, then it is not perfectly right to propose the divine indwelling as a formal effect of sanctifying grace, on a par with our sharing in the divine nature of our adoptive divine filiation.[85] It is rather the root of all these formal effects, belonging as it does to the very idea of the formal cause of our justification. Accordingly the consideration of the divine indwelling should precede that of the formal effects of grace.

There is a good deal more in this relative aspect of sanctifying grace. If created grace and Uncreated Grace are correlatives, then it should not sound surprising to say that the priority in importance and efficiency belongs to Uncreated Grace. The divine indwelling is *the* important factor in our sanctification. God alone can divinize; no created reality can do so. It is by dwelling in us that He changes us and unites us to Himself. Both Holy Scripture and patristic tradition are explicit and clear in their emphasis on God-in-us. Moreover, if it is true that the essence of the supernatural order lies in God's self-gift to His rational creatures[86] while in the natural order He as it were gives the creatures to themselves, then obviously the divine indwelling is the primary reality in our sanctification.

Perhaps it is good to note that the emphasis on the divine indwelling in no way involves a twofold formal cause of our justification — which would be in opposition to the teaching of the Council of Trent.[87] There is only one inherent cause of our justice and sanctity, namely, sanctifying grace. The indwelling Trinity is in no way inherent in us by way of a form, nor

---

[83] P. Galtier, *De SS. Trinitate in Se et in nobis* (Paris, 1933), 288: "Communior in dies est sententia quae tenet specialem illam in anima habitationem esse de ratione causae formalis iustificationis nostrae."

[84] Cf. for example, St. Athanasius, in Rouet, *Enchiridion*, 780; St. Basil, *ibid.*, 949; St. Cyril of Alexandria, *ibid.*, 2107; cf. P. Galtier, *Le Saint Esprit en nous d'après les Pères grecs* (Rome, 1946).

[85] This is commonly done in our manuals; cf. Van Noort n. 151: the fourth among the formal effects of sanctifying grace is, "nos facit templum Spiritus Sancti et totius Trinitatis."

[86] K. Rahner, "Zum scholastischen Begrifflichkeit der ungeschaffenen Gnade" in *Zeitschrift für katholische Theologie* (1939), 137–157, reprinted in *Schriften zur Theologie*, I (1954), 347–375; also our article "Created Actuation by the Uncreated Act" in *Theological Studies* (1957), 61–92, esp. 62.

[87] Denzinger 1529, "unica causa formalis (iustificationis)."

is the divine justice imputed to us. The Trinity only terminates the relationship of which sanctifying grace is the real foundation.

Grace in this conception, appears to entail of necessity a complex of new relationships to the indwelling divine Persons. The question then arises of how to conceive these relations to the Father, the Son and the Holy Spirit. The explanation prevalent in theological tradition at the time when the divine indwelling did not take the central place which it is being given today, is by way of *appropriation*.[88] That is to say, the divine indwelling in just souls is said to be one common effect of the three Persons but attributed rightfully to the Holy Spirit, or to each of the other Persons in a special way, because of the similarity obtaining between this effect of the divine Love and the proper way of existing of the Persons within the Trinity. In this opinion, there are no proper distinct relationships of just souls to each of the divine Persons; these distinct relations exist only in the intentional order, not in the objective reality. And the reason for saying so is that all divine operations *ad extra* or all efficiency and production are common to the three Persons, because of the unity of their essence and nature.[89]

Today there is a definite tendency to go beyond the appropriation theory and to conceive our relationships with the Father, the Son and the Holy Spirit as special and proper to each, not only by way of speaking but in reality.[90] These distinct relationships do not suppose any special efficiency of each of the Persons — the traditional principle which says that every efficiency is common to the Three is fully accepted. But they are conceivable (and so we may take the sayings of Holy Scripture and of Tradition in their proper meaning), because of the essentially relative character of sanctifying grace. Sanctifying grace presents a two fold aspect: it is a perfection produced in the soul by God, and in this regard it refers to God as One; and it is also a link uniting to God, the foundation of relationships that terminate in the Triune God, and in this regard grace unites to God as Three, because God as Person is not One but Three. In this manner distinct and proper relationships to the divine Persons are acceptable.[91]

This idea of grace brings out what contemporary theologians love to call the personalistic concept of grace,[92] that is, the concept of grace as involving a set of relationships between persons, in particular, at this point of our study, between the created persons in a state of grace and the divine Persons. It is said that the notion of person as of the self-

[88] Cf. S. Th. I, q. 43, a. 3 and 5. Further, P. Galtier, *L'Habitation en nous des Trois Personnes* (Paris, 1950).

[89] Cf. S. Th. I, q. 32, a. 1; q. 45, a. 6; III, q. 23, a. 2; Galtier, *De Trinitate*, nn. 430 and 435.

[90] Cf. De Letter's article "Sanctifying Grace and the Divine Indwelling," in *Theol. Studies* (1953), 242–273, esp. 249.

[91] Cf. *ibid.*, 250 f., 261 f., 276 f.

[92] Cf. *art. cit.*, of P. De Haes; *Clergy Monthly* (1957).

contained and incommunicable individuality of a spiritual being includes relationships of opposition and union with other persons. A person exists not only for himself but also for others; his perfection unites these two aspects. In the life of grace, the supernaturalization of the human person places him in relationships of opposition and union with the divine Persons. Here lies the reason of the trinitarian pattern of the life of grace.

4. In Christ and in the Church. The relationship to Christ and to the Church which springs from sanctifying grace is another prominent theme of the contemporary theology of grace. When grace is viewed, not merely as a perfection in us, but as the reality of the Christian life proposed in the New Testament and further developed by the Fathers, then the life of grace shows its necessary connections with Christ and with the Church. These relationships further reveal its structure and its contents.

In Christ. Our life of grace is related to the Redeemer in two ways; it originates in Christ and incorporates into Him. It is *ex Christo* and *in Christum*. It comes from Christ from whose fulness we have all received. He came that we might have life, and He died and rose again from death that we should live in Him — *in Christo*.[93] These teachings of St. John and St. Paul were further developed by the Fathers when they explained the purpose of the Incarnation. The Son of God became the son of man

that men might become sons of God or be deified.[94] He came to communicate to us His own divine life. Accordingly, our life of grace is a sharing in that of Christ. Whatever was in Christ, St. Cyril of Alexandria said, derives into us.[95] And St. Augustine too said that the grace which sanctified the humanity of Christ is the one that makes us Christians.[96]

Scholastic theology, particularly that of St. Thomas, systematized these ideas of Holy Scripture and the Fathers by distinguishing in Christ a threefold grace: the grace of the hypostatic union which is incommunicable; His personal habitual grace which sanctified His humanity as a principle of supernatural life and which was absolutely perfect and infinite in its kind; and His grace as Head of all the justified, whether actually or potentially, which is, so to speak, the overflow of His own sanctifying grace.[97] Our life of grace, then, is a sharing in the sanctifying grace of Christ Himself, who as Head of mankind imparts to us, His members, to live by His own life.

---

[93] Cf. Jn 1:16; 10:10; Rom 4:25; 2 Cor 5:17.

[94] St. Athanasius, "Verbum Dei homo factus est ut nos deificaremur" (*Or. de Incarnatione Verbi Dei* 8; Rouet 788). St. Augustine, ". . . ille Filius qui, cum esset Filius Dei, venit ut fieret filius hominis, donaretque nobis, qui eramus filii hominis, filios Dei fieri" (Epist. 140, *ad Honorat.*, 3, 9; Rouet 1433).

[95] "Quaecumque enim Christo insunt, eadem in nos derivantur" (P.G. 75, 333).

[96] "Ea gratia fit ab initio fidei suae homo quicumque christianus, qua gratia homo ille ab initio suo factus est Christus" (P.L., 44, 982).

[97] Cf. S. *Th.* III, q. 2, a. 10; q. 6, a. 6; q. 6, aa. 1 and 3; q. 8, a. 5.

Because our grace is a continuation of that of Christ, it entails a second relationship to Him: it incorporates us into Him.[98] After the teaching of Scripture and the Fathers, this incorporation involves a twofold reality. Grace actively unites us with Christ after the manner in which the members are linked with the head whose influence they receive uninterruptedly, or of the branches which live by the sap of the vine; and this incorporating grace says identity of the flow of life which courses through the head and the members, or the vine and the branches.[99] The Council of Trent used the Scriptural metaphor of the vine and the branches to express the constant influence of Christ on those whom He reaches by His grace.[100] And the just-mentioned Thomistic theology of the *gratia capitis*, as being the overflow of Christ's personal habitual grace, expresses the same twofold reality of our incorporation into Him. This idea of incorporation also expresses the unity between the members of one Body, and this leads us to our relationship through grace with the Church.

In the Church. The *locus* of our union with Christ through grace is the Church, His Mystical Body. Here again our relationship with our fellow members springing from grace is twofold: grace is *per Ecclesiam* and *in Ecclesiam*.

All grace comes through the Church, whether through her sacramental action or through the intercession of her prayer, particularly her sacrifice, the Mass.[101] The Church as a body intervenes in the distribution of grace either through her official ministers or through the influence of her members. Our grace is social in its origins. It may not be easy, and in many cases it is impossible, to put the finger on a visible action of the Church in the dispensation of all graces and so detect her visible causality, especially for the graces given to those outside the fold. But if these graces also, as Pius XII said in his encyclical *Mystici Corporis*, orientate their recipients to the Church,[102] that is undoubtedly because these graces are not independent of the Church. And we can well visualize how her power of intercession is operative in her liturgical prayer or in the private prayer of her members, and more particularly

---

[98] There are different degrees in this incorporation, sanctifying grace being susceptible of increase, and faith eventually remaining when grace is lost; and different ways, sacramental or extrasacramental (i.e. by the votum of the sacraments of baptism or of the Eucharist).

[99] I Cor 12:27; Eph 4:15; 5:30; Jn 15:5. — This does not mean that our grace is numerically one with that of Christ, as the metaphor of the 'overflow' might suggest; our grace is only a participation in it; cf. the encyclical *Mediator Dei*, transl. of CTS, n. 216.

[100] Denzinger 1546.

[101] This effective intervention of the Church in the dispensation of graces, particularly through the offering of the Mass, is a point that needs further clarification in the study of the "Extra Ecclesiam nulla salus"; cf. A. Piannazzi, "Outside the Church no Salvation" in the *Clergy Monthly* (1942–1943), 41–45; and an unpublished study on "The Universal Mediation of the Church" by J. R. Lerch.

[102] AAS (1943), 243 "inscio quodam desiderio et voto . . . ordinantur."

in the sacrifice she offers *pro nostra et totius mundi salute*. It constitutes a truly universal causality in the order of grace, co-extensive to that of her Head, Christ Himself.

Grace is of the Church, and also for the Church. It links together in a communion of supernatural life all the members of the Church — our life of grace is social of its very nature. When we say that grace incorporates into the Church and makes us members of one another, we mean to say that the grace of each profits all the members, after the manner in which in a body the health of each organ and limb makes for the well-being of the others and of the whole. This is the social aspect of the life of grace which the study of the Mystical Body draws into forceful relief.[103] Concretely it is expressed in charity, the activity of the life of grace, in which love of God or Christ and love of the neighbour are inseparable, by virtue of the mystical identification of Christ with His members.[104] Brotherly love, then, not surprisingly, is Christ's special commandment and the hallmark of His disciples.[105] All this goes to show the essentially social nature of Christian grace.[106]

3. P. De Letter, S.J.,[107] surveys contemporary theology on the divine indwelling in the postwar years 1945–1951 and studies the interdependence of our incorporation in Christ and the inhabitation of the Trinity.

Sanctifying grace and the divine indwelling.[108] During these last few years speculative theology on sanctifying grace has mostly centered upon the mystery of the divine inhabitation in the souls of the just and upon the connected questions — created and uncreated grace, appropriation, divinization and divine sonship. By reviewing, therefore, current theology on the divine indwellings we necessarily touch on most of what has been written recently on sanctifying grace. . . .

F. J. Trütsch's[109] . . . classification of recent theories differs from Michel's.[110] Contemporary theology on

[103] Cf. both the historical and theological studies of E. Mersch.

[104] Compare the common teaching on the twofold material object of the one theological virtue of charity: God and the neighbor; and the gospel on the two commandments, Mt 22:36–38, with the "Mihi fecistis" of Mt 25:40, 45.

[105] Cf. Jn 15:12.

[106] Another manifestation of the social character of the life of grace are the communal graces or *gratiae gratis datae*; cf. *Clergy Monthly* (1955), 201–207, 294–300.

[107] P. De Letter, S.J., cf. ch. XIV, n. p. 35. These excerpts are from two of his articles in *Theological Studies*, "Sanctifying Grace and the Divine Indwelling" of June, 1953, pp. 242–272, and "Grace, Incorporation, Inhabitation" of March, 1958, pp. 1–31.

[108] This survey is limited, with but rare exceptions, to the postwar years 1945–1951.

[109] F. J. Trütsch's doctoral thesis, SS.

[110] A. Michel, "Trinité (Missions et habitation des personnes de la)," DTC, XV, 2 (Paris, 1950), 1830–1855. *trinitatis inhabitatio apud theologos recentiores* (Trent, 1949); the work was actually written in 1946.

the inhabitation can be grouped in two main classes of opinions. The first looks for an explanation in God's presence as principle of the supernatural life; the other considers His presence as term or object of it.

The first class comprises three subgroups. (1) One group considers God as efficient cause of sanctifying grace, and this efficient causality explains His special presence in the inhabitation, either by itself alone (as Vasquez thought, but hardly anyone today), or as a partial principle of explanation together with God's presence of immensity (so, after John of St. Thomas and Gardeil, who presupposed it to objective presence, Garrigou-Lagrange, Elfes, Lange, Koenig, and others), or by the special way of efficient causality proper to the production of grace, namely, such as involves immediate presence of the divine Persons (Galtier, Retailleau, Dumont, et al.). (2) Another group explains the inhabitation by exemplary causality, that is, through assimilation or a divine operation that is formally assimilating the just soul to God (Galtier, Joret, Chambat, Martinez, Gomez, Rudloff), either under the aspect of nature (Gardeil), or of deity (Retailleau, Garrigou-Lagrange) or of Trinity (Galtier, Chambat). (3) A third group considers quasi-formal causality as the explanation of the divine indwelling (de la Taille, K. Rahner).

The second class of explanations of the divine inhabitation, in the Suarezian line of thought, considers God's objective presence through knowledge and love as the reason of His indwelling in a special manner (Froget, Pesch, Gardeil, Garrigou-Lagrange, Lange, Delaye, Rudloff, Retailleau, Menendez-Reigada). As is apparent from this tableau of opinions, many authors unite more than one opinion in an explanation of their own. . . . Against this background of opinions current theology reveals a desire to seize the speciality of God's presence in the soul through grace and manifests some sort of dissatisfaction with the appropriation theory.[111] This desire and this dissatisfaction are apparently inspired by the thirst for realism and the aversion to nominalism which are characteristic of our time. . . .

The *proprium* theory of the divine indwelling continues to find followers. F. Taymans d'Eypernon, S.J., for example, in an inspiring book on the mystery of the Holy Trinity[112] rallies to De Regnon's position that each of the Divine Persons plays a special role in sanctifying the just soul and that the just soul has a special and distinct relation to each of the Divine

---

[111] The desire and the dissatisfaction do not date from today. Petau and De Regnon have always had their admirers, some hesitant, others more daring; cf. H. Schauf, *Die Einwohnung des hl. Geistes: Die Lehre von der nichtappropriierten Einwohnung des hl. Geistes als Beitrag zur Theologiegeschichte des neunzehnten Jahrhunderts unter besonderer Berücksichtigung der beiden Theologen Carl Passaglia und Clemens Schrader* (Freiburg i. B., 1941), and the review by J. Bittremieux in *Ephemerides theologicae Lovanienses*, XIX (1942), 147–149.

[112] F. Taymans d'Eypernon, S.J., *Le mystère primordial: La trinité dans sa vivante image* (Paris, 1941), pp. 109–128.

Persons. So does Fr. G. M. Dupont, S.J., in a spiritual book on devotion to the Holy Trinity.[113] He even goes further. Even in the order of creation he detects some sort of special relations to each of the Three Persons, a view which not all theologians or students of St. Thomas will share. . . . The desire to present the *proprium* theory of the inhabitation in an acceptable manner inspires two articles of Fr. M. J. Donnelly, S.J., in *Theological Studies*[114] in which he draws his principle of solution from de la Taille's concept of grace as created actuation by uncreated Act. . . .

A new approach: our incorporation in the Mystical Body. A new approach to the problem of our union with the Three Divine Persons is taken in the remarkable dissertation of Fr. H. F. T. Borgert, C.SS.R., on God's indwelling in the soul.[115] The author faces the contrast between the explicit statements of Scripture and Tradition on the ontological indwelling of the Three Divine Persons, and the minimizing theory of appropriations. The latter does not seem to render all that is implied in the former. He accordingly begins by examining the doctrine of the New Testa-

ment and of the Fathers in order to detect there a possible new way of approach to the problem. His findings lead him to the conclusion that according to the revealed doctrine the Three Persons inhabit the just souls as three distinct Persons; the same doctrine hints clearly that the entrance to the inhabitation of the Divine Persons lies for men in the union of their souls with Christ, in their membership in the Mystical Body.

Scholastic theology in general failed to exploit these hints of the sources of revelation; it rather followed St. Augustine who, on this particular point, did not synthesize his teaching on the divine indwelling with that on the Mystical Body of Christ. . . . Fr. Borgert accordingly approaches his study of the mystery from the new angle indicated in Scripture, that is, the mystery of our incorporation in Christ. He proposes his own hypothesis, as a probable theory of the divine indwelling. . . . The central starting point is Christ, God-Man. His humanity, because of the hypostatic union, is the *instrumentum coniunctum* of the divinity and the universal principle in the dispensation of grace. Through faith and baptism we are in real relation to Christ's humanity and so *ipso facto* to the Verbum, for it is through Christ's humanity as instrumental and quasi-principal cause that we receive faith and the sacramental character. By the very fact of this relation to the Verbum we are in a real relation to the Father and the Holy Spirit. In this precisely

113 G. M. Dupont, S.J., *Foundations for a Devotion to the Blessed Trinity* (Calcutta, 1947).

114 M. J. Donnelly, S.J., "The Indwelling of the Holy Spirit According to M. J. Scheeben," *Theological Studies,* VII (1946), 244–280; "The Inhabitation of the Holy Spirit: A Solution According to de la Taille," *ibid.,* VIII (1947), 445–470.

115 H. F. T. Borgert, C.SS.R., *In Geest en Waarheid: Over de Inwoning Gods in de Zielen* (Nijmegen, 1950).

consists the indwelling of the Divine Persons. Faith and baptism unite us with Christ; then follows the un-created Gift; then the created gift, grace, which completes our incorpora-tion in Christ and the divine indwell-ing. And so the inhabitation properly consists in a relation to the Verbum, and in the Verbum to the Father and the Holy Spirit, with the grace and virtues. That relation with the Verbum does not coincide with our relation to the divine nature *ratione creationis*. To this link with the Verbum grace ans-wers as a participated similitude of the natural filiation. . . .

Fr. Borgert is not the first to attempt this new approach to the mystery of our union with the Divine Persons. In 1944, Fr. E. Mersch, S.J., incor-porated in his *La théologie du corps mystique*[116] (now available in the Eng-lish translation of Fr. Cyril Vollert)[117] an earlier study of his "Filii in Filio"[118] in which this approach was made. His idea in its main outline is as follows. Grace unites us to, or incorporates us in, Christ. "Christ is the Son of the First Person; He is the Second Person Himself; He is the co-princi-ple of the Third Person. When we are united to Him, therefore, we are, in Him and through Him, adopted sons of the First Person; with regard to the Second Person, we are mem-bers of the Word and share in His intellectual sonship; and with regard to the Third Person, we are associated in the work of love that has its ter-minus and its summit in the Holy Spirit."[119] This is exactly St. Paul's teaching, which Mersch sums up by quoting Prat: "From the supernatural being received at baptism, special rela-tions with each of the three divine Persons are derived: a relation of son-ship with the Father; a relation of consecration to the Holy Spirit; a relation of mystical identity with Jesus Christ."[120]

It is grace, the grace of adoption, which unites us to Christ and to the Verbum. This grace, inasmuch as it is *ad extra*, is a common effect of the Trinity. But it is not only *ad extra*, because and insofar as it unites us to the Word it is in a way *ad intra*. It belongs to the order of that which is "interiorized."[121] Grace, moreover, is essentially an "entity of union." It unites us to Christ, to the Person of Christ who is the Word and the Son of the Father, and so makes us also (adopted) sons of the Father, in the Spirit. And as we share in Christ's sonship, which is the natural sonship of the Word, so also we share in His spiratorship and have a special relation to the Holy Spirit. Grace, therefore, is a special relationship to the Trinity. This is Mersch's way of reconciling the common and certain doctrine, ac-

[116] Brussels, 1944; 2 ed., 1946.
[117] *The Theology of the Mystical Body* (St. Louis, 1951); cf. Book IV, pp. 325–452; also, on the supernatural, pp. 455–478; and, on sanctifying grace, pp. 594–621.
[118] *Nouvelle revue théologique*, LXV (1938), 551–582, 681–702, 809–830.

[119] *The Theology of the Mystical Body*, p. 330.
[120] Fernand Prat, S.J., *The Theology of St. Paul*, II (London, 1934), 320.
[121] Mersch, *op. cit.*, p. 373.

cording to which all operations of the Trinity *ad extra* are common to the Three Persons (and so also grace insofar as its efficiency or production is concerned), with the possibility and reality of special relations to each of the Three Persons. Nor does he require for these three relations a threefold foundation in created grace; grace need not be a miniature of the Trinity. All that grace does is immediately to unite us to Christ, to the Word, and make us share in His sonship. The relations to the Father and to the Holy Spirit follow necessarily on our relation to the Word, just as Christ the Word is necessarily related to the Father and to the Holy Spirit.

Mersch's explanation of our union with the Trinity through our union with Christ and the Word or our incorporation in His Mystical Body by means of grace, "entity of union," which takes us into the "order of the interiorized," appeals to new concepts, other than those in which the common Scholastic explanation of created grace as the foundation of relations is conceived. Perhaps that is the only way. Some may desire, however, to see this new trinitarian concept of grace expressed in the traditional categories. Can it be shown, in Scholastic terms, how the grace of sonship places us in a special relation to the Father and to Him alone, not to the Trinity as one? . . .

It would seem then, that a close union of positive, that is, biblical and patristic theology on the indwelling, with the speculations of Scholastic

theology on this august mystery, the one tempering and guiding the other, together with contact with other mysteries of the faith (for instance, that of our union with Christ in His Mystical Body), hold promises for further fruitful research.

Grace, incorporation, inhabitation. [122] Among the points of doctrine emphasized in the contemporary theology of sanctifying grace, two themes are particularly prominent: the Christological character of grace, and the Trinitarian. Our life of grace is nothing but the life of Christ in us, our life *in Christo* (since our sanctifying grace is our sharing in His capital grace, *gratia capitis,* the overflow into our souls of His own habitual grace).[123] In that manner we are sons in the Son, *filii in Filio*:[124] grace incorporates us in Christ, the Son of God incarnate. Simultaneously, and apparently as a consequence of our union with Christ, sanctifying grace places us in a new relationship to each of the three divine Persons in a way which, contemporary theology is inclined to say, goes beyond mere appropriation.[125] Christian grace is es-

[122] Cf. De Letter's article, "Sanctifying Grace and the Divine Indwelling," *Theological Studies,* March, 1958, p. 1 ff; cf. also "Contemporary Theology of Grace," *Clergy Monthly,* 21 (1957), 288–297.

[123] S. th. 3, q. 8, a. 5; cf. e.g., W. Grossouw, *In Christus, Schets van een theologie van St. Paulus* (Utrecht and Brussels, 1948).

[124] Cf. E. Mersch, "Filii in Filio," *Nouvelle revue théologique,* 65 (1938), 551–582, 681–702, 809–830.

[125] Cf. "Divine Indwelling," pp. 244, 249, 261 f., 277 f. Further, F. Bourassa, "Presence de Dieu et union aux divines

sentially Trinitarian in structure by relationships to the Persons which are not purely of the intentional order[126] but are objective and ontological, and which are distinct despite the oneness of the divine efficiency by which the Trinity produces created sanctifying grace, the one created foundation of this new relation of union with the Persons.[127]

The interdependence, however, of these two features of grace seems rarely to have been examined closely; yet both speculatively and practically it gives rise to real problems. Speculatively, it raises the question whether the Trinitarian structure of our grace, or the triune relationship to the Persons of the Trinity that results from grace, is so linked with its character of grace of Christ that it results from this as from its necessary prerequisite, in such a manner that an economy of grace without Incarnation is not conceivable. Practically, it points to the difficulty experienced by not a few Christians who are aware of these two aspects of our life of grace, aware of the place that should be given, in the conscious living of the spiritual life, to Christ on the one hand and

to the Blessed Trinity on the other. Accordingly, a study of the interrelation between our incorporation in Christ and the inhabitation of the Trinity should be rewarding. After recalling and explaining each of these two glories of divine grace, we shall endeavor to sketch an answer to both the speculative and the practical problem.

Our triune relation to the indwelling Trinity. We begin with the explanation of our triune relation to the indwelling Trinity.[128] On a former occasion we pointed out the contemporary endeavor to propose a truly Trinitarian concept of grace, that is, one which reveals the structure of grace as essentially involving relationships to the three divine Persons, not merely of the intentional order, or resulting only from our conscious acts of prayer, adoration, love, and the like, but also objectively or antecedently to these acts and arising from the very essence of grace.[129]

The reason for this endeavor is, no doubt, to be looked for in the return to the sources of revelation which is characteristic of the present-day theological revival. As Père Prat wrote a number of years ago, "the common explanation which sees in the indwelling of the divine Persons only different

---

Personnes," *Sciences ecclésiastiques* 6 (1954), 5–23 and "Role personnel des Personnes et relations distinctes aux Personnes," *ibid.*, 7 (1955), 751–772.

[126] Even theologians who do not go beyond the appropriation theory hold special relations to the three Persons in the intentional order, relations of a moral and religious order which arise from our acts of faith, adoration, prayer, love; cf., e.g., P. Galtier, *L'Habitation en nous des trois Personnes* (Rome, 1950), p. 130 f.

[127] Cf. "Divine Indwelling," p. 268 f.

[128] To say it at once: our incorporation in Christ will be explained differently by one who admits a triune relationship to the indwelling Trinity and by one who does not. Incorporation as such does not involve but rather presupposes this triune relation.

[129] Cf. "Divine Indwelling," pp. 244, 249, 261 f., 277 f.

degrees of appropriation, does not seem to harmonize sufficiently with the language of the Fathers and the Scriptures.[130] His remark has been echoed by many a theologian after him. And so we are told that "we are to admit relations from person to Person which go beyond the nominalism of a pure appropriation, without however denying the oneness of the divine action in natural and supernatural creation."[131] Even theologians who feel reluctant to part company with St. Thomas, or rather to go beyond his explicit teaching on the question, seek to give the Scholastic theory of appropriation a meaning that is not liable to this objection of nominalism.[132]

Our present endeavor is an attempt at proposing a properly Trinitarian concept of grace and establishing proper relations to the three divine Persons. This can be done, not a few theologians maintain, while fully respecting the traditional Catholic doctrine which is recalled by Pius XII in *Mystici corporis*[133] when he mentions the theological explanation of the divine indwelling: that the absolute distinction between Creator and creature persists undiminished also in our divinization through the divine inhabitation, and that every divine efficiency or production of reality *ad extra* is common to the three Persons.[134] But within this Catholic context, a Trinitarian concept of grace supposes certain theological ideas about the essence of the supernatural or of grace which we have first to state before explaining the concept of a triune relationship.

Presuppositions of a Trinitarian concept of grace. The first and perhaps the most basic presupposition is the idea of a divine quasi-formal causality as the specific explanation of the essence of the supernatural. It would seem that only within the theological context of the self-communication of God by way of quasi-information or actuation can a Trinitarian concept of grace be held. A theology of the inhabitation which refuses as unacceptable this species of causality proper to the order of grace[135] cannot consistently conceive of distinct relations to the three divine Persons.

The reason for the last statement should not be hard to see. If every Catholic theologian must admit that the divine efficient causality is common to the three Persons, and if on the other hand God's exemplary and final causality with regard to creatures is closely connected with or even measured by that efficient causality, then it seems to follow logically that within the setting of such causality no proper or distinct relations to the Persons can arise. The divine action

---

[130] F. Prat, *Theology of St. Paul,* tr. J. L. Stoddard, 2 (London, 1927), 291.

[131] G. Philips, in *Marianum,* 14 (1952), 15.

[132] Cf. "Divine Indwelling," p. 255 f.; Bourassa, "Adoptive Sonship," pp. 318 ff., 332 f.

[133] Cf. Denzinger 3814.

[134] Cf. Bourassa, "Adoptive Sonship," p. 309.

[135] Some Thomists do so; cf. De Letter's article "Created Actuation by the Uncreated Act: Difficulties and Answers," *Theological Studies,* 18 (1957), 60.

and the perfection that results from it in the creature, which should be the source and foundation of these relations, are of necessity common to the three Persons who produce them by virtue of the one divine essence or nature which they possess in common. Only by appropriation can they be attributed to one Person in preference to another. Accordingly, if grace and the relationship between the soul and God that results from it are said to rest only with the divine efficient causality, together with the exemplary and final causality that goes with it, then a Trinitarian concept of grace would seem to be excluded a priori. If, however, the order of grace consists essentially in God's self-communication to His creature by way of actuation or immediate union in the order of formal causality (this causality of course being not that of a form but only of an act, and in fact of the pure Act), then a different relationship than that which unites to the Trinity as one is not inconceivable.

Theologians who hold this quasi-formal causality agree that it is necessarily attended by an efficient causality, namely, by the production of a new reality in the creature to whom the divine Act unites Himself; and this production *ad extra* is, according to the above-mentioned principle, common to the three Persons, as is the exemplary and the final causality inseparable from and commensurate with that efficiency. We have here a first reason why our relationship to the Trinity through grace should be

called triune and not simply threefold or three distinct relations. But it is important to note, this efficiency is not the reason and cause of the supernaturalness of grace to the extent namely that it is of the same order as the divine efficiency in the order of creation or of nature. It differs, however, from the natural divine efficiency in its being inseparably linked with a self-donation of God as Act of the creature, in such a manner as to be subordinate and secondary to this. The only reason for its existence is that without it the actuation or quasi-information of the creature by the divine Act would not be real but only nominal.

It is not surprising that theology has appealed to this quasi-formal causality as the explanation of what is specific to the order of grace. Both the indications of Scripture and tradition, which speak of our divinization and union with God through grace in such a manner as to say that these are not found outside the reign of grace (Jn 14:23 Rom 8:9) and the common teaching about the order of creation or of nature, which is defined by the threefold causality mentioned above and to which the order of grace is irreducible, are of a nature to suggest a causality specifically proper to the supernatural. The data from the fonts of revelation, no doubt, are of themselves insufficient to require quasi-formal causality as the only plausible explanation of the order of grace. A theology of the inhabitation which finds no room for this concept of causality also claims to offer a satisfactory explanation of the sayings of Scripture and tradition.[136] Yet revelation insinuates a discontinuity and disparity between the order of grace and that of nature, or between the divine and the human, such as to constitute a gulf which God alone can and did bridge. And common theological doctrine, interpreting that teaching of revelation, understands the transcendence of grace with regard to nature in such a manner that nature is in no way a beginning of grace,[137] despite a real sort of continuity with grace expressed in the natural desire of, or at least its inherent obediential potency to, the supernatural. These two teachings naturally suggest that we seek a concept of the supernatural which derives from a proper and specific causality of its own. . . .

A second presupposition to a Trinitarian concept of grace, a sequel to the first, is the essentially relative character of grace. Sanctifying grace is no doubt a quality, perfection, form, or habitus which inheres in the soul, but it is not only that. It is a created and accidental perfection which involves a transcendental or essential relation to the indwelling God.[138] . . .

As a consequence of this relative character, sanctifying grace presents of necessity two distinct, though inseparable, aspects.[139] As a quality or habitus which perfects and inheres in the soul, it is produced by God by way of efficient causality, and therefore by the three Persons as one efficient cause. As foundation of a relation of union with God as quasi-form of the soul, it unites us to the indwelling Trinity. This unitive aspect is not of the order of efficient causality. Union as such means only a relation, not a perfection which is produced. Union only calls for a term to terminate its relation, not for a cause to produce it. In a union with God in Himself, or with God as quasi-form, the term of the relation is God in Himself, who is three Persons. Since terminating a relation is not efficient causality but belongs reductively to the order of formal causality, there is nothing against saying that it refers us to the Persons as Three.

The third presupposition to a Trinitarian concept of grace — actually only a different manner of envisaging the second (namely, considering the absolute and relative aspects of grace no longer statically but dynamically) is that one conceives the divine inhabitation or the work of our sanctification not merely as an action of God ad extra, but secundum quid ad intra. . . . If one says — as perhaps few if

---

[136] All that such an explanation affirms of the supernatural order of grace holds good for the aspect of production of grace or of the divine efficient causality. But it is incomplete, because it leaves out the aspect of union (which belongs to the quasi-formal causality).

[137] Cf. S. th., 2-2, q. 24, a. 3, ad 2.

[138] Cf. G. de Broglie, De gratia (unpublished manuscript) p. 139, who says that grace is also "relatio transcendentalis ad Deum ut actuantem nos."

[139] It would seem that it is because the Scholastic explanation generally neglects one of these two aspects (that of union) that it cannot have a properly Trinitarian concept of grace (except by appropriation).

any theologians actually say but many take for granted[140] — that there is in the divine work of our sanctification nothing else than the divine action *ad extra,* then a priori a Trinitarian concept of grace in the sense of a triune relationship to the Persons is unacceptable. But if grace, besides being a perfection produced by God, is a link of union with Him as quasi-form of the soul, then the divine work of our sanctification is not only a productive efficiency but also, and in the first place, a unitive divine initiative which draws us to Himself as to the uncreated Act[141] fulfilling our natural desire of Him or obediential potency. Uniting us to Himself does not, as such, mean any efficient causality but only quasi-formal causality, no production of a perfection but only the origination of a relation of union with Him as quasi-form or of union with Him as He is in Himself. . . . This therefore, since it does not, as such, produce any new reality is not *simpliciter ad extra;* it can truly be said to be *secundum quid ad intra.*[142] . . .

A triune relationship. What do we mean by a triune relationship to the three divine Persons? . . . This term

intends to express the junction of the two aspects of our union with God through grace: its oneness and its threefoldness, after the analogy of the Trinity which is triunity. The oneness of the relationship to the indwelling Trinity springs from two factors that go to originate this relationship: the created reality of sanctifying grace as a perfection of form in the soul (this is one and not threefold)[143] and the uncreated Act or absolute esse or absolute perfection which, by uniting itself to the soul as its quasi-form or Act, and so to speak impressing in the soul its own likeness, produces the created actuation. Considered from these aspects, the relationship of grace is one. There is one created foundation of a relationship of union with the one uncreated Act.

But this way of envisaging that union with God is, as it were, extrinsic; it does not touch on what is characteristic of the union with God as quasi-form or with God in Himself. The uncreated Act to whom grace unites by an immediate union . . . is both one and three, or triune. Consequently, that union regards at the same time one term, the uncreated Act, and three terms, the three divine

---

[140] As St. Thomas says that we should do.

[141] Perhaps it may be more suggestive, if not more correct, to present the union of God with the soul through grace as His attracting us to Him, rather than as His self-donation to us. But in both cases the reality expressed is the same union with Him as quasi-form or actuating Act.

[142] This phrase, therefore, expresses that this union with God, unlike an *opus Dei ad extra,* does not as such produce any new reality, and in that sense and to that extent (*secundum quid*) is not *ad extra* but *ad intra.*

[143] If there is any distinction in the gifts of grace (as the common, especially Thomistic, theory holds: grace and the virtues or gifts are really distinct from one another), this distinction does not originate in a diversity or distinction in the divine action that produces them, but in the multiplicity of the creature, in which essence and potencies are really distinct: the supernaturalization of the essence is also really distinct from the supernaturalization of the potencies.

Persons, but each of these three terms is in His own way identical with the one term. The relationship of union with God, actuating Act, is therefore both one and three, indivisibly and by equal right or necessity. . . . The best manner of expressing the necesary junction of this oneness and this threefoldness of our relationship to the indwelling Trinity seems to be to call it triune.[144]. . . .

If one were to say that this seems too static a conception of the inhabitation . . . then we must turn for an answer to the consideration of the divine operation itself: of the Trinity sanctifying our souls by producing sanctifying grace and so uniting us to Itself as uncreated Grace or actuating Act. . . . For the divine Persons, their very presence in our souls, even apart from the efficient production of sanctifying grace which does not distinguish but unites them, is dynamic and has a transforming effect on our human personality: we really are in communion with the Father as Father and the Son as Son, and the Holy Spirit as our hallowing Spirit; and this communion, without any move or as it were agitation on their part, is the ontological call for us to live as sons of the Father, brothers of the Son, and living temples of the Spirit. The role of Persons, therefore, apart from their common causality in producing created grace, is to move us

without being moved themselves (as the immovable Mover of Aristotle) to the affections and actions which befit our communion with them. On this ontological Trinitarian grace naturally follow the intentional relations to the three Persons in our religious attitude.[145] So it appears that this Trinitarian structure of sanctifying grace, or the triune relationship to the divine Persons which is inherent in grace of its essence and before any actions of our own, is the ontological foundation of a Trinitarian spirituality such as we find in the liturgy of the Church and in the lives and writings of mystics. . . .

Our incorporation in Christ. Our sanctifying grace, in the present economy of the Incarnation-Redemption comes to us through Christ, the Word-Incarnate Redeemer. He is, the Council of Trent defined, the meritorious cause of our justification[146] and Scholastic theology, particularly St. Thomas, explains further that He is also the universal instrumental cause of our sanctification and so has an efficient causality in the distribution of grace.[147] On that score, our life of grace involves a special relationship to

---

[144] Let us note here that such a triune relationship is not to be found in the order of nature (except by appropriation) because every relation to God in that order is based on efficient causality or on an *opus Dei ad extra* which regards God as one.

[145] Here lies the difference between a Trinitarian concept of grace by appropriation only, which holds distinct relations to the Persons of the intentional order only, and a Trinitarian concept according to which the triune relationship exists before any operation of ours.

[146] Cf. Denzinger 1529.

[147] Cf. *S. th.*, 3, q. 8, a. 1 ad 1. On this question cf. Malmberg, "Onze Eenheid met den Godmensch in de Kerk," *Bijdragen der Nederlandsche Jezuieten* 5 (1942) 6, 61 ff; H. F. Th. Borgert, C.SS.R., *In Geest en Waarheid: Over de Inwoning Gods in de Zielen* (Nijmegen, 1950), esp. p. 320 ff.

Christ, commonly expressed by saying, after St. Paul and patristic tradition, that by grace we are incorporated into Christ. The phrase is meant to express something more than the causality of Christ in giving us grace. It says that our grace is not only *ex Christo* but also *in Christum*, though the second idea flows from the first. And this orientation to Christ, essential character of Christian grace, involves a twofold reality: sanctifying grace is a link with Christ, and it is a communion of life with Him. . . . In what sense does sanctifying grace link us with Christ in a communion of life, and what is our relationship to the Word, or to the divine Person of Christ, which arises from this communion?

Communion of supernatural life. Our life of grace is the life of Christ in us, or our life in Christ. . . . When, then, we say that our grace incorporates us in Christ, we mean that our sanctifying grace is a permanent link of union with the humanity of Christ (for Christ is its cause not only of becoming but also of being)[148] and that it is nothing else but a sharing in His sanctifying grace.[149] The efficient causality by which Christ produces grace in us is, considering His humanity, instrumental[150] and sub-ordinate to the divine efficient causality which He has in common with the two other Persons of the Trinity. . . .

Our relationship to the Word. Does our communion with Christ — which is an ontological dependence of our grace on the causality of His humanity, the instrument of the divinity communicating to us a share in His sanctifying grace — involve a special relationship to the Person of Christ, the Word or Second Person of the Trinity?[151] If it does, then we touch here on the inner structure of our triune relationship to the Trinity, and grace must be said to be Trinitarian because it is the grace of Christ. The question has been answered in the affirmative by several recent authors, as Mersch, Malmberg, Philips, Borgert, De Haes.[152] Perhaps somewhat hastily. There is something to be said for the many theologians who, after St. Thomas, refuse to conclude that, being sons in the Son, by our union and incorporation in Christ we share in Christ's filiation and are sons of the Father and not of the Trinity.[153]. . .

It would seem that only the consideration of the specific divine quasi-

---

[148] Cf. Malmberg, *art. cit.*, 6,251; and Denzinger 1546 "iugiter virtutem influit."

[149] *S. th.*, 3, q. 8, a. 5: "eadem est secundum essentiam gratia personalis . . . et gratia eius, secundum quam est caput ecclesiae justificans alios."

[150] Cf. Malmberg, *artt. cit.*, 6, 61, for a list of references to the *Summa theologica*, e.g., 3, q. 8, a. 1.

[151] Our incorporation in Christ, as explained so far, regards Christ as man. The question now is whether it involves a union with Christ as God, i.e., with the Person of the Word.

[152] E. Mersch, *op. cit.*, p. 330 (cf. "Divine Indwelling," p. 267); Malmberg, *art. cit.*, 6, 253 f.; G. Philips, "Notre filiation dans le Fils," *Ephemerides theologicae Lovanienses* 24 (1948), 50–52; *ibid.*, 29 (1953), 306 f.; P. de Haes, "Filii in Filio," *Collectanea Mechliniensia* 38 (1953), 674–678.

[153] Cf. *S. th.*, 3, q. 23, a. 2c; ad 2; ad 3.

formal causality, that goes of necessity with the production of sanctifying grace, can account, as far as is possible, for our special relation to the Person of the Word and for our adoptive sonship regarding the Father which arise from our incorporation in Christ. If the divine quasi-formal causality is left out and only the efficiency of God producing sanctifying grace is considered, then a priori there can be no room for a special relationship to the Word or to any of the divine Persons.[154] This is apparently the reason why St. Thomas and his followers on this point say that by grace we are sons of the Trinity and not of the Father as Christ is: they consider the adoption as efficient causality only and as an *opus Dei ad extra*; to that extent their conclusion is justified.[155] . . .

Conclusion. If the above considerations are right, then we must say that our triune relationship with the Trinity through grace is not absolutely linked with our incorporation in Christ as with its necessary prerequisite. It is so only de facto. The

Incarnation belongs to the present economy of grace, as far as we can see, not of necessity but for reasons of fittingness.[156] When our sharing in grace is to follow the pattern of our social and corporal nature, as we may expect it will since grace perfects nature after the manner of nature, then it is fitting that we enter the life of grace and share in the divine life through incorporation in Christ, God made man. In the context, our union with Christ both effects and reveals our triune relationship to the Trinity and our special relation to Him as our Head and Brother. Thus incorporation and inhabitation meet in the triune relationship born from the grace of Christ.

As to the practical difficulty about the place which Christ and the Trinity should take in a balanced Catholic spirituality, we can do no better than refer to the liturgical prayer of the Church. She generally prays to the Father through our Lord Jesus Christ in the Holy Spirit.[157] It is not unnatural, however, that Christ, the God-man should take a more prominent place in the devotional life of Christians than the Blessed Trinity.[158] As was remarked in the review of *Foundations for a Devotion to the Blessed Trinity*, perhaps it is best that

---

[154] Cf. *supra*, the first of the presuppositions of a triune relationship with the Trinity. The determination of these special relationships (filiation with regard to the Father, brotherhood with regard to the Son, and possession of the indwelling Spirit), explained in the body of the article, supposes, as we have it from revelation, that our elevation to the supernatural order happens by way of regeneration; it does not, however, according to our present argumentation, suppose that this regeneration takes place in the Son of *necessity*, though in *fact*, in the present economy of grace, it does not take place except in Christ.

[155] Cf. S.T., III, q. 23, a. 2c; ad 2, ad 3.

[156] The sacramental economy of grace itself is based on reasons of fittingness; cf. S. th., 3, q. 41.

[157] Cf. the conclusion of most orations in the liturgy.

[158] If for no other reason than that the Christian life consists in the imitation of Christ, who in His life on earth set the example of a supernatural life lived on the human level.

this exalted mystery "be the subject of an all-pervading homage, as indeed it is, rather than become in some sense rival to other devotions"; rather the foundation and general background for the whole of Christian spirituality than an object of a particular devotion.[159] Yet it may be well to follow the example of Mother Church and thus to grow more conscious of the Trinitarian structure of our union with God in Christ.

4. **K. Rahner, S.J.,[160] studies the relation between created and uncreated grace and seeks to harmonize better the Scriptural and scholastic ways of viewing them by using the concepts of formal ontology that appear in the *visio beatifica*. Thus the communication of God to the creature is by way of quasi-formal causality and involves nonappropriated relations of the creature to the three Persons.**

Grace in scholastic speculation. This is not the place to set out in detail the various scholastic theories about the relationship between created and uncreated grace. We wish to draw attention only to that common feature which concerns our present discussion, being clearly conscious of simplifying matters somewhat and leaving aside other approaches (which will be indicated later). However diverse they may be among themselves, it is true of all the scholastic theories that they see God's indwelling and his conjunction with the justified man as based exclusively upon created grace. In virtue of the fact that created grace is imparted to the soul God imparts himself to it and dwells in it. Thus what we call uncreated grace (i.e. God as bestowing Himself upon man) is a function of created grace. It is not difficult to see the basis of this conception: 'uncreated grace' (God's communication of Himself to man, the indwelling of the Spirit) implies a new *relation* of God to man. But this can only be conceived of as founded upon an absolute entitative modification of man himself, which modification is the real basis of the new real relation of man to God upon which rests the relation of God to man. This absolute entitative modification and determination of man is created grace, which has in consequence a twofold aspect: it is ontologically the formal basis of the analogical supernatural participation in God's nature through entitative assimilation of man to God's spirituality and holi-

[159] Cf. the review of G. M. Dupont, *Foundations for a Devotion to the Blessed Trinity* (Calcutta, 1947), in *Month* 184 (1947), 192.

[160] K. Rahner, S.J., perhaps the most influential theologian in German-speaking Catholicism today, editor of Denzinger's *Enchiridion Symbolorum* and coeditor of the new *Lexikon für Theologie und Kirche,* is the author of many books and articles. This excerpt is from his book, *Theological Investigations*, Vol. I (Baltimore: Helicon Press, 1961), and is selected from pp. 324–346.

ness (*consortium formale*), and it is the basis of a special relation (union, indwelling) between man and God himself (*consortium terminativum*). For our purposes it makes no difference how the various theories go on to explain the way in which created grace provides a basis for a new relation between man and the God of grace: whether for instance it is said that God's new efficient causality in respect of grace makes Him present in a new way in the object of His activity (in virtue of the identity of being and operation in God and His immensity); or whether the view is put forward that the entitative elevation of man as regards his spiritual powers, which are thus orientated to the beatific vision as last end, gives him a new capacity (of an actual or potential kind) to take possession by knowledge and love of the God who is present in him by immensity; or whether one sees a perfect friendship with God established by grace, a friendship which provides anew and in itself sufficient basis for the presence of God in man (already there in fact). For in each case the indwelling of the Spirit in the justified man by grace is seen merely as a *consequence* of the bestowal of created grace, as the end-term of a (categorical) relationship of man to God given with created grace.

Hence the question arises how the two ways of looking at things, that of Scripture and the Fathers on the one hand, and that of scholastic theology on the other, may be brought into harmony: there created grace as

a *consequence* of God's communication of Himself to the man whose sins have been forgiven, here created grace as the *basis* of this communication. There is not the slightest question of contesting the soundness of the positive aspect of the scholastic theory. Our only intention is to complete it by elaborating in more explicit terms a pattern of thought (already in principle to be found in scholastic theology) and applying it to our problem in such a way that the admissibility of the patristic formula should become clear too, and hence make available a more adequate appreciation of the nature of uncreated grace. . . .

The statement of the solution. The possession of the Pneuma (and thus primarily uncreated grace) is conceived of in Scripture as the homogeneous germ and commencement of the beatific vision. And therefore we have the right to apply to uncreated grace in this life the concepts of formal ontology relating to the possession of God in the *visio beatifica*, at least in those cases in which the theological statements concerning this grace themselves suggest it. Now it has been seen that one fails to do justice to the essence of uncreated grace as this is declared in the sources of Revelation, if one sees it as exclusively founded upon a categorical relation to God of the man to whom grace has been shown, which relation rests merely (in some way or other) upon the accidental created modification of man's soul. This difficulty is resolved when we transfer to uncreated grace the concepts of formal ontology which appear in the *visio beatifica*: God communicates Himself to the man to whom grace has been shown in the mode of *formal* causality, so that this communication is not then merely the consequence of an efficient causation of created grace. Thus it becomes clear that the proposition no longer holds good which maintains that man has uncreated grace because he possesses created grace; on the contrary, with Scripture and the Fathers the communication of uncreated grace can be conceived of under a certain respect as logically and really prior to created grace: in that mode namely in which a formal cause is prior to the ultimate material disposition.

In what more precisely the communication of God by way of formal causality to the creature consists — this almost purely formal ontological account says very little expressly about it — may be determined in terms of the *visio beatifica* only negatively. Just as grace in general as an entitative supernatural elevation of man can be described in more precise detail only in terms of its definitive unfolding, the *visio* (though this 'unfolding' and 'disclosure' are not *just* a 'growth' to a final stage arising out of an inner impulse but are also a new eschatological intervention of the God who is still in Himself concealed), so too uncreated grace is only to be determined in terms of the *visio*: it is the homogeneous commencement, already given though still concealed and still to unfold, of that *communication* of the divine Being taking place *by way*

of formal causality to the created spirit which is the *ontological presupposition* of the *visio*.[161]

Firstly, then, this union, so far as it takes place by way of formal causality, is not simply a consequence of created grace — indeed it precedes the

---

[161] Cf. Leo XIII, "Divinum illud munus," ASS XXIX (1896), p. 653: "Haec autem mira coniunctio, quae suo nomine inhabitatio dicitur, condicione tantum seu statu ab ea discrepans, qua caelites Deus beando complectitur . . ." As is well known, Pius XII, in the encyclical *Mystici Corporis*, AAS XXXV (1943), p. 231 f.; Denz. 3815) has once more referred to this text as a starting-point for a consideration according to the *analogia fidei* so as to achieve a deeper understanding of the indwelling of the Spirit in the grace of justification. The Pope points out more clearly than before that the divine activity *ad extra* is common to the three Persons (Denz. 800; 1331) in the sense that this is to be understood of efficient causality (Denz. 3814); and at the same time draws attention to the *visio beatifica* as the starting-point for a more profound theology of grace. In this way he clearly points to a theology of grace which seeks to make full use of that notion of God's formal causality with respect to the creature which is a traditional possession of the schools in the theology of the *visio beatifica* and is quite inescapable in the doctrine of the hypostatic union. The circumstance that Pius XII clearly seems to wish to leave open the question whether the relations to the three divine Persons of the man to whom grace has been shown are really only appropriated cannot be discussed here. There is hardly any need to establish the fact that the solution here proposed respects the Pope's warning against every kind of pantheism ("omnem nempe reiciendum esse mysticae huius coagmentationis modum, quo christifideles, quavis ratione, ita creatarum rerum ordinem praetergrediantur, atque in divina perperam invadant, ut vel una sempiterni Numinis attributio de iisdem tamquam propria praedicari queat"). Compare here Trütsch, *loc. cit.*, p. 112 f.

created grace to the extent that this grace, as the ultimate disposition to the union, can only exist when God's formal causality is actually being exercised. Secondly, so far as it is the ontological *presupposition* of the beatific vision, this union is already posited independently of an actually exercised apprehension of the three-fold God by man in knowledge and love, whether this should be through the supernatural acts of the theological virtues or through the beatifying vision and love of fulfilment. Thirdly, this ontological union is posited as a presupposition of the *visio*. By this is meant that this immediate, ontological union, in spite of or even because of its basis in formal causality, should not be conceived of vaguely as some sort of "unity of nature," in which God and the created spirit are thought of as flowing into each other along arbitrarily adopted causes. This onto-logical unity arising out of the exercise of formal causality is nothing but the presupposition and the ontological aspect of the unity of the created spirit with God in the act of immediate loving contemplation, an act therefore which implies the highest degree of unity in the fullest distinction. And here our interpretation once again reaches a point at which it can either rejoin the traditional interpretation of God's indwelling in the line of St. Thomas, Suarez, John of St. Thomas or Gardeil,[162] or adopt the

categories of a more personalist metaphysics of the relationship between God and the creature through grace. For in the last resort this interpretation of ours seeks nothing else than to focus more sharply for the human understanding the highest and most intimate union with God which is possible to a creature in the gaze of love, and to do so by grasping as precisely as possible the ontological presupposition of the union in the categories of formal ontology.

We need not attempt to decide here how we should interpret the distinction between the communication of the divine Being to man by way of formal causality in grace and in the *visio*: whether we should interpret it as a difference in the degree of this increasing communication *in itself*, or as a difference derived from the difference in the material *disposition* to this communication.[163] In other words, we do not intend to take up the question whether the growth from un-created grace to the possession of God as the basis of the *visio beatifica* is

---

[162] At any rate, it is quite unjustified, on the basis of the fact that the created grace of the "pilgrim" state (*status viatoris*) is distinct at least in degree from the light

of glory, to conclude with B. Froget (*De l'habitation*, p. 155 f.), M. Retailleau and others (cf. Trütsch, *passim*) that if the divine essence is already united immediately with the pilgrim's spirit as it is in the visio, he would have to possess the *visio* already. Such a conclusion presupposes that this immediate union is the unique cause of the vision. But if a *created* supernatural disposition (grace or the light of glory, which are capable of growth) is a necessary presupposition of the vision, the fact that it is deficient can explain why the *visio* is not posited, although an immediate informing communication of the divine Being to the created spirit has already been posited.

[163] Cf. Galtier, *De SS. Trinitate in se et in nobis* (Paris, 1933), n. 443 f.

an inner growth of this possession in itself or just the 'growth' (always understood with the restriction indicated above) of created grace into the light of glory — or whether this either-or is really not justified at all in a more precisely worked-out ontology of the relationship between *causa formalis* and *causa materialis*. . . .

Does not our view, with its emphasis on the relative independence of uncreated grace as regards created grace, endanger the significance of created grace for justification, adoption, etc., as Trent sees them? We need not here go into the familiar controversy conducted above all by Scheeben and Granderath as to the meaning of Chapter VII of the Sixth Session of the Council of Trent in the matter of the *unica causa formalis iustificationis*. In this question too we may surely have recourse to the concepts developed in scholastic theology in its treatment of the *visio beatifica*. Just as there the light of glory is seen as the *dispositio ultima quae est necessitas ad formam*," so here an analogous relationship may be assumed to hold between created and uncreated grace. In this regard created grace is seen as *causa materialis* (*dispositio ultima*) for the formal causality which God exercises by graciously communicating His own Being to the creature. In this way the material and formal causes possess a reciprocal priority: as *dispositio ultima* created grace is in such a way the presupposition of the formal cause that it can itself only exist by way of the actual realization of this formal caus-

ality. From this objective reciprocal priority there follows further the logical justification for inferring the presence of one reality from that of the other. Because created grace as *dispositio ultima* can only exist along with the actual formal causality of the form for which it is the *dispositio*, it is correct to say: If created grace is given, so too necessarily by that very fact uncreated grace and hence the whole grace of justification, is communicated to man.

Thus on our view of the relationship between created and uncreated grace there does not exist even the beginning of a possibility of thinking of created grace apart from uncreated grace, and so of thinking of uncreated grace as a fresh gift arising out of a new and independent demonstration of God's grace. We must remember furthermore that created grace alone (as a finite determination of the subject) can be called *forma* in the strict (categorical) sense of the word (as opposed to the divine Being itself, which remains transcendent with respect to the creature in spite of its formal causality); and we must remember that the Council only wished to meet the imputation theory of the Reformers, Seripando and others, but did not wish to determine how created and uncreated (inner!) grace (of which latter it also says precisely "signans et ungens Spiritu promissionis Sancto . . .") are related to each other and together constitute the *single* grace of justification. In view of all this we may say that the Council's teaching on created grace as the *unica causa formalis* of justification does not exclude our conception of the relationship between created and uncreated grace. For in this conception too created grace remains the "unique" formal cause of justification, in so far as it alone is the genuine (categorical) "form" of the justified man, and once it is posited, justification as a whole is really posited with it already. In addition it must be said that Chapter VII of the Tridentine decree on justification only teaches explicitly that the *causa formalis* of justification is wholly *interior* (and thus not an *imputed* "causa formalis extrinseca"), and that conversely therefore the *causa formalis* of justification is interior grace *alone*. It is true that the Council describes this interior grace in terms which in the theology of the schools hold good primarily of created grace, but it nowhere says that *interior* grace, as the unique formal cause of justification, must be understood *exclusively* of *created* grace.[164] . . .

There can be absolutely no objection to maintaining on the basis of the positive data of Revelation that the attribution of determinate relations of the recipient of grace to the three divine Persons is not merely a matter of appropriation, but is intended to give expression to a proper relationship in each case. In Scripture it is the Father in the Trinity who is our Father, and not the threefold God.[165] The Spirit dwells in us in a

particular and proper way.[166] These and like statements of Scripture and Tradition are first of all "in possession." It would be necessary to prove that they may be merely appropriated, on the grounds that they can be understood merely as such and that the contrary is impossible; it cannot be presupposed. So long as this has not been achieved, we must take Scripture and the expressions it used in as exact a sense as we possibly can. There is another point which should not be forgotten. In the history of Western piety an attenuation of the 'Trinity of the economy of salvation' into a kind of pre-Christian monotheism (and that is what the doctrine of bare appropriations in the theology of grace really amount to) has not merely diminished the significance of the Holy Trinity in concrete religious life. In itself (i.e., logically, and if the contrary were not already defined) this attenuation could also endanger the "interior Trinity" to the benefit of a rationalistic monotheism for which the three divine Names would only be for us three aspects under which to regard the one divine Essence. For in Scripture the interior Trinity and the Trinity of the econ-

---

[164] Cf. *Ibid.*, n. 413.

[165] See Rahner, "*Theos* in the New Testament," *Theological Investigations*, Vol I.

[166] By this it is not of course meant that the Spirit alone makes his dwelling in us. Each Person communicates Himself and dwells in us in a way proper to Him. And because the indwelling ascribed to the Holy Spirit in Scripture (as a Power who sanctifies, consecrates, moves, etc.) corresponds precisely to the personal particularity of the Spirit and of His going forth from the Father and the Son, there is absolutely no objection to saying that in *this* way only the Spirit dwells in man.

omy of salvation are seen and spoken of in themselves with such simultaneity that there would be no justification in itself (logically) for taking the expressions literally and substantially in the first case and only in an "appropriated" way in the second. We should like to think that here our proposed theory of uncreated grace in terms of the concepts of scholastic theology offers the possibility of determining man's relationship in grace as a non-appropriated relation to the three divine Persons, without doing injury to the principle of the unity of efficient causality in the creative action of the threefold God *ad extra,* and without making the indwelling conjunction of the three divine Persons into a hypostatic union.

5. J.-H. Nicolas, O.P.,[167] indicates why he prefers to explain the Trinitarian presence in the just soul not through divine efficiency in producing grace nor by the simple union of love but by means of full supernatural knowledge.

For a long time past, theologians have endeavored to solve this problem. They were anxiously preoccupied with the task of providing for themselves and for others that understanding of the faith which corresponds to the deepest need of Christianity and which consists in such a precious light for the soul that it would be senseless and very un-Christian to despise it. They asked themselves, therefore, what new presence of God in the soul could produce grace.

Explanation of the Trinitarian presence through divine efficiency in producing grace. Certain of them have thought that this novelty is sufficiently insured by the divine action which produces grace in the soul. . . .

Grace being an entirely new perfection in the creature, not to be compared to any other, to produce grace would be a completely new and incomparable way of making himself present to his creature. *Criticism.* This solution, as it stands, appears inadequate if we reflect on the fact that God's productive action belongs to a unique category, however diverse the perfections which it brings about . . . so that the presence resulting from this action is always of the same type. . . .

Explanation of the Trinitarian presence by the simple union of love. Other theologians, having reflected on the whole spiritual and living content of the idea of presence, have attempted to approach the question from an altogether different angle. . . . Presence is a relationship between two persons. . . . Thus, the theologians we have just mentioned sought the reason of the new presence of God

---

[167] J.-H. Nicolas, O.P., an outstanding present-day Dominican theologian, first published this work in French under the title *Le Mystère de la Grâce.* This excerpt is from the English version, entitled *The Mystery of God's Grace* (Dubuque, Iowa: The Priory Press, 1960), pp. 68–81.

in the just, in the new intercourse of knowledge and love established by grace between the soul and God, and, more especially, in charity which is a friendship, and like all friendships implies a personal union between friends. *Criticism.* We answer them by stating that friendship of itself is not presence; it arouses the desire and tends towards it with all its momentum, but it does not create presence. The affective union which it establishes between those who love each other is not the effective union which they desire, so that, being purely intentional and representative, it can be in no way real.[168] Now the Trinity is present in the soul of the just in a real and special manner. . . .

Explanation of the Trinitarian presence by means of full super-

[168] We must draw attention however to the thesis upheld by Father Dockx, O.P., which, were it established, would checkmate our argument. In his book *Fils de Dieu par la Grâce* (Desclèe, 1948) and in an article in the *Nouvelle Revue Théologique* (July, 1950), this theologian has striven to find the necessary and sufficient reason for the presence of the Trinity in the conditions proper to this unique love which constitutes supernatural charity. This thesis has not yet emerged from the sphere of technical theology and its discussion would draw us into considerations which are too difficult and austere to find an appropriate place in our present work. For the benefit of the reader who is astonished at these discussions between theologians, it is well to note that, in reality, they are merely concerned, at least here, with the rational explanation of a fact which is of itself of much greater importance than all ideas which we may form about it: all theologians agree not only about recognizing the fact of the Trinitarian presence in the souls of the just — which is an article of faith — but also that it is in the love of charity

natural knowledge. God, then, is present to the soul. First, God is present through his creative action, by which He is wholly in the interior of every being — and that holds for every creature, material or spiritual, sinner or just, damned or beatified, because He is the omnipresent Creator for each and all. God is present also by reason of the personal relations of knowledge and love which grace establishes between the soul and Him — and that holds good for the just alone. This is the explanation which we must support. But it still calls for much clarification. . . .

How are we to conceive of the combination of these three elements which appear at first view so divergent? If we search the *sphere* of love, we shall discover nothing. . . . But it is otherwise where knowledge is concerned. To know is, in every case, to unite ourselves immaterially with the thing known; to make the thing itself enter into our consciousness, yet in an unrealized manner. When I know an ant, it is as though it were in me, but it is not there in a material sense, its real life unfolds outside me. Such a union alone could not constitute a real presence, since it can come about without physical contact. I can think intensely about an absent friend without thereby making him present. If this contact, nevertheless, exists, knowledge itself may be modi-

that the explanatory principle of this presence must be sought. If they argue, it is for the sole purpose of ascertaining how this connection between charity and the divine presence should be precisely understood.

fied by it, the immaterial union which it constitutes always receiving, by means of this contact, the character of reality which it lacked, while inversely, the physical contact itself, owing to its elevation to the rank of knowledge, receives the mark of spirituality which it does not possess of itself. Such knowledge, combining in a single union, at once immaterial and real, on the one hand the physical conjunction of the thing known and the knower, and on the other hand the spiritual presence of this same thing in the consciousness of the knower, is of a well-known type; it is experimental knowledge. It is conditional on the physical contact being at its origin and at its end. In short, that means that the act of knowing is determined by the real action of the thing known on the knower, and that it joins up with the thing at the point where it is in real contact with it. The typical case of this mode of knowing is sensible perception.

Does grace produce an experimental knowledge of God? If it does, the problem will be solved: through such a knowledge the real contact of the soul with God will be changed into a personal presence which grace, in its turn, will render real. But can we affirm this?

It is through faith that we know God, and faith does not consist in an experimental knowledge. Moreover, the sinner may have faith; he may know that God is present in his interior, at the root of his being, and he may know that God is Trinity, without that fact giving him the Trinitarian presence. Faith of itself is a knowledge through ideas, that is to say, non-experimental, in which the real contact between the knower and the known, whether it is realized or not, plays no part.

Thus, if supernatural knowledge merely brought faith into play, we would have to abandon the notion of regarding it as the origin of the Trinitarian presence, which would thus become inexplicable, since it could be explained neither by the creative contact nor by knowledge, nor by love, nor even by the three combined; for they would appear merely juxtaposed, incapable of combining with each other, of really uniting. But the just man tends towards the God in whom he believes with his whole strength, and he loves Him. Love, then, penetrates knowledge and modifies it profoundly: Is a woman's knowledge of her child only what she could read in any manual of pedagogy? Thus, the soul knows God with a knowledge of faith completely impregnated by love — the knowledge of connaturality. . . .

What, indeed, does it lack in order to be experimental? Only that the thing known should be at its origin and at its end. As soon as it is there, existentially joined to the knower, his knowledge will become experimental. It is the thing known in its concrete and living reality which affects this knowledge; so if this thing is there, in real contact with the knower, it will find its natural complement in this contact and will identify itself with it. We find this complement realized in supernatural knowledge: God is at its origin, effectively causing grace in the soul, together with faith and love, whose exercise He activates; God is at its end also, effectively united to the soul by this very action.

If it were merely a question of the knowledge of faith, this contact with God would not make it experimental knowledge, for it would remain outside the soul, faith of itself being a purely intellectual and abstract knowledge, a knowledge through ideas, which is indifferent to such a contact. But we are dealing with plenary supernatural knowledge, with faith impregnated with love, with a concrete knowledge entirely directed, precisely as knowledge, towards this contact, completing itself in it and at the same time raising it to its own level, which is spiritual. By virtue of this knowledge and of the love which animates it, the creative contact of the soul with God becomes a personal presence, the Trinitarian presence, on which, on its side, it confers reality. The synthesis we sought of these three elements of the divine indwelling is, therefore, insured, and we see that this presence is the effect of grace, since it is the fruit of the love of charity, of which grace is the immediate and unfailing source.[169]

Thus expounded, the Trinitarian presence is not confined to mystics. An objection which is often raised against this solution is that, in this case, the divine indwelling is truly realized only in the Christian who ac-

tually unites Himself to God, or, more exactly, in the mystic. Now, it is absolutely certain that the state of grace implies this divine presence, even in the mediocre or distracted Christian, even in the newly baptized little infant. . . . This objection does not stand up to close scrutiny. . . . We have seen that, if grace is undoubtedly a participation in divine nature, it could not be in the sense of something of God coming into us. God is absolutely simple; He can only be wholly where He is; and the idea of any composition between the divine being, who is infinite and pure without any mixture, and a created being is altogether inconceivable. Grace, considered in itself, can only be a created form. It is only through their operations that two beings, while remaining distinct, can communicate in such a way as to fuse together as one in perfect community, in a good which is the total good of each. It is in this way that the soul of the just man communicates with God, sharing his life. If grace can make us divine, it must be because it constitutes within us the source from which the actions of a divinized life arise. And grace *is that* from the very first moment, before these actions may, in fact, be performed; it is certainly the source even when these actions are not pro-

---

[169] Since we cannot give a full exposition of the doctrine of mystical knowledge — which we have termed plenary supernatural knowledge — we have not referred to the role played by the gifts of the Holy Ghost. In reality, charity does not exist without the gifts which render the soul more and more docile to the inspirations of the Holy Ghost. Faith infused with love is what the theologians call "faith illuminated by the gifts."

duced, even in those in whom they are produced in a merely intermittent manner. Once grace is present, the soul becomes through it capable in its depths of God, turned towards God and placed on a level of divine life.

What, then, is left of our objections? All the conditions for this presence are realized as soon as grace is produced, even before it becomes actual in operations of supernatural life. Indeed, a very simple example will help us to understand this.

A mother is present to her little child with a true presence which cannot be compared to a purely material one by which she may be present to her cat, nor even to that by which she is present to somebody else's child. Yet, this little being asleep in his cradle does not love or know her much more than the animal or the other child. But, on the one hand, he is completely enveloped in maternal tenderness, and on the other hand, his filial love is still pregnant in his dulled sensitivity — in his mind, which is as yet completely shrouded and incapable of performing its operations. Between himself and his mother there is not the least spiritual intercourse in action, but there exists in him all the sources from which this intercourse will come as soon as the conditions necessary for spiritual action are realized. The presence of which we speak is, therefore, comprised — if we suppose physical proximity, which is the basis of all true presence — of the actual love of the mother and of the potential love in the child. It is very unphilosophical to deny the reality

of potency; to do so commits the mind, in every sphere, to difficulties from which there is no issue.

The "coming" of the Trinity into the soul. The objection is raised that, in such circumstances, it is not the Trinity which comes into the soul, as is stated in the Gospel, but the soul which brings about God's presence through its own acts. That amounts to a gross misunderstanding of things! Did we not see above that grace was, originally and above all, the privileged love with which God loves a spiritual being as His child. Under the radiation of this love, created grace flowers in the soul and becomes actual in this plenary supernatural knowledge composed of faith, love, and all the illuminations of the Holy Ghost, which knowledge insures the Trinitarian presence. For God, who never displaces Himself in any way because He is always there and everywhere, coming into a soul means loving it with that new love which determines the Trinitarian presence by creating grace. By thus loving the soul, God comes into it and begins to dwell in it without waiting until the soul has been able to begin loving Him in return.[170]

The Christian is never alone as long as he is faithful to grace. He has only to seek refuge through faith and love in that core of his soul where the three divine Persons . . . live in him and with him in unutterable friendship.

---

[170] For a more detailed examination of these objections, see *Revue Thomiste* (1950–1951).

INDEX

Abelard, and Aristotelian idea of virtue, 177; and Baius and Pelagius, 174 f; and progress of theology, 175

Abercrombie, N., on grace in Baius, Molina, Dominicans, Jansen, 261 ff

Abraham, election, faith, justification by faith, 8 ff; justice a gift, 73; a just man, 73

Actuation, by Uncreated Act, 379

Adoption, and Holy Spirit, 358

Agape, divine and brotherly love, 41; self-giving love, 41

Aheb, Hebrew word for love, God's love, 1 ff

Alivisatos, H., on sacramental grace in Orthodoxy, 344 ff

Alliance, new, created by spirit, 4 f

Ambrose, and original sin, 109

Ambrosiaster, and Augustine, 109

Amiot, F., on grace in St. Paul, 60 ff

Analogia entis, as discovery of Antichrist, 324 ff

Analogy of being, and analogy of faith, 325 f

Anglicans, and justification by faith alone, 310 ff

Anthropology, for Orient and Occident, 349 ff

Anselm, St., on grace, liberty, predestination, 173

Approximation, of adoption, 200; Aquinas and two traditions, 356; and divine indwelling, 369, 390 f; doctrine of, and Petau, 355 f; Greek tradition, and Augustine, 356; and Nominalism, 378; and *proprium* theory, 373 f

Aquinas, and actual grace, 188; and adoptive filiation, 199 ff; and appropriation, 356; and created and uncreated grace, 195 ff; and deification, 181; and fallen nature, 193 ff; and gift of integrity, 194; healing and elevating grace, 193 ff; and irresistible grace, 190; and last end of man, 192 f; and liberating grace, 189; and man as Son of Trinity, 356; and mission of Son and Spirit, 197 ff; and Mystical Body, 191; only one kind of grace, 201; and original sin, 187; and Pauline *Charis*, 195; and physical pre-

motion, 286; a precursor of Baius?, 187; and psychology of justification, 188, 196; and Semipelagianism, 188; a static construction of Augustinism, 188; synthesis of Augustinian and Aristotelian data, 182 f; synthesis of Augustine and Greek traditions, 180 f; synthesis built on supernatural end, not fall, 181; synthesis open to criticism, 191; and theology of created grace, 195; the Thomist synthesis, 181 ff; Thomist synthesis and Augustinian synthesis, 191; on uncreated and created grace, 367

Aristotelian, ideas of virtue, 177 f

Aristotelianism, and firm notion of nature, 179; and theological speculation, 178

Aristotle, and Luther, 232

Asceticism, for Orient and Occident, 351 *n*

Athanasius, on active presence of Spirit in souls and Church, 89; and divinization by grace and participation, 102 f; divinization by participation in Word and Spirit, 104; on man's identification with Christ, 89; and Mystical Body, 90 *n*; on regeneration, adoption, gift of Holy Spirit, 89; and synthesis of theology of salvation, 90

Augustine, and actual grace, 129 f, 134 ff; and *auxilium quo et sine quo non*, 129 f; central core of his teaching, 139; and divinization, 120 f; and divinizing grace, 127 f; doctrine of sin and grace preeminent, 120; and efficacy of grace, 136 f; on fallen man and liberty, 125 f; and formation of doctrine, 124 f; and formation of his ideas, 122 ff; and God's will to save only elect, 148; grace doctrine still important, 119; and grace of Christ, 124; and grace of justification, 126; and gratuity of grace, 130 f, 135; his doctrine and that of Church, 156 f; and his grace doctrine, 143 ff; his grace themes long dominant, 354; and human liberty, 139 f; and inhabitation of Holy Spirit, 128; and invincible grace, 147; and justification, 128 f; and liberating grace, 121 f; and loss of freedom in fallen man, 146; and Luther, 232; and man's destiny, 114 f; master from fifth to